The Encyclopaedia
of World Costume

THE ENCYCLOPEDIA OF WORLD COSTUME

Doreen Yarwood

CHARLES SCRIBNER'S SONS · NEW YORK

Copyright © Doreen Yarwood 1978

Library of Congress Cataloging in Publication Data

Yarwood, Doreen.
Encyclopedia of world costume.

    1. Costume – Dictionaries.   I. Title.
GT507.Y37   391'.003   78–3726
ISBN 0–684–15805–1

1 3 5 7 9 11 13 15 17 19 $^{1}/_{C}$ 20 18 16 14 12 10 8 6 4 2

Printed in Great Britain

Preface

Bearing in mind that more than one dictionary of costume is available in the English language, the publishers and I felt that it would be more useful to handle the considerable quantity of material in this book in an encyclopaedic manner. This is a more difficult as well as more ambitious approach which constantly involves the author in decision-making about the best way in which to present a section of the material. Since costume historians and students would differ greatly in their individual interpretation and preference, such decisions are bound to reflect a personal viewpoint: in this book I accept responsibility for the result.

The articles in the encyclopaedia reflect this broader concept of handling the material so that related subjects are discussed together in one larger entry. Such descriptions cover the history and development of the garment as it was worn in various parts of the world at different periods as well as the many forms and designs which it might take. Thus, under cloak, all the main garments of this type which have been worn are discussed, regardless of place or time of origin. Similarly, under trousers, the discussion ranges from Scythian, Persian, Chinese and Indian versions to western blue jeans.

One of the problems in presenting the material in this manner is that different people have different ideas regarding the heading under which they would expect to find the item upon which they require some information. Because of this a comprehensive index has been supplied, not grouped in subjects, but arranged in simple alphabetical order making it easy to find any subject, large or small, which is discussed in the book.

The term 'world encyclopaedia' has been used in the title because the book includes costume worn in most parts of the world, but it cannot be claimed that the coverage is equally comprehensive for all parts of the globe. The encyclopaedia is intended for use in the English-speaking world so is geared primarily to those needs, though the coverage of other regions is fairly wide. Even in a large volume a limit has to be drawn somewhere; in this case, an attempt has been made to handle civil dress and textiles; military and ecclesiastical dress have been omitted.

In a work of this complexity it is impossible to acknowledge *in situ* the source of each illustration. The drawings have been made from original sources in museums, galleries and libraries over a period of many years. I would like to express my sincere gratitude for the generous assistance which I have received everywhere during this time from the directors and staffs of these institutions.

In particular, I would like to express my appreciation to the staff of the Victoria and Albert Museum and Library, London; the British Museum, London; the Science Museum, London; the Museum of London; the Lewis Textile Museum, Blackburn; the City Museums and Art Gallery, Birmingham; the Saffron Walden Museum; the Bankfield Museum, Halifax; the Central Museum, Northampton; the Lace Museum, Nottingham; the Pitt-Rivers Museum, Oxford; the Gallery of English Costume, Manchester; the Museum of Costume, Bath; the Welsh Folk Museum, Cardiff; the Royal Scottish Museum, Edinburgh; the National Museum of Antiquities, Edinburgh; the Industrial Health and Safety Centre, London; Borg Textiles Ltd; Musée du Costume de la Ville de Paris; Centre d'Enseignement et de Documentation du Costume, Paris; Kostuummuseum, the Hague, Netherlands; Openluchtmuseum, Arnhem; Centraal Museum, Utrecht; Bayerische Nationalmuseum, Munich; Historisches Museum, Frankfurt-am-Main; Museum of Decorative Arts, Budapest; National Hungarian Museum, Budapest; Rocamora Museum, Barcelona; Museo del Pueblo Español, Madrid; Nordiska Museet, Stockholm; National Museum, Copenhagen; Rosenborg Palace, Copenhagen; Musées Royaux d'Art et d'Histoire, Brussels; Musée Royal des Beaux Arts, Antwerp; the Louvre, Paris; the Prado, Madrid; the Tunisian Embassy, London; the Indian High Commission, London; the National Aeronautics and Space Administration, Washington D.C.

DOREEN YARWOOD
East Grinstead 1977

The author and publishers would like to thank the following for permission to reproduce illustrations: the Trustees of the British Museum (fig. 5); Musée du Louvre (figs 4 & 6 © by S.P.A.D.E.M. Paris, 1978); the National Gallery (fig. 3); the National Portrait Gallery (fig. 2); the Royal Scottish Museum (figs 7 & 8); Victoria & Albert Museum (fig. 1).

Contents

Doctor of Medicine, Oxford
Bell sleeve, 1770

Present day Bachelor's gown,
London University, open sleeve

ABA, ABAYEH
Arab dress, Syria. Red and
white kaffiyeh with agal. Cream
wool abayeh with gold and
silver edging over cream silk,
embroidered waistcoat and
white cotton tunic. Red leather
boots

Present day Doctor of Medicine,
Oxford
Scarlet gown with crimson bell
sleeves and facings. Black velvet
bonnet

Present day Master's gown,
Sussex University, closed sleeve

Biretta, sixteenth century

Pileus, modern

Ladies' cap. Present day, Oxford

A

Aba, Abayeh

A simple, loose gown worn over other garments as a cloak or blanket in Turkey, Persia, North Africa and Arabia. It can be made of plain or striped wool, camel or goat hair, or silk. The word *aba* is the name of a coarse woollen fabric.

Abaca

Native name given to the fibre and also the plant from which manila hemp is obtained in the Philippine Islands. Used chiefly for cordage, hats and matting.

Academical dress

Academical dress worn today in Western universities consists of garments fossilized in the style of an everyday costume – partly lay, partly ecclesiastical – of a past age. These garments date from the later Middle Ages and the early Renaissance; small alterations have taken place from time to time and the details of hood and sleeve styles as well as headcoverings and colours of materials vary from university to university.

In Europe, including Britain, the early universities of the twelfth and thirteenth centuries were closely associated with the Church. Most of the Doctors and Masters were in Holy Orders so ecclesiastical dress was normal wear. This was then similar to that worn by everyone else, consisting of long, loose tunics, one over the other, a hood with shoulder cape, hose and shoes. A round hat derived from the Roman *pileus rotundus* was also worn; this had a stalk or tab, like a beret, on top.

In the later Middle Ages, when the general fashion trend was towards short, fitting tunics, the lay academics retained their voluminous gowns – now sometimes shorter than previously – and wore them on top of their everyday clothes. This is what academics have been doing ever since; at least, on formal occasions.

Modern academical dress consists of a gown, a hood and a cap or hat. The gown is basically of the design which was fashionable in the early sixteenth century and is chiefly based on the Spanish and Italian modes of the time. It is calf-length and worn open in front, the edges being turned back and sometimes faced with a different colour and material, according to the university concerned. There is no collar but the fabric is gathered into a yoke at the back which derives from the original square collar. Depending on cost, the gown is made from rayon or corded silk and is black, except for the Doctors' full dress, which is usually scarlet, though in some universities it is purple, maroon, claret or crimson (at Cambridge it is black). The custom of the wearing of brilliant colours by recipients of higher degrees dates from the sixteenth century. The undergraduate gown is a shortened version of the graduate one.

Sleeve styles vary greatly but all derive from the early sixteenth century. In general, Bachelors' gowns have some form of open sleeve which is very wide and hangs down nearly to the hem of the gown. The closed or glove sleeve is more usual for Masters' gowns; this is the design which was fashionable in England in the reign of Henry VII, where there is a slit in the front of the sleeve at elbow level and the arm is passed through, leaving the tube of material to hang down behind the arm. In Doctors' gowns the full, bell sleeve is the most usual.

There are two principal designs of *hood*,

ACADEMICAL DRESS
Oxford University, late medieval

Oxford University, B.A., 1670s

Full shape hood with caul, cape and liripipe stump

Simple hood with caul and liripipe stump

the full shape and the simple shape. In the former style, as worn at Cambridge and London, for example, there remains a vestige of all three parts of a medieval hood and, though the hood is never worn on the head but hangs in elongated, stylized form down the back, these can all be discerned: the shoulder cape, the cowl or head portion, and the truncated end of the liripipe. In the simple shape, as worn at Oxford, for instance, the hood has remains of only the cowl and the liripipe. It is in the colours and materials of the linings and edgings to these hoods that the degree and university are designated, and in the universities of the world there is a wealth of variety, from coloured silk to fur, as academic dress is worn in many countries; notable European exceptions are the Soviet Union and Scandinavia.

The most general head-covering today is the *mortar-board*, trencher or catercap. This has a stiffened round cap or head-piece with a square board on top to which a tassel is attached. This unusual head-covering derives from a square form of the *pileus*, which was adopted by the University of Paris in the early sixteenth century (before this, the round *pileus* or the stiff *biretta* were worn). Known in Latin as the *pileus quadratus* and in French as the *bonnet carré*, the fashion soon spread in Europe. Its early form was a soft, flat, square cap worn on top of a skull cap. In the seventeenth century the two parts became attached to one another and the flat, square part was stiffened into a board to prevent the corners flopping over the face. By 1665 the centre tump had appeared and a tassel was attached to this in the eighteenth century.

The *Doctors' bonnet* is a sixteenth century Tudor style introduced at the Reformation. It has a small, stiffened, oval brim and a soft velvet crown with a band of cord or ribbon. Some universities in Britain adopt different headgear, as at Oxford, for example, where there is a ladies' cap, and at Sussex, where the *pileus* is worn by Doctors.

Afghan dress
Costume strongly influenced by neighbouring India, but also by Turkish and Persian styles. In the mountain areas in winter, sheepskin coats and mantles worn with the wool to the inside. Legs usually covered in full trousers (*chalvar*) and, for street wear, women were enveloped in the *chadri* (*boorka*), with embroidered headpiece incorporating a mesh panel to peer through (see also *Chādar*).

Agate
A semi-precious stone, one of the variegated chalcedonies, its colours blended in clouds or defined in stripes. Widely used in costume jewellery.

Aglet, Aiglet, Aiguillette
A lace with a metal tag used in the costume of both sexes. In the fifteenth century such tags were known as points and this method of fastening was used to attach the edges of one garment to those of another – for example, the hose to the gipon or doublet or the codpiece to the hose.

In the sixteenth century aglets or points were commonly employed all over the costume to join decoratively the slashed edges of caps or hats, sleeves, doublets and gown skirts. The tags were often of gold or silver, chased or jewelled, and the cords were of coloured or gold silks. Sleeves, especially in Italian dress, were attached by points to the armholes and the upper sleeve was fastened thus to the separate, lower one at the elbow. Seventeenth-century aglets or aiguillettes were generally ribbons with metal tags sewn on in bunches as decoration round the waistline of the masculine doublet or the feminine gown.

Agraffe
Originally a hook fastening to a ring to form a clasp for clothing. From the late Latin *grappe*, meaning hook. In the eighteenth and nineteenth centuries a decorative clasp of jewelled metal used in turbans and hats, gown bodices and to fasten cloaks at the throat.

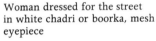

White veil and trousers.
Coloured tunic, brightly-
coloured, striped jacket

White tunic and trousers.
Sheepskin coat, fur inside.
Turban and cummerbund.

Woman dressed for the street
in white chadri or boorka, mesh
eyepiece

Dark wool cloak, white tunic,
striped cummerbund. Leather
boots, turban

AGLET
Swiss, 1514. Holes
in edge of gipon to
be attached to lace
tags in the top of
the hose.
Unfastened

Flemish, 1530–5.
Velvet cap with
gold points

French, c.1630.
Aglets at doublet
waist

ALBANIAN DRESS
Nineteenth-century dress worn today for festive occasions. All in white except for black and gold jacket and black shoe pompons

Peasant dress still in use. Colourful embroidered blouse, skirt and apron with long fringe. Trousers and footwear of coloured wool all in one, leather soles

Everyday dress of woollen cloak, felt hat, blue and white striped waist sash and white shirt and trousers with black decoration worn over soft footwear

Costume, *c*.1910. Red cloak taken up over head, embroidered panels. Worn over black and gold sleeveless coat and white chemise. Loose black trousers, gold anklets, leather footwear. White face veil

Alb

A long, white tunic, in ancient Rome the *tunica alba*, worn as secular dress until the later sixth century AD. After this time it became exclusively a liturgical garment.

Albanian dress

The traditional costume of this mountain people is colourful and decorative and – probably due to the twentieth-century isolation of this small country – peasant dress has continued to be worn longer than in most parts of Europe. The style, materials and ornamentation have much in common with the garments of other Balkan peoples, notably Greeks and Montenegrins, and in Albania also, the dress varies from region to region and even, sometimes, from village to village. The especially decorative costumes, such as the man (illustrated) wearing the *fustan* (skirt), are now reserved for festive occasions only – a wedding for instance – but many of the other costumes, like those shown, are still in everyday use. Typical are the decorated *tirqe* (leggings) with dark strips of material appliquéd on to white or dark fabric; also the warm *broutza* (woollen cape) worn by the mountain herdsmen.

Women's dress is more colourful than men's and many garments are elaborately embroidered in silk and cotton thread, predominantly in black or red. This is especially so with the blouses, which are decorated all over the areas round the neckline and over the breasts and sleeves. The aprons, which are even more elaborately ornamented, are an essential part and focal point of the whole costume from all the regions. On top of the blouse is worn a woollen dress or coat and, sometimes, a cloak. Often the Oriental influence, stemming from the long period of Turkish dominance, is seen in the wearing of full trousers, separate or attached to the boots or shoes, which have turned-up toes. The traditional decorative motifs are geometrical, but in urban areas, more modern designs, using floral motifs, can be seen.

Alepine, Alapeen
A mixed fabric of either wool and silk or mohair and cotton. Used in the eighteenth century.

Alnage
Measurement by the ell, particularly employed in woollen cloth. An English measure, now little used.

Alpaca
An animal of the camel family, the alpaca resembles the llama, both species being domesticated breeds of the wild guanaco. Raised in flocks in the high Andes since the days of the Incas, the alpaca is now bred in Peru, Bolivia and Chile. Its strong silky fleece is generally black or brown.

Alpaca wool was introduced in Europe first in Spain and then Germany and France. First attempts to spin and weave alpaca were made in England in 1808 but, despite experimentation over the years, the material was discarded as too difficult to work. Sir Titus Salt, the Bradford manufacturer, developed in 1836 the method of using a cotton warp with an alpaca weft and this proved a great success. Bradford gained a reputation as a manufacturing centre for alpaca and exported both yarn and cloth in quantity, especially to the USA. This success led to a great demand for the fabric, a demand which could not be fully satisfied by the existing flocks in South America. Attempts were made to raise the animal in Europe and Australia but these failed as the alpaca – its normal habitat some 15,000 feet above sea level – did not acclimatize to the lower altitudes.

The word alpaca is applied to both the animal and the material which is made from its wool.

Alpine dress
The traditional and peasant dress of the Alps, which has survived in remote valleys and is sometimes still worn, especially for festive occasions, possesses a number of characteristics which are to be seen regardless of whether the costumes come from southern Germany, Switzerland or Austria. The costumes are colourful and decorative; they are gaily embroidered, most frequently in cross-stitch, with varied motifs which most often include stags, pairs of birds and flowers.

The men wear knee-breeches or shorts, and these can be of woollen cloth or leather and are supported by cross-bar leather braces and waistbelt, both of which are often decoratively embroidered. The leather breeches and shorts are called *lederhosen* and are warm and very hard-wearing. A short jacket accompanies the breeches and this sometimes has a collar; a waistcoat can be worn as well. The white shirt has full, long sleeves and its collar is held at the neck by a broad tie or kerchief. The wool stockings, often white, are knitted in decorative patterns. Shoes are of leather, and hats of felt with ribbon and feather decoration.

There is great variety in the styles of women's blouses and their head-dresses, the latter especially differing from region to region. These include felt and straw hats with feather and ribbon decoration, kerchiefs, caps and hoods, and some elaborate designs in lace, velvet or straw. The Swiss *schlappe* is one of these; it is a white embroidered or lace cap with pleated, stiffened, black and white gauze or lace wings shaped like a fan and attached to it on each side, and with ribbons hanging from it down the back. This head-dress derives from the Appenzell area.

The white blouses with their varied sleeve styles and neck finishes are worn under a traditional, fitting bodice, often of velvet, which is laced tightly across the chest under the breasts. The full skirts are colourful and ornamented; the aprons plain or decorated with lace or embroidery and are usually white. Stockings, again mainly white, are decoratively knitted like

Green hat and jacket, white apron, brown, embroidered skirt. Austrian.

Grey and green jacket and lederhosen, red waistcoat. Bavarian

Black hat with yellow ribbons. White blouse and apron, dark blue skirt. Bavarian

Green hat with flowers. White blouse, grey apron over black skirt, white stockings. Austrian

Black hat. Green jacket and lederhosen, green braces. White shirt and stockings. Austrian

Black hat and breeches, brown jacket, green braces and belt embroidered in red. White stockings. Austrian

White blouse, white embroidered apron, red bodice and decorative skirt, schlappe headdress, Swiss those of the men and shoes are usually of leather. For festive occasions garments are richly embroidered and a quantity of jewellery is worn, especially earrings and necklaces.

Amber
A fossil resin, yellow to brown in colour, which, when rubbed, becomes electrified; indeed, its Greek name is 'electron'. Used for jewellery and ornament from the earliest times, chiefly in necklaces and bracelets. Found in several parts of the world; for example, in the Mediterranean and Baltic coastal regions.

American shoulders
A name given to the padded shoulder-line of men's coats tailored in the USA from about 1875 until 1940. The padding gave a broad, square silhouette to the shoulders.

American vest
A single-breasted waistcoat made without collar or lapels. Fashionable in the second half of the nineteenth century.

Amethyst
A semi-precious stone, used in jewellery, of quartz coloured by manganese or a mixture of iron and soda to shades of bluish-violet and purple. Beautiful stones are found in India and Brazil, especially those with the deeper, more valued tones.

Amulet
A charm worn (usually around the neck) to protect the wearer against misfortune, illness or witchcraft. In ancient Egypt it was widely believed that the wearing of a specific amulet would ensure magical protection against a specific evil. Amulets were enclosed in the wrappings of the mummy when it was placed in the tomb in order to provide such protection in the life to come. Egyptian amulets were made from semi-precious stones, faïence or, less commonly, gold or bronze.

Angora
1) The name of a *goat*, bred from early times in Asia Minor, which has a white,

strong and lustrous coat with hairs up to six inches in length. Named after the city of Angora in Turkey, in north-central Asia Minor, angora was used as a fur in the nineteenth century but has more usually been imported for weaving, sometimes mixed with other fibres, as mohair.
2) The angora *rabbit* is bred in England and elsewhere. Its fur, often mixed with wool, is used to produce soft, fluffy scarves, gloves and knitwear.

Anklet
1) Ankle *socks*, worn for sport or by children, generally with a turned-down cuff.
2) An ankle *bracelet*, worn from earliest times, especially in hot climates where legs were bare.

ANKLET
Brass anklet, India

Heavy metal anklet, Central Africa

Anorak
The modern garment of this name derives from Scandinavia. It is made of light-weight cotton, silk or nylon and is lined, and often padded, to give resistance to wind and is water-repellent. It is worn for sport such as sailing, ski-ing, mountain walking and climbing. The garment is hip-length and fits snugly at wrists and hips. It has a hood which fastens closely under the chin. All fastenings are adjustable in order to accommodate several layers of woollies underneath. The modern anorak stems from the Eskimo garment known variously as anorak, amout or parka, according to its country of origin (see *Eskimo dress*).

AMULET
Glazed amulet.
Winged scarab beetle
Egyptian, *c*.700 BC

Djed pillar, represents stability

Papyrus bundle, represents success

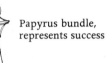

The heart, represents conscience of man and seat of his intelligence
Egyptian amulets

ANORAK
Modern anorak

Apron

A garment with a long history, worn for four chief purposes: as protection for the clothes beneath, as a decorative feature, as part of a traditional or regional dress, and to indicate particular status.

Protective aprons were worn by both men and women and the colour, design and material often varied according to the occupation of the wearer. For example, leather aprons were worn by blacksmiths and stone masons, green baize aprons by furniture removers, check-patterned ones by barbers and blue-and-white striped ones by butchers. The man's apron was generally cut in one piece, rising up from

Egyptian triangular apron, *c.*1125 BC

Man's working apron

the waist to cover the chest also, and it was tied with strings at the back with a loop added over the head. Most designs had one or more pockets in front to hold tools. Women's working aprons, both in town and country, were long and full, gathered closely into a waistband and tied at the back. Some had a bib or upper part to protect the bodice of the dress. They were made of white linen or cotton or could be of heavier materials, like the Welsh flannel examples in darker colours, striped or checked.

In many countries peasant costume has developed into a regional or even national dress and the feminine apron is usually part of such attire. It derives from the working apron which was an essential part of the dress, whereas the festival or holiday version is generally only decorative, ornamented with embroidery and appliqué work. The Hungarian *kötény* is one such example, where each region of Hungary has its own design of apron, some beautifully embroidered for use on festive occasions (see *Hungarian dress*).

In some ancient civilizations the apron was worn as a decorative symbol of rank or authority. The Egyptian triangular apron, seen in the paintings and sculpture of the Pharaohs, is one such example. These aprons, like the pendant designs, were attached to the waistbelt and hung down in front over the loincloth or skirt. The triangular ones were of pleated material, the pleats radiating from a lower corner. The pendant aprons were richly decorated, made of gilded leather, embroidered materials, metal plaques and beads.

Purely decorative aprons have been fashionable wear in certain periods and countries. Minoan statuettes show such ornamental aprons, decorated by embroidery and quilting. In more recent times, the elegant apron was worn as an item of high fashion by European ladies in the seventeenth and eighteenth centuries. Some of these aprons were quite tiny, others nearly full-length, but all were dainty and elegantly embroidered and/or lace-edged.

Egyptian pendant apron, *c.*1250 BC

White apron with
black embroidery.
Swiss, 1552

French ornamental
apron. A child,
1714–15

English, c.1690.
Decorative apron

Minoan dress,
seventh century BC

Dutch working
apron, 1625–30

Zürich woman in
plain apron, 1700.
Little boy, 1657, in
embroidered apron

Hungarian kötény,
c.1652

ARMLET
Bronze armlet. Bronze Age,
Scotland

Silver armlet, Indian, *c*.1880

Aquamarine
A beryl of pale blue or blue-green.

Arisard
An ancient term for a feminine robe or
tunic which was girded at the waist.

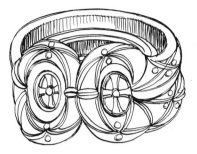

Bronze armlet. Ireland, second
century

ATTIFET
Czech noblewoman with attifet
head-dress, 1615

Mary Queen of Scots, 1578,
wearing an attifet head-dress

ARO
Spanish dress, 1470–80,
showing the aros in the
vertugado skirt

Armlet
An ornament like a bracelet but encircling
the upper arm. Worn by men and women,
especially in ancient cultures such as the
Minoan, Greek and Roman; also in Bronze
Age and Iron Age northern Europe.

Aro
The hoops of wood which were inserted
at regular intervals into gown skirts in
Spain in the later fifteenth century to form
the bell-shaped *vertugado* skirt.

Arrowhead
The embroidered mark in the shape of an
arrowhead sewn on tailored garments at
the junction of pleats or at pocket edges to
prevent tearing and strain.

Asbestos
A fibrous-textured mineral which is woven
into other material to make an incombust-
ible fabric. Used primarily for clothing
where protection against heat is necessary
(see *Industrial and Protective Clothing*).

Astrakhan cloth
A material manufactured to imitate astrakhan fur.

Attifet
A heart-shaped head-dress worn by ladies
in the sixteenth century. The front edges
were wired to hold the shape which dipped
to a point over the forehead and curved up
and back in an arc on either side. The head-
dress was usually white, of silk or linen,
and was embroidered and trimmed with
lace edging. The hair was dressed in tiny
curls or, as was more usual in France,

puffed out in rolls at the sides, arranged over pads termed arcelets. This was a style of coiffure and head-dress favoured by Mary Queen of Scots and was also to be seen in the widow's hood (in black) worn by Catherine de' Medici.

Aune

Like alnage, a measurement of an ell; an old French cloth measure.

Aztec dress

The Aztecs (also called Mexica) came to the valley of Mexico sometime in the twelfth to thirteenth century. A warlike people, they gradually built up an empire centred on their capital city of Tenochtitlan, which they constructed during the fourteenth and fifteenth centuries on the site of the present-day Mexico City. The Aztecs were conquered by Hernando Cortes and their lands were annexed to Spain in 1521.

In the hot climate a minimum of clothes were worn; lioncloths by the men and simple tunics and skirts by the women. The Aztecs possessed a flourishing cotton industry and this material was used for many garments, in quilted form when extra protection was needed. Important citizens wore richly decorated cloaks and a quantity of metal jewellery. Gold and fur were used for ornamentation, also the feathers of exotic birds such as the quetzal; the Aztecs called the tail feathers of this bird *quetzalli*. There was much in common between Aztec dress and that of the Maya (see *Maya dress*).

AZTEC DRESS
Aztec dress, c.1500 AD

Babies' and infants' wear

From the Middle Ages until the seventeenth century, babies in the West were *swaddled*; that is, wrapped in bandages from neck to toe, over a chemise, the arms and legs bound tightly to the body to protect the fragile limbs and make the baby easy to carry. The baby remained in swaddling bands, looking like an Egyptian mummy, until it was weaned, though at about four months the arms were freed. The medieval method of swaddling was by criss-cross bands; by the seventeenth century the bands were wrapped horizontally round the baby. In the eighteenth century swaddling was still customary for young babies but, in the upper classes at least, after about six weeks the baby was unbound and dressed in *long clothes*. Before this, in the sixteenth and seventeenth centuries, the baby had been dressed in long clothes on top of the swaddling bands. These long clothes consisted of a short-sleeved long gown, about three feet in length, like a christening robe, and a cap, both elegantly decorated with embroidery and lace. A mantle, also richly decorated, could be added on top for extra warmth. When the baby was old enough to sit up and crawl, he or she (for both sexes were dressed alike until four or five years old) wore a dress reaching to the feet, an apron, a bib and a cap. The style of these followed that of the adults of the period, with appropriate stiffened petticoats, ruffs, falling bands and other fashionable garments.

In the early nineteenth century, swaddling was replaced by long clothes which were retained for a few months. After this clothes were short but, by 1850, a great many layers were wrapped round the long-suffering baby; there seemed to be excessive anxiety in case the child should catch a chill. The baby's outfit included a

Baby boy, c.1570. Embroidered silk cap, brocade over-dress with crimson lining. Silk under-dress, white ruff

Seventeenth-century mother holding her baby which is dressed in long clothes

Dutch family, 1621. Little boy seated wears white cap, ruff and cuffs, a black dress with gold stripes and gold and brown underdress. Older child, standing, has a green apron over a white, patterned dress

Baby in cap and swaddling clothes, c.1605. White with gold embroidery

Eskimo mother and baby. Both are dressed in white and brown furs. Mother has sealskin boots

Flemish mother with three children, 1655–60. The baby, in a walking-cage, is dressed all in white

Canadian Indian cradle board, covered in buck-skin embroidered with beads and decorated with brass tacks. Baby holder is laced with buckskin laces chemise, stays to support the spine, a flannel stomach-band for extra warmth, flannel and other petticoats, a dress and a coat; two caps were worn night and day. White was the usual colour for baby clothes in wool, cambric, linen, muslin and lace. As the century advanced materials became heavier and layers were numerous, so that in 1900 babies were wearing more layers than they had in 1800. Also in the nineteenth century the *barrow*, or barrow coat, was worn by the young baby. This was a flannel or knitted-wool cloth wrapped round its body and the material turned back in a deep fold over the feet, making a bag. More sophisticated examples had caps attached and were held in place by pins and ribbon ties. Modern versions are often of quilted nylon and have zip fastenings.

In many areas of the world, in simpler cultures, babies have to be carried safely and warmly while the parents travel around in their work or on seasonal journeys for food. *Eskimo* women, for example, wear extra large fur hoods to carry the baby on their backs. In America, the Indians used a *baby frame* or *cradle board* made from a piece of flat wood covered in decorated buckskin with a pouch designed to fit the baby. The board was then strapped to the parent's back.

During the twentieth century, freedom of movement has gradually arrived for Western babies. Layers of clothes have become fewer, the garments shorter and the fabrics more practical for washing, hard-wearing qualities and ease of play. The all-in-one romper suit has been popular for many years, as also the little girl's dress with knickers to match. Dungaree suits are now made for the smallest toddler so that they can have fun and yet be clean and attractive. The widespread use of easy-care man-made fabrics has solved the busy mother's washing problems.

Bag: almoner, pouch, purse, reticule, handbag

From earliest times some type of bag or purse has been carried or worn to contain money, keys and other necessities. In Europe, for long periods, such containers were superfluous because the costume itself was so voluminous that it was easy to insert many pockets which would hold all such valuables and personal items. These periods included much of the sixteenth century and the seventeenth and eighteenth centuries until about 1780, and then the nineteenth century from about 1835 onwards. Bags and purses are to be seen in dress especially in the Middle Ages, the years 1780–1830 and in the twentieth century.

In the *Middle Ages*, purses, pouches and bags were usually attached to the belt or girdle. This was the custom for both sexes and the pouch might be visible, hung or slung on or from the belt, or might be attached to the belted undertunic for safety and so was not visible on the exterior to attract the notice of thieves. These bags were of leather, silk, wool or linen and were often embroidered, fringed or tasselled. They were known by various names: the *almoner*, worn by nobles or used especially for alms, the *gipser* (*gipcière*), the *scrip* or wallet, or merely purse, pouch or bag.

In the *later eighteenth century* the bag was revived since the costume for both men and women was fitting and slender. The *stocking purse* was popular, a long knitted purse which had a good capacity. For ladies the *reticule* (also known sardonically as a ridicule or indispensable) was fashionable, especially in the years 1795–1820. At a time when the costume was flimsy and the silhouette slender, pockets were small or non-existent so the reticule was carried over the arm. It was dainty, made of delicate fabrics – velvet, silk or satin – and was embroidered or beaded. The top was often gathered in with a draw-cord. The reticule contained a handkerchief, perfume bottle, a fan and a purse.

The ample crinoline and bustle skirts of the nineteenth century, with their many full petticoats, made easy the concealment of purses, handkerchiefs, etc. in pockets, but after the First World War, in the 1920s, with the reversion to the slender silhouette, the *handbag* came into its own. Styles

MODERN BABY WEAR
Carry bag.

One-piece playsuit

Romper

Baby dress with
knickers to match

Almoner or purse.
German, c.1310

English purse,
c.1450

Velvet purse with
silver clasp. Gold
cord and tassels,
fourteenth century

Italian belt purses,
1490–5

French First Empire
reticule

Suède handbag,
1950. Zip fastener

Velvet handbag,
1960

Embroidered,
beaded, silk
handbag, metal
mount, 1927

Handbag,
English,
1941

Shoulder bag,
Spanish, 1945

Maroon silk
reticule, c.1806

English envelope
handbag, 1929

varied in the succeeding years from reticule designs at first to flat *envelope bags* in the 1920s and early 1930s then to *shoulder bags* in the 1940s (revived in the 1960s) and to zip-fastened box shapes and a tremendous variety in forms by the 1960s and 1970s. In the twentieth century there has been a spread of designs made specifically for certain occasions and functions: the *evening bag* of gold, silver or brocade, the *beach bag*, the *shopping bag*, the *casual bag*, the smart *town bag*, etc. Interior fittings have become important with compartments for mirror, comb, lipstick, purse or wallet, compact, passport and cigarettes. Summer and sports bags are made in a variety of materials, including all kinds of plastic, and are decorated in many different ways.

Baku, Balibuntal
A fine straw, like flax, grown in the Philippines and woven in China. Used for hats and toques.

Balaclava
A woollen, knitted head-covering, like a helmet, extending over the head and shoulders. Worn, especially by soldiers, in the 1890s and again in the First and Second World Wars. Named after the site of the Crimean battle in 1854.

Balandrana
A wide, long, full cloak with a hood, worn as protection against the rain by travellers in the Middle Ages and in the sixteenth and seventeenth centuries.

Balayeuse (sweeper)
In the late nineteenth century, pleated, stiffened dust-ruffles, called sweepers or balayeuses, were sewn to the underside of the hems of ladies' long, trailing gown skirts to act as dusters to absorb the dirt from the floor or street and to protect the gown fabric on top (see *Petticoat*).

Baldric, baldrick
A leather belt or silk sash, richly ornamented, slung round the body from one shoulder to the opposite hip to carry a

BALACLAVA

BALDRIC
Black leather baldric embroidered in silver thread, 1650, English

Decorated leather baldric, *c*.1640, Swedish

Blue silk baldric with gold bells, 1400–1415, English

sword, dagger, powder-horn, pouch or bugle. It was worn in the Middle Ages from about 1340 onwards, also in the seventeenth century. Medieval baldrics were often ornamented with a row of metal bells attached to the lower edge. A similar broad belt worn in the sixteenth and eighteenth centuries was called a *bandoleer* or *bandolier*.

Ballet dress
Until the 1830s, ballet costume was adapted by the theatre from the fashionable dress of the day. In 1730 Marie Camargo had broken with tradition by wearing an ankle-length skirt with knickers beneath when she introduced the *entrechat* into the

BALLET DRESS
Design for 'La Sylphide', 1832

Classical ballet dress, 1882

Modern classical ballet dress
(tutu), 1976

ballerina's dance vocabulary. Gradually dances became more energetic and demanding and a freer costume was essential. It was Marie Taglioni who wore the first classical ballet dress designed for her in the title role of *La Sylphide* in 1832. This was a white dress with low neck, fitting bodice, short, puff sleeves and a bell-shaped skirt reaching to mid-calf level. The only decoration was a flower garland round her head, a posy at her bosom and a bracelet round each wrist. The theme of the costume was a dainty ethereal femininity, and the resounding success of the design established the supremacy of the ballerina over the male dancer.

After this the skirt was gradually shortened to a lampshade-shaped design, especially from the 1880s as Russian dancers introduced more demanding, acrobatic movements. The modern ballet skirt is the *tutu*, the word derived from the French child's term for bottom. It was first applied to the short petticoat worn under the skirt but was later adopted for the very short classical ballet skirt, though it is also sometimes used for the longer 'Sylphide' skirt. The tutu was made from tarlatan in the form of briefs to which several rows of tarlatan frills were attached, each longer than the one below. Over this were added two more frills, decorated with embroidery, beads and sequins, the edge stiffened with wire. The tutu was attached to the fitting bodice at a tight basque. With the tutu were worn tights and satin shoes. Male dancers continued to wear tights and a decorative shirt and short jacket.

Dancing *sur la pointe* also became a part of classical ballet in about 1830. At first the toes were padded with wool, but later in the nineteenth century were blocked and the ends darned to give support.

Balmoral
In 1852 Prince Albert purchased the Balmoral estate and supervized the demolition of the modest Balmoral House and

then the building of the palace in 'Scottish baronial' style for his dear Victoria. From this stemmed the renewed interest in Scottish fashion which ranged from tartans to garments and ornament. In the 1850s and 1860s several items of wear were prefixed by the name 'Balmoral'. These were garments which the Queen and Prince Albert liked to wear at Balmoral Castle and which were suited to country use. They included the *Balmoral boot*, which was a lace-up shoe for men and an ankle-length boot for women; the *Balmoral cap* based on the traditional Scottish blue-bonnet; and the *Balmoral petticoat*, made of striped or patterned wool and acting as an under-skirt when visible as the gown skirt was looped up for easier walking in the hills. There was also a *Balmoral cloak*, which was short and hooded; a *Balmoral mantle*, which was longer, more voluminous and had shoulder capes; and the *Balmoral jacket*, which was fitting and waist-length, ending in points in front like a waistcoat. (See also *Scottish highland dress*.)

Band

The word was used in the early sixteenth century to refer to the *shirt neck-band*. During the decades of the wearing of the ruff in the remainder of the sixteenth century, and also the elegant collars of the seventeenth century, the word band referred to all the variations in these types of neckwear, both masculine and feminine.

In the sixteenth century the *band-box* was used to store the ruffs. As these ruffs became larger, so the band-box increased in size also. It was circular and often beautifully decorated (see *Ruff*). The band-box continued in use in the seventeenth century for the elegant and valuable collars which were fashionable until they began to be replaced by the cravat in the 1660s.

The word band, in the seventeenth century, referred equally to an upturned or horizontal collar – when it was called a *standing-band* – or to the soft, unstiffened collar which was carefully draped over the shoulders of the doublet or gown and was termed the *falling-band*. Such collars were white, of lace or lace-edged cambric or

Falling band,
French, 1635

Falling band,
Prince Rupert,
1635–40

Falling band,
Queen Henrietta
Maria of England,
1634

Falling band,
English, 1645

Standing band,
James I of England,
c.1620

silk, and were tied at the throat, as the ruffs had been, by *band strings*. These terminated in tiny tassels or crochet-covered balls. The seventeenth-century falling-band, known also as a *rabat*, continued for ecclesiastical use in its smaller, linen strip or tab form. Such strips were known as *short-bands* and were worn well into the nineteenth century by ministers of religion, academics and members of the legal profession. Nonconformist ministers continued wearing short-bands until comparatively recently.

Bandanna, Bandana
From the Hindi word *bãndhnũ*, which refers to a method of dyeing wherein the cloth is tied in places to prevent it from receiving. In the eighteenth century, large silk – and later cotton – squares were imported from India. These had a dark red or blue ground and white and yellow spots left by this process. They were used as neckcloths or headkerchiefs. Later, nineteenth-century cotton bandannas had spotted patterns produced by chemical means.

Bandeau
1) A narrow ribbon or jewelled fillet encircling the hair at the brow.
2) In the early years of the twentieth century, a narrow band sewn inside a woman's hat to make it possible to adjust the hat to the desired angle.

Bandle
An Irish measurement of two feet in length.

Barathea
In the nineteenth century, a black fabric, used for mourning, made of a mixture of silk and wool. In modern times, a worsted or synthetic fabric with a pebble weave. The worsted barathea is traditionally used especially for military uniforms of quality.

Barbette
In France usually refers to the veil fixed above the ears to the hair or head-dress and which then fell in folds to hide the neck (see also *Wimple*). In England, in the thirteenth century, it more commonly

BARBETTE
English, mid-thirteenth century.
Barbette

c.1190. French style of barbette. With the veil or couvrechef this forms the wimple

refers to the strip of white linen worn under the chin and drawn up at each side to be fastened on top of the head or attached to the hair at each side above the ears.

Barège
A gauze-like semi-transparent fabric originally made at Barèges in the French Pyrenees in the 1850s. Made of silk and wool, wool, or cotton and wool. Sometimes printed with floral designs and referred to as Barège de Pyrenées. In the later nineteenth century, Barège-Grenadine was a cotton version.

Barracan
In the seventeenth century, a coarse camlet, the word of Arab or Persian origin. Later refers to a coarse cloth of Spanish goathair woven in with a mixture of wool.

Basque
An extension of the bodice below the waist to form a short skirt or tabs. Seen in men's sixteenth and seventeenth-century doublets, when it derives from Basque dress. Also in the nineteenth century in feminine gowns with crinoline and bustle skirts.

Basquina, basquine
An outer petticoat or skirt made of heavy, rich material, worn in the sixteenth century over farthingale hoops; a wide skirt, usually open in front. In Spain, where it originated, the two edges were often brought together in the centre front and held by decorative points (*puntas*). Alternatively, the basquina was open in an inverted V displaying its rich decoration with large-motif design.

Bathing dress
Men and women enjoyed bathing in fresh water lakes and rivers for centuries. They used to prefer to bathe naked as the only available bathing costumes were of coarse, heavy material, of similar style to their normal clothes, and were therefore most uncomfortable when wet. In the eighteenth century bathing in the sea became popular; it was advocated for health reasons and

BASQUE
Spanish, 1550. Basque doublet
and jerkin

English, 1863. Basque jacket

BASQUINA
Spanish, 1564. Basquina

people began to enjoy it. The sexes were separated for such sea-bathing, but it was not easy to maintain privacy for this and the ladies tended to be spied upon by interested males.

Men continued to bathe naked until after the mid-nineteenth century. Indeed, they strove furiously to continue the practice, but nineteenth-century propriety got the better of them and, one by one, the town councils of fashionable resorts began to insist that men should wear a costume. Such costumes, made like shorts, had been available since the 1840s but as they were fashioned from non-elasticated serge or worsted, as soon as they became saturated they descended to the ankles, not only failing in their purpose of maintaining modesty, but becoming an actual hazard in struggling out of the sea and up the beach. Many men used the bathing machines which enabled them to plunge in and out of the sea without being visible to public gaze, but as others continued the practice of running

over the sands and through the shallow waters, the town councils issued their edicts: bathing suits or no bathing.

The problem of the descending shorts was solved by 1880 with the all-in-one costume which completely covered the torso and had a round neck and short sleeves and encased the thighs. At first such costumes were striped horizontally but soon plain costumes in a dark shade were usual. They were made of flannel, serge or worsted until a knitted, jersey fabric was introduced, which was a great improvement. Gradually, in the twentieth century, the top part of the costume was abandoned with the introduction of elasticated fabrics and, later, synthetic fibres led to the hip-hugging, abbreviated trunks of today.

The history of *women's bathing suits* is a longer one. From the later eighteenth century women had worn a covering, despite the fact that they bathed from machines and so entered the sea unobtru-

Flannel bathing
gown, cap, 1830

Red and white
bathing suit,
c.1880

Edwardian bathing
costume. Check
cotton. Cap with
bow, stockings and
shoes

Blue serge bathing
costume, 1885–90.
Shoes, stockings
and cap. Lace and
braid trimming

Black and white
bathing costume,
1920s
Belt, braid, edging.
White rubber cap

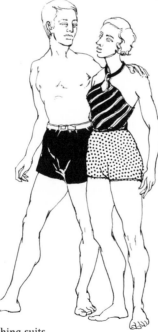

Bathing suits,
early 1930s.
Halter neckline

Bikini and trunks.
Modern bathing
attire

sively, descending the steps of the machine and immediately entering the water. Ladies undressed in the machine hut and donned a shapeless flannel gown which was fastened by a draw-string at the neck and covered the whole body. As they descended the steps they were hidden by an awning, known as a 'modesty hood', so it is difficult to imagine what any wandering males might glimpse, especially as the machines were guarded by fully clothed female attendants who scared off such lingerers. These ladies were often referred to as 'dippers', as one of their functions was to make sure that nervous bathers took the plunge quickly and without fuss.

About the time that the men's complete bathing costume was introduced, the ladies also were provided with a suit designed for them. This was a complex outfit, bearing a marked resemblance to normal day wear. Made of flannel, serge or worsted, it consisted of pantalettes to the knee or ankle and, on top, a dress with a collar, short sleeves and a skirt nearly to the knee. Colours were sombre and decoration excessive, from lace-edging to braid and embroidery. The costume was completed by dark stockings, tie-on-shoes and a bathing cap. In the 1880s and 1890s, bathing dresses became more elaborate. Ladies wore elegant hats, and even had corsets under their bathing costumes to preserve their slim waistlines. Decoration included ruching and ribbon bows and sashes.

In the twentieth century fashions changed slowly at first. Edwardian bathing suits were elaborate and over-dressed but colours became lighter and more varied and fabrics were less heavy. It was just before the First World War that the clinging one-piece suit was accepted and this still had sleeves and reached to the knees with a skirt. The famous Australian swimmer Annette Kellerman had worn a sleeveless, one-piece suit ending above the knees at this time* and, in 1920, Jantzen introduced in America a one-piece, elasticized, rib-knit wool suit which became popular so that slowly, costumes became more daring. In the 1920s suits were all sleeveless and only covered the hips. One-piece suits were in clinging jersey and pieces began to be cut out from the sides; this led to the backless designs with narrow shoulder straps of the 1930s, also the two-piece of halter-neck top and pantees. Colours became gay and suits were made of varied materials, often patterned. In 1947 the French introduced the *bikini* with the smallest of bras and briefs, fashionable especially on the beaches of the south of France, but for some time banned by such strongly Roman Catholic countries as Spain and Italy. Elasticized, synthetic fibres have since made a tremendous variety of design of suit possible for all ages and tastes.

Batik

A Javanese word meaning wax-painting. It refers to an ancient method of resist-dye process which is thought to have originated in India. In Java, among ruins of temples some 1,200 years old, there have been found sculptured figures wearing garments similar to those worn there today and decorated with the same traditional patterns.

In Java, the resist is made from beeswax, some animal fat, paraffin and a little resin to make it adhere well to the fabric. Cotton is generally used, or sometimes silk, and the wax is applied hot so that it flows easily and is absorbed by the material. A *tjanting* is used to apply the wax; this is a small copper cup with a slender, curved spout on one side and a handle on the other. The wax protects the parts of the design which it is desired to leave uncoloured so that the material cannot absorb the dye when it is applied. In Java, the wax is removed and replaced in a different section of the design for each new colour to be dyed, whereas in Europe and America it is more usual to dye one colour over another, only removing the wax when this becomes too difficult. Here batik is also used in a greater variety of fabrics – on wool or velvet, or even straw. Batik was introduced into

* In 1907 she was arrested on a beach in Boston for wearing a brief one-piece swimsuit in defiance of accepted conventions regarding bathing wear.

Europe by the Dutch. In modern practice, a finely pointed brush is often used to apply the wax instead of a *tjanting*.

Batiste
A finely woven linen fabric named after Baptiste Chambrai, the French weaver from Cambrai. It is the French term for cambric. In the nineteenth century it was applied to a cotton muslin. There was then also *batiste de laine*, a wool batiste which was a lightweight, fine wool, sometimes mixed with silk, similar to challis (see *Challis*).

Batting
Cotton or wool fibre prepared in sheets for padding garments and bed-coverings.

Baudekin, baudkin, bodkin
A rich, decorative fabric originally made with a warp of gold thread and a weft of silk. Also called *cloth of baudekin*, first introduced into Europe from Baghdad to Cyprus and Sicily, and from thence brought westwards by the Crusaders in the thirteenth century. The name stems from the Italian *baldachin*, later *baldacchino*. Afterwards the word acquired a wider interpretation as a rich brocade or shot silk.

Bayadere
A striped fabric in silk and wool, the stripes being alternately matt and shiny. Also the name of a Hindu dancing girl.

Beachwear and seaside dress
Days out by the sea and seaside holidays became increasingly popular during the nineteenth century. Children played and adults sat on the beach; there was paddling and swimming, but there was no sign of costume designed for enjoyment on the sands in the sun – everyone wore their normal clothes. For ladies, this was petticoats and flounces, crinolines and bustles, hats with flowers and ribbons, even veils, gloves and parasols. They wore corsets with boning and their necklines were high at the throat. For men also, hats and gloves were essential, worn with a three-piece suit, boots, a stiff collar and tie. The children, too, were dressed – or rather over-dressed – as usual. Even in the 1890s beachwear for a child would include woollen underwear and stockings, serge knickerbockers, skirt and jacket and a high-necked blouse, boots, hat and gloves. For men and boys there was a faint lessening of the strictures in the 1880s and 1890s; a straw hat could replace the bowler and a striped blazer and plain flannels the suit. But for ladies and little girls, there was no let-up.

By 1870, rubber-soled canvas shoes were being produced for wear on the beach. These were called sand-shoes but the popular name, *plimsolls*, stuck when the manufacturer added a strip of rubber round the shoe to cover the join between sole and upper. This was likened to the then topical plimsoll line on ships.

It was in the 1920s that the cult of sunbathing began and by the early 1930s beaches in the south of France were strewn with sun-worshippers. *Sun costumes* of all kinds were designed; skirts with backless tops and jackets or capes and floppy hats to match and, especially fashionable, *beach pyjamas*. These were slimly cut over the hips, then flared or were gored at the bottom, not unlike the so-called 'French cut' of ladies' trousers in the 1970s.

Beadwork
Can be done by embroidery, knitting or weaving. Woven beadwork is produced on a small loom where the beads are threaded, one row at a time, upon the weft. Each row of wefted beads is then laid below the warp threads and the weft returned above the warp and threaded through each bead. Thus beads lie between two warp threads and are supported by two lines of weft.

BEADWORK
Beadwork weaving

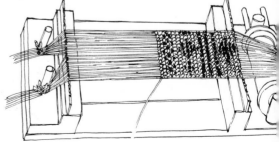

Sea-side dress in 1826, English

Mother and daughter. Sea-side
dress in 1870, English

Beachwear, 1938. Printed cotton
sun suit, English

Sea-side dress in 1885, English

Beach pyjamas, French, 1931

Beard

All imaginable permutations have been experimented with over the centuries in the growing of beards by men. In some cultures the wearing of a vigorous beard, curled, perfumed, even sprinkled with gold dust, was a symbol of virility; in others it was regarded as unhygienic and characteristic of the lower orders and the well-born man would therefore take care to be clean-shaven. In most periods peasants grew natural beards, partly for warmth and partly to avoid the problems of shaving with cold water, no soap and most inadequate razors. Beards, particularly stylish ones, were, through the ages, carefully tended by the upper classes and became the prerogative of certain professions or occupations as well as having religious significance. The Jews have been one example of a race which has used the beard, together with the coiffure and certain items of clothing, to differentiate between themselves and other races and religions. Through the centuries the Jew was urged never to shave or trim the corners of his beard but to grow it full along the whole jaw-line (see *Jewish dress*).

Although beards have, at all times, been grown by the lower classes and by elderly men, there have been many civilizations and ages which have preferred to be predominantly clean-shaven. Among these were the *Sumerians*, the *Minoans* and *Mycenaeans* and, to a large extent, the *Greeks* and *Romans*, the latter especially in the eastern Byzantine empire. In *Europe* and the *West* men were more usually clean-shaven in the later Middle Ages and early Renaissance, in the eighteenth century when wigs were deemed incompatible with the growing of beards, the early nineteenth century and most of the twentieth – apart from enthusiasm among the hirsute young in the post-war years.

Of the ancient cultures, the *Egyptians* were usually clean-shaven but kings and high officials often wore a false beard or postiche, made of plaited hair. This was held in place by a decorative strap attached to the headdress or round the ears under the wig. In *Mesopotamia*, the Assyrians, the Babylonians and later the Persians took great pride in their beards, which were long and waved, the ends curled into tightly frizzed ringlets. If the natural growth were not adequate, false hair was added to achieve a vigorous, bushy effect. Black hair was favoured, dyed if necessary, and perfumes and oils were used freely. In *Greece* and *Rome* beards were worn chiefly by older men, peasants and slaves. When grown by Greeks and Romans of note, beards were usually short, curly and styled to extend round the jaw. The *Etruscans* are frequently depicted in sculpture and wall-paintings with beards. These are also curly and short and extend round the jaw-line; they are dressed to a point at the chin.

In Europe, in the centuries which followed the collapse of the western Roman Empire, full beards were generally worn. In the primitive living conditions of the so-called *Dark Ages*, especially in the colder northern areas, it was more natural to grow a beard than to carry out the painful process of shaving. The beards were roughly trimmed to varying shapes so that a Saxon beard might differ marginally from a Frankish or Gallic one. In the *early Middle Ages* beards continued to be the norm and in the twelfth century in particular were especially long and often trained into two points or forks. In these years, the more distinguished the gentleman, in general, the shorter, neater and curlier his beard.

The *later fourteenth*, the *fifteenth* and the *earlier sixteenth centuries* were years when most men of rank and position were clean-shaven. In the *second half* of the *sixteenth century* in Europe the beard returned as a fashionable characteristic. The Spanish were the pacesetters of the European mode at the time and the typical Spanish beard was small, pointed and confined to the chin. From about *1550 until 1650* there were many fashions of beard, all fairly small and neat but shaped differently and known by a variety of names. There was a *pencil beard*, little more than a narrow tuft on the chin, the *Cadiz beard*, called after the expedition to that city in 1596 and the *Roman T beard*,

Roman emperor,
AD 200

Twelfth century,
English

Egyptian pharaoh

Greek, sixth
century BC

Assyrian, ninth
century BC

Persian, fifth
century BC

Etruscan, seventh
century BC

Carolingian, 850 AD

Roman T, 1590

Austrian spade
shape, c.1610

Charles I. Van
Dyck beard, c.1640

Spanish style, 1580

Edward I, c.1300

Edward VII style,
1895 (when Prince
of Wales)

Napoleon III,
imperial beard

Swedish, 1640

Swallow's tail
beard, c.1560

Russian boyar,
sixteenth century

in the early seventeenth century, which was neat and pointed. Similar was the *Van Dyck beard*, popularized by the painter's portraits of Charles I and his court. The sixteenth-century *spade beard* was larger and shaped like a spade on a playing card and like the actual implement of that period. There was also a *square cut beard*, which was bushy and trimmed straight across at the bottom; the *cathedral beard* was large and imposing and frequently worn by academics and churchmen; a *stiletto beard* was a very slender strip of hair, and the *swallow's tail beard* was forked at the end and brushed out bushily like a Swiss lansquenet's style. All these were of the later sixteenth century. To tend them, men carried a small beard brush and comb, and starched, oiled and perfumed the beards to maintain their shape and attraction. Some men even slept with them in curlers or with cardboard boxes over them to protect the grooming.

By the *second half* of the *seventeenth century*, the interest was centering on the wig and beards were not fashionable again until the later *nineteenth century*. The middle years of this century were a heyday for facial hair, but this was generally in side whiskers rather than beard form (see *Moustache* and *Whiskers*). Napoleon III popularized the *imperial* in the second half of the century. This was a small, tufted beard in the centre of the chin. In the 1890s Edward VII of England, then Prince of Wales, helped to make the pointed, but fuller, spade shape fashionable again, but with the coming of the twentieth century, beards, though still worn by some, have never returned to high fashion.

Bearer

1) Used in the years 1670–1720 to denote a padded roll worn by ladies round the waist to give the desired shape to the skirt.
2) Used in the mid-seventeenth century for stiffening inserted in boot hose tops.

Beauty patch

In Europe, beauty patches had been worn in ancient Rome and were re-introduced by the Italians in the sixteenth century.

Made of black silk or velvet, the patches were adhesive on one side and, by the seventeenth and eighteenth centuries, when they were extremely fashionable, they were cut into different shapes of stars, crescent moons, hearts, etc. They were carried on the person in exquisite, dainty *patch boxes*, each with a tiny mirror in the lid – a forerunner of the twentieth century powder compact. The patches diverted attention from the smallpox scars which marred the complexions of the majority of people. The patches were carefully placed for maximum effect near the eyes, on the cheeks, the forehead, the throat and the breasts. In France the word *mouche*, meaning fly, was used for these patches.

Beaver

1) An amphibious *rodent* with a coat of soft, warm, brown fur. The best quality comes from the North American continent and from the USSR. In the Middle Ages the fur was used chiefly for gloves; in modern times it is popular for gloves and hats (see *Fur-bearing animals*).
2) The *beaver hat* was originally made from beaver skin but, from the sixteenth century onwards, the hats were fabricated from a felted wool and rabbit fur, with a nap of beaver hair.
3) *Beaver cloth* is a thick-napped woollen cloth, used since the eighteenth century and sheared on one face to produce a close, dense surface to simulate fur. Used chiefly for warm overcoats.
4) *Beaver fustian* was a coarse, rough, over-coating fabric made chiefly in Philadelphia, since about 1800, in a dark blue shade.

Bedgown

A loose, comfortable gown worn only in the bedroom or the house for relaxation and designed for both sexes (see *Welsh dress*).

Bed-jacket

A modern garment designed as a pretty jacket to wear over a nightdress for warmth and elegance while in bed.

BEAUTY PATCH
Lady of the French Court of
Louis XIV wearing beauty
patches

BELT-BOX
Detail of belt-box

BEDOUIN DRESS
Man and woman in home-made garments of white cotton and coloured wool woven from camel and goat hair. Leather boots.

Bronze Age Danish dress. Bronze belt at waist

Bedouin dress

The true Bedouins are the desert Arabs, hardy herdsmen, nomadic and tent-dwellers. Their tents are made of woven goat-hair strips sewn together and hung over a ridge pole. Bedouins inhabit much of the desert area of Middle Eastern countries, with some tribes claiming an ancient lineage back to Abraham.

Bedouin dress is clearly Arab in the shape and type of garments worn, consisting chiefly of a kaffiyeh on the head held in place by the agal (see *Kaffiyeh*), a basic robe (see *Aba*) and, on top, a djellaba or gallibiya (see *Djellaba*). Bedouins generally make their own cloth, much of it woven from camel and goat-hair, and this is brightly coloured. Women, particularly, wear a quantity of metal jewellery – necklaces, earrings, bracelets, anklets and finger rings. Leather boots, shoes and sandals are worn.

Beetling

A textile process for embossing fabrics by means of a beetling machine. As a finish for cotton and linen, which creates a lustre obtained by hammering the fabric over rollers.

Belt-box

Through the ages a bag or purse has been attached to the belt to hold valuables and necessities. Among the finds of the peat bogs of Denmark have been costumes from the Bronze Age which include a bronze belt disc or box attached to a woven, tasselled belt; this was large enough to contain sewing necessities or valuables. The example illustrated, from the Egtved grave, has a central, protruding spike.

Bengal

A cotton gingham fabric, originally imported from Bengal in India. A version woven in coloured stripes was popular from the seventeenth century and was known as 'Bengal stripes'.

Bengaline

So-named because of its similarity to a fabric imported in the seventeenth century from Bengal to England. Later, the (French) word was used to describe a poplin, a mixture of silk and worsted, which was characterized by a wool weft and a corded effect.

Beret, 1830

Basque beret

Tam-o'-shanter

BERET
Beret, Sweden, 1440

BETSIE
Betsie, English, 1810

Beret

This simple form of head-covering has a long history. It is made of a circular piece of woollen cloth or felt which is drawn up round the edge by a thread or a leather thong to make it fit the head. Some designs are very full and have a semi-stiff head-band. Most berets have the characteristic tail in the centre, which is sewn on to cover the central eye of the woven fabric.

Berets were worn by the Cretans, and in Greece and Rome as the *pilos* and *pileus* respectively, and throughout the early Middle Ages related to the biretta. In the sixteenth century, velvet or wool beret-styles of hats were fashionable; these had a turned-up brim. In the 1820s and 1830s, ladies began to wear a beret-style of hat, which also had an upturned brim, this time like a halo. The beret was lavishly trimmed with feathers and, again, velvet was the fashionable material. The hats were especially popular for evening wear. Children, both girls and boys, in the 1890s, wore sailor berets with their sailor suits.

The modern beret takes many forms, most stemming from the Basque design popularized by the French in the 1920s. It was worn by everyone but is most closely associated with the French working-man. In western Europe, in general, berets of this type were fashionable for ladies, worn with suits or coats, during the 1920s and 1930s, though the style has never died out and re-appears from time to time. Another well-known form of the beret is the Scottish

woollen *tam-o'-shanter*. This is a woollen cap in several colours worn at a jaunty angle. Named originally after a poem by Robert Burns, it was very popular in the nineteenth century for both sexes and has been consistently revived for feminine winter headwear in the twentieth. (See also *Greek*, *Roman* and *Scottish Highland dress*.)

Bertha

In the 1840s a deep fall of silk or lace finishing the neck and shoulders and sometimes extended to the waist in ribbon and lace.

Beryl

A transparent, precious stone of great beauty and hardness. In colour bluish-green, yellow, pink and white. Beryl is a silicate of beryllium and aluminium of which varieties include aquamarine and chrysoberyl. The silicate is crystalline, usually in the form of hexagonal prisms.

Bespoke tailoring

Tailored clothes, predominantly for men, which are made to measure. In the USA the equivalent term is 'custom-made'.

Betsie

A tiny ruff or collarette of several rows of lace or lawn, fashionable in the early nineteenth century. Named after the ruffs of the time of Elizabeth I of England.

Bias

Woven fabric cut obliquely across the warp and weft. A term used since the Middle Ages to describe fabric cut on the cross. Medieval hose and, later, underwear cut in this way fitted and clung better to the limbs and figure. Bias binding, also cut on the cross, is suited to finishing hems and edges of a curve or a gored skirt.

BIEDERMEIER STYLE OF DRESS
Biedermeier dress, 1834

Biedermeier style of dress

The name applied to a style of furnishing and furniture in Germany in the years 1825–45. The furniture was luxuriously cushioned and padded and the furnishings were of heavy, tasselled draperies. The name was also given to the style of dress in German-speaking countries at the time which displayed similar characteristics of fullness and decoration.

Biggin

The word comes from the French *béguin* which, in turn, stems from the coif-like cap worn by the Béguines, who were members of lay sisterhoods initiated in the Low Countries in the twelfth century. The term biggin was used to apply to a baby's bonnet, a child's cap, like a coif, in the sixteenth and seventeenth centuries, also to a man's night-cap, worn in bed. In the seventeenth and eighteenth centuries the biggin, still in the form of a close-fitting coif or cap, was worn under the heavy wigs.

Blanchet

White flour or powder for the face (see *Cosmetics*).

BLIAUD
Bliaud with embroidered borders at neck, sleeves and hem, *c.*1070

Bliaud

A long, belted overtunic worn by both sexes between the eleventh and early fourteenth centuries. Noblemen wore a calf- or ankle-length bliaud, usually decorated at hem and neck, and with the skirt slit at the sides to facilitate riding. A shorter, knee-length bliaud was worn by men of other classes. Ladies were dressed in a ground-length bliaud, similarly decorated but cut to be more close-fitting over the breasts and waist and having wide, open sleeves over the lower arm. The word derives from the German *blialt*, meaning cloth.

Bloomers

The word was coined from the *Reform Dress* initiated by *Mrs Amelia Jenks*

Bliaud with double girdle, *c.*1140

BLOOMERS
The Reform Dress. 'Bloomer'
costume.

BOA
Feather boa, 1805,
Dutch

Blouse

Introduced into the feminine costume of western Europe and America in the second half of the nineteenth century. A separate, loose bodice of different colour and material from the skirt, usually finished with a belt or sash. Blouses became especially fashionable in the 1890s when tailored suits were popular for holiday and less formal wear. Blouses were of shirt design with high collars, tie or bow and full sleeves with fitted cuffs, or were softly feminine with flounces and lace ruffles. The American *shirtwaist* was a development from the masculine shirt and was generally white. The *Edwardian blouse* was an important part of a lady's wardrobe. Several designs were fashionable but all were beautifully stitched and elegantly draped in front over a tightly drawn sash. They had high collars and intricate decoration in embroidery, lace, pleating and flounces. *Evening blouses*, with short sleeves, were introduced in the 1890s.

In the twentieth century, especially in the years 1925–40, many styles of blouse were worn, such as the *middy blouse*, based upon the midshipman's white and navy seaman's blouse, and the *sash blouse*, which had long ends crossed over in front and tied at the waist at the back. The *peasant* style, worn for many years in central and eastern Europe, was introduced in the 1930s and has been revived in fashion from time to time since. It is very full and made of a white, thin fabric such as voile, lawn or silk and is stitched with coloured silk smocking at neck, wrists and waist. In the post-war years the longer, *tunic blouse* has become fashionable, worn outside the skirt or trousers, and is especially popular with the latter.

Boa

Long, round tippet of feathers, fur, tulle or lace, fashionable especially in the early and late nineteenth century. The boa was long enough (about 7–8 ft long) to wind round the lady's neck so that the ends hung down to the knees. The fashion was revived in the 1920s. The name clearly derives from the South American family of serpents which kill by constriction.

Bloomer, a mid-western American. Mrs Bloomer was an ardent campaigner in the mid-nineteenth century for a more sensible and healthful attire for women and one which would give them freedom of movement, a facility seriously lacking in the corseted, petticoated, crinoline gowns of the day. The Reform Dress consisted of a jacket and knee-length skirt worn over full Turkish-type trousers. It was these trousers which were called bloomers, and the women who supported Mrs Bloomer in her defiance of convention by wearing the outfit were also referred to as bloomers. Mrs Bloomer travelled to London and to Dublin in 1851, dressed in the new mode, to hold mass meetings to popularize it. The exercise was a total failure, despite the spasmodic efforts of a few brave women who, for a while, continued to wear the dress in the streets.

The word bloomers was revived in the 1890s when women began to wear the full style of knickerbockers with a jacket and blouse for sports and leisure activities such as cycling and walking. These bloomers were also known as *rationals*. (See also *Sports and Recreational Dress*.)

Evening blouse of
silk and lace with
black velvet ribbon
decoration and
sash, 1907

Silk and cotton
blouse with ruched
trimming, 1865

Mauve silk blouse
with ruffles and
tucks, 1895

Striped jersey
blouse worn
outside the skirt,
1960

Striped shirt blouse
worn with tie for
sport, 1893

Middy sleeveless
blouse. White with
navy and white
collar and navy tie
and belt, 1930

White voile
peasant-style
blouse with
smocking in
coloured silks.
Worn with dirndl
skirt, 1934

Crêpe de chine
blouse with shirred
and embroidered
decoration, 1904

Bobbin

1) An article round which thread or yarn is wound. A wooden or metal cylinder, flanged at one or both ends, perforated so that it may revolve on a spindle for use in spinning or weaving. A bobbin is also the small spool used in the shuttle of a sewing-machine (see also *Weaving* and *Spinning*).
2) In lace-making, the bobbin is a small pin of wood with a notch (see also *Lace*).

Bobbinet

A net of twisted cotton or silk yarn originally made with bobbins. Used especially for lace grounds.

Bodice

The upper part of a woman's dress above the waist. The word derives from the later medieval garment which was in two parts and known as a pair of bodys (bodies). These were made of leather or canvas and boned, the two portions being hooked together at front and back. From this developed the laced underbodice or corset (see *Corset*).

Bodkin

1) A long pin used to fasten up ladies' hair in ancient Greece and Rome, also in Europe until after the eighteenth century.
2) A pointed instrument for piercing holes in cloth.
3) A short, pointed weapon like a dagger.
4) Since the eighteenth century, a blunt-ended needle with a large eye for threading ribbon, cord or elastic through loops, eyelet holes or a hem.

Bombasine, bombazeen

A twilled dress fabric made of cotton and worsted or silk and worsted. From the seventeenth century it was generally woven in black and used for mourning fabric.

Bombast, bombace

A padding used to distend garments, made of raw cotton or cotton wool, in the sixteenth century. From the 1580s the Spanish style of peasecod-belly and padded trunk hose led to stuffing with cotton rags and wool as well as flax and bran. These styles were fashionable all over Europe but especially in Spain, France and England (see *Peasecod-belly*).

Bonded fabric

A comparatively recent process where differing fabrics can be bonded back to back, thus doing away with the need for a lining; or, alternatively, the fibres of one type of fabric are held together by plastic and adhesive, making a warmer, more durable material which tends to keep its shape better in garment form after dry cleaning.

Bonnet

From the Middle Ages until after the sixteenth century, the term was used to describe many types of small, soft head-covering. In the early sixteenth century men wore a bonnet (bonet) which was usually made of black or dark velvet. It had a soft crown and a brim which was turned up all round and slit or cut at intervals, the edges being fastened by aglets and the brim decorated by a brooch or jewel. Because so many fine bonnets of this type were made there, it was often called a *Milan bonnet*. An alternative style, the *necked bonnet*, had the brim on the back portion pulled down while the front part was still turned up.

The traditional *Scottish bonnet* was recorded from the seventeenth century onwards. It was made of wool, woven in one piece and, most commonly, blue. The wearer's ribbon cockade showed his allegiance by its colour, and feathers were worn to denote rank.

The *feather bonnet* of the North American Indian is a spectacular creation (the one illustrated is in the Royal Scottish Museum in Edinburgh). Such bonnets are a late development and were reserved for wear by chiefs on special occasions only. The example shown has a skin cap decorated by bead embroidery, scalp locks and owl feathers. The tail is of white cotton, bound with navy serge. The dyed buzzard feathers are wrapped and bound on with red wool. Like the impressive example in the Birmingham Museum and Art Gallery, the

Chignon bonnet, 1800

Scottish bonnet, c.1800

From hat to bonnet, c.1786

Tudor or Milan bonnet, c.1500

North American Indian feather bonnet (Sioux)

Gipsy bonnet, 1808

Beehive bonnet, 1803

Tall bonnet, 1815

Early Victorian bonnet, 1839

Mary Stuart bonnet, c.1820

Poke bonnet, c.1819

Drawn bonnet, c.1840

Wide bonnet, c.1835

Large-brimmed bonnet, 1828–30

Bibi or cottage bonnet, c.1850

Spoon bonnet, c.1863

Silk bonnet, 1857

Gipsy bonnet, c.1867

Silk bonnet, 1872

Chip straw bonnet with ribbon, lace and plume decoration, 1883

Scottish Indian bonnet stems from the Sioux American Indian.

The *nineteenth century* was the age of the bonnet and it was then entirely a feminine head-covering. The fashion started in the later years of the eighteenth century, at which time the demarcation line between a hat and a bonnet was undefined but, in general, a bonnet was tied under the chin with ribbons and had little or no brim at the back. Late eighteenth-century styles either followed the very large hat designs or were small and dainty.

By 1800–10 a number of hat styles were being adapted into bonnets by the addition of a scarf or ribbons tied round and under the chin. There was a *gipsy style*, usually of straw, and the small-brimmed *Grecian chignon* design. The *beehive bonnet*, also usually of straw, was so called because of its characteristic shape. The *conversation bonnet* had one side of its brim coyly turned back, the other side primly pointing forwards to hide the cheek.

After 1810 a clear distinction was now apparent between hat and bonnet designs. The latter had no brim at the back and were tied under the chin with wide, long ribbons. In the years up till 1850, the bonnet increased in popularity, though there was competition from the large hats of the 1830s. Between 1810 and 1820 the crown of the bonnet extended upwards to accommodate the more complex hair-styles and the brim became wider. With the 1830s came the immense brims and a tremendous variety of styles, fabrics and decoration in the form of ribbons, plumes and artificial flowers. In the early years of the century, a cap had still been worn under the bonnet, as in the *Mary Stuart* design illustrated. This bonnet was so called because of its brim dipping in a heart shape in the centre front. By 1830 the wearing of a cap was generally abandoned in favour of displaying the elegant coiffure.

From 1830–35 onwards, the bonnet, often called the *capote*, was the most fashionable head-covering. The brim remained large until 1840, after which time, with the smaller, neater coiffures, it

diminished also. There were many designs of bonnet, but most popular was the *bibi* or *cottage* style in which the crown was small, like a baby's bonnet, and formed a continuous line with the brim. The brim sides curved downwards from the back of the crown to hide the cheeks. In the 1840s the bonnet was worn straight and almost enclosed the wearer's profile but, in the 1850s, the style was more open and worn further back on the head, displaying ruching inside and flowers, lace and ribbons outside. The *drawn bonnet* was fashionable from about 1835. This was made of a series of cane hoops covered in silk and gathered between, like an eighteenth-century calash (see *Calash*). This style, like the poke (poking) bonnet, remained fashionable for many years. The term poke bonnet described the style wherein the open brim projected forward over the face. From 1830 onwards, bonnets were designed with a gathered curtain attached to the brimless back of the garment; this was called the *bavolet*. The popularity of the bonnet continued in the 1860s but it was a smaller design, set back on the head and with the brim curving high above it displaying lace ruffles and flowers inside. This design was referred to as a *spoon bonnet*. The bavolet at the rear was full and fairly long. After 1865 the bonnet became steadily smaller, the bavolet disappeared and, by 1870, designs were tiny – perched on top of the complex, elegant coiffure – the ornamentation of lace, flowers, plumes and ribbons being more extensive than the bonnet itself. Gipsy bonnets returned, this time just a tiny, flat plate covering only the crown of the head. By 1880 hats had more or less replaced, or become indistinguishable from, bonnets.

Boot

Boots have been worn by men from earliest times, at first made in a primitive manner with fur and hides roughly sewn or threaded together with thongs. Through all ages, in most parts of the world, they have been an important item of the wardrobe for travelling, horse-riding and doing

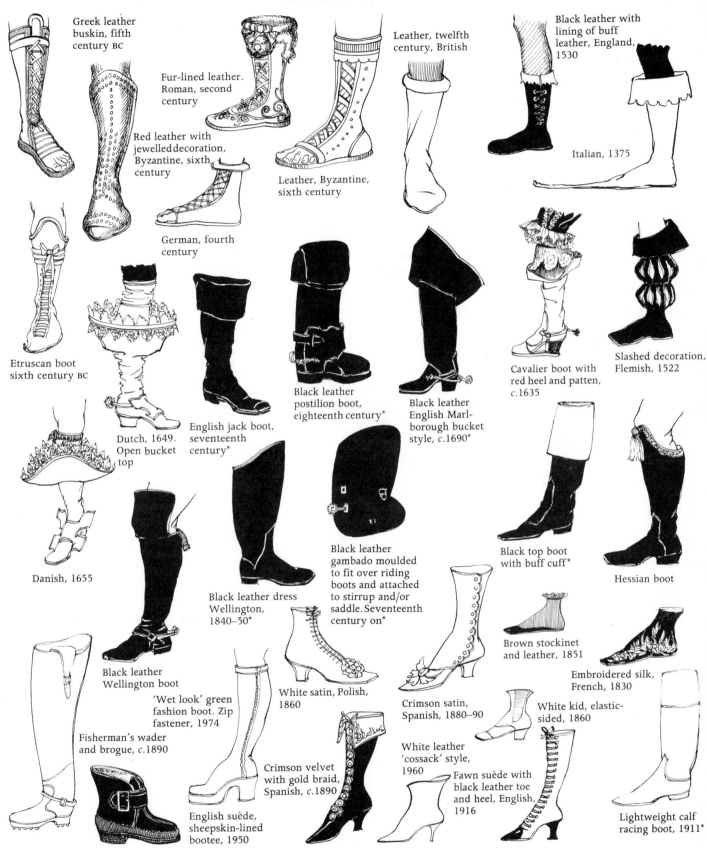

Greek leather buskin, fifth century BC

Fur-lined leather. Roman, second century

Red leather with jewelled decoration, Byzantine, sixth century

Leather, Byzantine, sixth century

German, fourth century

Leather, twelfth century, British

Black leather with lining of buff leather, England, 1530

Italian, 1375

Etruscan boot sixth century BC

Dutch, 1649. Open bucket top

English jack boot, seventeenth century*

Black leather postilion boot, eighteenth century*

Black leather English Marlborough bucket style, c.1690*

Cavalier boot with red heel and patten, c.1635

Slashed decoration, Flemish, 1522

Danish, 1655

Black leather dress Wellington, 1840–50*

Black leather gambado moulded to fit over riding boots and attached to stirrup and/or saddle. Seventeenth century on*

Black top boot with buff cuff*

Hessian boot

Black leather Wellington boot

'Wet look' green fashion boot. Zip fastener, 1974

Fisherman's wader and brogue, c.1890

English suède, sheepskin-lined bootee, 1950

White satin, Polish, 1860

Crimson velvet with gold braid, Spanish, c.1890

Crimson satin, Spanish, 1880–90

White leather 'cossack' style, 1960

Fawn suède with black leather toe and heel, English, 1916

Brown stockinet and leather, 1851

Embroidered silk, French, 1830

White kid, elastic-sided, 1860

Lightweight calf racing boot, 1911*

* Footwear in the Central Museum, Northampton

Russian boot of red
and black leather.
Stitching in black
and yellow

Lapland boot of
natural-coloured
leather. Indented
decoration

Chinese man's boot.
Grey-blue and
white brocade.
Rust-red brocade
cuff
White kid foot

Black cotton
Chinese man's boot.
White felt sole

Kurdish leather
boot

Greenland Eskimo
boot of tan leather
and sealskin. Thigh
length

Yellow leather
Syrian boot. Green
tassel. Red cloth
lining

Canadian Cree
Mukluk (woman's).
Tan moose hide
and beaver fur.
Coloured bead
decoration.

Bedouin riding
boot. Natural-
coloured leather
with stitched
decoration

Light tan pigskin
cowboy boot.
USA, 1965

Black leather
Cossack boot,
c.1850

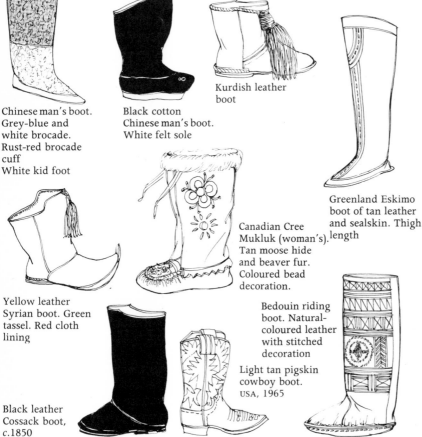

All the footwear on this page is in the Central Museum, Northampton

all kinds of outdoor work; while in colder climates they have proved essential for protection and warmth. Equally, even in hot areas of the world, boots have been essential footwear where the terrain was inhospitable, as in desert or mountain country.

Apart from this utilitarian purpose, boots have, in certain ages, been fashionable footwear equal to, or paramount over, shoes or sandals. In the West, in Britain and Europe, this was especially so in the first half of the seventeenth century, the later eighteenth century and much of the nineteenth, though, in the latter case, the boots were only partly visible for much of the time as they were worn under the trousers. In all these instances, boots were masculine wear but, in the nineteenth century, ladies wore boots also, designs varying from ankle-boots in the early years to high-buttoned footwear at the *fin de siècle*.

In general, the style of the foot part of the boot has followed that of other footwear of the period and country. For example, in Europe, the extended toe of the later fourteenth century is echoed in long-toed boots, while the broad-fronted shoes of the earlier sixteenth century had their counterpart in broad-toed boots. Likewise, in the Balkans and the Middle East, for instance, where toes tend to be turned up at the ends, boots follow the same trend as shoes and sandals.

Boots were worn by the men of *ancient Greece* and *Rome* for travelling and for out-of-doors wear in cold or wet weather. The soles were shaped to each foot and most designs were of leather and about mid-calf in height. They were laced up the front and could be fur-lined and/or decorated with the animal's paws and tail hanging over the top. The *cothurnus* (Latin), *kothornos* (Greek) was a higher boot used primarily for hunting. The name was also applied to the boot with especially thick soles worn by tragic actors in the theatre. Soldiers and peasants wore a heavy boot of undressed hide called a *pero* or *crudus*. *The Etruscans* often wore boots; either short, ankle-length ones or reaching to mid-calf. An Oriental influence shows in the styles which, like their shoes, had upturned points at the toes. The boots were made of cloth or leather, brightly coloured, especially in red, green and brown, and fastened by straps round the ankle or front-lacing. In *Byzantium*, too, the boot was normal footwear for men. Leather was the usual material, in black for everyday wear, while at court, and for important occasions, red leather was *de rigueur*, embroidered and with pearls.

Boots were an important article of clothing in the *Middle Ages*, particularly before about 1350. They were vital as protection against the cold and wet, and for difficult travelling conditions, as well as for life in a house which lacked any comforts and had only bare necessities. Women as well as men wore boots out-of-doors and for travelling. Many styles were mid-calf height, laced up the side and with turned-down or roll tops. A higher boot, reaching up to the knee, was generally called a *buskin* or *brodequin*. Elegant designs worn at court could be in bright colours and made of soft leather, silk, embroidered or brocaded. For riding, boots were usually of leather. In the later four-teenth century, when the toes of footwear were extended to great lengths, boot designs tended to follow suit. A cruder, knee-high boot worn by peasants and labourers was known as a *cocker*. The tall, leather boots with heavy soles, but which left the toes uncovered – like the Greek and Roman designs – were also worn in the early Middle Ages. Known as *heuze* or *houseaux*, they were of varying height from mid-calf to mid-thigh and were in use from the ninth century to the fifteenth.

Boots were not fashionable in the fifteenth and sixteenth centuries. They were worn for travelling and out-of-doors in bad weather, in which case they were of leather, in black or brown, and followed the general footwear designs. In the 1530s and 1540s broad toes were usual and slashes appeared in the leg part of the boot. Later sixteenth-century designs had normal-shaped toes and the boot fitted the leg closely, often to mid-thigh level. In the first half of the *seventeenth century* the boot became an article of high fashion for men; especially between 1625 and 1650, when boots were worn on all occasions, indoors and out. They were made of soft leather and were high, with a funnel top which covered the knee for riding. For town wear this funnel was turned down, giving the open bucket top so characteristic of Cavalier dress. The weight of this top caused the boot to sag and crease across calf and ankle (see also *Boot hose*). On the instep, the leather flap, called a *surpied*, was cut into the familiar butterfly or quatrefoil form. It and the spur were held in place by a leather strap, the *soulette*, fastened under the boot. The boots had heels and, often, platform soles as well.

For riding or military wear the *jack boot* was worn in both the seventeenth and eighteenth centuries. In the seventeenth century it generally had the instep flap of leather. It was made of hard 'jack' or 'bend' leather, which means that the waxed leather was hardened by coating with boiling pitch. It was a heavy boot with square toes, deep square heels and a funnel top to cover the knee. In the eighteenth century the back part was often cut out to facilitate bending of the knee; and a softer and lighter-weight jack boot was also available without an instep flap and with a lighter top.

With the introduction of petticoat breeches in the 1660s, and then the gradual change-over in men's dress from these to coat and breeches, the boot went out of fashion and until the 1780s was retained only as functional protection for bad weather and travelling. In the 1780s it returned to favour as a fashionable item in a man's wardrobe and there was a choice of several styles. All of these, worn with fitting breeches, were also well-fitting, of polished leather in black or light shades of brown, and were generally knee-length or just below. There was the *top boot* (also known as a *jockey* or *jemmy* boot), which was of soft black leather, turned down in a deep fitting cuff at the top to display the light brown leather lining. In the 1790s the *Hessian boot* (known as a Hussar boot in France) became fashionable. Taken from the style worn by the troops of Hesse in Germany, it was of hard, black, polished leather and had a tassel hanging from the top in front.

In the early *nineteenth century* the *Wellington boot* (named after the Duke, but a style also worn by Napoleon and sometimes called a Napoleon boot) was introduced. In military wear it was a high, black leather boot extending above the knee in front and cut away at the back in a square to enable the knee to be bent while on horseback. A somewhat shorter version was worn under the trousers by most men for much of the nineteenth century. This was also of black leather, but softer, and reaching to just below the knee. It had a slender, square toe and a low heel. The waterproof rubberized version of the Wellington boot in half or full length is of similar style but can now be obtained in all colours.

BOOT HOSE TOPS
Boot hose tops,
English, 1640

During the whole of the *nineteenth century* men wore boots rather than shoes, and after about 1820–30, they were worn under the trousers. Apart from the Wellington, styles were buttoned or laced (these last often known as *high-lows*) and were made of black or brown leather with black patent leather for dress wear. There were also *elastic-sided boots* which had an inset of rubberized fabric at each side at the top. These were made possible by the work of *Thomas Hancock* who was studying the problem of elasticizing rubber material from 1820–47. An elastic cloth woven with rubber was developed from his work.

A lady's boot (termed a *bottine* or a *jemima*) was first designed for the young Queen Victoria and it became a popular style for ladies in the 1840s. It was a short boot, made of cloth or leather, with no heel and, often, a patent leather toe-cap. Such boots, which needed no fastenings as the elasticated gussets made them hug the ankle, remained fashionable for most of the nineteenth century, the style changing in tune with the footwear of the time. From about 1830 until the outbreak of the First World War, boots became as fashionable for ladies as shoes or slippers and were the most accepted outdoor wear. In style of heel, shape of toe and fastening, they followed the trend of shoe or slipper. In general, boots worn earlier in the century were short, ankle-length or a little higher – the *Balmoral* was one of these (see *Balmoral*) – while by the 1890s they reached to mid-calf and the highest designs were of the years 1909–13. Ladies' boots were made of all kinds of materials – leather, suède, brocade, silk, velvet, satin – and they could be fastened (apart from the elastic-sided designs) by buttons or laces at the side or up the centre front.

Since 1920 the boot has been largely a feminine article of wear. Not particularly fashionable between the wars, it returned to favour in the 1950s, and since then designs have been as varied as are the materials from which they are made, both natural and man-made. Apart from these fashion boots – particularly appreciated during the Second World War and the austerity years which immediately followed it – there were also the short suède or leather, sheepskin-lined, styles often termed *bootees*.

Beyond this brief survey of boot styles in Europe there are also designs which have been evolved from specific needs or climatic conditions in different parts of the world, as well as traditional methods of using and decorating the materials available to hand in order to make a boot suitable for and attractive to the people using it. From these designs which have been developed in response to specific requirements are the thigh waders for *fishermen*, the warmly-lined boots for *aviators* (especially in the early days of open cockpits), and protective boots for *firemen* and certain industrial workers (see also *Industrial and protective clothing*). The need for a boot to withstand the extreme cold in Arctic regions has led to the Canadian, Eskimo, Norwegian, Finnish and Lapp types. Among these are the *Finnsko* or *Finnesko* boot, as worn in Norway and Lapland, which is made of birch-tanned reindeer skin with the hair left on. Such boots were worn by members of Scott's last expedition to the Antarctic in 1912 and there is reference to this in Scott's diary. A similar boot is the *mukluk*, made of sealskin, moose or walrus hide with the hair left on and turned to the inside. The Indian design of moccasin front is common to such boots (see also *Moccasin*). Some of the Eskimo boots are very high, reaching to the thigh for extra protection. In the *Middle East* and the *Orient* boots follow the general trend of footwear and often have turned up toes. Decorative designs and materials also illustrate local traditions, as in the *Bedouin* boot (illustrated) and also the beautiful *Russian* example of stitched red and black leather. Certain *Chinese* boots are characterized by the thick felt sole, also sometimes with turned-up toes. In contrast, *cowboy* boots are generally of heavy, tough leather with a heel to hold the foot in the stirrup. They are sometimes decorated, as in the example illustrated, by stitched and/or appliqué designs.

Boot hose

Cloth stockings worn inside the boots to protect the valuable silk knitted stockings beneath. In the first half of the seventeenth century, when the open, bucket-top, soft leather boots were fashionable, boot hose were finished at the top edge with lace, ruffles or fringe loops which hung over the top of the boot. Known as *knee-pieces* or *boot hose tops*, they could be costly, embroidered in silver or gold thread. (See also *Hose*).

Boot jack

Used particularly from the eighteenth century onwards. A V-shaped device of wood or iron which holds the boot steady and enables the wearer to withdraw his foot.

Boot-lacing studs

Date from the late nineteenth century. Oval-shaped brass hooks which held a cross-lacing in men's boots. They replaced the earlier eyelet holes which needed to be threaded by the lace.

Boot, pegged

Where the sole of a boot is fastened by wooden pegs.

Bosom (breast)

-bottle In the second half of the eighteenth century ladies tucked a small, slender glass or metal bottle into a pocket made in the top of the stomacher, in front, between the breasts. The bottle contained water and a posy of fresh flowers.

-flowers A posy of artificial flowers similarly placed and also worn in the eighteenth century.

-knot A perfumed ribbon knot or rosette attached to the top of the gown at the bosom. Fashionable from about 1750–1820.

Bourrelet

Old French for burlet or birlet. In the Middle Ages a roll, padded with cotton or cloth waste and used chiefly for hoods and head-dresses (see also *Hoods*). In the sixteenth century referred to as a roll support for a ruff, also for the flock padding or wadding inserted into a man's doublet.

BOSOM-FLOWERS
Bosom-flowers, French, 1776

Bracelet

An arm ornament usually worn round the wrist or lower forearm. Made of metal, jewelled, incised or enamelled, sometimes in a continuous ring, at other times made of chain design. Some modern bracelets have charms attached.

Silver bracelet with gold strip decoration, Indian

Gold bracelet, Phoenician, seventh century BC

BOSOM- OR BREAST-KNOT
Bosom- or breast-knot, Swedish, 1782

BRACELET
Silver bracelet, Anglo-Saxon

Gold bracelet, Celtic, Spain, seventh century BC

Gold bracelet from Petrijanec. Ancient Rome, fourth century AD

Gold bracelet, Entremez, Portugal, third century BC

Braces

From the later eighteenth century, straps over the shoulders with button attachment, to support breeches, pantaloons or trousers. Decorative braces are traditional wear in many forms of peasant or national dress for trousers, shorts and skirts (see also *Alpine dress*). In England, also called *gallowses* and *galluses*. In the mid-nineteenth century the braces often divided at the lower ends to attach to two buttons on each side, back and front. Later, the straps were crossed at the back and sewn together where they intersected. Elasticized fabrics were introduced, also adjustment slides. The American term is *suspenders* and the French *bretelles*.

Braid

A narrow band of interlaced, woven fabric made from varied textiles. Used for trimming, binding or appliqué decoration. A common, traditional method of making braid is by *tablet weaving*. The tablets are flat squares of material – bone, card, ivory – and the warp is stretched between two fixed points, not wound upon a loom. The warp threads are grouped together and twisted to form a corded effect when the weft is run through them to hold them together. The warp is threaded through holes in the tablets, which are turned by hand to give the desired twist to the warp. These tablets are retained in a bunch together. A flat piece of wood acts as combined shuttle and beater-in.

Braies

In northern Europe, from the early centuries AD until the beginning of the Middle Ages, these were a loose form of shapeless trousers worn by men. They were held in place by a drawstring at the waist and could be knee-length or longer, the bottom edge being either tucked into stockings or

BRAID
Tablet braid loom

BRAIES

Merovingian dress, *c.*700 AD.
Braies and cross-banding

Costume in Gaul, fourth and
fifth century AD. Braies

bound with leg wrappings. The Teutonic tribes and the Celts generally referred to the garment as *bracchae*. From about the twelfth century, with the advent of the long tunic, braies became an undergarment and as the hose became more fitting and longer, the braies gradually shortened until, in the fifteenth century, when the hose had become 'tights', the braies were mere shorts or underpants (see also *Hose*).

Brandenburg

A greatcoat adopted by the French after 1674, based on that worn by the Brandenburgers when the French, under Louis XIV, were engaged with the Elector's army. The coat was noted for its braid ornamentation incorporating loops on one side and braided buttons on the other. This type of fastening, which was used on coats in the eighteenth and nineteenth centuries, became known as *brandenburgs*. In the eighteenth century, in particular, they were also called '*frogs*'. These fastenings, apart from their adoption in France and England, were also used extensively on greatcoats in Russia, Poland and Hungary.

Brassard

1) *Armour* for the upper part of the arm.
2) A *badge* worn upon the arm.
3) In the gowns *à l'italienne* of the early sixteenth century, the lower section of the *sleeve* from elbow to wrist, separated by laced points from the upper section.
4) In the nineteenth century, a mourning black *band* worn by men (see also *Mourning dress*) and a white ribbon and bow adopted by young first communicants to the Roman Catholic Church.

Brassière, bra

Pads or supports to suppress, uplift or alter the form of the breasts have been part of women's fashion throughout history. The ladies of Minoan Crete wore a stiffened corselet which uplifted their bare breasts, and in Elizabethan England, eighteenth-century Europe and many other periods, the corset was also used in this way. Only in certain ages was a garment worn over the breasts themselves. In the ancient Classical world, the Greeks and later the Romans wore a breast-band of linen or wool to support and contain the breasts; a band or tape was also worn on top of the chiton to delineate the shape of the bosom. Also, in certain periods, there were garments designed to enlarge or accentuate breasts which were not considered, by the fashion of the day, to be of adequate proportions. In the nineteenth century a *bust improver* was advertized which consisted of pads made of wool and cotton which could be inserted into a boned bodice. By the end of the century, when a full bust-line was fashionable, flexible, celluloid bust improvers could be purchased. A *bust bodice* was worn at this time, made of white cotton or calico and boned at the sides for support.

The word *brassière* was introduced from the USA in 1912. The origin of the word is obscure. The French word means a baby's vest, a shoulder strap or leading strings for a young child. The French term for brassière is *soutien-gorge*. In the 1920s the garment was a flattener and not an uplifter. It was made of strong white cotton and covered the body to the waist, with supporting straps over the shoulders. In the 1930s appeared the 'bra', made to delineate and uplift the breasts. Typical designs were of rayon or cotton, the elastic straps crossed over the back to fasten on buttons at the front. The elastic hook-and-eye closure at the back came later. Also at this time were available moulded pads of foam rubber which could be inserted into the brassière to amplify nature's creation; these were called '*falsies*'. The 1950s were the years of the *uplift bra* and 'sweater girl' image. A circular stitching was used to make the high, pointed breast line. A strapless bra was worn with backless evening gowns and beachwear. The padded or contour brassière had now obviated the need for 'falsies'. In the 1960s and 1970s a bra is still worn by most women, though the young tend to abandon it, but the uplift line is less prominent. The accent is on a natural form without delineation and each woman can interpret the fashion as she wishes. (See also *Underwear*.)

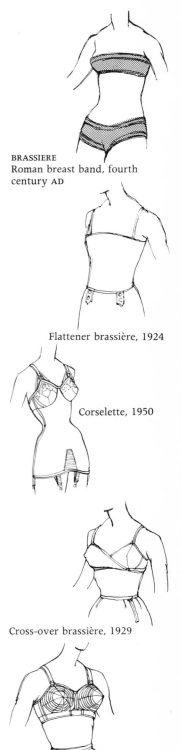

BRASSIERE
Roman breast band, fourth century AD

Flattener brassière, 1924

Corselette, 1950

Cross-over brassière, 1929

Uplift bra with circular-stitched cups, 1958

Breechclout, breechcloth
Traditionally, a covering for the loins and thighs (see also *Braies* and *Breeches*).

Breeches
A masculine outer garment covering the hips and legs as far as the knee. Until the early Middle Ages these were synonymous with braies (see *Braies*). During the Middle Ages, and for much of the sixteenth century, men covered their legs with hose (see *Hose*), but a looser form of breeches was sometimes to be seen. It was from the late sixteenth century that men began to wear breeches and they continued to do so until, in the early nineteenth century, these were slowly replaced by trousers. During this long period many different styles were fashionable but each one was characteristic of a certain age in fullness, length and cut, as well as in fabrics used, so that a specific style of breeches can usually be dated within a decade.

In the late sixteenth and early seventeenth century breeches were full and often padded. The full, loose designs were known as *slops* and were usually finished at the knee with a tied, fringed sash. Similar were the German *pluderhosen* and *Venetians*. These had a bouffant (generally padded) shape which narrowed in pear form towards the knee. *Cloak-bag* breeches were an early seventeenth-century design. Oval in shape, these were full, unpadded and were drawn in at a little above the knee, where they were finished by decorative points or lace. In the 1630s came the longer full breeches, unpadded and ending below the knee with ribbon loops. Sometimes this style – often known as Spanish hose – was pulled in close at the bottom, sometimes it was left open. Side seams were often decorated by braid and/or buttons.

In the second half of the seventeenth century, boots, which had earlier been so fashionable, were abandoned in favour of shoes as *petticoat breeches* became the rage in the 1660s (though the fashion lasted from about 1652–75). This was an unusual masculine fashion, either taking the form of a knee-length skirt, like a Scottish kilt, or resembling full, knee-length shorts with the appearance of a skirt. The garment was bedecked almost all over by ribbon loops and bows as well as lace ruffles, and a small apron of ribbon loops covered the front closure. There are several suggested origins for the style. It seems certain that petticoat breeches came from the Rhineland, since the proper name for them was *rhinegraves* or *rhinegrave breeches*. This derives from the German *rheingrafhose* which, in turn, comes from the Rhineland count – Rheingrafen Karl – who wore the costume and from whom it was taken up with enthusiasm by Louis XIV and his court.

With the later seventeenth century came the fashion for *knee-breeches*, which lasted until after 1800. In the eighteenth century, with the advent of the suit – the *habit à la française* – the breeches were often of the same material as the coat. The *culottes* (as breeches were termed in France) gradually became skin tight. A beautiful fit was obtained by cutting on the bias and extending the back to a high waistline. In front, the material which stretched across the thighs was sewn or buttoned on to a wide basque which hugged the waist. At the bottom, the culottes, which earlier had been concealed by stockings rolled up over the knee, were now pulled down over the stocking and buttoned or buckled there. In the late eighteenth century breeches or culottes were still fitting but worn longer to well below the knee. This was a fashion which stemmed from France, doubtless influenced by the climate of opinion engendered during the Revolution and the symbolism of the trousers worn by the Sansculotte movement (see *Sansculotte, Trousers*).

Breloque
In the nineteenth century, a small ornament fastened to a man's watch chain.

Broadcloth
In the Middle Ages broadcloths were so-called to distinguish them from single widths or 'streits' of one yard wide. By the nineteenth century the term was used more to define quality than width, though 54 inches was still the norm. Traditionally,

Venetians, 1620.
English

Spanish hose
design, Dutch,
*c.*1630

Teutonic
tribes-man,
second
century AD

Italian, 1530

Cloak-bag
breeches,
English,
1624

Knee-breeches in
habit à la française,
Dutch, 1780

Slops, Dutch,
1615–20

Rhinegrave
(petticoat)
breeches, English,
1665

Long knee-
breeches,
French,
1789–90

BRONZE AGE DRESS
IN EUROPE

Scythian, fourth century BC

Danish peat bog finds

Bronze Age, North German

broadcloth has been made from pure wool of high quality, plain in colour and weave and used for men's clothing. In modern times there is also a *cotton broadcloth*, made in plain and patterned material and used for the garments of both sexes. There is also a *broadsilk* which describes silk made in broader widths than usual.

Brocaded Material

A rich fabric woven with raised figures, originally in gold and silver thread (Italian *brocca* = boss); also a cloth of gold and silver, made in India. The European fabric was of silk, interwoven with the gold and silver threads. Later, the word applied to any flowered material with a raised pattern. In the eighteenth century the figuration was woven in coloured silks, raised on an extra weft (see also *Weaving*, Jacquard).

Brocantine

A self-colour pseudo-brocade of silk upon a fine wool material made in the late nineteenth century.

Brocatelle

An imitation of brocaded fabric made in a combination of yarns, most commonly of silk on wool or silk or linen on satin. Used in the eighteenth century for upholstery furnishings but later for costume also.

Bronze Age dress in Europe

The Bronze Age period in northern Europe, from 1500–600 BC, has yielded some interesting finds of jewellery and actual garments from the *tombs* and *peat bogs* of Denmark, northern Holland and Germany. The preservation of some of the oak coffins and their contents is remarkable, especially those from *Jutland* in *Denmark*. In the graves at Borum Eshøj, Muldbjerg, Trindhøj, Egtved and Skrydstrup (to name the most important), have been found four complete sets of men's garments and three of women's from the earlier Bronze Age. These are now in the Danish National Museum in Copenhagen. The *men's clothes* were of wool; they comprised cloaks, tunics and felted caps. The garments were simple and held in place by leather straps, a waist belt and horn buttons. The *women* wore jackets or tunics with elbow-length sleeves, and a metal belt. One skirt was made of looped cords fastened at top and bottom by woven bands and was long enough to be wrapped twice round the body and tied on by a belt below waist level. The belt was intricately woven and ended in decorative tasselling. This type of skirt is essentially a Bronze Age garment. It is thought to have been given up or worn over a longer skirt when later the climate became colder. Women wore their hair long, held in place by a fillet round the brow and often by a net of horsehair and wool cord as well. The garments in the graves were accompanied by ornaments and jewellery as well as toilet articles such as combs and razors.

Garments found in the *North German* and *Dutch* peat bogs show a style of short breeches or longer trousers, a tunic and a cloak. The lower leg was sometimes wrapped by bindings, and footwear was simple leather shoes fastened by a lace threaded through holes in the top edge. Remains can be seen in the Schleswig-Holstein Prehistory Museum.

The *Scythians* were a different people – a nomadic group of tribes who wandered the steppes which extended over Europe and Asia from Hungary to Manchuria. The western flank of these nomadic tribes had established themselves by 600 BC in European Russia round the Black Sea. By 400 BC they had moved westwards to Hungary, Bulgaria, Rumania and eastern Germany but, after 250–200 BC, all trace of them disappears, though their art forms lived on in Viking, Gallic and Irish designs. This nomadic society – with its various groups such as the earlier *Cimmerians*, the later *Sarmatians* and the *Parthians*, who occupied the area south-east of the Caspian Sea – travelled immense distances on horseback and they were magnificent horsemen as both warriors and hunters. Knowledge of them and of their dress comes to us from descriptions by the Greek historian Herodotus and the essays of Hippocrates (both fifth century BC). Excavations from the eighteenth century

onwards in Russia and Mongolia have supported the accuracy of these historic accounts. The Russian researches have been chiefly in the Ukraine, in the Dnieper valley near Kiev, and also in the Crimea. The chief city excavated there so far – Neapolis near Simferopol – was an important centre for the Scythians in the fourth century BC. Other Scythian burials have been found in the Balkans, Hungary, Rumania and eastern Germany.

The Scythians developed an original style of art, vigorous and, like their costume, related to their nomadic life. Gold was used a great deal, also bronze. Animals, especially stags, horses and lions, and also fish, feature in their designs. From their vases and plaques we have a clear picture of their dress. The group illustrated is taken from the plaques and vases at *Kul-Oba*, the originals of which are in the Hermitage Museum in Leningrad. *Men's dress* had something in common with the Teutonic styles of the time. Tunics were worn, often one or more on top of each other, open in front and belted at the waist; some tunics had short sleeves, some long. Underneath the tunic was a shirt. The trousers were loose, worn either wide and open at the bottom or tucked into the short boots and tied at the ankle. The men had long hair, beards and moustaches and wore round caps, often with a point in front like the Phrygians of Asia Minor (see also *Cap*). Their clothes were of wool, tanned leather or fur, simply cut and sewn, but rich in colour and decoration of embroidery and braid.

From the excavation of the burial chambers of the Asiatic Scythians in Outer Mongolia, *women's clothes* were shown to be more ornate than men's, with felt, fur-edged cloaks, decorated almost all over in intricate appliqué work in bright colours. The gown beneath, its bodice and sleeves fitted, was also ornamented. Women dressed their hair in plaits and wore a high head-dress or veil over the coiffure. They had decorative, white stockings mounted on leather soles; these might be covered by overboots, ornamented by fur strips dyed in colours.

Bronze mount, Scythian, fifth century BC

Danish Bronze Age. Horn comb from Borum Eshøj.

Greek spectacle
brooch, 700 BC

Gold, garnet
brooch, Russia,
third century

Silver Celtic pin,
Ireland, ninth
century

Silver thistle
brooch, Orkney,
Norse, tenth
century

Gold and amethyst
brooch, English,
nineteenth century

Sapphire and pearl,
gold brooch,
English, fifteenth
century

Incised silver
brooch, Ukraine,
seventh century

Brass and stone
brooch, Isle of
Gotland, seventh
century

Gold enamelled
brooch, 1000 AD

Gold brooch,
English, twelfth
century

Gold brooch,
fourteenth century

Visigothic bronze
brooch, sixth
century

Viking, bronze
tortoise brooch,
800 AD

Silver trefoil
brooch, 796 AD,

Anglo-Saxon,
sixth century

Bronze brooch,
Oslo, fifth century

Scottish silver,
gold and amber
brooch, c.700

Anglo-Saxon
Gold, jewelled
brooch, English,
thirteenth century

Silver brooch,
Scotland,
nineteenth century

The Scythians loved jewellery and personal adornment. They used precious metals and stones, also enamelling and cloisonné work. In addition to animals, their motifs included geometrical and floral patterns. Excavations have also revealed a wealth of accessories such as hand mirrors, combs, pins and needles.

Brooch

A functional and ornamental piece of jewellery worn by both sexes. Brooches were used to fasten garments by means of a spiked pin hinged to the back of the brooch. Designs have shown immense variety through the ages, extending from the huge circular, Celtic, silver brooches with their long pins for fastening thicknesses of animal skins or plaids, to the tortoise designs of the Vikings, the enamelled Visigothic bird shapes, the classical spectacle brooches and the superb craftsmanship of the late Middle Ages, the Renaissance and the eighteenth century.

Buckle

A fastening device used from earliest times in costume, consisting of a rim of metal with a hinged tongue, carrying a spike in order to secure a strap or belt which passes

BUCKLE

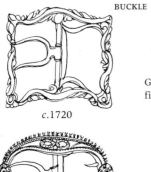

*c.*1720

Gold buckle, Hungary, fifth century

*c.*1770

Lady's shoe, Spain, seventeenth century

*c.*1800

Man's shoe, England, eighteenth century

Eighteenth-century silver and jewelled buckles

through the rim and is then pierced and held in place by the spike. As well as acting as a fastening device for belts and straps, buckles have been fashionable in certain periods in footwear, both masculine and feminine. The *shoe buckle* was made to be attached to the shoe latchets on the instep and could be removed for cleaning. It consisted of a *frame*, which was decorated on the upper surface and was curved to fit the instep, and the *chafe*, which included the pin, the spike and the hinge. Shoe buckles were especially fashionable from the second half of the seventeenth century until about 1800. During this time designs varied greatly from the small oval or rectangular buckles worn until about 1720, to the much larger ones which followed, reaching a peak of fashion in the 1770s. They were then square or oblong, curved deeply to fit the instep, and their extravagance of design conformed to fashion in dress at this date. After this period buckles declined in size, until the 1790s when they were gradually replaced by the shoe tie.

During the years 1650–1800, the buckle was one of the items of dress which denoted a person's status or wealth. A variety of metals were used, from gold and silver to Sheffield plate, iron, steel, copper, brass and tin. Wedgwood ceramic buckles were also available. Designs were chased, moulded and engraved and often set with jewels, from diamonds to garnets, or with marcasite, paste or glass.

Buckram

1) A fine linen or cotton fabric of the mid-sixteenth century.
2) A coarse linen or cloth stiffened with gum and used for linings and reinforcement from the sixteenth century onwards.

Buff coat or jerkin

A buff-coloured military coat of the sixteenth and seventeenth centuries, adopted for civilian use. Made originally from buffalo hide and, later, ox hide, the garment was tough and warm and cut in the fashion of the time. It was generally worn on top of the doublet and could either have sleeves or extend only to shoulder wings.

BUFF COAT
Buff coat, Dutch, 1637–40. Scarlet sash and white falling band and cuffs worn on top

BULGARIAN DRESS
Red cap with pearls over green kerchief. White blouse with red embroidery. Black jacket with coloured embroidery. White skirt, red and yellow apron Leather boots, *c.*1840

White shirt embroidered in colour, green and gold jacket, red sash, brown trousers. Legs wrapped in black and white banding, fur kalpak, leather shoes, 1890

White wool chemise with spot pattern, striped bodice and skirt, white wool underskirt. Multi-coloured apron. Fur-lined and edged coat. Black shoes, dark head-kerchief, 1873

Sheepskin coat or jube with wool inside, exterior embroidered in coloured wool. Light wool entari (robe), red wool sash
Black lamb kalpak (cap). Leg wrappings, rough leather moccasins, 1873

Bulgarian dress

Although, since the Second World War, Bulgaria has become more industrialized and many people now work in towns, a large proportion of the population still work on the land and many live in small village communities where they are almost self-sufficient, making their own clothes, embroidering and decorating them, from material which they have spun, dyed and woven themselves. The country styles of dress persist although the international, urban costume is more widely worn as time passes.

Bulgarian peasant dress varies from district to district and there are even distinctions from village to village, but in general it has much in common with that of other Balkan peoples. This can be seen in the warm sheepskin coat – the wool turned inside – which has over-long sleeves ending in fur mittens. It is usually decorated in brightly-coloured wools and appliqué work. It is worn over the *entari*, a loose robe bound at the waist with a broad cummerbund. The legs are covered in wide trousers (Turkish style) and bound below the knee. On the feet are moccasins, boots or leather shoes. The fur *kalpak* is worn on the head in cold weather. Women's dress is colourful and this is seen especially in the embroidered aprons and blouses. The Balkan style black jacket is often worn; it is short, fitting, richly embroidered and sometimes laced across in front. Bulgarian embroidery is an art form in itself – it is colourful and interspersed with beads and gold and silver thread. Complex appliqué designs adorn festive costumes.

Bum-barrel, bum roll

A protuberant part of a woman's dress. In the sixteenth and seventeenth centuries referred generally to the waist bolster, which was a padded roll tied round the waist under the skirt to give a full silhouette above the hips.

BUM-BARREL
Bum-barrel or waist bolster, *c.*1600

BURGUNDIAN DRESS
Young men with
short pleated and
padded tunics and
hose, *c*.1450

Fur-trimmed velvet
gown. Striped
plastron
Padded headdress,
c.1435

Couple, 1470.
Steeple headdress
with veil

Young man in tall
hat and richly
decorated
houppelande, 1475

Burberry
Trade name of cloth and clothing made by
Burberrys Ltd. A waterproofed fabric used
chiefly for raincoats. (See *Raincoat*.)

Bure
A coarse woollen material used for costumes of monks and nuns in the Middle
Ages. In the early twentieth century
French designers used a finer version of
the fabric and combined it with velvet to
make garments of fashion.

Burgundian dress
The Burgundians were people of Germanic
origin who first settled in what is now East
Germany. Under the later Roman Empire
they established themselves in Gaul in
present-day France. It was after 1360 that
the Dukes of Burgundy succeeded in expanding their kingdom dramatically to take
in Flanders, Lorraine and areas of France.
This rich, powerful state became the pace-
setter for much of European costume.

Until the fourteenth century, France had
been one of the chief leaders of medieval
fashion, but during this century became
too weakened by the Hundred Years' War
with England to develop to the full her
textile industries in an impoverished
country. It was Burgundy which possessed
the most beautiful fabrics of richness and
design – rich colours, gold and silver cloth
and jewelled embroideries. Especially in
the first three-quarters of the fifteenth
century Burgundian dress was admired,
copied and envied by the whole western
world. It was noted not only for the richness of its patterned fabrics and jewels, its
materials generously edged and lined with
costly furs, but also for its extremes as well
as elegance of style.

In *men's dress* the tunics were more
fitting, padding and pleats more excessive,
than elsewhere; skirts were shorter, displaying a larger area of tight hose whose
toes extended in ridiculous points. Young
men wore tall hats at a rakish angle over

fluffy, bushy hair. *Ladies' gowns* had more figure-hugging bodices and higher waist belts. Their fur-edged, plunging necklines were only saved from complete exposure of the breasts by the insertion of a decorative plastron. The costume was crowned by tall, bejewelled head-dresses of a rich variety of design which were capped by complex, wired veils. Both sexes wore their clothes with an air of elegance and insouciance, the men displaying their masculinity by gesture and stance, the ladies their attractions in a coyly-lifted skirt and tilt to the head.

Burka, burqa, boorka, burqu'

1) A long *veil* worn in public places by Asiatic and chiefly Moslem women to hide them from the view of men and strangers. (See also *Chadar*.)

2) In Moslem India, *burkha* signifies a *tent-like cloak* which envelops the whole figure, leaving only a mesh panel for the eyes to peer through.

3) A *short, round cloak* of coarse fabric worn by Russians, Poles and Moldavians: in Russian, *bypka*. The Cossacks wore long, full cloaks of black wool or fur, together with astrakhan caps on their heads.

Bushel

A tailor's thimble. *Bushelman* – a man or woman engaged in repair tailoring.

Bustle

A device for pushing out the skirts on ladies' gowns, at the back just below the waist. A recurring fashion through the centuries for supporting drapery and decoration concentrated at the rear of the dress. The means for providing this support have varied from padded rolls (see *Bum-barrel*) to starched flounces or whalebone and metal frameworks.

The most varied forms of bustle (*tournure* in France) appeared in the nineteenth century. In the first half these were generally wool pads tied on with strings round the waist. Later, as the circular crinoline declined in fashion the fullness was concentrated at the back and between 1865–75 crinoline petticoats in bustle form were worn, made of metal frameworks or whalebone bands inserted into the petticoat. These were gradually replaced by a wire basket or a horsehair and gauze pad with metal frame beneath, both of which rested upon the buttocks and were tied on round the waist. In the years 1878–82 no bustle was worn as the hip-line was sleek and the draperies of the skirt were concentrated lower down, but after 1882 the bustle returned, reaching its height of popularity about 1885 and diminishing again by 1888. Bustle petticoats accompanied these styles and these were made with rows of stiffened ruffles and pleats at the back. (See *Petticoat*.)

Button

A knob or disc sewn to a garment and which, when pushed through a buttonhole opening, serves as a fastening. In Europe buttons are mentioned from the mid-fourteenth century onwards but it is thought that at this time they were purely decorative, as, for instance, in the row of small buttons which ornamented the outer seam of the fitting sleeve of the forearm in both men's tunics and women's gowns.

Buttons were used as fastenings at least from the fifteenth century onwards and have been an essential item in costume continuously since that time. In certain periods, buttons have been especially fashionable, both as decoration and for fastening. In the eighteenth century, for example, decorative, costly buttons were sewn to men's coats and waistcoats – down the centre front as fastenings, and on the pocket flaps, cuffs and at the head of the skirt pleats as ornamentation. Buttons were widely used in the nineteenth century; apart from fastenings for men's coats, waistcoats and trousers, the bodices of ladies' gowns were closed by a row of many tiny buttons and ladies' boots were fastened by a row on the outer side. The button-hook was an essential piece of equipment for drawing the small buttons through the buttonholes of the leather.

Buttons are of two chief types, according to the means by which they are attached to the garment. In one type there is a shank, which is a metal hook or a tuft of

BUSTLE

Bustle petticoat, 1875

Bustle, 1887

Bustle petticoat, 1872–5

canvas or cloth; in the other design the button is pierced with two or four holes and is sewn on to the fabric by passing the needle and thread through these holes.

During the centuries buttons have been made of all kinds of material, from gilded metal and mother-of-pearl to the ordinary metal ring button covered in calico for sewing to underwear. Quality buttons for decoration have been made of gold and silver in filigree work or jewelled; there have been porcelain buttons with dainty pictures and motifs; and, in the later eighteenth century, Wedgwood jasper-ware buttons, painted silk pictorial buttons, ivory, pearl and cut glass. Brass buttons were made in England from the late seventeenth century and, in the second half of the eighteenth century, steel buttons cut with facets were produced and became very fashionable. Horn buttons were introduced at the same time, but were not produced in quantity from the hoofs of cattle until the mid-nineteenth century.

Advances in the manufacture of buttons were made throughout the nineteenth century. Of particular note was the introduction in Birmingham, by the Danish B. Sanders, of an improved design wherein the button was formed of two discs of metal locked together by having their edges turned back on each other and enclosing a filling material. In 1827 Samuel Williston initiated the mechanical manufacture of cloth-covered buttons in Massachusetts in the USA. Modern buttons are still made of a variety of materials but the most common designs today are in plastic. Many buttons are covered to match the garment, while the more costly decorative examples are of metal, wood, glass, pearl or bone.

Byssus
A very fine, high quality textile known to the ancients and applied to fabrics made from cotton, linen or silk. Originally referred to a kind of flax.

Byzantine dress
The Roman Emperor Constantine, impressed by the strategic situation of the Greek city of Byzantium commanding the waters between west and east of the Mediterranean and the Black Sea, transferred the imperial seat of government there in AD 330. He began the building of a great new city which he called New Rome. Later in the century, the Roman Empire was divided into two parts, eastern and western, and after the fall of Rome in the fifth century, the eastern empire ruled alone. Byzantium was renamed Constantinople (now Istanbul) after its first Christian emperor and remained the capital of a vast, polyglot empire until its capitulation to Mohammedanism in 1453.

Because of its geographical position between east and west, Byzantine culture, throughout the eleven centuries of its domination, was always a complex mixture of influence from both sources. The results of this blending are nowhere more striking than in costume. In the first few centuries the influence of Rome was still strong (see also *Rome* (*ancient*)) and draped styles of costume predominated in the cut of the dress. The fabrics and colour were, from the beginning, strongly eastern and the eastern style of costume began slowly to assert itself in the form of trousers, footwear, head-coverings and, above all, in decoration and jewellery.

During the long reign of the Byzantine Empire there were two periods of especial brilliance and prosperity when the dominance and influence of Constantinople were paramount. The first of these was under the Emperor Justinian in the sixth century AD, and the second was from the ninth to the thirteenth century. In the former period the influence of Rome was strong; in the second, Byzantine dress showed more features of Persian, Assyrian, Egyptian and Anatolian designs. The Byzantine Empire was immensely wealthy, due largely to its extensive commercial trade with east and west. The trade routes extended from Scandinavia and Russia to Armenia and Ethiopia. Luxury fabrics and jewels flowed into Constantinople and costume attained a richness of colour, fabric and ornament which far exceeded that of the great days of Rome. This wealth,

BYZANTINE DRESS

Emperor Justinian, sixth century

Empress Theodora, sixth century. Jewelled maniakis and headdress

BYZANTINE DRESS
Gold, decorated
gown with jewelled
belt and collar.
White palla and
undergown, sixth
century

Dalmatica with
clavi, sixth century

Richly jewelled
and embroidered
costume,
fourteenth century

Gold, jewelled
garments. Tablion
on cloak, tenth–
eleventh century

allied to the Oriental and Arabic craftsmanship and love of richness, produced
the most dazzling attire, envied and copied
by the rest of the world.

The chief feature which characterized
Byzantine dress was the beauty of the
fabrics. The development of the textile industry was responsible not only for the
costly magnificence of the dress but its
quality of stiffness and luminosity. These
fabrics introduced a new kind of cut which
displayed them to advantage; the draped,
full attire of the Greeks and Romans, so
suited to wool and linen, gave way to
simple, straight garments without folds,
giving a stiff, more formal appearance, at
once hieratic and dignified. The quality of
Byzantine fabrics stemmed from the beautiful woven patterns and from the extensive
use of silk. The designs were floral and
geometrical – the predominant motifs being
circles, palmettes, all kinds of flowers and
leaves – incorporating mythological and

dramatic animals and birds. Imperial dress
was characterized by a preponderance of
purple and gold. In the ninth and tenth
centuries the garments of the well-to-do
were especially vivid in reds, violets, gold,
yellow and green. The influence of Saracenic, Syrian and Egyptian imported textiles spread to the Byzantine workshops,
illustrated in the types of woven and
embroidered patterns. Caravans from the
Far East brought even more exotic, beautiful
fabrics and these too were studied and
copied. The overwhelming factor in creating the stiff, shimmering quality of Byzantine costume was the extensive use of silk,
which had been imported by both Greece
and Rome at fabulous cost – silk had thus
always been a rarity, preserved only for
the court and the very rich. It was the
Emperor Justinian who introduced the
manufacture of silk to Constantinople,
thus making its use more widespread (see
also *Silk*).

The dress of the imperial court is well documented and illustrations of it in glowing colour can be seen in numerous church mosaics. The Emperor Justinian and his noblemen wear knee-length tunics, belted low in the waist, and cut straight. The tunics had round necks and long sleeves and were worn over fitting trousers or hose. The long cloak on top was fastened on the right shoulder with a pin and displayed the ornamental *tablion* in front. This rectangular piece of jewel-encrusted material was inset and proclaimed the wearer to be a member of the royal house or a court dignitary. The Empress and her ladies are similarly attired but the tunic reaches nearly to the ground. Characteristic of the royal house is the wearing of the *maniakis*, of Persian derivation, a separate collar of fabric, embroidered in gold and encrusted with jewels.

These mosaics and frescoes show the changes that have taken place, even by the sixth century, from the Roman model. In Byzantine dress the limbs are always covered and sleeves extend to the wrists for both sexes. The tunic is loose-fitting but is not draped. It hangs straight, girded only at the waist, and its stiffer, plainer form admirably displays the richness of the fabric. Women's gowns are often patterned all over, though both sexes wore garments ornamented with panels and roundels of decoration applied to the material. While the masculine cloak was fastened on the shoulder, ladies generally wore a *palla*, which was draped around the shoulders and, when necessary, over the head also. In the fifth and sixth centuries both men and women still wore the *dalmatica* with its loose, long sleeves and clavus decoration.

As time passed Byzantine dress became richer and more glittering. In the second period of prosperity, from the ninth to the thirteenth century, the colours were deep and strong, with extensive use of violets and reds. Silk materials were encrusted with jewels and pearls. Imperial dress included a long panel of material with gold and jewelled embroidery, like a scarf tied round the body, its ends hanging loose.

There was a noticeable infiltration of eastern influence into the dress and the classical line had disappeared. For example, the Oriental *caftan* was adapted by Byzantium into a formal item of attire (see also *Caftan*). *Trousers* were generally worn by both sexes and were fitting, elegantly cut and often decorated by a jewelled, embroidered band running vertically down the limb at back or front. The trousers were tucked into high boots or worn over shoes.

Conversely, Byzantine dress had a considerable influence upon the costume of eastern Europe. This was especially so in southern Russia and in the Balkans, where the formal, richly bejewelled attire in stiff, encrusted silks became an integral part of the vestments of the church as well as the lay aristocracy. The knee-length or ankle-length tunic – worn over tight trousers tucked into high boots and covered by a fur-collared caftan, worn loose or belted, established in such countries as Bulgaria and Turkey – became the staple dress for centuries. In turn, with the westward advance of the Ottoman Empire after 1453, these styles of dress, at least for men, were brought to countries in central Europe – Hungary, Poland, Czechoslovakia – and became part of the traditional costume until the nineteenth century.

The leather boot, in black or coloured, was normal *footwear* for men. At Court, red leather was the most usual, embroidered and with pearls. Sandals were also worn, especially by ladies, and soft ankle-clinging shoes with pointed toes for general indoor use. These were brightly coloured and decorated in gold and jewelled embroidery.

Men were often bare-headed or wore the Phrygian cap or a hood. *Ladies* encased their hair in a silk cap or pearl net and this could be accompanied by a veil. Imperial head-dresses for both sexes were heavily bejewelled. Pendant chains hung from the royal diadem on each side of the face in Oriental fashion. The ladies' coiffure was encased in a jewelled silk coif with the diadem on top, decorated with an aigrette or star. Jewellery was elaborate and varied. Perfume was liberally applied and handkerchiefs were carried.

Red cap, tunic and shoes. Dark grey cloak with gold edge, light grey patterned trousers, Byzantine, sixth century

Empress, sixth century. Jewelled silk cloak with tablion. Manlakis and jewelled headdress

Persian candys, first century BC

Hungarian dolman, derived
from the caftan, c.1670

C

Caffa
1) A rich *silk* made in the sixteenth and
seventeenth centuries.
2) A painted *cotton* made in India.

Caftan, caban, candys, kandys
The caftan is of ancient origin and came
from Asia. It was an open garment, sewn
and made of several shaped pieces of
material seamed lengthwise. It was worn
over other garments and was crossed over
in front, often being girded to hold it in
place. It is the prototype of the European
coat. The caftan appeared in the dress of
many different cultures, first in Asia, later
being introduced into Europe. We can see
it illustrated in Scythian dress – a long coat,
with long sleeves, belted at the waist,
worn on top of tunic and trousers. In more
elegant, fashionable form it appeared 1,500
years later in Byzantine attire as a long coat,
buttoned down the front, shaped and of
rich material.

In general, the caftan developed, with
various modifications in cut and decoration, into a useful garment worn throughout Asia, in the Middle East, in India,
Persia, Mongolia, China and Asian Russia.
Fundamentally it remained a simply cut,
coat-like garment, with sleeves (generally
full) and two panels crossed over in front.
The caftan was introduced into Europe in
the Middle Ages, first from the spread of
the Mongolian Empire in the thirteenth
century as far as the Danube, and then the
Ottoman encroachments of the fifteenth
century which came even further west to
Hungary, Czechoslovakia, Poland and
Yugoslavia. Varied in detail, the caftan
retained its main characteristics and became a vital garment in the whole of
eastern Europe, where it was worn (as in

Hungary and Russia) until well into the
nineteenth century.

In western Europe, of more direct line of
descent towards the coat was the *caban*,
which appeared at the end of the fourteenth century. Similar to the caftan, and
clearly its close relative, it also was an open
outer garment, crossed over in front,
belted, with long sleeves and with an
attached hood. It was certainly derived
from styles of caftan, first introduced into
Italy in the thirteenth century via Venice,
and continued to be used, as an outer
garment, until the sixteenth century. It
re-emerged, in its modern form as a coat,
in the later seventeenth century.

Another close relation to the caftan was
the Persian candys or kandys. This type of
long coat developed, like the caftan, from
the fitted garments of the Asiatic horsemen
from the Scythians onwards, and in Persia,
as in earlier ages, was worn with trousers.
The fuller design, inherited from the earlier
Medes and used on formal occasions, had
full, pleated sleeves, but another design,
with fitted, long sleeves, was in more
everyday use; soldiers wore a shorter
version of this. (See *Persian dress*.)

Cairngorm
A yellow or reddish-brown rock crystal,
widely used in ornamenting Highland
dress; also for jewellery in general. The
stone is named after the Scottish mountains,
the Gaelic Carngorm meaning blue cairn.

Calamanco
A glazed woollen fabric made in Flanders
in the sixteenth century. Often checked in
the warp so that the checks are visible on
one side of the material. By the nineteenth
century, highly glazed and made of a
mixture of cotton and wool.

Russian caftan, sixteenth century

Modern Egyptian caftan of white silk striped in grey. Tie fastenings

Turkish caftan, sixteenth century

Calash, calèche, thérèse

Worn outdoors as a protection for the high coiffures, especially of the years 1773–83, the calash was a large, articulated hood made as a hooped frame covered in ruched and padded silk. This could be pulled up or folded down over the coiffure as required, in the manner of a carriage or perambulator hood. It was tied with a ribbon bow under the chin. In France it was originally known as a *thérèse* but later as a *calèche*, a word of Slav origin, used from the seventeenth century to denote a light carriage which had a removable, folding hood.

Calendering

A process in finishing cloth where it is passed through a calender in order to smooth and glaze the fabric. The process can also be used to produce a watered or moiré effect. A calendry is the place where the process is undertaken and a calenderer the operator.

Camaca, camoca

A rich silk fabric derived from the Arabic word *kamkhā*. Used extensively in Europe in the Middle Ages but imported originally from China, later Persia.

Camelaukion, kamelaukion

A hemispherical, dome-shaped crown worn by the Caesars of Rome and by Byzantine emperors. Related to the round tiara crown of Mesopotamia (see *Mesopotamia*).

Cameo

A precious stone such as onyx, agate or sardonyx, with two layers of different colours. The lower colour serves as a ground while the upper is carved in relief, often in the form of a portrait.

CALASH, CALECHE, THÉRÈSE English calash of black silk, *c.*1775

CANEZOU
Canezou of white muslin worn over dark floral dress, French, 1830

Camlet

Appears in English in different forms – *camblet, chamlyt, camelot*. In early European history the word was associated with fabrics made from camel's hair, but before this it probably originated from the Arabic words *khamlat* or *khaml*, meaning the nap or surface of the cloth. In the seventeenth and eighteenth centuries camelot, according to Samuel Johnson, referred to a fabric of a mixture of silk or velvet with camel's hair. By the nineteenth century camelot refers to fabrics made from fibres of the angora goat. In early times the name was given to some beautiful, costly fabrics of silk and wool. It is not established whether camel's hair was employed in the material, but certainly that of the angora goat was incorporated.

Cane

Canes or sticks have been carried or used to assist walking during many centuries in costume. The word *cane* is commonly applied to any slender walking-*stick*, but strictly is made from the hollow, jointed, ligneous stem of certain reeds or grasses,

CANNONS
Cannons of lace attached to petticoat breeches, 1665

Richly patterned cannons, English, 1575

such as bamboo, or the solid stem of plants such as palms (the *rattan* is one of these). Very popular, especially in the nineteenth century, were *malacca* canes, which are made from the rich brown stems of a palm grown in the Malacca district of the Malay peninsula

In general, the use of canes and sticks became especially fashionable as the wearing of swords declined. The seventeenth and eighteenth centuries in Europe were years when men carried short canes or long sticks and, in the later eighteenth century, fashionable ladies also carried long sticks with ribbon bows and tassels tied to the gold or silver top, which could be opened and contained perfume or powder. Throughout the nineteenth century men carried canes, often gold-headed. These were mainly short canes but, by mid-century, the walking stick tended to replace the swagger cane, though the latter returned to favour towards 1900.

Canezou

A ladies' fashion which originated in the 1820s but was especially in favour between 1830 and 1835, when it took the form of a cape covering the shoulders, sometimes in two or three tiers, and held in place by long ends tucked into the waist belt in front. The canezou was usually white and was made of transparent material, edged with lace, embroidery or pleating.

Cannons, canons, canions

In the second half of the sixteenth century these were tube-like breeches, worn by men, tightly-fitting over the thigh and extending from the lower edge of the short trunk hose to the knee. Cannons were generally made of a different material and pattern from either the trunk hose or the stocking and in the 1570s and 1580s could be ornately embroidered in coloured silks, gold or silver thread. In the seventeenth century, especially in the 1660s when petticoat breeches were fashionable, deep linen or lace flounces were attached to the lower end of the cannons, appearing to act as a full, ruffled extension of the rhinegraves themselves. This was a fashion to be seen in France and England but especially in Holland and Germany (see *Hose* (trunk) and *Breeches* (petticoat or rhine-grave)).

Cap

The distinction between a cap, a bonnet and a hat is sometimes blurred. In general, a *bonnet* is usually tied by a ribbon bow under the chin and has no brim at the back (see *Bonnet*), a *cap* fits closely to the head, often without any brim, and is made of a soft material, while a *hat*, though varied in shape, with brim or without, is usually a grander head-covering of richer and stiffer fabric (see *Hat*).

More primitive cultures tended to wear caps rather than hats; caps were easier to make and fit. In cold climates and mountain areas the cap of fur skin is the common and necessary head-covering; examples are numerous from the Eskimo, the Cossack, the Hungarian, the Chinese and Mongolian, the Indian sub-continent – Pakistan, Kashmir, Tibet and Nepal – to the frontiersman of North America. A round, fitting cap was worn, in different forms, by all the ancient civilizations. The Greek *pilos* was typical and almost identical was the Roman (and Etruscan) *pileus*, both usually made of felt. Similar caps were worn in the early centuries AD throughout Europe, as can be seen in Gallic, Merovingian and Carolingian dress. A variant was the *Phrygian cap*, which originated in Anatolia but was to be seen over a wide area from very early times till the Middle Ages. It is a generalized term which was used to apply to a cap which came to a point in front, a point which was then allowed to fall forwards from the top. Caps of this type can be seen in ancient Persian, Etruscan, Scythian and Byzantine dress, among others, as well as being commonplace in Europe in the Middle Ages. The *conical* cap was also widely used by ancient cultures. This can be traced, for example, in sculpture and paintings of Persian, Hittite, Assyrian, Minoan, and some classical dress; its use also extended till the Middle Ages.

The *skull cap* was widely used in medieval times from the twelfth until the fifteenth century and it has continued to be worn in later periods as a nightcap or smoking cap, also in ecclesiastical dress. A skull cap is small and round, closely fitting the top of the head and with no brim or peak, although it can have a short tail. Also known as a *calotte*, it was often worn under another cap or hat. A version of the skull cap known as a *zucchetto* was adopted by the Church as a round cap to cover the tonsure. Another variant of the skull cap was the *biretta* which, by the fifteenth century, developed into a stiffened, square shape with three or four raised ridges on the crown radiating from the centre, which could be marked by a tail, pompon or tassel. It was worn by the clergy and also the lay academicians of the universities (see *Academical dress*).

Small jewelled and embroidered caps have been worn in many ages by *women* to decorate and contain their plaited or coiled long hair. Made of varied materials, but often in velvet, muslin, lace, silk or lawn, these were frequently richly ornamented with pearls, jewels, gold and silver thread as well as coloured silks, and could be accompanied by a veil. They were especially fashionable in the later Middle Ages and the early Renaissance in Italy, while pill-box designs, perched on the back of the head, were characteristic of the later sixteenth century in central and western Europe. Modern versions of both styles can be seen in the evening *juliet cap* and the out-door *pill-box hat*.

The *stocking cap* – the knitted woollen cap with turned-up brim and a long end hanging down the back, sometimes ending in a tassel – has been used as a working-man's head-covering by many peoples in different ages. It has traditionally been associated with the sea, worn especially by sailors and fishermen, particularly round the Mediterranean as in Spain, Portugal, Italy and Greece. The medieval cap worn by the *jester* or professional fool was a version of this, though the single or multiple ends were padded to stand up or curve over and were finished by bells. The cap was traditionally ornamented with a donkey's ears and was attached to a shoulder cape as in a medieval hood.

Black fur cap,
Daghestan, USSR

North American
frontiersman,
nineteenth
century

Teutonic tribesman,
Roman Empire

Fur cap, Cherkess,
USSR, c.1850

Hungarian fur hat
(kucsma), c.1650

Greek pilos, fifth
century BC

Felt skull cap,
c.1200

Etruscan cap,
sixth century BC

Blue calotte worn
under beaver hat,
1510

Felt cap, 1470

Phrygian cap,
Byzantine, c.530

Jewelled cap,
Italian, 1550

Assyrian conical
cap, c.850 BC

Jewelled cap,
Sweden, 1590

University biretta

White cap
decorated with
pearls, Florence,
c.1460

Black jewelled hat
over jewelled cap,
German, 1550

Velvet, jewelled
cap, Italian,
1450–60

King Henry VIII,
c.1538. Velvet flat
cap

White cap, French,
1785

Butterfly cap, 1776

Black velvet cap,
1543

Stocking cap

Man's negligée
cap, 1760s

White cap with
lappets, 1725

Baigneuse cap,
1780

Dormeuse cap,
1770

White cap under
straw hat, 1785

Mob cap, 1775

Lace-edged cap,
1782

Man's tweed cap,
1910

Turkish fez of red
felt

Man's deerstalker
cap, 1885

Astrakhan cap,
Persia

Red tarboosh with
black tassel, Egypt

CARACO
Caraco and skirt of silk with
gauze flouncing, 1775

Women wore caps *indoors* from the sixteenth century onwards until the later nineteenth and, out-of-doors, often placed the currently fashionable hat or hood on top. These indoor caps varied considerably in style during the centuries, mainly due to changes in the manner of dressing the hair. They were nearly always white, made of lawn or cambric, and were sometimes stiffened. They were decorated by lace bordering, embroidery, pleated or ruffled edges and ribbon bows and loops, the latter usually in colour. The greatest variation probably existed in Dutch caps which differed in design from region to region. Especially in the seventeenth century, ladies wore more than one cap, one on top of another, and with an increased quantity of decoration. The *eighteenth century* was the great age for ladies wearing indoor caps. In the earlier years these were small, perched on the top or the back of the head and with dependant lappets at the back. With the advent of the large coiffures and wigs of the 1770s and 1780s, so the caps became larger and larger and more and more elaborately decorated. There were several types: the *baigneuse*, worn originally in the bath, but later in use for daytime fashion; the *dormeuse*, originally designed for night-time use, but again later worn in the day also. Both styles were elaborate, tied under the chin with ribbons and held closely to the cheeks with ruching and pleats. The *mob cap* was a particularly English design which had a full puffed crown with ribbon band decoration and a flounced edge. Until about 1750 it was tied under the chin and had side lappets. After this it was generally worn unfastened. The size varied with the coiffure styles and it remained in use until the nineteenth century. The *butterfly cap* was perched on the head; it had a flat back, a frilled front edge and no fastening. The *round-eared cap* was similar, though it sometimes had single or double side lappets.

Men also wore caps when relaxing at home in the later seventeenth and the eighteenth centuries because, in these years, where they adopted heavy wigs for appearing in public, they shaved or closely trimmed their own hair. At home, therefore, they wore a *negligée cap*. This was full, pleated or gathered into a band, and was made of a rich fabric and worn with a dressing or relaxing gown. At night men wore a *napkin cap*, which was a plain nightcap to cover the head and to avoid taking chill in cold weather in ill-heated rooms.

The wearing of a cap began to have a social connotation from the sixteenth century onwards. In Europe this indicated that for men and boys a cap was worn by servants, schoolboys and apprentices, and for women it became a mark of the domestic servant as ladies ceased to wear it in the middle of the nineteenth century. However, when in the nineteenth century gentlemen began to wear a cap for country and sportswear, this gave a lift to the garment, and a cap, with vizor or peak, became *de rigueur*. The *man's cloth cap* with vizor was worn with the Norfolk jacket and knickerbockers, while the *deerstalker* design, with ear flaps tied up over the crown, was especially fashionable from 1870–90. The *montero cap* was worn from the seventeenth to the nineteenth centuries. This was a peaked cap with side flaps which was in use for travelling, for mountain wear and for extreme cold. The flaps could be let down over the ears to protect the traveller.

The *fez*, said to be so called after the town of Fez in Morocco, was a brim-less cap shaped like a truncated cone. Made of cloth or wool, it was generally dark red but could also be in dark blue or black and was decorated by a silk tassel on top. It might be worn alone or be part of a turban head-dress. The fez was made part of the national dress of the Turks in the early nineteenth century and all Turks wore it until Turkey became a republic in 1923 and the cap was proscribed. *Tarboosh* is the Arabic name for this cap, which is worn by Moslems of both sexes in the Middle East. It may be draped with a scarf or be part of a turban. It was introduced into India in the nineteenth century. Similar is the *checia* (*checchia*), also generally red, which was worn by Arabs and by French troops in Africa.

Dark green silk caraco and skirt with apple green edging and flounce, 1786

Capote

1) A nineteenth-century *bonnet* (see *Bonnet*).

2) Name given to different designs of *greatcoat* and *cloak* worn during the eighteenth and nineteenth centuries by both sexes. Generally a full, long garment with a collar and, sometimes, a hood; made of heavy cloth.

Caracalla

A knee-length tunic worn in Gaul in the first century AD. It was fitting and had long sleeves; the skirt was slit centre front and back and a hood was attached at the neck. The name caracalla was given to the garment when it was introduced to Rome, where it was usually worn ankle-length.

Caraco

During the eighteenth century ladies wore jackets which were of the same design as the current gown but were cut off at hip level. Early examples, generally referred to as *casaquins*, were fairly fitted in front but loose at the back, based on the sack gown. In mid-century the *caraco* was a shortened form of the *robe à la française*, while by the 1780s it was fitted to the waist and flared to a full basque at the back. This style, often like a shortened redingote, was also called a *juste*, and a pierrot style of jacket was similar, though also fashionable earlier in the century. Worn with a skirt in current fashion, such outfits were referred to as *caraco gowns*.

Cardigan

Named after the Earl of Cardigan who fought in the Crimean War in 1855. A knitted wool waistcoat or jacket without collar and worn with or without sleeves. The modern cardigan has no collar, long sleeves and is buttoned centre front (see also *Jersey* and *Sweater*).

Carmagnole

A short jacket worn by the sansculottes of the French Revolution in 1792. The jacket was a workman's garment worn in Carmagnola in northern Italy and was adopted by the revolutionaries in Marseilles and later Paris (see *Sansculotte*).

Carnelian, cornelian

A deep or orange-red or reddish-white variety of chalcedony used in jewellery.

Carolingian dress

In AD 768 Charlemagne became joint king of the Franks with his brother, and sole ruler from 771; in AD 800 he was crowned Holy Roman Emperor by the Pope. Charlemagne generally wore normal Frankish dress, though he appeared in full Byzantine splendour on state occasions. Like other Frankish noblemen, his usual attire comprised a linen undertunic and braies, the latter cross-gartered to the knee with leather strips; these were often coloured and decorated with metal studs. His shoes were of leather. The belted overtunic was of linen or cloth and had a coloured border. The cloak, pinned on the shoulder, was lined with fur or silk and was bordered. In cold weather he would also wear a sleeveless short jacket and a round cap. Some noblemen wore sock-like calf-length boots or a fabric hose pulled up over the braies. For formal occasions the ankle-length *dalmatica* tunic with wide sleeves was worn with a long cloak on top.

Caraco of dark, flowered material over light, cotton gown, 1780

CAROLINGIAN DRESS
Carolingian aristocratic dress. Byzantine influence in gown decoration and draped scarf

Carolingian king wearing Byzantine dress for state occasion. Bordered dalmatica over undertunic, cloak, ankle boots

Women wore similar underwear of chemise and braies, also similar footwear. Their gowns were long and full and usually decorated by bands of embroidery at the neck and down the front. A long, crossed scarf, like the Roman *palla*, was draped round the body and over one arm. The hair was dressed in nets of woven beads and precious stones with veils worn on top. Both sexes wore decorative and functional jewellery made in gold, silver, bronze and iron, set with stones of all kinds and decorated with incised lines, embossing and enamel. Beads of amber, garnets and other stones were often worn.

Carroting
A process used in preparing hat furs for felting. They are treated with a solution of nitrate of mercury.

Cassock, casaque
1) In the sixteenth and seventeenth centuries the *cassock* was a long *coat* or *cloak* worn chiefly by soldiers or horsemen or for hunting. It was unbelted and buttoned down the centre front. The word stems from the French *casaque*, related also to the Italian *casacca* and Spanish *casaca*.
2) In *ecclesiastical* dress the cassock is a full-length garment with sleeves and a standing collar. It can be worn loose or with a belt or sash.
3) In modern, feminine dress the *casaque* refers, in French, to a *blouse* worn outside the skirt or trousers; also to the brightly-coloured silk *tunic* worn by jockeys.

Caucasian dress
The people of the Caucasus and surrrounding regions have had a long and turbulent history and have developed a rich culture which is independent and indigenous, yet strongly influenced by the neighbouring empires of past and present – notably those of Persia, Ottoman Turkey and Russia – and their costume reflects these factors.

The *Circassians* (the Russian word *Cherkesses*) have different origins and language from other Caucasian peoples. Now part of the USSR, they lived for centuries under their own feudal system and developed their own customs and clothes. Characteristic of their costume is the long caftan-like coat with sleeves falling over the hand, worn over loose trousers and collared tunic. *Georgia* (Russian word *Gruzia*), a kingdom for 2,000 years, was occupied by Russia in 1801 and became part of the USSR in 1920. This land of varied climate – Mediterranean in the west and extreme in the east – encouraged a different development of the life and customs of the people in different regions and costume and language varied accordingly. Heavy wool and fur garments were worn in the cold winters of the east and full trousers and boots were normal wear for both sexes.

Modern *Armenia* is smaller than, and has different boundaries from, the ancient Armenia. Like neighbouring Azerbaijan, it became part of the USSR in 1920, while much of the older country of Armenia remained part of Turkey. The Armenians have been strongly influenced by all major sources of the area, from the sixteenth century occupation by the Turks, the earlier and later incursions from Persia and, since 1800, Russia. Their costume shows all these influences, especially in the full trousers, long caftans and leather boots with turned-up toes. The extreme winters have led to extensive wearing of heavy wool and fur.

The lands of *Kurdistan* are today divided between three countries – Iran, Iraq and Turkey. The nearly two million Kurds, who have successfully defended themselves from their neighbours since earliest times, are still a warlike, nomadic mountain people, now slowly losing the struggle for their independent way of life under the pressures of the modern world. The chief industries are the production of wool, fur and hides and these products are made into carpets and garments, the high quality wool being especially prized. Kurdish dress, though it has much in common with that of the rest of the Caucasian area, is distinctive. It has to cater for an extreme climate and for a hard nomad life, much of it spent on horseback, yet the quality of decoration and of the actual garments is colourful and original.

Georgian dress.
Shaggy wool burka
(mantle). Coat and
trousers, boots,
fur hat

Circassian in typical
national long coat,
fur-edged hat and
loose trousers

Armenian. White
turban and red hat.
Red leather boots.
Silk sash over cloth
tunic

Kurdish noble-
woman.
Embroidered caftan
over gown with
sash

Kurdish horseman
in caftan (djubbah)
decorated in black
silk and silver
embroidery.
Leather boots

Armenian girl.
Decorative coat
over full trousers.
Boots. Wide sash

CAUL
Gold, jewelled caul,
1240

White linen head-
dress and metal
caul, c.1300,
Danish

White headdress
with caul, France,
thirteenth century

Caul headdress,
France, fourteenth
century

Padded headdress
and jewelled caul,
1445

Jewelled cap and
net, Spanish, 1515

Gold caul and ear-
plate, Flemish,
1505–10

Navy straw hat,
veil and snood,
1945

Reticulated head-
dress with wired
veil, 1420

Gold, jewelled,
cylindrical cauls
and fillet. White
veil, 1350

CAVALIER DRESS
Cavalier dress, 1640–9, England

Caul

A netted cap was worn by women in different ages, but especially in the medieval period. The cap was of silk or wool and covered with a trellis or net of cord made of coloured silk, wool, or gold or silver thread, jewelled at the intersections. In the Middle Ages there were many differing designs of these reticulated head-dresses, such as the cylindrical cauls held in place one on each side of the face by a band round the brow in the fourteenth century, or the box shapes over the ears which preceded these. Such designs were attached to rigid metal frameworks but other, softer designs were worn earlier as well as later in the fifteenth century.

Decorative cauls or nets to hold the hair were adopted by men as well as women in widely dispersed communities and periods, such as those depicted in Greek and Roman dress, seen in Bronze Age remains from northern Europe, or shown in portraits of Italian Renaissance beauties. Cauls also appear in nineteenth-century dress, particularly in the early years when Greek modes are being emulated. The final phase appears in the 1930s with the snoods and hats with attached nets at the back; these were often made of chenille.

Cavalier dress

The term cavalier was applied to the followers of the royalist cause of Charles I of England in the 1640s. The dress worn by the cavalier was the same as that of the aristocrat or well-to-do man in the remainder of western Europe, comprising, as in the illustration, a gaily-coloured silk, satin or velvet matching jacket and breeches decorated with braid; a lace falling-band, cuffs and boot hose tops; a cloak; plumed, swashbuckling hat; gloves; cane; and soft leather bucket-top boots with heels and butterfly surpieds. Hair was natural, worn long and in ringlets or curls. The shirt was of fine white silk or linen and visible on the chest with the open jacket, and on the sleeve.

Ceinte

In the fifteenth and sixteenth centuries, a girdle. From the old French *ceint*.

Moslem woman from Trebizond,
Turkey
Tcharchaf of white silk
decorated with silver thread.
Black net petche (veil) with
border of gold passementerie,
1875

Moslem woman from Van,
Turkey. Tcharchaf of check
wool with dark panels and
borders

Moslem woman from
Afghanistan, late nineteenth
century. Chadri and chalvar of
cream-white cotton, shoes
attached to chalvar. Rū-band
mesh opening for the eyes in
white silk drawn thread-work
and embroidery

Cestus

1) In classical dress a waist *belt* or *sash*. In classical mythology referred especially to one worn by Aphrodite (Venus). Also a nuptial girdle. From the Greek κεστός and the Latin *cestus*, meaning embroidered.
2) A boxer's *glove* made of thongs of bull-hide loaded with strips of iron and lead, used in ancient Rome.

Chādar, chadri, çarşaf, burka, izār

Various names from different languages to denote the all-enveloping covering worn by Moslem women on top of their other garments to go out in public. Traditionally, it was Moslem women throughout the Arab and eastern world who veiled themselves in this way, but there were the exceptions of some Christian and Jewish women in Asia Minor and Syria who adopted the enveloping garment (though without adding the face veil), while in Malaysia and Indonesia Moslem women were not veiled. Moreover, the custom of veiling women in public began before Islam – in ancient Persia, for instance.

Instruction in the Koran on the subject of women's behaviour and attire in public is not dogmatic and provides guidance rather than rigid rules. Women are enjoined to look away from temptation and to preserve their chastity; they are not instructed to veil their faces so that they may not be seen. Because of this, each society has interpreted the guidance according to its age and former traditions. Thus societies with a history of rigid male domination interpreted the Koran to mean a strict veiling of their women in public, others were more tolerant in their understanding of the question. There were two items of clothing concerned with veiling. The names listed above refer to the all-enveloping cloak which was simply a very large piece of material – indeed, in a number of languages the word refers equally to a sheet or bedcover – and this was draped around the body, leaving only the face free. It was held in place by the hands or could be girdled.

Chādar is the Persian word and *chadri* the Afghan (see also *Afghan dress*). Both of these were often worn with a face veil, or the garment could be made to cover the face also and a fine threadwork lattice was embroidered at eye level for the woman to see where she was going. *Çarşaf* (or *tcharchaf*) is the Turkish word, while *izār* is Arabic. In the time of Mohammed the *izār* referred to a wrap for men, but from that period until modern times has described an enveloping cover for women, similar to a *tcharchaf* or *chadri*, which is accompanied by a *rūban* (a mesh panel for the eyes to peer through). In Moslem India the word *burka* (or *burkha*) also describes the enveloping cover, though the Arabic *burqu'* refers to a face veil.

The colours and materials from which these sheets were made varied greatly from country to country and according to the wealth of the wearer. Among the poor, black cotton was general, but ladies of wealth wore wraps of rich fabrics lined with satin or silk and bordered with embroidery and lace.

The veils which accompanied the enveloping sheet were even more varied in size, material and method of draping and were known by many different names – among these, from Turkey there was the *yasmak*, the *petche* and the *mahramah*; in Arabic the *burqu'*, the *rūban*, the *maqna'*, the *niqāb*, the *khimār* and the *wiqāya*; while in Persia there was the *pīcheh* and the *rūband*. Some of these words are clearly related, though the veils may differ in size and draping or fastening. The *yaşmak* was a veil worn in Istanbul. It consisted of two pieces of fine muslin, one of which was placed across the bridge of the nose and covered the lower part of the face, falling to the breasts, and was then tied or pinned at the nape of the neck, while the other was placed over the head, being brought down as far as the eyebrows while, at the rear, it

was pinned to the first piece or hung down the back loose. The veil was semi-transparent and allowed free vision but it was considered essential for most of the nose to be covered. In the rest of Turkey veils were heavier. Typical was the *petche* (*peçe*) in black material, sometimes made of horsehair; or the *mahramah*, which was of calico, thrown over the head leaving just the upper part of the face free and this was then covered by a dark square of material. The *burka* was imported from Egypt and was a large piece of black muslin which was draped over the eyes and fell in folds nearly to the ground.

In the Middle East in general, many types of veil were prevalent. They could be of muslin, cotton, linen or silk in white, black or, occasionally, coloured. The *burqu'* (*borkou*) was of linen in black or white or, occasionally, silk. It was attached to the hair on the temples and left the eyes free, or they were covered by a *rūban*. The *khimār* was small and was pinned to the crown of the head and covered the face. The *wiqāya* was of soft thin material and much larger, generally falling nearly to the ground in front. The *maqna'* was even larger but covered the head and was allowed to fall open in front. Persian veils included the *rū-band*, which was generally white and incorporated the fabric mesh panel for the eyes to peer through. The *pīcheh* was more like the Turkish *petche*, being black, often of horsehair, and covering the face completely.

Chainse

A white linen undertunic worn by both sexes in the early Middle Ages under the bliaud, the overtunic (see *Bliaud*). The chainse had sleeves fitting at the wrist, where they were visible below the shorter, wide sleeve of the bliaud. In women's dress the ground-length chainse also often showed below a shorter bliaud. Some writers assert that the chainse was the same garment as the chemise or shirt but some early descriptions refer to the wearing of both garments, chainse over a chemise (see also *Chemise*).

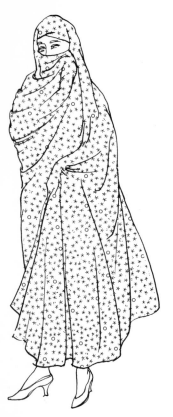

Persian chādar of patterned cotton, twentieth century

CHAINSE
Noblewoman, *c*.1000 AD. White chainse under dark, bordered bliaud

CHALVAR ETC.
Woman from Damascus, Syria,
1875
Chalvar and dress of satin,
striped in pink and purple
Bare feet in leather strapped
pattens (kub-kobs). Silk and
muslin headdress

Woman from Angora, Turkey,
1870. Fez with kerchief. Cotton
robe and jacket
Satin chalvar. Leather shoes

Modern Egyptian use of chalvar

Chalcedony, cassidoine

A variety of quartz with a wax-like lustre; either transparent or translucent. Other varieties of different colours are known in lapidary work under the names of agate, cornelian, onyx and chrysoprase. The use of this material in jewellery is an ancient one (see Bibilical reference: Revelation 21 v.19), but the sometimes quoted assertion that it stems from the Ancient Greek city of Chalcedon is not proven.

Challis

A fine silk and worsted fabric of soft, pliable texture used chiefly for ladies' dresses, negligées and children's wear. Introduced at Norwich in 1832. Now made of fine wool or wool with rayon or cotton.

Chalvar, chalwar, şalvar, shalvar

The full, baggy trousers worn in the Balkans, Asia Minor, the Middle East and Persia. Suitable for both men and women, the garment is about three yards or more in width at the waist and is drawn in by cords or a girdle. The leg portion, which is also very full, is either looped up and tied below the knees to fall in loose folds to the ankles or is ankle-length and tied there.

The chalvar or şalvar is thought to have originated in Iran and it is believed that the Arabs first saw this type of dress when they invaded Persia in the seventh century, though legend has it that Mohammed himself wore the şalvar before this. In the Moslem world, especially under the Ottoman Empire, women were encouraged to wear the şalvar; portions of the Koran were quoted to reinforce the view that, since the garment so thoroughly encloses the body from waist to ankle, it is suited to the maintenance of feminine chastity.

In Asia Minor the salvar was worn chiefly by women and was an important item in national dress. It was accompanied by a blouse or chemise, waistcoat and caftan (see *Turkish dress*). The garment is still worn today for work in the fields, which is traditionally and presently carried out chiefly by women. The suitability of such a garment can be appreciated when one observes a farm-worker weeding or planting crops. She bends over from the waist downwards, the legs apart and not bent at the knees. The ṣalvar keeps the body protected and covered, with no gap at the waist, where a chill may be taken, yet it gives complete freedom of movement. For similar reasons the ṣalvar was worn for centuries by men in the fighting forces.

The chalvar (ṣalvar) is generally worn by peasant women over the whole Balkan and Middle East area without the linen drawers underneath. When adopted by urban women of greater wealth or standing, linen under-drawers were put on first and the chalvar on top was of a rich fabric such as satin or brocade with gold and silver threads, and many yards of material were used to give great fullness and grace of drapery.

Chamarre, simarre, chimer

A loose gown, generally of rich material and heavily decorated. The French word *chamarre* refers to the masculine gown introduced about 1490 which was fashionable in Europe in the first half of the sixteenth century, especially in France, Germany and England. It was wide, loose, open in front, generally with a turned-back, large collar and had sleeves which were puffed or very full at the top and sometimes hanging behind the arm. It was richly ornamented with braid, passementerie and fur and was lined with fur or with silk of contrasting colour, hence the French word *chamarrer*, which means to bedeck or decorate gaudily. The English word is *chimer* or *chimere*, taken from the medieval word chimera.

This garment for the well-to-do stemmed from the coat made of sheepskin traditional to Spain and known there as the *chamarra* or *zamarra*; similar was the *acciamarra* of white sheepskin in Sardinia. The Italian word is *zimarra*, and a garment known variously as *simar*, *simarre* or *cimarra* appears from early medieval times in the Middle East, especially Persia and Arabia, where it refers to any loose, rich gown, and it is probably from here that it was introduced into Europe.

CHAMARRE
King Henry VIII of England, 1538, dressed in red velvet chamarre decorated in gold thread and trimmed and lined with brown fur.

Chamois

An agile antelope indigenous to the high Alps, Pyrenees and other mountain areas. *Chamois-leather*, which is very soft, pliable and strong, was originally prepared from the skin of the chamois, but now comes also from the skins of sheep, goats and deer. Of a deep yellow colour, it is used chiefly for gloves, linings and pockets. *Chamois-cloth* is a cotton fabric made to imitate chamois-leather and is used for the same purposes. (See *Leather*.)

Chaplet

A wreath or garland of leaves or flowers worn round the brow as a mark of esteem. Also known as a *capulet, capelet* or *anadem*. Could also be, in the Middle Ages, a circlet set with gems.

Chatelaine

A gold or silver chain to which were attached keys, scissors, penknife, thimble-case, button-hook, tape measure, handkerchief or smelling salts; worn by ladies round the waist.

Chausses

Anglo-French term for medieval hose. Referred to the lower part of the hose covering the foot and lower leg. From the seventh to the eleventh century was generally criss-crossed by gartering to the knee.

Chemise

An undergarment made of white linen or silk in the form of a shirt for men and a smock or shift for women. It appeared in the fourth century AD as body linen, rather than the tunic, under the name *camisia* and replaced the earlier loincloth. It continued to be worn until the end of the nineteenth century and for much of this time was a full garment, gathered into a round or square neckband, where it was embroidered and finished with a frill. Sleeves were long and full and ended in wrist ruffles.

The chemise or shirt was visible during many periods of costume – at the neck above the tunic or gown, at the wrists and,

CHEMISE
White chemise, *c.*1500

White chemise, *c.*1515–20

Robe à l'italienne, *c.*1500.
Chemise shows at neck and
between gown sleeve sections

sometimes, on the sleeves, as in the fifteenth and sixteenth-century *robe à l'italienne* which had finestrella gown sleeves in two separate sections for upper arm and forearm. These were fastened together by laces or points and the fullness of the chemise sleeve puffed out between and at the shoulder, where the gown sleeve was fastened in a similar manner to the armhole. In the decades when the gown neckline was very décolleté, the chemise neckline was often low also, with its lace or frilled edging seen just above the gown. This was the fashion in the fifteenth century and again in the later seventeenth and the eighteenth century. With the three-quarter or elbow-length gown sleeves of these years, the chemise sleeve showed below ending in lace ruffles.

With the scanty feminine attire of the early 1800s, layers of underwear had been drastically reduced and the chemise was left off or a simpler, sleeveless design was substituted. With the gradual return of normal underwear in the years 1810–12, the chemise was returned to favour with the petticoat.

Chemisette

A white underbodice or fill-in of muslin or cambric with lace trimming. It had a high neckline ending in a small collar and could be sleeveless or have long or short sleeves. Fashionable especially in the later nineteenth century, ladies wore it under a day dress with a low neckline like a pinafore style.

Chenille

French word for a hairy caterpillar. Refers to a velvet or plush cord made with fibres of silk and wool protruding round a core of thread or wire and resembling the tufts of a caterpillar's back. Used for trimming, fringing and embroidery.

Chiffon

A lightweight transparent fabric, strong despite its fragile appearance. Made of silk, rayon or cotton.

Italian dress, 1774. Chemise frill
above gown neckline

Children's dress

Until the later eighteenth century children wore the same type of clothes as adults. Girls and boys of all ages are depicted in sculpture and paintings from the ancient civilizations of Egypt, Assyria, Persia, Greece, Rome and Byzantium side by side with their parents, and their garments are diminutive versions of the adult ones. Compared with modern children they also wore a greater quantity of jewellery and used cosmetics, just as their elders did; this was especially so in Egypt and Rome. *Medieval* sources of illustration, from illuminated manuscripts, tapestries, paintings and sculpture, evidence the same trend. Increasingly often portrayed by the fifteenth century, especially in Italy, are children beside their parents, dressed in diminutive renderings of their attire. The boys wear fitting hose with the fashionable tunic of the day, hoods and hats; cloaks and footwear like those of their fathers. Little girls are often bare-headed, their hair loose, and do not wear such elaborate head-dresses as their mothers, though they might be seen in a small turban or a coif with a veil.

By the *sixteenth century*, little boys up to about five years old were dressed in skirts like their sisters. After this they were 'breeched' and wore adult male fashions. These included all the trends of the day so that, in the first half of the century, they can be seen depicted in the square silhouette of the wide gown or robe and with wide, square-toed footwear; while in the second half they adopted the vagaries of trunk hose and bombast, peasecod-belly and large ruff. Little girls wore wide skirts with petticoats to maintain the fashionable full silhouette but, after the age of 10 or 11, wore some type of farthingale petticoat and restrictive bodices, French hoods and, in the second half of the century, ruffs or open, framed lace collars.

During the *seventeenth* and much of the *eighteenth century*, the custom continued of dressing children like their parents, but from the later 1770s garments for children began to show a divergence from adult dress and in many aspects the child's clothes were prototypes of designs adopted later by the adult.

The general trend for children's clothes in the years *1775–1830* was towards comfort and a greater freedom of movement. The liberalization of thought and the ideas and themes of philosophers such as the seventeenth-century Englishman John Locke and the eighteenth-century Frenchman Jean Jacques Rousseau were bearing fruit. It was not until the French Revolution of 1789 that adult dress changed so completely from the over-decorated and corseted artificial silhouette to a freedom of attire based upon classicism, though the trend in costume was perceptible in the previous decade.

In children's dress the development towards a greater suitability and freedom of movement in clothes began much earlier. This was particularly so in *boys' dress*. The baby boy was still dressed in petticoats and skirts in his early years – indeed, this custom lasted about 400 years, until the early twentieth century – but, after the age of five, instead of being put into knee-breeches, coat and waistcoat, the young boy was, from the 1770s, dressed in what was termed 'skeletons' or a skeleton suit. This consisted of a frilled shirt and trousers. These trousers, which originated from country peasant attire for relaxation, were nankeen ankle-length styles and usually buttoned on to the shirt. A short, fitting jacket, with two rows of buttons extending from shoulder to waist, was often worn on top of the shirt. White socks and flat, black shoes completed the costume. Sometimes a sash was worn on top of the costume, round the waist. The interesting item of dress here was the trousers which were introduced for boys a generation before their use was accepted by men. After about 1830 the short jacket without waistcoat continued to be worn by boys over a shirt whose frilled collar was gradually replaced by a turned-down plain one. This jacket was the basis for all designs for boys and followed on from the skeleton suits of the older boys. It was only waist or hip-length and, though open in front and without collar and revers, was the

Maximilian Sforza as a boy, c.1496 Tunic and skirt in gold and white, red and blue sleeves. Red hose and hat

Ancient dress. Diminutive of parents

Child in striped gown, 1377

Boy in floral patterned houppelande, dagged edges, c.1420

Italian girl aged 4. Jewelled dress and cap, 1562

Small boy in child's chair, German, 1531

Italian boy in dark velvet gown with gold banding and fur lining, c.1550

Small boy, Italian, 1560

Flemish girl in blue dress with black velvet trimming. French hood, 1520

Italian girl in gold cloth dress and high ruff, 1581

Very small child in grey dress and black banding worn over wheel farthingale, Flemish, 1590

Italian small boy in doublet, jerkin and trunk hose, 1581

Czech boy in dark green jerkin with silver decoration. Red trunk hose, white shoes and doublet, 1580

Two Spanish boys, the elder in jerkin, doublet and trunk hose, the younger in dress and petticoats. Rich embroidered and jewelled fabrics, 1577 forerunner of the Eton jacket. In the 1830s, young boys alternatively wore loose tunics which were belted at the waist by a broad band. These were the child's version of the man's full-skirted coat, but the garment also derived from the countryman's smock. The tunic was of different materials – cotton, wool, tweed, velvet and was nearly knee-length. It was worn over trousers, while the shirt beneath still had a frilled collar worn outside. Trousers were usually supported by braces worn on top of the shirt or blouse. Boys wore hats like their fathers' or, between the ages of five and ten, wore soft, flat-crowned caps with peaked brim.

With *girls' dress*, the change from corseted waists and layers of petticoats and underskirts towards the Empire style of high-waisted simple dresses came, similarly, earlier than with adult design. This freedom of movement and attire stemmed, as with boys' dress, from the social and philosophical ideas of the day, and began to affect children's clothes in the 1780s. Girls wore white or light-coloured dresses, usually with short sleeves and with sashes encircling a high waist. This ankle-length dress was based on the designs for small children and was worn over a minimum of underwear. Materials varied according to season and time of day. Light wool was usual in winter, cotton in summer; for evening, muslin or silk were worn. As with the later adult Empire dress, a variety of cloaks, capes, spencers, tippets and pelisses were added on top for warmth.

Pantaloons were fashionable during the nineteenth century. In the early years they were not seen, being hidden by the skirts, but after about 1820 it was fashionable for the lace-trimmed pantaloons to show below the shorter dresses, for boys under five as well as girls. As children's dress from 1800–50 followed adult modes and skirts widened, both boys' and girls' skirts became shorter and so did the pantaloons, so that only a few inches of embroidered frill showed below the dress hem by mid-century. The drawers or pantaloons could be full-length – that is, with bodice, shoulder straps and legs – or could extend from a waist-band downwards. Some

examples, pantalettes, were just leglets and were tied on by tapes at the knee (see *Pantaloons* and *Pantalettes*).

By the later 1830s, clothes for children, as for adults, moved once again towards restriction and artificiality of line and silhouette. In the mid-century very young *boys' clothes* tended towards the effeminate and boys were kept in skirts as long as possible. These skirts were worn over flounced petticoats and displayed lace-trimmed pantalettes or knee-length trousers beneath. With the older boys, some public school uniforms, such as that worn at Eton College, established a pattern for boys' dress in general. The short, open jacket of the early nineteenth century was the basis of this *Eton suit*, worn with trousers, a white shirt, white, stiff, turned-down collar, black tie and waistcoat. Originally the jacket was coloured, differing from school to school but, with the general tendency towards dark clothes for men, the Eton jacket became black and this pattern was generally followed. Trousers were usually grey. Until mid-century the head was covered by a low, peaked cap; after this a round hat and, later, a top hat, were worn.

In the 1840s, dresses for *girls*, like the adult ones, began to have fuller skirts and flounced petticoats were worn underneath, generally displaying lace edging below the dress hem. In the 1850s, girls were put into boned bodices from the age of about 11, and stiffened petticoats or crinolines were worn under the increasingly full skirts. The length of these varied according to the age of the child. In little girls the skirts were just below knee-length and the petticoats showed below. The styles of dresses, boots, hair and bonnets were miniature versions of adult ones.

From about *1860–65* there was more variety and choice in clothes for *boys*. Younger boys wore full knickerbockers fastened at the knee (see *Knickerbockers*) – while older boys were clad in long trousers – together with a short jacket which fell open from a single fastening at the neck. *Knickerbocker suits*, introduced from the USA, became fashionable, with the two garments made of matching material. *Blazers* came in in 1880, there were also

German boy, 1629. Gold brocade doublet and breeches

Italian little boy in red dress and sash, 1607

Spanish little girl in farthingale, c.1656

Italian little girl, 1700–5. Fontange headdress, embroidered apron

Small boy, Czechoslovakia, 1605. Dress over farthingale skirt

Dauphin of France, 1610. White satin doublet and red breeches, blue baldric

French children – 1751, small boy in blue dress trimmed with black fur.

Small boy in grey silk coat and breeches, 1763.

Girl in cream satin dress and lace apron over paniers, 1752.

Louis I of Spain as a boy, 1692. Blue silk jacket and petticoat breeches. Powdered periwig

Swedish boy, 1626. Doublet and breeches. Lace falling ruff

Flemish girl, c.1655. Red dress and white apron

Italian boy and girl, 1752. White powdered hair. The boy dressed in blue, the girl in pink

French little girl, 1645. White, lace-edged apron over blue and gold dress

German little girl, 1625. White silk dress piped in blue

reefers (both worn with long trousers), and soon boys were wearing belted *Norfolk jackets* with their knickerbockers similarly designed to those of their fathers (see also *Jacket: blazer, reefer, Norfolk*). From the 1880s young boys were often dressed in knitted woollen *jersey suits*. These, which were warm and comfortable, were popular until well into the twentieth century.

In Britain there was an extended vogue from the 1840s onwards for children's clothes (and adults') to be made in tartan fabrics. Winterhalter's painting of the royal children in 1849 helped to popularize the tartan vogue, and Queen Victoria's taste at Balmoral and Prince Albert's interest in Scottish designs were also a strong influence. *Highland dress* styles were also very fashionable for boys and girls, both of whom wore kilts; with this boys had a fitted jacket and glengarry cap, girls a blouse and tam-o'-shanter.

Sailor suits were very popular for boys for much of the second half of the century, and especially in Britain and Germany for both countries possessed a powerful navy which was held in high esteem. In Britain, the royal family's close links with the Royal Navy during these decades helped to popularize the fashion, which stemmed from Winterhalter's portrait of Prince Edward (later Edward VII) at the age of five – mothers wanted their sons to be dressed similarly. In mid-century the sailor suit for boys had long trousers, a blouse with a large square collar edged with blue and white stripes, and a circular straw hat. These hats were based on the flat-brimmed style worn by sailors but the children's version had a turned-up brim. Variations on the design of the sailor suit were incorporated as time passed. Young boys wore knickerbockers instead of trousers and caps replaced straw hats in winter. In general, the winter suits were of navy serge with cotton shirts and navy cap; in summer, white drill with straw hat was the vogue. Girls too wore sailor blouses with large square collars, together with pleated skirts, reefer jackets and straw hats. These blouses were fashionable in the early years of the twentieth century in the USA

where they were known as *middy blouses*; the term was used in Britain also.

Of quite different design for boys was the somewhat effeminate dress based on *Little Lord Fauntleroy*. The Fauntleroy style was a 'best suit' favoured by mothers (but not usually by their sons) in the 1880s and 1890s. The dress, which was elegant and somewhat extravagant, was based upon the Cavalier style of the 1640s and was quite unsuited, even as a party dress, to the later nineteenth century. It became fashionable through the influence of the Aesthetic Movement of the time. *Little Lord Fauntleroy* was a book written by Frances Hodgson-Burnett, an English-American novelist, and published in 1886. It was immensely popular and ran to many editions. This style of dress for boys had been evolving before the book's publication but the illustrations in it, by Reginald Birch, of Cavalier dress, set the seal on the fashion and it was enthusiastically adopted for the rest of the century. It consisted of a black or coloured velvet jacket and knickerbockers tied with a broad sash at the waist, and was decorated by a white lace falling-band on the shoulders. Hair was grown long and curled. White stockings and black buckled shoes completed the ensemble.

Girls' clothes from the 1860s were closely patterned on those of their mothers. In the 1870s and 1880s, styles of dress for girls were at their most restrictive of the century. They wore tightly-laced, boned corsets, despite ever increasing warnings from doctors of the dangers of constricting the bodies of growing children into these cages. The damage which could be caused by impeding circulation and breathing by restricting the development of the muscles of the chest and abdomen, and even the displacement of vital organs, was described and publicized, but most mothers continued to dress their daughters in the fashions of the day – the wasp waist, emerging from its swathes of bustle draperies, remained supreme. In contrast to this, and a parallel to the Fauntleroy theme, was the *Kate Greenaway* costume. Catherine (Kate) Greenaway (1846–1901) was an English artist and illustrator who produced

Little boy in skeleton suit, 1785, English. White blouse and trousers, blue sash

Little boy, 1851, English, plaid dress

Swiss girl, 1805. Pale green dress with black and white stripe. Black velvet sash

Swiss little girl, c.1805. White cotton dress with white embroidery

English girl, 1840. Green and fawn shot silk dress with braid decoration. Embroidered white drawers

Austrian boy, 1835. Gold-brown coat with black belt. White trousers

Spanish boy, 1830–40. Black jacket and grey trousers. White blouse with red bow tie

French boy and girl, 1855. Girl in grey dress with pink stripes. Boy in darker grey dress with brown velvet banding

French girl, 1878. Brown wool dress and black boots

French boy, 1857. Black velvet suit and cap

French girl, 1899. Pink suit and hat. Beige and pink check blouse and ribbons

Swiss girl, c.1876. White piqué dress with white lace decoration.

French girl, 1858. Blue silk dress over crinoline. White lace decoration. Blue boots

French boy, 1844. Black jacket and top hat. White trousers with blue stripe. White blouse

French little boy, 1863. Brown jacket and trousers. Brown boots original children's books illustrated by herself. Typical were the annual almanack, published from 1883–95, and the Kate Greenaway Birthday Books. The children in her pictures were, like Little Lord Fauntleroy, dressed in fashions from a bygone and more romantic age – in this case, Empire dresses with high-waisted sashes, puff sleeves, shoulder capes, ankle-length skirts edged with lace and dainty bonnets, often worn over a frilly cap. She depicted little boys in skeleton suits. In the late 1880s and 1890s, the smocked-yoke style of dress became fashionable for girls and it was also comfortable and practical. Based upon the countryman's smock, the material fell loosely from the stitched smocking on the chest. Soon, blouses, pinafores and dresses were made in this style with gaily-coloured stitching carried out on light shades of washable fabrics. The fashion was especially popular for young girls and lasted well into the twentieth century.

As with adult dress, the events of the two world wars effected an acceleration of the trends in children's fashion and changes towards dress designed especially for the young were hastened. Between 1918 and 1939, *boys* generally wore a suit of short trousers, jacket and waistcoat or pullover. The outfit was completed by a shirt and tie, woollen socks to just below the knee with leather laced-up shoes and a peaked cap. In school uniform, coloured blazers and grey flannel shorts were worn; out of school suits were made of tweed or worsted. This attire was comfortable and hard-wearing, the only drawback being the coldness of bare knees in winter.

Girls in the inter-war years wore styles which closely followed those of their mothers; clothes were now simpler and more comfortable. In the 1920s the waistline was low and the dresses shapeless. Skirts were short and the long hair had been bobbed or cut into an Eton crop. In the 1930s form returned, also a natural waistline. Adult skirts were cut on the bias and were longer, but this only influenced the dress of older children. Between 1918 and 1939, younger girls wore short skirts

ending above the knee; this applied equally to dresses, separate skirts and coats. Underneath they wore woollen tights* in winter and had bare legs with short socks in summer. Winter footwear consisted of boots or shoes with buttoned gaiters, and in summer it was sandals or light shoes. Very young children wore bloomer play-dresses where the abbreviated dress and knickers were of one material.

In the 1930s, the adult wardrobe became much more extensive with the introduction of clothes for different occasions, such as sports dress, sunbathing attire, swim-suits, dance dresses, holiday clothes, etc. Similarly, children's wardrobes expanded and clothes were geared to comfort, play and suitability.

The real revolution in dress for young people came after the Second World War when, finally, in the 1950s, the informal clothes worn in the USA came to Britain and Europe. Designers worked to produce clothes especially suited to the young form, whether child or teenager, and the resulting modes were not suited to the adult, though many tried to adopt them. Clothes were tight-fitting, yet informal. The prime garment was the fitting trouser, either stretch pants or blue jeans. The latter had been the working dress of the manual worker and was now re-introduced as a cult for teenagers and a symbol of their freedom. Once again boys and girls dressed alike. In previous centuries boys, when young, had worn skirts like their sisters; now, sisters wore their brothers' style of trouser and unisex was once more in vogue. Soon after the war girls grew their hair long and flowing, looking rather like old English sheepdogs peering out through a curtain of hair. Boys, in contrast, had crewcuts. By the 1960s things went into reverse – boys began to grow long hair, girls cut theirs short again.

New materials such as nylon and the many easy-care, non-crush fabrics made new fashions possible, as well as patterns and textile surfaces. For younger children,

* These were, of course, fitting, woven knickers and not the nylon tights of today.

White cotton summer sailor suit, 1890

Skeleton suit 1815–20. White blouse and socks

Jacket and trousers, 1811

Eton jacket with grey trousers and black top hat, 1895

Little boy in navy sailor suit. Straw hat, 1883

Tweed Norfolk jacket and knickerbockers, 1906

French navy and white sailor suit. Grey socks and black boots, 1880

White dress with embroidered decoration. White socks and black shoes, 1924

Winter coat and fur muff, 1915

Fur-trimmed winter coat and hat. Tights, 1966

Wool coat with fur collar. Worsted trousers, 1976

Pinafore dress over a blouse 1976

Little Lord Fauntleroy style velvet suit with sash and lace collar

Little girl in sailor suit of navy and white. Black stockings and patent shoes, 1912

Girl in red blouse and patterned cotton skirt, 1976

play clothes were designed especially but, for all ages of young people, trousers were most often worn, especially in cold weather. For boys, short trousers had disappeared with the war and, with American influence, long trousers were worn from a very early age, of similar design to those adopted by their young sisters.

Chinchilla

A small *rodent*, native to the Andes in Peru and Bolivia, with a very beautiful, soft, bluish-grey coat with black markings. The Incas hunted the chinchilla for its fur and also as food. Its name derives from an earlier culture, the Chincas, who were conquered by the Incas – chinchilla is a diminutive of chinca. Since the days of the Incas, the chinchilla has been ruthlessly hunted for its fur until, in the nineteenth century, it became almost extinct and is now protected. At present it is bred in North America but is still a costly, rare fur. *Chinchilla rabbit* was bred for its fur in the early twentieth century. It is descended from a black and white hare and is now bred in California.

Chinchilla cloth is not an imitation of the fur. It is a cloth with a long nap, gathered in small tufts, and is used especially for children's coats.

Chiné

A silk fabric which has a pattern that appears to have 'run'. *Chiné* is a French word which refers to the Chinese process of colouring the warp threads before weaving.

Chinese dress

Chinese culture has developed and flourished over many centuries, the land area of China is immense and the population enormous, yet the basic garments worn by the Chinese people have changed remarkably little. In both the cut and number of garments, dress is traditionally similar for both sexes as well as for all social classes. The difference between an emperor's or a mandarin's dress and that of a peasant is largely one of richness of material, decoration and quality of cut.

The Chinese have always worn sewn, closed garments for protection against the climate. In cold weather these might be lined, also padded, and one layer of clothes is added on top of another. Cotton is the traditional Chinese fabric and cotton wadding has long been used to make padded garments which were adopted as protection from the cold. For the wealthier members of the community, garments could be of silk, satin or velvet, padded for winter warmth with raw silk or cotton and lined with fur.

The chief garments are, traditionally, a tunic or jacket (*san*) worn over trousers (*koo*). For centuries the tunic was cut in a T-shape and was slipped on over the head. It could be hip-level or knee or ankle-level, according to status and occasion. It had a round neck and wide sleeves long enough to reach or cover the hand. The coat or jacket derived from the caftan (see *Caftan*) and could be fastened up the centre front or – more typically Chinese, especially in long robes – overlapped in front at an angle and was buttoned or tied on the chest and down the right side. The trousers were amply cut, especially at the seat, and were fastened at the waist by a soft girdle. They could be worn loose or bound at the ankles. For the peasant population these two garments have been traditional wear for both sexes for centuries. Higher social classes have worn skirts and/or robes on top of these.

Long *robes*, made of beautiful silk fabrics and richly embroidered in gold and silver thread with coloured silks, have been traditional wear for both sexes in the upper echelons of society. For over 1,000 years the dragon was the most important motif on these designs, recurring in dynasty after dynasty. The robes of the T'ang Dynasty (618–907) and the Sung Dynasty (960–1279) were amply cut with wide, long, flowing sleeves and very full skirts, slit at the sides. Complex belts made of heavy, jewelled, metal plaques were worn with these robes. The style of robe changed somewhat with the Mongol emperors of the Yüan Dynasty (1279–1368). Their dress was strongly influenced by their own

Manchu princess in informal court robe. Plum-coloured silk embroidered in coloured silks, peony and hydrangea motifs. Later nineteenth century

Chinese lady, ninth century. Silk gown with stole, T'ang dynasty

Manchu Dragon robe in dark blue silk embroidered in gold and silver thread and coloured silks. Late eighteenth century

Chinese woman, early twentieth century. Trousers and ankle socks with shoes for bound feet

Chinese lady in cheongsam, c.1930

Costume of Mongol warrior horseman. Yüan dynasty, c.1280

Well-born Chinese in tunic and trousers, c.1910

Chinese mandarin in silk robe with decorative square panel, nineteenth century

Jacket and tunic over trousers, cloth cap, late nineteenth century

Mandarin silk robe with decorative collar and square panel worn over embroidered silk long robe with 'hoof' cuffs. Silk hat with peacock feather, late nineteenth century

Flowered silk
cheongsam. Chinese
fashion in Hong
Kong, 1955

Chinese woman's
shoe for bound
feet

Manchu lady's
coiffure, *c.*1880

Chinese official in
summer hat, *c.*1910

tradition and background and these famous warrior horsemen needed a more practical robe, even for state occasions. They had single or double leather or cord belts drawn tightly round a less full robe which reached the ankles, displaying wide, long boots. With the succeeding Ming Dynasty (1368–1644) there was a reaction and a desire to return to the traditional indigenous Chinese cut of robes. The 12-symbol robes were introduced with a careful disposition of the symbols (sun, moon, constellation of stars, dragon, pheasants, etc.) on specific parts of the robe. Red was the dynastic colour of the Ming and was used for official wear at court.

The *dragon robe* (*lung-p'ao*) achieved its greatest status under the Manchus of the Ch'ing Dynasty who ruled over the greatest Chinese Empire from 1644–1912. The principal motif on these long robes, which were worn by courtiers and officials, was the dragon, now virtually the symbol of China and to be seen on coins and the national flag. The Manchus, like the Mongols, were foreigners, warrior horsemen, whose indigenous costume was more fitting and practical than the traditional costume of the Ming Dynasty. They introduced the wearing of the dragon robe as a formal part of official dress (it was previously a garment traditionally presented to officials by the emperor). They altered the cut of the robe to make it less full and flowing, and slit the skirt front and rear for convenience in riding. The wide, flowing sleeves were replaced by long, fitting ones, terminating in the 'hoof' cuffs which almost covered the hand and were so called because of their resemblance to a horse's hoof.

Over the centuries of Manchu rule the dragon robe assumed a prescribed design. At first it was decorated almost randomly with dragons, clouds, flowers, arabesques and other motifs. Gradually, the dynastic costume was formalized and sumptuary laws were issued in the eighteenth century specifying cut, colours and general design for robes worn by different ranks of officials. For example, the yellow robe was reserved for the emperor and it would be decorated by nine five-clawed dragons and

12 symbols, while the skirt was slit in four places – the two sides, centre back and front. Ground colours differed for princes, while those of lesser rank could only have four-clawed dragons and two skirt slits. The designs were symbolic, representing a philosophical concept such as the 'waves of eternity'. The most usual robe had a striped (waved) hem with wave borders with surf, above which were depicted stylized mountains with clouds floating overhead. The dragons were on the centre and above them were the sun, moon and stars. Women wore robes like those accorded to their respective husbands or fathers.

On special occasions, high born Manchus of both sexes wore jackets over their robes, similarly decorated but with wide, flared collars. The *mandarin robes* – those of the Chinese officials – were loose and long and had wide, flowing sleeves or sleeves ending in 'hoof' cuffs. A large, embroidered square, one in front and one at the back, denoted the office and rank held by the mandarin, as did also the feather depending from the hat and his bead necklaces.

The *hats* worn by Chinese officials were of pork-pie shape for winter wear, had upturned brims of silk, fur or velvet and a crown covered in crimson silk. A jewelled ornament decorated the top of the crown and from this depended a feather. Both ornament and feather denoted rank (see *Feathers*). Summer hats were conical in shape, generally of woven rattan decorated with silk. Before the Manchu dynasty men wore their hair long and tied up in a knot on top of the head. The pigtail became compulsory under Manchu rule.

In general, women did not wear hats. By the nineteenth century, *coiffure* styles adopted by Manchu women were elaborate. The hair was piled up on top of their heads and held in position by wire frameworks and a pomatum made from wood shavings (*pao hua*). The coiffure was enlarged with false hair and ornamented with flowers and ribbon. Chinese women also had elaborate coiffures but these were smoother on the top of the head with the interest centred on the fringe and the hair coiled low at the back. Face powder and rouge were heavily applied (see *Cosmetics*).

The *binding* of *women's feet* in China was a tradition thought to have begun about 1,000 years ago as a fashion among the palace dancers. The custom was slowly extended among well-born women and it is believed that the chief reasons for the widespread and lengthy practice of this barbaric custom were for status, for a woman whose feet had been so treated quite clearly could not be a member of the labouring classes and, equally, she could not stray far from her place in her husband's home. Over this long period bound feet acquired the characteristic of a national fetish. The binding of a woman's feet began when she was a child of about six. The small toes were turned back under the sole and the foot was drawn tightly towards the heel. The foot continued to be bound always and gradually it became quite deformed, with the heel pressed into the instep. The shrivelled stump was then thrust into the tiny pointed shoe (see also *Shoes*). It was the fashionable Chinese women whose feet were bound, especially during the nineteenth century. Manchu women did not indulge this custom but wore normal-sized slippers which were mounted on a high wood block which had concave sides. This gave extra height, regulated the stride to a dainty, lady-like one, and kept the shoes out of the dirt of the streets (see also *Chopine*). Well-born men wore shoes or boots with broad toes mounted on deep white felt soles (see *Shoes, Clogs* and *Boot*). The ordinary citizen wore flat-soled slippers of black cotton or felt over white cotton socks.

In 1912 the rising tide of change swept aside the Manchus. The dynasty had been declining during the nineteenth century and Western influences made it impossible for China to be held back from emulating the developing world outside her boundaries. A republic was formed and the traditional Chinese culture began to give way to modern ideas. This was reflected in dress, but the country was vast and changes came only slowly. Women's feet were no longer bound but, for a generation

of women already bound, it was too late for freedom of movement. In the cities a mixture of fashions developed, with some taking to Western dress and others retaining the traditional Chinese garments. It was men who pioneered the wearing of Western clothes, but only in a small way. Men's clothes in the West in the 1920s and 1930s were unsuited to China's climatic extremes; they were too heavy for summer wear and not warm enough in winter so, in general, men took to Western hats, footwear and coats, but preferred their own style of jacket and trousers to the Western suit.

In the 1920s women in the cities began to exploit their new freedom to earn a living and to go about in public places. Having begun to adopt Western styles of dress, they went much further than the men had done, showing themselves to be more adventurous in responding and adapting to change. In the 1920s there was evolved the *ch'i p'ao*, or as it is better known in the West, the Cantonese word *cheongsam*. This proved an ideal compromise between East and West and, indeed, later became a European fashion also. It was a Chinese-looking dress but was also in fashion with the 1920s styles in the West. It suited the Chinese woman's slim figure perfectly and became so popular that by about 1930 this style of dress was worn by the majority of Chinese women. The *cheongsam* was a fitting garment made in one piece and fastened on the right side in Chinese style. It had a high stand-up collar and the skirt was slit at the sides to the knee or above. It was sleeveless or could have long or short sleeves. The dress was made in traditional Chinese materials and was padded in winter for warmth. The *cheongsam* began as a long dress but the hemline gradually rose so that by 1947–48 it was in line with Western fashion. It has continued to be fashionable to the present day, though it was not permitted to wear it in mainland China after the Communist takeover.

In rural areas, changes were very slow to come and traditional Chinese garments, which are eminently suited to the climate and to work on the land, continued to be

Modern dress in mainland China

CHOKER
Black velvet and lace choker
neckline

*c.*1902
Lace and velvet choker
neckline

worn. The blue cotton jackets and trousers, with straw sandals or black cotton felt-soled shoes, and the wide-brimmed straw hats, survive outside mainland China. Since the 1950s, in the towns, Western clothes are more widely adopted in a Chinese version of a suit – jacket and trousers for men or, for women, a blouse and skirt. The young wear jeans as elsewhere.

In *mainland China*, the Communist revolution of 1949 brought reforms and directives in dress as in the rest of life. Everyone was to wear the same dress, men and women, all types of workers. A drab uniformity was established very quickly and this sameness was based upon a blend of peasant and military dress. The new style of dress was a jacket with high collar, buttoned down the centre front, worn over long trousers. Men's hair had to be cut short, and a peaked cap covered it. Women's hair had to be straight and longer; their shoes had flat heels, and they could wear no make-up or jewellery. The garments were made of traditional Chinese cotton and the colour was prescribed according to the class of worker.

The attempt to erase any distinction of status could not last. Human beings are not equal and uniform in any society. The basic garments have not changed greatly since 1960, though dresses have been reintroduced for women and men's suits are more 'Western' than before. The main change is in differences according to status. The man or women in an important position wears clothes of better quality and cut than the peasant and of different materials and colours. Individuality is slowly returning.

Chintz

A painted calico imported over the centuries from India. From the Hindi word *chint*, it was originally written as *chints*, the plural of chint, and later acquired usage as a singular word. Present-day chintz is a printed, glazed cotton with brightly-coloured designs of birds and flowers.

Swedish, 1892. Pearl choker
necklace, 1905

Choker

Used to describe a necklace worn high round the throat, often in several rows of beads or pearls, or a high neckline to a gown or coat. Such necklines were especially fashionable in the later nineteenth and early twentieth centuries and whalebone strips were inserted at the sides to hold up the material.

Chopine

A sixteenth and seventeenth-century version of the patten. An overshoe – slipped on over the elegant, slippered footwear for use in the mud or dirt of the street – raised on high heels or stilts of cork or wood. Light in weight but decorative, covered in leather, velvet, silk or brocade and ornamented with lace and embroidery. Especially fashionable in Italy, and particularly Venice where the stilts extended up to 2 feet 6 inches in height. This made the Venetians unable to walk steadily in the street without assistance; wealthy ladies required a servant to lean upon and to hold up their skirt trains, which were exceptionally long. Such designs of chopine, made of wood, were termed *zoccolo*. Chopines were also fashionable in Spain and the vogue spread to southern Germany, France and Switzerland, but it was never popular in northern Europe.

Cloak, cape, mantle

The English word cloak derives from the medieval Latin *cloca*, meaning cape, and the Old French *cloke*, which was the same as the later *cloche*, meaning bell. The word was used because the most usual form of cloak in the early centuries AD, as well as in more ancient cultures, was a simple bell-shaped design without fastening, made from a roughly circular piece of material with a hole cut for the head. The German medieval design *Glocke* was similarly named.

A loose type of outer covering for the body has remained in use in all parts of the world since man first wore animal skins. Throughout the centuries the piece of fabric, large or small, was utilized by the ordinary man or woman as a blanket or bed-covering at night and a garment by day, its size and material varying only according to the climate in which it was being worn. Examples of this double use of the cloak stem most often from societies where a person had to spend the night in cold weather or in the open and required protection from the rain and wind. Roman soldiers used their cloaks for this purpose, as did the Scots who wrapped themselves in their plaid at night and pleated and draped it round themselves by day. In the Middle East, the Arab *burnous* and *hayk* have traditionally served the same purpose as they were essential in the chill of the desert night. The earliest cloaks were simply fur skins held to the body by a leather thong or fastened by a thorn or a crude pin at the shoulder. Later, the cloak became an outer garment worn over a tunic and hose; while in the more sophisticated times of the sixteenth and seventeenth centuries in Europe, this outer garment, still necessary for travelling, riding and keeping out the cold, had become an item

of fashion in its own right, with an elegance of line and beauty of fabric and lining.

The cloak has been made from every possible shape and size of material. In primitive times and in the ancient and classical cultures, it could be circular, semi-circular, a segment of a circle, a rectangle or a square; but it was simply a piece of material, not sewn, but draped or pinned about the person. Medieval mantles were similar and varied greatly in size; they were generally fastened by a brooch or cords at shoulder or neck. From the sixteenth century onwards, cloaks and capes were cut and shaped, sewn and lined.

In ancient civilizations in the warm areas round the Mediterranean and in the Middle East – in Egypt, Persia and Greece, for example – the cloak was often of fine linen or cotton and worn only on top of a loin cloth or short tunic. The *Egyptian cape* could be very fine, almost transparent, falling in pleats or small folds from the decorative neckband (see also *Egypt, ancient*). The *Cretans* wore cloaks in winter, but these were chiefly functional rather than decorative and were short, made of wool with fur edging. The coat or caftan was more usual in *Persian dress*, but the simple, circular cloak with a hole for the head, like the one illustrated, was worn by soldiers and travellers. The outer wear of *classical Greece* and *Rome* was entirely a draped style. Both sexes had large mantles or cloaks, such as the Greek *himation* and the Roman *palla* and *toga*, which were intended to provide warmth as well as to act as evidence of rank and position. The *himation* and *palla* were rectangular pieces of material and the *toga* was shaped as a segment of a circle. In both cultures there were also a variety of shorter, knee-length cloaks, such as the Greek *chlamys* and the Roman *lacerna*. These were generally fastened on one shoulder and were worn by men for travelling or by peasants and soldiers. Some designs had hoods attached, such as the Roman *paenula* (see also *Greece, ancient* and *Rome, ancient*). Byzantine cloaks and mantles followed similar lines (see *Byzantine dress*).

In *non-classical Europe* during the Bronze

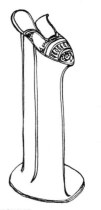
CHOPINE
Venetian chopine or zoccolo. Wood, about 2 feet high, sixteenth century

Velvet brocade chopine, Spanish, sixteenth century

German chopine. Leather with lace and fringe, c.1610

White leather chopine, English, seventeenth century

and Iron Ages and, later, during the early centuries AD, cloaks were the essential outer garment for both sexes. In the colder north, fur was widely used merely as a skin fastened by thorn or brooch at the shoulder, or as a lining to a wool garment. The shoulder fastening was more common than the brooch at the pit of the neck for, especially in the case of a man, it left the weapon arm free for action. Cloaks were semi-circular, square or rectangular and reached to the ankles or to the knees; some had hoods attached.

In the early *Middle Ages*, mantles for the nobility and wealthier classes were often very long and voluminous. Such mantles were worn over the ankle- or ground-length tunics of the eleventh to thirteenth centuries by both men and women. Sometimes the brooch shoulder-fastening was replaced by cords or chains across the chest, attached on each side of the garment to a metal boss. In the later Middle Ages, from the fourteenth century onwards, cloaks were worn less often, except if needed for warmth in travelling and riding. They had been rendered less necessary because of the introduction of the separate hood with attached shoulder cape, the varied designs of surcote, also the houppelande. Similarly, in the first part of the sixteenth century, the wearing of the loose, padded gown or chamarre made the wearing of a cloak superfluous on most occasions.

It was from about 1550–60 that the cloak returned to daily use, this time as a garment of fashion and not merely of utility. Capes and cloaks had long been traditional *Spanish garments*. In the second half of the sixteenth century, with Spanish dress paramount, they came into their own and spread all over Europe. Spanish modes were greatly varied – in length, in fullness, by the addition of hanging or open sleeves, and by the use of a wide collar or small turn-back or none. The method of wearing also differed as the garment could be worn round both shoulders or over only one, or might simply be draped over an arm or slung round the body by its fastening cords. The Spanish cloak was beautifully

cut and sewn; the materials used were rich and heavy; linings contrasted and edges and collars especially were luxuriously decorated. Earlier styles tended to be larger, later ones very short.

The cloak continued to be an item of fashionable dress for men in the seventeenth century until, in the last quarter, the advent of the *justaucorps* and the later *habit à la française* finally replaced the cloak with the traditional three-piece suit. In the 1630s and 1640s especially, the cloak was draped casually about the body, over an arm, over a shoulder, or suspended round the back by its cords – these were the most elegant ways of wearing what was a full, richly ornamented and beautifully lined article. In the early 1670s the cloak was still being worn for warmth in winter, slung round the shoulders on top of the coat, but after this it became an article reserved for wear in cold weather, at night, and for travelling and riding. Ladies had also been wearing cloaks for these purposes during the sixteenth and seventeenth centuries, but it had been an article of usefulness rather than fashion for them.

During the *eighteenth century*, greatcoats were more usual outdoor wear for men than cloaks, though the latter were worn for evening attire and for bad weather and travelling. There were several specific designs, such as the long, voluminous cloak with one or more shoulder capes, usually worn by men; and also the cardinal, which was a shortish cloak with a hood, for ladies. Some cloaks were named after persons who had made them famous for varying reasons; for example, the *Nithsdale*, a long, hooded riding-cloak, often fur-lined, which took its name from Countess Nithsdale who helped her Jacobite husband to escape from the Tower in 1716 disguised in her voluminous cloak. There was also the *Roquelaure*, named after the Duke who first wore it. This was a knee-length cloak with a skirt vent for riding on horseback. Worn all over Europe, and especially in the American colonies, it had a high or cape collar and was buttoned down the front.

The cloaks worn with masks at masquerades and carnivals derived from the

Pink silk lustring domino, *c.*1770–80, French design

Anglo-Saxon nobleman, tenth century. Dark red cloak

Greek dress. Tanagra terracotta statuette from Boeotia, 300–200 BC

Roman palla

Empress Theodora, sixth century Byzantine – purple mantle

Greek himation

English noble-woman, c.1310. Mantle fastened by cords

Green cloak with gold edging and ermine lining, German, c.1420

Nobleman, c.1105. Very long mantle

British cloak of dark wool lined with black fur. Bronze brooch fastening. First century BC

North African
wool burnous

fashions at eighteenth-century Venetian events. In Venice the custom was for both men and women to wear a loose cloak of rich, decorated material – a *tabarro* – and, on top of this, a *bautta* – a short, black net or lace cape attached to a black silk hood which covered the head and neck but left the face exposed. A white half-mask, called a *larva*, was worn with this outfit and a black tricorne hat was added on top. The *domino* was the equivalent dress in other areas of Italy and in Europe. This cloak was often black and was fuller and longer than the *bautta*; it was usually hooded and was voluminous. The Venetian attire is vividly depicted in paintings by Giambattista Tiepolo and Pietro Longhi.

In the *nineteenth century*, men more generally wore greatcoats of varied design for outer wear rather than cloaks, but voluminous cloaks were still in use for travelling, often with shoulder capes attached, and black *opera cloaks* were fashionable with evening dress, especially in the first half of the century. A bicorne hat accompanied these, or from about 1840, a Gibus, the collapsible opera top hat, named after its inventor (see *Hat*). The opera cloak was usually of velvet or cloth, fastened with silk cords and lined with coloured silk. The *crispin* was similar but had long cape sleeves. During the nineteenth century, as in the eighteenth, ladies frequently wore cloaks and capes of varied designs because their fullness and looseness was so suitable for wearing over the immense hoop and crinoline skirts. These cloaks, which had collars and/or shoulder capes, were made of all kinds of material suited to winter and summer fashion and varied in length from a mere shoulder cape to a ground-length garment. At the end of the century the multi-tiered shoulder cape with high collar was especially fashionable.

Apart from fashionable dress, certain types of cloak are traditional designs which have been worn for long periods in widely separated parts of the world and have continued in use for so many years because of their practical use for the protection which they offered from cold, rain or public gaze. The circular cloak, with or without a hood, but with a hole cut for the head and worn without fastening, has been referred to. This has appeared from earliest times and through the centuries from such widely separated periods and areas as the ancient Persian example illustrated, to the Alpine mountain cloak in Austria and Germany, its Pyrenean equivalent, and its near relation, the square-shaped Spanish poncho (see *Poncho*). Another design, most usually worn by women, is the full, long cloak made of heavy wool and with an exceptionally large hood; an Eskimo version of this, in fur, is described and illustrated under *Babies' and infants' wear*. A thick flannel design was worn extensively in Wales, especially in the eighteenth century. This was ankle-length, very full and was faced with silk. The large hood was gathered, then tailored into the stitched collar. A similar garment, usually in black cloth, was traditional to Ireland, where it was often termed a Kerry cloak. Sometimes the large hood was not cut separately and stitched on to the main garment but was part of it, draped or held in place by cords, brooches, or just the arms, and it thus enveloped the whole figure, head and body. This cloak is of ancient origin, dating back to the Arab world of the early centuries AD, where it took the form of the *haik* or *hayk*. It was imported into Spain by the Moors and was seen and illustrated by Christoph Weiditz in Granada in 1529, also in Flanders in 1532 (see bibliography).

From Spain, this design of cloak spread over Europe where it was especially popular with the women of Flanders and northern Germany in the sixteenth century, where it was known as a *heuke* or *huik*. Fynes Moryson, in his travels in Europe in the 1590s, describes this 'hoyke or veil' (see bibliography). There were several designs, chiefly the hooded *heuke*, the peaked *heuke* and the *heuke* with hat; Weiditz, in the 1530s, depicts the first two of these. In the hooded design, wire or whalebone was used to stiffen the upper part so that it projected in front of the head like a canopy. The peaked *heuke* had a wood or whalebone structure at the top

English gentleman,
c.1670. Silk cloak

Don Fernando
d'Aragon, 1575–80.
Spanish cape in
dark velvet

Blue velvet cloak
trimmed with
ermine, English,
1857

French gentleman,
c.1635. Dark cloth
cloak over the arm

woollen cloak
shoulder cape
own, red and
Blue ribbons
ringing,
sh, 1839

Gold cape, Flemish,
1580–5

Dark green wool
shoulder cape in
three tiers, white
satin piped edges,
English, 1900

Red silk cloak with
shoulder cape,
English, c.1775.

North African
hayk of striped
cotton

which projected in front like a duck's bill and the fabric of the cloak was held close to the face at the sides. The bill or peak acted as a counterbalance to the weight of the material of the garment. At first the bill was flat but gradually it became higher and concave on top and convex beneath. In the later sixteenth century the round hat with a spike on top was often worn on top of the *heuke* and held it in place on the head so that it could be draped in folds round the figure without a peak. The *heuke* continued to be worn in the early decades of the seventeenth century, when the material was often pleated, causing the fabric to fall in a multitude of folds.

The Arab garment, the *hāyk* – derived from *hak*, to weave – which was the prototype of these European cloaks, was an oblong piece of cloth (generally striped) which the Arabs used to wrap round their head and body over their other clothes. It was used for day or night wear and measured about six yards in length and five to six feet in width. The same type of garment survived – worn by the women illustrated by Weiditz – in Granada in 1529 and is also in use by Tunisian women of the twentieth century.

Another Arabic garment, related to the *hayk*, is the *burnous*, also used as an item of clothing by day and a blanket by night. This is a hooded cloak, worn extensively now and for centuries past by Arabs and Moors and also in Turkey. Often it is fringed-edged and a tassel decorates the lower edge of the hood. Usually it is made of wool and is often white. The Arabic word was incorporated into Spanish as *albornoz* which, in the seventeenth century, was a hooded travelling cloak.

Clogs

Shoes or overshoes made partly or wholly of wood with a thick base to protect the wearer either from mud and dirt in the street or from conditions of work in the factory or farm. The thick base or sole is usually of wood though it can be of leather.

Though there are many variations on the theme in different parts of the world, there are two basic designs of clog; the shoe and the overshoe. In the latter case, many types – especially in the Middle Ages and sixteenth and seventeenth centuries – were almost synonymous with pattens. That is, they consisted of deep wooden soles held to the feet by straps, ties or buckles and were worn on top of soled hose or soft shoes (see *Patten*). This type of clog continued in use into the eighteenth and early nineteenth century, where a clog might be designed to fit over and conform to the materials of the shoe, such as the brocade one illustrated. The wooden clog, attached to the foot by straps or cords, is traditional to the more primitive parts of the world with a warm climate. Here, the clogs were not worn as overshoes but on bare feet, the deep sole being necessary to protect the foot from stony ground. African examples, for instance, are of carved and brightly painted wood with decorative cords or leather straps. Similar are the Japanese *geta* or *gaeta*, which have deep wood soles some three to four inches in depth and are painted in bright colours and designs. The straps of velvet or cord are attached between the toes. Here, the *geta* is an overshoe, for it is worn in addition to the *tabi*, the sock-like Japanese footwear (see *Japanese dress*).

The clog which is in the form of a shoe has been worn for centuries in northern Europe and also in the East. The Chinese version has a very deep sole, more like the European chopine (see *Chopine*). This is of wood or, sometimes, felt or leather and the upper is decorative, made of richly embroidered silk.

In Europe, the working clog made entirely of wood is indigenous especially to northern France and the Low Countries. Known as a *sabot** in France and Belgium and a *klomp* (or *klompen* for a pair) in Holland, the clog is carved from a single block of wood and shaped to fit the foot. Everyday designs are left in the natural

---

* The wearing of sabots by French workers led to the term sabotage. The French verb *Saboter* means to make a noise with sabots or wilfully to damage. Sabotage therefore came to mean the wilful destruction of plant and machinery by dissatisfied workmen. The term came into general use after the French railway strike of 1912 when the strikers cut the shoes (*sabots*) holding the railway lines.

Heuke with hat, Dutch, 1580s.

Flemish woman wearing cloak like a heuke, 1531

Pleated heuke worn with hat over fashionable dress, Dutch, 1610

Ancient Persian circular cloak

Venetian nobleman wearing black tricorne and bautta of black net and silk over black cloak and fashionable dress. Eighteenth century theatre dress

Heavy black wool hooded cloak. Early nineteenth century, Welsh

Modern Tunisian street veil of style of Arab hayk

Moorish woman in Granada, 1529. Street dress of white cloak with grey fringe, based on Arab hayk, worn over yellow dress and white chalwar

Heuke with bill or peak. Black over purple dress, Dutch, 1580

CLOGS
Black leather, wood
and metal clog,
northern England

Woman's clog in
natural wood,
decorated in black.
Leather straps.
Nigerian, 1924

Child's carved
wood sabot with
leather strap with
dark blue cloth
edging. Breton

Man's clog with
leather and felt
sole, Chinese

Lancashire clog of
black leather with
wood sole

Shetland clog of
leather and wood,
1874

French sabot in
natural wood

Lady's clog covered
in black silk,
embroidered in
colours, Chinese

Japanese clog or
geta of wood
painted black with
straw sole and
black velvet straps

Boy's clog covered
in white silk
enbroidered in
blue and black,
Chinese

Japanese clog or
geta of wood
painted red with
gold design

Man's clog in
natural wood with
leather straps,
Nigerian, 1924

Lady's brocade
shoe with detach-
able clog,
c.1700–30

Child's clog of
wood, stained
black, Dutch

All these clogs are
in the collection
of the Central
Museum,
Northampton

wood but Sunday versions are stained or painted and decoratively carved and ornamented with coloured leather, velvet or cloth. In Britain, the tradition of the working clog dates from the Roman occupation and it has been worn in the country by labourers since that time. The British version has developed into a design with a leather upper and a wooden sole. This came into its own with the Industrial Revolution as it was eminently suited to factory work as a cheap, durable form of footwear which gave protection from the grease, oil and chemicals. It also continued to be widely used in the country, especially in the north. During the nineteenth century, clogs were the normal wear for the working classes, with one pair for work and a more elegant version for Sundays. The British clog was shaped to the foot, the black leather upper lasted and nailed to the wooden sole. A leather or metal strip was attached to the outer edge of the sole by brass nails to keep it watertight. Iron strips reinforced the under edge of the sole. The clog was worn over thick socks or bare feet and in the latter case it was first lined with hay, straw or bracken. Clog soles were made of alder, birch, sycamore or beech. They were turned up by about three inches from the toe to give a stride of a foot.

Cloisonné

From the French word *cloisonner*, to partition. An enamel process used in jewellery design. Thin metal plates are set on edge upon a foundation plaque and different coloured enamels are inserted into the compartments in powder form. The whole is then heated to a high temperature to liquefy the powdered enamels.

Cloqué

From the French word *cloque*, blister. Refers to a fabric which has a blistered effect. This is achieved by stitching an all-over pattern onto a material which has a thin backing or lining.

Cloud

A loose-knitted, filmy scarf of wool or silk, worn by women over the head and shoulders with evening dress, especially in the nineteenth century.

Clown, Pagliaccio, Pierrot

A character called *Pierro* appeared on the Italian stage in a comedy by Castelletti in the 1540s. His costume consisted of a long white tunic and trousers and he wore a straw hat. Later he appeared in French comedy as *Pierrot*. In the second half of the sixteenth century the character of *Pagliaccio* (the word means literally 'poor or inferior straw') became established in Italian comedy, clearly a close relative of Pierro. He was a teller of jokes and funny stories and was also dressed in loose white clothes with a deep ruffle at the neck. By the end of the century he was also known as Gran-Farina because his face was whitened also. Like the other characters in Italian comedy he wore a mask and had a skull cap topped by a tall hat.

The English version of this tragi-comic character is the *clown*, a much more fantastic and *outré* personality. From the eighteenth century onwards the clown has appeared in circuses and pantomimes. He is traditionally attired in a shapeless, loose, all-in-one costume confined at ankles and wrists. It is made of brightly-coloured material, decorated and appliquéd in diamond shapes and other motifs and usually with large buttons down the front. Like Pierrot and Pagliaccio, he wears a large neck ruffle, a skull cap and a hat and his face is whitened, but clowns generally also have red wigs, exaggeratedly painted lips and cheeks, and exceptionally long shoes which they pretend to trip over from time to time.

Coat

(see also *Overcoat* for outdoor coats)

It was in the second half of the seventeenth century in Western Europe that the coat began to replace the fitting tunics and jackets which had been customary men's wear for centuries. This coat, the *justaucorps*, emanated from France in the years 1665–70. At first it was a loose garment, reaching nearly to the knees and worn flared, its front edges turned back and decorated. Sleeves were fairly short, ending in deep cuffs. By 1680 the *justaucorps* had settled into its more traditional style. It was

CLOWN, PAGLIACCIO, PIERROT

Pagliaccio, *c*.1600 (after Maurice Sand)

Pierrot, late, seventeenth century

Modern English circus clown

English clown's shoe of black leather, nineteenth century
Central Museum, Northampton

Dark cloth tail
coat, Italian, 1815

knee-length and was buttoned at the waist where it snugly fitted the figure. Buttons and buttonholes, generally decorated by gold or silver braid and embroidered, extended the full length of the coat. There was no collar – this would only have impeded the fall of the curled periwig. Sleeves, now full-length, ended in immense turned-back cuffs which, like the pocket flaps, were decorated with buttons and embroidery. Often a rich sword baldric was slung round the body; also, deep waist sashes were fashionable. Towards 1700 the *justaucorps* became more waisted and the skirt fuller and flared. Fabrics were still rich – brocade, velvet, silk – and decoration equally so.

With the advent of the eighteenth century the *habit à la française* became the accepted attire for gentlemen all over Europe. This was a suit comprising coat, waistcoat and breeches. The same three garments were worn during the whole century, and though the silhouette changed slowly, almost imperceptibly, the process was continuous. The trend was towards a more slender, plainer and dignified streamlined effect. Fabrics became darker and less richly ornamented and there was a tendency towards making the coat and breeches of one material.

The coat, the *justaucorps* of the previous century, kept its flared skirts until about 1720. After this, the skirt fullness was arranged in a fan of pleats radiating from each hip seam, where a button was sewn at the head of the pleat – a fashion which survives in the tail coat. This fan-like spreading at the hip was the masculine interpretation of the feminine panier skirt. To maintain the desired shape, whalebone was inserted into the coat seams and buckram into the linings for stiffening. Until 1760 the coat remained full. It was made of rich fabrics in bright colours and was decorated by gold frogging and passementerie or coloured embroidery. Such ornamentation was centred on the pocket-flaps, the immense cuffs and the centre buttoning. After about 1760, the coat skirt lost its fullness; it was worn open and the front skirt edges sloped to the rear. Sleeves became

narrower and cuffs and pocket-flaps smaller. The skirt tails became shorter. A small collar and revers had developed since the wig was now tied neatly back away from the neck. Ornamentation was restrained and fabrics were often of wool rather than silk or satin, though velvet was still popular. Striped materials were fashionable. The simpler, English styles strongly influenced French male fashion in the 1780s. An example is the *frac* (*fraque*), the French version of the frock coat. This was a less formal garment than the *habit* and was quite plain; it had no pockets or cuffs and a flat collar. In the last decade of the century the coat was very slenderly cut and was restrained in design and material. It was worn open and had neat cutaway tails which now reached the knees at the back. Collars and revers were larger and the collar stood up at the back of the neck.

During the *nineteenth century*, colours for men's dress – most notably the coat – steadily became more sombre, fabrics became heavier and decoration more restrained. The years 1800–30 gave to the English gentleman the reputation of being the best-dressed man in Europe, and the supremacy of English tailoring was established at this time. For the first decade of the century the *tail coat* was cut straight across at the waist in front and fell to long tails at the back. The coat lapels were large, the collar high up to the ears and the sleeves were fitting. By 1820 two chief tail-coat styles had evolved, one double-breasted and cut away straight in front and with knee-length tails, the other single-breasted and cut away in a sloping line at the hips and with rounded tails. A *double-breasted coat* is one where the fronts overlap and there is a double row of buttons, one for closing and the other as decorative balance. In a *single-breasted* design the closure is central, fastened by a single row of buttons and buttonholes and there is no wide overlap of fabric.

Between 1810 and 1825 all coats became more waisted and fuller on the chest and lapels became smaller or were formed into a rounded, shawl collar standing away

Scarlet justaucorps with gold braid and buttons, English, 1695

Brown habit à la française with gold buttons, Italian, 1745–50

Blue satin habit à la française. Gold frog and button fastenings, English, 1735–45

Louis XIV in brown justaucorps with gold decoration and buttons, c.1685

Striped faille coat in light and dark green. Steel buttons, French, c.1789

Silk coat with gold stripe, French, 1790–5

Red cloth coat, German, c.1800

Green velvet habit à la française with gold braid and buttons, English, 1715

Red cloth coat with brass buttons, English, 1792

Grey tweed frock
coat and matching
trousers, English,
1899

from the neck at the back. Sleeves became fuller, especially at the top, and were pleated or gathered into the armhole. Materials became heavier, generally in wool, cloth or velvet, and colours darker – navy, brown, tobacco colour or dark green. From 1825–40 the waisted appearance of the coat was accentuated and the chest and hips were padded to make this more marked. Corsets were worn by many men to give the desired form. The tails were cut separately from the coat and seamed on, enabling this corseted look to be more clearly delineated. Collars were rolling, but many designs had pointed lapels also. The coat was generally worn open and the tails fairly short. Sleeves were full at the shoulder then fitting below. Blue, claret and fawn coats in cloth were fashionable. They had velvet collars and metal or pearl buttons.

In the second half of the nineteenth century there were four types of coat available for men, suitable for different occasions. Three of these had tails – the tail coat, the frock coat and the cutaway – the fourth was a jacket which, by the 1870s, was designed as part of a three-piece suit. All these, except the frock coat, still exist in present-day equivalents, though coats with tails are now reserved for formal occasions. The *tail coat* continued to be worn until about 1860 for use in town, but was seen less often after 1855. Like the other formal coats, it was now in black or dark cloth and had collar and revers buttoned high on the chest. The tails were knee-length or shorter. The style has survived in evening dress (see *Evening dress, men*).

The *frock coat* was worn into the twentieth century as formal city attire. Its full skirts were knee-length and level all round and there was a vent at the back. The skirt was seamed on at the waist. Most commonly double-breasted, the frock coat was often worn unbuttoned and it was the most characteristic style of the years 1850–1900. It was made of black cloth until later in the century when lighter grey versions became fashionable.

The *cutaway coat* also had tails. First introduced earlier in the century, when it

Sheepskin-lined
suède car coat,
English, 1960

was generally called a *Newmarket coat*, it largely replaced the tail coat in the 1850s and was preferred for less formal occasions and by younger men. It was black or grey, single-breasted, and was cut back in front to rounded, short tails. The edges were often finished with braid. By 1880 it had developed into the formal *morning coat*, now generally retained for weddings, racing and formal day wear.

There were two different styles of short coat. Early in the century the spencer was worn and, later, the sack coat. The *spencer* was only waist-length and had a roll collar and long, cuffed sleeves. It was worn by men from about 1790–1850 but developed into a fashionable jacket for ladies, especially to be seen in the years 1790 to 1825. The garment was waist-length only and this was very short as the waist-level of the time was high, just under the breasts. The spencer could have short puff or long sleeves and was of wool or velvet for outdoor wear or of lighter fabrics for use indoors and for evening. In the 1850s a short coat was introduced for informal wear and was accompanied by trousers made of a different material. The coat was plain, black or dark, and trousers were check, plaid or striped. At first known as *sack coats*, being shapeless and ill-cut, they were only worn indoors informally. By the 1860s they were regarded as suitable for street wear for informal occasions. The style had a high-buttoned, small collar and revers and generally only the top button was fastened high on the chest. The coat was single-breasted and its rounded front edges were finished with braid; some designs had velvet collars. After 1870 complete suits of jacket, waistcoat and trousers, all of one material, were introduced (see also *Suit* and *Jacket*).

In the 1890s a black dress sack coat was fashionable, worn with a black waistcoat and black and grey striped trousers. This attire lingered on as almost a uniform for city wear until the Second World War. Indeed, from 1900, men's fashions in coats changed very slowly with only minor alterations towards a looser cut and larger collar and revers buttoned less high on the

Dark blue cloth tail coat with black velvet collar, Austrian, 1826

Maroon cloth cutaway coat, German, 1845

Black frock coat, Russian, 1832

Blue silk spencer with white piped decoration, Italian, 1818

Black cloth frock coat, English, 1862

Black frock coat. Formal day dress, English, 1910

Morning formal dress, English, 1946

Dark brown tweed sack coat, English, 1862

Black cloth frock coat German 1873

Black cloth cutaway tail coat for formal dress, English, 1898

COD-PIECE
Cod-piece, English, 1505

Prominent padded cod-piece,
German, 1555

COIF
White coif, Danish, thirteenth
century

chest. Colours remained conservative, and worsted and tweed materials were usual according to whether the coat was for town or informal use.

In the years since 1950 men's dress has become much more varied and casual. Different forms of informal jackets and knitwear have tended to replace the sports jacket of the inter-war years. For formal wear the suit is usual. Innovations in coats have been more in materials – reversible and man-made fabrics, for example – than in style, though with the spread of private motoring, the short warm *car coat* made of suède lined with sheepskin, has become popular (see also *Duffle*).

Coat-hanger
The loop sewn inside the back of a coat at the neck so that the garment can be hung up. Introduced in the nineteenth century.

Coburg
A thin material of worsted and cotton or worsted and silk named after its German town of origin.

Cock
An upward turn of the brim of a hat or cap. The word applied to the angle of tilt, also to the peak or brim. An eighteenth and nineteenth-century term. (See *Hat, tricorne*.)

Cod, cod-piece
A *cod* was a bag. In the eighteenth century it became a slang term for purse. *Cod-piece* was the word used to describe the bag covering the fork of medieval hose or tights. This was laced to the hose by points. It was also used more and more during the fifteenth and sixteenth centuries to contain money and a handkerchief. In the sixteenth century the cod-piece was padded to make it protuberant and this custom was carried to excess by mid-century. Later, in the seventeenth century, after the bag or pouch had been discarded, the term was still in use to refer to the front fastening of the breeches. *Braguette* is the French word for cod-piece.

Coif
A white linen cap worn by both sexes, close-fitting to the head and tied under the chin with strings. Worn from the early Middle Ages onwards as a nightcap or under another cap, head-dress or hat. Also worn by professional men in the sixteenth and seventeenth centuries, by churchmen, lawyers and academics.

Cointise
A pendant scarf worn on ladies' head-dresses in the Middle Ages. Also a 'favour' as attached to the helmet of a jousting knight. Alternative word *quintis* or *quaintise*, meaning a quaint device or badge.

Collar
Until the early Middle Ages clothes were made without collars. From the thirteenth century a narrow strip of material began to be attached to the neckline of the chemise and/or tunic. On the latter garment this evolved, in the later Middle Ages, into

White valona worn over a golilla, Philip IV of Spain, 1525–30

Collet rotonde of lace and embroidery, Elizabeth I, 1589

Collet monté of lace, 1615

Collet monté, Flemish, 1625

Collet monté of lace, English, 1605

Fur-edged carcaille, 1385

White collar under striped scarf, English, 1831

Napoleon high coat collar, c.1799

Eton collar

High folded-down coat collar, 1787

Jewelled collar or carcanet, 1892

High standing collar, 1906

Standing collar, English, 1873

Shawl collar, French, 1830

Choker neckline,
English, 1905

High collar,
English, 1904

Peter Pan collar,
1935

Wing collar, 1915

Turned-down stiff
collar, 1916

Buttoned-down
collar, 1950

Open-neck
collar, 1951

Modern polo collar

Wing collar to shirt
blouse, English,
1895

Modern mandarin
collar

a stand-up collar, the height varying according to the date. In the late fourteenth century, for example, a high collar, known as a *carcaille*, was fashionable for both tunic and houppelande.

In the *sixteenth century* the collar became a separate article which finished the neck-line of the shirt or chemise; it was more usually known as a band and evolved in the early seventeenth century into the large lace collars known as falling-bands (see also *Band*). In the late sixteenth century the starched, wired and supported lace or lace-edged embroidered collars became fashionable. It began as a Spanish fashion, where it was a simple collar, open in front or encircling the neck. Called a *valona*, this was of white gauze, starched and generally plain. It was supported on the *golilla*, which was of card or stiffened material and set into the high doublet neckline.

Other nations adopted these stand-up collars but generally, especially in England, France, the Low Countries and Germany, they were much larger versions, made of or edged with lace, starched and supported at the back by a framework worn round the neck called a *rebato* or *supportasse* (see also *Ruff*). There were two chief designs of these collars, worn by both sexes; the circular one extending all round the neck without a break, which was called a *collet rotonde* or *whisk*, or the open style, which descended to a horizontal line in front, Flemish or Bohemian fashion, or, pleated and wired, framed the back of the neck only. This last style was fashionable with ladies, attached to a décolleté neckline; it was called a *collet monté* or *Medici collar*. In all these collars the back was supported to frame the head and the differing versions were modish into the 1620s.

During the second half of the *seventeenth* and much of the *eighteenth century*, the coat and waistcoat were collarless and neckwear was in the form of a cravat or scarf (see *Cravat* and *Neckwear*). In the later eighteenth century the small coat collar which had begun to develop by 1770 as the tied-back wig had replaced the full-bottomed style (see *Wig* and *Coat*), grew larger and, in the last decade, became a turned-down style worn high round the back of the neck with the wig bow tie hanging outside it. The collar was generally faced with velvet or satin or was embroidered. An especially high collar of this type was popularized by Robespierre and bore his name while, at the end of the century, the Napoleon style, with high collar and large decorative revers, retained the fashion until about 1810.

During the *nineteenth century* coats had varying styles of collars and lapels and, at the same time, the cravat was replaced by a detached shirt collar, which also took many different forms as the century progressed. In the first 30 years the coat collar was high at the back, standing a little away from the neck and was often of the *shawl* or *roll type* – that is, in one line from the back of the neck to the buttoning. In the 1820s the *M-cut* was introduced, where an M-shaped notch was made between collar and rever. In the mid-century collars and revers were small and the coat buttoned high, but after 1865 collar and revers became larger and were buttoned lower on the chest.

The detached *shirt collar* was white all the century and, for much of the time, starched stiffly. In the early years it was standing, with points rising high on to each cheek, but with a wide gap in the centre front to accommodate the chin. From the 1840s the collar was upstanding and very stiff; at first it was shallow but became deeper as time passed. Various names were given to slightly differing styles, such as the Piccadilly, the Rosebery (after the Prime Minister in the 1890s) and the Dux. In the later years of the century there was a tendency, especially in informal wear, for softer, turned-down collars, though white remained the usual colour. At this time ladies also wore similar collars with the shirt blouses which accompanied their tailored suits. The wing collar, with points turned downwards and outwards, was fashionable for both sexes in the 1890s and Edwardian years.

The day dress fashions for ladies between 1890 and 1908 had very high necklines. Elegant blouses and tea gowns had lace collars, boned at the sides to keep them up under the ears; these were *choker* collars. Other designs had deep velvet neckbands with a frill above. With evening dress the necklines were, in contrast, décolleté but the throat was still covered and decorated by a deep jewelled band, which was referred to as a dog collar or *carcanet*. This name derived from the eighteenth century term *carcan* which described an iron neck collar used for punishment. The carcanet was more elegant but some designs must still have been a punishment to wear.

The trend in men's collar styles in the *twentieth century* has been towards softer more informal wear. Until after the First World War the stiff white collar continued to be worn for most occasions, though the detached, softer, turned-down collar accompanied informal suits such as Norfolk jackets and knickerbockers. In the inter-war years there followed soft turned-down collars attached to shirts, also *buttoned-down* collars and, for informal and holiday wear, *open-necked* shirts. The slotted collar had slots on the underside to hold the plastic strips which maintained the shape of a soft collar and could be removed for laundering. For ladies, and for children, the *Peter Pan* collar was fashionable. Called after Sir James Barrie's perennially youthful boy, this was a round-ended, flat collar about two to three inches deep.

The trend towards informality and freedom of personal choice progressed at an increased pace after 1950. Informal knitted wear replaced, for men, the shirt collar and tie for many occasions. The *polo* collar which, at the end of the nineteenth century, had been a stiff, white stand-fall collar, now became a high, turned-down finish to knitwear, in use for both sexes. The *mandarin* collar was favoured for ladies' dresses and blouses. This design, of Asiatic origin, was a standing collar of about one-and-a-half inches high and with a small gap in front where the garment was buttoned across. For men's shirts of all kinds, formal or sportswear, the man-made fibres made possible the manufacture of stiffened, yet comfortable, collars which could be drip-dried and also appear attractively finished.

COLLARETTE
White lace
collarette, 1755

Collarette
A band of material such as lace, tulle or velvet, often ruffled and gathered, which encircled the lady's neck. Most usually worn with décolleté necklines or gowns with open, flaring collars, and especially in the sixteenth and eighteenth centuries (see also *Betsie*).

Colobium
A short-sleeved or sleeveless long, linen tunic worn by the Romans. It was later adopted as a liturgical garment but was afterwards replaced by the dalmatic (see *Dalmatica*). The colobium was also worn in Hebrew dress. A shorter garment, based on the Roman colobium and generally sleeveless, had an extended history as a loose blouse or open tunic for the ordinary man. It was in general use from the times of Ancient Gaul to the Middle Ages.

Conch
A shell-shaped head-dress and veil or cloak, worn in the later sixteenth and early seventeenth centuries. English versions were elaborate and of considerable size; they were often made of gauze mounted on a wire frame with a transparent veil behind. In France they were especially, but not exclusively, worn for mourning.

Cordelière

1) A knotted cotton *cord* worn as a girdle by Franciscan friars. Decorative versions with tasselled ends are fashionable in modern dress as ladies' girdles.
2) A wool and silk *material*.

Cordonnet

A fine cord of cotton or silk used to outline the edges of lace-work, also for fringes and tassels.

Cornet

A term applied to a varied selection of ladies' head-covering in different periods. First applied to the point on the early medieval hood, it was then used in the fifteenth century for a woman's cap with a point on top. Sometimes it was used to describe sixteenth and seventeenth-century caps with wired front edges or projecting crowns, also the term refers to caps with lappets which, in the later seventeenth century, lay on the shoulders. In the early nineteenth century a cornet was a day cap with frilled or ruffled front edge which was then tied under the chin and closely hugged the cheek-line. Out of doors such caps were worn under a hat, displaying the frilled edge. The term could also be used to describe the small hat style of the early years of the century.

Corsage

The upper part or bodice of a woman's dress which extends from shoulder to waist.

Corset

The corset has been the principal agent in aiding man in his desire to re-shape nature to conform to current fashion in clothes. For many centuries there was no attempt to do this; clothes were worn for warmth, for modesty, for religious significance, for sexual arousal and as a status symbol to denote rank and power. It was with the emergence of fashion, as distinct from costume, that man began to exploit the possibilities of variety offered by altering the shape of the human figure. A very early instance of this is recorded in the *Minoan* costume of *ancient Crete* where, from statuettes of the eighteenth century BC, we can see a corset formed of metal plates acting as a foundation for women's costume. This enabled the skirt to lie flat on the hips and accentuated the slimness of the waist; a boned bodice on top supported and lifted the bare breasts. It is the first recorded use in the West of metal for corseting and the restriction of the human figure. In the classical dress of *Greece* and *Rome* there was no attempt to re-shape the body. The natural line was followed and the figure delineated by narrow bands and girdles controlled the drapery. However, figure control was deemed important and literary evidence informs us that a *zoné* or girdle was worn around the waist and hips.

For centuries after the fall of Rome garments for both sexes were loose and full, held to the body only by a waist or hip belt. It was in the *twelfth century* that a corselet or shape-maker was worn, but this was an outer garment, not underwear, and was put on over the gown. This fitting bodice or corselet was sleeveless and extended from shoulders to hips, often being tightened by front lacing. It could be made of linen or soft leather and delineated the breasts, waist and hips in a natural form. In the thirteenth century garments returned to a loose, flowing style once more. By the middle of the *fourteenth century* the fitted tunics and gowns were being made for both sexes and fashion decreed a slender waist. Garments were tailored in sections to fit the figure and to display it, while under the tunic and gown was worn a stiffened linen underbodice whose purpose, as with the Greek *zoné*, was to control and show to advantage the natural figure. This underbodice was known as a *cotte*, an early French word used, like *côte* (rib), to describe a garment fitting closely over the torso. With the more figure-revealing clothes of the fifteenth century, the underbodice was further stiffened by a mixture of paste between two layers of linen. It was then known as a *body* or *pair of bodys*, a term which later developed into the word bodice. In France it was a *corps* or *cors* from which it is thought the modern word corset stems.* In the later fifteenth century this bodice was usually open in front and laced across to tighten as desired. The garment has survived in the national and regional dress of many European countries, worn outside and on top of a blouse, with a skirt.

It was in the *sixteenth century*, when an unnaturally long and slender waist became *de rigueur*, that the body evolved into a rigid corset-like garment. Reinforced at first with wood, then metal, strips in the seams and later with whalebone, it was still known as a *body* or *pair of bodys*. There exist illustrations and descriptions of corsets made of metal strips and plates, hinged at the sides, but these are thought to have been designed as special-purpose support for medical and remedial needs. In the second half of the sixteenth century, when Spanish fashions were paramount, the feminine waist became more slender and longer. The body or bodice, termed *basquina* by the Spanish and *basquine* by the French, became more severely restrictive. It was made of stiffened linen or of leather and, to maintain the rigidly concave line in front, a busk was introduced. This was a strip of wood, horn, metal or whalebone, wider at the top than the bottom, which was inserted in the centre front of the garment and extended from the bust nearly to the hips or at least as low as was compatible with being able to sit down (uncomfortably). This busk was the origin of the rigid boning in corsets which followed during the centuries and was only abandoned in the early twentieth century. By 1580 whalebone strips were also inserted into side seams and the body had become an agonizing straight-jacket to endure.

The *seventeenth-century body* was usually referred to as *stays* and, though still whalebone-stiffened and maintaining a slender waist, was much less unnatural and less of an instrument of torture than its sixteenth-century predecessor. It was shorter, extending only to the waist, where

* The word corset or corsettus used in the Middle Ages generally described a different, outer garment which was a tunic or robe.

it was finished with tabs or basques. It had shoulder straps, or sometimes short sleeves, to hold it in position and was laced up the centre back. The front panel was a stiffened and decorative stomacher, made of firm material to maintain the unnaturally slightly concave line of the rib-cage. Eighteenth-century stays were similar, though the slenderization of the waist was more pronounced in order to contrast with the hooped and paniered skirts.

Whalebone agony and tight lacing were joyously abandoned in the 1790s with the surge toward liberalization and natural, unfettered movement. Those with young and elegant figures wore no controlling garments at all, but the not-so-slim took to a girdle like a Greek *zoné* or long slender stays which supported a high breast-line and slenderized the stomach and hips without accentuating the waist, for, by this time, the gown waistline was just under the breasts and marked there by a ribbon sash. Such long stays were still whaleboned and had a front busk.

With the *1830s* came a return to a slender waist at a natural level and by the *1840s* a restrictive corset was being worn again and this became more and more extreme in the attempt to produce a tiny waist as the century progressed. In the *mid-nineteenth century* the corset was short, extending from the breasts to just below the waist. There was no need for it to be longer as the fullness of the crinoline skirt extended from waist downwards. As the crinoline gradually evolved into the bustle, so fashion – as well as demanding a slender waist – insisted on slender hips also, so that the corset had to become longer and extend over the hips. The nineteenth-century corset was a more sophisticated garment than its predecessors. It was tailored in fitting sections instead of introducing gussets into one-piece garments. The front fastening replaced back lacing from the 1830s, though the stiff front busk was still inserted. By 1870, *steam-moulding* had been introduced. In this process the finished corset with bones and busk inserted was heavily starched and then placed in a steam mould to set its shape to the

Minoan goddess with corseted bodice and tight waistbelt, *c.1600 BC*

Metal corset, early sixteenth century

Late sixteenth century metal and whalebone corset

Boned bodice, *c.1660*

Soft leather corset, embroidered and jewelled, *c.1700*

Brocade corset, eighteenth century

Linen corset with whalebone stiffening, *c.1720*

Corset, 1868

Fitted corset bodice, *c.1150*

Stays with long busk, *c.1810*

Cotton and boned stays, *c.1830*

Corset, 1878

Short corset, 1877

Boned corset with suspenders, 1890–5

Short corset with criss-cross front panel, *c.1914*

Corset, 1898

Corset 1903, with suspenders

Long corset, 1916

Long corset, 1909

desired figure. The mould was of copper and steam was introduced into it by pipes.

The corsets of the years *1880–1905* were the most rigid and agonizing of all. They were excessively restricting at the waist and were very long. They were made in many longitudinal sections with whalebone strips inserted into each seam; but such long corsets tended to ride up and wrinkle and whalebones would break at the waist as the wearer sat down. As the curve between breast and waist and waist and hips became more pronounced, this was a frequent occurrence, so steel replaced whalebone more and more. The centre front of the corset was now fitted with a metal spoon busk (*buse en poire*), so called because of its shape which was narrow at the top and widened below the curving waist into a pear shape. It was in these years that the storm of protest arose from the medical profession. Doctors tried to inform parents of the damage being done to young girls' bodies by encasing them in such an extreme form of corset, but the criticisms made little difference. Ladies, young and old, followed, or tried to follow, the fashionable silhouette, accepting as a natural unpleasantness of life the fainting fits and the 'vapours'. By 1878 the *suspender* had been introduced. Suspenders* were at first attached to straps or a belt worn over the corset, but by 1901 they were fastened to the corset itself. This was a great advantage, for the suspenders held down the long corset in position and did away with the constriction of garters. Also, since the corset was anchored down, it did not need to be so rigid at the waist to maintain its shape. *(Detachable garters in USA.)

In the early years of the *twentieth century* a new line appeared – the *S-curve* or bend. This resulted from the introduction of the straight-busked corset which had evolved from Dr Jaeger's health corset and the design of Madame Gaches-Sarraute, the corsetière who pioneered the straight front in order to give support to the abdomen but to avoid restriction of the thorax and consequent inward pressure on the diaphragm which had resulted from the curved, waisted designs of the

nineteenth century. But although the new straight-busked front was strongly recommended by the medical authorities who had been campaigning for years to abolish the concave corset front, the advice of these gentlemen was still unheeded in the feminine search for the tiny waist. The ladies laced up the new corset as tightly as the old and so created a new, and worse, figure distortion. Due to the intractability of the straight front busk, the bosom above it was pushed forward and the hips below it backwards. The new fashionable ideal was, therefore, achieved: a full, forward bosom, a tiny waist and generous, backward-slanting hips. If nature was inadequate to conform to these requirements, bust bodices and petticoats were suitably padded and lined with starched flounces. The bosom line was not uplifted but was worn low, to overhang the tight waist belt. The fashionably tall woman, dressed in the S-bend line, sailed into a room carrying all before her. The style was immortalized in the drawings of Charles Dana Gibson and became known as the 'Gibson girl'.

1905 was the zenith of the Gibson line. By 1908 the waistline rose and a more natural figure was allowed. The corset became longer but was less waisted and fewer bones were inserted in it. The desired figure was now more natural but was also slim at waist, bust and hips. A very long corset was fashionable between 1908 and 1914, so long that it was difficult to sit down. It was laced up the back and had a busk fastening in front. Suspenders were also long, attaching to stockings at about knee-level.

The flapper dress of the 1920s brought about the end of the restrictive, boned corset and its place was taken by flatteners and girdles (see *Underwear*, 1920 onwards). Corsets were still worn by the not-so-slim until after the Second World War, but they became less restrictive and less heavily boned as time passed and the natural figure re-emerged in the 1930s. The development of elasticized and man-made fabrics with softer, more comfortable means of figure control have, since 1950, all but eradicated the 'corset agony'.

Cosmetics

Many diverse substances and preparations used to beautify the hair, skin and complexion, to adorn and display the body. From the Greek word *kosmetikos*, to adorn.

The whole of recorded history shows that the human race has always, to a greater or lesser degree, used paint, perfume, powder and dye on the face, hair and body. In primitive societies this has been done in order to strike fear into the heart of an enemy – as with the North American Indian or the woad of the early Briton – to indicate rank or position, to protect the skin, or, sometimes, as part of a ritual in connection with the onset of puberty, the practice of religion or the making of magic – tattooing, painting and ritual cuts on the skin were examples of these. In more advanced and sophisticated societies the use of cosmetics was usually to make the sexes more attractive to one another, to beautify in general, to cleanse or give medical aid to the skin, or to hide the imperfections of nature or the onset of old age. The quantity of cosmetics used and the extent of the attempted alteration or improvement upon nature has varied immensely from age to age and from one culture to another. For instance, in Europe, an excess of artificiality was indulged in in the eighteenth century, while the swing of the pendulum brought an abhorrence of the use of make-up and the appreciation of a clean, washed, shining face as the ideal of the mid-nineteenth century. In periods when 'naturalness' was in fashion, this was due largely to a religious conviction and restrictive morality, but a factor which also loomed large, especially in the strictures of the medical profession, was the fact that, prior to the twentieth century, cosmetic preparations contained harmful substances such as mercury and lead and could disfigure or even kill.

It is not certain when people first painted their faces or bodies. It is thought that the custom originated in the East, but our earliest evidence comes from the Middle East. There are references in the Old Testament and in the Koran to the use of cosmetics and aromatics, as in the description of Jezebel – 'she painted her face' (II Kings 9 v.30) – and in the reproof of Aholah and Aholibah by the Prophet – 'Thou paintest thy eyes and deckedst thyself with ornaments' (Ezekiel 23 v.40). However, long before this we have archaeological evidence in the finds of palettes for the grinding and mixing of powders used for painting the eyes in ancient Egypt, dating from 10,000 BC. It is from *Egypt* that we can trace the extensive use of cosmetics because of the custom of burying comforts and luxuries with the dead, and these included toilet articles, paint, powder and herbs. Examples of these can be seen in a number of museums; in Cairo, in Edinburgh and especially in the British Museum in London. They include alabaster palettes and paint pots, jars of porphyry which contained unguents, kohl tubes and vessels, eye sticks, metal mirrors and ivory or wood combs. When the tomb of Tutankhamun was discovered and opened in 1922, some of the cosmetic vases contained quantities of aromatics which were still fragrant, while others contained a skin cream which was still usable.

In ancient Egypt both men and women used cosmetics. They applied rouge to their cheeks and ladies softened this with a yellow cream, men with a deeper orange one. They used a red ointment on the lips and a preparation of henna on the nails, the palms of their hands and the soles of their feet. Ladies traced the veins of their temples and breasts with blue paint and sometimes tipped their nipples in gold. The chief focus of make-up on the face in Egypt was the eye, where two colours were used. A green eyeshadow, generally made from powdered malachite, was applied to both upper and lower lids, while the eye lining and touching up of lashes and eyebrows was done with black or, sometimes, grey or darker green. This substance, called kohl (kohol), was made from powdered antimony, carbon, black oxide of copper, dark ochre and other materials. The powder was stored in pots or tubes and, moistened by saliva, was applied with an ivory, wood, glass or metal kohl stick, like a modern eyebrow pencil. Many kohl

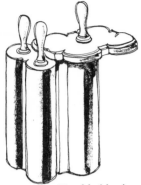

Wood kohl tubes
in group of four
with a lid which
slides over

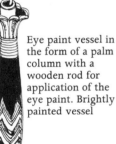

Eye paint vessel in
the form of a palm
column with a
wooden rod for
application of the
eye paint. Brightly
painted vessel

Turquoise
cosmetic jar
with gold
banding.

Cosmetic dish

Shell for containing
cosmetics – eye
shadow and liner
and rouge,
Sumerian

tubes have been found and these were often grouped in sets of different colours as well as being used singly.

The hot dry climate made the frequent use of oils and ointment a necessity. The Egyptians bathed regularly in artificial baths, then liberally applied oils and unguents to keep the skin soft and elastic. These were all perfumed and the processes for making these perfumes and cosmetics were kept secret. It is thought that the experts were the priests who made up the compounds and this was considered to be a mysterious art of great esteem. The oils were derived from several sources, chiefly palm, flax, almond, olive, sesame and animal fats, while perfume ingredients included thyme and origanum grown in Egypt and myrrh, frankincense and spikenard, which were imported from Arabia.

Various treatments were advised for care of the hair. Restoratives for falling or languid hair included preparations made from date flowers, while the possible preparations for dyeing and tinting were numerous. Among the more *outré* recommended were the blood of a black cow or warm oil in which either crushed tadpoles or the uterus of a cat had been blended.

Although the Egyptians probably led the ancient world of the Middle East in the sophistication of their cosmetic art, they were by no means alone in the extensive use of it. At Ur, Sumerian make-up equipment has been found, including hair tweezers, toothpicks and ear scoops as well as cosmetic cases and jars. The ancient *Assyrians* and *Babylonians* dyed and curled their hair and beards and made up their eyes heavily with eyeshadow, eye-liner and lash and brow blackener made from powdered antimony. Both sexes painted their faces with white lead and rouge, reddened their lips and used henna on their nails and palms. They took perfumed baths and anointed themselves afterwards with perfumed oils. The *Medes* and *Persians* also made lavish use of perfume, creams, ointments and coloured make-up. Their hair and beards were oiled, curled and dyed with henna.

Further east in the *Indus* valley (now

Pakistan) have been found cosmetic jars and kohl pots containing black eye make-up with kohl sticks from a culture which existed there 5,000 years ago. The jars are of alabaster, ivory and earthenware and the eye maquillage is of an earth green with lamp black mixed with fat for eye-lining. Other containers show traces of earth creams for rouge and lipsticks. Nails were coloured and polished and a red colouring was applied to the finger tips and to the soles of the feet. It is thought that both sexes used cosmetics, which were kept in boxes made from ivory, horn and shell. Body perfumes, especially sandal-wood, were widely used, and oils, creams and ointments were perfumed also. Scissors and razors were used to trim and define beards and body hair was removed by small cosmetic razors. Waxes and oils were employed in dressing the hair. As in ancient Rome, people regularly visited the public baths where they could bathe in hot or cold water or take a steam bath. Scrapers, like the Roman strigils, were used for cleaning and stimulating the body.

In ancient *Greece* a natural appearance was favoured for many centuries, but by the fourth century BC it became fashionable for women to paint their faces with white lead and a rouge which could come from a natural substance such as mulberry, or a mineral one such as red sulphide of mercury. In addition, a compound of arsenic was used as a depilatory. The use of these substances, which had been common for centuries, aroused the medical profession to warn of the dangers inherent in these customs, but their advice in ancient Greece, as in sixteenth and eighteenth-century Europe, went unheeded. The Greeks also applied eye make-up like the Egyptian kohl, and bleached and dyed their hair. Blonde hair was especially fashionable and they also added false hair and eyebrows. They cleaned their teeth carefully, bathed, and then perfumed and oiled their bodies. Oils, as in ancient Egypt, were derived from the olive, the palm, almonds and sesame. Favourite perfumes came from violets, myrrh, mint and marjoram.

Republican *Rome* did not take a great

interest in beautification but, under the Empire, with the example of Greece and Etruria, the Romans began to take advantage of cosmetics. In the first century AD it became the mode to cultivate a pale complexion. Fashionable women used different kinds of preparation to achieve this, preparations which could take days to make. A paste derived from a mixture of narcissus bulbs, honey, gum arabic, wheat, barley, lentils and eggs was most used. Face packs applied at night were made from perfumed meal. In the evening, a maquillage of chalk and white lead tinged with rouge was applied, with carmine for the lips, antimony to blacken the lashes and brows and blue tints to delineate the veins. Various substances were recommended for different purposes – crocodile excrement as a mud pack, pumice stone to whiten the teeth (and false teeth were supplied where needed), barley flour and butter to cure pimples and spots and depilatory plasters to remove surplus hair. Nail colour was supplied by a mixture of sheep fat and blood, and hair was bleached to a fashionable blonde shade. Beauty spots were added and wrinkles were attacked with various astringent preparations.

The Roman baths (named *thermae* from the Greek *thermos*, meaning hot) were an institution which was an integral part of life in the days of the Roman Empire. For many, living conditions at home lacked space and comfort and the public baths provided a free or inexpensive daily means for many people to relax, chat, carry out business or social affairs, bathe, receive massage and medical treatment, as well as to eat and drink and be entertained. In Imperial Rome alone there are estimated to have been over 800 *thermae*, supplied by the 11 great aqueducts which poured into the city bringing in over 340 million gallons of water a day. The bather undressed, then went to the *unctorium* – the anointing room – where his body was treated with oil, then he was covered in powder or sand and probably engaged in some athletic exercise. After this he went to the *caldarium* – the hot room – which was divided into small compartments with hot water baths. He received a rubbing-down treatment, which included scraping with a strigil. Afterwards he plunged into a cold water swimming-bath – the *frigidarium* – and was massaged, perfumed and oiled. The baths provided a warm room in winter – the large, moderately heated *tepidarium* – and cool, shady gardens in summer, where strollers could walk or sit and relax under the roofed peristyles which surrounded the open courts. People spent many hours, even all day, at the *thermae*.

Despite the strictures and teaching of the early Christian Church and the Jewish traditions, the use of cosmetics continued. In Europe, perfumes were hardly used during the *Middle Ages* and cosmetics were applied more sparingly. The fashionable appearance was to have a pale complexion, and to attain this the lady painted her face with water soluble paints and added white and pale pink powder, or else she was regularly bled. Only women of ill-repute used rouge or carmine for the lips to excess. The natural look was sought and, though eye make-up was seen, its use was sparing. It was *a la mode* in the fifteenth century to pluck the eyebrows to a thin line, also to remove the hair on the forehead, the temples and at the nape so that it did not show beneath the head-dress. The use of perfume was re-introduced to Europe by returning Crusaders who brought back Oriental perfumes. The use of these was quickly adopted and new perfumes were made, especially in Italy and France. The Moors also brought back the use of perfume to Spain in the eighth century.

With the *sixteenth century* there came a revival in the heavier use of cosmetics and the custom continued to grow so that in the last third of the century, in England and Europe, nearly all ladies painted their faces and used a variety of preparations for their teeth, complexion and hair. Most ladies had 'sweet coffers' in which they kept their ointments and creams made from their own special recipes, and these were numerous and varied. Many beauty aids were harmless and were derived from the garden, such as rosemary for a hair tonic, elder flowers for toning up the skin, geranium leaves for colouring the cheeks and sage for whitening the teeth. It was also popular, if expensive, to follow Mary Queen of Scots' example and bathe in wine. Other frequently-used cosmetic aids were less harmless and some very dangerous, causing decaying teeth, terrible skin conditions and sometimes terminating in a poisoning of the whole body. Among such substances was white lead, applied by ladies in one coat on top of another to whiten their faces, neck and bosom and to eradicate wrinkles; also mercury sublimate (obtained from the ore cinnabar), applied in an endeavour to remove skin blemishes; also a rouge for the cheeks made from mercuric sulphide.

The Church and the medical profession opposed the extensive and heavy use of such cosmetic compounds on both moral and health grounds. Some women heeded their advice and used lemon juice, rain water or barley water for their skins, but for many others, from Queen Elizabeth and the court downwards, the advice went unheeded and the fashion continued for an artificial red and white complexion and dyed hair. The complexion extended to the bosom because of the fashionably décolleté necklines, and red hair was popular in imitation of Elizabeth's wigs. To obtain the shade, ladies were advised to use a mixture of lead calcined with sulphur and quicklime mixed with water.

The condition of people's teeth was not good and it was not improved by the use of poisonous cosmetics on the face. Various substances were employed to try to keep them clean and white, not with notable success. Many different herbs were blended to make up the recipes, and these were pounded into a paste and mixed with crushed flowers, honey and wine to rub on the teeth. Skin conditioners were also advised, not surprisingly, popular ingredients being egg-whites and honey. Late in the century beauty patches came back into favour. At first applied to the temples because they were thought to relieve the pain of toothache, the fashion developed in the succeeding centuries into a complex ritual of meaning.

There were public baths in England and Europe, also steam baths known as hot-houses, but they had an unsavoury reputation and most people avoided them and indulged in a minimum of bathing and washing, instead coating the skin with yet another layer of make-up and overpowering insanitary odours with an increasing use of perfume. Most ladies wore a pomander swinging from the girdle, and this contained solid perfume.

For much of the *seventeenth century* the use of cosmetics was restrained. Men used make-up to a limited degree and ladies contented themselves with painting their face and neck with ceruse, which was a cosmetic base of white or pale pink colour. With this was used a rouge and a reddener for the lips. Eye make-up was at a minimum. Perfumes of all kinds were applied liberally – made from flower essences such as violets, roses and lavender but with the addition of derivatives from ambergris, musk, bay and cinnamon – and the application of these was still preferred to regular bathing.

From 1670 onwards cosmetics were more heavily applied and men of fashion began to use them more openly. A basic light-coloured paint was applied to the face and a white powder and rouge were added on top. Reddened lips and dark hair were fashionable. Beauty patches were now at their height and modishness and, in France especially, enunciated a silent but clear language according to their shape and position. Generally seven or eight patches were worn, cut out as moons, stars, suns, hearts, crosses, etc. Patch boxes were carried containing replacements and a tiny mirror was set in the lid. For example, a patch placed near the mouth indicated flirtatiousness, one on the right cheek that the wearer was married, on the left that she was affianced and one at the corner of the eye that the lady was passionate. 'Spanish wool' was available from the seventeenth century. This was a wool saturated with white lead and chalk and used as a face powder. A later version, called 'Spanish papers', was in the form of small books of leaves made of wool laid on paper impregnated with red or white paint. These, which could be carried in the handbag, were an early version of the powder compact.

In the earlier part of the *eighteenth century* the full blooded, richly carmine-lipped, dark-haired beauty gave place to the Dresden china, pink-and-white lady of the Rococo. Face painting continued, for men also, but it was delicately applied in moderation. Home recipes of incredibly time-consuming complexity were utilized as few cosmetics could be bought as yet. Beauty patches were worn more than ever, 10 or 12 at a time, and the shapes were more varied than before. Patch and rouge boxes were always carried. The second half of the eighteenth century was, like the second half of the sixteenth, a time of artificiality and excessive use of perfume and cosmetics. Face painting was practised widely, by men and children as well as by ladies. The fashion was for a white face, achieved by a heavy application of ceruse which was made mainly from white lead, to which was added bright red cheek and lip rouge. Washing and bathing were considered to be unhealthy and to expose one to the dangers of a chill in winter or sunburn in summer. A little eau de cologne applied to the hands and face was thought to be adequate for cleansing purposes and perfume was sprinkled in quantity to offset any unfortunate odours. The heavy face-painting attempted, therefore, to cover both the scars of the 'pox and the layers of dirt. Gentlemen also spent a great deal of time and care on their toilette. Each gentleman kept a dressing box which was fitted with sections for perfume bottles, powder and rouge, combs, brushes and hair oil, as well as curling irons and scissors. After shaving he would apply face lotions, powder, rouge and beauty patches.

Both sexes wore powdered wigs, but while those of the gentlemen were neatly curled and small, those of the ladies, from 1765 onwards, became very large and tall (see *Wig*). The tremendous height was achieved with the aid of pads and false hair placed under the wig. The coiffure

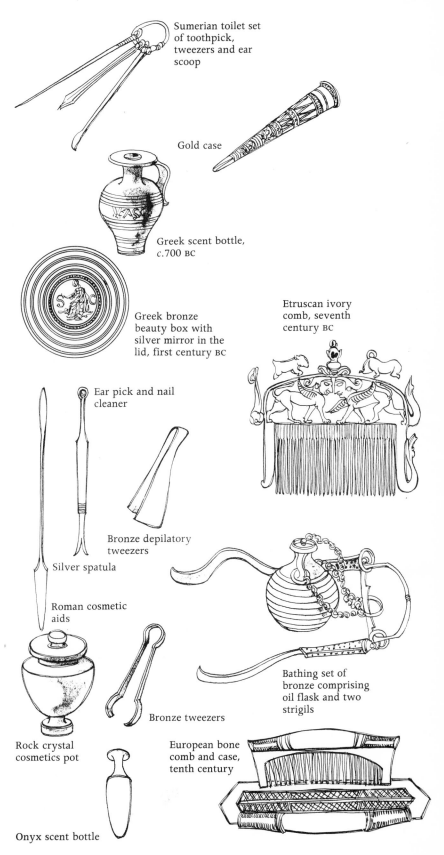

Sumerian toilet set of toothpick, tweezers and ear scoop

Gold case

Greek scent bottle, *c.*700 BC

Greek bronze beauty box with silver mirror in the lid, first century BC

Etruscan ivory comb, seventh century BC

Ear pick and nail cleaner

Bronze depilatory tweezers

Silver spatula

Roman cosmetic aids

Bathing set of bronze comprising oil flask and two strigils

Bronze tweezers

Rock crystal cosmetics pot

European bone comb and case, tenth century

Onyx scent bottle

was then decorated by pearl ropes, ribbons, plumes and flowers. Ringlets fell over the shoulders and bosom and the back hair was dressed in a chignon or cadogan; at the sides were enormous sausage curls. Extremes of style were reached by the aristocracy, especially in France. The constant application of pomatum with rice or wheat powder sprinkled on top led to the wigs becoming verminous, with consequent discomfort – an occasional tap was necessary to evict the 'visitors'. The hair powdering also caused a deterioration in the skin of the face and it was necessary to add further paint and powder to the complexion.

Home-made cosmetic preparations were now most varied, as also was the advice given on aids to beauty. It was possible, too, to purchase ready-manufactured preparations more easily than hitherto. Many cosmetics continued to be dangerous to use and yet were widely applied. White lead was still the most common agent in face whiteners and was used in nearly all complexion paints. It hastened the ageing of the complexion, damaged the teeth and caused skin complaints. Other cosmetic aids were less harmful, even if they did not live up to the claims made for them. Such aids included coloured powders made from earth shades, pastes from almonds or honey, toilet waters from lemons, lavender, jasmine or roses, pomatum from such varied substances as cucumbers, snails or sheep's trotters, and oils from poppies, almonds or hazel. There were, in addition, countless recipes for curing baldness and removing unwanted hair.

While the increasingly sophisticated societies of Europe were using cosmetics heavily, in the more *primitive cultures* cosmetics were employed with equal enthusiasm but in a different way and for different reasons. Among such societies painting or tattooing of the whole body was usual and, in contrast to Europe, it was the men who did this rather than the women. Christopher Columbus found on his travels to the New World that the inhabitants oiled or greased themselves all over and then applied coloured paints made from earths, vegetables and minerals.

Red and white were especially used but also other hues. The paints were partly for protection of the skin and partly for decoration. The North American Indians developed a sophisticated manner of face and body painting (see *North American Indian*). In the New Hebrides, also, natives painted both face and body in black, red and brown patterns. The colours and pigments used varied according to availability. Coloured clay, leaves, soot, blood, dung and vegetables were the most common. In other areas and times, such as the Mayan cilization or the Maori (see *Maori dress* and *Maya dress*), tattooing was more common than painting. The purpose was beautification but the process also denoted status and was carried out for religious purposes. In this the skin was punctured and paint or dye introduced into the wounds. In the *Far East*, a sophisticated form of cosmetic application was used from early times. Japanese and Chinese ladies painted their faces white and used rouge on their lips. They painted their nails and shaved or plucked their eyebrows and also painted their teeth black or gold.

In Europe, the *nineteenth century* brought an abrupt swing of the pendulum over the accepted attitude to the use of cosmetics. Even during the first decade, washing and bathing were becoming usual practice and, as a concomitant, the heavy application of cosmetics was considered to be 'fast' and unladylike. During the nineteenth century cosmetics were used sparingly and with the aim of preserving the natural appearance. Men liked to believe that their womenfolk did not use cosmetics at all and the ladies made sure that their use of make-up was so skilful and so subtle that their menfolk were able to continue in this belief. Needless to say, the ladies did not entirely give up the application of cosmetic preparations. The fashionable look was a pale complexion and, though a tint of rouge on the cheeks was acceptable, lip rouge was not; ladies were advised to bite their lips vigorously before entering a room. 'Spanish papers' were widely used and most ladies carried a pocket book of these in their reticule. An alternative was provided by

Chinese boxes of colours which contained papers of different hues – white for the face and neck, black for eyebrows and rouge for the cheeks.

It was now easier to purchase cosmetics and some famous firms were established – for example, Guerlain in Paris, 1828. Mme Rachel was a London beauty specialist who gave her name to a shade of face powder, still in use. Many different preparations were advised to preserve the natural beauty of the complexion or hair, such as cold cream for the face, macassar or olive oil for the hair, fine oatmeal with water as a face pack, glycerine and rose water for the hands, as well as walnut oil soap, perfumes from flower extracts and powder for the teeth. Many anti-wrinkle remedies were sold. One recipe recommended that the lady should sleep with her face bound up with slices of raw beef.

Harmful and, indeed, dangerous substances continued to be employed in the manufacture of cosmetics. Paints and powders to whiten the complexion still included such substances as zinc oxide, mercury, acetate of lead, nitrate of silver and a powder made from seed pearls dissolved in acid. Since the quantity of cosmetics applied was much less than in the eighteenth century, the harm done was proportionately less. Though in Western Europe cosmetics were now applied with restraint, such practice did not pertain further afield. In Russia, face paint was heavily applied, like an enamel mask. In China, rice powder covered the face, and the cheeks, lips and tongue were rouged. Japanese make-up was a mask of pink and white paint, dusted heavily with rice powder, white lips were carmined and eyes heavily made-up. Facial cosmetics on the ancient Egyptian pattern were still customary in Persia and Arabia.

The twentieth century brought to Europe a freedom and convenience in the use of cosmetics and also a tolerance of those who either desired to keep a natural appearance or to make up to excess. In the first two decades there was a gradual increase in the use of make-up, and convenient means of carrying the materials for making running repairs were being developed. *Papier poudré* replaced 'Spanish papers' and were tiny books of papers impregnated with peach-coloured face powder. *Rouge en feuilles*, similar paper leaves impregnated with red powder, were also carried in the handbag. Bottles of liquid rouge were available, as were red pencils or tube lipsticks and also eye make-up and complexion milk for the arms and neck. Liquid nail-polish was bottled for easy application, and small carrying boxes for the handbag contained all these preparations packed for easy transportation. The hazards of early motoring, with road dust penetrating even the motoring veil and hat, led the way to the introduction of a motoring vanity case which contained all cosmetics, including soap, for suitable repairs.

By 1915 the cosmetics industry was becoming big business, especially in the USA. The powder compact appeared, using loose powder, puff and mirror. Talcum powder was becoming an essential toiletry. By 1925 there were kiss-proof lipsticks; by 1928, Kleenex. From 1930 the mass market was being challenged. Different decades saw the popularity of varying shades and tones – in the 1920s garish colours were fashionable; in the 1930s deep and bright red lipsticks and nail polish; in the 1960s there was the pale look, with no rouge, light powder or none, and silver grey or cold purple lips. By the 1970s a more normal colour scheme was resumed and everyone was 'doing their own thing'.

The great names in the cosmetics business were mainly established early in the twentieth century. Helena Rubinstein came from Poland, arriving in America in 1915, where she built up an empire creating her own cosmetics. She travelled widely to Europe, India and Egypt, to learn about the preparation and use of cosmetics. By 1945 she offered 700 different items of face make-up, toiletries and perfume. Elizabeth Arden opened her first beauty shop in 1910 and was followed by Yardley, Max Factor, Gala, Pond and Innoxa and, after the Second World War, Mary Quant. Strangely, it was not until after 1940 that the first serious attempt was made to regulate the substances which were used in the manufacture of cosmetics, as well as to legislate regarding the veracity of advertising claims. This was done in the USA. Up to this time, substances used in making cosmetics had gradually become less harmful but materials such as mercury, Epsom salts and dangerous dye colours were in use even after 1920. By the 1930s, substances for many products were, in general, quite different from those used in earlier ages. For example, lipsticks were made from lanoline, almond oil, white paraffin jelly and cocoa butter, with carmine added for coloration; rouge was manufactured from carmine, starch, kaolin and perfume. On the other hand, some products had changed little from the days of ancient Egypt – cold cream and eyebrow pencils were among these.

Since the Second World War the great and lucrative cosmetic empire has attempted to cater for everyone's needs and to bring the entire population within its range, extending from talcum powder for babies to rejuvenating creams for old age. Cosmetics for teenagers, especially eye make-up, begin at a younger and younger age, despite the cult of naturalness which remains strong. Cosmetics become more sophisticated all the time and the emphasis is on persuading the purchaser that the product will enhance, even create, personal beauty and attraction, but that she will retain a natural appearance. However, in the twentieth century the accent is not entirely upon 'her'. During the Victorian age the idea of men using perfumed cosmetics was frowned upon in Anglo-Saxon countries; such effeminacy was for Latin peoples. This attitude died hard, and though the cosmetics business in the USA and France conducted vigorous advertising campaigns for cosmetics for men, only gradually was the idea accepted that deodorants, anti-perspirants, hair creams and perfumed after-shave lotions were attractive to women without making them feel that their men were not still 'men'. In order to overcome the effeminacy phobia, cosmetics manufacturers produced 'masculine' perfumes for their toiletries or, more accurately, perfumes with names

associated with masculinity, such as 'tweed', 'tobacco', 'ocean freshness', etc. The campaign was a great success and nowadays no beauty salon or toiletry and perfumery department in a store is complete without its section for men. Presumably because the quantity sold is still less than that for women, the individual, comparable prices are still much higher.

Costume plates

Engravings illustrating what fashionable people were wearing in individual countries at a given date. Unlike the later fashion plate, which depicted a design for costume, costume plates were merely a record, but they are a valuable source material for the student of costume. Early examples, showing especially regional and national dress, had been drawn by such famous artists as *Albrecht Dürer* in 1494 and *Giacomo Franco* in 1610. *Romeyn de Hoaghe* produced a set of drawings in Amsterdam soon afterwards.

There were a number of artists working in the seventeenth century who produced costume plates. The best known artist of this time to draw accurately, and to a superb standard, the costumes of the people he saw was the Bohemian *Václav* (Wenceslaus) *Hollar*, born in Prague in 1607. He fled from the city where he was practising law because of the Thirty Years' War and worked as an engraver in Frankfurt, Strasbourg and Cologne, before living for many years in Antwerp and, later, London. From 1640 he made many plates in England, showing individual costumes (he was especially fascinated by furs) and details of accessories, as well as figures set in a background of famous and typical London scenes, which form interesting and invaluable records. In the years before his death he produced 2,740 plates, working at the rate of 4d per hour, timing his work by an hourglass on his desk. He died in poverty in London in 1677.

After Hollar other artists produced interesting, useful costume plates. Of note was *Jean Dieu de Saint Jean*, whose work concerned the years 1678–95, also *A. Bonnart* and, in the last years of the century, *Antoine Trouvain* and *Nicholas Arnoult*. In later examples, actual fabrics were glued to the engraving, like a type of collage.

Cotehardie

A term used extensively for an outer tunic or gown worn by both sexes during the Middle Ages between about 1300 and 1430, and especially in Italy and France. Despite the frequent mention of the word, the exact form of the garment is not clearly defined. In general, in the early years of the fourteenth century, the term refers to a three-quarter length tunic for men, with a round neck, open down the front and buttoned and with fairly wide sleeves. By about 1340 it was a shorter, fitted tunic with elbow-length sleeves ending in tippets. The feminine cotehardie was a full-length gown, often worn ungirded. It had a low, wide neckline and was fitting on the torso, then flared out to a full, long skirt.

Cotton

From the Middle English *coton* and the Arabic *qutun*. The soft, white, fibrous substance which envelops the seeds of the cotton plant (*Gossypium*, a member of the mallow family). One of the most important of the natural textile raw materials; used to make cloth and thread. Grown in over 60 countries in many parts of the world, especially in the USA, Egypt, India, Brazil, the USSR and China.

Cotton has been grown since ancient times. From tombs in India, samples have been found which date back to 3000 BC. The ancient Egyptians grew and spun cotton, as did also the pre-Inca Peruvians and the ancient Chinese. Explorers of the New World in the fifteenth and sixteenth centuries discovered cotton being grown and manufactured in Peru, Mexico and the southern part of North America.

From the seventeenth century, painted cottons were imported into Europe from India and became very popular. Supplies were limited, so the fabrics acquired a scarcity value and became the 'in' mode with the well-to-do. Elegant society, with a sense of inverted snobbery, prized such

COTEHARDIE
Cotehardie, 1370, Italian

Cotehardie, 1380, Italian

cottons more than silk and used them especially for dressing-gowns, which became known as 'indiennes'.

The manufacture of cotton in England developed rapidly with the textile industry in general during the second half of the eighteenth century (see also *Spinning, Weaving* and *Textiles*). By 1800 the cotton industry had surpassed the woollen trade. The British cotton industry, which had expanded enormously since the mid-century, was established in Lancashire. Cotton was grown in the southern states of North America and this accelerated the already flourishing slave trade. Trading of negroes to the New World had been in operation since the early sixteenth century and the British had gradually acquired a larger share of this. By 1700 the so-called 'triangular trade' was well established. In this, the merchants (based in Bristol) sailed to Africa to exchange their manufactured goods of arms, hardware, jewellery, spirits and tobacco with the African chieftains for negro labour. The second leg of the journey took the slaves to America where they were sold, at great profit, to work in the plantations. The ships then returned to England laden with raw materials. The development of the cotton industry caused the centre of the trade to move to Liverpool and it also rapidly accelerated. In 1791 the British transported 38,000 negroes to America, more than half the total European trading for that year.

In fashion, cotton completely changed European styles, colours and decoration worn in the later eighteenth century. Silks and satins were slowly abandoned in ladies' clothes in favour of the thin, clinging cottons, though the former returned to favour in the mid-nineteenth century.

SPECIFIC COTTONS

Calico – a cotton cloth originally imported from India and named after its city of origin, Calicut, on the Malabar coast. In England the name refers to a plain white cotton cloth, in the USA to a printed cotton.

Cambray – a type of gingham named after its town of origin in France, Cambrai.

Cottonade – a nineteenth-century term for several coarse cotton fabrics.

Dimity – in the fifteenth and sixteenth centuries a coarse cotton or flannel. From the Greek *dimitos*, meaning of double thread. Dimity had weft threads twice the thickness of warp threads. Now a cotton cloth woven with raised stripes and patterns used for furnishing fabrics and garments.

Galatea – a strong, white cotton twill, often printed or striped.

Gingham – a cotton cloth woven of dyed yarn, generally in stripes and checks.

Hickory cloth – a coarse, heavy, twilled cotton with striped or check pattern. Used for shirts and working garments which receive hard wear.

Jaconet – a plain, light-to-medium weight cotton. Name a corruption of Jāgannathī, Urdu form of Cuttack, its town of origin in India. At first imported, later made in England.

Moleskin cloth – a heavy, strong, twilled cotton with a nap backing. Used for working and sports clothes.

Muslin – a plain, soft cotton first made in Mosul in Mesopotamia, now Iraq (see *Muslin*).

Percale – fabric imported from the East Indies in the seventeenth and eighteenth centuries. Since 1850 a firmly woven, smooth, plain cotton.

Percaline – a nineteenth-century glazed, coloured cotton cloth.

Regatta – a strong, twilled cotton for shirting made in narrow blue and white stripes (nineteenth century).

Sea island cotton – a fine lustre cotton with long fibres, traditionally grown on the islands off the coast of Georgia, Florida, South Carolina and Texas. Now grown in quantity in the West Indies.

Ticking – a closely-woven, heavy cotton (sometimes linen) used chiefly for mattress and pillow covering. Usually narrowly striped.

Cottoned

Fabric of which the nap has been raised.

Cottonize

To reduce the staple or fibre of a material, such as flax or hemp, to a short one resembling the cotton staple.

Counterchange design

A pattern where a certain colour of the motif and its ground are reversed in another part of the design. A form of decoration especially fashionable in the fourteenth-century parti-coloured garments.

Couvrechef, coverchief, headrail, kerchief

Names used at different periods and in different areas to denote a draped head-covering for women. The headrail was, in general, an Anglo-Saxon term for a veil which was draped around the head, then hung loose or was tucked into the neckband of the gown. *Couvrechef* was the Norman term for a similar article, then it was anglicized into coverchief. This was worn in different ways and was of varied dimensions during the early Middle Ages, then was largely discarded by the upper

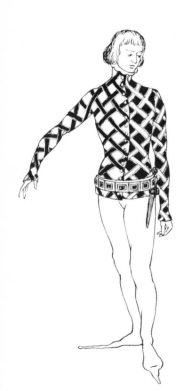
COUNTERCHANGE DESIGN
Counterchange trellis design on tunic, English, 1380

COUVRECHEF, COVERCHIEF,
HEADRAIL, KERCHIEF
Anglo-Saxon headrail

Norman couvrechef,
c.1070

Medieval coverchief, *c.*1200

classes in the fourteenth and fifteenth centuries in favour of the more shaped, stiffened head-dresses. The draped head-coverings remained the everyday wear for peasant and working classes throughout the centuries, becoming later the kerchief, still worn in the nineteenth century in industrial towns in Europe, as well as in country districts; and, in modern times, the headscarf.

Cowboy dress

A functional attire, established in the USA in the nineteenth century, of a shirt with neckscarf, a waistcoat and denim trousers or Levis (see *Trousers* and *Levis*). For protection in riding through thorny brush and scrub, the cowboy wore 'chaps' on top of his Levis. These 'chaps', popular abbreviation for the Mexican Spanish *chaparreras*, were of leather, hide or skin, often with the fur left on the exterior surface. They were open at the back, allowing freedom of movement for riding. Under the Levis were the calf-length leather boots with Cuban heel to hold the foot in the stirrup. A large-brimmed hat protected the wearer from the hot sun.

COWBOY DRESS
American cowboy wearing
'chaps'

Lace fall cravat,
Spanish, 1690–5

Steenkirk
(steinkirk), 1696,
French

Louis XIV cravat,
c.1680

English lace-edged
cravat, *c*.1755

Flemish cravat,
1663

Crash

From the Latin *crassus*, meaning coarse-woven. A coarse linen or wool interwoven with heavy, uneven yarns of cotton, linen or rayon.

Cravat

In men's neckwear the cravat took the place of the falling-band (see *Band*) from about 1645–50. At first it was simply a length of white linen or lawn, lace-edged, folded and tied loosely round the throat. The name is derived from the Croatian word *crabate* and the fashion from Croat soldiers serving at the time with the French army, who wore scarves tied round their throats for protection.

With the advent of the *justaucorps* in 1665–70, the cravat style became more sophisticated and was tied round the throat in a bow, its ends hanging formally in folds over the chest; these were decorated with lace or fringe. A later version of the cravat, worn in the 1690s and early eighteenth century, was termed the *steenkirk* or *steinkirk*, its name being derived from the Battle of Steenkerke in Belgium in August 1692. In this style the loosely twisted ends of the cravat were tucked into the shirt front or passed through a loop or button-hole in the coat edge. Towards 1720 the seventeenth-century cravat was replaced by the folded stock and this, in many and varied guises, was fashionable neckwear for men for much of the eighteenth and nineteenth centuries, though the word cravat was also sometimes used for this article (see *Stock*).

Crêpe

From the French word *crêper*, to crimp or frizz. Used to describe all kinds of fabrics – wool, cotton, silk and rubber – which have a crinkly, crimped surface. Crêpe was woven in the East in ancient times but not in Europe until after the Crusades when, in the thirteenth century, the Italians began to manufacture it. A dull, black crêpe was traditionally used for mourning garments, especially when made in silk gauze or wool. The word *crape* is used in England for crêpes used for this purpose. Quality crêpe

fabrics include silk and silk mixtures such as crêpe de chine, crêpe georgette, crêpe macrocain, crêpe meteor, crêpe poplin, crêpe royal and crepon.

Cretonne

The French name of a strong fabric made of hemp and linen (nowadays also of rayon). The name is said to derive from the village of Creton in Normandy where linen was made. The cloth is printed in bright colours in bold floral patterns and is used for informal summer garments and overalls. In England the term is generally applied to a strong unglazed cotton fabric, similarly printed and used chiefly as a furnishing material.

Crinoline

From 1830 a fabric made of horsehair and cotton or linen. The name derives from the Latin *crinis* (and the French *crin*) for hair and the Latin *linum* for thread. The material was used from the early 1840s for making stiffened petticoats, worn by women to support the weight of the other petticoats under the increasingly full, bell-shaped skirts of the day.

By 1850, even the layers of stiffened petticoats were insufficient to maintain the gown skirt in its desired form so that the crinoline petticoat was devised. At first this was like its predecessors, the sixteenth-century farthingale and the eighteenth-century hoop (see *Farthingale, Panier* and *Petticoat*), an underskirt of quilted material with whalebone hoops inserted at intervals to maintain the shape. But, unlike its predecessors, the crinoline did not stop at its proportions of 1850. Despite all criticism and ribaldry from the medical profession, men in general and humorous illustrated magazines, the crinoline skirt grew larger and larger and its popularity with all classes increased. It was the feminine status symbol of the 1850s. So, in 1856, the *cage-crinoline* was patented and by 1857 was in production. It was a framework of flexible steel hoops, joined together by vertical bands of tape or braid, which provided the requisite shape without the weight and avoided the need to wear so many layers of

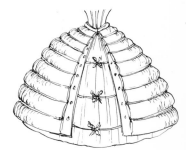

CRINOLINE
Horsehair crinoline, 1858

Cage-crinoline, 1862

Assyrian mitre

Crown of ancient
Egypt

Assyrian crown or
mitre, 880 BC

Ancient Greek
stephane, fifth
century BC

Ancient Rome,
200 AD

Anglo-Saxon
crown

Byzantine crown,
twelfth century

Byzantine crown,
sixth century

Saxon crown

Medieval king's
crown, c.1230

Queen's crown,
1380

petticoats. It was taken up with enthusiasm by all classes of women. It was cheap and a great success. The skirt circumference grew greater. 1859–60 was the zenith of the circular crinoline, after which the shape gradually changed to an oval. Then the front was flattened, also the sides, and the fullness was concentrated more at the back, leading to the bustle skirts (see *Bustle*).

There were several versions of the cage-crinoline – most notable were the *Cage-Américaine*, where the upper part was in framework skeleton form and the lower was covered in material; the *Cage-Empire*, which was designed to support the extra flounces of a ball dress and had extra hoops and framework for a train; and the later *Victoria Cage*, which was of bustle form.

Crochet

The craft of crocheting was introduced in the nineteenth century; it was a form of chain-stitch embroidery in which a crochet hook manipulated a single thread to produce crochet lace. In the 1840s a crochet industry was established in Ireland, with its centre at Cork, in order to assist in the unemployment difficulties of these years. Later in the century the craft became more sophisticated and some famous antique laces were successfully imitated.

Cross-gartering

Having the garters crossed on the legs, as in the years 1565–1620 when the garter was bound round the stocking below the knee, crossed over at the back and was tied in front above the knee.

Crown

A fillet or wreath encircling the head, usually of metal, ornamented and jewelled. A symbol of monarchy, honour or exalted rank. A *diadem* is also a crown. A *coronet* is a lesser crown denoting inferior status. The *stemma* was the ancient Greek and Roman garland which encircled the brow; under Byzantium it took the form of a jewelled circlet worn by emperors, from which depended jewelled ornaments. A *stephanos* was also a Byzantine crown. This and the *stephane* worn by the Greeks derive

from the Greek word στέφανος, a crown. A *tiara* when worn by the ancient civilizations – Persia, Assyria, Babylonia, for example – was a head-band or tall head-dress in the form of a crown. *Tiara* or *mitre* is also used to describe the head-dress of the high dignitaries of the Roman Catholic and Anglican churches and of the Jewish High Priest. A modern tiara is a jewelled, ornamental head-band rising above the forehead and worn by ladies with formal evening dress.

CUFF
Double lace cuffs, Swedish, 1640

Cuff

The decorative part at the bottom of a coat, tunic or dress sleeve, either turned back or with a facing of material added on. In some periods, for example the seventeenth century, separate decorative lace cuffs were worn on top of the jacket or gown sleeve. In the early Middle Ages cuffs were made so that they could be turned down over the hand for warmth and these were often fur-lined. In certain ages cuffs have been decorative features of display as in, for instance, the later seventeenth and early eighteenth centuries. Whether on a coat or shirt, cuffs have been fastened at various times by buttons or links.

Large decorative turned-back cuffs, Spanish, 1710

CUMMERBUND
Bulgarian. Red wool
cummerbund over sheepskin
trousers with black embroidery,
1873

Cummerbund

From the Urdu *kamar-band*, meaning loin-band. A broad sash worn round the waist, traditional in many countries of the Near and Middle East and in Asia to protect and keep warm the susceptible lumbar region of the body. Worn wrapped round on top of the join of shirt and trousers. A black, pleated cummerbund became fashionable in the West for men's evening dress in the 1890s. This mode has been revived in the second half of the twentieth century but is now fashionable in coloured velvet or silk to match the tie.

Cyclas

A tunic of the thirteenth and fourteenth centuries worn by knights over their armour. It was made of rich material and reserved for ceremonial occasions. This tunic or surcoat was about knee-length but shorter in front than behind. Women also wore a cyclas but this was generally a more fitting gown, still of rich fabric. The name is sometimes applied to the material itself.

Dagges

A medieval form of decoration introduced in the fourteenth century and lasting into the fifteenth. In this, the edges of a garment were cut into diverse jagged forms varying from simple V-shapes to complex leaf designs and imitation of torn leather. Except for the hose, no external garment escaped the dagges – the shoulder cape, hood, tunic, gown, sleeves, hem and tippets all received attention.

Dalmatica

A loose tunic worn by the ancient Romans from about AD 190. Made of white Dalmatian wool (hence its name), the dalmatica or dalmatic had long, wide sleeves and was usually worn ungirded. It was ornamented by vertical stripes in colour (*clavi*). In the Byzantine period both sexes continued to wear the dalmatica, but in the sixth century it ceased to be fashionable lay dress, though it continued in use throughout the Middle Ages as a liturgical garment.

Damask

In the Middle Ages a rich silk fabric figured in elaborate designs, originally worn in Damascus. The word was later also applied to figured fabrics made of wool, linen or cotton which displayed light and shade effects by the use of contrasting shiny and matt surfaces. The word *damascene* was also used to describe such treatment and designs.

Dandy, beau, masher

A dandy is one who gives undue attention to dress and fashion: a fop, an exquisite. In the eighteenth century the English dandy (under the soubriquet 'beau') acquired a European reputation for his imperturbability, nonchalant grace and elegance; in the late century he set the seal upon English manners and tailoring.

The first of these dandies was *Robert (Beau) Feilding* (died 1712), who became an arbiter of fashion at the court of Charles II. More famous was *Richard (Beau) Nash* (1674–1762), who studied law at the Temple. He became accepted there as an authority on dress and manners. The best-as 'Buck' Brummell. Later, under the patronage of the Prince Regent, Beau Brummell attention to his dress from his earliest years, first as a schoolboy at Eton and then as a student at Oxford, where he was known as 'Buck' Brummel. Later, under the patronage of the Prince Regent, Beau Brummel set the stage for the aristocratic gentleman's bearing and manners. He dressed simply and plainly, in subtle colours, with unobtrusive ornamentation but with exquisite care and attention to detail; he became the arbiter of the correct way to tie a cravat. Typical of his attire was the blue tail coat with brass buttons, worn over a fawn waistcoat and accompanied by white or light-coloured buckskin pantaloons and black Hessian boots. His evening dress had a white waistcoat and blue stockinet pantaloons strapped over black slippers. He certainly helped to popularize the wearing of trousers instead of knee breeches.

In his late thirties his gambling and extravagance took him heavily into debt and, losing the support of his patron, he fled to Calais in 1816 to escape his creditors. In his last years in France his appearance was in marked contrast to that of his salad days and was slovenly and dirty. He died destitute in 1840.

The dandy of the later nineteenth century was known in England as a 'Masher' or a 'Piccadilly Johnny'.

Dart
A dart-shaped tuck either taken up in the fabric or cut out and the edges sewn together in order to shape the material to the body and improve the fit and hang of the garment.

Delaine
An abbreviation of the French *mousseline de laine* which was a lightweight dress fabric resembling a woollen muslin. Originally of wool (*c*.1840), later of wool and cotton.

Denier
The denier was a tiny French silver (later copper) coin, its name derived from the ancient Roman silver denarius. In the early nineteenth century the name denier was given to a unit of weight, equal to about eight troy grains,* by which silk yarn

* Derived from a weight used at the fair at Troyes in France.

DAGGES
Houppelande with dagged sleeves, Flemish, 1476

Double dagged gown sleeves or tippets, Italian, 1445

was weighed and its fineness classified. In modern times the denier is used to define the fibre filament of synthetic fabrics as well as silk; the higher the denier number, the thicker the filament. The sheerest nylon stockings have the lowest denier number.

Denim
The name derives from *serge de Nimes*, a serge fabric which was made in that region in the south of France. Present-day denim is a twill weave washable material with a white weft and coloured warp threads. Though generally in use for jeans and overalls, it has now become a more fashionable fabric and is made up into suits and dresses.

Department store
In the nineteenth century, with the techniques and machinery developed in the Industrial Revolution, the mass production of clothes for a wide market began. For such production, mass retail outlets were

DALMATICA
White dalmatica with gold clavi, Byzantine, *c*.530

DIRECTOIRE DRESS
Merveilleuse.
White muslin
dress, red silk
stole

needed and for this purpose the department store was first initiated in France where, in Paris, *Ville de France* was opened in 1844, followed by *Grand-Halles* in 1853 and *Bon Marché* in 1876. The example of Paris was followed in all the great cities of Europe and the USA. Liberty's, in London's Regent Street, was a famous example. Such stores sold not only the Paris modes from the great fashion houses, but also popularized the simpler, practical gowns for everyday wear.

Dernier cri
A literal translation from the French 'the last cry'. Denotes the very latest fashion.

Diamanté
Derived from the French, meaning decorated or scintillating with diamonds or powdered crystal. Usually applied to buttons, buckles, brooches, etc.

Diamond
A colourless or tinted crystalline precious stone consisting of pure carbon. It is the hardest substance known and when cut for mounting in jewellery possesses an incredible brilliance because of its high refractive index; it has always been rare and costly. For many centuries the diamond was reserved for royal wear but was incorporated into jewellery for more general wear from the fifteenth century. For centuries India was the main source of diamonds, however it is now South Africa.

Diaper
Derived from the Byzantine Greek word διασπρος (diaspros) meaning white in parts or at intervals. The word diaper refers, in this sense, to a fabric, a design and an article of clothing.
1) A *fabric* of linen (or sometimes cotton) woven with patterns made visible by opposing reflections from its surface. The pattern consists of small geometrical or floral motifs set in a diamond-shaped framework of lines.
2) A *design* based on the diamond pattern.
3) Since the sixteenth century, a *baby's clout* or breechcloth made of white towelling or linen.

Directoire French dress, 1795–7.
Mauve tulle embroidered dress over white satin undergown
Gentleman in black cloth coat and fawn breeches. Leather boots
Child dressed all in white

Incroyable.
Flowered silk waistcoat and embroidered stockings

Dickey, dicky
In the nineteenth century a
1) Stiff, standing, shirt *collar*.
2) Detached *shirt front* more elegantly made and of finer material than the flannel shirt beneath. Worn by the less well-to-do members of the community.
3) A woman's *under-petticoat*.

Directoire dress
The Directory (*Directoire*) in France only lasted from 1795–99, but it is customary to use the term to refer to the architecture, arts, furniture and costume design of the years 1792–1802 – that is, between the fashions of Louis XVI and those of the First Empire.

In dress, the classical styles of ancient Greece and Rome were the inspiration, though the eighteenth/nineteenth-century version was quite different from the original. The classical influence is seen chiefly in feminine dress in Greek motifs in border ornamentation, in hair styles and in loose, softly draped garments made from thin, white or light-coloured fabrics. The French styles were sewn, however, not draped and pinned. The emphasis was on the unrestricted figure, the very high waistline just under the breasts, and a minimum of garments. Men's dress was restrained, elegantly cut and fitting, and without ostentatious decoration or colouring.

The dandy of the Directoire period, known as an *Incroyable*, affected an extravagant, exaggerated form of dress. His hair was raggedly cut, his hat large and worn at a rakish angle, his cravat and collar were extremely large and high enough to encroach on chin and cheeks and his coat and waistcoat had excessive revers. The feminine equivalent, a *Merveilleuse*, wore a dress extravagantly long and full, with sandals on bare feet and an exaggerated bonnet or hat over wildly flowing hair.

Djellaba, djubbeh, gallibiya, dishdash
A voluminous outer gown worn throughout the Middle East in the Arab world, also in Turkey and, further east, in India (*jubbah*), as a fuller, draped outer garment. There are many variations on the name of this garment according to the language and the country.

Grey silk and wool gallibiya, scarf and white turban with cap, Egypt

White cotton dishdash, Oman

White turban and gallibiya over striped silk waistcoat, Egypt

White headcloth over silk turban. Fawn djellaba with braid and buttons, Tunisia

Light coloured wool djubbeh over striped waistcoat and sash, turban, red leather boots, Syria

The *gallibiya*, for example, is Egyptian; it is long and full, with long, very wide, set-in sleeves. There is no collar. The garment has slits for the hands to pass through to pockets in the trousers or undergown beneath, or there are large patch pockets on the hips of the gallibiya. The skirt is generally slit at front or sides. In other Arab countries, Syria for example, the *djubbeh* is usually open in front like a coat and is turned back on either side of the opening. The garment might be only knee-length. The Turkish version is similar, often called the *jubbeh*, and this word was coined in European languages for various medieval and Renaissance jackets, tunics and skirts – for instance, the Spanish *jubon*, the French *jupe* or *jupon*, the Italian *giubba*. in southern Arabia, in Oman, the ubiquitous masuline gown, the *dishdash* is of a similar simple design. Here, as in all the Arab countries, the garment is much the same in cut and style for all classes of the population. What denotes a man of wealth and differentiates his garment from that of a peasant is the quality of the fabric from which it is made and the ornamentation of edges and front. Some winter garments are fur-lined.

Doeskin

Apart from the skin of a doe (see *Leather*), a soft, fine, closely-woven woollen cloth used for suiting, especially men's trousers.

Dogaline

A Venetian fashion of the fourteenth to sixteenth centuries (from *dogale*, apertaining to the Doge), where a very wide long sleeve was turned back and fastened up to the shoulder, displaying its rich fabric or fur lining from shoulder to knee, also the undersleeve of material of contrasting colour.

Dolman

An Oriental garment of Turkish origin worn in Hungary for many centuries in the form of a coat. Made from a rich, ornamental fabric, which was worn shorter as time passed. The skirt portion was cut to overlap at an angle.

English, 1888. Dolman coat of woven Paisley design in reds, green, blue, yellow and black

DOLMAN
Silk embroidered Hungarian dolman, gold fastenings

Hungarian dolman with sash belt, 1690

The dolman mantle or coat was fashionable in ladies' dress in Western Europe in the 1870s and 1880s. It was cut to fit over the bustle style of gown and had part sleeves. Heavy fabrics such as velvet, plush and cashmere were used and were in decorative patterns, especially Paisley. Trimmings were in velvet and fur, while padded, quilted silk linings made the coat a warm one for winter.

D'Orsay, Count Alfred Guillaume Gabriel (1801–52)

A famous Parisian dandy (see also *Dandy*), society leader and artist. Several items of clothing were named after him, notably the d'Orsay overcoat, top hat and slippers.

Dot patterns

The spot or dot has long been used to make a decorative pattern where the motifs are employed evenly or randomly, either light on a dark ground or vice versa. The most common variations are the birdseye, which is a small geometric pattern with a dot in the centre resembling a bird's eye, the *coin* dot design with large dots about half an inch in diameter, the *confetti* design, which is a more random arrangement, and the *polka* dot, where the spots alternate.

Doublet, gambeson, gipon, pourpoint, jerkin

Worn by men between the fourteenth and seventeenth centuries. It was usually fastened up the centre front, most often by a row of buttons. The garment derived from the *gambeson*, which was a padded thick cloth or leather tunic worn by soldiers under body armour or shirt of mail from the early Middle Ages. In the fourteenth century the garment passed into civilian wear for men.

The doublet varied in style from age to age and different names were given to the garment at different dates and in various countries. In the fourteenth and fifteenth centuries the words *gipon* (*jupon*), *paltock* and *pourpoint* were used. These referred to the high-necked, hip-length tunic of the fourteenth century and, more especially, to the shorter, waist-length version of the

DOUBLET
Pink waist-length doublet slashed to show white shirt beneath. Swiss, 1516

Patterned doublet and skirt. Sleeves puffed and slashed. Fashionable young Spaniard, *c.*1530

Silver cloth doublet, slashed at sleeve and chest, points at waist. English, 1630

Doublet and skirt banded with black velvet. French, c.1490

Short doublet open in front to show white shirt. German, 1480

Edward VI in black velvet doublet with gold, jewelled embroidery. Trunk hose and gown to match, 1555.

Elizabethan doublet, slashed and gold embroidered. Ruff above high neckline. 1565. Earl of Leicester

later fourteenth and the fifteenth centuries. From about 1490–1530, the pourpoint or doublet had a square neckline and was worn with a knee-length skirt and held in place by a sash or waist-belt. In appropriate periods the garment was slashed and/or padded and puffed.

In the second half of the sixteenth century this skirt became shorter so that in the Spanish modes of 1560–1600 it was merely a row of tabs at the waistline which then dipped low in the centre front. The neckline was very high to support the ruff. Early seventeenth-century doublets were concave in form over the torso (a line enforced by whalebone in the seams) in contrast to the protuberant stomachs of the 1580s (see *Peasecod-belly*). A natural line, with higher waistline, returned by 1630 and the doublet skirt was visible once more in the form of large tassets decorated by ribbon points. The doublet was replaced by jackets and coats in the second half of the seventeenth century.

Doublets in all periods could be either sleeved or sleeveless. The sleeveless types ended at the shoulder and the full shirt sleeves were then visible. In the second half of the sixteenth and early seventeenth centuries a garment called a *jerkin*, of almost identical cut and design to the doublet, was worn on top. This was generally finished at the shoulder by a padded roll or tabs (see *Piccadilly*) and the doublet long sleeve showed below. Although the two garments were so similar, one was generally of a fabric and colour which contrasted with the other.

Douillette

A padded and quilted winter outdoor garment worn by ladies in the early nineteenth century, like a pelisse in style (see *Pelisse*). From the French *douillet* (-te), soft, downy.

Drab

From the French *drap*, cloth. In English, refers to a linen or woollen cloth of a dull, light or yellowish-brown colour.

Drabbet
A drab twilled linen.

Drawboys
In the early eighteenth century a drawboy was the boy employed to pull the cords of the harness on a loom in order to operate the treadles in figure weaving. The word was then used also to denote the figured fabrics produced in this way and, later, the mechanism in the Jacquard loom which carried out the process (see *Weaving – Jacquard*).

Drawers
An undergarment for the body and legs which could be 'drawn' on. Men have worn washable undergarments under their breeches and hose since ancient times. In ancient Rome the troops serving in the colder northern European areas wore a knee-length type of drawers which fastened at the waist and were known as *feminalia* (see *Rome*, ancient); the term was also used in Carolingian dress. Early medieval drawers were tied just below the knee and at the waist; later, with fitted, longer hose, the drawers became shorter, more like trunks.

From the sixteenth century a knee-length design was most usual, though trunks and a warmer, ankle-length cut were also worn. Eighteenth-century drawers were cut like the breeches, knee-length and with a deep, buttoned waistband. Drawers were traditionally of white or natural coloured linen until the later eighteenth century, after which silk, cotton flannel or wool stockinette were also used. At this time, with the introduction of trousers, long drawers were usual and remained customary wear for much of the nineteenth century.

Only isolated references are made over the centuries to the wearing of drawers by women. It was not until the early nineteenth century that European fashion journals described such garments, whose use had become necessary because of the fashion for thin, transparent dresses. The drawers were generally cut like the masculine garments or with separate legs attached only to a waistband (see *Pantalettes*); they were of linen, cotton or muslin. As the wearing of thin dresses continued, the cold of European winters forced women to adopt warmer underwear, and drawers could be of silk, cloth or wool and were full and long, some examples even having attached feet for extra warmth. Many designs extended from waist to knee, but some were attached to a bodice with shoulder straps above a high waist. With the full crinoline skirts and ample layers of petticoats of the mid-nineteenth century, drawers were generally of flannel, often red; the legs were now joined to make a complete garment and were calf-length and, later, knee-length. In the last 30 years of the century, drawers, like other garments, became over-ornamented with tucks, embroidery and lace and flounce trimming (see *Underwear*).

Drawstring
A cord, ribbon or tape passed through a channel sewn in the edge of a garment; used to pull together the fullness of the material at waist, neck, wrist or ankle.

Dress improver
A term used in the 1880s to describe a bustle.

Dress protector or shield
Two crescent-shaped pieces of silk, rayon or cotton seamed together with rubber inset; could be sewn into the under part of the armhole of a garment to protect it from underarm perspiration. In use from the mid-nineteenth century on, but especially between 1880 and 1930.

Drill, drilling
A strong twilled linen or cotton fabric used for summer uniforms, trousers, shirts and overalls.

Drugget
1) Formerly a wool, or wool with silk or linen, *fabric* used for making clothes.
2) Now a coarse woollen material used for *covering* floors and furniture.

DRAWERS
White cotton drawers with muslin decoration, English, 1815–30

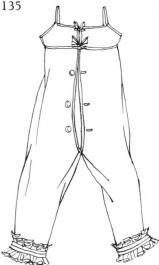
Boy's cotton drawers to be buttoned on to a waistcoat, English, 1820–35

Drawers, French, thirteenth century

Dungarees

Workmen's overalls. Made formerly of a fabric called *dungaree* (from the Hindi word *dungrī*) which was a coarse, poor quality Indian calico. Such overalls are now usually made of denim.

Dyeing

An ancient art, known to most cultures in some degree, wherein fabrics are coloured in such a way that the colour appears to be an integral part of the material and not merely a surface toning as in painting. The aim of the dyer through the centuries has been to produce a fabric whose colouring is impervious to washing, rubbing or exposure to sunlight. Prior to the seventeenth and eighteenth centuries few, if any, dyes passed this test and, due to a lack of co-ordinated research and communication, the work of each dyer had something of a hit-and-miss quality so that the colouring was sometimes successful, sometimes not.

Various dyeing processes and substances from which dyes were obtained were known to the ancient and medieval worlds. In the most primitive societies, natural substances such as berries, leaves, flowers, fruit and wood were mixed into a soft paste with the addition of albumen or blood and simply pressed into the material. This method of dyeing was highly impermanent, being simply a staining which quickly faded with exposure to light or was washed out. When this happened the dyer repeated the process, probably with a different colour. It was found that some mineral substances were fast to light. These included iron earths (reds, yellows, browns), lime, gypsum and clay (white and cream) and soot and coal (greys and black). Experiments were made with different binding agents – chief of these were blood, saliva, albumen, wax and glue. Experience showed that solvents such as urine, sea water and saliva gave more permanent results. More advanced civilizations discovered that dye substances which were soluble in water led to more satisfactory processes and lichens are the most suitable substances for this. Others which are soluble in alkaline liquids were then made

fast by oxidization in the air.

All these processes produced only temporary colouring. Experiment showed that a more permanent effect could be obtained from natural dye substances if an auxiliary chemical was employed to unite the dye with the material. The chemical needed varied according to the dye substance used and trial and error decided which chemical gave the best results. Such chemicals were known as mordants, from the French *mordant*, present participle of the verb to bite. The chief substances from which good natural dyes were obtained in ancient and medieval times were as follows: plants and trees – woad (leaves, blue), saffron (crocus, yellow), sumach (leaves and twigs, yellowish-brown), madder (root, red), henna (root, red), walnut (shells and roots, brown), tree galls (black), pomegranate (fruit, yellow); the mollusc Purpura (Tyrian purple); and the insects kermes (red), cochineal (reds) and lac (scarlet).

Dyeing with substances such as madder and indigo was practised extensively by the peoples of China, India, Persia and Egypt several thousand years ago. The earliest dyed textiles found come from the tombs of ancient Egypt. The most valued dye in ancient Greece and Rome was Tyrian purple, so called because the centre of the industry was at the twin cities of Tyre and Sidon (now in Lebanon) and because the dye was obtained from the mollusc Purpura. There was great demand for this colour, which was a deep crimson rather than purple, but it was a costly rarity because it was contained only in a small gland in the mollusc. These glands had to be extracted, crushed and prepared. Fabric dyed in a vat of this dye emerged yellow but became reddish-purple on exposure to sunlight. Stronger tones were obtained by a second dipping. Purple became the imperial colour under the Roman Empire and dyeing of these textiles a strictly controlled state monopoly. Production sites were established on the Greek islands, especially Crete, on the mainland and all along the coast of Asia Minor and Sicily. At Taranto there exists a hill composed of mollusc shells from the industry of this time. Purple dyeing from this and similar molluscs was carried out in West Africa, by the Incas and Aztecs of South America, and also in south-west Britain.

In Europe in the early Middle Ages, Florence was the chief centre for dyeing. The importance of the industry here was reflected in the custom of taking the names of dye substances for streets in the city as well as for families. The family of sculptors, della Robbia (madder), is one such example. In the thirteenth century the Florentine Federigo had carried out considerable research into the preparation and use of lichens from Asia Minor for the dyeing of purple. For this work he was accorded the privilege of adopting the family name of Rucellia, from the lichen *Roccella tinctoria*. By this time other large centres for dyeing and the marketing of dyes were being established: Genoa, Lucca, Frankfurt, Cologne, Venice and Istanbul became important city centres for the trade between East and West.

With the discovery of America and the opening up of the sea route to the East Indies, new dye products and processes were introduced into Europe. Cochineal was imported by the Spanish from Mexico where they had observed the skill of the Aztecs in using this insect for dyeing purposes. The Incas also were skilled in such arts at this time. In Europe it was discovered how to produce a brilliant scarlet by using tin as a mordant for cochineal. In the seventeenth century in a number of countries in western Europe there developed a new approach towards research and study into dyes and towards a collation and publication of the knowledge so far gained. A number of eminent chemists investigated the dye processes and published treatises which attempted to clarify and explain them. In France, Colbert, Louis XIV's Comptroller-General of Finance, published a code of instructions to dyers and manufacturers, while of the chemists whose contribution did so much to improve the knowledge of methods of dyeing should be mentioned the Frenchmen Dufay de Cisternay, Hellot, Berthollet and Chaptal, and the Englishmen Bancroft, Henry and Home.

The great step forward in producing fast and brilliant dyestuffs was in the mid-nineteenth century with the research into *aniline dyes*. In 1841, C.J. Fritzsche obtained aniline, a colourless, aromatic, volatile oil, by distilling indigo with caustic potash. Aniline was so named by Fritzsche from the Sanskrit word for the indigo plant. In the 1850s there was widespread investigation by many scientists to discover substitutes for natural dyestuffs. Sir William Henry Perkin was experimenting with a synthesis of quinine in 1856 when he oxidized impure aniline with potassium bichromate and obtained a black tarry substance which contained a purple precipitate. This was the first synthetic aniline dye which became known as mauveine. Further research in England and other European countries produced other brilliantly-coloured synthetic aniline dyes from coal tar, including alizarin, magenta, blue, green and fuchsia. (Magenta and solferino (fuchsia) were both named after battles in 1859 in the Franco-Austrian war.)

Research continued during the rest of the nineteenth century and in the twentieth towards dyes which were brilliant, varied and fast. Today the scope of synthetic dyes is vast and the subject complex. Different dyes are suited to specific fabrics. The reactive dyes of the 1950s presented a further step forward in that they form a chemical linkage with cellulose fabrics; the colours are brilliant and the fastness extensive even when obtained by cold-dyeing methods.

Pattern dyeing

Apart from straightforward printing, there are a number of traditional methods to obtain patterns on textiles by means of dyeing. These come under the heading of *resist processes*. *Batik* is the chief of these, where a resist substance such as wax is painted on the textile so that the dye does not penetrate that area of the design (see *Batik*). Secondly, the *tie and dye process* has been practised in almost all parts of the world. It is one of the oldest forms of making a design on textiles and, due to its

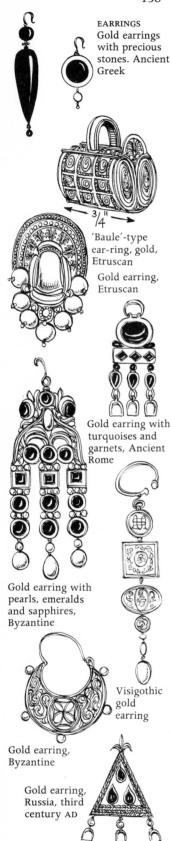

EARRINGS
Gold earrings with precious stones. Ancient Greek

'Baule'-type ear-ring, gold, Etruscan

Gold earring, Etruscan

Gold earring with turquoises and garnets, Ancient Rome

Gold earring with pearls, emeralds and sapphires, Byzantine

Visigothic gold earring

Gold earring, Byzantine

Gold earring, Russia, third century AD

simplicity of technique and equipment needed, can be practised by primitive societies. In this process parts of the material are tied up, knotted, plaited or stitched up before dyeing so that the dye cannot penetrate to these areas, thus creating a pattern on the textile when the cloth is undone. Drawn-thread pleating and folding can also be used to create patterns. Tie and dye methods have been practised chiefly in Africa, India, Japan, Indonesia and Cambodia. Alternatively, the yarn can be tied instead of the material. This technique, called *ikat* (a Malayan word), can be applied to warp or weft or both. The variation in the weave then produces further alterations in the pattern. This ancient technique was especially used in Turkey, South America, Japan, Africa and India.

Other forms of resist dyeing include stencils sewn on the textile or the clamping of the fabric between plates. There is also the negative pattern system where mordants are painted over the design areas so that, when the textile is dyed, the part treated with the mordant will be coloured while the rest of the colour fades away.

E

Earrings
A form of jewellery in use from earliest times. Both men and women had their ears pierced, and decorative, pendant earrings were a sign of rank in a sophisticated society. In Renaissance and Baroque Europe often only one earring was displayed. Only in periods where the wig, coiffure or head-dress obscured the ears were earrings out of fashion. In the twentieth century the spring clip and the screw earring gradually replaced the earring set in pierced ears.

Eau de Cologne
A perfume first prepared by *Paul de Feminis* who brought his recipe for it from Milan to Cologne, where he settled and sold his product under the name *Eau admirable*. He left the secret of its preparation to his nephew *Giovanni Maria Farina* who lived in Cologne from 1709 and marketed *Eau de Cologne*. The original perfume continued to be manufactured by this family over the centuries in Cologne and also in Italy. It was originally prepared from a precise blending of oils from certain herbs, drugs and spices dissolved in alcohol and distilled; the distillate was then diluted with rose water. Later, the original perfume was simulated successfully with artificial preparations.

Échelle
French for ladder. A form of bodice decoration fashionable in the later seventeenth and earlier eighteenth centuries, where a row of ribbon bows, diminishing in size from bosom to waist, decorated the centre front of the stomacher.

Egypt (ancient)
It is perhaps surprising that the costume of ancient Egypt altered comparatively little in view of the great span of years in which the culture was dominant. In the 3,000 years of this civilization the style of dress remained a draped one. This was in common with the basis of costume in other ancient civilizations of the Mediterranean and Middle Eastern peoples – Greece and Rome and Mesopotamia, where the Assyrians, Babylonians and Sumerians lived.

The ancient Egyptian dress was composed of loincloths or skirts, capes and robes, all held in place by knots tied in the material, waist belts, sashes and collars. This was in contrast to the Oriental styles of Persia, India and China, where the peoples wore sewn, fitted garments based on coats, tunics and trousers.

During the 3,000 years of the ancient Egyptian culture the style of the garments slowly evolved and became more complex, and a greater number were worn, either in combinations with one another or on top of one another, as time passed. There is ample evidence of what people wore from the wealth of wall and sarcophagus paintings, sculpture, ceramics and jewellery which survive. The illustrations from these sources are somewhat stylized but are clearly understandable. A certain amount of care is needed, though, in relating this illustrative material to the periods when the dress would be worn as, in certain later ages, pharaohs, gods and persons of rank are sometimes depicted in the dress of an earlier age, one which was nostalgically in vogue at the time – rather as in eighteenth-century Europe famous people were portrayed in figure sculpture wearing Roman togas, items of clothes which they fairly certainly never wore.

By 4000 BC a civilized way of life had developed in ancient Egypt and in about 3200 BC Upper and Lower Egypt were united under one crown (a fact which is recorded in the dress of kings by their wearing of the double crown which combines the two different types – the tall, white one had been worn in Upper Egypt and the lower, red one, rising to a point at the back, in Lower Egypt) (see also *Crown*). After 3200 BC there were three chief periods of prosperity and peace in the ancient Egyptian civilization (interspersed with invasions, wars and times of unrest) and these are referred to as the Old, Middle and New Kingdoms.

The *Old Kingdom*, its capital at Memphis and ruled by the kings of the first to the eighth dynasties, prospered until about 2500 BC. Dress at this time was simple and consisted of a short *skirt* for men and a

slender sheath type of *dress* for women. The man's linen skirt was generally tied at the waist or held in place by a belt. As time passed, variations were introduced into the skirt design and it was often pleated or gathered. Important persons wore an ornamental pendant hanging down from the waist-belt in front. This was made of leather, embroidered materials and beads. Sometimes men wore shoulder braces or a *corselet* on the torso. The feminine dress covered the body from below the breasts to the ankles. It was held up by shoulder straps and these and the hem could be decoratively banded. Both sexes wore woollen cloaks.

The deep, decorative *collars* were introduced early. These were brightly coloured, embroidered and beaded and were worn by both sexes. Men and women also shaved, or cut, their hair short and wore long, thick, dark *wigs*. Apart from the pharaoh's crown already mentioned, *head-dresses* were rare at this time. Ladies generally tied their wig back with a ribbon or metal circlet round the brow. Most men, especially those of rank, were cleanshaven, but kings wore the *false beard* which was held in place at the chin by straps attached to the crown or over the ears.

The *Middle Kingdom* prospered from 2200 BC until 1785 BC, its capital at Thebes and ruled by kings of the ninth to the seventeenth dynasties. Costume developed slowly and steadily. To the man's skirt was often added a *cape* draped round the shoulders and tied in a knot on the breast. The skirt could be either short or ankle-length. Some short skirts were now of heavier material and the pendant in front was more decorative, as were also the deep shoulder collars. The *jewellery* of this period is especially fine, delicate, yet varied. Much of the best is of gold, jewelled and inlaid. Semi-precious stones such as lapis lazuli and garnets were widely used.

The *New Kingdom* extended from about 1580 BC until the Egyptians were conquered, successively, by the Assyrians in 671 BC, the Persians in 525 BC and Alexander the Great in 332 BC. Egypt finally became part of Rome in 30 BC, after which time the

Assyrian earrings

White chalcedony and gold earrings, English, 1850

Gold earring, Phoenician, seventh century BC

Gold earring, English, 1875

ECHELLE
White satin gown with lace stomacher, sleeve ruffles and underskirt. Blue velvet échelle, 1690

Sheath dress, blue with embroidered borders. Decorative collar, wool cloak, wig. Old Kingdom

White linen pleated skirt, black wig. Old Kingdom

New Kingdom, Sari-type of draped gown in fine linen. Collar and bracelets, wig

White fine linen robe with fringed waist sash tied on hip. Collar, wig. New Kingdom

Pharaoh in striped headdress. Robe in white linen with decorative belt, collar and pendant apron. Sandals. New Kingdom

Collar, corselet, skirt with belt and pendant. Fur tail at the back. Old Kingdom king in red crown of Lower Egypt

White linen robe knotted at breast. Collar, headband and bracelets, wig. New Kingdom

White linen cape and skirt. Wig. Middle Kingdom

New Kingdom queen. Fine linen cape and skirt with decorative head-dress, collar and waistbelt. Sandals, wig characteristic form of Egyptian dress gave place to Roman. Egypt prospered and extended her empire under the eighteenth to the twenty-second dynasties with the capital still based on Thebes. During the centuries under the New Kingdom the same basic garments were worn as before, but there was more variation in size and draping, and to them were added new items of dress which were introduced from the East when Egypt extended her borders, acquiring lands in Asia and Africa. The chief of these was the robe or gown worn by both sexes. Of Persian origin, this was rectangular in shape, about five feet in length and four feet wide. The sides were left open and the fullness of the fabric held in place by pins and a waist-belt to form wide, elbow-length sleeves. Often, instead of a decorative leather belt, a wide sash, some ten feet long, was tied round the body in various ways with its fringed ends hanging down at side or front. Women usually wore the gown without a waist-belt or sash; the edges of the fabric were tied in a knot at the breast.

The skirt and cape of the Middle Kingdom continued to be worn, especially by women. The *cape*, also a rectangular piece of material, was tied in front on the bosom and the decorative collar generally worn on top. The ankle-length *skirt* was also a rectangle, this time very wide. It was held in place by being gathered in with a draw-thread knotted at the waist or by a decorative girdle, the long end(s) of which hung down in front. Another type of feminine gown was provided by a very large rectangle of material, some four feet deep and 13 feet long, the wearing of which was of Oriental origin and it was draped in a similar manner to the Indian sari (see *Indian dress*). The Egyptian style of draping was, however, aimed at producing folds which all radiated from one point at the waist.

The production of fabrics in Egypt was by this time of a high standard. Widths of up to five feet could be woven and the linens were so fine as to be nearly transparent. Most garments were made of pleated or gathered materials. There was

now also a much greater variety in decoration on the costume and in styles of wig and head-dress. The deep, ornamental *collars* and *pendant aprons* were foci of decorative treatment. Gilded leather, coloured embroidery and jewelled, inlaid metals were used in these; colours were brilliant (see also *Apron*). The two chief decorative motifs were the *lotus flower* and the *papyrus* bundle, both appearing in various stylized forms. Other typical motifs included the *sun's disc* flanked by outspread wings and the sacred emblems of the *hawk* and the *scarab beetle*. The symbol of power was the *uraeus* (pl. uraei), the sacred asp (cobra), the head and neck of which appeared on the head-dress and pendant aprons of sovereigns and divinities.

Such persons also wore a variety of complex head-dresses which included such motifs. There was the tall, white crown of Upper Egypt with plumes added at the sides, or a design of sun's disc, horns and tall plumes. The term *Atef* crown and head-dress were sometimes applied respectively to these. Other head-dresses were caps and hoods topped by complex creations of goats', rams' or cows' horns and metal and wool decoration representing bundles of papyrus and different types of plumes. Especially characteristic was the striped linen headcloth, the *khat*, which was bound round the brow and was then folded

Tutankhamun in striped linen khat with uraeus, c.1350 BC

King Menthu-hetep, wig with bands and uraeus, c.2100 BC

Queen Nefertiti. Shaved head and crown, fourteenth century BC

Wig with ribbon band, fourteenth century BC

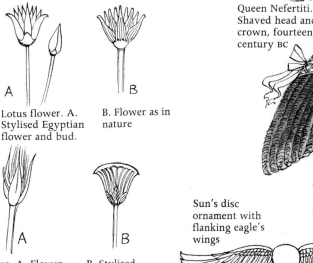

Lotus flower. A. Stylised Egyptian flower and bud.

B. Flower as in nature

Papyrus. A. Flower as in nature

B. Stylised Egyptian motif

Sun's disc ornament with flanking eagle's wings

Uraeus

Pharaoh wearing double crown and false beard

Prince with Horus lock. Headdress of goat's horn, plumes and papyrus bundles. New Kingdom

White crown of Upper Egypt with plumes. Atef. New Kingdom

to hang down on each side of the face to the shoulders. The material was tied at the rear and hung down in a tail. This was a royal head-dress which has been made familiar by the gold mask of Tutankhamun.

The head was still generally shaved and a wig was worn. A lock of hair was permitted to be grown over one ear by princes of the blood and this hung down under the wig; it was known as the *Horus lock*, from the youthful God Horus. Ancient Egyptians are most commonly shown in paintings and sculpture to be barefoot. Illustrations of footwear worn by persons of rank show sandals made from palm leaves and papyrus (see *Sandal*). Persons of rank also wore gloves.

Elastic, elasticized materials, elastomers
The raw material of natural elastic which, incorporated with woven or knitted fabric, was used in elasticized materials, was rubber. This is a substance which has been known to man for centuries and the natural rubber came originally from a number of different trees and plants, though it was developed as a commercial proposition from the rubber tree, grown in plantations chiefly in Malaya.

Until the nineteenth century this rubber was simply a solid substance which would erase, but in order to use it widely it was necessary to give it elasticity and make it resistant to extremes of heat and cold. Much of the early work on this, mainly by mixing it with sulphur, was done by the Englishman *Thomas Hancock*, who took out a patent in 1820 for a process to produce an elastic cloth, which was a mixture of rubber and fabric. An important contribution was then made by *Charles Goodyear*, the American inventor who, having spent years trying to find a suitable method of carrying this work further, in 1839 accidentally dropped some of the rubber and sulphur mixture on to a hot stove and discovered that a satisfactory means to vulcanization was to hand. His first patent for the process was granted in 1844.

The new elasticized material of fabric and rubber was used at first for footwear – for elastic-sided boots and, later, for over-

shoes and for boots. *Elastic thread* was slowly developed and continued to be used chiefly by the boot trade during the nineteenth century, though a limited use was made of it in corsetry manufacture. The chief deterrent to its large-scale use in corsetry was in the transportation of the latex (rubber-tree sap fluid) to provide lengths long enough for manufacture into foundation garments. Until the 1930s the *latex*, which quickly hardened on contact with the air, was sent out to Europe and America in hard sheets which were softened and cut into strips on arrival. After this a method was evolved so that the latex emulsion could be shipped in that form in tankers direct to the factory and the Dunlop Rubber Company developed a process to extrude long lengths of fine elastic thread. Improvements followed so that in the 1930s, *Lastex* was produced in as great a variety of lengths and fineness of thread as other fabrics and this made possible its very wide use in the manufacture of corsetry and underwear of all kinds.

A new revolution in elasticized materials took place in 1959–60 with the production of artificial elastic. These Spandex fibres contain no natural rubber and are now called *elastomerics*. The chief of these fibres, invented in the *Du Pont Laboratories* in the USA, is *Lycra*. It weighs much less than its rubber equivalent and is much stronger. By 1970 Lycra was being manufactured in printed tricot fabrics which, with stretch and non-stretch areas in one garment, could be made into panteegirdles, bras, briefs and a variety of underwear (see also *Underwear*). The term elastomeric has now been replaced, under EEC regulations, by *elastane*.

Ell
An old European measure of length, used for cloth, which varied from one country to another. For example, the English ell was 45 inches but the Scottish just over 37 inches.

Embroidery
The art of ornamenting textiles with figured patterns by means of a needle and

thread of wool, silk, linen or metal.

Embroidery can be self-coloured (white embroidery) – where the decorative quality is provided entirely by the stitch – or coloured work, where the interest is two-dimensional, colour and form. Outline embroidery relies for its interest upon bold lines depicting the pattern and the stitches used are clear and decisive. Shaded embroidery has a pictorial quality, blending the colours in masses to give light and shadow. Many fine embroideries in this category are needlework pictures, copies or interpretations of paintings or worked from cartoons designed by well-known artists especially for the needlework interpreter. A third form is flat mass embroidery where the design is depicted in solid masses and lines. An outline is made to the shapes, which can be filled in by embroidered stitches or appliqué work. Colour plays an important part in embroidery but, from earliest times, metal thread has also been used to give richness and brilliance to the work. In the use of gold and silver in embroidery, the metal threads were usually laid on the surface of the textile only, in order to conserve such valuable material, and were secured by small stitches in another thread. Later, fine metal wire was wrapped around the embroidery threads themselves.

The art of embroidery originated in the East, in China and Japan, Arabia and Mesopotamia, and seems to date back to before 1200 BC. In *China*, silk embroidery had been practised from early times, though the most ancient actual examples date from the first century BC. The finest embroideries were of silk for both ground and pattern, but peasant workmanship was of silk and wool embroidered on a linen ground. Motifs and designs showed great variety and traditional patterns continued to be used for long periods. Convention dictated the use of motifs and these were only slowly modified. Characteristic were the mythical dragon, the phoenix and the unicorn, also the symbolic motifs representing mountain ranges, waves of the sea, heavenly bodies and clouds in the sky. There were landscape scenes and motifs from nature –

animals, birds, flowers, trees and fruits. Most typical were the magnolia and lotus blossom, the pomegranate, peach and the bamboo, the duck and the peacock, the deer and the elephant. The practice of embroidery in silk spread to *Japan*, where Chinese craftsmen were working in the early years of the first century AD. In both countries embroidery in gold and silver thread was also worked as well as the unusual technique of combining embroidery with weaving.

In the ancient civilizations essential needlework and decorative stitchery developed together, one evolving from the other. Garments needed mending and patching, and from this came ornamental stitching and more complex designs. Needlework was an early art form carried out by all classes of the community. Examples have come from Egyptian tombs and there are references in Hebrew literature, from Indian writings and, later, from the classical world of Homer, Ovid and Virgil.

Indian embroidery is thought to have developed contemporaneously with that in ancient Assyria and Babylon. From early times embroidery was worked in gold and silver thread, first as flat metal strips, later with metal wire twisted round threads. Beads and jewels were introduced into these embroideries which were worked on fine cotton materials. Characteristic motifs include the elephant, the peacock, the lotus and the mango. Some of the most beautiful embroideries have come from Kashmir, where the motifs and designs were most varied and colourful. Typical were patterns based on natural forms of flowers, fruits, butterflies and birds and these show a marked affinity with contemporary Persian and Chinese embroideries. Dominating many designs is the classic shawl motif (like the Scottish Paisley version) which, it is suggested, derived from the cypress cone or the almond in Kashmir.

As in India and Persia, gold and silver embroidery in *Europe* seems also to have ante-dated that in silk. Archaeological researches in the Crimea have revealed remains of robes dating from the third century BC embroidered in metal thread

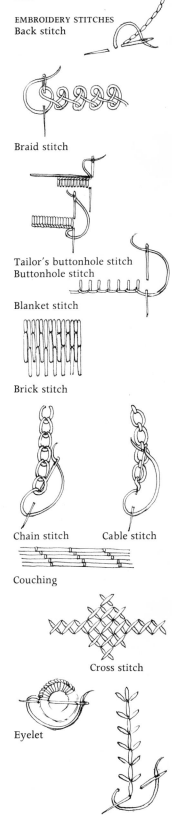

EMBROIDERY STITCHES
Back stitch

Braid stitch

Tailor's buttonhole stitch
Buttonhole stitch

Blanket stitch

Brick stitch

Chain stitch   Cable stitch

Couching

Cross stitch

Eyelet

Fly stitch

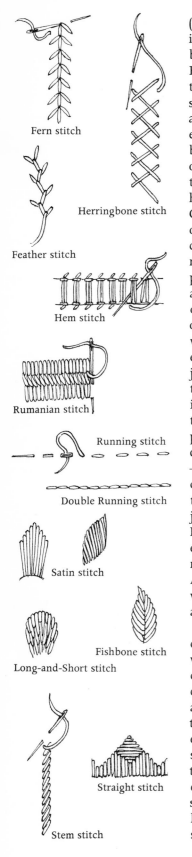

Fern stitch

Herringbone stitch

Feather stitch

Hem stitch

Rumanian stitch

Running stitch

Double Running stitch

Satin stitch

Fishbone stitch

Long-and-Short stitch

Straight stitch

Stem stitch

(these are now in the Hermitage Museum in Leningrad). Many embroideries have been recovered from the tombs of ancient Egypt. These are often of coloured wool thread on linen and illustrate pictorial scenes as well as geometrical patterns. Here also there are examples of gold and silver embroideries, the threads made of thin beaten metal strips. The Jews learnt the art of embroidery from the Egyptians during their captivity and the skill also seems to have been introduced to Greece, via the Greek Islands, from Egypt. The influence of the Orient upon the embroideries and designs of Mediterranean countries was most marked. Both Greece and Rome imported costly embroidered fabrics as well as employing Asiatic embroiderers. Schools of needlework were set up and copies made of Oriental designs. In Imperial Rome there was continuous demand for rich fabrics embroidered all over with gold thread and jewels. With the collapse of Rome, Byzantium continued the tradition and the inspiration for designs was more eastern than before. Geometric patterns were employed, also natural motifs. Typical were designs based on flowers, trees and animals – especially lions, tigers, elephants, peacocks, eagles, unicorns and palms. Gold thread was widely employed and pearls and jewels incorporated into the embroidery. Further impetus was given to the use of eastern motifs by the advent of Mohammedanism in the seventh century. The Arab conquests in Sicily, Spain and northwest India introduced new themes to these areas.

In *medieval Europe* embroidery was considered to be an important art. Designs were made by well-known artists, particularly in Italy and France. These were drawn on paper and the lines pricked with a needle. When the paper was placed on the stretched material which was to be embroidered, powder was applied to the surface so that it passed through the holes to mark the material beneath. To make embroidery easier, the material was then stretched on a frame. Some frames were large, rectangular constructions but, for smaller projects, a circular tambour frame

was used. The main subject of inspiration for embroidery was the Christian religion and a great deal of the work was for the Church. Furnishings in the castle and the home were also given enbroidered decoration. In the later Middle Ages, when costume was richly decorated, embroidery was an important means of providing such ornamentation. Heraldic motifs were used a great deal, but so also were geometric and floral patterns. Most garments received embroidered decoration but belts and purses especially so. These purses or pouches were attached to the belt for security. Those made in France were particularly decorative and were called *tasques*.

The majority of embroideries in the early Middle Ages were worked on linen with wool or silk thread. Gold and silver work was only sparingly introduced. The outstanding example of the eleventh century is the Bayeux Tapestry, an embroidered hanging over 200 feet long, worked in coloured wools on a linen ground, and vividly illustrating scenes from the Norman Conquest. As a result of the Crusades, richer materials were imported into Europe and in the later Middle Ages there was greater variety in design, a richness of colour and an increase in the use of silk. This was especially so in Italy and in Spain, where the Saracenic influence was strong. In Sicily, the art of weaving silks and gold cloth had been developed in the twelfth century and the island's textile industry became famous for its silks, velvets and brocades. Embroidery in silks and precious metals developed at the same time. Typical were Saracenic cut cloths where two materials were used. The design was cut in one of these, then fastened on to the other by silk embroidery stitches. The Moorish influence was very strong in the Iberian peninsula. Fabrics were rich and embroideries contained spangles after the Saracenic custom, as well as gold and silver threads in all-over designs. Fine quality embroideries were produced by the wealthy city states further north in Italy. Much of this was on linen, in open-work manner.

In the thirteenth and fourteenth centuries, English embroidery, *opus angli-*

canum, was the finest in Europe. The quality of the stitchery was so fine that the work was highly sought-after. Figure scenes and pictures of animals, birds and flowers were naturalistic and well-drawn. Silver thread and seed pearls were introduced into the embroideries and appliqué work was widely used. In the fourteenth century velvet grounds were favoured.

In the *sixteenth* and *seventeenth centuries* the quality of embroidery in Europe was very high, designs and colour were subtle and sophisticated and materials were richer. In the sixteenth century especially, secular embroidery reached a higher standard and a greater richness in quality than before, and the craft of embroidery was highly esteemed. In France, particularly, the royal house lent energetic patronage under Catherine de' Medici and, later, Louis XIV. Cut work on white linen was developed, also drawn-work designs. In Italy, many embroideries copied the paintings of great artists, and artists created designs especially for the needleworker. Linen grounds were favoured with drawn and solid embroidery used upon them. Colours were subtly blended and beads introduced to give body to the work. English embroidery had lost its pre-eminence by the sixteenth century. Elizabethan work was very rich in colour and materials. Silk was widely used and seed pearls and metal threads were introduced. Much of the work was for garments and large motifs predominated, mainly of fruit and flowers.

Spanish embroidery of the sixteenth century had a considerable influence on the rest of western Europe. The so-called Spanish work, or *blackwork*, became widespread. Probably derived from Moorish craftsmanship, this was originally an embroidery on white linen of black silk outline in arabesques and scrolls formed by climbing plants and tendrils. Gold and red silk threads were introduced to give brilliance to the design. The method particularly lent itself to designs based upon woodcuts from the newly printed books of the period. The work was especially fashionable in England where it had been introduced at the time of Catherine of Aragon and, later, of Mary's marriage to Philip II of Spain.

Of especial richness and excellence of quality in the fifteenth and sixteenth centuries were the embroideries of Flanders and Burgundy. Designs were derived from the paintings of the time – those of the Van Eyck brothers, Van der Weyden, Rubens, Van Dyck and others. Much of the work was in silk and gold thread in colours carefully blended to resemble woven fabrics.

With the coming of the eighteenth century there was a revival in the art of embroidery for practical purposes, and this included costume as well as furnishings for the home. In the seventeenth century there had been a stress, particularly in the fashionable stumpwork, to embroider pictures and portraits rather than articles to be worn and used. Embroidered designs and materials during the eighteenth century were a reflection of and subject to the same influences which determined design of garments and furniture. According to the period there was a vogue for Indian patterns, for chinoiserie, for rococo motifs, and for neo-classical and Egyptian themes.

In the first half of the eighteenth century motifs, which were predominantly floral, were large and designs were carried out in flat solid form in satin and long and short stitches, sewn with silk thread in beautifully shaded colours. Gold and silver thread, spangles, beads and chenille were incorporated. The decoration was most usually applied to the edges of men's coats, the pocket flaps and cuffs, all over the waistcoats and the ladies' panier gowns. *Crewelwork* was used for many garments and *quilting* was especially fashionable, also drawn fabric stitches combined with Italian quilting. White quilting was particularly in use for babies' clothes. In the second half of the century, motifs were smaller, in sprigs and arabesques. In the 1780s the trend, as in the garments themselves, was away from silks, satins and velvets towards wool and silk embroidery on light-coloured or white cottons and linen. *Patchwork* was in vogue.

A slow decline in the quality of embroidery set in in the last quarter of the eighteenth century and this continued throughout the nineteenth, though there was a revival of interest in quality craftsmanship in the 1870s and 1880s resulting from the work and ideas of William Morris together with his colleagues and fellow artists. In the early nineteenth century clothes were ornamented at borders and hems with simple embroidery using classical motifs in coloured silk and metal threads. By the 1820s the chief interest in embroidery had moved to needle-painting and copies of most of the famous paintings and masters were being worked for wall decoration. *Berlin woolwork* (from Germany) was all the rage; cross stitch and tent stitch were chiefly used and decoration was also applied to useful articles such as slippers, gloves, bags and shawls. By mid-century designs were large and predominantly floral, in bright or garish colours with beads lavishly incorporated. Whitework was also produced in quantity and this varied in quality and fineness from the Ayrshire christening robes to *broderie anglaise* and *Mountmellick* embroidery. Quilting was still widely worked, as were patchwork and smocking.

Meanwhile, as in other fields of craftwork, the machine was beginning to compete with the handworker. A machine to embroider was produced as early as 1828, and soon after mid-century machines were producing quantities of whitework which were affecting the livelihood of the hand-embroiderer. Much of the development took place in Germany and Switzerland, but after the introduction of Gröbli's shuttle machine in 1865, which perfected the combination of the sewing machine's continuous thread techniques with the principle of the embroidery machine, the industrialization of embroidery spread to most of western Europe. When, in the early twentieth century, the lock-stitch and chain-stitch sewing machines were adapted for embroidery (see *Sewing machine*), machine work had taken over most of the market and almost all embroidered garments were machine made.

Parallel to the mainstream of embroidery

developed in Europe there also evolved a peasant art form, much more nationalistic and regional, retaining its freshness and individuality over centuries in patterns which became traditional to a given area or race of people. Such embroidery has influenced the mainstream work from time to time, but it has mainly retained its separate identity and, in many areas, especially eastern and northern Europe, is still practised.

German-speaking regions have evolved a peasant embroidery as well as the rich embroidery of the medieval *opus teutonicum*. In the country districts garments were embroidered on linen with wool and silk in harmonious and brilliant colours. Designs were varied, incorporating geometrical and plant motifs, interlacing scrolls, figure compositions and landscape scenes inspired by the Bible, mythology and legend or village life. The work was unsophisticated but vital and beautifully embroidered. Sometimes, as in the Orient, embroidery was combined with a woven pattern. German wool embroidery became famous, in rich colours and incorporating beads. It was from this inspiration that the Berlin woolwork, so fashionable in the nineteenth century, spread to the rest of Europe and the USA. *Swiss* linen embroidery was equally vigorous and of high quality. For many centuries the linen ground was dark, blue or brown, and the pattern was embroidered in white thread. There was a wide range of stitches and colour was later introduced to give emphasis and richness to the design.

The embroidery of *eastern Europe* has always been more strongly influenced by the Orient, in particular that of Turkey and Persia. The peasant work was colourful and vigorous, a development of the popular art of the people and widely employed on garments for both sexes for festive occasions. Embroidery was chiefly used to decorate blouses and shirts, belts, sashes and braces, caps, shawls and kerchiefs, skirts and trousers. The work of *Czechoslovakia* and *Alpine Austria* shows considerable affinity with that of Germany and Switzerland. *Hungarian* embroideries are especially colourful and elaborate and leather is ornamented as well as linen. Red and black are most often used. *Rumanian* embroidery is particularly varied as the country has been subjected to influences from so many directions: from Byzantium and the Greek Orthodox Church, from Turkey and from Russia. Geometric patterns and stylized motifs were widely used and colours were strong and rich. Black and white work became popular after the quality of fast dyeing was improved. The cross stitch was in general use here as in most peasant embroideries.

The cross stitch was especially to be seen in *Scandinavian* work. In the extreme north of Norway, and in Finland and Iceland, subjects were taken from local life – reindeer, lake and mountain scenes, the midnight sun – all conventionalized to make patterns for garments. National dyes from lichens, bark and plants were used to give soft colours. Both Norwegian and Swedish embroideries show designs like those of the carvings on the wooden stave churches, of interlaced ornament blended with animals and plants. White work was traditional to Denmark, such as Hedebo embroidery on hand-woven linen. Russian embroidery, due to the vastness of the country, varies greatly from one part to another, but in general there is an Oriental approach to the work and an extensive use of gold and silver threads. In the north the work resembles that of the Finns.

EMBROIDERY TERMS AND STITCHES

Anglo-Saxon work – an early embroidery where the design is outlined by stitches and filled in with silk couching.

Appenzell work – named after the Swiss canton where it originated. A very fine drawn-work on white lawn or linen, used as decoration for aprons and caps.

Appliqué (or applied) work – embroidery where a design is made by sewing (with different stitches) one piece of material on to another. This gives a bold, colourful effect. *Inlaid appliqué work* is where an identical design motif is cut from both ground and second fabric, then the material from the latter is sewn into the empty shape in the former.

Arrasene work – an embroidery using chenille cord.

Assisi embroidery – a traditional form named after the Italian city where it was, and is, practised. The design is left unmarked in the ground fabric and the background is covered with cross stitch, usually in blue or rust-brown. The design is boldly outlined in black or a dark colour in double running stitch. The ground is generally of natural colour and the embroidery is worked by counting threads.

Ayrshire work – a Scottish embroidery worked in white cotton or linen in tiny patterns of flowers with eyelets.

Back stitch – a single row of stitches worked to give a continuous or broken line.

Berlin work – a wool and bead embroidery worked on canvas with various stitches, but chiefly cross stitch, in bright, strong colours. Especially popular in the nineteenth century.

Blackwork – a form of embroidery practised especially in the sixteenth century, consisting of black silk stitchery on white linen; used mainly for shirts and lingerie. Sometimes the work was enhanced by the addition of red silk and gold threads. Widely used in Spain.

Braid stitch – a plaited type of edging stitch (see illustrations).

Brick stitch – a flat stitch of different lengths used for filling and shading.

Broderie anglaise – like Ayrshire embroidery, also called Madeira work since it originated on that island. Usually whitework, its design punctuated by cut out shapes and eyelets, the edges buttonholed or overcast. Very fashionable in the late eighteenth and early nineteenth centuries for babies' and children's wear, collars and cuffs.

Buttonhole stitch – a looped stitch used for finishing cut or turned edges. There are several variations, such as the tailor's buttonhole stitch used for buttonholes and the open type, blanket stitch, still used to finish blanket edges (see illustrations).

Canvas work – stitches may be worked on single or double-mesh canvas and the background is completely covered. The mesh varies in size and the threads in thickness to correspond (see *petit point* and *gros point*). Stitches most commonly employed include Gobelin, Tent, Cross, Florentine, Brick, Web, Crosslet and Jacquard.

Chain and cable stitches – descriptive terms for looped stitches (see illustrations).

Cording – used for bold outlining of embroidery designs. A heavy thread or cord is placed along the line to be delineated and this is held in place by oversewing.

Couching and laid work – a filling method for solid embroidery where the threads are laid on the design, then couched (tied down) at intervals by small stitches worked in a finer thread. Gold and silver embroidery was often couched in order to economize on the costly metal thread.

Crewel work – bold, decorative embroidery, also called Jacobean, worked in coloured wools in varied stitches and filled-in designs.

Cross stitch – one of the simplest and most effective stitches widely used in several variations of crossed threads especially in peasant embroideries.

Cut work – embroidery generally on white material with parts of the design cut away and edged with buttonhole stitch. Richelieu work (named after the French cardinal) was a seventeenth-century version where parts of the cut-out design were united by embroidered bars. In Italian cut work the cut-out portions were filled in with needlepoint work.

Drawn thread work – where certain warp or weft threads are drawn out and decorative stitches are used to secure and make a lacy design with the remaining threads.

Eyelet embroidery – floral designs with small circular cut-out or pierced holes finished by satin stitch or buttonholing (see also *Ayrshire work* and *Broderie anglaise*).

Feather, fern and fly stitches – descriptive terms (see illustrations).

Florentine work – a canvas embroidery shaded in different colours by the use of vertical satin and brick stitches into zig-zag or diamond patterns. Also known as Hungarian point or flame stitch (*punto fiamma*), because of its resemblance to the tips of flames.

Gros point – a canvas embroidery worked on a larger mesh, generally in cross stitch.

Hardanger embroidery – a drawn thread embroidery named after the Norwegian fjord of that name. An ancient type of work carried out over the centuries in Persia and Asia in coloured silks on gauze. The Norwegian embroidery was generally of white cotton or linen, its design based on squares and diamonds, with a variety of stitches used to secure the drawn thread work.

Hedebo embroidery – a traditional Danish embroidery often with cut and drawn work. The name derives from the Danish word *hede* (heath), where the peasant embroiderers originally practised their craft.

Hem stitch – widely used in drawn thread work in most forms of peasant embroidery in Europe (see illustrations).

Herringbone stitch – a type of crossed thread stitch with a number of variations.

Knots – used as punctuation and emphasis in embroidery. Several types, notably French, bullion and Chinese knots.

Mountmellick embroidery – an Irish white embroidery of floral designs in cotton thread on a cotton ground.

Needle weaving – decorative embroidery in drawn thread work where coloured silks are woven in and out of the remaining threads by a darning stitch.

Opus anglicanum – work from the great period of English embroidery between the mid-thirteenth century and the end of the fourteenth.

Patchwork – pieces of varied materials in all colours, shapes and sizes sewn to a bleached calico base with decorative stitching.

Petit point – canvas embroidery worked on a small mesh, often in tent stitch (needlepoint).

Quilting – two pieces of material with a layer of padding between are stitched or quilted together by a running or back stitch making a floral or geometrical design. In Italian or Florentine quilting a cord is threaded through a channel made in the design by two parallel rows of running stitches, giving a raised effect to the design.

Rumanian stitch – a filling stitch, like Cretan stitch (see illustrations).

Running stitch – the simplest of stitches,

worked horizontally. The double running stitch, or Holbein stitch, produces a continuous line (see illustrations).

Satin stitch – a simple flat stitch for filling in. There are a number of variations in direction and length such as fishbone, long and short, brick and darning stitches.

Shadow embroidery – a design worked on the underside of a transparent fabric to give a shadow effect on the right side.

Smocking – a decorative stitching which holds together a material gathered into tiny pleats so providing shaping to a garment. Used chiefly on blouses and shirts. Traditional to most peasant embroideries.

Stem stitch – an angled outline stitch.

Straight stitch – a filling stitch embroidered horizontally or vertically over counted threads.

Stump work – a form of raised or padded embroidery generally in white satin. Fashionable in the seventeenth century.

Tambour work – embroidery worked while held in a small circular frame. From the French *tambour*, drum.

Tent stitch – a canvas stitch used in *petit point*. Like a sloping satin stitch or half a cross stitch.

Emerald

A precious stone of a variety of beryl (see *Beryl*) in a brilliant green colour due to oxide of chromium. In ancient times emeralds were mined in Egypt; later, the Spaniards obtained large amounts of emeralds in their conquest of Peru. In more modern times emeralds have been found in Norway, Australia, the Ural mountains, the USA and the Salzburg Alps, but chiefly in Colombia in South America.

Empire dress

An expression usually referring, in Europe, to dress worn during the French First Empire of Napoleon Bonaparte from 1804–15.

Fashions were noted for simplicity, the natural line and elegance based on classical sources. Dress for men was modelled on English tailoring, which was then supreme in Europe, and upon English elegants such

as Beau Brummell and Lord Byron. Men wore the tail coat cut away square in front at the waist, showing an inch of waistcoat below. It had a high collar and revers, sleeves full at the shoulder and tight at the wrist and was elegantly waisted. Knee breeches and stockings were still in fashion, particularly for formal occasions, but more and more they were being replaced by the wearing of pantaloons or trousers which were strapped under the instep to hold down the fitting portion over the lower leg. The outfit was completed by a shirt with upturned collar, cravat, gloves, cane and hat. The top hat was gradually ousting all other styles from favour.

For ladies, the Empire line meant décolleté gowns with the 'waistline' immediately under the breasts, where they were usually belted or girdled. The skirts then fell full and long to the ground where there was also often a train. Because fabrics were so light and thin, a variety of tunic overdresses, capes, stoles, scarves and short spencer jackets were worn on top and, generally, the dress was white or very light in colour and the garment over it of a richer tone and heavier material. There was an accent on the natural figure, with a

FRENCH FIRST EMPIRE DRESS
Straw-coloured tunic, white lingerie gown. Pale blue spotted stole, white gloves, 1812

Brown coat, sage-green trousers strapped under instep. Black top hat and boots. Cane, gloves, 1810

Promenade dress of white India muslin with cotton embroidery. Brown overdress. Silk hat, fur muff, 1804

Bright green satin redingote with spot pattern in darker green. Tulle betsie. Silk hat and gloves, 1815

minimum of underwear and petticoats, and the emphasis was on a graceful femininity. It was a style eminently suited to the young and the slim and those who possessed a graceful carriage and ease of movement.

Napoleon, like Louis XIV, actively interested himself in French industry, including textiles. He re-introduced a court apparel of a richness of quality, style and decoration not seen since before the Revolution. Such garments were made of velvets, silks, brocades and gold and silver cloth. Ladies were adorned with diamond necklaces and lace and wore trains and nodding plumes. This richness of dress had an influence, to no small degree, on fashionable clothes for more mundane occasions.

Ensemble
From the French, meaning together or at the same time. In dress it is applied to two or more garments designed together to make a complete outfit; in particular, it has referred from the 1920s on to the three-piece of jacket, skirt and matching top coat. It can also be applied, in modern dress, to a variety of garments which can be alternated to make a complete outfit — top, jacket and skirt, trouser suit with top, etc.

Eolienne
From the Greek word αἰόλος, meaning with a sheen. A lightweight fabric of silk with either wool or cotton.

Epaulet
The Anglicized version of the French word *épaulette*, meaning a shoulder strap. Used in English to refer to a decorative strap or band at the shoulder, used most often in military dress, but is also applied to ornamental features in civil costume.

Esclavage
French word for slavery. Applied in costume to slave bangles and necklaces. The bangles are solid bands and the necklaces made up of several rows of chains or beads, both resembling the fetters of slaves.

Escoffion
A sixteenth-century net or coif of silk or gold thread for containing a lady's coiffure. From the Italian word *scuffia*, meaning a cap.

Eskimo and Siberian dress
The aborigines of the American continent came from Siberia across the Bering Strait. It is thought that the first of these waves of settlers arrived about 25,000 years ago and, by the time of the voyages there of the first Europeans (the Norsemen) in the tenth century, these Asiatics had percolated to all parts of the Americas from the Arctic coast of Canada to Tierra del Fuego (see also *North American Indian dress*). Those who settled in the Arctic regions became known as Eskimos; this name is said to have come from the Indians living further south and means 'a people who eat their food raw'. The Eskimos settled first in Alaska about 3,000 years ago and spread across the north of Canada to inhabit the coastline and islands there as far as Greenland and Labrador. They adapted themselves to the cold and the dark winters and their clothing as well as their way of life display marked similarities to those of the people living in the Arctic regions of Siberia, from whence the Eskimos originally came.

Most Eskimos have broad faces with slit eyes, a yellowish-copper complexion and straight, coarse, black hair; they are not usually tall. They wear tailored clothing in order to protect them from the wind and intense cold, and this clothing is made almost entirely of hides and skins with the fur turned to the inside or worn on the exterior. (In summer the modern Eskimo may wear garments of wool or cotton.) The skins are sewn together by the women who are expert at doing this in a manner designed to keep out both wind and water from the seams. Thread was of sinew and needles of bone or ivory but nowadays steel needles and thread are sometimes used. Different furs are used according to availability in any given area: most usual are caribou reindeer, polar bear, deer, antelope, sheep, dog and fox. Birds are also used, both for their skin and the feathers for decoration. Because of its quality of waterproofing, sealskin is generally reserved for boots; the fur is usually worn inside (see *Boot*). It is the women who prepare the skins for use as clothing. They skin the animal, using a special knife, and scrape the hides. These are then treated and softened (though not actually tanned) by soaking and manipulation, using urine and ash. Waterproof capes, tunics and coats are made from strips of seal or walrus intestine sewn together.

The garments are very much the same for both sexes. These are a hooded tunic or coat with trousers which are tucked into or worn outside boots. Usually men tuck them in and women wear them outside. The women's hoods are often extra large so that a baby may be carried inside them (see *Babies' and Infants' wear*), and sometimes their boots are wider at the top to carry personal necessities there. In winter two of these tunics may be worn, one with the fur turned inside and the other turned outside. In the Aleutian Islands this hooded tunic is called a *parka*, in Greenland, an *anorak* (see *Anorak*). The outer tunic or coat is called, in some areas, a *kuletak* or *kooletah*; the trousers are *kallik* and the boots, *kamik* or *kommik*.

Eskimo from the Aleutian Islands (Alaska). Hooded coat made of strips of seal intestine sewn together (waterproof). Wooden hat to protect eyes from the sun's glare at sea. Sealskin trousers, fur moccasins

Canadian Eskimo from Baffin Island. Fringed and hooded tunic and short trousers of caribou hide. Boots and mittens of sealskin fur. Fur inside on the boots

Eskimo woman in hooded tunic and trousers of caribou skin. Sealskin boots with fur inside

Eskimo in waterproof coat (as above). Leather boots, pinewood sun goggles

Eskimo in suit of caribou skin in two shades of brown. Sealskin boots (fur inside)

Man from northern region of the Yenisei river, Siberia. Hooded jacket of reindeer skin decorated with white fur and appliqué of red and green felt. Sealskin boots

Samoyed child, Siberia. Hooded coat of reindeer skin trimmed with white fur and coloured felt. Fur boots and mittens

Tunic and short breeches

Gown with over-skirt

Mantle over gown and pleated under-gowns

Long pleated tunic and cloak

Greek style of robe

Etruscan dress

The Etruscans lived in central Italy in the area between the Po and the Tiber from the eighth century BC. By 700 BC the culture had developed extensively and the Etruscans inhabited fine cities with wealthy citizens creating buildings of a high standard and displaying a mastery in the visual arts.

It seems certain that they were not indigenous to Italy; their artistic work and dress show a strongly eastern Mediterranean influence. From their burial places we have a clear idea of Etruscan costume which, though retaining similarities to the Greek styles, shares many features with the Minoan costume of Crete. We cannot be definite about the origins of their design of dress but the influences which bore upon it were clearly varied. Their garments are frequently shown to be sewn and fitted like Cretan ones; and there are further affinities, like the bright, exotic colouring, rich decoration and abundance of jewellery. At the same time many figures are illustrated in the tomb wall paintings in draped costume, pinned at the shoulders and falling, Grecian manner, in folds of drapery. There is also a type of *toga*, presaging the Roman garment, and decorative collars which ante-date the Byzantine ones. Etruscan style in dress displays a marriage between eastern and western themes, blending eastern features from Egypt, Syria and Crete with a later, Ionian flavour gained, possibly, from the contemporary Greek colonists in Italy.

Men wore a tunic which corresponded to the Greek *chiton* (see *Greece, ancient*). Often it was sewn and fitted, knee or calf-length. Alternatively, it appeared as a double-girded classical garment, knee or ankle-length, often pleated in the Greek manner. Several types of cloak or coat were worn, the former semi-circular or rectangular in shape. Some resembled the Greek *chlamys* (see *Greece, ancient*) others were more like the Persian *candys* (see *Caftan*), with sleeves falling wide from the shoulder. There was also a large, rectangular cloak based on the Greek *himation* (see *Greece, ancient*). The larger cloak could,

ETRUSCAN DRESS

Tutulus

Coiffure

Classical-style
dress with cloak
and tutulus

Long tunic cloak
and shoes

Bordered cloak of
style of tebenna

Male tebenna with
fringed edging

alternatively, be semi-circular and was then draped more as a Roman *toga* (see *Rome, ancient*), though the Etruscan garment pre-dated the toga and was called a *tebenna*.

Women's gowns were long and generally sewn and fitted to the figure. They were made of brightly coloured fabrics, decorated by patterned borders at neck, sleeves and hem, Oriental in theme. Sleeves were usually elbow-length, fitted or flaring at the bottom. The dress hugged the breasts, waist and hips but was then flounced or pleated in the skirt. In later years a draped Grecian-style *chiton* was, alternatively, worn. Cloaks were like those of the men and had richly ornamented borders.

Both sexes wore shoes or boots in brightly coloured cloth or leather. These had Greek *petasos*-style hat (see *Greece, ancient*) again for both sexes, were complex and great care and attention was given to the coiffure. Hair was worn long, curled and in ringlets held in place by pins and a fillet round the brow: people were generally bareheaded. In bad weather men wore a

Greek *petasos*-style hat (see *Greece, ancient*) and women draped the folds of their cloak over the head. Both sexes also wore the conical hat with roll brim; this was an Oriental style known as a *tutulus*. The quality of Etruscan *jewellery* was very high, being technically very fine and of great variety in design. It was worn in abundance (see *Jewellery*).

Etui
A French word for a small case or box, which was used from the seventeenth century on to contain small toilet and sewing articles. Women wore it attached to the lower edge of the bodice or hung from the belt.

Evening dress (men)
The establishment of a specific costume for evening wear for men originated in the nineteenth century. Before this, evening clothes were of the same design as day wear, simply made of richer, more colourful materials and decorated more extensively with gold braid, passementerie and lace.

The traditional white tie and tails type of formal evening dress, which has survived until our own day, originated in the elegant, plainer fashions adopted by the English dandies of the early years of the nineteenth century. Beau Brummell, for instance, wore an evening outfit with white waistcoat and blue tail coat with stockinet pantaloons to match strapped over black slippers. By 1820 evening tail coats and trousers were black, the latter very fitting, ankle-length and buttoned part-way up the side of the leg.

In the early Victorian years, with the fashion trend towards darker, more sombre colours, the accepted evening dress for men became stabilized as a black and white outfit and remained so until after the First World War. The actual garments have varied marginally over a century, the only changes being minor ones in size and shape of lapel, the cut of sleeve and coat and the width of trousers; all these factors have simply reflected the alterations in style in the day dress of the period, as can be seen in the illustrations. Equally, the design of neckwear was comparable to that of day attire. At first the white shirt and collar were accompanied by a white stock, later a white tie. Until after the First World War white gloves were always worn with evening dress and an opera hat was worn or carried (see *Hat*). Out of doors, a black overcoat could be worn; alternatively, a black opera cloak, usually with coloured lining.

By the 1860s evening dress had become a uniform with no irregularity being acceptable. The coat and trousers were of black worsted, the former with black silk revers, the latter with braid outside seams. A black piqué or satin waistcoat, in this period, temporarily replaced the earlier white one. The shirt front was stiffened and had pleated or frilled edges; a flat white tie was worn. Apart from the return of the white waistcoat and the adoption of a wing collar and wider bow tie, this outfit has remained the evening dress for formal occasions until the present day, though its use has been more restricted since the Second World War. It is colloquially referred to as *'white tie'* or *'tails'*.

The *dinner jacket* was introduced in the 1880s for informal wear, though there is some dispute as to whether this was in Monte Carlo, London or New York. It was first called a 'dress lounge' in England and until after the First World War, was never worn at any function where ladies were present. The early dinner jacket had a continuous roll collar, faced with black silk or satin, and it was worn open over a black waistcoat and with a black tie. Later it was fastened with one button and, in the 1920s, the double-breasted dinner jacket was introduced, which made a waistcoat super-fluous. In America it is known as a *tuxedo*, because it was first introduced in the millionaire region of Tuxedo Park, New York, for small dinner parties. It could be made in black or midnight blue material. The dinner jacket has always been more popular in the USA than in Europe due to its greater informality and comfort. The complete outfit is often referred to in America as *'black tie'*, in distinction from the formal *'white tie'*.

After the First World War, the formal 'white tie and tails' was worn less often than before, but a dinner jacket was normal wear for all evening functions until after the Second World War. Since 1950, the wearing of evening dress has declined still further and in recent years colour and rich-ness of fabric have returned as part of the general livening-up process in men's clothes, especially among younger men. For dress evening wear, a velvet jacket is now acceptable in black or a dark colour with matching tie and cummerbund. These might be of velvet, silk or satin and the tie is generally of a large bow pattern. The shirt is often coloured and decorated by embroidery and/or pleated or frilled front edging; black evening dress trousers are generally worn.

Eyeglasses and spectacles
In Europe, the wearing of spectacles or holding of a lens or lenses to the eye to assist in reading dates from the late thirteenth century. In England, Roger Bacon suggested that it might be possible

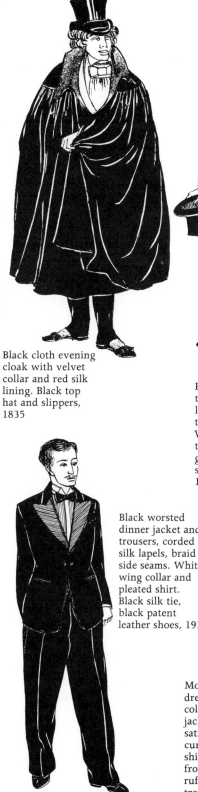

Black tail coat with silk revers. Black trousers with braid side seams. Black satin waistcoat. White shirt, collar, tie and gloves. Black slippers and hat, 1865

Black overcoat over tail coat. Black silk hat, white gloves, 1890

Black tail coat and trousers. White waistcoat, shirt cravat, collar and gloves, 1850

Black cloth evening cloak with velvet collar and red silk lining. Black top hat and slippers, 1835

Black tail coat and trousers. Black silk lapels and braid trouser side seams. White shirt, collar, tie waistcoat and gloves. Black slippers and hat, 1910

Black worsted dinner jacket and trousers, corded silk lapels, braid side seams. White wing collar and pleated shirt. Black silk tie, black patent leather shoes, 1939

Formal evening dress 1941. Black tail coat with trousers. Semi-stiff white shirt. Pearl and gold studs. White stiff wing collar, white piqué tie and waistcoat. Black patent leather shoes

Modern evening dress. Plum-coloured velvet jacket. Cherry red satin tie and cummerbund. Pink shirt with frilled front and wrist ruffles. Black trousers and shoes

Black worsted tail coat and trousers, braid side seams. White collar. Black patent leather shoes, 1937

EYEGLASSES AND
SPECTACLES
Metal frames,
Italian. Early
fifteenth century

Double reading
glass. Fifteenth
century

Reading glass,
c.1360

Chinese method of
keeping glasses in
place with
weighted cords,
sixteenth century

Cords tied round
ears. Italian, 1575

Perspective glass,
c.1630

to improve sight by such means, but the credit for the making of such equipment belongs to Italy. This achievement has been ascribed to several different Italians, among others Alessandro Spina and Degli Armati, but it is more likely that the inventor was none of those put forward but a glass-worker who was bound to secrecy for commercial reasons. Definitive evidence shows that Fra Giordano di Rivalto stated in a sermon in 1306 that spectacles had then been made for nearly 20 years and that he knew personally the man who first achieved this. The earliest report of spectacle-making comes from the Venetian guild of workers in rock crystal and glass in 1310, while the earliest portrait depicting a person wearing such eyeglasses dates from about 1352.

It is accepted that spectacles were first made in Italy about 1286–87 and that other countries in Europe followed suit in the fourteenth and fifteenth centuries. The suggestion that spectacle-making in China ante-dated that in Europe appears to be without foundation and was based upon misconceptions and inaccuracies derived from the accounts of later historians and the misinterpretations of contemporary writers. Earliest evidence in books of the wearing of spectacles in China dates from 1430 and this indicates that it was then a rarity. The statement that Marco Polo saw such spectacles being worn while he was travelling in China is without corroboration as he does not mention this in his own accounts. Clearly spectacles were introduced into China from Europe, though tinted glass and the magnifying glass were known earlier in China. The Chinese preferred, in general, to use rock crystal for spectacle lenses instead of glass.

The lenses in these early eyeglasses were convex, not so much to aid hypermetropia (long-sightedness) but to assist the middle-aged and elderly, who suffered from presbyopia, to read; no provision was made for myopia (short-sightedness) until the mid-sixteenth century. At first the single magnifying glass was most common or, soon, two magnifying glasses with the handles riveted together. Since their purpose was to make

reading easier and they were not for wearing continuously, it was not too inconvenient that the glasses had to be held in the hand. From the fifteenth century many attempts were made to solve the difficult problem of spectacles – how to keep them in place on the nose. Surprisingly, this was not satisfactorily accomplished until the eighteenth century. Medieval frames were of metal – iron, brass, gold or silver – horn, bone or leather. The frame could be split to allow the lens to be inserted. Early lenses were of beryl or quartz, later of Venetian glass.

During the sixteenth century, concave lenses were introduced for myopia. Because of the invention of printing, cheap spectacles began to be made and sold. Previously they had been costly and the prerogative of the well-to-do and these quality eyeglasses also continued to be manufactured. There was as yet no support from the medical profession for the wearing of glasses and therefore no eye-testing. The customer simply chose from the shop a pair which he felt enabled him to see better. No satisfactory way had been discovered to keep spectacles on, so the single reading lens – a spectacle – was still popular; if one has to hold the glass by hand, one glass is easier than two. Various methods were evolved for spectacle wearing. The chief of these were leather straps fastened round the back of the head or cords tied round the ears. A Chinese method was to weight the cords so that they lay upon the chest. Many people simply allowed the spectacles to slide down the nose until they came to rest at the most bulbous part. Seventeenth-century alternatives were chiefly based upon the single eyeglass rather than spectacles. They included the *perspective glass*, worn round the neck on a cord, and the *prospect glass* (*lorgnette* in France), which was a miniature telescope. Tinted lenses were available and tortoiseshell frames were fashionable as well as gold and silver ones.

At last, in the eighteenth century, came the *temple spectacles* which were held reasonably firmly in place on the nose by side arms terminating in rings which pressed against the sides of the head. These rings were generally hidden by the wig or hair. The first practical pair of temple spectacles was brought out by Edward Scarlett, a London optician, in the 1720s, and the idea quickly spread to other countries. During the eighteenth century, despite this advance in practical spectacle-making, it remained unfashionable to wear spectacles. The poor and the unfashionable continued to use them and, indeed, the elegant would wear them in private, but it was not the done thing to be seen in them in public, especially for ladies. People continued to use various designs of magnifying glass or spyglass. A double eyeglass was fashionable, called *scissors glasses*. When the single handle of this was held in the hand it resembled a pair of scissors. The *quizzing glass*, hung round the neck by a cord, was like the earlier perspective glass, though often in the form of a mirror. *Prospect glasses* were still very fashionable. Great ingenuity went into the making of these tiny telescopes and they were incorporated into all kinds of articles – the top of a walking stick, a snuff box, a watch, a fan – a little mirror being set at an angle so that the user could spy without being spied upon. In France such a spyglass was aptly termed a *'lorgnette de jalousie'*.

It was in the nineteenth century that the much-needed *bifocal lens* was first made in practical form, the term bifocal (and trifocal) being first coined by the Englishman John Hawkins in 1827. Prior to this, elderly people who needed reading and distance lenses had to have two pairs of spectacles, and many attempts had been made from the mid-eighteenth century onwards to provide a satisfactory means of combining the lenses in one pair of spectacles. There were examples of spectacles with four lenses, two of which were hinged so that they could be swung away from the eye when not needed. Another design had two of the four lenses suspended from above the eyes by a rod across the forehead. In yet another type two of the lenses were pushed up to rest on the forehead when not in use. Despite further variations no design was produced which made it

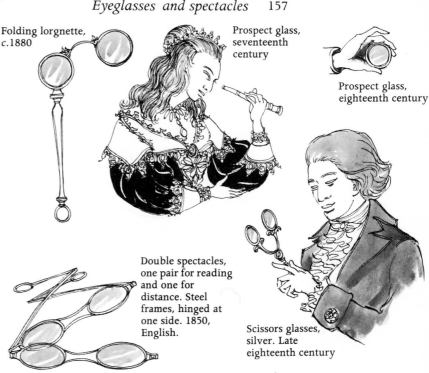

Folding lorgnette, *c.*1880

Prospect glass, seventeenth century

Prospect glass, eighteenth century

Double spectacles, one pair for reading and one for distance. Steel frames, hinged at one side. 1850, English.

Scissors glasses, silver. Late eighteenth century

comfortable and convenient to switch from distance to reading. In 1784 Benjamin Franklin experimented with an early bifocal idea. He ordered each lens to be cut and put half of each in his spectacle frame, looking through the top half for distance and the lower for reading, but this idea was not followed up until John Hawkins patented his trifocal of three lenses, divided horizontally, in one circular frame. Experimentation continued throughout the nineteenth century to develop a satisfactory method of attaching one lens to the other which was robust yet easy to use. By the 1880s, two methods were employed, one which cemented the join and one which keyed one piece of glass into the other.

During the nineteenth century it was still not fashionable to wear spectacles, though most people did so, as necessary, in private. The ornate and ingenious spyglasses and quizzing glasses were abandoned to give place to more practical eyeglasses. Scissors glasses were in use for a few years and were then replaced by *lorgnettes* or *lorgnons*. These were a pair of spectacles attached to a handle at the side; the former had a long handle, the

Temple spectacles, steel frames, *c.*1790

Englishman with monocle, 1863

Double glasses, hinged design, *c.*1800

Temple spectacles with trifocal lenses, *c.*1840

Spring pince-nez,
gold frames, 1895

Rimless pince-nez,
1925

Gold frames, 1930

Plastic frame and
lens sunglasses,
1966

Plastic frame half-
moon reading
glasses, 1972

latter a short one. They could be folded to the size of a single glass. The *monocle* was very fashionable in the nineteenth century. Unlike the quizzing glass, this was retained in the eye socket, not held in the hand. Often the wearer would have two monocles, one for reading and one for distance. In general, the monocle was fashionable for men and the lorgnette for women. A modish replacement for spectacles was brought in from the 1840s; this was the *pince-nez*. It became the most common design of the later nineteenth century.

The twentieth century has brought tremendous variety in spectacle frames and general design, but it is only since the Second World War that it has been considered acceptable, especially for girls, to wear glasses. Indeed, in reversal of past traditions, in the 1960s it became the fashion to wear them as part of a costume when they were not optically necessary. Until 1939, though, the adage 'men don't

make passes at girls who wear glasses' held firm. It is only since the use of plastic for frames, and the infinite variety and attractiveness of the designs made possible by this material, that the attitude to the wearing of spectacles has changed. Contact lenses were first suggested in the mid-nineteenth century and were made in Germany before the end of the century but, again, it is only since the Second World War that such lenses have been perfected for easy and convenient use.

Eyelet, oilet
Other spellings, oylette, olyet, eylet, all derived from the Middle English oilet and the French *œillet*, diminutive of *œil*, eye.

A lacing-hole in cloth or leather for the passage of a lace, cord, ribbon or tape, originally bound with thread (buttonholed), later finished by a metal ring, especially in footwear and corsetry.

F

Facing(s)
In the Middle Ages usually referred to an edging of fur or rich material sewn to the hem, neck or sleeve of a garment. Later applied to a piece of material sewn to face a part of a garment. This could be in a decorative fabric, as in a cuff on the outside of the sleeve, or of a plainer material when used on the edging on the inside, as at a hem, collar or cuff, to provide a neater, firmer finish.

Faille
A light, soft, ribbed fabric woven in silk or rayon.

Fair Isle knitted patterns
A traditional type of knitted design from the highlands and islands of Scotland, Orkney and Shetland, but named after Fair Isle, the most southerly of the Shetland Isles. It became fashionable in the whole of Britain in the years between the two world wars, when women hand-knitted pullovers, jumpers and cardigans for themselves, their husbands and children, following a printed pattern and instructions. The work is carried out in stocking stitch in bands of coloured geometrical designs of considerable complexity, set in a natural coloured background. (See *Knitting*.)

Faja

Spanish word for sash. Applied specifically to the wide sash worn in country areas where this was traditionally an important part of peasant dress to avoid taking a chill in the lumbar spine after becoming overheated while working in the fields. The *faja* has also been a traditional item of decorative dress, at the fiesta for instance, and as part of a bull-fighter's costume. (See *Spanish dress*.)

Falderal, falderol

A trifling ornament, a trinket, a gewgaw.

Faldetta

A voluminous, hooded cape, usually made of black material, worn by women in Malta. Of Moorish origin, the *faldetta* is a close relative of the Arab *haik* (see *Cloak*).

Fall

A pendant form of decoration in dress such as a cascade of lace or silk ruffles or a bunch of ribbons.

Fan

The fan has been used in costume as a decorative article for creating a current of air to cool the head since very early times; the majority of advanced cultures have employed either the small hand fan or a larger one mounted on a long handle, operated by a servant, and made of feathers, leaves or grasses. Among the ancient civilizations of *Egypt, Assyria, Persia* and *India*, the *long-handled fan* was a symbol of rank and power. This was especially so in Egypt, where the office of royal fan-bearer was an important one, and many illustrations of these colourful, semi-circular feather fans, mounted on decorative wood and metal handles, can be seen in wall paintings and reliefs. Smaller feather hand fans were also much in use. *Feather fans* were widely employed in ancient *Greece* and *Rome*, also by the *Etruscans*. The long-handled type, held by a servant, was to be seen in ceremonial use and in large households, but the hand fan was in common use. There were many designs, from the peacock feather fan on a metal

mount to smaller heart or palm-shaped ones made in a variety of materials such as silk, cane, wood or straw. These were flat and rigid, like a small board, and were ornamented with painted, embroidered, jewelled and enamelled designs.

The earliest use of the fan known to us was in *China*, where it is thought to date from 3000 BC. Such fans were of pheasant or peacock feathers mounted on a handle. Soon the hand fan of a flat, screen type evolved, made of palm, bamboo or silk stretched over a wood board or frame and decorated. This type of fan was introduced into Japan in the sixth century AD and has continued in use through the years in both countries.

The *folding fan* was invented in Japan in, it is thought, about AD 670. It soon became an indispensable item of dress and ritual and has continued to be so until modern times. The folding fan consists of a mount and sticks. The mount (or leaf) is most commonly made of paper, silk, lace, parchment and a thin kidskin called chicken-skin. It is generally painted or embroidered and is pleated and then

FALL
(*left*) Ribbon falls on doublet and breeches, German, *c*.1665

(*right*) Ribbon falls at sleeve and knee. Lace fall of cravat at throat, Austrian, *c*.1670

Folding fan, English, 1875

Ancient Greek peacock feather fan

Ancient Egyptian feather hand fan

Ancient Egyptian long-handled feather fan

Ancient Greek painted hand fan

Ancient Greek long-handled feather fan, brass handle

Chinese painted silk board hand fan

Lacquered ivory *brisé* fan, nineteenth century, Japanese

Carved ivory *brisé* fan, eighteenth century, Chinese

Black lace folding fan with tortoise-shell sticks, English, 1865

Queen Anne with feather fan, 1610

Folding fan with painted vellum mount and ivory sticks, English, 1755

Queen Elizabeth with feather fan, 1580

Pink ostrich feather fan, English, 1922

Folding fan with painted skin mount, Italian, nineteenth century

Spanish circular fan, *c*.1850

stretched over the sticks. These are a number of blades, also made from a variety of materials – carved wood, ivory, mother-of-pearl – fastened at the handle end by a rivet. At each side of the fan is a guard stick, which is slightly heavier and larger than the rest and also fastened to the rivet. In Japan there were many varieties of folding fan, each with a different name and used for specific occasions. There were dancing fans, battle fans, court fans, and tea fans which were used at tea ceremonies. Many of the finest Japanese fans were decorated with painted scenes done by the greatest of Japanese artists.

The folding fan was introduced to China in the tenth century AD and has continued in use since then. But China also developed the chief alternative hand-fan design (apart from the rigid board type already described), which was the *brisé* fan. Although superficially similar in appearance to the folding fan, the *brisé* fan has no mount. The blades are generally beautifully and intricately carved and decorated; they are fastened at the handle end by a rivet but, nearer to the outer edge of the fan, are connected together by ribbon threaded through each blade, so making a broken (*brisé*) type of structure. China developed especially the ivory fan of this type, producing the most superb examples from the seventeenth century at the Imperial ivory manufactory in Peking Palace.

In *Europe*, the feather hand fan was in use from the Middle Ages and was especially fashionable in women's dress of the sixteenth and early seventeenth centuries. Designs were varied, colours bright and mounts of wood or metal, beautifully carved and set with jewels. This type of fan, on a large scale, was revived as a fashion for evening wear in the 1920s. Also in use in Italy in the sixteenth century was the rigid, board hand fan. A particular Venetian version of this was flag-shaped, carried on a carved stick. The folding fan came to Europe in the sixteenth century, brought from the Far East and India by the developing trade with Portugal and Spain. From here it was introduced to Italy, then France and England. It became an important costume accessory from the seventeenth century until the First World War. It was in the *eighteenth century* that the greatest elaboration of the fan took place; materials were costly, workmanship superb, the greatest artists of the day were commissioned to paint scenes upon the silk or skin mounts. Sticks were beautifully carved and decorated with mother-of-pearl or encrusted with enamel and jewels. In the later eighteenth century the carved ivory *brisé* fan became fashionable and in the nineteenth century the exquisite black lace fans from Spain. In general, in the nineteenth century, there was great variety in fans – in materials, design and quality. Circular folding fans on a stick were popular, as well as the more traditional semi-circular ones. Some of the circular ones were rigid like the board fan and did not fold up.

Farthingale

The first of the hooped framework skirts which recurred from time to time in women's fashions. The farthingale originated in Spain in the 1470s and this form was usually referred to in England as the *Spanish farthingale* to distinguish it from the later, wheel designs. Farthingale is the English word for the *vertugado* which was first worn in Castile about 1470. This was a bell-shaped underskirt of heavy, rich material into which circular hoops of pliant wood, known as *verdugos* (see *Aro*), were inset at regular intervals. These *verdugos* steadily increased in circumference between waist and hem in order to maintain the shape of the skirt. The dress skirt on top hung over the framework in a creaseless, flat manner but was sometimes open in front in an inverted V shape to display the underskirt.

Many stories have been related to explain why the hooped skirt was first introduced and nearly all attribute it to different female members of the royal houses of Europe who wished to conceal an unwanted, embarrassing pregnancy. Possibly all such stories are apocryphal, though understandable. The farthingale was suited to such concealment but it is

Palm leaf fan with bound wire edge and wood handle, Chinese

Chinese painted silk fan with embroidered decoration

Nigerian leaf and wood fan. Handle bound and stitched

doubtful if the accompanying boned bodice and unyielding corset were of equal benefit to the mother-to-be.

The Spanish farthingale was introduced to France and the fashion was popularized by Eleanor of Castile, the second queen of Francis I, about 1530. In France, the skirt was called the *vertugade* or *vertugale* and, later, *la mode vertugadin*. By this time the mode of wearing the hooped skirt had changed. Whereas in fifteenth-century Spain the hoops had been plainly visible sewn into the underskirt, the French *vertugale* was a canvas skirt inset at intervals with wicker hoops covered by taffeta. It was tied on at the waist with tapes, then underskirt and gown skirt were worn on top so that the structure of the garment was completely hidden and only its form was evident. In France, the sides were straighter than the bell shape of Spain, while in England, the same type of *vertugale* – the farthingale – had totally straight sides making a cone shape. In all cases the rigid form enabled the skirt to fall without creases, apart from at the back where folds were concentrated to descend to the ground in a train. This creaselessness encouraged the development of the large motif floral patterns of the day as they could be displayed to advantage in raised velvet or rich brocade. In England and France the gown was usually open in front in an inverted V shape to display an equally decorated contrasting underskirt. A heavily jewelled metal girdle encircled the tiny waist and fell in front to a pendant jewel or pomander (see *Pomander*). In Spain the girdle usually encircled the waist only and had no pendant end; also, the skirt was more generally closed in front, the edges held together by jewelled clasps set at intervals.

As the sixteenth century progressed the farthingale became wider at the hem and a greater number of petticoats was worn on top to give increased fullness to the gown skirt. By the 1570s the fashion evolved for a padded roll to be tied round the waist under the dress so that a much fuller silhouette was obtained (see *Bum-barrel*). The gown skirt therefore had much more material in it and fell in folds all round the figure. Other countries, notably England, Germany and Flanders, followed suit, though Italy and Spain tended to retain a more slender, straighter silhouette.

Soon even the bolster roll proved inadequate to support the desired wide skirt, so the *wheel* or *drum farthingale* was evolved in France and in consequence the style is generally referred to as the French farthingale. Like its Spanish predecessor, it was a canvas or linen petticoat with circular hoops of cane or whalebone set at regular intervals from waist to ground. In the wheel type the hoops were of equal diameter and the flat top of the cartwheel was also of canvas, pleated or gathered, and with a hole for the waist where it could be drawn tightly and affixed with tapes. Gowns worn on top of the wheel farthingale had an excessively slender, corseted waist, the bodice of which was formed with a long, boned busk in front which descended to the drum ruffle which usually covered the canvas top of the farthingale. This ruffle was less commonly worn in France than in England, where the very full skirt fell directly over the drum shape, the material gathered in at the narrow waist. Skirts with this farthingale were often only ankle length. The fashion for the wheel farthingale lasted into the 1620s when it gradually disappeared.

In Spain, however, where the farthingale had originated, the fashion survived longest. The Spanish had retained their own style throughout, which became wider as time passed. By 1645 the last phase evolved. It was then an immense size but, instead of the original bell shape, was now flatter at front and back and wide at the sides at hip level; this was ancestor to the mid-eighteenth century panier skirt in Europe (see *Panier*). These immense skirts are pictured in the many Velasquez portraits of the mid-century. Even high-born little children had to be encased in these monstrous frames with corseted bodice and padded sleeves.

Spanish farthingale petticoat

Spanish vertugado skirt, 1477

Queen Isabella. Black velvet gown lined with white satin. Gold and pearl clasps. Spanish farthingale. Spain, 1565–70

English princess, 1546. Brocade gown over cut velvet underskirt and Spanish farthingale

French or wheel farthingale petticoat
White satin gown embroidered in colours worn over wheel farthingale, English, 1600

Silk gown over wheel farthingale without circular drum ruffle. Jewelled embroidered borders, English, 1610

Queen Elizabeth, 1585–90. Black velvet gown decorated with pearls and ribbon bows. White satin undergown with decoration by gold thread, pearls and jewels. Worn over Spanish farthingale and waist bolster

Evening gown in
silk and lace.
Doucet, 1908

Trouser suit in
turquoise and
cyclamen with
black fur trimming.
Poiret, 1911

Fashion designers: haute couture

The story of couture, led by France, began in the time of Louis XIV. This, the *Grand Règne*, lasted from 1643–1715 and in these years *Louis le Grand* established France as the great power of Europe and, as a natural corollary, all Europe modelled its dress upon French fashions. France was confirmed as the arbiter in dress, a process which had begun tentatively about 1635. At this time most of women's as well as men's clothes were made by men, the tailors and male dressmakers. In 1675 women dressmakers petitioned the king to be allowed to make feminine underwear, skirts and petticoats, peignoirs and accessories, on the grounds that this would accord with feminine modesty and propriety. Louis XIV granted the petition and the dressmakers founded their own corporation and guilds.

Although France had led the fashionable world for several decades, the names of the leading designers had not been especially noted. The first designer with marked influence was *Rose Bertin*. In the 1770s design consisted largely of decorating the complex, silk gowns with flowers, ribbons, lace and ruching. Mlle Bertin (born Marie-Jeanne) came from Abbeville and was a milliner. In this age of immense overdecorated wigs and coiffure styles topped by hats or caps, the milliner was vitally important to the world of fashion as the head was the focal centre of the toilette. Rose Bertin was very successful and came to Paris where, with the assistance of her patronne, the Duchess of Chartres, she set up her salon in the fashionable Rue Faubourg Saint Honoré in 1773. In a short space of time Mlle Bertin's eye for design, colour and proportion had made her indispensable to the Parisian aristocracy and she became milliner and dressmaker to the Dauphine, later Queen, Marie Antoinette. With the Revolution, Rose Bertin went to Germany and later opened an establishment in London where French émigrés flocked to patronize her. She returned to Paris in 1800, but died 12 years later in poverty and obscurity; the fashionable world had discovered new ideas and modes and she was out of date.

Louis Leroy was the next designer of note and one whose adaptability and capacity for survival was high. Born in 1763, Leroy became a coiffeur, a milliner and then a tailor. Before the Revolution he was, like Rose Bertin, a designer for the aristocracy but he curried favour with the new régime and was asked by the Convention to design clothes for its members. With the return of the émigrés he re-adapted to garments displaying more extensive decoration and specialized in draped Greek ensembles; then assiduously sought the patronage of the Empress Josephine by dubious backstairs means. He became Josephine's couturier and the fashionable designer for the *Merveilleuses*. Leroy was at the height of his fame during the First Empire but, with the fall of Napoleon, adapted once more and established himself as the chief couturier for the Bourbon Court as well as the English aristocracy. He organized his establishment in a manner not unlike that of the couturiers of the twentieth century, selling not only garments and ensembles which he had designed but also perfumes, and accessories.

Haute couture had its beginnings in the mid-nineteenth century. Until that time dressmaker or tailor designers had controlled the design and production of ladies' garments, creating one ensemble, bespoke, for one individual client. In haute couture, models are created by the designer, bear his or her name and are protected by copyright from indiscriminate reproduction. The official definition given by the Paris *Chambre Syndicale de la Couture* is: 'Haute couture is any undertaking whose most important activity consists in creating models with the object of selling them to a professional clientèle which thereby acquires the right to reproduce them. An Haute Couture concern of this nature also reserves the right to repeat these models for private customers.' France, and particularly Paris, was the natural source for haute couture. The Parisian had always possessed an intense interest in clothes and personal ornament. This absorption has attracted craftsmen in the world of dress

Pale blue brocade evening gown with plain sash, gloves. Worth, 1904

Promenade costume, Paquin, 1905

Pale green taffeta gown. Skirt in three fabrics: train in green taffeta, overskirt in green velvet patterned in gold, centre panel darker green. Worth, 1885

White satin with silver and crystal embroidered overdress, Lanvin, 1919

Black patterned silk dress. Black feather fan. Worth, 1922

Cream silk chiffon evening dress. Vionnet, 1931

Deep blue sequined evening dress. Chanel, 1932

White evening dress with musical notation design in blue, black and red. Schiaparelli, 1939

Chiffon and fur
tiered dress. Poiret,
1913

Winter coat with
fur trimming.
Patou, 1922

to come to Paris so that the designer has found such expertise to hand when he has needed it. In French, the word *couture* means sewing; a *couturier* is a male tailor or dressmaker; a *couturière* a feminine one. An haute couture establishment, therefore, is a first class designing and dressmaking concern. There is, because of all this, a certain irony in the general acceptance that Worth was the first haute couturier, for Worth was an Englishman.

Charles Frederick Worth was born in 1825 at Bourne in Lincolnshire. His father was a lawyer, impoverished through gambling, so that young Charles went to work with a printing firm at the age of 11 to help to support the family. A year later he travelled to London and sought a position in the drapery trade, where he became apprenticed as a counterhand to Swan and Edgar. Worth worked in London for eight years, rising to become cashier. He learnt about the drapery business, about quality fabrics, of how they were made up into shawls and dresses, also about the commercial and accountancy side of the business. He decided that his future lay in the design and handling of fashion garments and that, since Paris was the centre of the mode in Europe, that was where he must go. So, at the age of 20, with a small sum of money obtained by his mother from her relatives, and speaking no word of French, he set off for France. Worth found a job in Paris in a draper's shop where he cleaned out the premises and worked for 12 hours a day serving customers also. Having gained some experience and learnt some French, he obtained a position at the Maison Gagelin in the Rue de Richelieu, selling fabrics to dressmakers. He worked at Gagelin's for 12 years, learning the trade, making designs and producing ideas for innovations. He was valued by the firm so that, when he suggested that he should set up a small dressmaking section there to make some of the clothes which he designed, they agreed. He married a sales-girl on the staff, Marie Vernet, who modelled his dresses and became his collaborator as well as the first live mannequin. At the Great Exhibition of 1851, Maison

Gagelin won a Gold Medal for France and much of the credit for this was due to Worth, as was also the extensive business carried out as a result. The triumph was repeated at the Paris World Fair of 1855.

Worth became dissatisfied. The firm was making money as a result of his designs but he was not profiting greatly from this; also, his ideas for setting up a department for high quality, made-to-measure gowns were not encouraged. So, in 1858, he left Gagelin and, with the backing of a Swede called Otto Bobergh, set up his own establishment and his home in the Rue de la Paix, then a good quality residential quarter but soon to become, with the building of the Opera House, a centre for fashion and elegance. Many of the Gagelin clients followed Worth to the Rue de la Paix and he quickly built up a good clientèle. The House of Worth was the first fashion house to use live mannequins to display the creations and, with his flair for elegance and originality of design, Worth acquired the monopoly of dressing the wealthy aristocrats of Europe. It was in 1860 that Marie, his wife, approached Princess Pauline de Metternich, newly-arrived in Paris as wife of the Austrian ambassador, with some of her husband's designs. The princess ordered two crinoline gowns and when the Empress Eugénie later saw these at the Tuileries Palace, she was so enchanted with the style and attractiveness of the designs that she became Worth's most famous patron. This set the seal on the House of Worth which came to number nine European queens among its clients.

In his early forties Worth had become the first couturier of France, a position which he held until his death. He was an innovator and, like all great fashion designers, kept just abreast of fashion needs, anticipating intuitively what would be desirable next and producing a change just as demand was about to grow. Though he had long been associated with the design of crinoline gowns, in 1866 he introduced the princess line, and soon he was the leader in the creation of the tunic or apron front, the train and the draped-up skirt, all of which developed into the bustle styles. He was the first designer to run his house as a commercial business, making a great deal of money and enhancing the status of his profession. By the 1860s he was employing over 1,000 workers and a great luxury industry was being created. He had strong links with the French textile industry, especially the silk manufacture of Lyons. Indeed, it was these merchants who protested most strongly about his abandonment of the crinoline, for it was a style they approved of because of the immense quantities of material needed in the making up of the gowns. Worth's showrooms were luxuriously appointed. The 'king of fashion' also lived in luxury and entertained lavishly. His collections were shown in palatial interiors. It was Worth who set a new business pattern for couture by not only producing model designs for private clients but also for sale to dressmakers, manufacturers and stores in Europe and America – this was the establishment of haute couture.

After Worth's death his fashion house continued business in the hands of his two sons Gaston and Jean Philippe and later was controlled by his grandsons; but, despite the knowledge, experience and superb taste of Jean Philippe, in particular, the inventive genius of the concern had died with Charles Frederick. The first fashion tycoon, he had reigned over Parisian couture for nearly 50 years; no other couturier ever gained such complete supremacy.

By 1900 Paris fashion had become big business and a number of fashion houses had been established. *Jacques Doucet* was a well-known couturier in the later nineteenth century, though his business had been founded by his grandparents as early as 1824 as a haberdashery and lace shop in the Rue de la Paix. *Callot Soeurs* was founded by three sisters in 1895 and was especially successful from then until the First World War, known for its elegant creations in lace and tulle, georgette and chiffon. The English *House of Redfern* had been established in Paris in the Rue de Rivoli in 1881; this was followed by

branches in New York and London. *Caroline Reboux* ran the Maison Reboux in the Rue de la Paix, the millinery house where she was patronized by clients of Worth.

Mme Paquin, who opened her house in 1891, was the first woman to become a leading designer; on the business side she was advised by her husband, the banker. She was a supremely elegant woman, highly professional and with superb taste. Her creations were renowned for their beautiful fabrics and their elegance, and the evening gowns for their rich fur, braid and gold trimming. By 1902 Mme Paquin had opened a branch in London and this was followed by ones in Madrid and Buenos Aires. In London, another woman was becoming a leading couturière. *Lucile, Lady Duff Gordon* was Canadian born and of Irish/Scottish stock. She had begun in a very small way in 1890, designing and making clothes herself, but by 1900 had established Maison Lucile in Hanover Square. Lady Duff Gordon was an innovator with a vivid, determined personality. Maison Lucile expanded to become an empire which included branches in New York and Chicago as well as Paris.

The years 1905–18 were dominated by the most colourful personality of the world of couture at that time, *Paul Poiret*. Poiret was more than an innovator; he was a rebel, a man of brilliance, forceful to the point of arrogance. He was born at Billancourt. From an early age he was absorbed in the subject of women's dress. He was employed by Jacques Doucet in 1896 and went on to work for Jean Philippe and Gaston at Worth. In 1904 he opened a small shop on his own account near the Place de l'Opéra, employing eight workers. His designs were revolutionary but, like Worth before him and Dior after, he had sensed that the moment had come for change and he soon became highly successful. The impact of his original ideas was enormous. His creations freed the feminine figure from corsetry and whalebone and abandoned the flounced and frou-frou petticoats so typical of the turn of the century. Poiret's clothes were extravagant and luxurious, simple in line yet feminine and exotic. The Orient with

Grey and white silk suit with black tie, Lelong, 1925

Evening dress and cape in black silk crêpe with gold decoration and pink silk lining, Molyneux, 1926

Winter coat with
fur trimming,
Vionnet, 1929

Jersey suit. Chanel,
1929

its exquisite fabrics and brilliant colours held a fascination for him and many of his designs were based on eastern themes: his sultana trouser creations with Oriental turbans, his harem skirts, his kimonos, his gold fabrics, fur trimmings and Persian embroideries.

But Poiret was not creating the liberated woman or the unfeminine flapper of the 1920s. His women were still shackled but in a different way. While he freed the waist and hips from corsets and the ankles from petticoats, he hobbled the legs with skirts so tight from knee to ankle that ladies could hardly walk. Though a revolutionary in his creations so completely different from what had gone before, Poiret's themes were not divorced from the movements of his day. They had affinity with Art Nouveau design in the arts and, although Poiret denied that his ensembles and colour schemes derived from the Diaghilev Ballet, it was clear that the visit of the Ballet to Paris in 1909 displayed costumes and choreography which bore a close resemblance to Poiret's brilliant shades of cerise, flame, emerald, royal blue and violet, as well as an Oriental and Art Nouveau flavour.

Poiret also had a genius for showmanship. The House of Poiret was luxuriously extravagant in its décor and presentation. He toured the capitals of Europe in two cars to sell his creations, accompanied by his secretary and nine mannequins. But Poiret's world died with the First World War. In the 1920s he was still playing the ageing *enfant terrible*, designing clothes in garish colours, Oriental in theme and richly embroidered and be-furred. The world had changed, simplicity and the liberated woman were 'in' and Poiret was 'out'. He died a penniless eccentric on the French Riviera in 1943.

Immediately after the First World War, designers such as Lanvin and Patou, who had been known as couturiers before 1914, became active once more. *Jeanne Lanvin*, eldest of ten children, came from a modest home and began work as an apprentice at the age of 13. At first she specialized as a modiste but then began to design clothes for children, in the beginning for her own daughter, initiating fashions especially for children, attractive yet suited to their age. This was a new departure in the 1920s and Lanvin designs were popular. She went on to design clothes for young girls and then into general fashion, though the House of Lanvin retained a department for children's wear. Lanvin gowns were elegant, made from beautiful fabrics such as gold and silver materials and brocaded silks. The Paris house was in the Rue Faubourg Saint Honoré but branches were opened in other cities, especially on the French Riviera. *Jean Patou* was also known as a couturier before 1914, but set up on his own account just after the war. His designs were also elegant and he endeavoured to retain femininity in his creations when, in the 1920s, the trend was towards freedom and simplicity. He was particularly noted for his designs of the early twenties, also for an early return to a natural waistline and longer skirts in 1929. Another designer whose hallmark was femininity was *Lucien Lelong*, who set up his house in 1919 and was especially known in the 1920s.

These designers were, by preference, working in the classic field, but by 1920 the pattern of life for many women had altered irrevocably and they continued to seek interesting careers outside the home. As time passed, younger women especially entered professions and fields of work hitherto open only to men. Many such women learned successfully to combine a career and homemaking. In the 1920s this emancipation went to their heads and reaction against Victorianism was acute. Women demanded functional, comfortable clothes, a freedom to do as men did – smoking, free love, equality of opportunity – and, therefore, freedom of attire. Many women mistakenly felt that to work as successfully at a job as a man, they must appear to be masculine or, at least, unfeminine. For ten years women hid the attributes given to them by nature: breasts, sloping shoulders, small waist, ample hips and flowing hair. To assert their new-found freedom they emulated masculinity with flattened breasts, tubular, unwaisted dresses and shingled hair; they exposed their legs instead. A specific carriage was adopted – the pelvis was thrust forward to accentuate the flatness of the bosom and hips, while arms were thrust akimbo low on the hips (a most unladylike gesture by nineteenth-century standards) and eyes peered out mysteriously under a hat pulled down well over the eyebrows.

The boyish look was in. Pyjamas were worn as well as nightdresses, trousers appeared on the beach. The fashionable figure was thin rather than slim. One must have a slender neck, no bosom, no hips and twiggy legs. It was the age of the flapper. If one's figure did not conform, one must diet. Skirts rose nearly to the knee, and the waistline – or rather its suggestion – was low on the hips. Trimming and decoration were at a minimum. This revolution in feminine dress was not at first accepted by Parisian haute couture. The rank and file of ladies had run away from their leaders and were dictating their terms. The couturiers attempted to win them back with eclectic designs, recreating styles from the past. However, they had to accept, as designers have several times had to accept later in the twentieth century, that a fashion which is not in tune with public demand will not 'go', no matter how good the product and the marketing.

All efforts to put back the clock having failed, the couturiers followed the tide and designed for it. They produced clothes for all occasions, informal and holiday as well as evening and dress attire, and the quality of dress improved. The negative ugliness of line of the 1920s dress could not be obscured but it could be given a little elegance and quality. Unless its wearer had chic and was slim and beautiful, the results were likely to be unfortunate at best and hideous at worst, but a good designer with a feeling for colour, cut and fabric can work wonders.

The famous names of the pre-1920 years were joined by new ones and the years 1920–39 became great ones for haute couture. The return to a vestige of femininity was helped immensely by the bias

cutting of Vionnet and the easy-to-wear suits and dresses in jersey materials by Chanel – two of the outstanding women innovators in the couture world of the inter-war years – while the classic cut was preserved by couturiers such as Lanvin, Molyneux and Alix. Madeleine Vionnet and Gabrielle Chanel epitomized the Twenties and Thirties. It was the cross-cutting of Vionnet which, adopted by other couturiers, made possible the draped, clinging gowns of the 1930s.

Madeleine Vionnet came from a modest home in the Jura. She was brought up by her father as her mother had left home when Madeleine was only three, and when the child showed herself unsuccessful in academic studies at school, she was apprenticed to the local dressmaker where she worked for five years. At 16 she went to Paris to work, was married at 18, had a child who died and was divorced at 19. She then went to London to work in a tailoring establishment for five years and returned to Paris at the age of 24. Her design career then began while she spent some further years at the house of Callot Soeurs under Mme Gerber, then at Doucet, where she created some early designs which disconcerted this traditionally classic house by their severity and restraint.

It was in 1914 that Madeleine opened her first establishment in Paris, but after the war, backed by Bader of the Galeries Lafayette, she re-opened with a larger establishment in the Avenue Montaigne. For 20 years, until her retirement in 1939 (though she died only very recently), she was highly successful, having built up a wealthy clientèle who appreciated the ascetic classicism of her designs. Madeleine Vionnet believed that the feminine figure was all important to successful design and couture and that the natural form should not be disguised or distorted. Like Poiret she eschewed corsetry and padding but, unlike him, permitted little trimming. She was an artist in handling materials, in cutting and constructing; her creations were sculptured and individual to each client. She introduced a new technique of bias cutting, cutting on the cross of the

Wool dress with fur. Velvet and fur hat. Schiaparelli, 1933

Light wool jacket and dark pleated skirt. Molyneux, 1938

Black hat, skirt and gloves. Striped bodice of black with sequins and pearls. Fath, 1949

White suit and boots with tartan hat. Courrèges, 1964

fabric so that it would follow the lines of the body. Many of her designs were draped classical gowns which looked best on the statuesque woman. Typical were her day dresses and skirts of heavy crêpe, while for evening she used sheer fabrics which would float and drape; such designs were especially typical of Vionnet in the Thirties.

Coco Chanel was a legend in the world of couture. In the 1920s she introduced casual-looking, comfortable wear which was ultra chic – a characteristic of dress which women take for granted today but which in the early Twenties had never been heard of. Her designs were the antithesis of Poiret's contemporary extravagantly trimmed fabrics in brilliant colours and patterns. Chanel's were deceptively simple jersey suits in quiet tones, only slightly decorated. Poiret's creations were overstatements, Chanel's understatements, but it was Chanel who was in tune with the times and from the early Twenties until the war she was a resounding success. Then she made couture history; after 15 years of retirement, she re-opened in 1954, designing much the same simple little suits and 'little black dresses' in the current line and cut, and she recaptured her popularity, cashing in on a fashion world ready for change once again in reaction from Dior's New Look of 1947.

Gabrielle Chanel was born of a peasant family in the Auvergne in 1886. She suffered a number of personal losses in childhood and adolescence which seemed to make her retreat later in life into a fiercely independent, solitary mode of living. Her mother died when she was six years old and her father soon left her in the care of an aunt while he emigrated to America. Her sister died when Gabrielle was 18 and soon afterwards her fiancé was killed in an accident. At the age of 19 Gabrielle became a night-club dancer in Pau where she met an Englishman who backed her first venture, a hat shop in Paris. In 1914, with the war, she went to Deauville. While working for the Red Cross there, she noticed how unsuitable the fashions were for women undertaking war jobs, work normally done by men.

She tried adapting men's jackets to her own use and set up a small shop, making and selling jackets, skirts and jersey tops, which were very popular.

After the war, Chanel returned to Paris and opened her fashion house, and by 1924 had become a great success. Her easy-to-wear suits became a wardrobe classic, made of soft tweeds or jersey wool and consisting of a plain or pleated straight, short skirt, a jersey top and a jacket which was often collarless. She also designed simple dresses and skirts, all with great care and attention to detail. She made wool a dress fabric; often it was plain but jackets usually had a silk or quilted lining to match the blouse or jumper. The Chanel figure was slim and straight, the *gamine* type, a reaction from the grande-dame of the pre-war era.

Chanel creations were deceptively simple in appearance but great attention was paid to cut and length. Trimming was restrained, limited to carefully chosen fancy buttons and edging. The principal ornamentation was in the chunky costume jewellery which, until then, had been considered to be in poor taste. The double string, long necklace of pearls, jade or amber, the lapel pin, the earrings, the bracelets and pendants were essential parts of a Chanel ensemble, the ostentation only setting off the plain garments. Chanel, now usually known by her nickname 'Coco', popularized short, shingled hair and sun-tanned skin set off by white summer clothes. She launched her famous perfume in the late Twenties. She believed five to be her lucky number (she was born on August 5th) and she kept to her tradition for simplicity. Chanel No 5 became the best-known perfume for non-French speaking foreign visitors to Paris.

In the 1930s Chanel visited Hollywood where she designed creations for film stars in a number of films. She adapted her clothes to the new line, lengthening her skirts and re-introducing the waistline, but her simple style remained. She closed her house in 1939 and lived on the proceeds from her enormous perfume sales until 1954, when she decided to return to couture. Once again, her designs were adapted to a new line but they were still chic and plain; she was most successful. She died, still at work, in 1971 at the age of 85.

One of the interesting facts which emerges from a study of the lives of the couturiers is that, from 1930 onwards, few of them were first trained for dress design but nearly all began one or more different careers first. The most colourful personality in the couture world of the 1930s was the Italian *Elsa Schiaparelli*. Born in 1896 in Rome, she came from an academic, professional family. She married young, a daughter was born, but the marriage did not succeed. Schiaparelli worked in America for a time in the antique business, then came to Paris and tried dress design without much success, until 1928 when she discovered her métier. A number of small factories employing foreign workers were making sweaters and jumpers. Schiaparelli became interested in the peasant motifs and fabrics from the simple communities in Eastern and Alpine Europe. She had had no training in cutting and sewing but began to design garments to be made in the factories. Her designs were unusual and they interested a fashionable world which wanted a change from the plainness of the *gamine* ensemble.

Throughout the 1930s and 1940s Schiaparelli was a great success, exporting much of her work to England and America. She made use of materials unusual in the fashion world – hessian and tweeds, for example; she designed for knitwear and collage-decorated fabrics using bizarre and original motifs such as skeletons and music notation; she travelled extensively searching for new ideas which she brought back to Paris and incorporated in her schemes – these included the North African burnous and djellaba, Tyrolean and Russian garments and Peruvian embroideries. She sought inspiration in negro art forms, Cubism and Surrealism, and she employed artists such as Salvador Dali and Picasso to design textiles for her.

Elsa Schiaparelli was a volatile personality, sometimes crude and vulgar, rarely subtle, but full of vitality. Her work reflected these qualities and her clothes were fashionable with the smart, hard women of the 1930s. She used strident colours – the term 'shocking pink' derived from her use of this bright colour (and the name which she had given to her perfume, 'Shocking') though, of course, the colour itself was not new. Schiaparelli went on from knitwear to skirts and dresses. She promoted the padded shoulder line and slim hips fashionable in the 1930s and designed a number of elegant evening gowns, some eclectic, some very contemporary. She was successful during the war but during the 1950s her fashions were becoming dated and had lost their vitality. The flair which had carried her through two successful decades had waned and she retired in 1954.

There were also, in the inter-war years, a number of talented couturiers who were designing for the woman who wished to be elegant and smart but not to draw attention to herself. There were many such women – wealthy, of royal houses, of the aristocracy, wives of industrialists. One leading designer of this type was *Edward Molyneux*, an Irishman who had been a captain in the First World War. Apart from Worth, before the 1920s couturiers in Paris had been of French origin, but the world of couture between the wars acquired a more international flavour. Molyneux was the first of these foreigners to make a great reputation; Mainbocher and Schiaparelli followed. Captain Molyneux, as he continued to be called, went to work with Lucile, Lady Duff Gordon when he came out of the army, but he was out of sympathy with her creations which to him still seemed to be part of the pre-war world of tea gowns and large over-decorated hats. Molyneux, like Chanel, was of the new, no-nonsense generation of couturiers, with a feeling for simplicity and for designing clothes in which people could work and travel as well as taking part in the social round. He soon set up on his own, backed by Lord Northcliffe who displayed his collections in the *Daily Mail*. Molyneux's creations were in perfect taste, classic, ageless and suited to all ages of women. There were no extremes of length, waistlines, shoulder lines – all was understressed, impeccable yet supremely elegant. Few Molyneux ensembles survive; they were worn not discarded.

In the same tradition was the American designer *Mainbocher*. Like so many later couturiers, he followed other careers before taking up dress design. He was born Main Rousseau Bocher in 1890 in Chicago. He first aspired to be an artist or an opera singer and studied art and music in Europe before becoming a journalist, in which capacity he was appointed fashion editor of *Vogue*. He entered the field of couture in 1931, designing clothes which had an elegant simplicity. In the 1930s his creations had broad shoulder lines and his jackets were half-belted. Very popular was his day dress with high-necked, fitted bodice and short flared skirt. His evening gowns were slim-waisted and svelte with flared skirts and short puff sleeves or strapless bodices. In 1939 Mainbocher closed his Paris house in the Avenue Georges V and re-opened in New York where he continued his work.

Also in the classic trend was *Mme Alix Grès* who was designing in Paris in the 1930s. She was a sculptor before taking up dress design and her creations had a sculptural quality. She always worked directly with the material, not using a pattern, but cutting at once and moulding and draping the fabric to the model. Like Madeleine Vionnet, she used the bias cut a great deal and would not put any padding or reinforcement in her garments, which were designed so that the client should wear neither corset nor bra. In 1942 Alix became Mme Grès; she continued to produce beautiful classically draped gowns, many made in clinging jersey fabrics. Like Molyneux and Mainbocher, her creations were ageless, superseding fashion; they were still being shown in the late 1960s.

Haute couture had become more international in the 1930s but, although a number of famous designers were not French, the centre of the fashion world was still Paris. After the Second World War, among the proliferation of couturiers came more non-French designers as well as centres of fashion emerging in other countries. Italy was one of these, with its fashion centre in Turin, and typified by such designers as *Marchese Emilio Pucci*, a scion of one of Florence's oldest families who showed his collections in his family's beautiful palace. Several countries concentrated their designs on their natural products: Italy with its silks, knitwear and footwear; Spain its richly coloured fabrics, embroideries and leather goods; Switzerland beautiful linens and decorative knitwear. In England, the Incorporated Society of London Fashion Designers was founded in 1942, of whose members *Norman Hartnell* and *Hardy Amies* were the leading couturiers. In Ireland, *Sybil Connolly* designed garments which utilized the traditional Irish tweeds, linens and crochet-work and translated them into couture.

The best-known of the post-war couturiers was *Christian Dior*, who erupted into fame with his first collection in 1947 which presented his New Look. The majority of new trends in fashion appear gradually; the designers work individually in their own houses and do their best to keep their work secret until the collections are shown, but since each is presenting ideas current at the time and endeavouring to please the clients of that year, the same trends appear in a number of collections around the same time. Only occasionally does or can a designer present a startlingly new fashion and, if he does, he often meets opposition from commercial interests and/or the public who do not like his ideas. As, for instance, when Worth gradually abandoned the crinoline skirt – royalty did not like the change, nor did the silk manufacturers. Again, when Poiret abandoned corsets and layers of petticoats, he offended the corsetry firms. Christian Dior's New Look was one of the rare occasions, as were the later Quant mini-skirts and the earlier Chanel jersey suits. In each case, the designer had perceived the right moment to launch that particular fashion and the receptive public received it with acclaim.

Christian Dior was born in Normandy in 1905 and was brought up in a prosperous

Evening dress in light, patterned fabric. Mainbocher, 1939

The New Look. Dior, 1948

White brocade evening gown. Dior, 1950

Full coat. Balenciaga, 1951

White silk evening dress with black polka dot pattern. Black gloves, white silk handbag and shoes. Balmain, 1952

Trapeze line dress in navy organza. Dior (St Laurent), 1958

Revival of 1920s line. Laroche, 1958

Bubble silhouette dress with black bodice and skirt patterned in large roses. Cardin, 1959

Golden brown and
white dress, mini
length. Quant, 1967

White wool trouser
suit with black line
check design.
Courrèges, 1965

middle-class home. Following his parents' wishes he began studying for the diplomatic service, but his interests were in the arts so he became an art dealer in Paris. His parents lost much of the family fortune in the slump of 1929 so Dior sold his business and kept himself by selling fashion drawings to, among other clients, *Le Figaro*. He spent the war years in the army but afterwards, in 1942, returned to Paris to work for the House of Lelong. It was in 1945 that Dior was introduced to Marcel Boussac, the textile tycoon, who saw a bright future for the designer and backed his venture to open his own house. With ample capital behind him, Dior established himself on a large scale, beginning with a staff of 85 over whom he presided, looking – as many great artists have done – more like a diplomat than the popular conception of an artist. But there was no doubt that Christian Dior was an artist and that he had his finger posed gently but with precision upon the public pulse.

Dior was not the only couturier to have sensed that feminity was in the air again in 1947. Women were tired to death of austerity, uniforms, practical clothes and a shortage of beautiful fabrics. A number of designers had tentatively introduced tighter waists, fuller and longer skirts and sloping shoulders – Mainbocher, for instance, in the USA, and Marcel Rochas who introduced the *guêpière*, a new corset, in 1947, to produce a tiny waist – but it was Dior who launched his first collection entirely in the new feminine form. He staked his whole career on making women elegant and beautiful again. In February 1947 he presented this first collection, which he called *Corolle* (corolla, a botanical term meaning the delicate ring of petals opening in the centre of a flower); the American press called it the New Look and it has been ever since.

The new creation, which was further developed in 1948, had long, full skirts using yards of material, a tiny waist and feminine, sloping shoulders. It was applied to dresses, coats, suits and skirts and was accompanied by elegant hats and high-heeled shoes. The new fashion was im-

mediately popular but it took a year or so for everyone to acquire it as it was impossible to make a straight, short dress into a long, full one. By 1950 Europe and America were dressed in the New Look and Dior went on to other things – always feminine but a little more practical, especially for working girls: the H-line, the A-line, the Y-line, the tunic dress in 1956, and, in 1957, the chemise dress. Suddenly, in 1957, Dior died. The House of Dior, then employing 1,600 workers, continued, first under the young Yves St Laurent, then Marc Bohan.

Cristobal Balenciaga was a contemporary of Dior but very different both as a personality and a couturier. He was born in 1895 in a small fishing village on the Bay of Biscay near San Sebastian, and his father was captain of a fishing vessel. He learnt tailoring and sewing in his village and saved up enough money to open a small dressmaking shop in San Sebastian. Much later, at the age of 42, he was able to come to Paris and open a salon on the Avenue Georges V. From then until he retired in the late 1960s, Balenciaga ran a unique house. He shunned publicity and the press; his success was built on private clients who were interested in plain, starkly simple, elegant clothes. He was a perfectionist and, above all, a superb tailor. Balenciaga's designs were not influenced by other couturiers or contemporary fashion; his work was individual, unique, with classic quality. He was particularly noted for his coats, suits and designs in quality fabrics. He died in Valencia in 1972.

Like Dior, *Jacques Fath* died young at the height of his fame; he was only 42, a victim of leukaemia. He was born in 1912 and, also like Dior, began his career in a respected profession to please his parents – in this case it was stockbroking. He soon gave this up and started a small couture salon on his own just before the Second World War. Jacques Fath was an innovator, both for men's and women's clothes, and initiated a trend towards informality in the 1940s. Both in his own clothes and those he designed for others he was presenting roll-necked sweaters, blazers, shorts for men before these were generally fashionable and, for evening wear, he introduced frilled shirts and tartan dinner jackets.

Pierre Balmain was a contemporary of Jacques Fath. Born in 1914 in the Haute Savoie, he began his career in architecture, studying at the Ecole des Beaux Arts in Paris. After two years he turned to fashion drawing and spent some years working first for Molyneux and then Lelong. After the war Balmain opened his own house. His designs are noted for their clear lines, discreet features and what might even be termed an architectural feel.

Hubert Taffin de Givenchy was born at Beauvais in 1927. He started by studying law in Paris, then took up couture, working for a number of different houses – Lelong, Fath, Schiaparelli. A perfectionist, de Givenchy's designs are original and dramatic.

Pierre Cardin, a Frenchman born and brought up in Venice, came to Paris to work at the houses of Paquin and Schiaparelli and was with Dior when the New Look was launched. Cardin started up his own house in 1949. He designed for men as well as women and made a reputation in the 1950s with his original designs which included slim coats with immense cape collars (often double) and his Oriental styles. He introduced a number of ideas which were not popular at the time but which later were taken up: for instance, thigh-length boots; coloured, patterned stockings; and the wearing of a maxi coat over a mini dress.

Another generation of designers was working in the 1960s and 1970s, using new materials and presenting revolutionary ideas, many of which were aimed at the young. Couture was less exclusive and the ready-to-wear market an important one. New designers were numerous. Elegant, feminine creations, up-to-date but not necessarily way out, continued to be produced by a number of the couture houses – *Nina Ricci, Jacques Heim, Madeleine de Rauch, Jacques Griffe, Guy Laroche* and many others. *Yves St Laurent*, who had been employed as a young assistant by Christian Dior, took over the house when Dior died and his first collection, when he presented the trapeze line planned by Dior, was an immense success. The collections which followed were not so well received and St Laurent eventually broke away and set up on his own, developing his individual style which, for some time, was almost anti-fashion.

The modern look to the fashion scene, and one which was especially an appeal to youth, was initiated in the early 1960s by such designers as Courrèges and Ungaro in France and Quant in England. *André Courrèges* began his couture career working for Balenciaga. The two men had much in common; both were Basques (Courrèges was French, Balenciaga Spanish) and both were superb tailors, perfectionists and uncompromisingly severe in design. Courrèges started up on his own in 1961 and for a year or so his designs reflected those of his master. Then, in 1964, he presented a completely new approach in what was quickly referred to as the Space-Age Collection. The clothes were beautifully tailored, starkly plain, clean-cut in line, and chiefly in white and silver, using colour sparingly. Short-skirted dresses with tent shape and high waists were included in the collection, but predominant were trousers, cut to fit closely and finished at hip level with, in many cases, bare midriff and back. These were worn with sleeveless or short-sleeved bodices or jackets in two or three-piece suits intended for all occasions. Calf-length leather boots accompanied most ensembles.

Meanwhile, in London, *Mary Quant* was bringing about a revolution in providing clothes for the young, by the young – a trend which culminated in the mini-skirt of 1965, when girls wore mid-thigh length skirts and even the middle-aged were buying knee-length dresses. The mini-skirt was the symbol of youth in the 1960s. It does not seem clear who presented it first: Courrèges says that he did; in England, it is accepted that Mary Quant did but, like the crinoline a century earlier, having been introduced, the feminine public liked it so much they were reluctant to let it die.

Simple, space-age type clothes, in light

Space age unisex attire. Pinafore mini dress over wool top. Lace-patterned tights, black boots. Cardin, 1971 and bright colours and using a variety of materials including PVC, were presented by a number of different designers after this: Cardin, Patou, Ungaro were among them. With the 1970s, new names in fashion are legion and it becomes more difficult to discern current trends.

Fashion doll

The precursor of the fashion journal; served to make known the current modes as far afield as possible. These fashion or mannequin dolls were especially made and dressed in Paris, most widely in the seventeenth and eighteenth centuries, and sent out each month to the capitals of Europe. The dolls were large, sometimes life-size, and were beautifully and correctly dressed in the latest fashion.

Fashion journal, fashion plate

Fashion dolls continued to be made and sent out until well into the nineteenth century, but the information which they could provide on the current modes was supplemented, from the second half of the eighteenth century, by the fashion journal. This was a publication which gave news and illustrations of fashions which were being worn as well as those which were new and likely to become very fashionable. It was not a pattern book or a fashion plate but a magazine to inform both sexes of what was popular in Society.

Although French fashion was supreme and the French were still issuing their fashion dolls and had begun to produce such journals as *Le Cabinet des Modes*, it was the English who seriously promoted, at this time, the production of journals from the fashion world. *The Lady's Magazine* was the chief of these, dating from 1770 and published at first in black and white and, later in the century, in colour. Between 1770 and 1800 a number of such journals appeared, illustrated by good artists and giving reliable drawings of the leading fashions of the time. They appeared in France, England, Germany, Holland and Italy. These should not be confused with the publications which featured caricatures of fashion and were for amusement only. The outstanding publication of the end of the century was the *Gallery of Fashion*, begun in 1794 by Niklaus Wilhelm von Heideloff, a German from Stuttgart who had worked for Ackermann, the bookseller and publisher of quality prints. The *Gallery of Fashion* was a superb production on quarto-size paper; its annual subscription was three guineas though it issued only some 20 plates a year. The plates, which came out monthly, had two or three figures and accessories on each, with descriptions of the garments. Though in plate form, they were still a record of existing modes, not future designs.

The nineteenth century was the most important time for the publication of engraved fashion plates and journals. They were hand-coloured until the last quarter of the century, when printed colour work began to be published. Until about 1830–40 most journals were still published in France and England. Some famous publications were produced in the years 1800–40, such as the French *La Belle Assemblée*, *Le Petit Courrier des Dames*, *La Mode* and *Le Bon Ton*, and the English *The Ladies' Cabinet* and the *Ladies' Gazette of Fashions*. Some publications were illustrated by first-class artists; for instance, *Sulpice Guillaume Chevalier*, who worked for some time for *La Mode*. He signed himself 'Gavarni', a practice which stemmed from a printing error early in his career when, on one occasion, his name was confused with that of the subject of his feature – Gavarnie, a French Pyrenean village.

After 1830 there was a tremendous increase in the number of publications and nearly all European countries produced one or more. From 1860, Germany's *Die Modenwelt*, published in Berlin, was an important journal. It had a wide circulation and was published in 14 languages under different titles; the English version was *The Season*. In the 1870s Vienna, until then not an important fashion centre, became so at a time when France and Prussia were engaged in war. *Wiener Mode* and *Wiener Chic* were outstanding publications of the 1880s and 1890s. In the second half of the century the Americans entered the field and several papers which later became world-famous were launched – *Harper's Bazaar* and *Vogue*, for example. Also in this period were published some famous English journals, such as *The Queen* and the *Englishwoman's Domestic Magazine*. Both of these were started by Samuel Beeton, husband of the Mrs Beeton of *Book of Household Management* fame.

Feathers

Used for decoration from earliest times, also a symbol of rank. The tail feathers from rare and brilliantly coloured birds, such as the peacock, quetzal and bird of paradise, have been reserved for the ornamentation of head-dresses and coiffures of the ruling classes in society. In some cultures feathers have also been used to make garments and bedcovers, either because of the warmth of the natural product in a cold climate or, again, as a badge of rank.

The *eider duck* has long been used in the former category; its breast down, which is exposed when the feathers are plucked, is one of the warmest and softest of all natural materials. The tremendous number of birds which were destroyed to make the eiderdown quilts of the nineteenth and twentieth centuries made prohibition necessary in many countries to ensure the bird's survival. The eider also supplied feathers for making hats in northern latitudes (its natural habitat); these were made from the whole skin of the bird in countries such as Greenland and Iceland.

Throughout *Polynesia* the *cloak* was a garment of ceremonial and of importance. In Hawaii, for example, and in Maori society (see *Maori dress*), the feather cape or cloak denoted high status. Such cloaks had a flax net foundation to which small feathers were attached all over in different colours to form a geometrical pattern. Red was the colour denoting a chief's cloak, or one of yellow with a red design. The best of these were made from parrot feathers, less important ones from pigeon, quail or parakeet. The one illustrated is a typical chief's cloak, forming a segment of a circle and made in red and yellow feathers

tied to a net base. Now in the Royal Scottish Museum in Edinburgh, it belonged to the first king of Hawaii to visit Britain in 1824.

Feathers were, perhaps, most widely used for garments, decoration and status symbols by the Indians who inhabited *North* and *South America* before the coming of the white man. Exotic head-dresses with long plumes, especially those of the brilliantly-coloured quetzal bird, denoted rank in the South American Indian civilizations (see *Aztec, Inca* and *Maya dress*). In North America feathers were used extensively, the type and means of decoration varying according to tribe and district (see *North American Indians*). Beautiful robes, denot-

Persian feather crown, sixth century BC

Chinese hat with feather, nineteenth century

Hawaiian cape of red and yellow feathers, 1824

Mayan feather headdress, sixteenth century

North American Indian headdress of eagle feathers, nineteenth century

Maori coiffure with feathers and comb. Tattooed face, greenstone earring

ing high status, were made of the iridescent feathers of the wild turkey, the plumes completely covering the foundation as in the Polynesian examples. A common head-dress for many Indian races was the head-band ornamented by a few or many beautiful plumes, most importantly of the eagle or turkey. The bonnet, with its plumes affixed round the edge from top to halfway down the back, was originally worn to war by western American and Canadian Indians, but in the nineteenth century it became a festive head-dress for many tribes (see *Bonnet*). Each feather represented a particular act of courage performed. The quill was plucked from the golden eagle by the chief and the bird had to be captured, then later released after the feather had been plucked. It was not to be harmed as the Indians regarded it as the monarch of the bird world. Feathers were also inserted directly on the complex coiffures and top knots adopted by a number of Indian tribes.

Most of the *ancient civilizations* used feathers as decoration, especially for head-dresses. The peacock tail-feather with its brilliant eye was a favourite, its use generally reserved for persons of royal or priestly status or the right to wear it was awarded as a mark of high merit. The *Egyptians* wore many different plumes on their head-dresses, as did the *Minoans*, the *Assyrians* and *Persians*. The *Chinese* also used plumes attached to the crown of the hat by a jade tube as a mark of rank. Under the Manchus a peacock feather was the chief plume, graded so that one with three eyes was of highest merit, descending to a plume of one eye; a pheasant feather was of lesser status.

In *Europe* feathers were used to decorate hats, head-dresses and coiffure styles; those of the rarer, imported birds being reserved for the nobility. Men's hats in the later Middle Ages were decorated by tall feathers of all kinds, but especially the tail feathers of the peacock, pheasant and cockerel. In the sixteenth and seventeenth centuries ostrich tips and plumes were worn in men's hats, curling on or around the crown and brim. Often these were blended with other feathers to provide variations in colour and form. By the later eighteenth century the large hats of the ladies were similarly ornamented, while in the early nineteenth century, very tall plumes adorned the coiffure for evening functions. Feathers of all kinds were worn in ladies' hats and bonnets throughout the nineteenth and early twentieth centuries. This was especially so in the decades of large designs such as the 1830s, 1890s and early 1900s. Particularly fashionable were ostrich feathers from the wings and tail, marabou feathers from the African stork, pheasant and bird of paradise tail-feathers, and aigrettes from the egret, the white heron. Feathers were also widely used in ladies' dress during the eighteenth and nineteenth centuries for dress trimmings, boas and fans; the ostrich and marabou plumes were most usual for this purpose. In the early twentieth century, plumage laws were passed in order to restrict the indiscriminate slaughter of birds for decorative purposes and belated efforts were made to preserve some species which were in danger of extinction. Since 1920 feathers have been used in ornamentation in a much more limited way.

Felt

A material made by rolling, pressing and hammering combinations of fibres from wool, hair and fur, which are moistened, then heated (see *Fulling*, under *Textile processes*). Felt is one of the earliest of materials, made even when woven cloth was little known. Felt caps and garments from the Bronze Age have been found in the Danish and German peat bogs; felt was used extensively by the Greeks for caps and cloaks. The material has proved especially suitable in cold, damp climates, due to its qualities of impermeability. In more recent times felt hats have been made from fur fibres, manipulated and pressed, then subjected to shrinking processes. Especially suitable for this are the pelts of beaver, otter and muskrat.

Cavalier felt hat with white ostrich plume, 1630, English

Charles IX of France. Black velvet hat with gold embroidery. White ostrich plumes

Polish nobleman, 1532, ostrich plumes

Felt hat with brooch and plume English, 1470

Italian young man, 1590. Black hat with black and white plumes

Black hat with plume and jewelled band. English, 1577

The Priest-King from Knossos, Minoan, Crete, c.1500 BC

Maroon silk hat with grey plumes. Austrian, 1914

Straw hat with velvet ribbons and dark ostrich plumes. English, 1904

Purple silk bonnet with purple and cream plumes. French, 1872

Velvet hat with ribbon and white ostrich plumes. Swiss, c.1520

Mrs Siddons, English, 1784. Black hat, ribbons and plumes

FERRONNIERE
Italian, c.1530. Ferronnière

Feridjé, feridgi, ferigee

A Turkish garment worn by women out of doors. Like the çarşaf, (see *Chādar*, etc.), it completely enveloped the body as a cloak (see also *Cloak*) but had loose sleeves and a large square cape at the back. Women of limited means wore a *feridjé* made of black cotton or alpaca, but the garment adopted by the wealthy was of rich fabric, decorated by embroidery, tassels and braid and was lined with coloured satin or silk. A similar garment was worn in the Middle East, the Arabic *feredíyah*.

Ferronnière

A fine chain worn round the forehead with a small jewel set in the centre. A Renaissance fashion in Europe, especially in Italy and France, worn with the Madonna style of coiffure, the name was taken from the painting 'La Belle Ferronnière', believed at one time to be by Leonardo da Vinci. The fashion was revived in England and France in the 1830s.

Festoon

A garland of flowers and leaves suspended in a curve between two points. In costume, festoons are of flowers, soft material or lace, usually decorating a full skirt, as in the eighteenth-century panier skirts or the nineteenth-century crinoline ones.

Fibula

A clasp, buckle, pin or brooch. From the Latin word to fasten. Used in ancient times to fasten garments, especially the cloak and the tunic. Many designs resembled the modern safety pin in structure and appearance.

FESTOON
Festooned skirt, English, 1771

FIBULA
Gold fibula with ducklings,
Etruscan, seventh century BC

Silver fibula, Spain, fourth
century BC

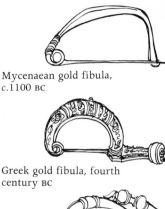
Mycenaean gold fibula,
*c.*1100 BC

Greek gold fibula, fourth
century BC

Greek bronze fibula, third
century BC

Silver fibula, Spain, fourth
century BC

Roman gold fibula, first century
AD

Roman bronze fibula, first
century AD

Bronze fibula, third century AD

Fichu

A French word which, in English costume, is taken to refer to a neckcloth or neckerchief worn by women between about 1780 and 1880. The material was loosely draped around the neck and tied in front or back or fastened with a pin or brooch at the breasts. In the late eighteenth and early nineteenth centuries the fichu was of white, soft, fine fabric, usually lawn or muslin, and was often lace or ruffle-edged. In the 1780s it was softly bunched over the breasts giving a pouter pigeon effect. There were a number of nineteenth-century versions known by different names. The *fichu-antoinette* was trimmed with black lace and velvet ribbon and was crossed over in front to fasten under the waistbelt; the *fichu-corday* was crossed over at the breast but tied at the back; the *fichu-la vallière* was not crossed over but joined at the waist in the centre front. Some fichu styles were in the form of a canezou or a pélerine (see *Canezou* and *Pèlerine*).

There is more than one theory for the origin of the use of the term fichu in costume; one suggests that it is derived from the French meaning 'to drape or throw carelessly' round the shoulders; another states that the term derives from part of the medieval horse harness. In French costume a fichu refers to a black lace scarf which is draped round the neck and knotted at the breasts. The type of white muslin fichu in soft folds giving the puffed-out effect as seen in the later eighteenth century is known in France as a *fichu-menteur*.

Fillet

A band of any material, from ribbon to metal, worn round the head to keep the hair or head-dress in position, also for ornamentation. Fashionable in dress from the earliest times and, though seen chiefly on women, men also, especially in more primitive cultures, wore a fillet round the brow. Different names were used for such bands as, for example, the ancient Roman *vitta*.

FICHU
White lawn fichu, English, 1790
White muslin fichu, French, 1788

Fitchet

A medieval term for a vertical opening at the hip of a gown or surcoat, made so that the hand could be passed through to the belt and purse which were worn, for security reasons, out of sight beneath.

Flannel

An open, woollen material, usually without a nap. In Britain it was of Welsh origin and was being made there before the sixteenth century in a plain – later also twill – weave. During the nineteenth century flannel became a popular material, used for underwear, scarves, shawls, dresses and jackets. A wide range of weights and textures was developed and flannel was produced in a variety of colours; for example, the red flannel for underwear.

Flannelette

A cotton material made in imitation of flannel. *Canton flannel*, originally made in China, is a heavy, warm flannelette, as also is *Kimono flannel*, though this is finer and is often printed with Japanese motifs.

FLEUR-DE-LIS
Counterchange design of heraldic
lions and fleur-de-lis, 1360

Outing flannel is a type of flannelette used chiefly for underwear and sleeping garments where, sometimes, wool is incorporated. A similar fabric, called *Shaker flannel*, is usually reserved for baby garments because of its soft fineness. It was originally made by the Shakers, a religious sect of eighteenth-century origin.

Fleur-de-lis

Modern French term for the lily-flower, a plant of the genus iris. (Many other spellings, such as the older fleur-de-lys and flower-de-luce.) In textile design the fleur-de-lis stems from the conventionalized motif which was borne upon the royal arms of France under the monarchy. This was the heraldic lily which derived, according to one school of thought, from the iris or, an alternative theory, from the head of a sceptre or battle-axe. The fleur-de-lis appeared frequently in medieval costume ornament and has remained a traditional and popular motif ever since.

Flounce

Strips of material gathered or pleated, one edge of which was applied to a garment with the other left free to flare. Especially fashionable on women's garments of the mid-eighteenth and mid-nineteenth centuries.

Flower-bottle

In the second half of the nineteenth century men wore a tiny glass bottle containing a fresh flower in the left lapel of the morning coat. A ribbon fitting was sewn to the back of the lapel to hold the bottle in position. (For ladies, see also *Breast-bottle*.)

Fly fringe

A cord fringe with silk tufts and tassels attached. Used as a decorative edging to women's dresses in the eighteenth and nineteenth centuries.

Fly-front closure

A closure where buttons and buttonholes or zip fasteners are hidden by an overlap of the material extended over them. Rare

FLOUNCE
Ball dress of pink and white
striped gauze. Flounced skirt
over crinoline, 1862

before the nineteenth century, then introduced for men's trousers and breeches. Also employed in some styles of centre-front fastening overcoats.

Fontange

A ladies' head-dress named after Mlle de Fontanges, mistress of Louis XIV, and worn from the 1680s until about 1710. Towards 1680 the feminine coiffure had begun to be dressed higher in curls and ringlets in sympathy with the masculine periwig of the time. To provide the desired height, the hair was supported on a silk-covered wire framework called a *commode* or *palisade* (see also *Hair-styles*). The fontange head-dress, the *bonnet à la Fontanges*, was a white lawn or linen cap decorated with ribbon loops and bows, while on the crown of the head were fluted and pleated wired ruffles of lace or lawn, set one row behind and above one another like a tower of organ pipes. The whole was ornamented with lappets of lace and ribbon bows. The head-dress reached its greatest height about 1700, echoing not only the men's wigs but also the tall chair and settee backs of the time. After this, accompanied by considerable ridicule, the fontange diminished to a lace crowned cap.

Foulard poile de chèvre

A fabric resembling foulard (see *Silk*), but made from goat hair.

Frankish dress

The Germanic tribes were known by the generic name of Franks from about AD 250. They comprised a large group of peoples inhabiting a wide area of Europe from the Baltic Sea to the Danube and from Poland to the Rhine. In the early fifth century they moved westwards into Gaul and annexed Flanders and part of France. They were a warrior people and chiefly of great stature. They are described by Sidonius Apollinaris as having red hair knotted in front on top of their heads, shaved at the nape and with long moustaches. They wore a fitting tunic, often striped, with a wide belt decorated with metal studs and having a dependent sword and dagger. On top was a coloured cloth cloak with different lining. Legs were bare and boots laced at the ankles. This description was given in AD 470 in Lyons and is similar to those of Tacitus writing in the first century AD. Agathius, writing in the sixth century, describes the linen or leather trousers which they wore, tied to their legs by thongs, like those of the Gauls of the first and second centuries (see also *Merovingian dress*).

Fringe

1) A decorative *edging* sewn to the garment by a narrow braid on one side while the other, of single or corded threads, knots or tassels, is free. In general use from the Middle Ages onwards, but also widely employed as an ornamental finish in the ancient civilizations, especially the Babylonian and Assyrian.
2) *Hair* cut short on the forehead and combed straight to resemble fringing.

Frontlet

A band or decorative item worn on or round the forehead. The word has been applied through the centuries to different

FONTANGE   German, 1695–1700

FRANKISH DRESS
Wool tunic and mantle, fur over-tunic. Bare legs, leather boots. Bronze armlets, brooch and buckle

Queen Mary II of England, *c*.1694

FRONTLET
Frontlet loop under headdress with butterfly veil, 1480

Catherine of Aragon. Gold, jewelled frontlet to gable hood, *c*.1520

Gold, jewelled frontlet to French hood. Flanders, *c*.1530

parts of feminine head-covering within this context. For example, in the second half of the fifteenth century, when the hair was pulled tightly back to display a fashionably high forehead, the loop of velvet or silk attached to the skull cap or net which concealed the hair and was worn under the elaborate head-dress of the day was termed a frontlet. Later, in the first half of the sixteenth century the word was used to refer to the metal jewelled band worn round the forehead which fronted both the gable and French hood styles.

The word frontlet has also been applied to the *forehead cloth* which, smeared with cream or medicament, was worn at night hopefully to prevent or remove wrinkles.

Fully fashioned
A term applied to modern machine-knitted fabrics designed for underwear, stockings, tights, socks and jumpers, cardigans, pull-ons etc., where the flat material is shaped as necessary by adjusting the number of stitches to fashion the sections of the garments which are afterwards seamed together. In the case of hose, some designs are made without seams.

Furbelow
English word derived from the French term *falbala* which, in the eighteenth century, was used to describe all forms of flounces, frills and pleated edging employed to decorate garments. In more modern usage the term is more commonly seen in the plural – furbelows – and refers to ornamentation in general and overdecoration or decoration in poor taste in particular.

Furs
The story of costume begins with the wearing of hides and furs; there has never been a time anywhere in the world when animal skins have not been employed, in the colder regions as garments for warmth and protection and in the torrid zones for status and display. Fierce struggles, even wars, have been undertaken from time to time in order to control an area naturally rich in fur-bearing animals; the invasion and early settlement by the white man in North America was one example of this, the sixteenth century conquest of Siberia, another.

The earliest, most primitive dress of man in the colder regions of the world consisted, at first, only of animal skins, held together solely by thorns piercing the fur at the shoulder or a leather thong tied round the waist. With the making of bone needles and gut thread, man began to sew the skins together to make garments. Bear and reindeer were the animals chiefly used at this time, followed later, in Europe, by the wild deer, boar and ox. As man learned to herd and domesticate animals, the skins of goats, sheep, donkeys and cattle were used for clothing. Sheepskin became the commonest material in use in the lands round the Mediterranean as can be seen in the early paintings and sculpture; the 'kaunakes' garments of Sumeria are one example (see *Mesopotamia*).

In the warmer areas furs from specific animals, moreover a particular part of the animal such as the head, paws or tail, were used to denote rank and for display. It was also believed that by adornment with a part of such animals the wearer might inherit the physical qualities of that animal, such as fleetness of foot, ferocity or courage. In ancient Egypt, for instance, a lion's or wolf's tail was worn hanging from the belt (see *Egypt, ancient*).

All the early civilizations, as well as the more primitive cultures, used hides and fur for their costume. The Egyptians, Assyrians, Babylonians, Persians, Minoans, Greeks, Etruscans and Romans all treated hides to make leather for use as footwear (see *Boot, Leather, Sandal, Shoe*), helmets, shields and military tunics. They used costly furs as trimmings, decoration and linings. They became skilled in cutting and shaping the pelts to make fitting, warm garments. Expensive, warm and beautiful furs were always prized, both for their utility and their attractiveness (see *Minoan Dress, Mesopotamia, Etruscan Dress, Greece, ancient,* and *Rome, ancient*). Nomadic and more primitive peoples made whole costumes from skins, the fur generally turned inside, and these garments have become

Sable antelope, about 4 ft. to shoulder. Southern Africa

Jaguar, 6 ft. long. South America

Fallow deer, 3 ft. to shoulder. Europe

Markhor goat. Largest of the wild goats, over 3 ft. tall. Himalayas

Marten. Weasel family, like sable. Europe, America, Asia. Size varies from 26 inches to 3 ft long, including tail

European brown bear. Total height erect 5 to 8 ft.

Common red fox, Europe and Asia. 15 inches high to shoulder

Otter, Europe and elsewhere. 2½ to 3 ft. long

Timber wolf, North America. 4 ft. long

Moufflon wild sheep, Europe

Grey squirrel, America and Britain. 18 inches long

Mink, Europe and America, weasel family. Up to 18 inches long

European wild rabbit. Up to 18 inches long

Common badger, Europe and Asia. Up to 3 ft. long including tail

Beaver, Europe and North America. 27 inches long

North American bison or buffalo. Up to 6 ft. in height to shoulder

European weasel, about 7 inches long

traditional over the centuries. The Scythians and Parthians wore tunics or caftans and trousers of pelts as did also the North American Indian and the Eskimo (see *Eskimo Dress, North American Indian Dress* and *Scythian Dress*).

From the sixth to the seventeenth century in Europe furs were widely used for warmth and decoration. Garments were edged and lined with fur but the fur was not worn to the outside. Fur linings were employed chiefly on cloaks, tunics, gowns, underskirts, nightgowns, boots and mittens, both for outdoor and indoor wear. During the Middle Ages the wearing of specific furs indicated a distinction of class. Sumptuary laws were passed from time to time regulating which furs were permitted to be worn by diverse classes of society. The costly furs, reserved for use by royalty and the wealthy aristocracy, included sable, ermine and vair. Ermine had been known to the Greeks and Romans and was thought to be a species of white rat – they called it 'Armenian rat'. It was not until the eighteenth century that it was recognized as a member of the weasel family. In medieval times wearing ermine was a prerogative of royalty; it was Edward III of England who ordered that the black tipped ermine should be a royal fur. Sable and vair could be worn by the nobility. Vair was the Siberian grey and white squirrel. The skins were sewn together to make the garment and were known as menu-vair (small skins) and gros-vair (large skins). Descending the fur social scale, one comes to marten, otter, muskrat, fox, beaver, lamb, rabbit, cat, goat and wolf. The peasants' cloak continued to be made of sheepskin or wolfskin. Most of the softest, richest furs came from the cold, northern, near-Arctic regions of Russia, Siberia, Scandinavia, Lapland and Canada. In the East, in the Byzantine domains, the Ottoman Empire, China and India, fur was used as a decoration and symbol of status on hats, collars and boots.

By the sixteenth century the enormous quantities of furs which had been used, especially those from the small animals such as sable, vair and marten, had begun to create a scarcity, making some species rare in Europe. Exploration of the New World indicated the possibilities of rich new fields to plunder. The French began trading with the Indians in Canada and the Spanish and the English, along the Atlantic coasts of America. At the same time the Spanish were discovering the rich furs of South America, where the Incas hunted the little chinchilla for its beautiful fur and bred the great herds of vicuña and llama for their wool.

With the seventeenth century the exploitation of the fur-bearing animals of the North American continent began in earnest. The Indians made all their clothing from animal skins but were also eager to trade their furs for the beads, knives, guns, cloth and liquor which the white man brought. Trading posts were set up to which the Indians brought their pelts, which included great quantities of fox, mink, marten, badger, raccoon, wolf, lynx, beaver, bison or buffalo, opossum, bear, seal and otter. North America was explored by the white fur trappers from Hudson Bay to New Orleans. Most of the nations of Western Europe took part in this profitable trade. Despite the vast quantity of animals available, the unsparing hunting of certain animals whose fur became fashionable, such as the beaver and mink, soon began to threaten the existence of the species. The pelts were sent back to Europe to make immense fur hats, hoods and muffs and to line garments. Even the supply of the New World began to dry up before the greed of Europe and the traders. Fashions for certain furs waxed and waned during the eighteenth and nineteenth centuries, threatening yet more species, in particular the chinchilla, the sable, the white fox and the wolf.

Despite the quantities of furs used to line garments and the different fashions which came and went, it was nearly the middle of the nineteenth century before it became customary to wear the fur surface on the outside of a coat; it was always a lining. From 1840 Europe led the mode for fur coats with the fur to the outside, first with seal then other furs. It was in the twentieth century that fur was worn in the greatest quantity. This was the time for the fashion for fur coats, capes and jackets. More adequate heating in the interior of buildings did away with the need to line garments with fur but a coat to wear to go out in the street became more desirable. Now the fur was on the exterior of the garment and the lining was of satin or silk. Fur coats were no longer the prerogative of the rich, the middle classes were able to afford this status symbol. This extension of the wearing of fur coats to a larger percentage of the population, as well as the mode for fur collars, cuffs and tippets, began to threaten the survival of a greater number of species. The chinchilla was in danger, the silver fox, also the Alaskan seal.

Since the mid-twentieth century there has developed a strong body of opinion against the killing of animals for their fur. At the same time the research into synthetic furs has been accelerated. With natural furs there has been an extensive augmentation of supplies by means of ranch-raised animals and, at the same time, an increase in the custom of dyeing of furs so that a lower quality pelt is coloured to imitate a costlier one.

Apart from the inroads made on a species of animal due to killing to obtain its fur, the modern world of the fourth quarter of the twentieth century is also affecting the habitat of animals, so that the existence of many fur-bearing ones is further threatened. For instance, because of the spread of rabies on the Continent of Europe, the red fox has almost disappeared there so that, from being an ordinary fur, the survivors in Britain are now regarded as animals more costly than the silver or black fox. Because of the mechanization of agriculture in Europe, moles have been severely reduced in numbers. Because of motorway construction, the hedgehog has almost disappeared. Because of oil drilling in watery districts, the musquash has now become rare. Finally, because of the disturbance of marshy ground due to airfield and dam construction, many marsh-dwelling animals are threatened.

The fur trade classifies animal skins, which it terms peltries, into four types. These are hides from cattle and horses, pelts from sheep and lambs, furs from fur-bearing animals and skins from goats and kid. Fur-bearing animals are covered by a soft underfur or wool which acts as insulation from extremes of temperature and an outer fur or hair, called guard hairs, which protect the animal and stop the underfur from becoming a wet and solid mass. In some animals, such as the beaver, coypu and seal, the guard hairs are coarse and are removed before the fur is used. The softest, silkiest and densest furs belong to animals which inhabit the Arctic areas. The most valuable furs, partly because of their beauty and partly because of their scarcity (factors which are interactive) include that of the chinchilla, the sable, the ermine and the black fox. Fine furs which are rather less rare are those of the mink, the seal, the beaver, the marten, the muskrat and the skunk. Of the hardest-wearing furs should be mentioned the karakul lamb, the raccoon, the coypu (nutria) and the mink.

Today the principal countries which produce natural furs are Canada, the USA and Siberia. The Soviet Union has collectivized its fur industry, which is one of the most valuable in the country. The auction sales at the Fur Palace in Leningrad are large-scale and world-wide.

The preparation of furs for clothing is complex and has evolved from the ancient craft practised over the centuries in many parts of the world. Animals are killed in mid-winter when their fur is at its best and are carefully trapped so that the fur is not damaged. After the pelt is taken from the animal, the skin is fleshed, that is, the thin flesh membrane is skilfully removed by a very sharp fleshing knife. The pelt is then soaked in a tanning fluid, washed, dried and finished. It is then stretched out and softened by the application of grease to put back the natural oils in order to produce a lastingly soft skin. Today the skin is put into a machine which gently beats the oil into the pelt. Earlier societies used simpler methods; the North American Indians, for example, trampled the skins with their bare feet, while Eskimo women chewed the skins, the saliva providing the necessary chemicals for preparation (see also *North American Indian Dress* and *Eskimo and Siberian Dress*).

Different processes are followed for skins intended for use as leather, called tanning, or for their employment as fur, termed dressing. In the latter case, the processes can be numerous and vary from furrier to furrier. Costly furs are treated by hand but machines are used for the majority of skins. Every care is taken to maintain the softness of the pelt so that it will hang well when it is made up into a garment and to retain its natural oils while complete cleansing is carried out. Some pelts, such as beaver and seal, need more work on them than others. Present-day processes also include dyeing, which is no longer regarded as a deception, and it is thought that all furs are improved by judicious dyeing with chemicals to give greater lustre to the natural colour. Such dyeing processes can involve complete immersion or the dye can be applied to only the upper hairs by a brush. Bleaching is similarly handled.

The excessive demand for furs, especially in the later nineteenth and the twentieth centuries, has forced country after country to impose protective legislation on certain species of animals, the chinchilla and beaver, for instance. At the same time there has been a rapid extension of fur-farming, the breeding of species of animals in captivity particularly for their fur. Experiments began before 1870 and continued spasmodically in North America until the twentieth century. Early experimentation, begun by the North American Indians, was with the fox, white, black and silver, which had become rare and costly. During the twentieth century farm- or ranch-raising of animals for their fur has become an industry and concerns many species, in particular, the chinchilla, mink, sable, beaver, skunk, muskrat and karakul lamb. Farmed animals have as good and, often, better skins than wild ones. The animals are generally larger and they are protected so the skins do not suffer damage from fighting and accident. Better and

specially blended colours can be achieved. Mutations and hybrids have been obtained by cross-breeding two animals of a different colour. In the case of mink, for example, some beautiful blue and silver tones have been produced. Of the 15–20 million skins of mink produced per year in the world, about 15 per cent are farmed. (This does not include any figures for Russia which are not published.)

THE PRINCIPAL FUR-BEARING ANIMALS

Antelope – numerous species, varied in size, including gazelles. From Africa, India and Asia.

Badger – up to three feet in length including tail. The European badger has a grizzled coat, each hair being yellow at base, then black and grey nearer the tip. The head is white with two black lines running longitudinally from the snout to behind the ears. Also found in America and Asia.

Bear – brown, black and white (polar). Found in remote, mountainous regions in Europe, America and Asia. Five to nine feet long, the Himalayan black bear has particularly lustrous fur.

Beaver – found in a few places in Europe but mainly in North America and Siberia. The pelage consists of strong guard hairs amongst which is a thick, silky underfur, rusty brown in colour, much valued in the fur trade.

Bison (*buffalo*) The European buffalo, now found in Greece, Italy, Asia Minor and Egypt, is the Indian or *water buffalo* and is similar to an ox. A related species is to be found in many parts of Africa, while the *Cape* or *Black buffalo* inhabits Central, South and East Africa. These buffalo have all been used for leather. The North American bison, often called buffalo, is a larger animal with dark brown hair growing all over its immense forequarters.

Cat – the best fur comes from the wild or semi-wild animal which has a thicker fur than the domestic cat. The European wild cat is found in the north and east of Europe, also in the Scottish Highlands. It is a forest-dweller and has a yellowish-grey fur with black markings.

Chinchilla – one of the most beautiful furs in the world, soft, pearl-grey with black markings; it has more hairs per square inch than any other animal. Like a squirrel in size and form, the chinchilla lives high in the Andes; it has been hunted for centuries from the days of the Incas and is now protected in Chile. It is widely bred for its fur on farms in North America and Europe. About 200 skins are needed for a full-length coat.

Chipmunk – North American squirrel with black and yellow striped markings.

Coypu – an aquatic rodent about 18 inches long, native to South America but also found in Europe. Famed for its fur known as *nutria*.

Deer – many different kinds, of which, in Europe, the most common are the *red deer*, the *fallow deer* and the *roe deer*. In the northern regions of Scandinavia, Siberia and North America the larger *elk*, the related American *moose*, the *reindeer* and its American counterpart, the *caribou*, can be found. The reindeer and caribou, in particular, have provided clothing as well as food, milk and transportation to the Laplanders and Eskimos for centuries.

Dog – the dog is not normally used for its fur though the wild dog has fur similar to that of a poor quality fox. The Siberian wild dog, which is like a heavy Alsatian and is about three feet long, was most often used.

Dormouse – a small animal about five to six inches long, intermediate between a squirrel and a rodent. Common to Europe, the dormouse's fur varies from grey to tawny yellow; it is used chiefly for trimming.

Ermine – the white winter coat of the stoat. Found in Russia, Scandinavia and North America. About ten inches long, with a black tip to its tail. Used from medieval times as a royal fur (see Stoat).

Fox – Member of the canine family, native to Europe, North America and Northern Asia. The *red fox* is found in all these regions. The *grey fox* is an inhabitant of America as is also the wild red fox which is sometimes marked on the back and shoulders with a black cross. Most valued

for its fur is the *silver fox*, which is a black fox with silver-tipped guard hairs. It is to be found chiefly in the far north of Canada, especially Labrador, as is also the *Arctic fox* which has a white winter coat and a summer one of dark brown or smoky blue. In the fur trade this is known as the blue fox and it inhabits the northern coast of North America from Alaska to Greenland. The *silver blue fox* of today is a mutation and is the most costly of fox furs.

Goat – *Markhor*, the largest of the wild goats inhabits the Himalayas. The *Mongolian goat* has long silky hair in white and greyish blue. The angora goat has a pure white, curly, silky coat (see also *Angora goat*). The skin of *kid*, the young goat, is widely used in dress accessories. Finely marked skins are imported from China, Africa and India.

Guanaco – member of the camel family which lives in herds in the Andes. The guanaco is a wild animal of the species of which the llama is the domesticated equivalent.

Hamster – a rodent-like small animal (about one foot long) inhabiting Europe and the Middle East. The fur is brown and black or a golden brown.

Hare – the same family as the rabbit, but larger, about 23–27 inches long. The brown hare is common in most of Europe while the Arctic hare is Canadian.

Jaguar – one of the big cats native to America, the jaguar has a short-haired coat shading from white to yellow to orange and marked with black spots arranged in rosettes round a brownish centre. A hard-wearing fur used for coats, jackets and trimming.

Lamb – Karakul is the breed of sheep which produces the most famous fur from its young lambs. Known as 'Persian lamb' because it was originally introduced as a fur by Persian traders, the karakul sheep is native to Southern Russia in the Bukhara region though, in England, the fur is also referred to as astrakhan after the Russian town on the edge of the Caspian Sea. During the Russian Revolution many owners drove their herds over the border into Afghanistan to protect them and the sheep are still bred there. After 1918 several attempts were made to breed karakul sheep in Germany but, though the sheep survived, the fur lost its remarkable curly quality. The curl lasts only a few days in the karakul lamb and, because of this, there are several qualities of fur depending upon the age of the animal. The most costly, prized skin is *broadtail*, which derives from a still-born lamb and has a moiré or watered silk appearance. This is a natural birth and affects about 2 per cent of lambs. The stories which are prevalent, describing the removal of the lamb prematurely from its mother or of torturing the mother in order to make her drop her lamb prematurely are fictitious. There would be no point in treating the mother so in order to obtain broadtail as the sheep is worth more than the lamb. The second grade of skin comes from the normal karakul lamb and is taken when it is from two to five days only and when the pelt has an even, tight curl. About 20–28 skins are needed for a full-length lady's coat and these are sewn by machine, except in the case of broadtail, when they are sewn by hand. The karakul lamb is naturally black but is also dyed black after dressing to add lustre to the pelt. There is also a beautiful mutation in soft brown.

In 1905 a flock of Russian karakul sheep was shipped to South Africa to be crossbred with sheep there. The result was a beautiful black tightly-curled pelt which is a flatter, lighter-weight skin. This is now much more fashionable than the Russian heavier, curlier pelt so is more costly. The largest world production of the lamb now comes from South Africa and Namibia. There is also a natural grey pelt from here and this is becoming more fashionable than the black.

Less expensive furs are produced from the Krimmer lamb from the Crimea, a greyish-mixture coat, and the South American lamb which has white fur.

Leopard – similar to the jaguar but smaller and a native of Africa and Southern Asia.

Llama – domesticated descendant of the guanaco, with a coarse, woolly fleece.

Lynx – a member of the cat family, with tufted ears, found in Europe, Siberia, Mongolia and North America. The Canadian lynx is the largest species and has the most valuable fur.

Marten – member of the weasel family, indigenous to Europe, Asia and America. Larger than the weasel and with a fine, soft, valuable fur. The most highly prized is that of the *sable*, a marten found in Northern Asia, from Russia and Siberia to Japan. The most esteemed fur in the world, sable is a small animal, about 15 inches long, and has a superb, silky, dense fur varying from brown to black. Used primarily, because of its cost, for trimming and collars. It has traditionally been used for coats and gowns for the Russian monarchy.

Mink – a semi-aquatic member of the weasel family with a valuable dark fur. The mink is indigenous to Europe and Northern Asia from Siberia to Japan. The North American mink is larger and its fur most valued for its thickness and softness. The mink is widely farmed in both North America and Europe.

Mole – found all over Europe, in Africa and North America. A very small animal, the mole has a thick, short, velvety fur of a dark bluish-grey.

Muskrat – a species of aquatic vole indigenous to North America. About one foot long, the muskrat has a thick, soft, shiny, brown and grey fur; it was introduced to Europe in 1905 because of the value of its fur, which is sometimes called *musquash*, from the North American Indian name.

Ocelot – a native of America and member of the cat family. The ocelot is marked like the leopard but is smaller (nearly three feet long).

Opossum – an American marsupial, about 27 inches long, with a thick fur ranging from white to black.

Otter – an aquatic animal of the weasel family with a short, dense, dark fur. The river otter is found in Europe, North Africa, Asia and North America. The Canadian otter has the most valued fur, especially the animals from Labrador and Alaska. The sea otter is a larger animal, about four to five feet long. It is found in the Pacific and has a dense, rich, long, most valued fur. The animal was almost exterminated because of extensive hunting but, due to protection, its numbers are now increasing.

Polecat – a member of the weasel family and a close relative of the mink. Found in many parts of Europe and Asia. It is up to two feet in length but the Russian polecat, which has the finest, silkiest fur, is smaller.

Pony – a fur fashionable in the first part of the twentieth century for coats. Taken from young colts or foals which have a flat fur with moiré marking. Imported chiefly from China, Poland and Russia.

Rabbit – a rodent of the hare family now found in most parts of the world. A soft grey, white, brown or black fur generally dyed to imitate costlier furs. Used widely as trimming (see also *Angora rabbit*).

Raccoon – an American mammal about the size of a badger with a grey-brown fur and black-ringed tail. The colloquial name for the animal and its fur is *Coon* and it was widely used by the American frontiersman, especially for hats and trimming.

Rat – a cheap fur used as trimming.

Seal – marine aquatic mammal of many different types and sizes found in many parts of the world but especially in northern waters. Of particular interest in costume use are the *Greenland* (*Harp*) *seal*, where the white and white and grey pelts of the young seals are used to make coats, the *sea-lion* (*hair seal*), which is used chiefly for leather and the *fur seal*, which is the most important. Fur seals are smaller, up to six to seven feet long, and have a brown or black, thick, hard-wearing fur with coarse guard hairs which have to be plucked out. The *Alaska seal* has the best fur.

Sheep – the *moufflon* is the European wild sheep, found now in Corsica and Sardinia. It has a short wool coat used for costume. The *merino sheep* is the most important breed for fine wool. It is sheared and dyed to imitate more expensive furs. The breed originated in Spain but is now found all over the world.

Skunk – an American member of the weasel family about two feet long with a glossy, black fur. The *spotted skunk* or *civet* is smaller.

Squirrel – a small rodent found nearly all over the world. Many different species, notably the European *red squirrel* and the American *grey squirrel*, which has now almost supplanted the smaller red species in Britain. A soft, silky fur with long hairs in the tail. *Vair* was the medieval name for the grey and white Russian squirrel. In England the fur was called *miniver* in the thirteenth and fourteenth centuries: a corruption of the French *menu-vair*.

Stoat – a little larger than its close relative, the weasel, it has a body about ten inches long and a tail of five inches. Its fur is brown with white underbelly, but, in northern areas, its winter coat is pure white and it is highly valued as ermine (see *Ermine*).

Vicuña – like the guanaco, a wild llama inhabiting the Andes but a smaller animal with a finer, silky coat.

Weasel – the European weasel is so small (six to seven inches long) that it is not much valued for its fur. The larger members of its family, on the other hand, are highly valued. See marten, mink, skunk, stoat (ermine), wolverine.

Wolf – member of the dog family to be found in Europe, Asia, Africa and America, especially in the northern regions where the fur is best. The European wolf is now found only in Scandinavia, Eastern Europe and in the wilder parts of Western Europe; it resembles an Alsatian. The larger North American *Timber Wolf* or *Grey Wolf* is still to be found in numbers in Northern Canada and Alaska.

Wolverine – the largest member of the weasel family, it is found in the northern areas of Europe and America. About four feet long, including its tail, it has dark brown fur which is thick and hard-wearing. It is particularly valued in Arctic regions for the warmth of its dense fur.

SYNTHETIC FURS In the first half of the twentieth century several developments took place to make a less costly fur coat available to a larger percentage of the population as well as introducing a greater variety in furs: fur-farming provided a larger quantity of desirable animals and new colours were produced by mutations and dyeing techniques. Since the Second

Guanaco (wild llama). South America, 5¼ ft. tall

Wildcat, Scotland

Chinchilla, Andes. 9–12 inches long

Mole, Europe. About 6 inches long

Polecat, Europe. About 15 inches long

FUSTANELLA
Royal palace guard, Athens

World War the accent has been on producing the imitation fur. At first, plastic filaments were attached to a base of shorn sheepskin. Such 'furs' were hard-wearing, resistant to moths, were cheaper and could be made in a wide range of colours and surfaces.

The modern approach took the imitation fur a stage further to a totally synthetic fur which was made entirely from natural and synthetic fibres and could imitate a genuine fur or give a totally different result. The more bizarre shades and textures were a characteristic of the 1960s. Now the accent is more on a successful imitation of a prized fur. Among such successes are synthetic broadtail, chinchilla, pony, squirrel, beaver, leopard, mole and ermine.

There are several types of pile from which fur fabrics are made. They can be woven, tufted, flocked and sliver-knit. In the last-named, rapidly expanding industry, the fabric is made from three component parts: the fibre, which produces the surface 'fur', the yarn which makes its backing and the chemical emulsion which is applied to coat the backing in order to ensure fibre adhesion and fabric stability. The fibre is made from a knitted process and is then slit and sheared to give the desired pile. Variations in texture pattern such as waves, curls and movement of the pile can be created by heat tumbling processes. Different materials can be used for the fibre, of which acrylics and polyesters are the most usual.

Fustanella

A full, stiffly pleated skirt of white cotton or linen worn by men in Greece as in, for example, the Highland soldier (*evzone*) or the royal palace guard. Derived from the diminutive of the Greek word φουστάνι (foustani), Albanian, *fustan*.

Fustian

In Britain fustian dates from Norman times; it was a coarse cloth made from cotton and flax. More recently it is a heavy, twilled cotton material, dyed in a plain dark dull green or brown. *Fustian of Naples*, or *fustianapes*, was a mock or cotton velvet, made in Naples from the time of the Middle Ages.

G

GAITER
Gaiter, 1880

Gabardine, gaberdine

1) A fitted *coat* with sleeves introduced to Europe from the Orient via Venice during the Middle Ages. The sleeves were wide and the coat, which was buttoned up the centre front, was often held by a sash or belt at the waist. The word stems from the Arabic *gaba*. Such a loose overcoat continued in general use in Europe until about 1550, after which time it became a garment for the poor, used as a covering in inclement weather. The English word seems to stem more directly, during the fifteenth and sixteenth centuries, from the Spanish *gabardina*, meaning a cassock or cloak, and the garment was looser and wider at this time.

2) A similar *outer covering* was worn by the Jews from the Middle Ages onwards. It was generally of black cloth or silk and was ankle-length.

3) In the twentieth century the word is given to a cotton or rayon *fabric* which is waterproofed before weaving. The term can be used for the fabric and also for the rainwear made from it.

Gaiter

A covering for the ankle and lower leg made of cloth, leather, cashmere or elasti-

1 European medieval dress: The tapestry depicts women wearing the voluminous
houppelande and the heart-shaped turban headdress with dangling liripipe. Note the
men's chaperon hoods and neckchains. (*The courting scene from Falconry, one of the
Devonshire Hunting Tapestries c.* 1430)

2 Queen Elizabeth I: Typical of the richness of Elizabethan court dress is the pearl and embroidered ornamentation, the padded sleeves, the wide farthingale and the stiffened white lace circular collar. (*Elizabeth I 1533–1603* by or after George Gower *c.* 1588)

3 Dutch costume 1627–30: Showing the transition in men's dress in Western Europe between the constricted doublet, trunk hose and ruff of the early 17th century and the casual, romantic, Cavalier attire of the years 1630–45. Note the falling ruff, soft boots and carelessly draped cloaks. (*Constanijn Huygens and his (?) clerk* by Thomas de Keyser)

4 A domestic breakfast scene: The women are wearing the *robe à la française*. Note also the children's dress and that of the doll. (*Le déjeuner* by François Boucher, 1739)

5 Japanese dress: 18th-century dress showing kimono, hakama and obi. Note coiffure styles. (*The artist, painting a landscape* by Utamaro)

6 The garden scene: Illustrates the later crinoline gowns of the 1860s when the fullness was directed towards the back, foreshadowing the bustle of the 1870s. The seated figure elegantly displays how a woman should descend to the level of the lawn. (*Au jardin* by Claude Monet)

7 Chinese dress: Manchu woman's informal court robe (Ch'ang-fu) in satin embroidered in coloured silks. Late 19th century

8 North American Indian dress: Plains Indians, Blackfoot tribe; man's buckskin shirt and leggings decorated with aniline-dyed quills, horsehair tassels, strips of serge cloth and thong fringes, with rank markings of white weasel skin. Late 19th century (Reservation period)

cated material. Worn intermittently by both sexes from the late eighteenth until the early twentieth century. Such a covering was fitting at the ankle and was generally buttoned down the outer side; it extended over the top of the boot or shoe (see also *Spats*).

Gallant, galant

In the seventeenth century the ribbon loops, bows and clusters which decorated the entire costume of both sexes, but especially that of the men, from the hair and hats to the ties on the shoes.

Galligaskin

1) Wide and/or padded hose or breeches worn by men in the sixteenth and seventeenth centuries.
2) In the nineteenth century the term was applied to a type of fitting leggings or long gaiters, made of leather, which reached to mid-calf and were buckled and strapped under the foot.

Galloon

A narrow, closely woven braid of silk, cotton or gold or silver thread. Used for finishing, edging and decorating garments.

Galoshes

A wooden shoe, patten or clog fastened to the foot with leather straps to protect the elegant shoes from mud, dirt and rough pavements. Worn from ancient Roman times onwards. In modern form galoshes serve the same purpose but are overshoes of rubber, lined with canvas. The man's galosh is a complete overshoe, the woman's is generally lighter, of a plastic material, and can be tied at the ankle by a drawstring or zipped up the side. The most common rubber design has a sling back.

Gamashes

A kind of long leggings worn to protect the wearer, whether riding or walking, from the mud and wet. Made of cloth and buttoned or laced down the outer leg. Gamashes were in use from the late sixteenth until the eighteenth century; during the seventeenth century a sole was added

to the foot portion. A rougher, loose gamash, made of coarse linen, was worn by peasants and farmers.

Gambado

A protection for the rider's leg while mounted on a horse. The gambado was made of a heavy, usually black, leather and resembled a wide outer half of a boot, which was attached to the saddle and harness (see illustration under *Boot*).

Gamurra

The woman's undergown worn in Renaissance Italy in the fifteenth and sixteenth centuries. It had long sleeves and a bell-shaped skirt while the overgown, the *cioppa*, was of richer material, elegantly embroidered. This had a train, falling from the high waistline, and the sleeves floated behind the arm which displayed the gamurra sleeves.

Gandura, gandoura, gondourah

An East African undergarment made of white linen, silk or wool. Worn under a burnous (see burnous under *Cloak*).

Garde-corps

A thirteenth century garment which was

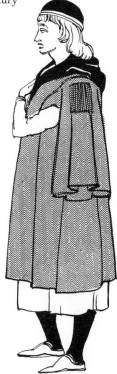

loose and unbelted and worn over an under-tunic. It was three-quarter or ankle-length and had wide sleeves which were pleated or gathered at the shoulder then slit in front to allow the arm to pass through, while the remainder of the material hung in folds behind. Such garments might be fur-lined for winter wear.

Garibaldi blouse or shirt

The visit of Giuseppe Garibaldi to England in 1863 gave impetus to the fashionable mode in Europe and America of the time to adapt his famous red shirt and pill-box hat to feminine modes. There were a number of variations on the Garibaldi blouse or shirtwaist but they were all of red wool decorated with black braid and had full sleeves gathered into fitting cuffs at the wrist, a small, turn-down collar and were buttoned up the centre front.

Garment

Now, any article of wearing apparel. Derived from the old French word *garnement*, which was the term for denoting each of the items of wear comprised in the medieval word *robe*; this term referred to the clothes possessed by a person – later, *wardrobe*.

Garnache

A medieval outer garment or surcoat worn in cold weather. It was ankle-length and had wide, elbow-length sleeves cut in one with the garment, like a cape. The fourteenth century version, with two tongue-shaped fur tabs on each side of the neck opening is more usually referred to as a *housse*.

Garnet

A crystalline gem-stone used widely in jewellery, of which the favoured colour is a deep, transparent red. The name is thought to have derived from pomegranate, because the colour resembles that of the fruit pulp.

Garniture

Ornament or trimming added to costume, for example, flowers, ribbons, jewellery.

GARIBALDI BLOUSE
Garibaldi red blouse, 1864

GAUGING, SHIRRING
Dress decorated by gauging, German, 1880

GARTER
Gold, jewelled garter, English, 1380

Garter

A tie or band fastened round the leg to hold up or in place a sock or stocking. Worn by both sexes until they were replaced, late in the nineteenth century, by elastic suspenders. Men's garters, being visible, were, in several periods of costume, ostentatiously decorative. In the seventeenth century especially, they took the form of ribbon, silk or velvet sashes with fringed ends, tied below the knee in large bow knots with long, hanging ends. Later in the century, ribbon clusters finished the outer side of the garter.

Gauge

A scale of measurement or a standard measure to which an article must conform. In costume the term is used particularly with regard to stockings where the gauge is the number of stitches in a given measured section of fabric: the higher the gauge number, the stronger the stocking.

Gauging, gaging, shirring

A series of close parallel lines of running stitches sewn in a garment to make the material between set in gathers. A form of decoration popularly employed in the nineteenth century for dresses and bonnets.

Ribbon loop garters, French, *c.*1660.

Fringed sash garters, French, 1637

White ribbon garters, English, 1602

Gauze

A sheer, transparent fabric of cotton, silk, linen or rayon. Used since the early Middle Ages for veils and overdresses.

Gem

A term used to denote certain materials which possess a beauty inherent in their colour, brilliance, hardness and rarity which has led to their use through the ages as items of personal adornment. A gem is a stone which has been cut and polished to be placed in a setting and used as jewellery. In the natural state such minerals are called gem-stones.

Specific gem-stones are termed precious stones; these include the diamond, ruby, emerald and sapphire. Others, such as amethyst, opal, aquamarine and topaz, are called semi-precious stones. Hard natural materials, some carved in relief or intaglio, are also classed as gems. The pearl is one example, in this case of animal origin; a cameo, carved in relief in the shell of a molluscous animal, is another. All the precious stones have been successfully synthesized. Such synthetic gem-stones, though made artificially, possess the ap-

pearance as well as the physical and chemical properties of the natural mineral.

From the times of the ancient civilizations gem-stones have been carved and cut to increase their beauty. Lapidary work is the name given to this art of cutting, polishing and engraving gem-stones. The Assyrians and Babylonians carved engraved seals in cylindrical form while the Egyptians carved ones in scarab design. Greek cutters reached a high standard of craftsmanship, carrying out their best work by hand with a sapphire point, though they also used a bow-drill fed with sapphire dust. Such bow-drills had been in use much earlier in Mesopotamia. Quality of lapidary craftsmanship declined in the later Roman and the Byzantine periods but revived markedly with the Renaissance.

Until the later Middle Ages stones were generally polished and cut *en cabochon*, that is, in a smoothly rounded convex form, then mounted in circular or oval settings. The cabochon method is still used, cut and polished, but not faceted, especially for opaque, translucent and transparent stones, such as opals.

Plane faceted cutting is a later develop-

GIBSON GIRL
Gibson girl, 1904

GIRDLE
Double girdle of leather and silk cord, French, c.1150

ment; it gives brilliance to the gem by enhancing internal reflections of light. Numerous facets are cut to bring out the colour and quality of the stone to the best advantage. Some of the material of the stone has to be sacrificed as it is cut away to give the desired form. Among the many possible designs in cutting, developed from the sixteenth century onwards, the baguette, the brilliant, the rose or rosette and the table-cut are the most commonly employed. The baguette cut has a flat top and is shaped in a long rectangle, cut with four or more facets. The brilliant is in the form of a double pyramid or cone, with a truncated top and the sides cut into more than 50 facets. It is especially used for larger diamonds. Smaller diamonds and quality garnets are often cut in the rose, which is in the form of a lower pyramid with grouped facets. The table-cut is used especially for emeralds, rubies and sapphires. The stone is generally cut in a square or rectangle, with facets cut on the under side of the gem. Modern cutting is most usually done by a lathe, fitted with an iron point dusted with powdered diamonds.

The unit of weight for gem-stones is the carat. For centuries there was no standardization of the carat weight as the weighing was originally done by grains or seeds. Since these were not of uniform size and weight, the carat standard set up varied from one gem centre to another. Just before the First World War the USA adopted the metric carat weighing 200 milligrams and this has since been a general standard throughout the world.

Genappe

A worsted yarn used in the manufacture of braid and fringing, where it could be combined with silk. Named after Genappe in Belgium, its original place of manufacture.

Geneva

This Swiss city gave its name to several items of clothing worn by Swiss Calvinists of the late sixteenth and early seventeenth centuries; chief of these were:
1) *Geneva hat*: a tall-crowned, black, Puritan style.

2) *Geneva bands*: a pair of plain white lawn bands worn at the neck.
3) *Geneva gown*: the black, clerical gown which accompanied the bands.

Gew-gaw

A pretty, showy trinket or bauble of no value.

Gibson girl

A fashion created in the drawings of the American artist Charles Dana Gibson (1867–1944). She represented the modern American girl of the years 1902–8 and was illustrated wearing a tailored skirt and blouse, belted tightly at a tiny waist and with a tie or scarf at the neck. She wore the fashionable pompadour hairstyle and was often shown in an outdoor attire in jacket, straw hat and gloves. The fashion was short-lived but immensely and internationally popular.

Gilet

French word for waistcoat. In present-day dress, a lady's gilet is a sleeveless blouse or bodice front worn under a suitjacket.

Gimp, guimp

1) An edging *braid* made of cotton, silk or wool with a metal thread running through it and used as a trimming for garments. Beads and spangles are often threaded into the gimp edging.
2) The coarser *thread* which outlines the design in lace-making.
3) In the Middle Ages a *neckcovering* worn especially by widows and nuns (see also *Wimple*). In the late nineteenth century referred to a tulle, gauze or lace inset or bodice front to a gown.

Girdle

A belt for the waist or hips worn from the early Middle Ages, made of metal, leather, fabric or cord and often with one or two hanging ends. In the sixteenth century in particular, the lady's girdle hung down in the centre front of the dress and terminated in a pomander, jewel, mirror or book (see also *Pomander*). Often articles were attached to or were suspended from the belt, especially a purse, keys and a mirror. In modern times, a girdle is a lightweight, stretch belt or corset, worn as underwear and to which, before the advent of tights, suspenders were attached to support the stockings (see *Underwear*).

Glazed fabric

A material to which a gloss has been applied by means of treatment with paraffin then passage through heated rollers.

Gloves

A shaped covering for the hand with usually a separate sheath for each finger.

Gloves have been worn from ancient times as protection and for ornamentation, but in Mediterranean climates were not necessary for warmth. In ancient Egypt, Greece and Rome gloves were worn by both sexes for protection at work. Gloves were also necessary for hunting and for military use.

In Europe, in the early Middle Ages, gloves were a symbol of power in ecclesiastical and civil dress. This was especially so with royalty and high dignitaries of the Church, where such gloves were usually made of deerskin or sheepskin. They played a part in the formalities of investiture of a knight or a bishop and were presented to holders of civil appointments on specific occasions. From a more practical viewpoint gloves were worn for hawking and falconry. Here, a strong leather gauntleted glove was adopted, partly to provide a perch for the bird and partly as a protection from its talons. Decorated tassels often depended from such gauntlets. In the early Middle Ages, in general, most people wore mittens rather than gloves, with the hand in one section and a separate part for the thumb. Indeed, gloves were only seen with medieval dress on the wealthy, as sleeves were long, covering the hand to the first row of knuckles.

With the Renaissance, Italy led with such elegant items of dress as perfumed gloves. As early as the fourteenth century Venice had established itself as the meeting place

Queen Jane Seymour, 1536. Gold and jewelled girdle

Black jewelled girdle with leather purse, Spanish, 1450

Jewelled metal girdle, English, *c*.1360

Gold girdle with dependent gold bells and chains, German, *c*.1465.

between east and west and from here luxury goods flowed westwards. It was, therefore, in Venice and in Genoa, that the nobility were first seen wearing such items as perfumed gloves made of fine coloured leathers.

By the sixteenth century in Europe gloves were more often carried or worn by the nobility. These were wrist-length in general, made of leather, suède or kid. For special occasions or for men of particular rank, gloves could be gauntleted, embroidered, jewelled and fringed. Spanish leather was especially favoured and perfumed gloves were very fashionable. Among those designed particularly for working use, archery gloves were of a special pattern. Made to be worn in conjunction with normal gloves, these possessed three reinforced leather fingerstalls, which were buttoned round the wrist from a cross-strap in order to provide protection to the fingers where needed.

In the seventeenth century the nobility wore gauntleted gloves as an essential part of their costume. Such gloves were embroidered, tasselled and fringed and were made of the finest leather with gauntlets often of satin or stiffened silk. Velvet or knitted silk or wool gloves were also worn. The best examples were imported from Spain and were perfumed. They were in use with both sexes. Such styles of gloves, wrist or gauntlet-length, continued in fashion in high society during the eighteenth century but in the later years, with the classical influence on dress at the time of the French Revolution and Directoire years, ladies wore long gloves with the sleeveless or short-sleeved dresses of the time. These gloves were usually white or in pastel shades, in kid or silk, and they reached to above the elbow. They were fitting and often buttoned down the outer side.

The nineteenth century was very much an age when gloves had to be worn by gentlemen and ladies, indoors and out. Strict rules of etiquette were laid down with regard to the colour, length, material etc. for such gloves, as well as when they should be worn or carried. For men, gloves were short and, normally, coloured for day wear and white in the evenings. For ladies, the length depended upon the costume; during the day, with long-sleeved gowns, gloves were wrist-length, but with the short sleeves of evening dresses gloves reached to the elbow or above. Black silk or net mittens were also worn indoors in the day-time. Etiquette prescribed that a lady's hand should be covered at all times.

Until the nineteenth century most glove styles were of the pull-on type with no fastening, but after 1800 the short, wrist-length gloves were generally buttoned or fastened by cords. Men's gloves were more usually held in place by a clasp or stud. The glove-band or glove-string was a strap or ribbon used in the seventeenth and eighteenth centuries to confine the glove at the wrist or arm; it was tied or buckled to hold the glove in place.

A glove-stretcher is a pair of wooden or ivory scissors or tweezers made to stretch the fingers of elegant, closely-fitting gloves before donning.

The method of sewing a glove is for the seams to be raised on the outside of the material and raised with stitching on each side. This is known as the glover's stitch and is referred to in surgery where the lips of a wound are sewn upwards in glover's style.

Many customs and superstitions have grown up over the ages with regard to gloves. For example, it has been customary to give a pair of gloves as a present or claim them as a forfeit. Gloves have traditionally been distributed as favours at a wedding. In the Middle Ages gloves were worn as favours in a knight's helmet at a tournament. Gloves have been used as a pledge and have been thrown down as a challenge.

Gold, gold cloth, gold lace

From earliest times gold has attracted man by its lustre, its brilliance, its density and its immutability. It was mined and used to make beautiful objects, which included jewellery, by all the ancient civilizations, who valued it highly. After Bronze Age man had discovered the art of melting

Velvet sideless
gown (surcoat)
with fur edging,
worn over fitting
gown (cotehardie),
English, 1385

Dark velvet gown
with fur lining in
the skirt buttoned
up at the back,
English, c.1495

Flowered silk gown
over French (wheel)
farthingale,
English, 1610

Black gown with
gold and black
underskirt, gold
sleeves, Danish,
1635

Dark red gown
with white collar
and jewelled belt,
English, c.1435

Dark silk gown
with lace band
(collar) and pink
taffeta underskirt,
English, 1638–49

Deep rose velvet
gown with fur
edging and cuffs
worn over Spanish
farthingale,
French, c.1575

Dark velvet gown
with grey fur
trimming over
Spanish farthingale,
English, 1560

Robe à la Polonaise, French, 1781

Robe à l'Italienne. Gold and blue, patterned over plain underskirt, Flemish, 1515–20

Robe battante or sacque gown, English, 1730

Red gown with gold all-over pattern, white lace collar and sleeve ruffles, French, 1685

Cream silk gown with lace overlay. Self-colour ribbon decoration, Spanish, 1820

Contouche or sacque gown in lavender silk, dark green velvet bows, English, 1720

Robe à la Française or Watteau gown. Pink silk, embroidered in sprig pattern, English, 1750–60

Classical style of gown in white with blue belt and decoration. Cashmere shawl in red, gold and black, English, 1800

Robe à l'Anglaise of white and pink muslin over dark green satin petticoat, white fichu, English, 1783

Blue silk afternoon dress with white spot pattern. Bustle gown with apron front. Black and blue banding and fringing, English, 1870

Crinoline ball gown of white tarlatan with flounces and rosebud trimming. Amber taffeta overskirt and bodice, English, 1859

Blue silk tunic gown with kimono bodice and peg-top skirt, English, 1913

Evening gown of white poplin with self-colour sprig pattern, English, 1844

Afternoon dress of blue and white striped silk, English, 1847

Day dress in satin damask of blue and gold. Bolero jacket, leg-of-mutton sleeves, English, 1896

Dark brown silk afternoon dress draped up to show lining of floral pattern in apple green, brown and red. Underskirt of pale copper silk, fringed and pleated, English, 1875

Printed georgette
gown in brown,
orange and yellow,
English, 1936

Printed chiffon
afternoon gown in
shades of pink,
black satin
trimmings, French,
1926

Cerise and white
satin afternoon
gown. Double
tiered tunic skirt
with peg-top
underskirt,
English, 1914

Silver grey nylon
net evening gown,
English, 1958

Pale blue rayon
gown with white
spot pattern,
English, 1943

the ears by stiffeners inserted in the side seams. Sleeves were long and full and skirts extremely long. Gowns were elaborately decorated with lace, embroidery, fringe and fur. Typical of the age was the Edwardian tea gown.

In the second decade of the century gown styles changed quickly; fashions came and went before they had time to become established. There was a desire for change, but the direction of this was not yet clear. All kinds of unsuitable, uncomfortable and outré skirts were designed, ranging from the peg-top, the hobble, and the lampshade to the harem and tunic styles.

After the War, in the 1920s, reaction against nineteenth century restriction in dress was acute and women demanded functional, comfortable clothes and a freedom to work and behave as men did. They got their comfortable, ease-of-movement clothes but, over-anxious to appear as capable as men, adopted clothes which were unfeminine. For 10 years they hid the attributes of femininity given to them by nature: breasts, sloping shoulders, small waist, ample hips, flowing hair. To assert their new-found freedom, women flattened their breasts by bands, wore tubular unwaisted dresses, exposed their legs and cut their hair. The fashionable figure was thin rather than slim, one needed a slender neck, no bosom, no hips and twiggy legs.

Throughout the 1920s, gowns were straight and tubular; there was little decoration. The chief variation was in the hem-line which was the same for day and evening wear. In 1920–1 the skirt was ankle-length; from 1922 the hem rose steadily, reaching its shortest level, just covering the knee, in 1927. Designers then tried to lower it and give variety by introducing longer panels of draped fabric at sides and back, especially in evening gowns. The actual skirt hem-line did not begin its descent until 1929–30. The natural waist-line was unmarked between 1921 and 1930. The bodice was tubular and loose and a belt was worn low on the hips; it was decorated by a cockade or plaque. Sleeves were long and fitting, very short or the dress was sleeveless with, probably, a floating panel of material hanging behind the arm. Necklines were quite plain in a low V, bateau or square. Some evening gowns had low V backs also.

Femininity returned with the 1930s. The slim figure was still fashionable but the waistline was marked at its natural level and clothes were cut to cling to the figure, in pleats, gores or on the cross. Breasts were no longer flattened and, by 1937, the uplift bra had begun to define them. The hem-line descended by then to about eight inches above the ground. Evening gowns were long, often backless and halter necklines were fashionable; in 1938–9 the strapless evening gown with boned bodice was introduced.

War-time styles in the 1940s were strongly influenced by the need for practicability and by women's uniforms. The hem-line rose to just below the knee, skirts were straight, shoulders were padded to make a square silhouette, dresses were belted at a natural waistline. Gowns were comfortable and summer and party dresses provided some femininity in their swathed bodices and gathered skirts.

Sensitive to the yearning of women all over Europe for a return to pretty, feminine clothes, Christian Dior launched his 'New Look' in 1947. His designs could not have presented a greater contrast to the clothes of the war years. The new line was feminine, the shoulders unpadded and sloping, the waist closely defined, the bosom uplifted, the hips stressed and the skirt full and long, extending to 12 inches above the ground. Under these swinging skirts were worn flounced taffeta petticoats, a return of the frou-frou sound of the *fin de siècle*.

The 'New Look' gown was short-lived for it was not sufficiently practical for a new generation of women, most of whom now had jobs and professions, but it was a turning-point and there was no going back to padded shoulders and uniform appearance. Since 1950 gown design has changed quickly and there has been great variety in clothes to wear for day-time, work-time, parties and holidays and, above all, clothes for all age groups. There have also been

Lavender crêpe gown in 'New Look' style, English, 1947–8

Nylon jersey maxi gown in white, green and orange, English, 1971

Orlon knitted gown in sheath or shift style, orange and cream stripes, English, 1967

Sapphire blue taffeta dinner gown, English, 1948

GREECE (ANCIENT)
Man in double-girded chiton and chlamys, petasos slung on back of shoulders

Man in long chiton with himation on top

Himation type of cloak wrapped round body and head. Boeotian straw hat on top

Ungirded peplos

Girded peplos

Chiton and himation

contrasts in line and shape from the straight shift or sheath dress derived from the Chinese *cheongsam* (see *Chinese dress*) to the very feminine full-skirted cocktail dresses – ballet-length and long – of the 1950s, from the most abbreviated mini-skirted dresses to the long maxi. Specific lengths or necklines for day or evening wear, formal or leisure clothes, have been abandoned. A long dress may be an elegant, formal evening gown or it might be a summer design in cotton for a holiday; equally, a short, almost mini-length dress can be worn for cocktails or to do the morning shopping. It is the fabric, the colour, the style and the wearer which make the gown right for the occasion.

Grecian bend

An affected stance or posture where the body is pushed or bent forward at the hips. In feminine dress this occurred due to the excessive corseting practised in order to produce a tiny waist. Chief examples were in the 1870s with the bustle gowns and the early years of the twentieth century when the S-bend corset was adopted (see *Corset*).

Greece (ancient)

For centuries the different civilizations in mainland and island Greece, together with Asia Minor and North Africa, had co-existed, the costume of each influencing the others. Classical dress was the outcome by the sixth century BC. It had developed chiefly from the primitive Dorian styles and was then refined by Ionian influence. The Dorians invaded Crete and the Peloponnese from about 1200 BC. They were a northern race from Illyria, wearing a simple, primitive costume made of woollen cloth woven from the wool of the mountain sheep of the region from whence they came. Their unsewn garments were pinned on the shoulder and wrapped round the body. Later, the dress of the mainland peoples was influenced by those in Asia Minor who experienced more extreme temperatures and who introduced cloaks with hoods, the Phrygian cap with a point on top, the wide-brimmed hat and banded leg coverings. Later still a new culture established itself in Greece which was called Ionian. These peoples were much less primitive than the Dorians. They developed a quality textile industry in wools and linen, making fine materials which were suited to a draped costume.

Classical dress, with which we are familiar from the wealth of vases and sculpture to be seen in the museums of the western world, is the costume which had evolved by the sixth century BC and was worn until the second century BC when it was merged with Roman styles. It is a draped costume; one in which there is little sewing, the garments for both sexes being similar and consisting of different fabrics and sizes which are pinned on the shoulders and are held in place by girdles. The dress is of the utmost simplicity in basis but of the greatest variety in the method of wearing. There is no artificiality of silhouette in corseting or padding and no stiffening of the materials. The lines are entirely natural but sophisticated. The garments lend themselves to adaptation satisfactory to the personal taste of each individual. The only aids to draping are pins (see *Fibula*), girdles and weights for the hems and corners. There is a close affinity between the costume of the Greeks and their art and architecture. In all three modes of expression the basis is simple but the handling of the style requires precision and experience to reach perfection. The introduction of fine linens by the fifth century BC led to the pleating of material as well as simple draping. The rectangular piece of fabric was set into the required pleats, then twisted and tied at each end to maintain it in position, for several hours. The use of a thin starch and then allowing the fabric to dry in the sun assisted in the longer maintenance of the pleats when the garment was worn. This treatment was the most common for the feminine long tunic. With Alexander the Great's conquests in India, fine cotton and silk were introduced; these delicate fabrics were excellent for pleating and draping.

Not a great deal is known about the colours of Greek dress. Neither sculpture nor vases (which are in black, white and red) give information. There are only literary references to guide us and the knowledge that buildings and ornaments were originally brightly painted, so it is reasonable to believe that in a country with brilliant Mediterranean sunlight, costume would have been coloured also. From literary sources we have reference to white, yellow, red, different shades of mauve and purple, green, black, grey and golden brown. We also read of patterns and borders of flowers, stripes, circles and lozenges. Cloaks appear to have been in darker colours, tunics light.

The clothes worn by men and women were almost the same except that the masculine tunic was usually knee-length and the feminine one reached the ankles or the ground. Early Dorian tunics were simple rectangles of wool, fastened on one or both shoulders by a fibula so that material hung ungirded. Sometimes the garment was sewn at one side and left open on the other. Men of action wore the tunic pinned on one shoulder only to give freedom of movement. A short version of this tunic, open down the right side and leaving this shoulder bare, continued in use as the working man's and slaves' tunic: it was called the *exomis*. The later, Ionian tunic was the *chiton*, first made of wool and later of thinner materials in linen and cotton. Earlier examples were sleeveless, pinned at the shoulder and the material held at the waist by a girdle. Men often adopted the double girdle with one belt round the waist and a lower one at the hips with the material bloused in between. For men the *chiton* reached the knees, for women it was long and generally seamed at one or both sides below the waist. Later still the *chiton* was adapted to provide elbow-length sleeves by the use of wider rectangles of material which were fastened by fibulae at intervals between shoulder and elbow. Women wore this style of *chiton* a lot but for men it was generally reserved for ceremonial use when it was also ankle-length.

The feminine equivalent of the simple, loose Dorian tunic was the *peplos*. This was made of two pieces of fabric, pinned together on each shoulder and hanging loose to the ankles. In later years the ground-length *chiton* was worn and, often on top of this, a *peplos* which could hang loose to just below the waist or could be longer and be enclosed with the waist girdle. An alternative form of *chiton* was the *diploidion* where the fabric was very long so that the top part was folded over making the bodice section double. The extra material then hung loose over a waistbelt. The word could be applied to the whole garment or the folded portion only.

There were two chief forms of cloak or wrap; the *chlamys* of Dorian origin, which was of dark wool and pinned on the shoulder or at the throat and was worn chiefly by men, and the *himation*, which was larger and usually worn draped over the left shoulder and around the body. In earlier days this was the sole garment. It is also often seen in sculpture draped in this manner as the attire of the later period for philosophers and statesmen. Women wore the *himation* which they draped round the body in various ways and part of it was often used to drape over the head also. Both types of cloak could be weighted at the corners to assist draping and to hold them down in inclement weather.

Knowledge of undergarments worn is inadequate. Sculpture does not show these so we must rely upon literary sources which refer to a band of linen wound round the waist and stomach to control the figure and a similar breast band (see *Underwear*). For detailed information on footwear, hair and hat styles etc. in Greek dress (see also *Boot, Cap, Cosmetics, Hat, Jewellery* and *Sandal*).

Grenadine
A silk or silk and wool textile used during the nineteenth century for dresses, blouses and shawls.

Guimpe
In the late nineteenth century, a term used to describe the chemisette of white lawn, batiste or tulle designed to cover the neck of décolleté dresses. Worn especially in the USA by young people and little girls.

Gusset
Originally, in armour, a piece of flexible material designed to fit into the space between the joints of two sections of mail. In costume, a triangular piece of material let into a garment to give ease of movement or to strengthen or enlarge the area.

Haberdashery
The goods and wares sold by a haberdasher. From Anglo-Saxon times these comprised a variety of small wares. From the sixteenth century some of these wares, notably caps and hats, were handled by other tradesmen, such as the hatter, and haberdashery comprised small articles pertaining to dress, such as ribbons, tape, thread, wools and fastenings.

Habit
From early times denoted general dress or clothing. Later the term came to be used for the attire of a specific profession or rank. Still in limited use as, for example, a religious habit or riding habit.

Hair net
An ancient accessory made of silk many centuries ago in China. The hair has been

confined by nets in most ages since that time. The medieval head-dress included a net or caul (see *Caul*). The modern hair net for sleeping is made of nylon and an invisible type for day wear is made of very fine nylon thread or human hair.

Hair piece

The addition of a switch of false hair has been used to augment the coiffure of both sexes through the ages. This is distinct from a wig which describes a complete false hair cover (see *Wig*). Different names have been adopted from time to time as euphemisms for false hair: transformation, switch, fall, corner.

Hairpin

From earliest times women have used hairpins to hold their long hair in position. These have been made of various metals, bone, wood, ivory and shell in different designs based on a bodkin form. With the short hairstyles of the 1920s a hair grip (kirbigrip or bobby pin) was used instead. Fine wire crinkled hairpins in U-shape have persisted during the twentieth century for women who prefer to wear their hair long.

Hairstyles (coiffure)

WOMEN Throughout history, although women's hair has been dressed, curled, coloured and crimped in every conceivable manner and enhanced with every kind of embellishment, it was not until after the First World War that it was worn short. Previously parts of the hair framing the face had been stylishly trimmed to make a forehead fringe or to give side curls, but the main part of the tresses had been allowed to reach their full natural length and were then dressed in a variety of ways for, it is clear, not only is long hair more feminine in appearance, but it lends itself to greater variety of style. At certain times and under a number of cultures the hair of both men and women was cut very short, or even shaven, and a complete wig replaced the natural coiffure. These modes, which include the Egyptian designs and those of eighteenth century Europe, are described under *Wig*.

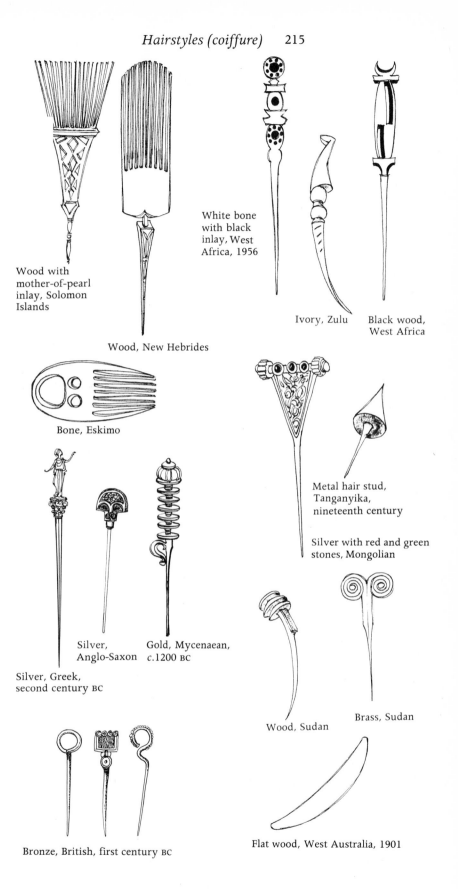

Wood with mother-of-pearl inlay, Solomon Islands

Wood, New Hebrides

White bone with black inlay, West Africa, 1956

Ivory, Zulu

Black wood, West Africa

Bone, Eskimo

Silver, Greek, second century BC

Silver, Anglo-Saxon

Gold, Mycenaean, c.1200 BC

Metal hair stud, Tanganyika, nineteenth century

Silver with red and green stones, Mongolian

Wood, Sudan

Brass, Sudan

Bronze, British, first century BC

Flat wood, West Australia, 1901

Ladies' hair was carefully and, often, elaborately dressed in the ancient civilizations. Assyrian women, like their menfolk, dressed their hair in a tightly curled and ringleted manner. The Minoans of Crete also built up an elaborate coiffure. The long hair was arranged in spiral curls and ringlets in front, falling on to the breasts and neck, while the remainder was piled high at the back, held in place by ribbons, flowers, jewels and metal pins. It then hung down the back loose or was braided. Greek women wore simpler styles. The hair could be curled on the forehead and at the sides or parted in the centre and drawn back in waves to a chignon at the nape. The word *chignon* refers to a manner of twisting the hair into a knot either at the nape or nearer the crown of the head. It is a style which has recurred during the history of coiffure design. Alternatively, Greek women wore a fillet round the brow and tucked the back hair into this. Hair was fastened by bone, ivory or gold pins. Many women wore wigs (see *Wig*) or false hair added to their own to alter the shape of the coiffure; they also dyed their hair and decorated it with flowers, jewels, stephanes and bands of material.

The Etruscans, like the Minoans, gave great care and attention to the coiffure, which was often dyed. Women dressed their hair in corkscrew curls on the forehead and temples, with the rest of the hair long, either confined in a net at the nape, hanging loose down the back or in plaits or ringlets over the shoulders and back. An alternative mode was a centre parting with hair waved back at the sides. Pins controlled the styles and decoration was by fillets, ribbons and plumes. Under the Republic, Roman ladies dressed their hair simply, in Greek styles, most commonly with a centre parting and a chignon at the nape. In Imperial Rome styles became more complex. The coiffure was dressed in a mass of curls on top in front or in rows of waves and was drawn back to ringlets and/or braided plaits. After a time noblewomen adopted such complicated coiffures that they required the daily attentions of several slaves and a stylist to dress it. The hairstyle was augmented by switches and pads, it was dyed and sometimes covered by a wig (see *Wig*), and was held in place by nets, combs, pins and pomade. Different colours of hair were currently fashionable; sometimes black was in demand, red was mostly favoured, while blonde was in vogue during the Gallic and Teutonic campaigns. Under the Byzantine Empire noble ladies more often encased their hair in a silk cap or a pearl net so that little of the hair was visible.

During the centuries that followed the collapse of the Roman Empire in Europe and through the early Middle Ages women grew their hair very long. In the earlier years it often hung loose, held in place by a band round the brow or covered by a kerchief or veil. From about the ninth century the hair was either swept back from the forehead or parted in the centre. The long ends were plaited and these braids were pinned up at the nape or hung loose over the shoulder or down the back. In the twelfth century it was customary to bind the plaits with strips of material and encase the ends in metal cylinders. During the thirteenth century the plaits were often pinned up round the head or coiled up at the back. Most often, in this period, little of the hair was visible: it was hidden under a wimple, veil or couvrechef. The typical fourteenth century style was to pin the plaits on each side of the head over the ears. They were held in place by a metal fillet round the brow and this was often attached to a mesh cylinder on each side of the head, which encased the plaits (see *Caul*). In the fifteenth century the hair was barely visible under the complex headdresses. Indeed, in the latter years of the century, offending hairs were plucked out on the temples and at the nape if they dared to stray beneath the head-dress edge.

For the first 30 years of the sixteenth century the hair remained hidden, encased in a coif which was in turn covered by the hood styles of the time (see *Hood*). After about 1530 the horseshoe-shaped French hood was set further back on the head so that hair was visible on the forehead where it could be seen to be parted in the centre

Greek, fifth century BC

Roman coiffure of teenage girl, first century AD

Minoan coiffure with pearls and ribbons, c.1450 BC

Chignon covered in coloured scarf, Greek, fourth century BC

Long plaits bound with ribbons, ends in metal cylinders, English, 1140

English, 1300

German coiffure, 1630

English, 1540

Curled coiffure decorated by jewels and plumes, 1590

Pearl rope decoration, English, 1640

Coiffure with plume, 1622

Coiffure decorated with jewels, English, 1620

Coiffure decorated by flowers and ribbon loops, Italian, 1680

Coiffure with ribbon decoration, Austrian, 1845

rled coiffure essed over pads. riped ribbon coration, Italian, 90–5

Queen Anne, 1702

Polish coiffure, 1820

and drawn back over the ears. The plaits were coiled at the nape under the head-dress. From about 1560 the hoods gave place to jewelled caps perched on the crown of the head so the hair could be seen once more. It was dressed in short curls all over the front and sides and the braids were coiled at the back. As the century advanced the coiffure became more elaborate (like the rest of the costume) and the curls were piled higher on top and dressed over switches or pads to increase the height. Decoration was elaborate, consisting of ostrich plumes, pearl ropes, jewels and ribbons.

Until about 1625–30 the coiffure continued to be dressed in tiny curls on the top and at the sides though less elaborately and without the padding. An alternative style was swept up in a simple pompadour with discreet jewel decoration. The characteristic style of the middle years of the seventeenth century, about 1630–60, was an innovation. In this the hair was worn in a short curly fringe on the forehead. (Such tight curls and waves, which were fashionable throughout the seventeenth century, were referred to as *frizz* or *frizzle*.) At the sides the hair was dressed in ringlets and curls. It was then drawn tightly back to a coiled plait or bun worn high at the back and usually decorated by a rope of pearls, some lace or flowers. It was an elegant and unusual style, associated with England and that worn by Charles I's queen, Henrietta Maria of France. From the 1660s to the 1680s the side ringlets were worn longer and they were wired to stand out from the side of the head, making the coiffure wider. Several different names were applied to such ringlets; for example, favourites were ringlets or curls hanging loose at the temples, heartbreakers were ringlets at the sides or the nape which trembled as the lady moved her head (the French term *crêve-coeur* was also used); confidents, were usually curls near the ears. In the last 12 or 14 years of the century the very tall coiffure worn with the fontange head-dress was fashionable (see *Fontange*). This high coiffure was reciprocal to the men's periwigs of the time, though

the ladies' hairstyle used natural hair, curled and ringleted up high over pads. Individual long ringlets were arranged on the shoulders also.

The high coiffure with natural curls continued in fashion for a few years into the eighteenth century. Soon the piled up appearance vanished and, for nearly 50 years, women wore their hair simply and neatly. Until about 1740 the hair was dressed plainly back from the forehead and in simple curls at the back. Flowers, ribbon bows and dainty caps were perched on top of the head. Towards mid-century the hair was dressed in side curls and was swept up off the forehead, sometimes over a pad to lift it higher, and was also swept up at the back. This was the pompadour style, named after Mme de Pompadour, mistress of Louis XV of France. It was a mode which recurred later, notably in the years 1898–1908. For evening or formal wear, false ringlets were added and flowers and plumes were used for ornamentation. From 1750 onwards the small neat coiffure disappeared. The hair was dressed with pomatum and powdered white. The coiffure grew larger, dressed up over pads, and, by 1760, wigs were sometimes worn (see *Wig*). In the later 1780s small neat heads with natural hair and curls returned.

In the early years of the French Revolution the classical theme became paramount in feminine dress. This affected hairstyles also; the Greek chignon style was fashionable, also the Roman studied, shaggy 'Titus' cut. Wigs also were worn and switches were fashionable for evening coiffures. From 1810–20 hair was worn longer, arranged in curls in front and over the ears. In the 1820s the design became more elaborate and in the 1830s was combed into loops and swirls which were piled up on top of the head. Evening coiffures were especially elaborate as was the decoration, which included ribbons, plumes and flowers. The 1840s brought a coiffure which was more demure and decorous. The hair was parted in the centre and pulled back sleekly to side ringlets. At the back a ring of plaits was set with curls depending from it. By 1850 the hair was grown very

Medieval, English, 1200

Norman, c.1070

Byzantine, ninth century

Emperor Augustus, Roman, 10 AD

Greek, fifth century BC

English, 1505

English, bowl cut, 1430

Spanish, 1525–30

Lovelock, Polish, c.1640

Cavalier, English, 1635

Spanish prince, 1565

English, 1857

English, 1845 1916

Chignon coiffure, 1874

1965

1911

1916

Page boy bob, 1944

Pompadour coiffure, 1901

1931

1922

Shingle, 1928 1949

1960

1965

1949

Roman, AD 17

long. It was still parted in the centre but was then drawn back more severely to a round bun or chignon at the nape. There were no curls or ringlets. By the 1860s the chignon was larger and set higher up the head. In the years 1870–90 the coiffure was feminine and elaborate. Hair was drawn up and back to display the ears. It was dressed in curls on the forehead and in complex ringlets and sweeps at the sides and back. The chignon was worn higher in the nineties.

There have been three distinct eras of design in the twentieth century: the styles before 1918, the inter-war years and the post-war period. In the first decade the hair was long, fashionably in the pompadour style, back-combed and piled on top of the head over pads and with a chignon at the nape. Large combs of tortoiseshell or amber held the hair in place. In the second decade most women still kept their hair long but dressed it differently, with waves and plaits coiled round the crown. It was during the First World War that the change to shorter, easier-to-manage hairstyles began to take over. Bobbed hair was introduced but did not become an established fashion until the 1920s, when a simple, straight cut was necessitated by the head-hugging cloche (see *Hat*). By 1922 the bob had become a modish shingle. This was a severe style developing into the 'Eton crop' which made girls look like young boys. Slightly longer styles came in at the end of the 1920s then, in the 1930s, the feminine coiffure reappeared, but long hair, dressed in a bun or chignon, did not return; by this time, the majority of women had cut their hair.

One of the reasons why so many women cut off their long hair was that it was now made much easier to manage because of the modern techniques of waving which gave body to straight, limp hair. Marcel waving had been introduced in the late nineteenth century. This method of making deep waves, which lasted for a day or two, by means of heated scissor irons, was named after Marcel, the Paris hairdresser who had introduced it. Methods of waving hair by using curling tongs or irons were, of course,

not new as the custom dates back to the ancient Egyptians. The people of these ancient civilizations in hot countries also had their own means of 'permanent waving'; they set the hair in waves and curls with wet clay then dried it in the sun and combed out the clay. A much more durable permanent waving was introduced in 1906 but did not become popular until the 1920s because it took up to 12 hours to do and cost over £200. Permanent waving in the inter-war years was by machine. The hair was put in curlers which were inserted in the machine where they were heated by means of electric dry heat or a steam method. The resulting waves lasted for many months but the actual perming was still a slow, hot process. It was succeeded by the cold wave which employed chemicals in lotions and which was faster and more comfortable.

With the aid of the perm, coiffures of the 1930s were longer and arranged in waves set close to the head and ending in neat curls at the nape. The style was hard and tended to frizz when the perm was new. During the war years longer hair was fashionable, probably in a desire to offset the masculine appearance of the square-shouldered box silhouette. The hair descended to the shoulders in waves and curls or was worn in a gleaming page-boy bob.

After the war the hair was dressed in softer, more natural ways. Permanent waving was still general but the advent of the home perm and heated rollers made it more of a 'do-it-yourself' operation. In the early 1950s hair was softly curled and worn in a variety of styles and lengths. Towards 1959 the high bouffant beehive look was fashionable with excessive backcombing to produce the height. The mid-nineteenth century coiffure, with centre parting and side sweeps, was also popular. Since 1960 styles have varied greatly. In general, they are soft and natural-looking; tight curls and waves are 'out'. Many young girls wear their hair very long and loosely flowing. Some teenagers, especially in the late 1960s, draped their tresses curtainwise over their faces, leaving the eyes to peer through like those of an Old English sheepdog. Women now follow their own bent, wearing what suits them; there is no set style. Many wear their hair straight, others take advantage of the softer perms to give their coiffure a bouffant or carelessly windswept appearance.

MEN Over the centuries men have taken as much care over the tending of their coiffure as women. The styles have not varied quite so much but long or fairly long hair has been more usual than a 'short-back-and-sides'. Men have tended to wear wigs more often than women, presumably because of the threat of baldness.

In the ancient civilizations Egyptian men generally cut their hair short and wore wigs (see *Wig*) but, in Mesopotamia, the Assyrians, Babylonians and Persians all set store upon and judged virility by a vigorous head of hair, which they carefully crimped into waves and curls, perfumed and sprinkled with gold dust (see *Mesopotamia*). The Jews have traditionally abhorred the cutting of hair, specifically the side locks on the temples; these (*peoth*) should be permitted to grow as far as the level of the jaw-line (see *Jewish dress*). In Crete, the Minoans wore their hair long, looped and braided and tied in various ways on top of the head and down the back, much as the women did (see *Minoan dress*). Greek men also tended their hair with care. In early years it was long but later it was generally short and curled. Blonde hair was admired so bleach was often used and pomades and perfumes were generously applied to give sheen and scent. Etruscan men curled their hair and often wore it in ringlets at the shoulders; they dyed and perfumed it (see *Etruscan dress*). The Romans spent a great deal of time on their toilette. The many barbers' shops did a good trade, washing, cutting and dressing the masculine coiffure. Hairstyles in the early Imperial period were short, arranged in studied naturalness of curls brushed forward over the forehead. Later, hair was worn longer in a curled, artificially crimped manner.

In the more primitive societies of Bronze and Iron Age northern Europe, men wore their hair long and flowing or cut to about shoulder-length. Styles varied but most unusual was, perhaps, that of the Teutonic races of the early centuries AD who, as described by Tacitus, the Roman historian, twisted and knotted their long hair on top or at the side of the head to make it stand erect (see *Frankish dress*). Side locks were grown long and the hair at the back cut short or shaved. This elaborate coiffure was apparently to give them greater height and to strike terror into the hearts of their foes when they went into battle.

During the early Middle Ages men wore their hair loose and varying in length from jaw-level to well over the shoulders. It was not curled but, generally, was combed over the forehead. Exceptional styles were the Norman of the time of William I, when the hair was short and the back of the head was shaved up to the level of the ears and, in contrast, the twelfth century when it was exceptionally long. In the thirteenth century the fashion was for a horizontal curl on the forehead and another at the nape. An unusual style of the years 1425–50 was the 'bowl cut', where the short hair was turned under all round and the head was shaved at the back under this. Later fifteenth century styles, especially in Burgundy, tended to be frizzled and bushy but, by the 1490s, the hair was long and curling on the shoulders.

Sixteenth century hairstyles were short and neat and, generally, subservient to the modes of hats, moustaches, beards and ruffs (see *Beard, Hat, Ruff* and *Whiskers and facial hair*). In the second half of the century the hair was carefully curled and beautifully tended. The seventeenth century, in contrast, was an era of long hair. In the first quarter the hair became restrainedly longer, but in the years 1625–60 the hair was grown as long as possible. In style it was tended naturally, flowing over the shoulders and falling back in gentle waves. This was the age of the Cavalier and the love-lock, also known as a heart-breaker. This was a lock of hair longer than the rest, generally dressed forwards and tied with a ribbon bow. In the second half of the century the wig slowly took over from natural hairstyles and this lasted almost until the French Revolution (see *Wig*).

During the nineteenth century men's hair was cut fairly short and the chief interest was in whiskers and beards. In the first 20 years it was worn in natural curls and waves and combed forwards over the forehead and ears. In the 1820s it was longer and bushier, in the 1830s a left-side parting was fashionable and curls were arranged over the ears. Short styles continued for the rest of the century with centre or side partings. From 1850 macassar oil was widely used to flatten the hair and keep it in place. Since it badly stained upholstery, the crocheted, embroidered anti-macassar covered all the chairbacks of the period in the average drawing room.

For much of the twentieth century men have worn their hair short. This was especially so in the 1940s and early 1950s when young men favoured the American crew cut. Originating from a university style, the hair is cut very short all over and stands up on top about an inch long like a bristly brush. In contrast, in the 1960s men began to adopt longer hairstyles once more. Again it was young men, especially students, who led the field at first and by the late 1960s were wearing their hair shoulder-length. By the early 1970s the majority of men, whatever their age, were wearing their hair longer than had been customary since the mid-nineteenth century. The old-fashioned barber dispensing his 'short back and sides' has almost disappeared.

For further illustrations of the coiffures of both men and women see also *Bonnet, Cap, Hat, Head-dress* and *Hood*.

Handkerchief

Formerly a hand-kerchief, meaning a smaller piece of silk or linen which could be held in the hand or placed in the pocket (pocket handkerchief). It could be purely ornamental or for use in wiping the eyes, nose or face or, a larger version, to be placed on the head or tied round the neck (neckerchief).

Handkerchiefs have been in use since Roman times but here, and for many centuries after, were so costly that they were decorative rather than useful. During the Middle Ages they were valued possessions and were often made of sheer fabric, ornamented with silver and gold thread and edged with fringe. Venice was the leader in this luxury type of accessory. In the fifteenth century the handkerchief was large and called a hand-couvrechef or napkin: it was still very expensive. By the sixteenth century handkerchiefs had become fashionable accessories for the wealthy of Western Europe. Still imported from Venice, they were of lawn, cambric or linen and often edged with lace. Seventeenth century handkerchiefs appeared in several sizes and in different shapes: square, round or even oval. The square format became accepted as the norm by the end of the century. It was during the nineteenth century that the handkerchief size became standardized at about 18 inches square for men and a smaller 12 inch square for ladies. Men's handkerchiefs were usually of white linen with a hemstiched edge and, often, the initial in one corner, though coloured and patterned handkerchiefs were also in use for day wear (see also *Bandanna*). Ladies' handkerchiefs were of cambric, linen or cotton and, for evening especially, were embroidered and/or lace-edged.

Hank

From a Norse word, meaning a coil or skein of thread or yarn. Of a definite length, which varies according to the type: cotton yarn 840 yards, worsted 560 yards, silk 120 yards.

Harlequin

A character in Italian Comedy called Arlecchino, whose appearance dates from the late sixteenth century, though earlier versions had been known in the previous century, such as Trivelino and Truffaldino. Arlecchino was an extrovert character, clowning and jesting; he was dressed in a jacket and fitting trousers of a light-coloured material, which was covered with patches of different, brightly-coloured fabric placed randomly to represent a tattered costume. He wore a soft hat, a neck ruffle, a black half-mask and had a black beard. With the seventeenth century the costume became more elegant and carefully contrived. The patches were now of blue, red and green or white, red and green triangles arranged symmetrically and sewn with a yellow edging.

From the Italian Commedia dell'Arte the character went on to appear in French Comedy and in theatres in Spain, England, Germany and Holland. The costume changed slightly according to period but the brightly-coloured, carefully arranged, triangular or diamond-shaped patches remained its chief feature. A feminine version, Arlecchina, appeared. This character derived from the earlier Columbine, in Italian Comedy usually the wife or mistress of Harlequin but, as Arlecchina, her costume was decorated like his.

Harlot

A term used in the fourteenth century to describe men's hose when the two legs joined to become 'tights'.

Hasp

A clasp for fastening together two parts of an item of clothing.

Hat

The distinction between one form of head-covering and another is not always clearly definable (see also *Bonnet, Cap, Head-dress, Hood*). In fashion in general the adoption of a hat denoted the importance of the wearer. Thus, in primitive societies, head-coverings were usually close-fitting caps or kerchiefs tied round the head. In Europe hats were worn by men from classical times onwards but were rare for women until the end of the sixteenth century. Of similar connotation was the custom for men to wear their hats indoors and in church until after 1660; a custom only abandoned because it was both superfluous and inconvenient to wear a hat at all over a full-bottomed periwig, the hat then being carried under the arm. As distinct from other forms of headgear, a hat had a crown, often quite tall, usually a brim and was made of a firm or heavy material; only in

limited cases was it tied on to the head by strings, ribbons or a scarf. Apart from fashionable purposes, hats have been worn for protection from sun and rain, by travellers and by agricultural workers in all ages and in all parts of the world.

It is surprising how many permutations have been achieved in the design of hats through the centuries, based upon shape, colour, material, ornamentation and method of wearing. The designs discussed in this article are those worn in Europe and the West from the fifth century BC to the present day. For hats worn by specific civilizations and in different countries see also individual entries, for example, *Alpine dress, Chinese dress, Hungarian dress* etc.

In classical Europe hats were worn chiefly as protection from sun and rain. In ancient Greece there was a wide-brimmed type, the *petasos*, which was often slung round the neck by a cord and hung down the back until needed, a truncated cone design of Egyptian origin and a brimless one, the *pilos*. These hats were made of wool, felt or fur; also, for summer wear, of straw, like the Boeotian *petasos* designs shown in the Tanagra statuettes. Etruscan hats were similar; they also wore an Oriental style, the *tutulus*, which was conical or

HARLEQUIN
Arlecchina, Arlecchino, seventeenth century. Red, green and white triangular patches (after Maurice Sand)

Arlecchino, eighteenth century

steeple-shaped. The Romans wore the *petasos*, also the *galerius* or *pileus*, based on the Greek pilos. This last-named style continued in use, with variations, during the Dark Ages and the Middle Ages as, for example, the *pileus quadratus* which became a professional headcovering (see *Academical dress*).

Hats were only worn during the early Middle Ages by men of rank and importance in the community; the most usual head-covering was the hood (see *Hood*) and/or a cap or coif (see *Cap, Coif*). It was in the fifteenth century, and especially the second half, that the fashionable man began to favour a hat instead of a hood. There were several styles; most popular were the tall sugar loaf shape, the hunting design with a turned-up brim and a long point in front, the round or flower-pot type pleated into a band or padded roll and, at the end of the century, the immense circular beaver hat with upturned brim, tied on with a silk scarf over a skull cap, and decorated with long, multi-coloured plumes. Apart from feathers of varied types, hats were orna-mented with jewelled brooches and, as with a hood, the liripipe could be attached at the back (see *Liripipe*). They were made from felt, velvet or fur.

The typical early sixteenth century hat was of black or dark velvet with upturned brim, which was ornamented by a jewelled brooch and, sometimes, plumes. The turned-up edges were usually slashed then held together by decorative cords or ribbons. The hat could be worn straight or on one side. This style had originated in the late fifteenth century. By about 1530 it was still of velvet but had a small stiff brim, no longer upturned, and a soft crown gathered into a decorative band of cord or jewels. The hat was decorated by one or more ostrich plumes and was worn at an angle. Spanish fashions dominated the second half of the century, so hats were generally black, of felt or velvet, still ornamented by a plume and jewelled band. Tall crowns were fashionable, either stiff or of soft velvet gathered into the band above the narrow brim. The hat was worn at a rakish angle. Late in the century women,

who up to now had covered their heads with veils, scarves and hoods (see *Hood*), took to wearing similar tall hats for riding and travelling.

Spanish styles continued in fashion until the pattern for costume began to be set by the Dutch, about 1620–5. With the new modes came the swashbuckling Cavalier hat which, like the Spanish sombrero, had a wide, curling brim and long, sweeping ostrich plumes. In the 1630s these hats became very large and looked most roman-tic worn in conjunction with the long, curling hair. In the second half of the century, as the wig slowly took over from natural hair styles, the hat became less swashbuckling. It was still usually of black felt but, after 1670, the decoration was more often in the form of a jewelled band and bunches of ribbons rather than long ostrich plumes. As the full-bottomed wig grew larger, the hat was more often carried than worn.

During the seventeenth century, a paral-lel mode of hat evolved, similar in style but stripped of its decoration and panache. Hair and hats were two of the parts of costume fashion where the differences between the Puritan's mode of dress and that of the modish aristocracy were most apparent. In northern Europe, the Puritan cut his hair short and wore it straight and his hat was high-crowned, of black hard felt and trimmed only by a ribbon and buckle. The design was also known as a Geneva, after the Swiss Puritans, while in Cromwellian England, as elsewhere in Europe, such hats were worn by both sexes, the lady's version usually over a white cap which covered her hair. In America they were referred to as Pilgrim's hats, as they were normal wear for the Pilgrim Fathers who sailed in the *May-flower*. In the second half of the century the crown became lower and the brim wider and turned up at the sides. This was termed in America the Quaker or Penn-sylvania hat, after William Penn, the English Quaker who founded Pennsylvania. It was also referred to as a Holland hat from its popularity with Dutch Quakers. By the 1680s this hat was made of grey or

Greek felt hat, fifth century BC

Etruscan hat, tutulus style, c.300 BC

Greek pilos, 440 BC

Greek straw hat, petasos style, 250 BC

Felt petasos slung round neck by a cord, Greek

Green velvet hat, jewel and aigrette, English, 1475

Red cloth hat, Italian, c.1480

Green wool hat, Italian, 1420

Felt hat worn on top of coif, English, 1260

Burgundian sugar loaf hat, c.1456

Beaver hat, tied under chin with scarf, plumes. Worn over silk skull cap, Flemish, 1490

Pearl decorated velvet hat, Hungarian, 1520

Velvet hat with ribbon tie, gold braid and plumes, Swiss, 1520

Black velvet hat with jewelled brooch, 1480

Dark brown hat with gold ornament, German, c.1525

Black velvet jewelled hat with white plume, 1550

Black hat with cream upturned brim, English, 1500

brown beaver or felt and was sometimes termed a 'wide-awake' hat. The style was revived a century later when it was adopted in France at the time of the Revolution. Ladies did not often wear hats during the seventeenth century, generally preferring hoods and veils to protect their hair out-of-doors.

Towards the end of the seventeenth century the vast periwigs which were fashionable made it impracticable for men to wear hats on top of them unless bad weather made this absolutely necessary. Custom, however, dictated that a hat must accompany the costume so, since the article had to be carried under the arm, the design gradually changed. The round crown became low and the wide brim was turned back. This evolved into the *tricorne* or three-cornered hat which became the chief design of the eighteenth century. In English, the turned-up brim was called a cock so these tricornes were called cocked hats. There were many variations on the theme during the seventeenth and eighteenth centuries and each was given a name, for example, the Monmouth Cock of the 1670s and 1680s named after the Duke of Monmouth, the Denmark Cock of the later eighteenth century where the back cock was lower than the front ones and the Dettingen Cock worn for most of the eighteenth century where all three cocks were of equal size. The tricorne was usually made of black felt and was trimmed with gold braid and/or white ostrich tips. In general it was a large hat in the earlier eighteenth century but as the size of wigs declined so did that of the hat. Because of the custom of powdering the wig, hats were still carried until the later eighteenth century. A particularly small version of the tricorne was affected by the English Macaronis.

An alternative to the tricorne in the second half of the century was the two-pointed hat, the *bicorne*. This was even easier to carry under the arm as it folded quite flat; the French termed it a *chapeau bras*. Primarily a military hat, it was worn in Switzerland and, later, by Napoleon. An unusually high cocked hat with a spout-like crease in the centre front was the Kevenhüller, named after the Austrian general Andreas von Khevenhüller, and worn chiefly about mid-century.

In the 1780s, with the return to natural hair or small wigs, men wore hats more often, though they never returned to the universal wearing of hats on all occasions as before. Certainly never again did they keep their heads covered indoors in the presence of ladies. The late-century hats (apart from the bicorne) were generally round, tall-crowned styles which originated in England. They were made of felt, beaver or fur and had ribbon and buckle or cord trimming.

Women did not wear hats in the eighteenth century until the 1770s; before this they wore dainty caps indoors with hoods on top out-of-doors. With the immense wigs of the 1770s, hats were small and flat, perched at an angle on the wig and worn over a cap. As the wigs subsided, very large picture hats were introduced from England in the 1780s; these had a wealth of ribbon, plume, lace and flower trimming. These styles were followed by elegant taller hats, echoing those of the men, but decorated more profusely with plumes and ribbons.

The bicorne hat was still to be seen early in the nineteenth century but its use was confined more and more to the military. The most usual hat until 1815 was the English round hat with the tall crown and small rolled brim. From 1820 the top hat (topper) became fashionable and this was to the nineteenth century what the tricorne had been to the eighteenth. The shape evolved during the century from the curved-sided version in the early years to the tall, straight-sided 'stovepipe' or 'chimneypot' design of the mid-century and to a lower crown in the later decades. At first it was made from beaver in grey, fawn or white. By the 1840s it was a black silk or polished beaver hat with a narrower brim. A collapsible opera hat of black silk was introduced which could be flattened by an internal spring so that it could be carried under the arm. This was the *gibus*, named after its inventor, the Parisian hatter, first

Purple velvet hat, Italian, c.1590

Black hat over cap, Dutch, 1619

Black velvet hat, crimson plume, jewelled band, English, 1578

Black hat with jewelled band over gold, jewelled cap, Czech, 1578

Black hat with coloured plumes, French, 1637

Puritan black felt hat, ribbon and buckle, 1655

Quaker style black hat, 1650

Black hat with striped ribbon over lace-edged cap, 1658

Black felt hat, white plume, 1665

Black tricorne hat, gold edging, 1748–50

Black tricorne hat, white ostrich frond trimming, 1720–7

Black, gold-edged Kevenhüller hat, 1750

Straw hat with black velvet ribbons, French, 1795

Brown felt hat, cord trimming, 1790–5

Silk hat with plumes and ribbons, 1777–80

Black felt bicorne, gold edge, English, c.1807

Silk and lace hat, 1788

Natural straw hat, white ribbons and flowers, Spanish, 1814

White silk hat with white lace trimming and flowers, French, 1830

Black felt bicorne with gold trimming, 1798

Conversation hat of cream straw, 1805

Fawn beaver top hat, 1811

Cream straw hat, black velvet ribbon and bird's wing trimming, 1875
Black silk top hat, 1860

Navy straw hat with white roses and magenta ribbons, 1909

Black silk top hat, 1860

Grey stovepipe top hat, 1855

Bergère white straw hat, pink ribbons, English, 1860

Straw boater, 1885

Tweed informal hat, 1880

White lace and tulle hat. Red ribbon and white plume trimming, 1897

Black Homburg hat, 1897

Straw boater with veil, ribbon and feather trimming, 1902

Grey felt trilby hat, black band, 1900

Black bowler hat, 1870

Blue velvet hat with black veil. Blue ribbons and pink roses, 1891

Grey chip straw hat with ribbons, lace and plumes, 1883

Straw hat with white ostrich plumes and black spotted veil, 1912

Felt hat with velvet bow and plumes, 1923

Grey bowler, black ribbon, 1890

Fur and felt cloche hat, 1927

Felt cloche hat, 1926

Black taffeta hat with white plumes 1907

made in 1823 and patented in 1837. It replaced an earlier, but less successful collapsible 'elastic' hat.

The top hat continued to be the formal fashionable wear until well after 1900 but, in the last 40 years of the century, alternative styles appeared for casual, summer and sporting wear. The bowler hat was the most fashionable of these. At first only adopted for casual wear, it soon became established for everyday use. Also known as a billycock, this round hard felt hat with rolling brim, in black, brown or grey, had been worn since the 1850s. In England it was named after its original hatter, William Bowler, but in America it was a derby and in France a melon. In the 1880s soft felt hats were introduced and, for summer, straw boaters. Tweed and wool soft hats were popular for holidays and travelling. The aristocrat of the felt hats was the Homburg, so-called after its town of manufacture in Germany. The crown was dented longitudinally from front to back and the brim, which curved up at the sides, was braided with ribbon to match the band. The hat was popularized by the Prince of Wales.

For much of the nineteenth century, at least until 1880, the bonnet was the principal headcovering for ladies (see *Bonnet*). In the early years turbans were also worn (see *Turban*) as well as small hats. Among these was the straw gypsy hat, a flat crown held on by a scarf tied round it and under the chin. There was also the conversation hat where one side of the brim was turned back and the other pulled forward. Large-brimmed hats were fashionable (like the large bonnets) from about 1820–35. These, made from straw or silk, were lavishly decorated by ribbon bows, flowers and plumes. In the mid-century the *bergère* or shepherdess hat, which had been worn during the eighteenth century, returned to fashion. This was a straw hat with a flat crown and a wide soft brim. Another contemporary fashion was for a pill-box hat copied from Garibaldi's own braided version.

Although small fussy bonnets were seen into the 1890s, ladies chiefly wore hats in the last 20 years of the nineteenth century. Shapes were extremely varied but, in general, hats of the 1880s were fairly small and tall in toque and flower pot shapes, while large hats were predominant in the nineties. Trimming was profuse all the time; it included ribbons, bows, plumes, birds' wings, fur, velvet, flowers and face veil. In the 1890s very large hats, often referred to as picture, Gainsborough or Marlborough apropos of the styles of the 1770s and 1780s depicted by the painter and worn by the Duchess of Marlborough, were very fashionable. These were laden with ornamentation and both the hat and the face were enveloped in a lace or spotted net veil.

During the twentieth century there has been a gradual decline in the wearing of hats. Before the First World War there was no indication of this; men continued to wear the top hat for formal occasions and a bowler, boater or felt hat, according to season, for everyday purposes. The Homburg was still seen but a plainer version without ribbon edging was more usual: in America this was called a fedora, in England, a trilby. (Both names derived from dramatic productions.) Ladies' hats were vast

HATS: 1934–1965
Light fawn felt hat, brown ribbon, 1934

Brown felt hat and ribbons, 1937

Red Tyrolean hat, 1936

Turquoise felt hat, ribbon edge, plume, 1936

White felt hat and ribbon, 1942

Grey felt hat and pink ribbon, 1948

White woven fibre hat, navy ribbon and elastic, 1935

Blue pill-box hat, 1965

Powder blue felt hat and ribbons, 1949

Tweed pork pie hat, 1955

HEADDRESS
Gold, jewelled and velvet
headdress, English, 1470

Black velvet and gold, jewelled
headdress, Italian, 1450

Transparent veil over green
headdress, Flemish, 1478

White double stiff veil over
steeple cap, French, 1470

creations surmounting the pompadour coiffure and, in turn, themselves crowned by a quantity of decorative trimming in the form of plumes, flowers and ribbons. Leghorn hats were fashionable, named after the Italian straw from which they were made which was imported from Leghorn (Livorno). Long hatpins were necessary to hold such hats in place. They were also useful as defensive weapons against what is now termed 'mugging'. With the coming of war, hats became more practical and were generally small and neat.

From 1920 onwards men wore the top hat only for rare formal occasions and, after 1939, the bowler was not often seen. The trilby hat became smaller with a narrower brim and ribbon band, then turned into the pork pie, with the centre, longitudinal fold in the crown becoming a circular one. Since 1945 there has been a steady decline in the wearing of hats by men.

Women's hats in the 1920s were all head-hugging, pulled down low on the forehead as far as the eyebrows. The cloche hat was typical. As its name suggests it was a close-fitting helmet or bell-shaped covering, though for summer wear, large picture hats were still fashionable, also pulled down to eyebrow-level. The 1930s brought tremendous variety to hat styles. Most popular were the halo, the Tyrolean, the pill-box and the sailor. Many hats, in contrast to the previous decade, were perched precariously on the head, like flat dinner plates. They were pulled down low over one eye and held in place by a strap or cap at the back; short face veils were popular. Since the Second World War there has also been a decline in the wearing of hats by women, particularly by the young. It is no longer obligatory to wear a hat in order to be well dressed. A variety of styles have been available, many of them informal. For winter wear fur hats are always popular, whether synthetic or genuine.

Head-dress

The elaborate and varied head-dresses of the fifteenth century cannot be classified as hats, bonnets, caps, turbans or hoods;

they are in a category of their own. The reticulated head-dresses of the early fifteenth century, made up of metal, jewelled cauls and covered by white veils hung over wire frames are discussed under *Cauls*. The typical form of the mid-century, worn from about 1430–60, was the heart-shaped head-dress, made from a padded roll covered in velvet or silk and decorated with pearls and jewels which was shaped to dip at the centre front and back but rise at the sides. A jewelled brooch usually ornamented the centre front of the roll. Under this was worn a jewelled caul and over it, often, a veil. In the years 1460–85 the steeple head-dress was most fashionable. Shaped like a dunce's cap, it was made of brocade, velvet, gold or silver cloth, stiffened into shape and attached to a black velvet frontlet just visible as a loop on the forehead. The cap was worn at an angle of about 40° from the vertical. Towards 1470 a wide black band of double material was draped over the top of the head-dress and two lappets hung down on the shoulders on either side. A transparent veil accompanied this head-dress; sometimes it was double and was generally wired to achieve a picturesque silhouette. A truncated form of this steeple shape was more fashionable late in the century. In the second half of the fifteenth century it was customary for all hair to be concealed by the head-dress. To this end the hair which grew on the temples and at the nape was plucked out.

Heel

A constituent added to the rear end of the sole of an item of footwear. The heel was first introduced for reasons of utility and comfort to raise this part of the foot from the ground. For instance, in the Middle East heels were added to footwear in Persia to lift the foot from the burning sand. Horsemen of nomad societies, especially in the East, found a small heel of assistance in keeping the foot firmly placed in the stirrup.

In Europe the idea of the heel developed from the clogs and pattens worn in the Middle Ages to keep the feet out of the filth of the street. It was in the late sixteenth

HEEL
Persian slipper with typical heel. Blue and yellow suède

Early wedge heel, 1585, German

Embroidered silk shoe, 1620, English

Fawn suède shoe with crimson bow, 1660, Spanish

Embroidered lady's shoe, 1690, Spanish

Silk brocade shoe, French heel, 1730

Brown and cream satin shoe, Italian heel, 1780

Cuban stacked heel, 1935

Wedge sole and heel, 1950

Platform sole and high heel, 1973

Stiletto heel, 1960

century that the embryo heel appeared, at first as a thickening at the rear of the sole, usually in stacked form, that is, layers of leather added one below another. (A modern stacked heel is one made up of layers of wood or leather while the covered heel is a block of wood or plastic covered with material.) By 1600 the heel had developed with a curve up under the arch

and in the 1620s heels were two to three inches high. Red heels were fashionable for the nobility in the second half of the century.

The high, curved, elegant French (Louis or Pompadour) heel evolved during the eighteenth century. By the 1770s this had diminished to become the lower Italian style, set far back under the sole. The nineteenth and early twentieth centuries saw a re-introduction of many variations of heel worn previously. Characteristic of the differing fashions since 1925 are the cuban heel, which is straight, of medium height and often stacked, very fashionable in the 1930s and 1940s, the wedge sole and heel is one of the 1950s, re-introduced in the clumping platform wedges of the 1970s and the spike or stiletto, introduced from Italy after 1953 and very fashionable by 1960.

HELMET
Pith helmet (sola tŏpī)

Helmet

A defensive covering for the head. Principally of military historical development and use (beyond the scope of this book), also as part of protective clothing for certain occupations (see *Industrial and Protective Clothing*). Other instances include the protective helmet worn by American footballers and the crash helmet now compulsory wear in Britain for motorcyclists. The *topi* or *topee*, the pith helmet worn by Europeans in the Indian subcontinent, was the *sola topī* in use as protection against the sun. It was covered in white cotton and lined in green. The name derives from the Hindı word *topī*, meaning hat.

Homespun

A cloth made from yarn spun at home. Also a coarse, loosely-woven fabric made from wool, cotton or rayon to imitate home-woven material

Hoods

The hood has long been a traditional and practical means of keeping the head and shoulders dry and warm in inclement weather. Most of the ancient civilizations wore such hoods, either separately or attached to a cloak as, for example, the Roman *cucullus* (see ancient *Rome*), which was handed down for medieval monastic use. In northern Europe especially, the hood continued in common use throughout the Middle Ages. At first it was simply a headcovering buttoned or laced at the throat. Soon it was extended to include a shoulder cape and this in turn became part of the fashion of the day being a subject for parti-colouring, dagged edges and heraldic designs.

In the fourteenth century the point on top began to lengthen into a padded sausage which hung down the wearer's back (see *Liripipe*). In the later years of the century, new ways of wearing the hood were experimented with. The common method was to place the face opening upon the head itself and to arrange the folds of the shoulder cape over the edge and to drape down the back, front or sides as the wearer wished and the liripipe hung loose on the other side. By the 1420s a more formal arrangement evolved. The *chaperon*, the name given to the hood and shoulder cape combined, was re-designed so that it was no longer necessary to re-drape the material each time that it was donned. Now the part set upon the head was made up into a padded roll, a *bourrelet* (see *Bourrelet*) or, as it was later termed, a *roundlet*. The shoulder cape was sewn to the inside of the bourrelet on one side and the liripipe to the other. The new style lasted for many years. A jewelled brooch generally decorated one side of the bourrelet, which was covered by velvet or other rich fabric. In the fifteenth century hats largely superseded hoods as fashionable headcovering.

Women also wore hoods, usually attached to capes for travelling purposes. During the first half of the sixteenth century various styles of hood became fashionable head-coverings. At first the design was simple, a velvet cap with hanging ends and back, worn over a white coif. The sides were flaps called lappets falling upon the shoulders and the back was a semi-circular piece of material hanging in folds and termed the fall. Most hoods were of black velvet lined with colour. Early in the century the hood then evolved into different forms. In England this was the gable hood, which was pyramidal in form and was alternatively referred to as a kennel or pyramidal hood. The head-dress was worn over a white coif and had a metal, jewelled frontlet to keep the shape and a velvet fall hung behind. Embroidered velvet lappets lay on the shoulders in front and the hair above the forehead was often encased in a coloured striped silk cap which showed in front under the gable form. By about 1515–20 one or both lappets were pinned up at the sides.

In the 1530s the English gable was gradually ousted in fashion in favour of the French horseshoe shape. This was set a little further back on the head to display the hair parted in the centre. There were one, or even two, metal jewelled frontlets, termed *biliments*, and these were separated by silk or satin bands between. The coif showed in front of the metal band. The velvet hood then hung in folds or a tubular shape behind the head. In the 1550s, especially in England, the horseshoe form became flattened on top to give a different shape. During the sixteenth century part of the hanging section of the French hood was sometimes brought forward to shade the complexion from the sun. This formed a rectangular peak or projection over the face and was called a *bongrace*.

Hoods were worn in the seventeenth and eighteenth centuries by ladies for out-of-doors and for travelling. These could be worn alone, tied at the throat with hanging ends or were attached to a shoulder cape or longer cloak. The long hood had two long streamers to tie under the chin, the

Red velvet chaperon, Burgundy, c.1450

Cloth hood, Greenland, fourteenth century

Hood and shoulder cape, English, c.1190

Hood attached cloak, English, 1155

Silk chaperon, Italian, 1449

King Henry IV of England. Red hood with gold border and jewel

Cloth hood, Italian, 1363

Queen Catherine Parr, 1546. Gold embroidered gable hood. Lappets pinned up. Jewelled frontlet, silk striped cap.

Queen Jane Seymour. Black velvet gable hood pinned up on one side. Gold and pearl lappets. Jewelled frontlet. Gold striped cap, 1536

Queen Elizabeth of York, 1500. Black velvet gable hood, gold jewelled lappets and frontlet

Princess Mary Tudor, c.1549. Black velvet French hood with gold jewelled biliments separated by white satin

Dark green silk hood, ribbon bow. Black silk mask, c.1644

Black velvet French hood with bongrace

Queen Anne Boleyn, c.1535. Black velvet French hood with pearl edging

Princess Mary of England, 1544. French hood with jewelled biliments, red velvet between. Black velvet fall

Red velvet hose cut in one garment as 'tights'. Italian, 1470

Upper and netherstocks gathered in bands and slashed, French, 1530

Soled velvet hose cut in one. Burgundy, 1450

Cloth hose in separate legs, English, 1340

Elizabethan abbreviated trunk hose with dark embroidered panes Canions and netherstocks differently coloured and decorated, English 1588

Hose striped in white, grey and red. Upper stocks banded and slashed, German, 1525

Elizabethan trunk hose with gold embroidered panes. Netherstocks gartered. English, 1567

Hose cut in one. Upper stocks striped, netherstocks in two colours, Flemish, 1490 short or pug hood was tied by narrow ribbons and its back was designed with folds radiating from a central point to provide the necessary fullness. The *capuchin* (capuchon) was lined with a contrasting colour and was attached to a deep cape. A fashionable hood worn in the American colonies in the later seventeenth century was called a *rayonne*. It was made of black corded silk lined with colour and the front edge was turned back to display this.

Hook and eye
A costume fastening consisting of a metal wire loop or eye sewn to one edge of a garment and a metal wire hook to the other edge to be fastened which engages the eye. A medieval form of fastening originally called a crochet and loop. The term hook and eye dates from the seventeenth century.

Hopsack, hopsacking
1) The material from which bags containing hops are made; a coarse fabric of hemp and jute.
2) In the nineteenth century a woollen dress fabric in plain weave. Also *hopsack serge*, which was a coarsely woven version. Cotton, linen and rayon hopsack weave is now used for dresses and suits.

Hose
A word of German origin signifying a covering for the legs; the term was used in the early centuries AD for a form of roughly-fitting trousers reaching to the ankle. The stocking, with or without foot portion, which was commonly criss-crossed with gartering on the lower leg was generally referred to by the French word chausses (see *Chausses*). It was pulled up to the knee over the braies (see *Braies*). Gradually the chausses became longer and the braies shorter. From about 1340, as garments were tailored to fit more closely, this trend also applied to the chausses. Now usually described as hose, they were made as two long stockings, each expertly cut longitudinally in four sections to fit the leg tightly from foot to crotch. They were made of velvet, silk or cloth and, in winter, could be fur-lined. Often the foot portion was soled so that shoes were unnecessary indoors. By 1360 the two legs of the hose were lengthened to reach the hips. They were kept up by being laced through eyelet holes all round the outer leg to the lower edge of the undertunic. These lacings were known as points (see *Aglet*). By 1370–80 the legs of the hose had joined to become 'tights' and soon extended nearly to waist-level, where they were laced to the undertunic all round the body (see also *Cod-piece*). Women wore similar hose but theirs reached only to just above the knee, like stockings, and were gartered there.

In the fourteenth century, with the general wearing of soled hose, the fashion for extended toes was introduced. First popular in Poland and Italy, the trend spread westwards, being especially exaggerated about 1380. Some toe points were so extreme that it became difficult to walk and the point had to be stuffed and stiffened with whalebone (see *Poulaine*).

In the fifteenth century hose had become so well-fitting to the leg that it was fashionable to wear parti-coloured or striped designs in order to display the masculine curves to advantage; sometimes one leg was covered in plain material and the other striped or, perhaps, the upper part was striped and the lower plain. With the sixteenth century the hose was often divided into two parts: the upper and lower stocks. The upper section, which covered the buttocks and thighs was, from about 1525, slashed and banded, in a similar manner to the treatment of other garments in this period, while the lower netherstocks were fitting, gartered at the knee, striped or plain.

With the Spanish fashions of the second half of the sixteenth century came the mode for trunk hose. These were upper stocks made in the form of full knickerbockers, which had a fitting waistband and thigh bands; the fullness of the material draped over the latter often hiding the bands from view. Trunk hose were slashed to display an undergarment of similar form but of different colour and material. The strips of the outer garment were known

HOUPPELANDE
Red velvet houppelande with jewelled girdle, gold bells and chains, English, 1420

Patterned houppelande with white collar and jewelled belt, English, 1445

Plain houppelande with cloak on top, Flemish, 1445

Pink houppelande with white lining, French, 1420

Plain houppelande with patterned baldric, Spanish, 1413

as panes and were usually richly embroidered, even jewelled. The lower leg was covered by netherstocks which were plain, fitting stockings. Towards the 1580s and 1590s the trunk hose became extremely short and were padded to give a wide, stiff silhouette at buttock level. Below these abbreviated trunk hose the fitted portion of the hose or stocks was divided into two parts: an upper section, which reached to the knee and which were called canions (cannons), and a lower stocking, of different colour and material, pulled up over them.

In the early seventeenth century trunk hose gradually gave place to loose breeches, after the style of Venetians or pluderhosen (see *Breeches*) and, after this, knee-breeches, so that stockings replaced hose (see *Stocking*). A form of over-stockings were worn during the seventeenth century called stirrup-hose. These were a protection for the costly silk stockings and worn for riding. They had an instep strap to go under the foot and were laced at the top to the breeches.

Hot pants
An abbreviated design of shorts fashionable, especially for girls, in the early 1970s.

Houppelande
A voluminous outer garment worn from about 1360–5 till the later fifteenth century but especially fashionable until 1445–50. The houppelande derived from Flemish styles and was worn by both sexes. Generally fitting on the shoulders it was very full and usually belted. In the fourteenth century it had a very high neckline, up to the ears; after this necklines followed current tunic fashion. The houppelande could be any length between mid-calf and sweeping the ground. It could be buttoned all the way up the centre front or, more commonly, was not open but the skirt was slit to knee level at the sides. A baldric was often slung round the body (see *Baldric*). The houppelande was always ample, draped in many folds; it was made from rich fabrics with contrasting linings, often fur. Sleeves were always wide, edges frequently dagged.

Hungarian (Magyar) dress

Situated in central Europe, Hungary has been subjected over the centuries to invasion and domination from different sources; the influences on Magyar culture, including dress, have come chiefly from Western Europe, Turkey and the Asian Orient. During the Middle Ages western influence on costume was strong, especially in the fourteenth century, when the Magyars enjoyed economic prosperity and a consequent high standard of art and culture. During the fifteenth century Hungary continued to prosper and the aristocracy adopted Italian Renaissance dress but Turkish pressure on her boundaries increased steadily.

The country fell to the Turks in 1526, who ruled over the greater part of it for over 150 years. The resulting influence on masculine dress was marked and from the sixteenth until the early nineteenth century, it was dominated by Ottoman fashion. The basic dress during these years comprised two coats, hose or trousers and boots. The coats were the *dolman* and the *mente*. The dolman was cut to fit closely to the body. It was waisted, made in light, richly coloured materials, often embroidered all over in gold or silver and had a flared skirt nearly to the knee (see *Dolman*). The mente was worn on top of the dolman but was often slung round the shoulders, unbuttoned, sleeves hanging free. It was fuller than the dolman and longer; it had wider sleeves and a broad collar spreading over the shoulders. Under these coats were worn a finely embroidered white shirt and hose which resembled tight-fitting trousers. Boots, over these, were more usual than shoes. Hats (*kucsma*) were generally of fur, decorated with plumes. They were traditional and were made from wolf, bear or sheepskin (see *Cap*).

Women's dress was much less affected by Turkish influence and changed more as time passed; it reflected more closely the international mode. Late fifteenth century fashions followed those of Italy; from mid-sixteenth, the mentor was Spain. Materials were rich and costly, embroidered

and jewelled. At the same time, a more national style was followed by many women which comprised an ample, embroidered white blouse with full sleeves and, on top, a traditional decorative bodice/jacket which was open in front and laced across the blouse. The full skirt was heavily embroidered and a decorative apron, the *koteny*, was tied round on top.

With the eighteenth century the influence of French fashion grew stronger. Stylish men still wore the dolman and mente but the cut of these garments slowly changed. The dolman was fitting on the torso but became longer-waisted and acquired flaring skirts: a parallel to the contemporary French coat. The mente also became slender in cut. Soon the dolman was designed in sleeveless manner like the French *veste* and later in the century most fashionable men abandoned fashionable garments and took to the *habit à la française*. Until about 1750–60 the Hungarian traditional style of feminine dress was still seen but after this the nobility followed the current mode.

Until the mid-nineteenth century Hungarian peasant costume had little colour. People were poor and made their clothes from their own coarse linen, rough cloth or sheepskin in natural grey-brown tones. Standards of living rose in the second half of the century and colour was introduced to fabrics which could now be purchased as well as homespun. There developed a liking for coloured embroidery on white cambric and wool, also for richly-coloured decoration on black garments, which were traditional for festive occasions, especially weddings; even bridal costumes were in black. A quantity of decoration was associated with wealth so the aim was to cover as much of the surface of garments for special functions as possible with bright, gaily coloured embroidery. In these traditional garments the Asiatic Turkish influence was marked as in, for instance, the high leather boots, the pantaloons and the decorative coats slung rakishly round the shoulders. An important material for winter wear was sheepskin, especially for the herdsmen of the plains. A traditional

Peasant dress. Sheepskin suba embroidered in wool with fringe ornamentation. White trousers tucked inside black leather boots. Black hat with red pompons

Peasant dress. Black apron over white gatya with white fringe. Embroidered coloured jacket over white shirt. Black fur hat

Embroidered szür with leather strap and buckle fastening. Black hat and boots

Fashionable fur hat and fur-collared mente with braid and cord button loops, worn over buttoned dolman, 1671

Fashionable dress, 1630–50. Man wears a dolman and mente, trousers and boots, kucsma (fur hat)

with plume. Lady in richly embroidered overgown and red brocade underskirt. White lace wired collar

Lady in fashionable dress of 1750. Man wears golden brown silk mente with brown fur trimming over

fitted dolman. Cap to match mente. Trousers and boots decorated with silver, c.1780

Modern festive dress in white decorated by coloured ribbons, lace and embroidery. Parta of flowers, lace and gold embroidery. Black boots

Modern parta of white lace and ruching decorated with pearls

Fashionable dress, 1685–90. Man in royal red mente with fur collar and frogged fastenings

over belted dolman. Dark red cloth hose, leather boots. Lady in fashionable attire of period garment, worn for centuries, was made from two sheep skins, one to cover the front and one the back. These were tied together at shoulder and waist, the legs of the animals being left to hang down. The long sheepskin jacket, the *ködmön*, evolved from this more primitive garment.

The peasant costumes illustrated, were worn in the later nineteenth century but also for festive occasions until modern times. For men the dress consisted of a white shirt with long, full sleeves and linen pantaloons called *gatya*. Two pairs were worn in winter, one on top of the other. Festive *gatya* are very full and wide, as are the shirt sleeves so that both are pleated or gathered. An embroidered jacket, high, black leather boots and a broad-brimmed hat or a cap were worn and, to complete the outfit, on feast days and holidays, was the *koteny*, the Hungarian apron decorated with embroidery and fringing, customary wear for the young of both sexes. Apart from the sheepskin *ködmön*, there were two types of outer garment for men: the *szür* and the *suba*. The *szür* is a charac-teristically Magyar garment. Oriental in cut and design, it is made from woollen cloth or frieze and is richly decorated by embroidery and appliqué work. The gar-ment has a large collar which is turned down all round and down the centre front. Though it has sleeves, the arms are never inserted. the *suba* is a cloak cut in circular pattern or section. It is made from sheep-skin with the wool turned inside and the exterior covered in cloth which is richly embroidered.

The traditional attire for girls and ladies, now reserved for festive occasions, is for a full white blouse with wide sleeves and a very full skirt, worn over petticoats, and gathered into a colourful belt at the waist. There is a kerchief at the neck and high boots on the legs. The whole costume is ornamented with colourful embroidery. The festive head-dress for girls is the *parta*, which is a coif of embroidery, ruching and lace, worn with a tall chaplet or tiara of flowers and with ribbons, streamers or lappets behind. In Hungary, the expression 'to stay in parta' means that a girl is un-married. Older women cover their hair with a coif or bonnet.

I

Ihram (Harem)

Penitence dress worn by Mohammedan pilgrims to Mecca. Consists only of two pieces of white cotton, one wrapped round the loins and the other draped over the left shoulder.

Inca dress

The Incas came from the highland valley of Cuzco in Peru and conquered earlier peoples in the remainder of Peru and Bolivia in the early Middle Ages. Their greatest era of power, wealth and culture was the fifteenth century when they ruled over what is now Peru, Bolivia, Ecuador and parts of Argentina and Chile, an empire comprising about five million people. They succumbed to Spanish rule in 1533 though today, descendants of the Incas still live in the high Andes and follow many of the traditions of their ancestors.

The dress of the Incas was ornamented by beautiful, brilliantly-coloured feathers and some cloaks were made entirely from these (see *Feathers*), and by jewellery; the Incas were particularly skilled at working in gold. Their garments were made from cotton, wool, fur and leather. They hunted the little chinchilla, both for fur and for meat (see *Fur: chinchilla*) and kept herds

INCA DRESS
Woman in white cotton gown under poncho-type tunic with decorated hem

of llama to supply food and wool. The finer wool of the vicuña was reserved for costlier fabrics (see *Fur: guanaco, llama, vicuña*).

The actual garments were simple. Men wore a loin-cloth and, sometimes, a short tunic or robe. Outer clothes were wraps or cloaks in the design of an Arabian burnous or a poncho (see *Cloak* and *Poncho*). Women wore an ankle-length robe with poncho on top. Headcoverings, if worn, were either woollen caps or turbans, the folds of the cloak or, for festive occasions, a feather head-dress. Feet were bare or sandals were worn.

Indian dress

The costume worn by the peoples of the Indian sub-continent, now comprising the nations of India, Pakistan and Bangladesh, is a simple one, which has developed slowly over many centuries, changing little. It is primarily a draped costume, consisting of pieces of material wrapped round the body, varying between the sexes only by the size and pattern of the material and the manner of draping and tying. Although the basic garments worn throughout the sub-continent are much the same, it is natural that, over such a vast area and with such a large population, differing customs and religious beliefs, the manner of wearing the garments varies considerably and, in the north, because of the cooler climate, there is a tendency towards the adoption of sewn garments rather than draped ones.

There have been three chief influences from which the form of Indian dress has evolved. The earliest stemmed from the Indo-Aryans who slowly established themselves in waves of immigration between 2400 and 1500 BC. From these people came the waist-cloth, breast-band and scarf or shawl. The first of these developed into the *dhoti* in all its varied forms and the breast-band into the bodice or *choli*. The scarf or shawl became a head-veil for women and, for men, evolved into a turban. From the Greek invasion of India in 327 BC came the influence of classical dress, the mantle or *orhni* stemming from the classical cloak and the shirt from the *chiton*. Even

the draping of a modern *sari* shows a clear derivation from the classical method of draping the *palla*. The third influence, from the horsemen of Asia, brought the sewn garments of coat and trousers worn, in mountain regions, with boots. The *coat* has had a long history in India and has changed its form considerably during the centuries. It was introduced by the Persians in the late sixth century BC and this style was later adapted by the warrior horsemen of northern India. The *jamal* coat worn by the great Moghuls, who came from Kabul in Afghanistan in 1525, was a long coat-gown with a very full, pleated skirt. It was double-breasted and cross-closed, tied with tapes high under the right shoulder, then encircled at the waist with a decorative sash or belt. It was made of rich fabrics and decoratively embroidered. The *angharka* was similar, very elegant and un-pleated. Under this coat were worn sheer, white muslin trousers, generally tied at the ankles, and embroidered leather slippers. The head was wrapped in a decorated, jewelled turban. There were several other coats or coat-cloaks, such as the *mirzai*, the peasant, quilted coat derived from the Asiatic horsemen's design, and the *choga* and *jubba* (*jubbah*), which were full and draped (see *Djellaba* etc.).

In modern dress men usually wear a loose, cotton *dhoti* and shirt. In towns a form of western clothes has been adapted to Indian needs so that a jacket can be worn over *dhoti* or trousers and shirt. For more formal dress, for the professional and well-to-do classes, the long coat with fitting trousers are more usual. Women wear a bodice-blouse and sari or a longer blouse with loose trousers.

The hip-wrap or waist-cloth is an article of clothing which can vary greatly according to the status, sex and region of the wearer. In its simplest form it is a rectangle of material wrapped round the hips, fastened at the waist and the ends passed between the legs to be tucked into the top to form a loincloth or is merely wrapped round the waist and tied to make a hip length skirt. In more elaborate versions the wrap can extend to the knees or the

Man of rank. Woollen coat decorated in bright colours. Loin-cloth underneath with hanging tassel. Turban type of cap. Sandals

Farmer. Embroidered wool loin-cloth under simple poncho. Wool cap

ankles, depending solely upon the width of the material; the length is commonly about five yards. The garment is worn by both sexes and is known by different names. The *lungi* is generally worn as a wrapped skirt, the two ends being gathered together then tucked in at the sides or left hanging loose. (The word *lungi* can also refer to a head-cloth or turban made from a similar rectangle of material.) The *dhoti* is wrapped round the hips so that the left end is longer than the right; the right end is then passed between the legs and tucked into the back of the waistband while the left end, in more complex drapings, is pleated and allowed to hang down in folds in front.

With the hip-wrap men generally wear a shirt or *kurta*. This has long sleeves and hangs loose to the hips or knees. Some styles have collar and cuffs and the garment is generally fastened at the neck in front. Masculine trousers or *pajama* are generally cut straight, of equal width, from waist to ankle. They are fastened by a drawstring at the waist and the bottoms are pleated and stitched to make them fitting on the lower leg. The *churidar* style is an upper class fashion, where the trousers are particularly long and fitting on the lower leg. White is most common for these garments. The professional and upper classes generally wear a long, fitted coat (cut similarly to the *achkan* pattern) with these trousers. This is like a slimly elegant version of the frock coat of mid-nineteenth century England, but it has an upstanding collar and buttons up to the neck and down to the waist; the skirt is generally slit at the sides.

The most usual wear for women is the blouse and *sari* or skirt, or a longer blouse with trousers. The modern *sari* is a piece of material six yards long and 45 inches wide. It is draped with the width of the fabric extending from waist to ground. It is put on over an ankle-length waist petticoat and the folds of the *sari* are tucked into this at the waist where they can also be pinned if desired. To drape, the material is wrapped width-wise round the body from the right side, the remaining length is then measured over the shoulder and

drawn to the ends of the fingers. The excess fullness is then gathered in at the waist in front and folded into at least four pleats which fall vertically just to clear the ground. The reserved section of material is then drawn across the front of the body and draped over the left shoulder, falling down the back at least to the hips. Alternatively, this material can be draped upwards over the head. There are a number of variations possible in draping a *sari*; the material can hang much longer at the back to form a train or this portion can be brought round the front of the body after passing round the back and be tucked in at the waist. In another version, the final length is allowed to hang down in front where it is then looped between the legs as in a *dhoti* and it is then tucked into a decorative waistband at the back. This gives a simulation of loose trousers at the ankles, between the looped up material. Such *saris* are particularly long, generally up to eight yards of material, but a *dhoti* or petticoat is not needed. For day wear *saris* can be patterned or plain and often have decorative borders; they are usually of georgette, silk or chiffon. For evening or formal wear they are made of heavier silk in order to drape more imposingly and are in rich or bright colours often ornamented with gold or silver thread. The *sari* is worn with a fitted bodice which acts as a bra to support the breasts and define them; the bodice lifts not flattens. Most commonly called a *choli*, this bodice is fastened up the centre front by hooks and eyes or buttons. It is short, finishing about two to three inches above the waist. Necklines vary from round to V or square and the garment can have long or short sleeves or be sleeveless. Necklaces are worn with the *choli*, which is often patterned to contrast with the sari.

In some parts of the Indian sub-continent, particularly the west and north-west, skirts were worn under a *sari*. These were of rich materials, full and pleated and fastened at the waist by a silk cord or a metal belt. The glittering material shimmered through the transparent *sari* on top. Also in the north, especially in Kashmir

White cap, dark cloth coat over white dhoti

Deep red silk sari with gold borders over floral choli

Moghul lord, c.1650. Striped jewelled turban, jamal with decorative belt, white trousers, gold leather shoes

Moghul dignitary, 1565. Angharka with gold edging and sash

Formal long coat and trousers, white cap

Silk sari over gold brocade choli, gold sandals

Lurex dress and salwar, white silk dopatta

White shirt (kurta) over white trousers. Turban (pagri)

Rose silk kurta over darker red silk salwar, both decorated with gold embroidery, silk veil

Silk gauze veil with gold ornaments. White sari tucked up like a dhoti.

Dhoti and turban

Kurta, pagri and dhoti

and the Punjab, trousers were and are worn, rather than a *sari*. These *salwar* (shalwar) were an adaptation from the Turkish design (see *Chalvar*) and were very full and long. In past centuries ten yards of homespun cloth was needed to make a pair of such Punjabi trousers, but modern versions are only fashionably full, usually of five yards of silk. The *kurta* or blouse is worn with the *salwar*. It hangs loosely to the knees and is decoratively embroidered.

A shawl or mantle (*orhni*) or a scarf or veil (*dopatta*) is often worn with the *kurta* and *salwar*, though not with a *sari*. This is a rectangle of silk or muslin about ten feet long and three feet wide. It is draped over the breasts and left shoulder and hangs over the right arm; it can be raised to drape on the head like a veil and can also be drawn across the face to screen it from public view. The Moslem lady still wears a more enveloping garment called a *burqa*. The modern version is in two parts; an upper section which covers the head and drapes to the waist all round and which has eye-holes to see through and an overskirt reaching from waist to ankles. The older form completely covers the body from head to foot falling from a pill-box cap and having only an eye-mesh to peer through (see similar designs illustrated in *Afghan dress* and *Tcharchaf*, under *Chadar*).

Women generally cover their heads with folds of the *sari*, by the *orhni, burqa* or by a separate veil made of very thin material which is embroidered and jewelled. Men wear a turban or a cap. The *turban* is more usually worn in southern and western India. It is made from a piece of cloth which varies in length from four yards to 20 and can be wound and tied round the head in an infinite number of ways. Its size is determined by rules of social etiquette. The larger turban, the *pagri*, should be neatly and carefully bound to produce an even silhouette and should cover both ears apart from the lobes. A tightly, smoothly wound turban is the mark of a cultured person. Sometimes one end is left to hang down the back or is looped up to be tucked in the top fold of the *pagri*. The *lungi* is much smaller and is generally tied on top

of a gold, embroidered skull cap. A number of different styles of cap are more usual as headcovering in the east and north-east of the sub-continent. The Gandhi cap of white or light material is widely in use; this is oval with a folded top. The red brimless fez with black tassel is worn by Moslems as is also the cylindrical grass cap.

While European footwear is now generally in use in India, the Indian style of shoe and sandal is still worn. The shoe has a low pyramidal heel and a flat sole. It is made of decorative leather styled with upturned pointed toes. Sandals have straps attached to a leather sole.

Though Indian garments are simple and few in number, ornamentation has always been rich and profuse, both in decoration of fabrics and in items of jewellery. Metal threads are widely used in weaving and embroidery, especially in borders. Jewellery is used to adorn every part of the body from the head-veils and turbans to earrings, nose-rings, necklaces, bracelets, armlets, finger and toe rings, anklets and girdles. Men wear jewellery also.

Indienne

A name generally applied in the seventeenth and eighteenth centuries to cottons imported from the East, particularly the Indian subcontinent. Supplies in the seventeenth century were limited so the fabrics acquired a scarcity value and became the 'in' mode with the well-to-do. Elegant society prized such cotton more than silk and used them for dressing gowns which they called *indiennes*. These fabrics were painted in traditional Indian manner but, due to scarcity and their popularity, they became expensive. In order to supply a larger, middle-class market, which could not afford the high prices, it became the custom in the eighteenth century to print the materials in imitation of the painted designs.

Industrial and protective clothing

Garments made to protect a worker and his clothes from corrosive or poisonous substances and any form of environmental conditions hostile to human well-being

INDUSTRIAL AND PROTECTIVE
Navy wool peaked cap with snood for containing men's long hair to reduce risk of hair entanglement

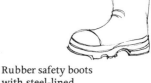

Rubber safety boots with steel-lined toe caps

Protective helmet

Munitions worker 1914–18. Rubber apron and boots. Cotton cap and overall dress. Protection against wet, oil, tar and acid

Munitions worker 1914–18. Boiler suit with puttee binding, cap and socks. For dangerous work where close-fitting clothes were essential

Yellow waterproof multithene suit. Face vizor, gloves, leather boots. Protection against acids, oil and solvents

P.V.C. brown suit, hood with vizor, rubber boots, gloves. Protection against corrosive liquids and sprays

Navy nylon suit lined with foam laminate for working in cold storage. Heavy duty rubber boots. Warm hood with ear flaps, gloves

American Apollo space suit designed for working on the surface of the moon

Fire suit of aluminized asbestos fibre. Protection against fire and radiant heat

Protective clothing for use where the product must be kept free of dust. Suit of multinolin (anti-static properties). Suit includes footwear, hand and head-covering

Protective clothing for bad weather on building site. Suit of dark grey melton and yellow waterproof P.V.C. fabric. Safety helmet and boots and safety. Protective clothing, especially in modern industry, also has the purpose of safeguarding the hygiene and quality of the industrial product from contamination by the worker.

The history of protective clothing in industry is a fairly recent one. Although the Industrial Revolution began in the mid-eighteenth century, there was little cognizance by most employers of any responsibility for the health and safety of their workers until the twentieth century. There were exceptions to this such as Josiah Wedgwood's insistence on protective aprons being worn by his lead workers and, of course, workers have always taken certain precautions themselves in the choice and suitability of clothes which they wore for work; the blacksmith's leather apron, the mill girls' heavy clogs, sacks tied round the body, were examples of this (see *Apron, Clog*). The early Factory Acts of the nineteenth century (1844 the first regarding safety) were chiefly aimed at protecting the worker from injury or death and were therefore concerned primarily with the guarding and design of machinery and equipment.

The First World War was responsible for the first great step forward in protecting workers, not only from injury, but also to ensure safety and health. Impetus was given by the influx of numbers of women workers, particularly to the munitions factories, where they were exposed to unpleasant conditions of dirt, noise, heat and damp as well as handling materials which could harm their skin or eyes. They were made to wear caps over their long hair, rubber aprons and boots as protection against oil, tar, acid or wet and trousers or boiler suits where close-fitting clothing was safer than loose garments.

Since 1918 extensive legislative requirements have been made of the employer and the altered attitude in social thinking and welfare have brought about a greatly increased appreciation of the protection in different forms of work. Long hair of both women, and recently, men, is confined in a cap or net; breathing apparatus is supplied where there are dangerous fumes or particles; helmets, vizors and goggles protect the head and eyes, heavy duty boots the feet, gloves and mitts the hands and fingers and ear muffs the ear drums.

The development of new materials and man-made fibres has widened the possible means of protecting the human body from fire, corrosive acids, extreme cold and heat. Suits are manufactured to give protective covering against all possible dangers. Perhaps the ultimate (so far) in helping man to survive in extremely hostile conditions is to be found in the space suit and breathing apparatus of the astronaut as shown in the drawing of the Apollo suit designed by the Americans for travelling and working on the surface of the moon.

Inlay

To set or embed into another material for the purpose of decoration. In costume this process is applied to jewellery, jewelled, metalled edging of garments, the handles of parasols and walking sticks, snuff and patch boxes and footwear.

Isfahanis

Name given to rich fabrics made during the years of Moorish domination in southern Spain. Derives from Isfahan, Iranian city and province, formerly capital city of Persia at the chief period of Arab supremacy.

Ivory

The hard white dentine obtained from the tusks of the hippopotamus, elephant, walrus and narwhal. Used for carved and inlaid decoration.

Check tweed
Norfolk jacket,
1891

Brown check tweed
sports coat,
hacking jacket
style, 1950

J

Jabot

A fall of cotton, silk or lace worn at the throat to conceal the closure of a man's shirt (seventeenth century) or as a finish to a lady's blouse (nineteenth century).

Jacket

An outer garment, like a short coat, for the upper part of the body. Evolved from *jack*, a term now obsolete, for a similar, short, fitting garment worn by both sexes. The word jacket is thought to be derived from the French *jaquette*, diminutive of *jaque* and the source of both words, jack and *jaque*, is probably the same i.e. the proper name Jacques. It is believed that the term came into general use because Jacques was such a common name in the country and the jacket, as a garment, was everyday wear, especially for men, for the peasantry of both France and England from the fourteenth century onwards. Later it became a garment especially worn by boys as, for example, *Eton jacket* (see *Children's dress*).

In fashionable costume, the chief body garment of the Middle Ages and Renaissance was the tunic, known by various names at different times – doublet, gipon, pourpoint, jerkin etc. (see *Doublet*). Jackets, which were less close-fitting and often shorter, were not generally accepted as part of modish dress until the nineteenth century though, for brief periods, they were adopted by both sexes. For instance, men generally wore an open jacket with their petticoat breeches in the 1650s and 1660s; this was an intermediate style between the longer doublet of earlier in the century and the *justaucorps* of the later years (see *Coat*). Dainty styles of jacket were fashionable for ladies in the second half of the eighteenth century, reaching to the waist and flaring out over the panier skirts.

Since 1800 varied styles of jacket have been worn by both sexes. For men the garment was used, chiefly from the 1850s onwards, to replace the coat for informal wear. There was the *sack coat*, the *dress lounge jacket*, the *smoking jacket*; the last-named was usually of a richly-coloured velvet, cloth or brocade, decorated by braid loops and buttons. It was reserved for use by gentlemen at home in the smoking room where they could savour their tobacco smoking without offending the ladies' susceptible nostrils in the drawing room. Later in the century there was also the *dinner jacket* to accompany evening dress (see *Coat* and *Evening dress*).

From the 1880s there were a number of jacket styles for men for sports and holiday wear. The *Norfolk jacket* was usually of tweed with knickerbockers and cap or hat to match (see *Children's dress* and *Knicker-bockers*). This was a belted style, buttoned down the centre front and was characterized by longitudinal box pleats. It was worn by men, women and children. The *blazer* was a light jacket, generally of brightly-coloured flannel, in use for sports and summer wear. Originally a scarlet, university jacket, the name was applied from the 1880s, to such a jacket of any bright colour, generally vertically striped and with the club badge on the upper pocket. The blazer, like the Eton jacket before it, was eventually adopted as part of school uniform (see *Children's dress*). The *pea* or *pilot jacket*, later known as a *reefer* jacket, was a naval short, double-breasted coat of heavy, dark blue cloth. It

Canezou jacket of
fur-edged velvet,
1802

Blue silk jacket
with gold banding,
1660

Hussar jacket with
braid decoration,
1813

Velvet jacket with
fur trimming, 1770

Plum-coloured
velvet jacket with
grey fur and tassel
trimming

Striped blazer

Striped bolero over
summer dress, 1938

Naval type reefer
jacket

Zouave jacket with
braid trimming,
1862

Mauve poplin
afternoon dress
with matching
bolero, 1905

was adopted for civilian wear, when it could be worn as a short coat or a hip-length overcoat. It was especially fashionable in the second half of the century. The *bush* or *safari jacket* was originally designed for use in the African bush. It was made of water-repellant corduroy or heavy linen and had four large flap pockets. The safari style, in all colours and materials, has become fashionable in modern times as a holiday jacket for both sexes.

Jackets of different styles were worn by ladies for much of the nineteenth century. In the early years these were very short, in *spencer* style (see *Coat*), extending only to just under the breasts and having short puff or fitting long sleeves. Typical was the sleeveless *canezou jacket* and the *hussar* style, which was decorated, like the military uniform dolman jacket, with brandenburgs or braid trimming. This style was reintroduced in the 1880s. The jacket was particularly suited for wear with the crinoline and bustle skirts of the years 1850–88. Fashionable in the middle years was the *zouave* collarless jacket worn open in front and having rounded corners. It was named after the uniform jacket of the Zouave regiment in Algeria. More typical of the 1870s and 1880s was the fitted outdoor jacket reaching to the hips and resting upon the bustle at the back. The *bolero jacket* has been a popular feminine fashion from the 1860s until the present day. It derives from the short, tailored Spanish jacket, which was worn open over a white shirt and a brightly-coloured sash. The bolero has since appeared with or without collar, sleeved or sleeveless. It is always worn open and is never longer than waist-length. Sometimes it is of matching material with the dress, sometimes of contrasting fabric; it is usually part of a summer ensemble.

Jade

A hard, partially translucent stone which can be highly polished. There are three minerals which are referred to as jade and these – nephrite, jadeite and chloromelanite – contain different materials; the first lime and magnesia, the others alumina and soda. High quality jade is often white but the beautiful greens and reddish browns result from other materials in the composition such as chromium and iron. Jade is chiefly found in Upper Burma but also in India, Silesia, Turkestan and Alaska. Although most of the beautiful carved jade comes from China, where the stone is traditionally reverenced, it had to be imported into the country.

Japanese dress

The early history of Japan is in the form of legends which are nebulous and disconnected. The Japanese appear to be a mixed race deriving from Central Asia, Korea, possibly Europe and probably Polynesia. The historical era began in the fifth century AD with the adoption of the Chinese script but, even before this, the Chinese and Korean influence upon Japan was extensive. With the introduction of Buddhism in the following century, these influences became stronger and Japanese dress developed from the Chinese prototype. As in China, the kimono (under different names according to the period of dress) was the fundamental garment. It was simple, square cut, comfortable to wear and to fasten and easy to adapt for riding and combat. The Japanese kimono was based upon a Chinese prototype which had been worn since the third century BC. It was open in front like a coat but cross-closed to a high rolled-padded collar and appeared to be a closed form as it was wrapped over to be of double material in the front centre panel. The garment was square cut and so were the wide sleeves. During the sixth and seventh centuries such kimonos were worn by both sexes, as in China, hanging loose in folds from the shoulder or belted with a sash tied round the body.

A formal court costume was established for both men and women by the beginning of the eighth century. This was based upon the Chinese dress of the T'ang dynasty, which had been worn for 200 years. But by the Heian–Fujiwara period in Japan (785–1185), the Japanese were establishing their personal interpretation of such formal

Court lady,
fourteenth century.
White kosode, red
silk hakama

Modern version of
Heian court dress
worn by members
of the Imperial
family at important
ceremonies.
Sokutai

Modern version of
Heian court dress,
junihitoe, in
coloured silks with
gold embroidery

Late eighteenth
century. Black obi,
patterned lining to
kimono

Late eighteenth
century formal
samurai dress of
kamishimo and
hakama over
kimono

Mid-eighteenth
century noble lady
in olive green
patterned uchikake
over white kosode
and red hakama

Twentieth century
kimono and obi,
tabi and sandals

dress and their costume design began to diverge from the Chinese model so that, towards the end of the tenth century, the national ceremonial dress was established. This was a very formal attire which almost obliterated the characteristics of the human form, especially in the feminine version which consisted of many layers of garments worn on top of one another, all visible in parts of the dress, and trailing on the floor. As in China, there was a ritual of certain forms and colours in dress reserved for specific status and rank, but the Japanese system was simpler. Fabrics were much less decorated than the Chinese, the ornamentation being confined to the corners, panels or borders and there was little or no jewellery. The men's dress was angular and stiff and strongly influenced by the warrior cult dominant in Japan's power structure.

Fujiwara was the name of the ruling family of these years, Heian the original name of its capital, Kyoto. It was a time of luxury at court, of lavish, rich costumes and great formality. This court dress exercised a tremendous influence on Japanese dress in general. Even in the twentieth century it has continued to be worn for the most formal and important occasions by the Imperial family, as for example, by the Crown Princess Michiko at her wedding in 1959. The nobleman's court costume (*sokutai*), like the lady's, consisted of many layers of garments. He wore a white linen shirt decorated with red and black silk at collar and wrists and, on top of this, a silk jacket, then a jacket with dependant train, a stiffly-starched robe, one or two dark-coloured, silk robes and, on the exterior, a double-breasted robe with high collar fastened on the right side. This outer garment was full length but it was held in place by a deep, decorative belt and the material was pulled up to hang over it. Under the robes were worn *hakama*, which were very full trousers, like a divided skirt, and these could trail on the ground or be bound up at the ankles. A skull cap or hat was worn on the head (the design varied according to rank) and this was tied with cords or pinned to the queue.

Behind was an erection to hold the queue and from this depended a gauze streamer.

The lady's costume was generally known as *junihitoe*, meaning 12 layers, though it could consist of more than this. Next to the skin a noble lady wore a white silk *kosode*, a lined kimono with short sleeves, the *hakama* (or *nagabakama*), the full trousers of red silk which trailed about a foot on the ground and were bound with a sash at the waist. On top of this came the longer, unlined kimono, the *hitoe* and then several layers of *uchiki*. These kimonos, up to 20 layers, were of silk in different colours, each one slightly larger than the one beneath so that each was displayed at the edges of the front, neck and sleeves; the colour combinations were carefully graded and chosen to blend in harmony. Then came the *uchiginu*, a lined *uchiki*, and an outer garment, the *uwagi*, which was made of richly decorated silk in colours and designs according to rank. The *karaginu*, a short jacket, was worn on top and, also, *mo*, the pleated train. The hair was dressed very long to hang down the back loose or tied at the nape. Aided by false hair, this trailed at the back even longer than the train. As time passed the court dress was simplified. It was still called *junihitoe* but the number of layers was reduced, generally to five, the extra layers being simulated by bands of coloured material inserted to show at the edges of sleeves and front. The shape of the garments was unchanged as was the heavy silk fabric in its varied colours.

For everyday wear the two garments generally worn, an upper and lower section, evolved into the characteristic *kimono*, worn by men, women and children. A kimono is made of straight pieces of silk about 18 inches wide, which are sewn together loosely so that they can be taken apart for cleaning or washing. For ordinary wear the kimono is simply cut and generally plain. Usually the small sleeve style, the *kosode*, is worn. This has a little opening to allow the hand to pass through. The wide, hanging sleeve, the *furisode*, is worn by geisha and young girls. On top of the kimono women wore the *uchikake*, which was a loose over-kimono of rich material, worn ungirdled. Men continued to wear the two-part garment (*kamishimo*) until the nineteenth century. The upper part was like a blouse or jumper, with wide, extended shoulders and the lower was loose *hakama*. The latter are now reserved only for formal occasions.

With the kimono, both sexes wore the *haori*, a three-quarter loose coat and the *obi*, bound round the waist. The *obi* is, by tradition, a most important part of Japanese dress and, especially for women, is a most decorative part of it. In the early years it was the belt or sash attached to the *hakama*, which was tied to fasten the garment at the waist. After the twelfth century the *obi* became a separate item of dress, at first a narrow sash, but becoming wider until, by the seventeenth century, it was 12–15 inches deep and up to 12 feet in length. It was made of rich fabric, often decoratively embroidered also, and was tied in a wide variety of ways in front, at the side or rear.

In the twentieth century the man wears an *obi* of soft silk wound round the waist and tied. For formal occasions the *obi* is of stiffer fabric and is fastened in a double knot at the rear. There are two chief forms for ladies; a large butterfly bow tie for girls and brides and a flat knot at the rear for married women. For full dress wear the *obi* is of still brocade and is about one foot deep. It is worn folded in half lengthwise with the selvedge edges uppermost, then wound tightly round the waist. These selvedges form a receptacle for the lady to keep her purse, handkerchief and cosmetics. The *obi* is then tied at the back in a complicated bow, the knot of which is bombasted by the insertion of a small pillow. These are maintained in the correct position by a silk cord which, having been passed through the knot, is then fastened in front with a jewelled brooch called an *obidome*. Until the late nineteenth century the *obi* was fastened by means of a *netsuke*. This was a toggle made in different forms. Often it was a circular button but it could be more decorative, carved into figure or animal form, singly or in groups, in bone,

Mid-nineteenth century white kosode with gold and silk embroidery. Ornamented obi. White silk uchikake on top

Haori over kimono and obi. Tabi and sandals

Carved wood netsuke, gold cords and lacquer inro

Modern wood sandals with leather straps

Dark silk kimono with embroidered panels and obi, *c.*1880

Working dress. Blue cotton trousers, white shirt, dark kimono. Tabi, straw hat

Lady's silk slipper

Black cotton tabi

Pale blue knitted twin set, double pearl necklace, 1937

Turtle-neck, cable-stitch, handknitted pullover, 1955

Handknitted pullover, 1930

amber, ivory, wood and shell. From the *netsuke* a silk cord passed down below the *obi* and from this depended a purse or an *inro*. This was a portable nest of small, decorative boxes, which fitted one inside the other to contain medicines, seals, tobacco, writing materials, perfume or other requisites.

In the present day western dress is normal everyday wear in Japan, but the traditional costume appears for festive and important occasions.

In modern Japan the hair, for both sexes, is also dressed in a western manner, but, until the early twentieth century, the coiffure was most formally and stiffly dressed. Until the mid-nineteenth century men shaved the front part of their heads and grew the back hair into a pigtail which they then knotted on the top at the rear. Ladies' hair was dressed in complex wings and sweeps, with a large puff on top. In both cases the hair was stiffened with oil and held in position by pins or ties.

Characteristic Japanese footwear includes the *tabi*, which is a sock with a separate shaping for the big toe and the deep clog, the *geta* (see also *Clogs*). Sandals and slippers were also worn.

Jasper

A hard, opaque variety of quartz which can be highly polished. It is found in many colours and is sometimes banded in stripes of several colours, especially red and green.

Jean

A strong, twilled cotton material: a type of fustian. The many different spellings include Janua, the medieval Latin word for Genoa, the Italian city where the material was made in the Middle Ages. It has been used widely since the sixteenth century for working clothes due to its hard-wearing quality. Though available in other colours, the fabric is commonly blue and is best known in the second half of the twentieth century for blue jeans, which are named after it (see *Levis*). The word jeans has been used since the early nineteenth century for trousers made from jean.

Jersey, jumper, pullover, sweater

These names, among several others, are used to describe knitted garments worn by men, women and children to cover the top half of the body. The name *jersey*, also *guernsey* or *gansey*, derives from the knitted shirts or tunics made by their wives for the fishermen of the Channel Islands from the seventeenth century onwards. These were of heavy wool, usually blue, from which the natural oil had not been removed so the garments were partially water-repellant. The island of Jersey had been famous for its knitted garments since the sixteenth century. By the 1580s the people there acquired a reputation for the knitted stockings and men's waistcoats which they exported to England and France; indeed, the name jersey then became synonymous with knitting and all such garments were called jerseys. It was only in the later seventeenth century that the term became localized as fisherman's jersey and the word later applied to just this one knitted article.

With the interest in sport in the second half of the nineteenth century and the growing desire to wear clothes more suited for participating, jerseys were introduced for playing football, hockey and other winter games by men and boys. These jerseys, usually striped horizontally, were hip-length and had long sleeves. By the 1890s the jersey was being worn for bicycling, mountain walking and golf. It was still long, with sleeves and had a polo neck. The term *sweater* was now used colloquially. This word had originated in America, coined by college athletes who, returning heated after some sporting activity, were inelegantly describing its effect upon them.

In the 1920s and 1930s knitted garments became fashionable and there were varied designs with names that differed from country to country. In England, the man's knitted top with V or polo neck and long sleeves or none was a *pullover*; it had no fastening. Ladies wore similar garments but called them *jumpers*. Those opened and buttoned down the front were *cardigans* (see *Cardigan*) and a matching set of the two was the very fashionable *twin set*. In America the *sweater* was generally now the fashionable term for such garments, in France it was *le pullover*, in Italy *il golf*.

Between the wars most woollen tops were hand-knitted and the gaily-coloured fair isle patterns were popular (see *Fair Isle Knitted Patterns*). By 1950 the fine quality machine-knitted garments were more readily available and these soon developed to a very high standard in a variety of materials from wool to all kinds of artificial fibres. New designs and fashions appeared (usually from the USA) and were established. In the 1940s and early 1950s there was the *Sloppy Joe*, a very long loose top with long sleeves, worn over a blouse which showed at the collar. There were *polo neck* designs (see *Collar*) and *turtle neck* patterns, where the neckline was finished by a wide collar rolled down like a tube and fastened down all round. In the 1960s *tank tops* became popular, especially with girls. These were usually sleeveless and had low, round necklines (see also *Knitting*).

Jersey fabric

Different forms of jersey knits were available in the 1950s and 1960s. These could be single or double (see also *Bonded fabrics*) and were made up into dresses, suits and other garments.

Jessamy

A corruption of jessamine, jasmine. In the seventeenth and eighteenth centuries referred to the perfume of jasmine, also the yellow colour of the jasmine flower as well as jessamy gloves, i.e. those yellow in colour which were given as a present to bride and groom.

Jester

A maker of amusement employed by a nobleman to entertain his household and guests. The jester originated in the Byzantine courts and flourished during the Middle Ages in Europe. His costume comprised a hood with dagged shoulder cape and fool's cap with ass's ears. He carried a cane topped by a miniature head, cap, cape and bells. Later his attire was referred to as motley or fool's dress (see also *Harlequin* and *Clown*).

Jet

A hard, dark form of lignite which could be highly polished. Known from prehistoric times. A dense substance, coloured blue to black. Used extensively in costume jewellery and decoration of garments, especially in the nineteenth century for mourning jewellery, buttons and ornaments.

Jewellery

The collective term for jewels and for the art of designing a piece or set of jewellery. Some items are practical adjuncts of dress decorated by precious stones and metals, for example, a brooch, clasp or pin, while others are intrinsically ornamental pieces only, such as earrings, necklaces, finger rings. The decoration of costume and the human body by such items is as ancient as the wearing of clothes. Human beings have always worn necklaces, bracelets and armlets, even in the most primitive societies and when they were wearing little else. These might be made of the teeth of animals or fish, shells and polished stones notable for the beauty of their colour, patterning or shape.

The ancient Egyptians made jewellery of fine quality, exquisitely fashioned, especially in the later dynasties when designs were varied and intricate (see *Egypt, ancient*). Turquoise, lapis lazuli and many precious stones were delicately set in gold to make decorative collars, armlets, bracelets, earrings and finger rings. Babylonian, Assyrian and Persian designs were more massive, made in bronze and gold, heavily encrusted with stones and jewels. As well as other items, men and women of rank wore heavily jewelled belts and hair fillets (see *Mesopotamia*). Cretan people loved jewellery and jewelled enrichment; they wore several bracelets on each arm, necklaces in rows with pendants, finger rings, earrings, pearl ropes in the hair and decorative metal waistbelts. The Minoans utilized gold, bronze and silver but the

Mycenaeans specialized in gold work. These metals were set off with precious and semi-precious stones, the cutting and polishing of which was a high art in Crete. They especially used amethyst, agate, cornelian, jasper, porphyry and lapis lazuli (see *Minoan and Mycenaean dress*). The Greeks, Romans and Etruscans all loved jewellery also and the quality of workmanship was especially high in Greece, where they used gold and enamels as well as filigree, which is a fine metal openwork of gold, silver or copper wire twisted into delicate patterns (see *Greece, ancient*). Etruscan jewellery was also of very high quality and was worn in abundance. The Etruscans specialized in the decorative process of granulation, where gold powder is applied to make patterns on the surface of the metal (see *Etruscan dress*). Roman jewellery designs were more derivative, based upon those of Hellenic Greece. They were elaborate, heavier and with a less fine quality of workmanship. As the Empire was extended there was an abundant use of gold and precious and semi-precious stones of all kinds, including diamonds (see *Rome, ancient*). Byzantine costume was even more richly ornamented, particularly in the use of gold and pearls (see *Byzantine dress*).

Because of the durability of jewellery and the value placed upon it by the owner, we know more of these items of Bronze and Iron Age Europe outside the classical world than we do of the people's dress. Jewellery was buried with the owner and many fine pieces have been discovered in tombs in northern and western Europe, the Dnieper valley and the Balkans. The Danish peat bogs have yielded bronze and gold necklaces, bracelets, brooches, armlets and finger rings. Scythian jewellery was especially fine, made in gold and bronze and decorated with sculptured animals and fish. They also used precious stones and developed cloisonné work (see *Cloisonné*).

After the collapse of Rome, the classical influence was still apparent on jewellery designs in Europe. Filigree work was still common, also enamelling and the actual pieces showed Roman influence as in fibula design (see *Fibula*). Derivation from Roman forms was especially strong in Italy and can be clearly seen in Ostrogothic work and Visigothic cloisonné pieces. Frankish jewellery shows more of a Gaulish and Teutonic derivation. Characteristic are the large circular brooches and square buckles. From southern Spain and Portugal come some fine, metal workmanship in gold and silver, both in chased, solid forms and in filigree; bird brooches, decorative bracelets and large, collar necklaces predominate, not dissimilar to Celtic torcs. Scandinavian jewellery is massive in scale and, after the fifth century, gave place to indigenous designs, such as the tortoise brooches. By the ninth century, the Viking style of jewellery had evolved and similar designs appeared in Scandinavia, Scotland and Ireland. Characteristic are the massive bronze armlets and the penannular brooches, which are very large, circular and have long pins which, when worn, pointed upwards. Some of these brooches, made of silver, are beautifully decorated with typical Celtic incised, interlacing patterns.

During the Middle Ages jewellery became more and more an integral part of dress as evidenced in jewelled necklaces and pendants, jewelled neck-edging, belts and girdles and decoration for the coiffure. The Roman fibula was replaced by the circular ring-brooch and especially characteristic was the pendant necklace. The trend of richness of dress with jewelled decoration continued and deepened in the sixteenth century and, by the 1580s and 1590s, much of the costume was enriched by jewels. During the seventeenth century the art of gem-cutting was developed (see *Gem*) and this strongly influenced designs of jewellery. Enamel-work reached a very high standard. Designs of jewelled pieces became complex with the precious stones grouped in intricate settings. Characteristic of eighteenth century work is the matching set of pieces of jewellery – necklace, brooch, earrings, bracelet, tiara – known as *parure*.

Artificial gems had been known for a long time. From the seventeenth century a high quality imitation stone was developed.

Paste, or strass, jewellery, as this came to be known, was made from a hard compound of glass which contained potash and white oxide of lead. This glass possessed such brilliance and French jewellers, in particular, became so skilled at handling it, that in the second half of the eighteenth century, paste jewellery became prized in its own right.

Costume jewellery is a twentieth century term for designs which have been popular since the 1920s in which the intrinsic worth of the piece may be negligible but the colour, material and form may be especially suited, indeed often particularly designed, for the garment being ornamented. This type of decoration is the twentieth century version of the seventeenth century temple jewellery, so-called because these artificial pieces were made in the Rue du Temple in Paris. Articles on individual items in jewellery can be found under *Anklet, Armlet, Bracelet, Brooch, Buckle, Cloisonné, Collar (carcanet), Earrings, Ferronière, Fibula, Gem, Ring (finger)*.

Jewish dress

In antiquity the Semitic race of people descended traditionally from the Patriarch Abraham and his son Isaac were called Hebrews. It is thought that Abraham came from Ur on the Euphrates and migrated to Canaan as part of a larger movement of tribes at the time. The word Hebrew in Aramaic and Hebrew signifies 'one from the other side (of the river)'. The Hebrews were also known as Israelites, from their descent from Abraham's grandson Jacob, later known as Israël.

During the centuries between the time of Abraham and the Birth of Christ the Hebrews inhabited different parts of the lands lying between the Nile and the Euphrates. In the early years they were still nomadic, then followed Jacob and his sons into Egypt from where, after oppression and persecution, Moses led their exodus back to the lands where their ancestors had lived. The tribes settled in Palestine, where the two rival kingdoms were later established; Israel in the north and Judah in the south. Israel lost its independence and many of its people to Assyria in the late eighth century BC; the Judaeans were later exiled to Babylon. It was on their return from captivity half a century later, that the Hebrews took the name Jew, signifying 'man of Judah'.

For much of the time during the centuries between the period of Abraham until the twentieth century, the Jews have constituted a race but have been part of other peoples and nations in the lands which they have inhabited. Because of this there is not a Jewish costume *per se*. The Jews have worn a similar form of dress to that of the other peoples of the area and time in which they were living. Thus they adopted Arab garments in the nomadic years in the desert, Egyptian dress in ancient Egypt, Assyrian, Babylonian, Oriental Asian, Persian according to time and place. Similarly, in Europe, since the days of ancient Rome, Jews have largely adopted the styles and types of garments of their host country. There have been differences though, distinctions of hair and beard styles, decoration, materials and colours worn, styles of hat and shawl. Some of these distinctions have been ordained by the Jews themselves in order to differentiate their people from the nation with whom they lived, some differences have been imposed by the host country for the same reason; the commandments of Moses as he led the Hebrew tribes out of Egypt were an example of the former, the orders of the Nazis in twentieth century Germany an instance of the latter.

It is not easy to trace Jewish costume from the days of antiquity. There is no written record of the early years and little pictorial evidence either, since their laws forbade representation of the human figure. Much of the data which we possess comes from the cultures with whom the Jews lived: the Egyptians, Assyrians, Babylonians, Persians, Greeks, Romans and, from the Middle Ages onwards, Europe and the Middle East (see *Egypt, Mesopotamia, Greece* and *Rome*). The Bible is a rich source of information but the data on costume can be misleading in nomenclature and ambiguous. It is implied here that the

Aramaeans were kinsmen to the Hebrews so Syrian dress shown in Egyptian paintings should give an indication of how Hebrew dress appeared. The earliest depiction of Israelite dress is shown on the black obelisk of Shalmaneser III, of the ninth century BC, now in the British Museum in London.

In general, in antiquity, the Jews wore the following basic garments. The Hebrew names are given in brackets.

A loin-cloth (*ezor*).

One or more tunics (*kethoneth*). These could be knee- or ankle-length and had short or long sleeves. They were generally belted or girdled and sometimes more than one belt was worn, to which purses, keys etc. were attached.

A cloak or caftan (*simlah*). Generally a large rectangle of material like the classical himation, draped in varied ways. The Assyrian and Babylonian design was often depicted having fringed edges and the garment wrapped round the body. The caftan, of Persian style, was worn open or held at the waist by a sash.

The *ephod* was a priestly vestment worn on top of the kethoneth. It was sleeveless, partly open at the sides and extended to the hips. It was made of rich material and bound by a sash at the waist.

For headcovering men had a turban or a cap, women a veil. For out-of-doors women enveloped themselves in a large mantle (*simlah*), in a manner after the Arab *hayk* or the Asian *chadri* (see *Chadar* and *Cloak*). Ordinary people went barefoot, the well-to-do wore sandals, shoes or slippers often with Oriental turned-up toes. Women protected their elegant leather slippers in the street by wearing pattens on the lines of the Arab *kub-kobs* (see *Patten*). Shoes were removed on entering a building. Women used cosmetics freely and wore a great deal of jewellery of all kinds, including the nose-jewel, the *nezem*. The Hebrew tended his coiffure with care. Men grew beards and side locks and the hair was uncut and uncurled. The feminine coiffure was long and elaborately curled and waved. It was held in place by a band or kerchief.

The Hebrews' attitude to dress was Oriental in that they wore a number of layers one on top of the other and wealth was indicated by the richness and multiplicity of the layers. Gold and silver cloth were woven and rich embroideries worked. Colour also indicated status as the dyes which were costly to produce, such as purple (see *Dyeing*), crimson, violet, black and dark blue, were favoured by the well-to do.

Some of the particular characteristics of Jewish dress date from antiquity. Among these are features which also applied to the dress of certain other peoples but some are mentioned in the Bible, referring to specific details of the costume which Moses imposed upon his people in order that the Hebrews should be clearly differentiated from the peoples with whom they would be living. For example, it was ordained that certain tassels should be attached to the corners of the cloak or veil. These tassels, called *tsitsith* were to be dark blue, attached to the garment by a blue cord. The tassels can also be seen depicted on the hems of tunics and, of course, tassels were an essential part of the decoration of Assyrian, Babylonian and Syrian dress, but they generally decorated the complete edge of a garment or hem. Over a period of time the cloak or mantle became the *tallith*, later the prayer shawl. This was a parallel development to that of the Roman pallium (see *Rome, ancient*). In both cases the garment had been a large rectangle of material used to drape round the body as a cloak. Gradually the rectangle became longer and narrower until it had become a stole or scarf and was worn chiefly as a liturgical or academic vestment. The Jewish *tallith*, worn round the shoulders, with its pendant *tsitsith*, became the most characteristic of Jewish garments. It was also ordered that a Jewish adult male should permit the hair on the temples and cheeks to grow at least as long as to the angle of the jaw. These side locks (*peoth*) were especially characteristic though this was a style which was also adopted by other ancient cultures, the Minoans of Crete, for example. The Jewish custom differed in that it has prevailed almost until modern times. A further injunction was a kind of sumptuary

Syrian dress from Egyptian painting. Cloak wrapped round body over tunic, c.1500 BC

Kethoneth with sash at waist. Fringed caftan. Felt hat. Peoth. Slippers, c.500 BC

Israelite, ninth century BC. Assyrian influence. Fringed simlah over kethoneth. Cap, peoth, shoes

Hebrew. Mantle (simlah) with tsitsith over kethoneth. Assyrian influence in fringing, headdress and beard. Oriental slippers, c.1000 BC

Tallith and simlah with tsitsith over kethoneth. Peoth. Oriental slippers

Hebrew turban

Sixteenth century barrette

Eastern Europe, nineteenth century. Caftan, fur hat and boots

Peoth and yarmulka, nineteenth century

Medieval Jewish hat

Turban and veil. Gown (kethoneth) with waist sash, c.500 BC

Embroidered, lace brüsttüch, nineteenth century

Jude

Nazi Germany badge for Jews. Black on yellow

Velvet and fur spodic, nineteenth century

law which forbade the wearing of garments made from a mixture of linen and wool.

The Jewish customs regarding the wearing of the *tallith, tsitsith, peoth* and *shaatnez* continued into the Middle Ages in Europe. It was also accepted that married women should cover their hair with a veil or cloak. Another particularly Jewish item of dress was the round conical hat, of which there were a number of variations in design. This appeared to derive from the tall Persian head-dress of antiquity. By the later Middle Ages the Jews had integrated to a large extent into the population, especially in western Europe, and began to relax their special costume regulations. In reaction to this the Roman Catholic Church in Italy, wishing to prevent a mixing of the races and religious creeds, decreed that the Jews must wear some distinguishing mark on their clothing. In various European countries it became customary for a badge to be worn. This varied in form but usually was shaped like a ring or a star and was added to the bodice, hat or belt. In the sixteenth century the Jewish elders introduced their own regulations for differentials in clothing, being of one mind with the Christian Church in its purpose. They reiterated the ancient ordinances taken from the Old Testament and insisted on adherence to the rules regarding *tsitsith, shaatnez, peoth* and veiling of women as well as introducing a number of sumptuary laws regarding modesty and humility in dress. In eastern Europe, by the sixteenth century, the Jews began to adopt some of the garments of the region, particularly the Oriental long caftan, often tied with a sash, and the fur hat. In the eighteenth and nineteenth centuries, as the upper classes of such countries as Hungary, Poland and Russia began to turn to French styles in dress, the Jews retained their Turkish-style caftans and fur hats (*spodic, kolpak*), so acquiring a characteristic Jewish dress once more. Other particularly Jewish items of costume included the masculine skull cap (*yarmulka*) and the feminine square veil and decorative plastron or blouse front (in German, *brüsttüch*).

Regulations were introduced from time to time in Europe, especially in the east, to force the Jews to wear distinctive clothing, special hats, for instance, or garments coloured yellow. In modern times Nazi Germany enforced the wearing of a triangular or star-shaped yellow badge on the person's back. During the Second World War Jews in Occupied Europe also had to wear such badges.

Joseph
A long coat or cloak worn by women in the eighteenth century chiefly for riding. It was usually of some shade of green; it was buttoned down the centre front and had a cape.

Jumpsuit
American term for a working suit of overalls worn by both sexes in the twentieth century. Made of cotton (denim) or man-made fibres, most commonly in blue but also brown, green or grey. This all-in-one garment has long sleeves and trousers and is belted on the waist with an attached belt of the same material. It is fastened from neck to crotch by buttons or a zip. In modern times the jumpsuit can also be made in more attractive materials, worn for comfort rather than working overalls; it is still an all-in-one garment but can have short trousers and short or no sleeves.

In Britain the working one-piece overall for men and women developed for industrial use. Generally referred to as a *boiler suit* it was worn from the First World War onwards. During the Second World War it was often called a *siren suit* because of its suitability as night duty wear, during air raids; it was popularized at that time by Winston Churchill.

JUMPSUIT
Siren suit, Second World War

K

Kabaya

A word of Arabic or Persian origin. A light, loose tunic worn generally in the East. In the present century refers specifically to one worn in Malay countries by peasant women.

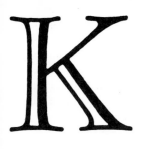

KAFFIYEH
Kaffiyeh with egal on top.
Present-day Saudi Arabia

Kaffiyeh

The traditional Arab head-dress made of cotton, linen, wool or silk, plain or patterned. Still worn today, even with western clothes. The material is folded to a triangular shape and placed on the head with one point falling down the back and the other two on the shoulders. The *kaffiyeh* is held in place by the *egal* (*agal*, *igal*), which is a decorative band made of cord or wool. The *egal* is usually two or three cords thick and these are covered by brightly-coloured material and can be decorated by beads and gold or silver threads.

Khaki

Urdū (Hindustani) word meaning dusty. Given to the dull yellowish-brown cotton material from which the uniforms of the army in India were made under British rule.

Kirtle

A word derived from various sources and with different meanings at various times.
1) From the Anglo-Saxon *cyrtel* and Old Norse *kyrtill*, a tunic. Refers to a man's tunic or body garment from the early centuries AD until about 1500.
2) From the Danish and Swedish *kjortel*, a gown, skirt or petticoat. From the late tenth century until the nineteenth, describes a gown or underskirt. From the late sixteenth century onwards the meaning of petticoat seems to have replaced that of undergown or underskirt.
3) Sometimes the word kirtle is used in the sense of a coat but this is generally a figurative reference.

Kissing strings

The strings for tying a ladies' bonnet or cap under the chin.

Knickerbockers

A loose form of breeches fastened by a strap and buckle or a tie at the knee. Worn from the 1860s onwards for comfort and ease on sporting, holiday and casual occasions. The jacket (often of Norfolk design, see *Jacket*) and the cap were generally of one material, making a suit, the outfit being completed by woollen socks, gaiters and boots.

The name is derived from Washington Irving's nom de plume for his *History of New York* of 1809, the fictitious Diedrich

KNICKERBOCKERS
Tweed suit with knickerbockers, 1890

Herringbone tweed jacket and plus fours, 1930

Knickerbocker. The Knickerbockers were a family of original Dutch settlers of New Amsterdam (later re-named New York). Cruickshank's illustrations of these Dutchmen in Irving's book showed a style of knee-breeches with ribbon ties which is said to have caused them to be named knickerbockers.

In the 1920s and 1930s a type of knickerbockers were popular for walking and cycling, which were called *plus fours*. They were rather fuller than the nineteenth century styles and had a deeper overhang over the band at the knee. They acquired their name because, in order to allow material for the overhang, the length was increased by four inches.

Knitting

A method of creating a fabric by the use of two needles and a continuous thread. Knitting has thus an affinity with crocheting and netting but differs from weaving in which two sets of thread are interlaced.

The word to knit derives from the Anglo-Saxon verb *cnyttan*. It is not known exactly how old the craft of knitting is but it is believed to date back at least to the second century AD. The craft was regarded as less skilled and important than weaving and few examples have survived from the early centuries and none from prehistoric times. Knitting came from the Arabian peninsula and the art was carried by the Arabs to Egypt, then eastwards into Asia to Tibet and westwards into Moorish Spain and Saracenic Sicily. Among the earliest surviving examples of knitting is a pair of socks of the fourth to fifth century found in Egypt which have separate sheaths for the big toes, suitable for wear with sandals; they resemble Japanese *tabi* (see *Japanese dress*).

Traditionally over the centuries brightly-coloured, patterned knitting developed in Egypt, Asia, in Tibet and further south round the north and east shores of the Black Sea, though the art does not seem to have penetrated in the early centuries AD to China, India or Africa. It is thought that the Spaniards introduced the craft to the Americas.

Knitting was practised in most of Europe from the Middle Ages onwards. From Spain it was introduced to France, to Germany and, by the later fourteenth century, to England. In the fifteenth century knitting and hosiery guilds were formed and by the later 1560s a high standard of work was being achieved in silk as well as wool and gold and silver threads were introduced especially to decorate stockings with clocks. The idea that knitting should be primarily a feminine pursuit is a twentieth century one. In general, before this, men were the professional, highly skilled knitters, apprenticed for five years or more to learn the intricacies of their craft and working within the guilds, while women worked within the cottage industry, at home, earning extra money in their spare time, even peripatetically while in the fields.

In the earlier Middle Ages, also in later, simpler communities, the material used was wool, often patterned, as in the traditional designs of Russia, Yugoslavia, Scandinavia and the Shetlands. Fancy stitches were incorporated into garments such as fishermen's jerseys, as in the Channel Islands (see *Jersey*). In colder and wetter climates wool was often felted to give protection. Typical garments made in this way were caps, socks, slippers, gloves and even cloaks. This method was widely used and survives today in the French beret and the Arab fez.

The character of the industry was altered by the introduction of silk knitting, especially for hose. Medieval hose had been cut from velvet or cloth into shaped sections which were sewn together. Knitted woollen hose appeared early in the sixteenth century and soon silk began to be used. Such silk stockings were not made in England until later in the sixteenth century but were imported from Spain and France by the nobility. A present was made to Queen Elizabeth in 1561 of a pair of silk stockings and she so much preferred them that she always tried to wear silk after this.

The British hand-knitting industry was at its peak in the sixteenth and seventeenth

KNITTING
Egyptian sock, fourth–fifth century

Shetland knitting pouch and needle

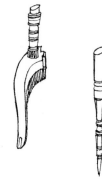

Knitting sheath and stick

centuries, mainly using wool and making caps, coifs, gloves, stockings, waistcoats and kerchiefs. The development of the spinning industry (see *Spinning*) led to more yarn being made available. Silk was widely used in the seventeenth century, while later in the eighteenth century, white cotton knitted garments were fashionable. These were knitted on fine needles in open-work, lacy patterns and included scarves, fichus, stockings and long mittens. Bead knitting was worked for bags and slippers.

Early knitting needles were hooked like crochet hooks; Arab ones were made of copper wire. In some methods one hooked needle was worked to take stitches from a blunt-ended needle, in others both needles were hooked. With the development of circular knitting four or five hooked needles could be employed. Medieval knitters used needles with pointed ends, as in modern work. These needles were homemade from a variety of materials: wood, bone, copper wire, iron, ivory or briar. They were called wires, skewers or woods and were tended carefully, kept in a leather pouch to preserve them undamaged and polished. Wood or cork stops were placed at one end of knitting needles until comparatively modern times, when these were replaced by plastic or metal knobs. Knitting needles were always made in different gauges and in the eighteenth century were very fine to knit silk and cotton. These were kept in carved or painted cases of ivory or wood.

From the sixteenth century onwards, when the cottage industry had become extensive, a hand-knitter tried to achieve great speed in her work in order to earn more and obtain further orders. A great assistance in this was the use of a knitting stick or sheath, which would hold the non-operative end of the right needle and so enable the right hand to be freed to handle the wool only and so attain a speed of some 200 stitches a minute. The sheath or stick was pierced at one end to take the knitting needle and it could be tucked into a leather waistbelt or held by the apron strings to keep it in place. The freed right hand could then act as a shuttle while the left hand maintained the balance of the work and controlled the movement of stitches up and down the needles. The knitting sheath or stick has continued in use as long as hand knitting is done to earn money.

During the nineteenth century machine knitting gradually ousted the hand knitter who, in Britain, retreated to the more remote areas: Scotland, Wales, Ireland, the Lake District and the Yorkshire Dales. The cottage industry here continued to be successful until the end of the century, producing a different article from the machine-made one and selling well in town markets. But in the twentieth century as machines were designed to be capable of more varied work, the hand-knitter retreated further and the remaining centres of the cottage industry were in Ireland and the Shetlands.

In the Shetland Islands in the twentieth century the hand-knitting industry continued to be practised as it had been in its seventeenth century heyday all over Britain. Children were taught the craft when very young and, as they grew older, achieved a great speed and rhythm in their work. The knitter tended her own sheep to produce her wool, cleansed, prepared, dyed and spun it into yarn. She used a knitting pouch or sheath held at the waist by a belt. The pouch works on the same principle as the sheath or stick; it is made of leather and padded and the leather covering is pierced with holes into which the knitting needle can be inserted and held in position. The peripatetic system of knitting in intervals of rest while working in the fields has traditionally been practised by the Shetland knitter, who kept her completed work round the back of her hips where it was held in place by a hook dependant from the waistbelt. This made it possible for her to take up the knitting in any free moment without the work becoming entangled. The Shetland Islands were famed during the nineteenth century for their lace knitting which they made especially into shawls (then so fashionable) copied from woven designs and using especially the same cone motif as the Paisley pattern. Coloured patterned knitting was traditional to the Shetlands from the late nineteenth century onwards; it became fashionable in the 1920s when it was practised in the home all over Britain, known as Fair Isle knitting (see *Fair Isle knitted patterns*). In the Shetlands (though not elsewhere) the colour range was limited to red, blue and white with a touch of yellow. In 1970 there were still over 2000 home knitters employed in the Shetland Islands and the work is in great demand but the hand-knitters are very poorly paid, an expert in Fair Isle or lace work earning about £5 for a 40 hour week in 1976. Under these circumstances and with the wealth and consequent full employment now reaching the Shetlands from the North Sea Oil industry, hand-knitting can only be a dying industry unless purchasers of the work are willing to pay a realistic price for the knitter's labour and skill.

MACHINE KNITTING A stocking frame which would knit hose by machine was invented at an early date, in 1589, well before other machines of the industrial revolution but, due to lack of official support, it was a long time before the frames were widely operative. It was the Rev. *William Lee*, curate of Calverton, a village a few miles north of Nottingham, who invented the machine to knit worsted stockings. He based this upon the operations carried out by the hand-knitter but used hooked needles which were devised to simulate the movements mechanically. His machine was enclosed in a wood frame, hence the term stocking frame, and was operated by a foot treadle and hand levers. Lee's stockings were knitted flat and had to be seamed but it was possible to vary the width of the fabric so that the stockings could be fully fashioned. The machine accomplished a row of knitting in one operation instead of only one stitch as in hand knitting.

Lee left the Church and came to London to work on his invention and made a number of frames. Queen Elizabeth came to see his machine working and was most interested in it but did not grant him a patent of monopoly because she feared for the widescale unemployment of the hand-knitters. She indicated that perhaps a machine which knitted silk stockings might find better favour. Disappointed but undaunted Lee returned to his researches and, by 1598, had developed a machine to knit silk stockings. He made a pair which he presented to the queen but, again, she refused his patent. A few years later James I also refused so Lee accepted an invitation by Henry IV to go to France. With his brother and a number of workers he set up his frames there and was successful. A few years later he died and his brother returned to England with the frames and workers and set up the machines in Nottinghamshire. By the mid-seventeenth century machine knitting had advanced so that the framework knitters acquired their own charter as a Worshipful Company.

During the seventeenth century framework knitting and hand-knitting prospered side by side. The machines began to produce other items besides stockings – gloves and sections for garments such as waistcoats. The machines were developed to make a greater variety of knitted fabrics in silk and wool as well as working at faster speeds. Nottingham was the important centre in England at this time but the use of stocking frames was becoming widespread in Europe also. In Spain machines were extensively employed for making silk stockings which were exported in quantity. By the late seventeenth and early eighteenth century the threat of competition by the framework knitters was seriously upsetting the hand-knitters and, seeing their livelihood threatened, they began to destroy the machines and attack premises and workers.

From the eighteenth century onwards Nottingham was the chief centre for the British stocking frame industry and the hosiery was produced from four types of thread: wool, linen, cotton and silk. Other, smaller centres continued machine knitting, such as Hawick and Edinburgh, but, as time passed, the concentration of the industry tended towards the Nottingham area. Both sexes worked on the frames, the men, in general, doing the more skilled work. The industry was organized by merchant entrepreneurs who generally supplied the frames for the stockingers (as they were called) to work upon. The stockingers worked in their own cottages or, more commonly, in larger buildings or groups of buildings. Typical were the three-storeyed structures with living accommodation on the ground floor, bedrooms in the first storey and, above, the workshops with the frames packed closely into them beside the characteristic long windows. Up to 20 workers knitted in a workshop which could, alternatively, be housed in a building adjoining the living accommodation or separate in a yard at the back.

From the mid-eighteenth century a number of refinements and improvements were made in the stocking frames though, even as late as 1900, Lee's frame still constituted the fundamental principle of design. It was *Jedidiah Strutt* who solved the problem of making a machine to knit ribbed hose as well as stocking stitch, which would give greater elasticity and firmness to the material. In order to create the knit one, purl one rib of a hand-knitter, it was necessary to reverse the needles to form the rib. Strutt took out patents for his design in 1758 and 1759 which was fitted with an attachment to turn the needles in order to reverse the loops. He set up a business in Derby and the stocking became known as *Derby-ribbed hose*. In the late eighteenth century further refinements introduced more decorative and lacy patterns. A *warp-knitting* machine was designed which produced a firmer fabric more like woven material, which could be cut and sewn into garments. In 1791 in Leicester *William Dawson* added a notched wheel to this type of machine, which was the first step towards a power-driven frame. Wider frames were made in the early nineteenth century to make fabrics of greater widths and, by 1816, there came the *circular knitting machine* or tricoteur, the invention of *Sir Marc Isambard Brunel*,

inventor, engineer and father of the famous Isambard Kingdom Brunel. Circular ribbed stockings followed in 1847 from a Nottingham knitter and a design for a power-driven machine from a Loughborough stockinger in 1855.

Late in the nineteenth century came the ability to widen and narrow automatically the fabric in power-driven stocking machines and fully fashioned silk and cotton stockings were being made before 1939. With the advent of nylon after the war, these machines were abandoned and new designs made, since it was then possible to knit a nylon thread circular stocking of equal width then set it with heat to retain a slender ankle and wider thigh. With the mini skirt came tights. These can now be made in one on a knitting machine starting at the toe of one leg and ending with the toe of the other, the whole operation taking three minutes per pair; in the middle is the body part with a finished opening for the waist. More often, however, it is convenient to make the two legs separately then sew them together. A further alternative system is to make one circular leg inside the other and, from this, then to open it up as tights. The operation of modern machines is now computerized.

Knots

Have acted as a means of fastening and decoration since early times, particularly in Oriental dress. In Europe ribbon knots were especially fashionable in the seventeenth century, where they could be seen ornamenting the hair of both sexes, the shoulder, the bosom, the sleeves, the bodice and the knees. Some of these knots were given names, such as the *button knot*, a small round knot acting as a button; the *lover's knot*, worn for remembrance; the *top knot*, hair or ribbon seen on top of the head; the *bosom knot*, placed in front on the neckline and the *duchess knot*, surmounting the fontange head-dress (see *Fontange*).

L

LACE
Bowed pillow horse

Pillow horse

Lace

Lace, like knitting, crochet and tatting, is made entirely of thread; there is no warp or weft, nothing exists until the lace-maker begins work. There are two types of hand-made lace: needle-point and bobbin. In *needle-point* or *needle-made lace* the work is carried out with a single needle and thread, worked one stitch at a time. The method evolved in Italy where it derived from drawn-thread work and cut-work, the spaces left by the pulled threads or cut-out pieces being sewn into a plain or patterned mesh. In true needle-point lace the design is drawn upon a piece of parchment which is then laid on material over a working pillow. A thread is placed on the lines of the design and is sewn to the parchment and material by frequent small stitches to hold it in place; two or three threads may be used if a heavier line is required and this process is called *cording*. The thread is then buttonholed all along its length, completely covering the thread or cords and the different parts of the design are then connected by ties or bars which are termed *brides*. The open spaces between the design are then filled in by needle-sewn fine mesh of looped stitches; the background is referred to as the *réseau* (netting). When the work is completed, it is detached from the parchment and pillow by cutting the original small, holding stitches.

Bobbin lace is an older method which evolved from passementerie. It is made by twisting and plaiting many threads together. At first, fingers of both hands were used as pegs to cross and twist the threads, then the bobbin system was developed which enabled a wider piece of material to be made. According to the number of bobbins used, the width of the fabric and complexity of design could be increased. The finger-made lace was only a narrow braid, while for a wide piece of lace, some hundreds of bobbins would be needed. Early bobbin lace was used only as edging for collars, caps and cuffs; it became a fabric in its own right from the later sixteenth century.

Bobbin lace is worked on a flattish, round pillow, hard-stuffed with straw to form a firm surface and covered with material. The pillow is supported partly in the lap and partly on a stand called a *pillow horse*; it can also be known as a lady or a maid. A parchment pattern for the design is sewn to the pillow. Bobbins are simply spools to hold some seven to eight yards each of thread. Early ones were made of animal bones and so early bobbin lace was known as *bone lace*. Later bobbins were mostly made of hardwood turned on a lathe though they could be of other materials such as bone or ivory. Each bobbin is designed

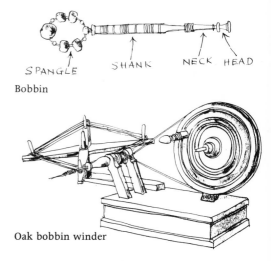

SPANGLE   SHANK   NECK HEAD

Bobbin

Oak bobbin winder

with a head which contains a groove for the thread to be looped around and a neck for the thread to be wound on to. At the other end of the bobbin is the spangle, which is a circle of beads whose purpose is to weight the end of the bobbin, this keeping it in place when not being handled and to give tension to the thread it is hanging by.

To commence making a piece of lace, a pin is pushed into the parchment and pillow at the top end of the pattern and two bobbins are fastened together and hung round the pin by their knotted thread. Further pins are inserted as needed to make the pattern and bobbin pairs hung on them. The twisting and plaiting of the threads is then begun, the fingers of both hands manipulating the bobbin threads. When the lace has completed the pattern across the top of the pillow – usually some 16–18 inches – the whole is removed, the completed lace being folded at the top and the pattern replaced, the whole process being known as setting-up. Modern pillows are often fitted with a cylinder containing the parchment which revolves in a recess to making a continuous process possible for the whole length of lace and obviating stopping for setting-up. Bobbin lace is sometimes known as *pillow lace* because of the pillows upon which it is made but this is not a precise term because other types of lace could also be made upon pillows.

Lace seems to have been first made in lands bordering the Mediterranean. There is pictorial evidence and actual remains of lace made in ancient Egypt, where it is believed that the threads were held on a wooden frame and plaited to make patterns. Literary evidence points to lace-making in ancient Greece and lace has survived from Asia Minor, Arabia and Armenia, where gold and silver lace has been preserved best; only later did such lace give place to flax thread.

In Europe the lace industry flourished from the sixteenth century until about 1800, the best work being done in the seventeenth century. However, in Italy, where lace-making seems to have devel-

Bobbin lace-making

Point de France, late seventeenth century

oped first, the finest work was a little earlier. Both needle and bobbin lace were being made in Italy from the later fifteenth century, first as an edging for caps, collars etc., then as reticella to decorate ruffs and cuffs and, finally, in the later sixteenth century as a fabric. One of the most

Bobbin lace from Milan, seventeenth century

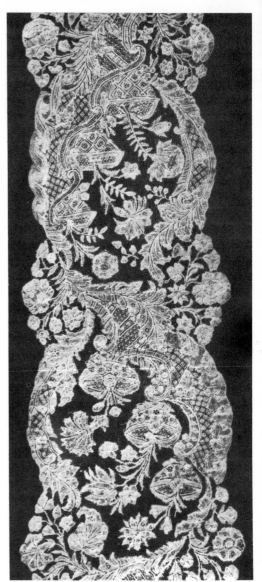

important lace-making centres was Venice where the most beautiful laces ever made were produced – *gros point de Venise, point de Venise à brides picotées* and *point de Venise à réseau*. Other centres making fine lace included Milan, Naples, Rome, Florence and Genoa.

The seventeenth century was an age of lace in costume. The falling bands and later cravats, sleeve cuffs and ruffles, the fontange head-dress, lace overlay and decoration for gowns all displayed to perfection the Baroque floral designs with free-flowing arabesques and their bold outline forms so characteristic of Italian lace, especially that from Venice.

From Italy knowledge of the craft of lace-making spread westwards, notably to France and Flanders. In France, in the seventeenth century, sumptuary laws had failed to curb the imports of vast quantities of costly lace from Italy and Flanders, so Jean-Baptiste Colbert, appointed Louis XIV's chief finance minister in 1661, decided that France should benefit from such expenditure by the nobility. He set in train extensive protectionist measures and at the same time encouraged Italian lace-makers to come to France to teach the French craftsmen. At first these foreign

Bobbin lace, Brussels, mid-eighteenth century

workers settled near Alençon and continued to make their famous *point de Venise*. Gradually the French lace was adapted to French design and influence and the name was changed to *point de France* (see Alençon point and Point de France). During much of the remainder of the seventeenth century the lace-making industry grew apace in France with many centres developing; chief of these were Le Puy, Argentan, Lille, Chantilly, Bayeux, Caen and Valenciennes. In Flanders, Antwerp, Bruges, Ghent, Ypres and Mechlin (Malines) were important centres but Brussels lace was one of the oldest established and finest in the country. Spain was

noted chiefly for its *point d'Espagne*, made using gold and silver thread from the sixteenth century onwards. In general, in Europe, needle-made lace was developed first, as a fashion edging and later a fabric, and bobbin lace followed; by the mid-sixteenth century both methods were being used. Needle-made lace was at its best in the mid-seventeenth century, then declined. Bobbin lace was of good quality all the century and only declined after 1800.

The revocation of the Edict of Nantes in 1685 was a disaster of the first magnitude for France's textile industries, especially silk and lace where Huguenot craftsmen played such an important role. It is estimated that France lost half a million such workers who, fleeing to other European countries in search of religious tolerance, were responsible for establishing industries there which soon competed with the depleted French ones to such a deleterious extent that France, from being an exporter of fine lace, became an importer once more. Huguenot lace-makers took refuge chiefly in England, Germany, Switzerland and the Low Countries; they brought their trade secrets with them and set up factories in their new countries. Ironically, one of the countries whose lace industry benefited most was Italy, where Venetian lace-workers once more monopolized the world markets with *point de Venise*, as they had done before Colbert's intervention.

Lace-making had been established in England in the sixteenth century mainly by refugees from Flanders, who set up in Devonshire in the Honiton area. The industry was reinforced after the revocation of the Edict of Nantes and also as a result of the French Revolution so that further centres were established in the Midlands as well as Wales, Ireland and Scotland.

Lace was a much less fashionable material in costume during the eighteenth century. The heavier Venetian and French laces were not suited to the mode and only the more delicate Brussels type of lace was made in quantity and was used for sleeve ruffles, neck and cap edging and lappets. Silk lace was introduced in the mid-century. This soft, shimmering, lustrous *blonde lace* was soon popular for ruffles and jabots. Chantilly was an important centre for this industry, also Bayeux and Spain, which produced some fine black and white mantilla lace in the Barcelona region.

During the nineteenth century machine-made laces had a disastrous effect upon the hand-made lace industry, apart from the silk laces of Chantilly, Bayeux and Barcelona which flourished because they were so superior to the machine-made equivalent but, inevitably, silk lace was also eventually made by machine.

MACHINE-MADE LACE As with the principal textile processes (see *Spinning, Textiles, Weaving*), attempts were being made to produce lace (formerly made by hand) by machine from the mid-eighteenth century onwards. These experiments were mainly conducted in Nottingham which, at that time, was not a lace centre but noted for its hosiery trade (see *Knitting*). In Nottingham were a number of stocking frame craftsmen (stockingers) who possessed imaginative ideas combined with considerable technical ability and they attempted to adapt the stocking frame to produce lace net. The earliest patent for such an adaptation was taken out in 1764 and a number of improvements followed. A great advance was in the machines to make *point net lace* in the 1780s. The chief drawback to all these stocking frame adaptations was that the net had to be made with a single thread, looped in various ways as in knitting and this meant that the fabric was so elastic that it could distort easily and, if a thread were to break, the whole would unravel. The *warp-frame* knitting system was developed from 1775 and was widely in use for lace by 1800. This was an advance on earlier point net in that a second thread was introduced but a stable, firm net was not possible until the Heathcoat twist net machine was patented in 1808.

John Heathcoat (1783–1861) was a stockinger in Nottingham who had great technical ability and considerable business acumen. At the age of 25 he invented a machine to make a hexagonal mesh net of the type customarily made by hand in the Midlands by the bobbin method. Heathcoat spent some time studying the bobbin lace-makers at work. He observed that, despite the apparent complexity of the multiplicity of threads being twisted and plaited, there was a general movement of one set diagonally across the lace from one side to the other and of another in an almost vertical direction. He decided to wind one set of his threads on to top and bottom beams, treating them as a warp (see *Weaving*) and used the second set as a weft, which did not merely pass over and under the warp threads but were passed round them and then moved across the fabric in a diagonal direction. When the warp threads were released from the tension under which they had been held by the frame, the fabric resembled lace net. From these experiments Heathcoat made his first lace-making machine, which he patented in 1808. This machine could only produce very narrow strips of net so he improved the design and his patent of 1809 was for a machine which would make a much wider strip. This *bobbin net machine*

was a great success and Heathcoat set up business in Loughborough, producing lace net in quantity. In 1816 his factory was attacked by Luddite rioters, because his produce was threatening the point net trade in Nottingham; his lace and his machines were destroyed. He was awarded £10,000 damages by the county of Nottingham on the understanding that he would re-start his factory in the area in order to employ local labour. Such a factory would give employment to many workers for the machines only produced plain net and the pattern demanded by fashion had to be run and embroidered by hand. Heathcoat refused and went to Tiverton in Devon, where he had already bought premises, and set up there in a large mill on the banks of the River Exe, where he installed 300 machines to be powered by water. Later he took out further patents for lace figuring and opened a factory in France which he ran on steam power.

Further improvements and inventions in lace-making machines followed during the nineteenth century, for example, in 1831 *William Sneath* patented a machine to make spotted net. The important breakthrough, however, was a machine to make patterned lace (which had been attempted for some time). The first machine which was capable of producing patterned twist lace was Samuel Clark's and James Mart's *Pusher machine* of 1812 and this imitated reasonably closely the bobbin lace system, but it was still necessary to work the pattern outlines by hand. It was the adapting of the machines to utilize the Jacquard system which finally brought machine-made patterned lace into full competition with the hand-made article (see *Weaving, Jacquard*). The first patent for doing this was taken out by *Samuel Draper* in 1835 and, in 1839, *James Wright* of Nottingham applied the Jacquard apparatus to the Pusher lace machine and from the 1840s this was very successful. By the 1860s Pusher lace was widely made, even imitating Chantilly silk bobbin lace most realistically in shawls, veils and trimmings for all garments. Meanwhile the Leavers machine had also been adapted to take Jacquard.

John Leavers had made his first machine to make lace net in 1813. By the mid-nineteenth century it had been improved and adapted to take Jacquard-controlled patterns. The last stage of mechanization, which did away with the need for lace-runners, the women who outlined the pattern by hand, was *Joseph Wragg's* invention which made it possible for the machine to introduce thicker threads which could outline the pattern.

By the middle of the nineteenth century most of the techniques and designs of hand-made lace from all parts of Europe could be imitated by machine and the centre of the English machine-made lace industry was Nottingham which had become the lace capital of the world. An interesting display of all kinds of machinery for making lace can be viewed in the Nottingham Industrial Museum in Wollaton Park near the city.

SPECIFIC LACES AND LACE TERMS

Alençon Point – the finest and most elaborate hand-made lace of France. First made in 1665 by French craftsmen taught by Italian lacemakers; the early work was based upon Venetian lace. By 1678 the lace had become a French product and was named *Point de France*. Usually a floral design on a net ground, the pattern was outlined by a cordonnet reinforced with horsehair: a heavy, firm, decorative lace (see *Point de France*).

Antwerp – a bobbin lace similar to but bolder than Mechlin.

Appliqué – needle-point or bobbin-made sprigs applied to a machine-made net ground.

Araneous lace, opus araneum – a cobweb type of design resembling a spider's web.

Argentan – a famous lace of the seventeenth century in Argentan, showing Italian influence in its design.

Argentella Point – an Italian lace made chiefly in Burano. A delicate lace similar in design to Alençon but without the raised cordonnet.

Arras – a bobbin lace generally featuring the mignonette motif.

Baby – a very narrow lace used as an edging for baby clothes, often Valenciennes.

Battenberg – a coarse hand or machine-made Renaissance lace using linen thread and tape.

Bayeux lace – similar to Chantilly, often black. From mid-eighteenth century silk lace was made in Bayeux.

Binche – an early bobbin-made Flemish lace.

Blonde – a very fine silk bobbin lace, originally cream-coloured, the silk being imported from Nankin, later white or dyed black. Made especially in Chantilly and Caen.

Bobbin, Bone, Pillow – lace made on a pillow with bobbins, the numerous threads being twisted and plaited to form a pattern. Bone was an early term for bobbin lace because the bobbins were made from animal bones. Pillow is an alternative, and usually nineteenth century, term.

Bride – a bar or tie to join the lace sprigs or motifs. *Bride picotée* is a bar in hexagonal form.

Bruges – a bobbin lace also called *Guipure de Bruges*.

Brussels – a very fine lace made from the fifteenth century onwards in Brussels from a fine linen thread derived from Belgian-grown flax. Brussels bobbin lace was known as *Point Plat* and needle-point as *Point à l'Aiguille* or *Point de Gaz*. Brussels was also known for an appliqué lace made from sprigs applied to machine-made net.

Buckinghamshire – a fine bobbin lace made from the sixteenth century onwards.

Bullion – a lace made from gold and silver threads.

Burano – an Italian needle-point lace made on the island of Burano in the Venetian Lagoon in the style of Venetian Point with cordonnet design. The centre flourished especially in the eighteenth century.

Carrickmacross – an Irish lace.

Chantilly – a bobbin lace of silk or linen thread, generally black but also white. Most famous for the silk blonde lace of the eighteenth and nineteenth centuries.

Chenille – a French lace with the pattern outlined in chenille.

Colbertine – a seventeenth and eighteenth century French net lace named after Jean-Baptiste Colbert.

Cordonnet – the cord or heavy thread used to outline the design in lace-making.

Cretan – lace made on the island of Crete from ancient times. Geometric motifs on a coloured flax or silk ground, also embroidered.

Cyprus – also made from ancient times. Then and in the Middle Ages made from gold and silver thread.

Dieppe – French bobbin lace similar to that of Valenciennes.

Duchesse – a bobbin-made lace of fine thread in dainty floral patterns, the sprigs made separately; popular for bridal wear.

Genoa – a lace-making centre from the fifteenth century onwards, known for its needle-point, bobbin, macramé and gold and silver laces.

Gold and silver – lace made from metal threads twisted into patterns was one of the earliest forms, known in ancient Egypt, Greece and Rome; a heavy material in simple, geometric designs.

Gros Point – see *Venetian lace.*

Guipure – a large-patterned, heavy lace with motifs raised by cords. In medieval times the word referred to a metal thread lace or passementerie.

Hollie Point – a needle-point lace made from the Middle Ages for church use. The term is a corruption of Holy Point.

Honiton – a wide area of Devonshire centred on Honiton which became important for lace-making from the sixteenth century onwards; established first by refugees from Flanders. Traditionally, Honiton lace was made from bobbin lace sprigs which were then sewn or appliquéd on to the net ground. Nineteenth century Devonia lace is a three-dimensional lace sculpture using flower or butterly motifs.

Italian lace – of the finest quality, made in Milan, Naples, Rome and many other centres, especially Venice (see *Venetian lace*).

Le Puy – oldest lace-making centre in France.

Lille – a French bobbin lace, very fine with delicate patterns.

Limerick – an Irish lace embroidered on net.

Macramé – derived from an Arab word for a striped cloth or fringe, macramé is a knotted point lace which was widely made in Italy and Spain during the fifteenth, sixteenth and seventeenth centuries. Unlike needle-point or bobbin lace, macramé is knotted, twisted and braided using the fingers only. It enjoys a modern popular revival.

Maltese – a bobbin lace made in simple geometric patterns and resembling a Greek guipure.

Mantilla – lace made for the Spanish traditional head-dress in France, also near Barcelona in Spain, white for special occasions, black for normal wear. From the mid-eighteenth century mantilla lace was generally silk bobbin lace (see *Manta*).

Mechlin – before the mid-seventeenth century this was a general term for Flemish lace, named after the town Mechlin (Malines). Traditional Mechlin lace is made in one piece by bobbins, ground and sprigs worked together; the cordonnet is of a shiny material. Mechlin lace was exported in quantity to England especially in the eighteenth century when it was used to trim the Indian cottons of the period.

Medici – French bobbin lace made of fine thread in intricate patterns with one scalloped edge.

Metal – a net lace with gold or silver thread design.

Mignonette – a narrow bobbin lace, sometimes called *Point de Tulle* or *Blonde de Fil*, used chiefly for trimming; very fine, resembles tulle.

Milan – one of the earliest Italian centres for lace-making, in the late fifteenth century.

Needle-point – lace made with single needle and thread and worked on a parchment pattern with outline cords and buttonhole stitching.

Nottingham – chiefly machine-made lace of the nineteenth century onwards (see MACHINE-MADE LACE).

Orris – corruption of Arras (see *Arras lace*).

Peniche – a Portuguese bobbin lace with pattern on large mesh ground.

Plaited – lace originally made in the Middle Ages with the fingers and using metal or silk thread. Worked in Spain and Italy where, later, bobbins replaced fingers and

(*far left*) Point de Venise, seventeenth century

Italian reticella lace, sixteenth century

designs became more complex.

Point – a term used in the craft to describe a needle or bobbin lace which is of exceptional quality of design and workmanship. Famous point laces include *Point d'Angleterre*, an English lace made in England but also, in the seventeenth century, made in Brussels and imported into England under this name to avoid payment of duty at a time when demand exceeded supply; *Point de France*, made in the Alençon region, its name decreed in the later seventeenth century by Louis XIV (see *Alençon Point*); *Point de Gaz* (see *Brussels lace*); *Point d'Espagne*, a Spanish lace; *Point de Venise* (see *Venetian lace*). *Point à Carreaux* is a French term for bobbin lace. *Point Tresse* was made from human hair, usually white or silver-grey from elderly people. *Rose Point* was an elaborate needle-point lace with conventionalized scrolls and flowers outlined with cordonnet and connected by brides. Made in Venice and elsewhere.

Polychromo – a nineteenth-century lace made with bobbins using multi-coloured silk threads.

Poussin – French word for a young chicken. A bobbin lace made in Dieppe, its mesh resembling chicken wire.

Power – machine-made lace or net of thin rubber. A modern fabric used for stretch corsets and girdles.

Punto – Italian for point. Punto Gotico was a Roman needle-point lace made with geometric motifs resembling those of Gothic architectural decoration. *Punto in Aria* (see *Venetian lace*).

Renaissance – lace made of linen tape or braid with brides attaching the sprigs or patterns and net infilling in larger spaces. A heavy, stiff lace, the bars or brides and tapes worked with blanket stitch. Similar to Venetian lace. A modern version was very fashionable in the early years of the twentieth century.

Réseau – French term for the net ground of a lace.

Reticella – an early needle-point lace deriving from the Ionian Islands and also known as *Greek Point Lace*. Fifteenth and sixteenth-century Italian work was made in geometric designs and widely used for edging ruffs and collars.

Russian – lace-making industry founded in Novgorod by Peter the Great to produce gold and silver work which was strongly influenced by Oriental motifs. By the nineteenth century most European laces were being imitated under the name *Point de Moscow*.

Schleswig – a fine, Danish needle-point lace of the seventeenth century.

Shadow – a transparent machine made lace with shadowy floral designs.

Shetland – an open-work lace made of fine Shetland wool in black or white for babies' shawls and coverlets.

Sprig – a detached piece of lace which is afterwards sewn on to a net foundation or joined by bars to join other sprigs.

Tatting – a nineteenth-century knotted lace made by means of a small shuttle and the fingers, the single thread forming small loops into varied openwork designs.

Teneriffe – a lace of the Canary Islands made in separate squares of stars, suns and flowers which are then joined together or appliquéd to a background fabric.

Torchon – a bobbin lace on a coarse net ground made by peasants of most European countries. Also known as *Beggar's Lace* and *Peasant's Lace*. The word *torchon* is French for dish rag or duster.

Trolly – an English bobbin lace known as trolly lace in Devonshire from the Flemish *trolle kant* (*trolle* means to pass round or cause to circle; *kant* is lace). In Buckinghamshire a trolly is a type of bobbin.

Valenciennes – a fine quality bobbin lace in complex floral designs, using a thousand or more bobbins, on a circular mesh ground. No cordonnet is employed. Bobbin lace-making began as early as the fifteenth century when Valenciennes was a Flemish town. The quality was exceptionally high in the seventeenth century although, by then, it was in French hands.

Venetian lace – needlemade lace was introduced into Europe by the Venetians who had probably learnt the art from Saracenic Sicily. The best work was carried out in the sixteenth and early seventeenth centuries when Venetian lace was imported by all of Europe to decorate costume. Its popularity declined in the later seventeenth century after Colbert had encouraged Italian lace-makers to work in France and *Point de France* was replacing the Venetian work, though there was a revival after the revocation of the Edict of Nantes caused the collapse of much of the French lace industry.

Among the fine Venetian laces were *Punto a reticello*, the Greek point (see *Reticella*); *Punto Tagliato*, cut-work; *Punto in Aria*, a very delicate seventeenth-century lace with an open design without mesh but connected by bars; *Punto a Groppo*, knotted lace like macramé (see *Macramé*); *Punto a Maglia*, darned netting. The most famous and remarkable Venetian lace was *Punto Tagliato Fogliami*, one of the best *Gros Point de Venise*. This was a heavy, high relief lace with a thick cordonnet made up of double, even treble, strands and beautifully stitched. Designs were Baroque, rich floral and arabesque patterns. The finest of this work appeared later in the seventeenth century and was used for cravats and fontanges all over Europe: it was the most beautiful lace ever made.

Lamé

A silk brocaded material containing flat threads of gold and silver. From the French *lame* = a thin plate or flake, usually of metal.

Lampas

A decorative flowered silk, originally imported from China. Can now be woven in silk and wool, like a damask.

Lansquenet, landsknecht

A Swiss or German mercenary soldier. The term originally applied to the serf put under arms by a nobleman. From *lands* = country (genitive) and *knecht* = servant. By the sixteenth century the word used to refer to a mercenary who carried a lance. In costume, the lansquenet dress displayed the most extreme form of the vogue of the years 1520–40 for puffs and slashes, where each garment was slashed so that the one beneath, of different colour and material, could be displayed through the cuts. These were finished by jewels and ribbon bows.

LANSQUENET
Swiss lansquenet, 1520–30.
White shirt pulled through
slashes on doublet

Lapis lazuli

A semi-precious stone of bright greenish-blue: a silicate containing sulphur. Used widely in jewellery by the ancient civilizations, especially in Egypt and Mesopotamia. Derives from the Latin *lapis* = stone and lazuli or azure from the Arabic and Persian terms for the brilliant blue colour.

Lappet

Pendant streamers, usually a pair, attached to the back or sides of a cap, crown or bonnet. Made of fabric, lace or ribbon. Especially fashionable with eighteenth century indoor caps.

Leather

The hide or skin of an animal, bird or reptile after it has been tanned or treated by a chemical process which preserves it; hides are derived from the larger animals such as buffalo, elephant, horse, cattle, and skins from smaller animals, birds and reptiles. Man has used the skins of animals from Palaeolithic times for making garments and utensils but *rawhide* is a much more perishable material than leather; it putrifies, it dissolves and disintegrates into a sticky mass with damp heat and, when used for clothing, is stiff and unyielding. Only in a hot, dry climate is the putrifying process slowed so that in ancient Egypt, for example, rawhide was used for containers and hangings but, even here, few articles have been found intact. When Howard Carter opened the tomb of Tutankhamun the rawhide base of his chariot was found to be glutinous.

It is not known exactly when, where or how man first learnt to transform raw animal skin into a non-perishable leather but articles of over 7,000 years old have been found in good condition. Early steps in the discovery of preserving animal skins were certainly the removal of the hair layer loosened by putrefaction and then a softening of the skins by oils, fat and brains, after which the inner, fat layer could be scraped away also, leaving the dermis, the central layer, which could then be tanned to make leather. Scraping tools of bone, flint and stone have been found at many ancient and primitive sites. Preserving and curing methods varied from the use of salt, alum, tannin from bark and smoking. Smoke curing was carried out by both Eskimos and North American Indians; the Eskimo women chewed the skin first to make it soft, wearing their teeth down to the gum, and the Indians used oils (see *Eskimo dress* and *North American Indian dress*).

The making of leather in modern times has become more a science than an art. Many different techniques and processes are used according to the type of leather to be produced and these are now fully mechanized, though industrialization came late to the leather industry and techniques did not change greatly over the years until the late nineteenth century.

Animal skins are composed of three chief layers, the outer *epidermis* which contains the hair, glands and blood vessels, the

LAPPET
White lace cap with lappets,
1720–7

fibrous centre *dermis* or corium and the inner, *fat layer*. The outer and inner layers must be removed and the centre one treated in order to preserve it and make it into leather. The outer epidermis is removed by soaking the skin in liquid in which chemicals such as lime has been dissolved, then scraping it off. The fat layer is cut off with a sharp knife, a process known as *fleshing*, now carried out by machine. The remaining, central layer is then washed and cleansed. Chemicals are used now but the traditional process over the centuries was to treat it with dung, preferably from dogs, hens or pigeons, to set up bacterial fermentation and so cleanse and soften the material.

Three principal methods have been used through the ages to transform this cleansed central layer of the animal hide into leather: tanning, tawing and chamoising and these processes produce different kinds of leather. *Tanning* has been the most important method in which the skins are preserved, by the chemical properties of tannin found in vegetable matter. The earliest way of doing this was to dig a pit and lay the skins in this one on top of the other with layers of oak bark and galls between each layer and on top; the pit was then filled with water. After two or three months the pit was emptied and refilled with new bark and more water and this was repeated, the whole process taking over a year to complete. An alternative source of tannin was introduced into Western Europe in the later Middle Ages in the form of sumac from the east. In modern processes, the tanning time is reduced greatly by the use of concentrated extracts of tannin.

The *tawing* method of making leather is a very ancient one. It was used in ancient Egypt, Assyria and Babylon and India; in Europe, the Greeks and Romans used tawing and it was widely employed in the Middle Ages in Europe. This is a mineral process using alum and salt and originally produced a white leather, though later it was dyed in colours. After the Moorish conquest of Spain in the eighth century in Cordova a process of tawing leather was practised which was made from the mouflon sheep (see *Furs*). *Cordovan* or *Spanish leather* became famous in Europe during the Middle Ages and most prized was the scarlet leather dyed with kermes. Eventually the process was carried out in all parts of Europe and the craftsmen known as cordwainers (from Cordova) though, due to specialization in footwear, the term was later retained for a shoe-maker or repairer (French *cordonnier*, English cordwainer).

Chamoising was a process using oil, especially cod-oil, which produces a soft leather. The term derives from the original use of chamois skins for the process and a soft leather later produced is known as wash-leather, which is derived from the underside of sheepskin, split so that the outer side can be used as a grain leather. Wash-leather is also called *shammy*, a corruption from chamois. The beautiful soft leathers of the North American Indian were produced by the chamoising process as also was *buff leather*, so-called because it was originally made in the Middle Ages from buffalo hide. The word buff applied to the colour derived from this leather.

After the tanning and cleansing was completed a number of finishing processes were carried out: working in fat or dubbin to give greater flexibility, rolling or hammering to consolidate the fibres, waxing to make waterproof, staining or dyeing to give different colours and patterning the surface. Among the patterning processes were nap-raising and boarding. The numerous processes and types of skins and hides from which leather is made include: *Alligator* – from the nineteenth century, chiefly the belly used for handbags and shoes. Most accessories marked 'crocodile' are usually alligator as crocodile skin is difficult to tan and preserve.

Boarded leather – a process employed in high-grade, smooth leathers to make a patterned surface by the use of a curved board rubbed over the folded leather. For example, goatskin develops a typical granular pattern if boarded while wet and is then known as *Morocco leather*. *Box calf* is calfhide boarded in two directions to give boxshaped creases; it is used extensively for shoes. *Willow calf*, rubbed only one way,

LEOTARD
Leotard

is finely creased in a long grain.

Buckskin – made originally from deer and elk, now sometimes from sheep. Used for shoes, gloves and some garments.

Cattlehide (bull and cow) – a heavy, fibrous leather used for soling and heeling footwear. The tanned hide is usually between four and six millimetres thick so it is split or skived into two or more layers by a splitting machine. The top layer carrying the grain is the most valuable, it is boarded and used to make shoes or bags.

Chamois – originally from the chamois goat but now made from sheep, lamb and goat. Made by chamoising: a soft leather for gloves and clothing.

Chrome – a mineral tawing process making leather for gloves and shoes.

Doeskin – when made into footwear is usually buckskin; when used for gloves comes from lamb or sheep, with a suède finish.

Elephant – made into bags, belts and shoes.

Glacé (glazed) – a glossy finish given to kidskin or goatskin to make soft, supple shoes and gloves.

Grain – a leather dressed on the grain side of the skin, often a split from cowhide. Scotch grain leather has a pebble marking.

Hogskin – a fine-grained peccary pigskin used especially for gloves. Has a distinctive grain marking from the hair follicles arranged in groups of three. Pigskin is similar but heavier.

Jack – wax leather coated with tar or pitch. Used, especially in the seventeenth century, for heavy boots with a high polish (see *Boot*).

Lizard – for shoes and handbags, chiefly from Java and India.

Patent – leather, generally cattle or horse, one side treated with successive coats of varnish and lacquer to give a highly glazed surface. Originally boiled linseed oil was used, now generally nitro-cellulose and synthetic resin. At first only black and white available but later colours also. Much 'patent' today is synthetic material.

Rawhide – untanned cattlehide softened with oil. Varnished to be moisture-proof.

Russia – a calf leather tanned with the bark of willow and larch, having a fragrant odour from the use of birch-tar oil as a lubricant. Originally from Russia but the term is used now for any leather processed in this manner.

Saddle – tanned cowhide used for bags, belts and shoes.

Seal – fine quality, soft and strong.

Shagreen – untanned leather originally made in Persia from the hides of asses, horses and camels and having a granular patterned surface made by pressing seeds into it while still damp, then dyed or stained green. Later, shagreen was made from sharkskin.

Silver and gilt leather – goatskin or kidskin finished with aluminium or gold leaf.

Suède – French word for Sweden, where the material was first made. Calf leather finished by buffing the flesh side into a velvety nap. Used for clothing, footwear and bags.

Synthetic leather – made from coated fabric and pasteboard, composition rubber and cellulose. *Leatherette* and *leatheroid* are trade names for imitation leather.

Lei

A large necklace made from fresh, tropical flowers, worn in Hawaii.

Leotard

A fitting, body garment with long sleeves worn by ballet dancers, acrobats and gymnasts for practice and exercising. Named after Jules Léotard, the nineteenth century French acrobat, who designed the garment for his own use. A modern version made of stretch nylon is now available which incorporates tights and so covers the body from shoulder to toe; this is also known as a body stocking.

Levis

Named after their creator Levi Strauss, who went to California in search of gold in 1850, and worn as working pants by American cowboys. In the USA these blue, fitting trousers made from strong cotton denim (jean), now everyday wear for young men, girls and children, are still often referred to as levis. In England they are jeans or blue jeans (see *Jean* and *Trousers*).

Body stocking

LEVIS
Blue levis, California, early twentieth century

Chaperon hanging
down the back by
liripipe, 1465

Liripipe attached
to velvet hat, 1475

Chaperon balanced
on shoulder by
liripipe, 1413

Hood with liripipe,
1375

Liripipe attached
to headdress, 1435

Linen

A fabric woven from flax. The cultivation of flax dates from ancient times. Evidence from specimens found of both the linen material and seeds and capsules of the flax plant show that linen was woven in Europe and the Middle East as early as 3000 BC. The flax fibres were strong and had good spinning qualities. Egypt was the chief producer of the fabric and some of the specimens discovered are of a fine texture and quality. White linen was greatly admired and became a symbol of purity, even divinity; it was widely used in the costume of priests and clergy in ancient times by the Egyptians, Greeks and Romans and, later, the Christian Church. The process of making a woven linen fabric from the flax plant is depicted in a number of tomb paintings in ancient Egypt; it is a process which has altered little over the centuries since that time. The flax plants, pulled by hand, were bound into bundles and dried. They were then combed to remove the seed capsules and soaked in water in order to separate the fibres from the hard centre. The fibres were then beaten, washed and dressed, spun and woven.

Over the centuries linen has been woven in varied qualities and textures from the finest lawns to the coarser burlap. Most notable were:

Book linen – a firm material used as a stiffening.
Burlap – originally finer but now a coarse linen, like *canvas*.
Butcher's – a coarse linen, often homespun – used for butcher's aprons and coats.
Cambric – a fine, white linen first made at Cambray (in Flemish, *kamerijk*).
Dowlas – a coarse linen made in the sixteenth and seventeenth centuries at Daoulas in Brittany. The name now applies to a strong calico of similar character.
Duck – a firmly-woven white linen used for washable trousers and sportswear.
Holland – a strong linen made in and named after the country. Often unbleached when it is termed brown holland.
Irish – bleached, fine, plain-woven linen.
Lawn – a very fine, white linen resembling cambric. Named after Laon in France where it was first made. Used widely over the centuries for shirts, handkerchiefs, ruffs and collars, blouses, aprons, dresses and clerical vestments. *Quintin*, a sheer, fine lawn, from its town of origin in Brittany.
Leno – a type of linen gauze.
Moygashel – trade name for an Irish linen of exceptional wearing qualities. Used especially for suits, dresses and coats.
Osnabrück (Osnaburg) – a coarse linen originally made at Osnabrück in Germany.

Linsey-Woolsey

Originally a coarse fabric of wool and linen said to have been first woven at Linsey in England. Later, a wool material woven upon a cotton warp, used in quantity in the American Colonies.

Liripipe

The peak or point on top of the medieval hood which began to lengthen into a pendant tail or padded sausage from the fourteenth century on. By the following century it had grown to five or six feet in length, when it could be held in the hand, hang loose down the back, be draped round the body or wound round the chaperon. Sometimes the whole chaperon was slung over the shoulder and hung down the back suspended by the liripipe, the other end being held in the hand. Also known as the tippet it could alternatively be attached to a hat or to a feminine headdress.

Lisle

A firm cotton thread used especially in the making of gloves and hosiery. Called after the French town of that name (now Lille).

Litham

A scarf or veil worn by Arab women in public to cover the nose, mouth and neck. Also worn, in a similar manner, by men of the Tuareg and other Moslem tribes in East African desert regions as protection against sand particles.

Chaperon and liripipe, *c.*1450

Litham

LOCKET
Gold locket enamelled in white,
green and purple. Contains a
mirror, c.1600

Gold locket enamelled in blue,
white, red and green. Set with
rubies, diamonds, sapphires and
pearl. Contains a portrait,
seventeenth century

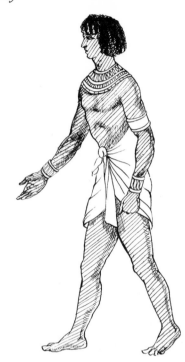

LOINCLOTH
White loincloth of ancient
Egypt

Livery

Originally the dispensing of food, allowances (in kind) and clothing to retainers and servants. Later referred more specifically to a suit of clothes or uniform given to a person serving in employ partly so that, by this costume, he or she might be recognized as being in the employ of a certain household.

Locket

A tiny decorative metal case hung round the neck by a chain or ribbon and containing a miniature portrait, lock of hair etc. The name derives from a small lock or clasp which was used as a fastening for necklaces and bracelets.

Loin-cloth

A piece of cloth wrapped and fastened round the loins, which was part of the basic dress for many primitive peoples. In warm climates, over the centuries, the loin-cloth has served as sole garment for ordinary and peasant peoples (see also *Egyptian, Indian, Maori* and *Minoan dress*).

M

Macaroni dress, 1772

Macaroni dress

In 1764 a group of young Englishmen founded the Macaroni Club in London on their return from the Grand Tour. The Macaronis, as they called themselves, professed an exaggerated form of the dress of the day which, by the 1770s, was elegantly foppish. Their coats were shorter and tighter than the norm and were cut away to sloping skirts; worn open, they displayed a striped, short waistcoat and elaborate, white linen. Their breeches were skin tight, with ribbon loops at the knee. Miniature tricorne hats were perched on the extravagantly high wigs or were held in the hand.

Madras

1) A vividly coloured silk and cotton kerchief, made in Madras in India and worn by the natives of the West Indies.
2) A turban made of a similar kerchief.
3) A black and white silk guipure lace made in Madras.
4) In the nineteenth century, a striped or checked muslin, named after Madras.

Mahoitres, maheutres

Pads to broaden the shoulder line of men's tunics and doublets; fashionable in Burgundy and France from about 1450.

Maillot

A French word used to describe a close-fitting, woven or knitted body garment, for example, a bathing costume or tights. The French also use the term for a young baby's first clothes.

Mancheron

Trimming or short over-sleeve placed near shoulder on the sleeve of a woman's gown.

Mandil

From an Arabic word for a sash, turban or handkerchief; in Persia, it is a turban.

Mandilion

A loose coat or jacket reaching to the hips and worn with the sleeves hanging free. Designs in the later Middle Ages resembled a tabard (see *Tabard*) in being put on over the head and could be sleeveless; they were chiefly worn by soldiers and ordinary people. In the second half of the sixteenth century the mandilion was a more fashionable garment, when it was buttoned at the neck, its sleeves hanging behind the arm. Like the Spanish capes of the day it could be turned partly askew, in which case one sleeve hung down in front and the other down the back. This was then referred to as wearing it Colley-Westonward, meaning awry.

Mannequin

French spelling of the English word manikin, which is the name for a tailor's or dressmaker's lay figure used for display, fitting and creating new designs of garments. The term, spelt in the French manner, is in general use for the display of new designs on a living model.

Manta, manton

Spanish word for blanket or large shawl worn during the centuries as an enveloping outer wrap. *Mantilla* is the diminutive applied more generally to the black or white lace, silk or cashmere head-shawl or veil traditional to more fashionable Spanish dress.

MANDILION
Mandilion worn Colley-Westonward, *c*.1585

MANTILLA
Black lace mantilla, Spain, 1640

MANTELET
Dark blue velvet mantelet with grey fur trimming, 1840

Mantelet

A short mantle or sleeveless cape which covers the shoulders. Worn from the Middle Ages onwards, mainly by women. Very fashionable in the nineteenth century as outdoor wear, particularly with crinoline gowns. These mantelets were in varied designs, some with a collar or hood and short, wide sleeves.

MAORI DRESS

Tattooing instrument

Face tattoo pattern

Flax cloak with brown knotted tags, reed skirt

Whalebone hair comb

Carved ear ornament

Dog skin cloak. Alternate strips of black and white fur

Greenstone tiki

Woven belt

Woven head-band

Cloak border

Mantua

A corruption of *manteau*, probably due to association with the Italian city of Mantua. Originally the name of a loose gown with unboned bodice worn by women from the mid-seventeenth to the mid-eighteenth century. *A mantua-maker* was a dress-maker who made such gowns.

Maori dress

The Maoris were of Polynesian stock. They came to New Zealand in several waves of migration between about 925 AD and 1350. The early voyagers discovered New Zealand by chance but the chief migration of the fourteenth century, from the Society Islands, arrived intending to settle and brought with them their families and plants and seeds to grow in their new land.

The climate in the Society Islands was warmer than that of New Zealand. In their original home the Maoris had needed few garments for reasons of warmth; men wore a simple loin-cloth, women a skirt. The loin-cloth was a strip of material about a foot wide which was passed between the legs then wound round the waist to be fastened there. The skirt was a similar piece of material but wider. It too was wound round the body and reached to just above or below the knees according to the age and status of the wearer. Another piece of material was used to drape round the shoulders in the evening.

In the Society Islands the Maoris had made these garments from tapa, that is, bark cloth (see *Tapa*), which was derived from the bark of the paper mulberry tree. The fourteenth century wave of settlers brought some plants of the paper mulberry with them and these would grow only in the north part of the North Island. The supply of tapa was too inadequate and not of sufficiently high quality for the Maoris so they were forced to abandon its culture and grow flax instead. The earlier settlers had also grown flax (having no paper mulberry plants) but had made their material by plaiting and tying. It was a long time before the Maoris abandoned this method in favour of weaving the fabric but, eventually, they were forced to adapt as the plaited flax was too rough and stiff for use in loin-cloths.

Descriptions and illustrations of the dress and customs of the Maoris were provided by the different European explorers in the expeditions to New Zealand, Tasman in 1642 and Captain Cook from his voyages in the second half of the eighteenth century. From these we can gain a good idea of what Maori dress was like before the missionaries of the nineteenth century brought Christianity to these peoples, which altered their way of dressing. For example, before the coming of Christianity women had left uncovered their bodies above the waist. Afterwards, they covered their breasts and men wore trousers instead of loin-cloths and cut off their complex top-knot coiffure.

From their arrival in New Zealand about 1350 the Maoris continued to wear the same basic garments: the men, a loin-cloth, the women, a skirt. They went barefoot and wore little or no headcovering but the colder climate made them adopt rain capes of grass, hemp or rushes, when necessary. Apart from this, they also wore cloaks for warmth. Everyday cloaks were of woven flax but the cloak became a status symbol so that certain materials, colours and decoration were reserved for important personages and occasions. Prized cloaks were of dog skins. Some were made up from whole skins, others of narrow, long strips sewn vertically; most valued ones were made from dogs' tails only. Such cloaks had a flax base and the dog skin was sewn to this, fur outside. Also prized were the feather cloaks made from the plumes of various birds, of which the red parrot feathers were especially valued. These feathers were interlocked or tied individually to the flax warp (see also *Feathers*). Other decorative cloaks were of flax ornamented by black cord tags or pompons of flax dyed in bright colours.

A particular form of Maori decoration was *taniko* work. This was a patterned weaving of strips which were sewn on to garments as borders or used as belts and headbands. The designs were geometrical, most commonly in black, red and white.

Fresh flowers and leaves were widely used as decoration in costume, generally as wreaths and necklaces. This was a Polynesian custom which survives as in the Hawaiian lei (see *Lei*). Personal ornaments for necklaces and pins were made from ivory, bone, shell and wood. The most prized material was nephrite or greenstone, which the Maoris carved into different shapes; the most characteristic of these was the *tiki*, carved in human form and worn on the breast attached to a flax braid hung round the neck. Especially valued were the teeth of the sperm whale which were made into cloak pins and necklaces.

Women wore their hair long held in place by a leaf chaplet or braid band round the brow. Men grew their hair long also but tied it up on the top of the head in a large knot and decorated this coiffure with feathers and whalebone or wood combs. Their ears were pierced for varied pendant earrings.

The art and practice of *tattooing* prevailed throughout Polynesia. The skin was deeply pricked to draw blood by a thin piece of bone fashioned into sharp teeth which had been dipped into a thick pigment of soot and water. The results of this painful process took some time to heal. In Polynesia the soot was obtained from burning kernels of the candle-nut but in New Zealand the resinous white pine wood was burnt. The Maori tattooing instrument was designed like a small hafted adze; the fine blade, made of bird bone, had a cutting or saw-tooth edge and it was bound by cord at right angles to a wooden handle. The Maoris had face and bodies tattooed with specific, complex designs. Each area, especially of the face, received certain, named designs.

Marcasite

A sparkling mineral – a crystallized form of iron pyrite – widely used in jewellery, buckles and buttons.

Martingale

A strap or belt attached by buttons to control fullness of material. The term can

MASK
Lady in mask and hood, 1643

apply to a belt at the back of a modern coat; it was also used in the sixteenth century to describe a panel between the legs of the breeches which was buttoned to a waistbelt. The original use of the term was a strap attached at one end to the noseband or bit of a horse's harness and the other to the girth to prevent the animal from rearing or throwing his head back.

Mask

Masks were worn, mainly by women, from the sixteenth century and were especially fashionable in the seventeenth and eighteenth centuries. They were intended as protection for the face against inclement weather in the street and while riding; they were also in use to conceal identity and for theatre and party wear. The mask could be shaped to the face and was pierced at the eyes, nose and mouth. From the seventeenth century half-masks, with slits for the eyes, were fashionable for

Modern maternity outfit of blouse and trousers

MATERNITY DRESS
Maternity dress, early sixteenth century. Front section open and laced across

Maternity jacket with adjustable buttoning and ribbon ties, 1870s

street wear with hoods. These were held in place by ribbons tied round the back of the head. Venetian half-masks were called loup masks, after the wolf, because they had a frightening effect upon children. This was anglicized to 'loo'. A lightweight mask covering the whole face was held in place by a button or bead held in the mouth.

Matelassé

A silk or silk and wool fabric woven with a blistered effect to resemble quilting.

Maternity and nursing wear

Before the twentieth century clothes were not designed specifically for maternity and nursing wear. The fashions of the day were adapted, usually by women in the home. For example, gowns were made to open in front with lacing across to accommodate a variation in stomach and hip size and, in the years when excessive corseting was fashionable, such corseting was abandoned or the whalebones were removed for greater comfort. In general, prior to the twentieth century, women tended to appear less and less in society as pregnancy advanced and to cover themselves with voluminous cloaks when venturing outdoors. For nursing wear gowns were designed to be opened at the breasts as required or to be slipped off the shoulder; this varied according to the fashions of the day.

In modern times dresses, skirts and trousers are specially designed to be expanded as necessary during pregnancy and smocks and tunics are usual wear over skirts and trousers.

Maya dress

The aborigines of the American continent crossed the Bering Strait from north-east Siberia to Alaska in successive waves of migration from about 25,000 years ago onwards (see also *Aztec, Eskimo, Inca* and *North American Indian dress*). These aborigines gradually spread southwards into Central and Southern America, reaching Tierra del Fuego about 9000 BC. The Maya were not the first inhabitants of Central America but formed and built up their culture there, in the area which is now Guatemala and the Yucatan Peninsula, from about 800 BC to about 300 AD. The flowering or classic period of their culture extended from then until about 900 AD after which it began to decline.

The Maya was a Stone Age culture so tools, mirrors and personal jewellery were made from materials such as obsidian, jade and iron pyrites. Their jade craftsmanship was especially fine, necklaces, pendants, decoration for nose and ears all carved, slowly and painstakingly, in low relief. The women carried out spinning and weaving and cotton and sisal were cultivated. It is believed that bark cloth (tapa) was in general use with cotton fabric reserved for the garments of priests and the upper classes of society. Brilliant colours were used, the yarn being dyed before it was woven. Fabrics were tie-dyed and woven in patterns; feathers were also woven into the material. Embroidery provided further colour and decoration.

In the warm climate the Maya wore few clothes except for ceremonial and religious purposes. The Maya peasant wore a loincloth which was a simple band of material wrapped round his waist then passed between the legs. A piece of material served as a cloak when thrown round the shoulders and, at night, in colder weather, a larger square of fabric was used as a blanket or more extensive cloak. Sandals and moccasins were both in use. Women wore a loose, sleeveless blouse or dress (*huipil*) cut straight and with holes for head and arms and, under this, a straight skirt. The nobility and priesthood wore an elaborate version of the peasant's dress that is, few garments but these richly patterned and ornamented. The men's loincloths and leather belts were brightly-coloured and patterned and ankle-length skirts were sometimes worn on top. Cloaks could just cover the shoulders or extend to waist or ankles. Important persons had cloaks of brightly-coloured feathers or of animal skins such as that of the jaguar. Ladies draped a stole round their bodies on top of the other garments.

Head-dresses for important occasions

and personages were elaborate, even fantastic. Feathers and carved decoration were mounted on a frame so that the head-dress could be several feet high or wide. Noble ladies wore elaborate coiffures also surmounted by feather ornamentation. Feathers were an important part of Maya decoration and it was mainly the women who carried out and were skilled in feather-work, tying the feathers into the weaving process (see also *Maori dress*). A wide range of birds of brilliant plumage were available to the Maya as to the Aztecs of which the finest and most valued was the quetzal

Loincloth and sandals. Bead necklace and feather headdress, *c.*700 AD

Coiffure and headdress of beads, feathers and jewellery, *c.*720 AD

Huipil, skirt and stole

Loincloth and skirt. Jaguar skin, sandals
Feather, flower and jade headdress, *c.*750 AD

whose tail feathers extended up to three feet in length in an iridescent greenish-blue. Feathers were also blended into bracelets and leg-bands.

The Maya adorned their persons lavishly; they painted their bodies and practised tattooing extensively. They filed their teeth into points and attached to them plates of jade or obsidian. Their coiffure styles were complex with forehead fringes and long hair plaited then coiled or hanging down the back. They wore an excess of jewellery made of jade, wood, stone, shell or bone as necklaces and bracelets but also inserted in their ears, noses and lips. The more important the person the more extensive the decoration of all kinds.

Mercerize

The process of mercerizing comprises a treatment of cotton fabrics with caustic soda which imparts to them a permanent high lustre. The process was named after the Englishman *John Mercer*, who patented the production of these effects in 1850. Later research in mercerizing has resulted in stronger cottons which also take dyes more successfully.

Merovingian dress

Merovingian was the name given to the first dynasty of the Franks. The name derives from an early king of the Salian Franks, Merovech, who lived in the fifth century AD; the dynasty was fully estab-lished under King Clovis. The Emperor of Byzantium awarded Clovis the title of Augustus, setting the seal on his conquest of Gaul. After this Frankish noblemen and their families adopted a Byzantine form of dress. Though their tunics were generally knee-length, these were bordered, belted and decorated with clavi. They retained their bracco leg-coverings, with boots on top or simply bound with strips of linen and often with the toes left bare in Teutonic fashion (see *Braies* and *Frankish dress*). They were usually cleanshaven or with moustaches and had moderate length hair or longer styles plaited on top of the head. Women dressed similarly to the modes of

MEROVINGIAN DRESS
Merovingian noblewoman,
*c.*650

Byzantium: a long gown with decorative neckband and clavi or a band of ornament down the centre front. They wore a veil and/or mantle, draped over head and body.

Mesopotamia (ancient)

The land covered by ancient Mesopotamia is now occupied by present day Iraq. Mesopotamia comprised a slightly smaller area dominated by the two great rivers, Tigris and Euphrates, which flow north-west to south-east across the land. Ancient Mesopotamia was bounded on the north by the mountains of Turkey, the south by the Persian Gulf, on the west by the Arabian desert and the east by the mountains of Persia.

Between 4000 BC and the conquest by Persia in the sixth century BC, Mesopotamia was inhabited by several great cultures whose domains and influences co-existed and overlapped one another during the centuries as the empires waxed and waned; chief of these were the Sumerian, Semitic, Babylonian and Assyrian. Inscriptions from the ancient cities of Ur, Kish and Lagash in southern Mesopotamia give evidence of

Sumerian king. Small cloth cloak and sheepskin-type skirt (kaunakes), c.2500 BC

Sumerian veil and headdress, c.2500 BC. Gold bands, rings and leaves. Beads

Kaunakes skirt and fringed cloak round torso, c.2500 BC

Kaunakes dress. Gold fillet and dog collar necklace, c.2000 BC

Linen cap, 720 BC

Leather helmet, cloth cloak and tunic with dagged edge, c.2500 BC

King Ashur-nasir-pal II. Tunic and apron shawl, felt cap, sandals. Assyria, 870 BC

Attendant temp. Sennacherib, Assyria, c.700 BC

Assyrian, temp. Ashur-nasir-pal II, ninth century BC

Tiglath-Pileser III. Gold embroidered crown, Assyria, c.740 BC

Semitic dress, c.2000 BC. Fringed shawl, wool cap, sandals

King of Babylon,
1100 BC

Woollen cap, *temp.*
Shalmaneser III,
ninth century BC

Ashur-bani-pal,
King of Assyria,
seventh century BC

a flourishing Sumerian culture before 4000 BC which reached a more advanced standard between about 2700 and 2370 BC. This was then followed by the Agade empire of the Semites under Sargon, whose Semitic language is known as Akkadian; a revival of Sumerian culture took place in the years 2110–2010 BC.

Early *Sumerian dress* for both sexes consisted of simple sheepskin skirts wrapped round the body like a kilt and held in place by a metal pin. Sometimes another piece of sheepskin was thrown over the shoulder like a cloak. The sheep's wool was worn to the outside and this appears to have been combed and trimmed into tufts. By about 2500 BC a woven fabric seems to have been made in which the tufted effect of the sheepskin was retained, either by weaving in loops or by sewing tufts of wool to the exterior of the garment. This tufted fabric was called *kaunakes* by the Greeks and it is illustrated in all the sculptures and mosaics of the period which show what the costume was like: for example, the standard of Ur, a mosaic of shell, red limestone and lapis lazuli which vividly depicts Sumerian life in peace and war (on display in the British Museum in London). Long cloaks were also worn, fastened on the chest; these, like some of the skirts, were of leather or felted cloth and cut into scalloped or dagged edges. Leather and metal helmets are also shown. Women appeared to have worn 'kaunakes'-style dresses, also ones of felted cloth. Men and women are shown barefooted. Men shaved their heads and faces; women dressed their long hair looped up or in a chignon and held it in place by a fillet or metal bands. Such gold bands which have been excavated show corrosion from woven veils or kerchiefs draped round the head. It is thought that large wigs, like those of the ancient Egyptians, were worn as many of the crowns and head-dresses found in the graves at Ur would have been too large otherwise. The Sumerians showed great skill in metal-working, especially in gold-beating. Their *jewellery* was of an exceptional standard for this period. Beautiful examples of beaten and chased gold made

into delicate leaf fillets and gold ribbons for the hair as well as elaborate, jewelled necklaces, earrings and brooches have been found at Ur (on display in the British Museum). Lapis lazuli and carnelian were widely used as well as other semi-precious stones.

With the influence of the *Semitic* rulers, then later the revival of Sumerian culture, between about 2370 and 2000 BC, the costume altered and became more varied. A *draped style* replaced the sheepskin tufted skirts, though the latter could also still be worn underneath the draped shawls. The newer style of garments had originated further north and east and a similar mode of dressing can be seen depicted in the sculptures of differing peoples in the years 2200–1300 BC, Semitic, Sumerian, Babylonian and Kassite. Both sexes wore a large rectangular shawl draped around the body. This piece of material was woven and edged with fringe and tassel. The draping varied but men usually adopted a method which left the right arm freely accessible, the folds of the fabric being contained by the left. Men no longer shaved their heads but grew their hair long and curled it in Assyrian and Babylonian fashion. Beards and sidewhiskers also were arranged in rows of corkscrew curls. Round hats with upturned brims or a type of turban were worn. Soft shoes and sandals were introduced. Women still had long hair, held by a fillet and, often, a veil. Dog-collar necklaces and earrings are shown in the sculpture.

The third stage in the development of the costume worn by the peoples of Mesopotamia had fully evolved by the eleventh century BC and is typified by the characteristic dress of the *Assyrian* empire of that time. Indeed, from the eleventh century until the fall of Babylon to the Persians in 539 BC, the styles and manner of dressing changed little. This was a more elaborate, advanced form of dress in which the men were attired in a more lavishly ornamented way than the women. In contrast to the time of Sumerian eminence, there is a wealth of information available on Assyrian and *Babylonian* dress of this era, especially in the great sculptured reliefs where, amidst the battle scenes, are also shown the clothes of captives, slaves and the great rulers of the age.

There were two basic garments: the *tunic* and the *shawl*. The tunic had a round neck and short sleeves; it was usually knee-length but for important occasions and for persons of rank it reached to the ankles. On top of the tunic were draped various shawls, rectangular and semi-circular in shape. Typical was the small square or rectangular one which was put on like an apron at the back, attached to the waist by long cords under the belt. This could extend to cover only the hips or it could reach the ankles. Another, usually semi-circular one, was draped round the upper part of the body, with one end tucked into the belt and the other thrown over the left shoulder. Often, in addition, a large shawl was wrapped round the body. Two belts, one on top of the other, were worn to hold the shawls in position; one was broad, of leather or linen, the other a narrow, brightly-coloured leather one. Some shawls, consisting almost only of fringe edging, could also be wrapped several times round the body. Women's dress was similar to the men's though less richly decorated. Women wore a short skirt as underwear, men a loin-cloth.

Garments were made from wool or linen in rich, strong colours. Decoration was by fringing and tassels and clothes were embroidered or printed in borders or all-over patterns. Coloured wool and gold and silver thread were used for embroidery. Motifs were mostly geometrical, particularly circles and squares; also characteristic were the rosette and palm. A quantity of rich and heavy jewellery accompanied the costume, especially earrings, armlets and bracelets. Footwear took the form of soft shoes in brightly-coloured leather or fabric, boots or sandals.

Both Assyrians and Babylonians took great pride in their hair and beards. These were grown long, tightly curled and ringleted. False hair was added if desired. Perfumes, oils and black dyes were used on the hair. Both men and women wore a metal fillet or band of material round the brow. There were several forms of head-covering. The everyday version was a wool or felt round cap or a style like the Middle Eastern fez. For important persons and occasions a jewelled fillet or headband was worn. The Assyrian royal head-dress was the tall, curved-sided crown or mitre surmounted by a truncated cone. Made of wool or felt, it was embroidered in coloured and gold bands and had pendant lappets at the back. The equivalent Babylonian head-dress was like a tall straight-sided crown of leather or felt, also with lappets. Royal crowns were surmounted with a row of feathers. Of especial significance was the horned cap of power, the symbol of divinity.

King of Babylon, 550 BC

Assyrian bracelet

Horned cap of power, Assyrian, seventh century BC

Assyrian hunter in tasselled tunic and apron shawl, embroidered belt, 720 BC

Assyrian queen

MINOAN AND
MYCENAEAN DRESS

Knossos, 1500–
1450 BC. Coiffure

Knossos, *c.*1600 BC.
Tall cap, fitted
bodice, ornamental
apron, full skirt

Knossos, *c.*1500 BC.
White loin-cloth
and apron with
blue bead net

Snake goddess,
from Knossos,
*c.*1600 BC, jewelled
turban headdress,
fitted bodice and
waistband, pleated
tiered skirt,
decorative apron

Tiryns, Mycenaean,
*c.*1400 BC. Red
bodice with blue,
black and gold
border and belt.
Orange apron.
Tiered skirt in
white, red, orange,
blue and black

Milliner

From *milaner, myllaner*, an inhabitant of
Milan in Italy. Someone who traded in
articles of apparel, especially bonnets,
which had been made in the city state or
Duchy of Milan. Later the term came to be
applied more specifically to the designer
and decorator of ladies' hats and bonnets.

Minoan and Mycenaean dress

Crete was inhabited from about 6000 BC
onwards. Settlers came to the island from a
number of areas further east, particularly
from North Africa, Syria, Asia Minor and
Palestine. By the advent of the Bronze Age
in the Aegean, which had begun about
2500 BC, the Cretan civilization was developing and, partly due to the origins of its
people and partly to extensive maritime
trade, it was strongly influenced by the
cultures of Egypt and Babylon. It was
especially in the years 1750–1400 BC that
the Cretan culture rose to a high level,
comparable with those of its mentors. This
was the time of the great palace of Minos at
Knossos, from which we take the name
Minoan to designate the culture. From the
wall paintings and sculpture from here,
from the contemporary palaces at Phaistos
and Mallia, also from the Mycenaean
citadel-palaces in the Peloponnese and
Santorin, we can gain a clear picture of
Minoan and Mycenaean dress over the
centuries. These display the desire of these
peoples for richness of dress in colour,
materials and jewelled decoration as well
as a great variety of design in the costume.
This was a culture of wealth and sophistication whose attire and enrichments were
increasingly copied elsewhere in the Aegean
and further afield. The Cretans conquered
the Cyclades and penetrated to Greece and
Cyprus, advancing as far as Syria. Their
style of dress was adopted intact or merged
with designs current in these areas. Trade
and contact with countries on the eastern
shores of the Mediterranean in turn influenced Cretan dress, which increasingly
displayed oriental features. The Cretans had
occupied the Peloponnese but here the
Mycenaean civilization evolved and, in
turn, became more powerful and later

destroyed centres in Crete.

Men wore few, simple garments but maintained an elegant appearance and a fastidious care of hair and bodies. All men, whether of noble or lowly birth, wore a *loin-cloth* belted tightly at the waist. The material and style of this loin-cloth varied according to the wealth of the wearer. The garment could be of harsh wool or leather but elegant men wore loin-cloths of soft linen arranged like a short skirt, formed in a point at the back (see illustration under *Feathers*), or with a point in front, weighted and finished by a triangular net of pearls or beads. The metal-decorated leather waistbelt tightly constricted the waist, as in women's dress, to contrast with the broad, masculine chest or full, feminine breasts.

This was the Cretan style of loin-cloth; on the mainland it was more often styled like short trousers with a piece of material passed between the legs and fastened to the belt back and front. Some Cretan illustrations show longer, broad trousers extending to the knees. The torso and the legs were generally bare though, for winter warmth, short, wool cloaks were worn, decorated with fringed edges or fur. They were fastened with metal pins.

Men wore their hair very long, dressed in loops and braids and tied in various ways on top of the head or down the back. They were cleanshaven and bathed frequently, oiling their bodies afterwards. They were conscious of maintaining a fine masculine physique, though elegant and slim. They often went bare-headed; *headcoverings*, if worn, were wide-brimmed hats, skin caps or turbans. Both sexes went barefoot indoors. Out-of-doors men wore sandals with leather thongs at the ankle, shoes or, in winter, calf-length boots.

Before 1750 BC women also wore the loin-cloth, designed as a short skirt, with the upper part of the body unclothed. After this a longer skirt was usual, of ground or ankle-length, and a tight-fitting jacket or bodice with elbow-length sleeves, still leaving the breasts bare. In the later Minoan period a metal corset acted as a foundation for the costume – the first recorded use in Europe of metal for corseting and the restriction of the human figure – and a boned bodice on top supported and accentuated the bare breasts with lacing beneath them. The waist-belt was tightly drawn, with rolled edges or in the form of a girdle wound twice round the slenderized waist. The skirt was designed in flounces which, in later years, dipped in the centre front at each level, like the masculine loin-cloth. These skirts were stiffened to a bell shape by bands sewn at intervals into the garment. This resembles the sixteenth-century farthingale skirt but it appears that the Cretan bands were, like the Spanish *vertugado*, inserted into the skirt itself, not set in an underskirt.

The whole Cretan feminine costume was characterized by vivid, rich colouring and elaborate, refined decoration, giving an impression of splendour and luxury. The skirts, in particular, presented a harmony of brilliant reds, purples, yellows and blues. Metal plates (like shingles) and embroidery were incorporated. The garments were elaborate, sewn and fitted to the figure, quite unlike the draped, classical Greek dress. Cretan costume was original and advanced. All kinds of decoration was used from fringing, ornamental aprons (back and front), embroidered banding, pleating, flouncing and inset panels. Typical embroidered motifs were the spiral, the trellis and the lozenge. Under the separate skirt and bodice Cretan women wore a shift and probably a simple loin-cloth also. Out-of-doors, for warmth, they wore capes or cloaks. Their footwear was styled like that of the men.

Women grew their hair long and carefully dressed it in spiral curls and ringlets in front then falling on the breasts and back (see *Hairstyles*). Head-dresses varied from the tall, cone-shaped hats to metal fillets, turbans and caps.

Cretan women, their men also, loved jewellery and jewelled enrichment. They wore several bracelets to each arm, necklaces in rows with pendants, finger rings, earrings, pearl ropes in the hair and decorative metal waist-belts. Gold, bronze and silver were used while Mycenaean costume

Bronze handmirror, Egyptian. Handle design based on the papyrus flower supported by two falcons

Bronze handmirror with incised decoration. Etruscan, fourth to third century BC

Bronze handmirror, Greek, fifth century BC (about 21 inches high)

Iron Age Celtic handmirror (Britain)

MITTEN
Black net mitten, embroidered in colours, 1850

specialized in gold work. The metals were set off with semi-precious stones, the cutting and polishing of which was a high art in Crete. Especially they employed amethyst, agate, carnelian, jasper, porphyry and lapis lazuli. In quality the Minoan work is the finer despite the greater use of gold by the Mycenaean peoples. Some beautiful examples of the work of both cultures are on display in the British Museum in London and the National Museum in Athens.

Mirror

Mirrors have been an important adjunct to costume from the times of the ancient civilizations. In ancient Egypt, Mesopotamia, Greece and Rome they were of polished metal, usually bronze. They were made to be held in the hand by an elegant handle and the reverse side was often decorated by incised designs, sculptural ornament or by inlaid stones and enamelling (see also *Cosmetics*). Glass mirrors were made in Venice in the Middle Ages. From this time onwards fashionable men and women carried tiny mirrors in pocket or bag or, as was typical of the sixteenth and seventeenth centuries, wore one attached to the long end of the decorative girdle. It was characteristic of all periods to carry a small mirror suspended by a cord or ribbon from the waistbelt. From the early nineteenth century onwards mirrors were normally carried in a reticule or handbag.

Mitre

From the ancient Greek μίτρα and the Latin *mitra*, a fillet or headband worn with classical dress. Also applied to the tall, conical head-dress worn in Asia and, especially, the Middle East (see *Mesopotamia*). Designated the headcovering of the Hebrew High Priest and, in the Christian Church, the episcopal head-dress.

Mitten, mitt

A covering for the hand where the four fingers are enclosed in one part and the thumb in a separate stall. Working mittens often leave the ends of the fingers and thumb uncovered, for easier manipulation.

For country use, these date from the Merovingian period, when they were called *moufles* or *mitons*. More fashionably, in some ages, notably the eighteenth and nineteenth centuries, ladies wore lace or net mittens indoors. These were often black and could be wrist or elbow-length (see *Glove*).

Modesty piece
A made-up frill of lace and ribbon attached to the top of the corset in front to conceal the cleavage when a gown with low décolletage is worn. Chiefly an eighteenth and nineteenth century fashion.

Modiste
A milliner or dressmaker who designs, makes and sells dresses and hats for women.

Mohair
Fabric woven or knitted from the wool of the angora goat (see *Angora*).

Moiré
Past participle of the French verb *moirer* = to water, when used in reference to silk, meaning that the material has a wavy, watered surface appearance. Other fabrics are also made in moiré form, for example, moiré velours (a velvet) or moirette, a watered worsted material. The term is also applied to a fur as, in particular, that of the very young karakul lamb (see *Furs*).

Montenegrin
A close-fitting outer garment worn by women in eastern Europe which was decorated by coloured embroidery and braid. Probably named after the area of Montenegro.

Mother-of-Pearl
The smooth, iridescent lining to some sea shells (nacre), used especially for buttons and buckles.

Motoring (Automobile) wear
The idea of designing clothes especially for use in motoring was an important, though short-lived, fashion. In the late nineteenth century, particularly before the

Fawn silk and alpaca motoring dust coat, adjustable veil tied over straw hat with ostrich plumes, 1905

Grey wolfskin motoring coat, wool cap with vizor and tinted goggles, 1905

Fur coat, hood and muff. Goggles of glass in metal and leather frame, 1908

Waterproof motoring coat and cap, goggles, 1908

Mary, Queen of Scots in white mourning with pleated barbe, sixteenth century

Mourning veil and barbe. 'Weeper', medieval

Pleated barbe and veil, medieval

Hungarian peasant mourning dress, all in white, black boots

Widow's peak, late sixteenth century

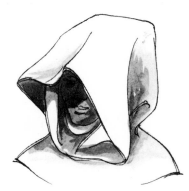

Fourteenth century 'weeper' hood

lifting of the 'red flag' restriction, the speed was so slow that the only problem was cold. In the early years of the twentieth century the motor car travelled much faster but it offered little protection from cold, wet, wind and dust. So, between 1900 and 1910, protective clothing was evolved for both sexes.

Men generally wore a cloth peaked cap and goggles which they pushed up on to the forehead when not needed. They covered their jackets, knickerbockers and stockings with long, full, fur or fur-lined overcoats, storm-coats or dust-coats according to season. On top of these rugs were wrapped round the knees and foot muffs could be worn also. The dust-coats, needed in hot summer weather, were of cotton, silk or alpaca and were recommended to be in grey or fawn in order not to show the dust. Women wore similar long, protective coats also goggles. On their heads they tied voluminous, specially designed veils round the fashionable hats of the day or took to hoods which also tied under the chin. Some women adopted the men's style of cloth, peaked cap or a woollen tam-o'-shanter. Some of the veils were adjustable so that, when motoring, they could be closed, leaving no portion of the head exposed, the lady peering out through a fine grey veil and a layer of fine grey dust, rather like a Moslem woman in her purdah dress.

Mourning dress

Black has been the most usual colour for mourning clothes in the western world since the days of Greece and Rome. White has also been a mourning colour, especially denoting virginity and innocence and so worn, in particular, by (and for) women and children. White had, at certain times, been customary wear for queens mourning their husbands; Mary, Queen of Scots wore white as mourning for King Francis II of France when he left her a widow at the age of 18. In parts of central and eastern Europe white has been traditional peasant mourning wear. Shades of purple and lavender have also been used for mourning dress, usually as a part rather than the whole of the costume, and to represent an emergence from full to half mourning. Although mourning clothes could be made from any material, certain fabrics have been considered especially suitable for this purpose, most particularly in the nineteenth century; these included black crape, serge, bombazine, cotton, cashmere and tulle.

Through the ages mourning garments have expressed sadness by falling or drooping lines in drapery. Examples of this were the medieval hoods and veils worn hanging over the face, called *weepers*. Also known as 'weepers' were the long or deep white cuffs worn in the eighteenth and nineteenth centuries; these were attached to the black sleeve and hung down over the hand. In the sixteenth and seventeenth centuries ladies wore trains at the front of their gowns as well as at the back, the material of which had to be pinned or held up to enable the wearer to walk. From the seventeenth century onwards long black cloaks were put on top of the other garments, long draperies and streamers of black crape were attached to the hat, head-dress, arm or belt or were tied round the waist on top of the coat.

The dress of a *widow* has traditionally expressed her loss and sadness to a greater degree than that of other mourners. In general, a widow's mourning dress was notable for its old-fashioned character. For example, the mourning *barbe* was worn by widows until the later sixteenth century though this derived from the thirteenth-century medieval barbette (see *Barbette*). Widows wore a white pleated barbe with the fashionable head-dress of the day – hood, veil, attifet – to cover the neck in front; sometimes, according to rank, the barbe displayed the chin, sometimes the chin was enclosed also. In the late eighteenth century the ruff encircled the neck above the barbe which then depended below, like a bib. The barbe has survived until modern times in a nun's head-dress. Another feature was the *widow's peak*. Originally a flap projecting in front from the hood or head-dress, this later was indicated only by a dip in the centre front edge of the head-dress. In the eighteenth and nineteenth centuries the peak was a triangle of black material set on the fore-

head under a veil. The use of the term *weeds* to denote the mourning dress of a widow dates from the sixteenth century but the word weed was used to describe any garment or raiment from the ninth century onwards.

Certain decorative features added to clothing, also accessories, have been adopted through the ages to indicate mourning. The black *mourning band* worn by men round the left arm was originally a service custom but was adopted by civilians early in the nineteenth century. An eighteenth century version was a knot of black ribbons attached to an armband. In the seventeenth century mourning bands of willow were worn round the hat and posies of rosemary were carried. Black fans were indicative of mourning. *Mourning jewellery* was customary from the Middle Ages onwards. Finger rings were most usual, fashioned as skeletons, coffins and skulls. Lockets and brooches, as well as rings, were designed as containers for a lock of hair from the loved one.

Mourning dress for all, tiny children included, was at its most extreme during the nineteenth century, when etiquette dictated the duration of mourning, which could last for many months, even years. Full mourning was for a totally black ensemble which included even leisure attire, bathing costumes, handkerchiefs, parasols and fans. This was relaxed, usually after 12 months, into half or modified mourning, when white, grey and lavender could be worn, still trimmed with black.

Mousquetaire

French for musketeer. A foot soldier armed with a musket, of particular fame in seventeenth and eighteenth century France, when such musketeers were part of the king's household troops and were of noble birth and of note as dandies. In the nineteenth century, in England, various items of dress were named after them, for example, mousquetaire collar, cuff, glove, hat, mantle and sleeve. These styles derived chiefly from the seventeenth-century musketeer dress.

MOUSTACHE
1620

1688

1915

1913

Army 1918

Mousseline

French muslin. In English refers to a fabric of cotton, wool or silk which is soft and generally very fine. *Mousseline-de-laine* was originally a fine woollen fabric, though later woven in wool on a cotton warp and generally patterned. *Mousseline-de-soie*, used particularly in the nineteenth century, was a silk fabric with a texture like muslin; later made of rayon, resembling chiffon.

Moustache

Hair grown on the upper lip. Not common when grown separately from beards or sidewhiskers except for brief periods (see *Beard* and *Whiskers*).

Mozambique

A dress material of wool or silk. In the 1890s referred specifically to a weave of mohair and silk.

Muff

A soft bag with an opening at each end into which the hands may be thrust to keep them warm. Muffs were carried from the later sixteenth century onwards. Until the 1790s both men and women used them but after this the muff was regarded as a feminine accessory. Muffs have varied greatly in size and materials. Most seventeenth and eighteenth century muffs were large, nineteenth century ones were smaller and by the 1880s they were dainty. Fur was the most usual material, padded, then lined with silk or velvet. Other materials used included embroidered or beaded silk, satin and velvet, feathers and down or gold and silver cloth. Decoration was by ribbons, lace and flouncing. Though always a useful accessory, muffs have also been carried as an item of elegance and fashion.

Muffetee

1) In the eighteenth and nineteenth centuries a type of muffler (see *Muffler*).
2) In the nineteenth century a pair of wool or fur cuffs or wristbands worn to keep the wrists and part of the hands warm.

Muffler

1) In the sixteenth and seventeenth centuries a square kerchief folded and worn round the neck and lower part of the face either for concealment or for protection against sun or cold wind.
2) From the sixteenth century onwards a long neckscarf most commonly of wool.

Mufti

Plain clothes when worn by a member of a uniformed service. Origin uncertain; possibly related to Arabic term *mufti*.

Mungo

A woollen cloth made from felted and hard-spun woollen rags. Similar to shoddy but of better quality (see *Shoddy*).

Muscadin

A pastille or comfit perfumed with musk. A Parisian term of derision applied to the bourgeois elegants in France in 1793 who used the perfume.

Muslin

Originally mussolo, named after the city of Mosul on the river Tigris in Iraq (near the ancient city of Ninevèh), where the fabric was made. Muslin is a general name covering a broad spectrum of fine cotton materials ranging from the sheerest organza to a heavier cotton for curtaining and, in the USA, for shirts and bedding (see *Cotton*). The French name *mousseline* derives from the early cotton fabrics which came from Mosul in the eighteenth century. These had an uneven texture which resembled foam (*mousse*). In the seventeenth century delicate muslins began to be imported into western Europe from India and became fashionable materials, especially in the second half of the eighteenth century. Particular named muslins include:
Adatis – a fine Indian muslin; the best quality came from Bengal.
Dorea – an East Indian striped muslin.
Madras – named after the Indian city (see *Madras*).
Mull – a lightweight material used in the nineteenth century which could be muslin or silk.
Nainsook – a heavier, soft Indian muslin, usually striped.

Organdie (Organdy) – a fine, plain muslin, slightly stiffened.

Organza – a sheer, slightly stiffened muslin used especially for diaphanous wedding garments.

Swiss – a sheer, crisp muslin ornamented with self-colour or contrasting dots.

Tarlatan - a thin, open-weave muslin, heavily stiffened. Widely used in the nineteenth century as a stiffening under full skirts.

MUFF
White swansdown muff with white ribbon, *c.*1810

Grey fur muff with violets, 1886, English

Fur muff with ribbon decoration, *c.*1670–80. English

Black fur muff with ribbon decoration, *c.*1635, French

Embroidered and painted white satin muff, 1775–1800, English

Indian silver necklace

Engraved gold triple collar necklace. Bronze Age Portugal

Queen Anne Boleyn. Pearl necklace, c.1535

Gold necklace, Etruscan, c.400 BC

Engraved gold lunula. Bronze Age Scotland

Mycenaean gold and carnelian necklace, c.1400 BC

Gold necklace. Celtic Spain, seventh century BC

Pendant necklace, Spanish, 1545

Jewelled necklace, German, 1531

Gold chain necklace, German, 1510

Gold necklace set with precious stones, Roman, first century AD

Queen Catherine of Aragon. Pendant, jewelled, chain necklace, c.1520

N

Mandarin neckline, 1952

Nail

A measurement for cloth, one sixteenth of a yard (two and a quarter inches). Possibly derived from the fact that one sixteenth from the end of the yard-stick was probably marked by a nail.

Nankeen, nankin

A yellowish-buff, strong cotton cloth, originally made in Nanking in China. It was widely used in the nineteenth century in Western Europe for men's pantaloons and trousers.

Necklace

Ornamentation encircling the neck in the form of shells, teeth, beads, precious metals or jewels set in precious metals. All peoples have adopted some form of necklace for decoration and reasons of status, the materials varying according to the standard of the culture and the substances available to it. In Europe the wearing of necklaces has been more usual when fashionable necklines have been low cut or when they have been very high, up to the chin, when the necklace or jewelled collar could be displayed on top of the garment. Both sexes have worn necklaces but more frequently the ladies. The torc (torque) is a type of twisted metal necklace (or bracelet) characteristic of the early Gauls and Britons; some of this Celtic workmanship is very fine. In Ireland and Scotland a flat version of the torc, called a lunula from its crescent shape, was more typical.

Neckline

Every conceivable line and cut has been applied to this part of the masculine and feminine costume during the ages. Designs include the arched, bateau, collared, décolleté, heart-shaped, halter, high, mandarin, off-the-shoulder, polo, round, square, strapless, turtle and V necklines (see illustrations).

Neckwear

From the sixteenth century onwards men have worn some kind of collar or other finish to the shirt, at first attached, later separate. This was generally tied in some way in front to adjust to the individual neck and personal preference (see *Band, Collar, Cravat, Ruff, Stock*). By about 1840–5, the stock was replaced by a striped, plain or patterned neckcloth or necktie. From then until well into the

Square neckline, 1911

Bateau neckline, 1967

Halter neckline, 1934

Off-the-shoulder
neckline, 1946

Arched square
neckline, 1565

Décolleté neckline,
1694

V neckline, 1450

Collared neckline,
1549

Strapless and heart-
shaped neckline,
1955

Round neckline,
1922

High neckline,
1380

twentieth century there was considerable variety available in the style of neckwear which could be tied in a bow or a knot and be a narrow band or wide and full, filling the triangular space between the collar and the coat revers. Wider scarf ties were also fashionable and some of these, like a proportion of the bow ties, were ready made-up. In the second half of the nineteenth century the Ascot and the Octagon were particularly modish. Scarf pins held these in position and tie pins or clips the knotted neckties. In the early part of the twentieth century the bow tie was more favoured, from about 1920, a knotted one. For a time after the Second World War neckties were very narrow, string ties they were termed, then the fashion pendulum swung the other way so that, in the 1970s, excessively wide knotted ties in a wide variety of materials, colours and patterns, are available. Tie tacks have largely replaced pins and clips.

Needle
Primitive sewing needles were made of bones or thorn and had no eyes; they were used only to make holes in the material and threads or thongs were passed through the holes to attach the two edges together. Bone needles with eyes were made in Stone Age Europe and with the Bronze Age came metal ones of bronze. The Romans used bronze and iron needles. Metal, eyed needles of iron, and later steel, were made in Europe, especially England and Germany, from the Middle Ages onwards. They were made from wire and one end was ground to a point.

Night clothes, night wear
Garments designed specifically to wear in bed were rare before the sixteenth century; people slept naked or in their day shirt or chemise. From then until the early twentieth century men and boys wore a *bedshirt*, *nightshirt* or *nightsmock* which had long sleeves, a round neck (with or without collar) and reached to the knees or ankles. It was generally of white linen or cotton and could be decoratively embroidered and trimmed with lace. Women wore a

Bow tie, 1849

Knotted tie, 1874

Striped neckcloth, 1855

Knotted tie, 1933

Silk scarf, 1865

Silk scarf, 1968

Silk neckscarf, 1885

Wide, silk patterned tie, 1975

Ascot tie or scarf, 1875

Narrow string tie, 1967

White cotton nightdress and cap, 1865

similar *nightshift* or *chemise* until the nineteenth century when the long voluminous *nightdress* was customary; this had long sleeves and a high frilled or collared neckline and was elaborately trimmed and tucked. Both sexes wore night caps. The designs for a cap to wear in bed were washable; men's caps usually had a point on top, ladies' were tied under the chin and were decorated by ruffles and ribbons. Other nightwear included slippers, a kerchief, a coif and a mask or forehead or chin-band to reduce the wrinkles (see *Cosmetics*).

Pyjamas (pajamas) had been introduced into England for informal wear, especially in the house, as early as the seventeenth century. This suit of coloured cotton or silk, consisting of a loose, buttoned jacket and trousers tied at the waist with a cord was borrowed from the Indian and Persian designs, the name deriving from the ancient Persian and Urdu *pāē* (foot, leg) and *jāmah* (clothing, garment). The fashion was only taken up by the aristocracy and was short-lived but was re-introduced as sleeping attire for men in the 1880s and gradually ousted the nightshirt. Pyjamas began to be made for women in the twentieth century, at first for little girls, then adults. By the later 1920s they were in strong competition with nightdresses. Both forms of sleepwear were made from this time onwards in comfortable, attractive designs with a variety of styles of neckline, sleeves, length and materials.

Nightgown, Indian gown, banyan, morning gown, dressing gown, negligée, peignoir, slammakin, tea gown

These terms were all used to denote loose, comfortable garments put on at home for public or private wear, that is, to receive in the drawing room or to relax in the bedroom. Often such coats or gowns were made of rich fabrics, were elaborately trimmed and lined and were not, as in the modern sense of the term dressing gown, merely intended for wearing between bedroom and bathroom. They were elegant, often ostentatiously rich and were meant to be seen. In an age (sixteenth to nineteenth centuries) when corseting and rigid clothes were the daily norm, the luxury of being able to shed a hot and irritating wig and *habit à la française* or paniered gown was fully appreciated. Men, in particular, so favoured themselves in their nightgowns and banyans that they sat so attired for their portraits to be painted, leaving to posterity a clear record of what such garments were like.

The terms nightgown, Indian gown, banyan and morning gown are almost interchangeable and their use varies from area to area. In general, the term *nightgown* refers to the earlier garment, describing a long, full coat, open up the centre front, with long, set-in sleeves; it is recorded to have been worn from the early sixteenth century onwards. It was intended for warmth and could be lined and trimmed with fur. It was made of velvet, silk, brocade or wool and could be drawn in by a sash tied at the waist. Nightgowns were worn by both sexes who also wore a nightcap; these caps were of varied design, generally embroidered.

In the 1630s there began to be imported from India a gown of slightly different cut. These *Indian gowns*, as they were called, became fashionable quickly. They were more fitting than the older nightgown and made of Indian silks and cottons, patterned, striped and plain. Both men and women wore them. By the 1680s many gowns were being made in Europe from Indian fabrics and, later, could be of any rich material. The fashion for things Oriental was satisfied by these gowns, which were accompanied, especially when worn by men, by an eastern-style turban or cap.

The term *banyan* (banian, banjan) was also used for these gowns. They were named after a loose jacket or gown worn in India which, in turn, derived from the name for a Hindu trader in the west of the country, particularly those from the province of Gujarat (now in Pakistan). During the eighteenth century these coats or gowns of rich material (referred to as Indian gown, banyan or morning gown), were worn in the house for comfort and

Negligée, *c.*1785, French

Striped nightgown or banyan, *c.*1680, French. Fur and velvet cap

Silk Indian or morning gown, silk sash and cuffs of different colour, *c.*1750, English

Persian-style silk dressing gown with cord girdle, French, *c.*1840

Dark velvet dressing gown with light silk lining, collar and cuffs, *c.*1860, American

Indian gown of painted cotton, *c.*1709, French

Silk dressing gown, 1865, French

NORTH AMERICAN INDIAN DRESS
Southern Plains
Indian. Shaved
head except for
roach feather and
back hair. Breech
cloth. Deerskin
apron and leggings

Kutchin Indian,
Alaska. Heavy skin
shirt with long tails
and leggings all in
one with moccasins.
Fringe and bead
decoration

relaxation by gentlemen all over Europe. They were elegantly cut on kimono lines, but fairly fitting at the waist then flaring out in the skirt and extending to the knees or ankles. They could be buttoned at the waist, tied with a sash or worn loose.

The *dressing gown* was also an informal garment to be worn indoors but this term was rarely used before the nineteenth century. The masculine style was almost ground-length and very full; it was tied with a sash or girdle at the waist and, in the second half of the century, had a rolling collar or lapels. Rich, decorative materials were still used. Towards the end of the century the dressing gown began to be relegated to its modern function of a gown to be worn in bedroom or bathroom.

From the eighteenth century onwards the informal wrappers, gowns and jackets worn by women in the house began to differ in styles and materials from those of the men. They were made from delicate as well as richer fabrics – cottons, silks, velvet and brocade – in more feminine styles trimmed with lace and ruffles. Though *negligé* was a term used for informal wear for both sexes, *negligée*, denoted more and more a lady's ensemble for relaxation at home. *Peignoir* was a robe of delicate material usually fastened at the neck. Literally a 'combing gown' since the name derives from the French *peigner* = to comb. The word *slammakin* (slammerkin) referred to an eighteenth century loose gown which had ruffled or pagoda sleeves and a sacque back (see also sacque and contouche under *Gown*).

The *tea gown* was a fashion of the later nineteenth century. It was so-called as it was worn by ladies when being entertained to tea in their hostess's boudoir (though, later, gentlemen were admitted also). The gown was a loose, unboned one, generally falling in graceful folds from a high waist-line or a yoke. It had long sleeves and was elaborately decorated with lace and ruffles; a matching cap was worn with the gown. The lady's *dressing gown* was generally a bedroom garment but, like that of the men, became a purely private gown by the end of the nineteenth century.

North American Indian dress

It is now accepted that the Americas were first peopled from eastern Asia and that migrations were recurrent starting from, it is thought, about 25,000 years ago. The Bering Strait provided the bridge between Siberia and Alaska, for it is narrow, shallow and frozen over for part of the year. Over a long period of time many Asiatic peoples found their way to the Americas forming, by the time of their discovery by the white man, a population which varied from the most primitive societies to the most complex, from the Eskimos in the north to the later Aztec, Inca and Maya high cultures further south (see *Aztec*, *Inca* and *Maya dress*). In general, civilization developed to a higher degree in South America and the population density was much greater; it is estimated that, by the fifteenth century AD, there were just over a million people living in North America and nearly 20 million in the South.

The American Indian has a light brown skin, dark eyes, jet black, stiff hair on his head and high cheek bones; body hair is sparse and it was customary to pluck out such growth. Some of the Indians were tall, others short, and features varied from aquiline noses to broad, flatter ones. These American aborigines were called Indians by the members of the Columbus expedition of 1492 when they reached the Bahamas (West Indies) and believed that they had made landfall on the Indian subcontinent. Similarly the aborigines were referred to as Red Indians or Redskins but this was not due to the natural colour of their skins, which varied from very pale brown to brown, but to their custom of painting their bodies with a red pigment.

The North American Indian developed a different degree of culture and a way of life which varied according to the area in which he lived. The parts of the continent where the most suitable climate and geographical situations were to be found were naturally occupied earliest, the woodlands round the Great Lakes and south towards Florida, the Pacific coast and the southwest. The Woodlands Indians lived in the eastern half of the country in an immense

Canadian woman of the Blackfoot tribe. Elkskin dress decorated with skin fringe and white, red, blue, black and yellow bead designs. Buckskin leggings. Moccasins

Blackfoot Indian. Buckskin shirt and leggings. Decoration by dyed quills, horsehair tassels, skin fringe and serge cloth. Moccasins

Child of Cheyenne tribe. Buckskin shirt and leggings with coloured bead and fringe decoration. Moccasins

War bonnet with buffalo horns, beadwork, head-band, ermine tails and feathers with horse hair tips

Mandan chief. Buckskin shirt and leggings. Quill embroidery and hair fringe. War bonnet of feathers, horns and ermine tails. Moccasins

North-west coast Indian hat woven from cedar bark and squaw grass. Painted design

Sioux Indian. Hunting shirt of buffalo skin decorated with quill-work, beads, fringe and human hair. Leggings, moccasins.

Necklace of four rows of dentalium shells and red serge spacers and tassels

Plains Indian woman. Skin dress decorated with fringe, paint and quillwork. Leggings, moccasins

North-west coast Indian. Split cedar woven hat painted in red, black and pale blue. Apron and cloak woven in goat wool weft on cedar bark warp. Black ground design in yellow, pale blue and white. Natural colour fringe

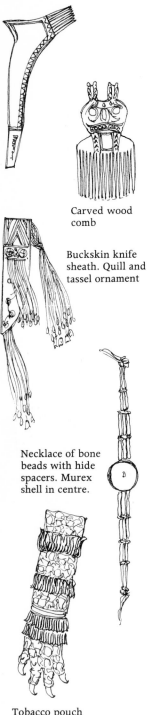

Moosehorn comb

Carved wood comb

Buckskin knife sheath. Quill and tassel ornament

Necklace of bone beads with hide spacers. Murex shell in centre.

Tobacco pouch made from alligator's foot

area extending from Hudson Bay to the Gulf of Mexico. These peoples, whose ancestors came as early as 2000 BC, lived by hunting and fishing, trapping and farming. Many of the tribes, such as the Iroquois, were war-like. Other peoples in the area included the Algonquin, the Mohawk, the Delaware, the Cherokee and the Chotaw. The Indians came to the Pacific coast from about 500 AD onwards and spread to inhabit the whole coastal strip from Alaska to California. Here was an ideal climate, warmed by the sea currents and rich in soil and in fish in both sea and rivers. In such conditions these north-west coast Indians developed high standards of culture as is evidenced in their high quality of North American Indian art. This can be seen in their painted totem poles, their masks and costumes for the dance, their sculpture, their metalwork in copper, silver and gold and their woven basketwork. Their decorative, woven blankets and aprons are characteristic, made from a mixture of cedar bark and hair from the dog and the goat, then patterned all over.

The Plains Indians inhabited a vast territory in the centre and south of North America from about 1000 AD onwards. These peoples included the Sioux, the Blackfeet and the Mandan in the northerly part and, further south, the Cheyenne, the Osage and the Comanche. Before the coming of the white man, these tribes practised agriculture on a small scale in the areas where rainfall was adequate and the climate least inimicable. They hunted the buffalo and grew beans, melon, corn and tobacco, but the poverty of this hostile land kept their standard of living depressed until, early in the eighteenth century, they began to trade their furs with the white man for horses and guns. With these two acquisitions the Plains Indians became mobile, establishing a new culture as horsemen nomads, spending their lives following the seasonal migrations of the animals on whom they depended for their food, clothing, shelter and all their domestic needs. This new culture was a dynamic one (the basis of so many American western

films), but it was short-lived. The white man had brought to them the means to a higher standard of life but his advance westwards across the continent brought it to an end little more than 100 years later. Further south-west, in the hot desert areas of Arizona and New Mexico lived the Pueblo tribes. Their ancestors had come as early as 2000 BC and, 1000 years later, they lived as cultivators, planting corn, making baskets and pottery and living in a close-knit society in adobe villages. Their dress and customs differed from the Indians of the other areas and they have been more successful in maintaining their way of life against the incursions of the white man.

The clothing of the North American Indian varied according to the climate in the areas he inhabited but, in general, apart from the Indians in the south-west, few garments were woven but were made from animal skins. Unlike the Eskimo, the Indian did not tailor his clothes but wore them draped, hanging loose in folds from the shoulder and sewn only minimally. Males wore a *breechclout* and females a skin wrapped round the waist to form a short skirt. In warm climates little else was worn on top apart from an apron back and front, though in wet weather a cloak or poncho was draped over the shoulders. For the cooler seasons or at night, a blanket of hemp or animal skin was wrapped round the body. In temperate zones men wore a skin shirt draped loose to the hips and skin leggings. The leggings reached the thigh and were tied to the belt of the breechclout. Both these and the shirt were mostly made from deerskin. Women also wore leggings but theirs were short, covering the lower leg only and were tied on with garters. Over these they had a long, skin dress, which was made from the skin of a larger animal, usually the elk. In the northern parts Indians followed the example of their Eskimo neighbours and wore fur garments and made their leggings in one piece with their moccasins to keep out the cold. The white man introduced woven cloth to the Indians, also his style of clothing; both of these had an influence in the eighteenth and nineteenth centuries but skin garments continued to be the most usual wear in the west.

The Indians had acquired great skill in tanning the skins of animals. Their process was an oil-tanning method in which they utilized the brains of the animal to produce the softest textured deer or buckskin in a chamois quality, which they successfully dyed in black or brilliant colours, especially red (see also tanning and chamoising under *Leather*). The garments were then very simply made from these beautiful skins. The whole skin was used and the shape of the animal utilized to avoid wastage. For shirts and dresses two skins were often used, the leg strips of the animal's skin left hanging down at the sides or back. They did not use eyed needles but pierced holes in the skin with a bone awl, then passed threads through these to tie the edges of the garment together. The thread was usually made of animal sinews. Women made and decorated all clothing as well as accessories. This ornamentation was brilliantly coloured, using white and black as a contrast to the colours and to the skin ground. The traditional Indian decoration was by porcupine quill embroidery. These quills were softened by chewing, then were dyed, using earth and vegetable dyes and incorporated into embroidered designs. Contact with the white man brought coloured glass beads which became an important embroidery material, and also introduced the Indian to the brilliance of aniline dyes. Garments were also decorated by cutting fringed edges to the skin and by adding hair tassels and bunches. Men's dress was further decorated by certain insignia denoting rank and achievement in combat. These included scalp-locks, feathers, ermine tails, teeth and shells.

The Indians used skins and pelts from all the animals available in their area. Apart from deer and elk, they hunted buffalo (bison), moose, beaver, otter, wolf, fox and squirrel and, in the north, the bear. It was along the Pacific coast and in the south-west that the Indians wore the beautifully designed blankets, cloaks and aprons which they used for wearing and wrapping themselves in. These were woven with a warp of softened cedar bark and a wool weft from mountain goat and/or dog. The edges were finished with fur or long fringing. The all-over designs are most distinctive; using animal motifs in an expressionist, symbolic, almost abstract form.

In many Indian tribes men paid great attention to plucking out both facial and body hair with tweezers and the decoration of face and coiffure. They painted their faces as part of their preparation for war. Both sexes used tattooing as a means of decorating body and face. Women usually confined this patterning to arms and legs but men, particularly the chieftains, could be elaborately tattooed all over. Vermilion was the colour most often impregnated into the pricked surface of the skin.

Men dressed their hair with care, often styling it in a dramatic manner. In general, Indians in the east, and especially the south-east, shaved much of the head apart from a ridge of hair running down the centre from the forehead to the crown. This was termed the *roach* and could be implemented with animal's hair and ornamented with feathers. In a feather head-dress a *roach spreader* worn here was made of carved bone, wood or antler and supported the feathers. In some styles the hair was grown long and dressed in a top knot on the crown or could be knotted at the nape while the rest of the head was shaved. In the north-east area Indians often plaited their long hair while in the Plains it was generally grown long and hung loose. Further north-west some tribes, the Blackfoot for example, grew a long lock in front which they dressed to hang down over the centre of the forehead. Women grew their hair long and tended it carefully; it was dressed loosely or plaited. Indians often went bareheaded or they wore a headband to keep the long hair back from the face. This band was of skin decorated with quillwork or beads. It held one or two feathers or a pair of buffalo horns.

The feather head-dress, the feather bonnet or *war bonnet*, was the head-dress adopted by the Western and Canadian Indians to prepare for war. By the nine-

Wood cradle board, painted on under side

Baby carrier of coloured basketry

Indian of the north-west in bearskin coat with claw and scalp lock decoration. Buffalo horn headdress. Skin leggings and moccasins

Bead work and quill porch in red, blue and white. Hair tassels

Strike-a-light pouch of buckskin decorated by orange and white quills. Contains flint and steel for making fire. Worn round neck

teenth century the Indians in the east wore it as a festive head-dress. The war bonnet was a symbolic head-dress. It was made of buckskin and coloured cloth, the feathers being taken from the living golden eagle. Each feather represented a deed of valour which had been performed either by the wearer or the whole tribe. Similarly, the horsehair tips symbolized the scalplocks of the warriors. The front of the band is generally decorated with quillwork or beads, and the side drops of a chief's war bonnet are of ermine (see also *Bonnet*).

The *moccasin* is the traditional Indian shoe. It is made in one piece of soft leather which encloses the sole, front and sides of the foot and is seamed to an inset piece on top of the instep. The leather is folded down in ankle flaps round the back and can be tied there. There is no heel. Moccasins are usually decorative and brightly coloured with the dyed leather embroidered with beads, quills and shells. Dancing shoes had tinkling metal tags attached. Both sexes wore moccasins; in the Woodland areas the soles were soft, in the Plains they were of heavier leather; in the south Indians went barefooted.

Indians, especially the nomadic Plainsmen, had few possessions and they carried essentials with them. These were contained, for safety, in a pouch hanging from the waistbelt or round the neck, or could be in a *bandoleer* (shoulder bag). These pouches and bags were beautifully made of dyed skin and decorated with brightly-coloured embroidery which incorporated beads and quills. Before the white man introduced his glass beads, the Indians made theirs from shells. In their pouches men carried tobacco, flint and steel to make fire, tweezer cases and small mirrors to do running repairs on their facial war paint. Women carried combs (which were not worn in the hair but used for dressing it), mirrors and articles for keeping the clothes of the family in repair. The baby was carried also, in a baby carrier of basket or buckskin, in the hand or strapped to his mother's back. The decorative cradleboards or baby frames could also be slung on a saddle, set on the ground or hung up in the tent – an ancient form of carrycot, in fact.

All the Indian tribes liked jewellery and personal decoration. Bracelets, necklaces, earrings and breastplates were worn, made of copper and silver. Bead necklaces were made from shells of all kinds and carved wood and bone. *Wampum* was an Algonquin term (meaning white) used by the Woodlands Indians of the north-east for purple and white beads made from clam shells. Wampum represented a symbol of friendship to these tribes, particularly the Iroquois, and wampum necklaces and belts served as a medium of exchange between the Indians and the white settlers.

Nosegay

A small bunch of sweet-smelling flowers worn on the person or carried as a posy or little bouquet. In the first part of the twentieth century placed by gentlemen in the buttonhole and, prior to this, adopted in eighteenth century France as a *boutonnière* (see also *Bosom-flowers*).

Beaded moccasin with ankle ties

Man's dancing shoe of red leather with white, blue, yellow and red bead decoration. Metal tags hanging to give tinkling sound

Moccasin decorated with moose hair

Oiled fabrics

A treatment of materials with oil and gum to make them water resistant or proof. *Oilcloth* is a heavy cotton fabric which has been painted and varnished. It is used in costume for caps, jackets and headcoverings. *Oilsilk* (oiled silk) is a lighter fabric, of silk, made waterproof by being soaked in oil; used for rainwear or as a lining. *Oilskin* is a cotton fabric treated with oil and gum and used for fishermen and sailors. In the USA *oilskins* are termed *slickers*. These materials are being replaced by plastic forms of waterproofing.

Ombré fabrics

From the French for shaded. Materials woven or painted with colours merging into one another.

Onyx

A form of quartz with layers of different colours giving banded markings. Used widely for cuff links, rings and brooches.

Opal

A hydrous silica which exhibits an iridescent colour glow in black, white or orange-red.

Orphrey

Gold embroidered bands or material. Derives from the Latin *auriphrygium* = gold + Phrygian; in ancient times Phrygia was famous for its gold embroideries. In Europe, in the Middle Ages, the term was widely used to refer to bands of gold or any rich embroidery sewn to ecclesiastical vestments and garments of royalty and the nobility.

Ottoman

A ribbed or corded fabric in silk, worsted or cotton. Ottoman satin and ottoman velvet are brocaded.

Overcoat, greatcoat, top coat, pardessus

These terms are largely synonymous and are used to describe an outdoor coat which is worn by either sex on top of indoor attire. All have been in use with this general meaning from the eighteenth century onwards, though a more specific definition is sometimes applied. The word greatcoat, the usual military term, is, in civilian dress, usually thought of as a heavy outdoor coat, worn over a suit, while overcoats and top coats can be of varied weights and styles worn over suits, jackets and ensembles. *Pardessus* is a French term which is generally used for a man's overcoat around mid-nineteenth century but in women's fashions can be applied to any nineteenth-century outdoor upper garment. Outdoor coats did not come into fashionable use until the eighteenth century; before this cloaks, capes and mantles of varying design and material were draped on top of both masculine and feminine indoor dress. Eighteenth-century *overcoats* were either of similar cut to the coat of the *habit à la française*, but made of heavier material and worn on top so that there were three layers – waistcoat, coat, overcoat – or were heavy-duty greatcoats, long and full, double-breasted, collared and often with shoulder capes. These designs were based on the coachman's greatcoat, suited for sitting in the open on the coachman's box, exposed to the cold, rain, wind and snow. The *Wraprascal* (or *Surtout*) was one such

Brown herringbone tweed informal overcoat, English, 1908

Russian fur shuba

long, loose, heavy greatcoat which had large buttons and, sometimes, shoulder capes; it was used also for riding in bad weather. The *Box coat*, a late eighteenth century introduction, was designed to be worn by the coachman or those passengers sitting on the outside of the coach, hence its name. Made of heavy cloth, it was full and long and generally caped. The *Redingote* was worn by men from about 1725 for riding and travelling, the name being the French version of riding-coat. In the eighteenth century this was a heavy, long coat, double-breasted with large collar and revers and often a short shoulder cape. A version of the redingote was introduced for women about 1785. This was a more elegant, lighter-weight coat and had the fashionably-high waistline, revers, collar and capes; below this it was worn open displaying the gown.

Much more variety in styles of overcoat was available in the nineteenth century. Men's garments were now more severely tailored and the overcoat was most suitable as outdoor clothing to wear on top. There were overcoats for smart town wear, for warmth while travelling and riding, for informal leisure purposes and for protection from different degrees of cold and wet. Among the heavy coats designed for warmth in bad weather and for travelling was the *Inverness coat* or *cape*, named after the Scottish city. This garment, of the second half of the century, was generally made of tweed or check or plaid cloth. It was long and full, belted, had a collar and an elbow-length cape which could be detachable. Sometimes the garment had sleeves, sometimes not; it could be cut as a cloak or a coat. The *Carrick* was also a bad-weather, caped coat worn for driving and travelling. This often had two or three shoulder capes; it was double-breasted and full and was worn from the beginning of the century onwards. A feminine version was fashionable in the later part of the century. This was made of thin material and often used as a dust (duster) coat (see *Motoring wear*). It was nearly ground-length and had tiered shoulder capes. The *Ulster overcoat*, generally called simply an

Ulster, was introduced from Belfast in 1867. It also was long and full, made of a heavy Ulster frieze. This full coat had a half or full belt and was often caped. *Shuba* is the Russian name for a capacious fur winter coat. In the late 1850s the *Raglan overcoat* was a loose, long coat named after Lord Raglan, British Commander in the Crimean War. It had a particular style of sleeve which was not inset in a round armhole but the seams continued from underarm up to the neckline. This gives a full, easy line which is very suited to an overcoat which has to be put on over another tailored coat sleeve; the Raglan sleeve has been in use ever since its introduction in 1857. (See *Sleeve*.)

Several designs of shorter coats were worn, of knee-length or less. These were suitable for more active pursuits or for less cold weather. For example, the *Covert coat* was designed for shooting or riding. It was cut straight to hip-level and made of a light material, generally waterproofed. The *Taglioni*, which was mainly in use in the first half of the century, was named after the family of ballet dancers; it was usually knee-length, its edges bound with braid. *Wrapper coats* were also generally short. Fashionable about mid-century, these were made in several styles, double or single-breasted, reaching to mid-thigh. Some were buttoned, others wrapped round the body and held in place by one hand.

There were a number of fashionable designs of overcoat for town wear for both men and women during the nineteenth century. One of the classic designs for men was the *Chesterfield overcoat*, worn from the 1840s onwards and named after the fashionable Earl of Chesterfield. A tailored coat, cut slightly waisted, the Chesterfield just covered the knees. It could be double-breasted but was generally single-breasted and fastened with a fly front. Black or dark cloth was the most usual material, with a black velvet collar (see also *Evening dress, Men*). The *Newmarket overcoat* was originally designed for riding and named after the English town. It was a fitting coat with long skirts and a velvet collar. Later in the century a similar style was worn by ladies

Redingote of blue wool, 1775, French

Brown Carrick, Polish, 1800

Redingote of pale grey cloth, French, 1780

Dark wool overcoat with gold braid and buttons worn over habit à la française, English, 1725

Red cloth redingote, English, 1789

Plaid wool Inverness coat with hat to match, English, 1885

Taglioni overcoat, English, c.1840

Cloth coat with fur collar and braid trimming. Polonaise-redingote style. French, 1834

Dark purple outer coat with shoulder capes, English, 1835

Dark blue cloth short overcoat
with velvet collar, English, 1845

Blue-grey paletot with shoulder
capes, English, 1880

Black cloth redingote, double-
breasted, silk collar, English,
1874

Dark cloth overcoat with muff
pockets, German, 1882

Polonaise style redingote with
fur collar and brandenburgs,
grey-blue cloth, English, 1814

Polonaise style of coat with
brandenburg fastenings, Polish,
c.1830

Ulster overcoat, German, 1882

Grey woollen coat with squirrel
fur trimming, English, 1902

Grey paletot trimmed with
claret velvet bands and buttons,
English, 1860

Grey cloth redingote with black
fur collar, English, 1830

Black cloth top frock overcoat, English, 1877

Cloth coat with fur trimming, French, 1923

Beige woollen winter coat with skunk fur trimming, English, 1917

Brown tweed herringbone overcoat. Raglan sleeve, English, 1950

Rust-brown cloth coat, grey fur, English, 1934

Black silk paletot with black velvet collar and cuffs over bustle gown, English, 1885

Three-quarter length coat, Dior, French, 1950

Nigger brown coat, astrakhan collar, 'New Look', English, 1949

Fawn cloth short overcoat, English, 1889

Dull red and black herringbone tweed coat with black velvet collar and cuffs, English, 1948 also. In the 1830s and 1840s a very long, full-skirted and exaggeratedly-waisted overcoat was fashionable for men. This often had a fur or velvet collar and was decorated, Polish style, with braid ornamentation or military-type Brandenburgs. Such coats were sometimes referred to as *Polonaises*. From the 1830s onwards fashionable men wore a *Top Frock* overcoat. This was a frock coat but was longer and made of heavier material. It was designed for wear instead of a frock coat but to appear as a smart town overcoat.

By the nineteenth century the *Redingote*, the caped travelling coat of the eighteenth century, had become a fitting, town overcoat. Single or double-breasted, it was waisted and had long, flared skirts. Sleeves were fitting and collars could be velvet or fur-trimmed. Ladies wore the Redingote also but, for them, its form changed considerably over the years. Early in the century it was a high-waisted coat but, during the 1820s, 1830s and 1840s, it was made of light fabrics and was a gown rather than a coat (see *Gown*). In the last quarter of the century it reappeared as an outdoor coat, tailored, with a fitted waist, a collar and flaring, long skirt. The *Paletot* was an outer coat worn by both sexes during much of the nineteenth century but the term seems to have been loosely applied to differing styles, varying from decade to decade. Thought to derive from paltock (see *Doublet*), the men's Paletot (or Paddock) appeared in the 1830s as a short greatcoat cut without a waist seam. By mid-century it had a much longer, flared skirt seamed to a fitting body. The full-length Paletot outer coat was fashionable for women from about 1860 onwards. It followed the fashionable line and was nearly always a waisted, fitting coat, often on princess lines without a waist seam. Most styles had collar and revers and tiers of shoulder capes could be added. In the 1870s and 1880s the Paletot was shaped to fit over the bustle gowns.

In the twentieth century men's overcoats followed the late nineteenth century pattern until after the First World War. In the 1920s and 1930s dark cloth, fitting styles were worn in town and tweed, full styles, belted or loose for informal wear. Since 1950 overcoats have been shorter and with the increasing use of the motor car, have been worn less and less, being replaced by the car coat (see *Coat*). Outer coats for women have followed the fashionable line of the period. In the second half of the twentieth century they have been available in flaring tent styles, princess line with full, gored skirts, straight loose types, belted, half-belted, full-length, three-quarter length or short car coats. One coat which is typical of the twentieth century, particularly for the young, is the *duffel* (duffle) *coat*. Named after the heavy woollen material from which it is made (see *Wool*), the fashion derives from the duffel coat worn by the Navy during the Second World War as protection against the cold. Soon after the war surplus duffel coats were sold very cheaply and became ubiquitous winter wear for young men and girls. The duffel is a warm, short coat, fastened in front with wood toggles; it can have an attached hood. The original colour was off-white but later duffels are made in various colours.

Oxford

1) A woollen cloth woven in black, grey and white.
2) A cotton fabric (a shirting) woven with narrow coloured stripes.

P

Paillette

Small, round, glittering pieces of foil in gold, silver or mother of pearl used to decorate women's evening dresses – a spangle or sequin.

Paisley pattern

This motif, characteristic of Paisley shawls, was based on the pine cone but is also related to the date palm motif of ancient Assyria, the anthemion of the classical world and the honeysuckle and cone of Indian designs (see *Embroidery*).

Palatine

A fur tippet worn by women in the seventeenth century. Named after the Princess Palatine, wife of the Duke of Orleans (1676).

Panier

From the late seventeenth century until about 1780 a framework was worn under the petticoats and feminine gown skirts to produce the required full silhouette and to support the weight of the layers of material. The framework was first established in England about 1690 and consisted of basket forms on the hips made into a petticoat and tied on at the waist. In England such frameworks were termed hoops but when adopted in France about 1718 the word *panier* = basket was used; this became the usual term.

   The panier skirt was fashionable for much of the eighteenth century but its form altered during these years. In the earlier decades the shape was circular and wide and these hoops lent a lilting, gentle motion to the skirt as the lady walked; it was a flowing movement, feminine and provocative. By the mid-century the silhouette had

PALATINE
Ermine tippet (palatine), English, *c.*1680

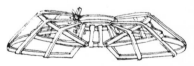

Whalebone and tape folding panier

PANIER
Side paniers

Panier skirt

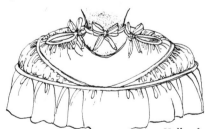

Holland panier, non-folding

changed from a circular hoop to an elliptical one, flatter at front and back but wider at the sides. This extreme width instilled a different motion. Here, the lady had to turn sideways to negotiate a doorway or enter a sedan chair.

By 1750 the sides were excessively wide and the front and back considerably flattened; it became difficult to sit in a chair despite furniture designed with extra width for this purpose. A new type of panier was made which consisted of several cane and whalebone hoops not inserted into a petticoat but strung together by tapes. This was tied on at the waist in a similar manner but was an articulated panier so, when a lady wished to negotiate an entrance, she only need lift the skirt upwards by placing her elbows under the paniers and this would reduce the width sufficiently for a passage. The system was equally useful for seating oneself in a chair or entering a sedan. Soon pockets and slits in the skirt enabled the wearer to slip her hands inside to raise the paniers. In the 1770s polonaise and similar gowns had three or more small paniers. By 1780 the fullness of the skirt was concentrated at the back and a bustle was worn.

Pantaloons, pantalettes

Pantaloon, generally used in the plural, has referred at different times in costume to various forms of covering for the legs. The term was used in the sixteenth century to describe a man wearing such pantaloons who was usually old, foolish and enfeebled as, for example, in Shakespeare's *As You Like It* in his description of the seven ages of man when he refers to 'The leane and slipper'd Pantaloone'. In Italian Comedy Pantalone was a Venetian character who was old and thin and wore such fitting trousers with jacket and slippers and with a black gown on top.

In the later seventeenth century pantaloons were synonymous with a style of breeches, then the use of the word was discontinued until it reappeared about 1790 to describe the tight-fitting trousers which were developing from knee-breeches. There was great opposition to the wearing of these long pantaloons, especially in England and France where breeches and stockings were considered to be more dignified but, by 1820, the popularity of pantaloons was overwhelming and the style ousted knee-breeches from fashion. Pantaloons were fitting and made from an elastic-type material such as stockinet or soft doeskin in grey, beige, lemon or white. Some were of finely-striped cotton and, especially fashionable, were those of nankeen (see *Nankeen*). They reached down to

Little girl in white dress and pantalettes, Austrian, 1840

Pantalone (Pantaloon), 1550. Black gown, red cap, jacket and pantaloons, yellow leather shoes (after Maurice Sand)

White pantaloons strapped under slippers, Austrian, 1826

White muslin pantaloons, c.1815

below the calf and just above the ankle, where they were fastened with buttons or buckle and ribbon. They could be worn with socks and shoes or tucked into tall boots. In the 1820s they became longer and were worn outside and strapped under the instep of the footwear. By mid-century pantaloons had become trousers.

The name pantaloons was also given in the early nineteenth century to feminine underwear. These were the drawers which were worn first by children and later by women (see *Children's dress* and *Drawers*). Pantalette was the diminutive of pantaloon and described the lace or frilled edged white leglets or drawers worn by children to the ankles and displayed below the skirt hem until the mid-century.

Pantoffle

An overshoe without back quarter covering the front of the foot only like a mule (see *Slipper*). Worn from about 1490 until 1650 but especially in the sixteenth century.

Paper clothes

Dispensable, inexpensive garments introduced in the 1960s: chiefly underwear and children's clothes.

Paper patterns

The production of paper patterns as a service and auxiliary trade to dressmaking was set up in England early in the nineteenth century. It is not known who first established this trade on a business footing but a firm was making such patterns on a considerable scale by the 1820s. Run by an Englishwoman (Mrs Smith of London) and her partner a Frenchwoman (Madame La Pouilli of Paris), this business produced full size paper patterns for dresses and millinery. The current Paris fashions were studied and a large stock of paper patterns based on these were supplied to dressmakers from London. Other firms followed suit.

In 1850 *World of Fashion* was the first journal to carry paper patterns for their readers' use and soon the idea was taken up by other magazines. In the USA Ebenezer Butterick, a tailor, made paper patterns in the 1860s and the firm of Butterick opened their English branch in Regent Street in 1873 and were quickly successful. By this time the paper pattern industry was well established both as a service to professional tailors and dressmakers and in magazines for the home reader and her private dressmaker.

Papillote

A hair curl paper used widely especially in the eighteenth century. From the French verb *papilloter* = to flicker, to blink, thought to derive from *papillon* = butterfly.

Paragon

A material similar to camlet made in Turkey and widely used in the seventeenth and eighteenth centuries in Europe (see *Camlet*).

Parti-colouring

A fashion prevalent in Medieval Europe from the late twelfth century until the end of the fifteenth century wherein garments were made in one colour and design on one half or quarter and a different colour or pattern on the other sections. Masculine hose was most often parti-coloured, divided vertically down the centre of the leg, front and back and, often, quartered at the knee also.

PANTOFFLE
German pantoffle of leather with cork insole, *c.*1530

PARTI-COLOURING
Parti-coloured hose, English, 1350

Parti-coloured gown, *c.*1360. Black velvet and gold brocaded fabric, English

PARTLET
Queen Elizabeth I, 1575. Black
lace partlet

PATTEN
Syrian kub-kob. Wood, mother-
of-pearl inlay, leather strap

Wood patten, Swiss, *c.*1400

Wood patten, leather straps.
German, *c.*1450

White silk partlet studded with
pearls, French, *c.*1550

Partlet

A detachable covering for the neck, chest
and shoulders worn in conjunction with a
low or wide décolletage : in different forms,
such as a chemisette or high collar.
Especially fashionable in the second half
of the sixteenth century when partlets
were generally of embroidered and jewelled
sheer fabrics or lace.

Passement, passementerie

A decorative trimming for costume made
of gold or silver lace, gimp or braid which
might include beads, cord or fringe.

Patten

An overshoe made of wood, leather and
metal, fastened to the foot by leather or
cloth straps. Worn to raise the boot, shoe
or soled hose above the mud and dirt of
the street. In the Middle Ages the patten
was usually shaped in wood with a block
under the heel and another under the ball of
the foot with a raised arch between. By
the early seventeenth century patten soles
were raised by a wedge support under the
arch while underneath was attached a

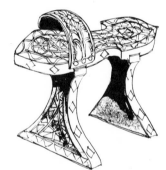

Turkish kub-kob. Carved wood,
inlaid with mother-of-pearl.
Appliqué decorated strap with
silk pompon

Wood patten. German, *c.*1390

Eighteenth century leather and
wood patten, iron ring, English

Wood pattens. Burgundy,
*c.*1447

piece of metal shaped in quatrefoil form; with the eighteenth century the quatrefoil became a circular ring (see also *Chopine* and *Clog*).

The pattens worn in Turkey, Persia and Arab countries had a similar purpose; they were also worn in the Turkish baths to keep the feet dry. These *kub-kobs*, as they are termed, were of carved wood soles on curving supports, inlaid all over in geometrical patterns using stones and mother-of-pearl. A broad decorative strap held the foot in the patten.

Pearl

Pearls are the result of a nacreous concretion of peculiar lustre formed inside the shell of certain molluscs, notably the pearl oyster and pearl mussel. Natural pearls are caused by pathological processes set in train by the introduction of an irritant. Such irritants vary but might consist of seaweed, a grain of sand or any piece of foreign matter which, when introduced into the shell, irritates the mollusc and activates the secretion of nacreous matter. The best natural pearls, as well as mother-of-pearl, are produced by the pearl oyster which is found in tropical seas all over the world. The ancient civilizations fished for pearls chiefly in the Persian Gulf and the Indian Ocean. The pearl mussel is a river mollusc found in the mountain streams of temperate climates in the northern hemisphere; British pearls were valued, especially from Scotland in Roman Britain.

The cultivated or cultured pearl is produced by introducing an irritant into the shell of the mollusc and so stimulating the secretion of nacreous substance. As long ago as the thirteenth century the Chinese discovered a means of introducing such irritants into the river pearl mussel. They used pellets of mud or tiny fragments of bone or wood, a process still extensively practised. It was the Japanese who experimented on such a process for the pearl oyster. Research into pearl cultivation was begun in 1891 by Mikimoto in Japan and this proved successful. Since then the Japanese have bred oysters for their health and strength, keeping them in cages in the

sea to protect them from predators. They are nurtured from spawn and operated on at three years old; seven years later the pearls are harvested.

Artificial pearls were first made in Europe in 1680 by the Frenchman Jacquin in Paris. A preparation made from the silvery scales of a small river fish called the bleak was introduced into hollow spheres of thin glass and the centre filled with white wax. A number of different processes are now used to produce quantities of imitation pearls which were at their height of twentieth-century fashion in the 1930s.

Pearls have always been desired as decoration for costume in jewellery and embroideries. Seed pearls, that is very small pearls often irregular in shape and, therefore, not of great value, were used in great amounts particularly in sixteenth and nineteenth century embroidery of costume and accessories.

Pearlies

London Cockney street traders who decorate their own clothes by sewing pearl buttons all over them in floral, geometrical and symbolic designs. They wear this costume to collect money for charity. The pearlies are mainly costermongers. The costermonger has been a street trader since the early Middle Ages. The word derives from costard the name of a large apple with ribbed markings, and monger, a dealer or trader. Costermongers were originally apple sellers who displayed their wares in the open street.

Since the early nineteenth century London costermongers have decorated their best clothes with pearl buttons, especially the men's waistcoats and the women's blouses. In the nineteenth century the men wore tie-up caps to protect their heads when carrying baskets of fruit on them, corduroy waistcoats with sleeves and large pockets and broad-ribbed corduroy trousers. The women wore large hats with ostrich plume trimming and cotton dresses or blouses and skirts with a long white apron on top. The pearl button decoration represented the poor man's

PEARLIES
Pearly coster girl, 1890s

PEASECOD-BELLY
Peasecod-bellied doublet,
English, 1580

PECTORAL
Gold pectoral ornament, Celtic,
seventh century BC

jewellery, imitating a costume studded with diamonds, and these buttons made from mother-of-pearl were inexpensive as oysters at that time were cheap food.

The custom for wearing full pearled costume was started by Henry Croft, a roadsweeper and an enthusiastic worker for charity. He sewed buttons on his own clothes to attract attention and to help to raise more money. The idea developed of covering the whole surface of the garments with pearl buttons. This made a magnificent display and hid any threadbare parts. Such outfits, which might contain as many as 80,000 buttons, were extremely heavy to wear, weighing up to 60 pounds in total.

Pearly royalty stems from the earlier coster royalty and the right to wear pearly suits is inherited. Suits are handed down from generation to generation, the style changing with the times. Difficulties are experienced in modern days because of a shortage in the number of pearl buttons available; plastic just will not do.

Peasecod-belly

A fashion of Spanish origin for men between 1570 and 1600 to pad the front of the doublet and jerkin into an artificial paunch shape, which was maintained by a wooden busk in front and whalebone strips in the seams.

Pectoral

An ornamental breast-plate or other decoration worn on the breast, such as that of the Hebrew High Priest.

Pekin

A fine quality striped silk textile originally made in China.

Gold pectoral plaques, Greek,
seventh century BC

PÈLERINE
White pèlerine with fringed
and ruched trimming worn over
an evening gown, English, 1845

Pèlerine

From the French *pèlerin* = pilgrim. In the Middle Ages referred to a pilgrim's cloak or mantle. The feminine form was a short cape with pendant ends worn by ladies in the eighteenth and nineteenth centuries.

Pelisse

A woman's mantle, usually fur-lined and fur-trimmed, worn during the eighteenth century; a re-introduction of the pelisson, the furred overgown of the Middle Ages. During the eighteenth century the pelisse had a large collar or shoulder cape and, sometimes, a hood. It could be of varied length from hips to ankles and had slits for the hands to pass through.

The pelisse continued in fashion during the first forty years of the nineteenth century. In the early years it followed the high-waisted line, generally belted there. It was ankle-length and had long sleeves. With the wider skirts of the 1830s there was a return to the pelisse-mantle style, which hung loose to three-quarter length and had a waist-long cape which formed hanging open sleeves. In the later nine-

Red velvet pelisse with white fur lining and trimming, 1777

Gentleman's pelisse, c.1875. Fur lining and trimming

PELISSE
Brown velvet pelisse with grey fur lining and trimming, 1814

PENDANT
Minoan embossed pendant, seventeenth century BC

Mycenaean pendant, c.1400 BC

Cretan gold pendant, c.600 BC

Gold filigree pendant cross, Byzantine, sixth century AD

Silver pendant cross, jewelled centre. Saxon, 814 AD

Gold and diamond pendant cross with pearls, English, c.1550

The Armada jewel, c.1588. Enamelled gold pendant with diamonds and rubies

teenth century a pelisse was worn by men; it was a long fur-lined coat with fur collar, cuffs and edging, favoured for winter use and chilly evenings.

Pendant

In costume, a decorative piece of jewellery hanging from a neckchain, ribbon, necklace, earring or bracelet.

Peplum

Derived from the ancient classical *peptos* (see *Greece, ancient*). In modern dress, a short flounce or overskirt attached to a waistbelt or the bodice of a dress or jacket. Nineteenth century examples hung longer at sides or back and front.

Persia (ancient)

The Persian Empire was built up in the sixth century BC under the great rulers Cyrus and Darius, absorbing the short-lived, earlier Median Empire which had developed on the fall of the Assyrian Empire at the end of the seventh century. From the sixth century until the conquest of Persia by Alexander the Great in the late fourth century a Persian costume was worn which had only little in common with the dress of the other great cultures of the ancient world: Egypt, Sumeria, Assyria and Babylon or, indeed, the classical dress of Greece and Rome. All these were draped styles. Persian dress had evolved from the central Asiatic type of wear based on the needs of the nomadic horsemen; it consisted of tunic, coat and trousers, fitted garments derived from the originals of skin, felted wool and leather, having affinity with the Chinese dress of the east and the Scythian of the fringes of Europe (see *Chinese dress* and *Scythian dress*).

In Persia men wore a knee-length tunic, belted at the waist and with long sleeves set in at the shoulder. Under this were trousers cut wide at the top and tapering to be more fitting at the ankle. Boots or shoes accompanied these, not sandals, and both styles fitted up high. A coat, when worn, was ankle-length and was fastened across the chest with ties. It was often worn open or slung round the shoulders without putting the arms into the long

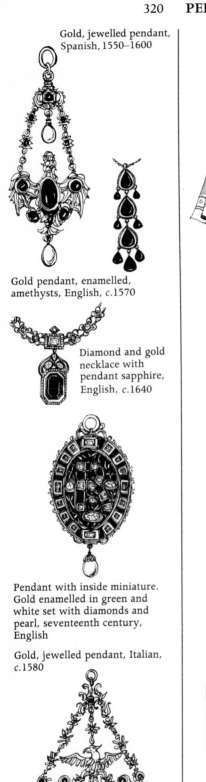

Gold, jewelled pendant,
Spanish, 1550–1600

Gold pendant, enamelled,
amethysts, English, c.1570

Diamond and gold
necklace with
pendant sapphire,
English, c.1640

Pendant with inside miniature.
Gold enamelled in green and
white set with diamonds and
pearl, seventeenth century,
English

Gold, jewelled pendant, Italian,
c.1580

Median robe,
buttoned shoes,
pleated cap

White headdress

King Darius.
Median robe,
crown, buttoned
shoes

Coat, long tunic,
trousers, shoes,
Phrygian cap

Felt cap, coat,
tunic, trousers,
boots

Buttoned shoe

Woman in shawl,
dress, underdress
and headcloth

sleeves. Caps of felt or leather were tall and cylindrical, round or of Phrygian design. Alternative headcoverings were the ribbed or pleated tiara and the white linen or wool draped cloth which was wound round in a conical or skull-fitting shape and was large enough to cover the shoulders also.

The chief source of information for men's dress comes from wall carvings and reliefs from the ruins of the palaces built by Cyrus, Darius and Xerxes in cities such as Persepolis. Here women are only rarely depicted. From the scanty evidence available it appears that their dress was similar to the plainer versions of the earlier Assyrian styles, consisting of an ankle-length dress or tunic and a shawl draped round the body; the head is covered and the mouth generally veiled.

One draped garment which the Persians adopted from their predecessors, the Medes, was their robe of honour, which became the imposing robe worn by Persian kings. This was a large rectangle of material about five feet by ten which was folded in two then sewn up the sides but leaving part unfastened at the top to give full sleeves; the garment was then slit at the top to provide an opening for the head. A belt or girdle tightly encircled the waist and the fullness of material was pulled up at each side over the belt to make the characteristic draped folds fall from these points. In some representations the fabric is shown pulled up at the left side only. Under this robe the king wore trousers and buttoned shoes. The characteristic decorative crown is worn on his head.

The Persians, like the Assyrians, were fastidious in the care of their coiffure. They adopted the same manner of curling the hair and beards into frizzed ringlets. Both sexes used cosmetics and liberally applied perfume and oils to their face and bodies. They wore a great deal of jewellery of designs similar to Assyrian work.

After Alexander's conquest Greek costume strongly influenced that of Persia with draped garments replacing fitted ones. With the return of Persian strength under the Sassanids in the third century AD there

PETTICOAT
Bustle-style petticoat with 'sweepers', 1878

PETENLAIR
Petenlair and petticoat of cream silk embroidered in yellow, red and blue, Swiss, 1750

Waist petticoat of silk with lace flouncing, 1905

Waist petticoat of crêpe de chine, 1910

was a revival of traditional Persian styles and fitted trousers, coats and tunics once more ousted cloaks and draped tunics.

Petenlair, pet-en-l'air
In the mid-eighteenth century, a French style of short jacket designed with a sacque back and worn with a petticoat; this was then the term for a separate, usually matching, skirt.

Petticoat
Originally two words petty coat, meaning a small coat. From the French *petit* and old French *cote*, becoming modern French *cotte* = petticoat.
1) From the fifteenth and sixteenth centuries a masculine garment, a short jacket or coat worn under the tunic or under armour. From the seventeenth century onwards this became the waistcoat.
2) As a feminine garment, an underskirt. Probably, originally, also a tunic, but from the fifteenth century onwards, the term referred to a garment covering the body from the waist downwards. From the sixteenth century until the early decades of the eighteenth century, this underskirt of rich, decorative fabric was visible as the

Princess petticoat trimmed with
ribbon and lace, 1913

Shaped slip trimmed with
ribbon and lace, 1940

Taffeta waist petticoat flounced
for 'New Look' style, 1948

Nylon slip, 1957

Embroidered satin slip, 1933

Queen Mary I, 1553. Brocaded
petticoat to match undersleeves

gown skirt was open in front to display it.
When gowns were no longer designed
with an open front the petticoat became
an undergarment and from about 1800
onwards the term referred only to underwear.

Petticoats as undergarments were usually
made of cambric or flannel. At certain
periods they were made of heavier or
stiffened materials to make the full skirts
stand out (see *Farthingale* and *Panier*). In
the early years of the eighteenth century,
for example, heavy petticoats were stiffened
with paste for this purpose. In France these
were called *criardes* (screaming, clamorous)
because of the noisy rustling which they
emitted on movement. Again, in the nineteenth century, from the 1840s to about
1870, several petticoats were worn, a red
flannel one on the inside then a corded
calico one, a horsehair one (see *Crinoline*)
and three or four starched calico or muslin
ones, flounced to support the weight of
the gown skirt. Typical of the elaborate
evening dress petticoats of the 1860s was
the empress petticoat which was gored and
fitting at waist and hips but fanned out

below this to a spreading hem with deep flounce and train. Quilted petticoats were also worn for warmth and to support the skirt; these were generally made of silk or linen lined with wadding or feathers.

The bustle gowns of the 1870s and 1880s demanded a different kind of petticoat support. These gowns were less full over the hips and down to the knees but then flared out at the back to a train; support was needed at the back just below the waist. Some complex designs of petticoats acted as an alternative to the bustle pad or basket structure (see *Bustle*) and incorporated many stiffened ruffles and pleats at the back, set in rows between waist and ground. At the hem were sewn pleated, stiffened 'sweepers' (*balayeuses*) which acted as dusters to absorb the dirt and keep clean the gown train on top. In the 1890s the hour glass silhouette needed only one silk or taffeta petticoat; this was fitted to the knee then, below this, flared, flounced and lace trimmed. Lined with taffeta, it produced the coveted frou-frou sound with movement.

In the twentieth century in the years before the First World War, taffeta or silk were widely used, with lace trimming, still making a frou-frou sound. Two petticoats were generally worn, a shorter one of wool (for winter) or percale (for summer) then a taffeta or silk long, outer one. This was flounced and ruched in tiers. The hanging petticoat or slip supported by shoulder straps and fashioned to the figure evolved in the 1920s with the introduction of shorter skirts and simpler clothes. Both this design and the waist petticoat followed the fashion line after this (see drawings and *Underwear*).

Piccadill, Pickadill, Picadil

The scalloped or tabbed edge at neck, armhole or waist of the body garments, fashionable in the late sixteenth and early seventeenth centuries. The name is thought to derive from Pickadilly Hall, in 1622 a house in the parish of St. Martin-in-the-Fields built by a Mr Higgins, a tailor who specialized in making garments decorated by 'pickadilles'. Later the name was perpetuated in the thoroughfare now known as Piccadilly. It is alternatively suggested that the name might derive from the fact that Pickadilly Hall was situated at the boundary or 'skirt' of the parish.

Picot

An ornamental edging to lace, braid or ribbon formed of tiny loops of twisted thread.

Pile

A material with a standing nap of threads, such as velvet or plush, which are produced by means of a secondary warp, the loops of which are cut and sheared.

Pin

Earliest pins were made of thorns or fish-bones, progressing to bone, bronze and iron. Medieval pins were a piece of metal wire with an end bent to form a head; the best quality pins were made of brass. After the Middle Ages pins were still luxury items. The head was made separately until nearly 1840; it was of wire, twisted round the shank and soldered in position. Machines for making pins with solid heads from one piece of wire were developed in the early nineteenth century in the USA. The safety pin derives from the ancient classical fibula (see *Fibula*). It has a loop at one end to provide a spring and the point is held in a protective sheath at the other. The modern safety pin was designed in America in the mid-nineteenth century.

Pinafore

In the nineteenth century, an apron-like covering of washable material worn by children and working women to protect the front of their dresses. So-called because originally it was pinned to the front of the gown. In modern fashion, a pinafore dress is sleeveless and has a low, round, V or square neck. In the USA this is a jumper. It is worn on top of a blouse or jumper.

Pinchbeck

An alloy of copper and zinc where the zinc only comprises about 15–20 per cent of the total metal, which then resembles

Bias cut crêpe de chine petticoat, 1927

PICCADILL
Piccadills to jerkin and doublet. French, 1610

PLEAT

Accordion pleated hem, 1876

Robe à la française. 'Watteau' pleats, 1770

Sunburst pleated skirt, 1947

Unpressed pleated costume, 1916

Kick inverted pleats in skirt of suit, 1943

gold. Introduced in the early eighteenth century by Christopher Pinchbeck, a London watchmaker, and named after him. Used for simulating gold in making less expensive jewellery.

Pinking
From the later Middle Ages until the early seventeenth century, a form of decoration by cutting small slashes or holes in footwear and garments. After this, a serrated pattern was given to the raw edge of a material to prevent unravelling. In modern times carried out by pinking shears or machine.

Pinner
1) The lappets or flaps of a coif or indoor cap (often pinned up), worn by ladies in the seventeenth and eighteenth centuries. 2) An abbreviation for the nineteenth century pinafore or apron with a bib.

Piping
An edging composed of a narrow binding containing cord.

Piqué
A stiff cotton material woven in a ribbed, figured or waffle pattern. Used particularly for men's waistcoats, collars and cuffs and ladies' dresses and blouses.

Placket
The fold of material sewn into the opening in a skirt or dress to which the fasteners – buttons, hooks and eyes or press studs – are sewn.

Plaid
In Gaelic, *plaide*, and Irish, *ploid*, meaning a blanket. A large rectangular piece of woollen cloth, generally in tartan or chequered pattern, used over the centuries as an outer garment also as a blanket at night in Scotland and the north of England (see *Scottish Highland dress*). The word plaid is also used to refer to the pattern of stripes woven to cross one another at right angles making a tartan design.

PLAIT
Plait coiled round crown of
head. Ancient Rome, 110 AD

Plait

Of the same source as pleat, meaning a fold
or series of folds of cloth. With hair, straw
or corded trimming, a plait is made by in
turn intertwining three or more strands to
make a chain of loops as in a pigtail or
braided tresses.

Plastron

In armour, a metal breastplate and a leather-
covered breast padding worn by the fencer.
In costume, an ornamental front to the
bodice of a woman's gown of contrasting
colour and material (see also *Stomacher*).

Platinum

A heavy, non-corrosive, silver-grey metal
with a high melting point used in jewellery.
Known in an impure state from early times,
the group of platinum (platina) metals
were not worked due to their high melting
points (that of pure platinum is $1755°C$).
Platinum is malleable and ductile. It can
be used in alloyed form, particularly with
one of its own group of metals, palladium
for instance, or with gold, silver or lead.
Platinum is found in Tasmania, Australia,
South America, California, Russia and
Southern Africa.

Pleat, pleating

Folds made and pressed in the material of
a garment to give fullness, to aid the fit or
purely as decoration. Certain designs in
pleating are named as, for instance, *accordion pleating*, where the material is folded
so that the same quantity of fabric is
allowed inward and outward. In *knife edge
pleating* only one crease is visible, while in
box pleating the folds are in pairs and point

in opposing directions. A classic eighteenth
century version was the *robe à la française*
with its so-called *Watteau* pleats. The folds
of these were sewn to the back of the neckline and at the waist, then fell free to the
ground. *Inverted pleats* are box pleats
reversed so that the folds face towards
each other. *Kick pleats* are short inverted
pleats, inserted at the hem of a fitting skirt
to give freedom for walking. A design used
especially in skirts is sunburst pleating,
where the folds radiate outwards; they are
narrow at the waist and become wider
towards the hem. Permanent pleating,
especially in man-made fabrics, is a feature
of modern dress but *unpressed pleats* are
also still in fashion and these give a softer
effect to the hang of the skirt. They are
fastened in pleats at the waistband then
left to hang in natural folds from here or
they can be sewn about five to six inches
down from the waist.

Plumpers

From the late seventeenth century, small,
lightweight cork spheres which ladies
carried in their cheeks to fill out the sunken
cavities caused by age and loss of teeth.

Plush

A soft fabric with a high pile which can be
made from most textile fibres.

Pocket

Garments did not contain pockets until the
sixteenth century; before this money, keys
and other small personal articles were
wrapped in a piece of cloth and tucked into
different parts of the costume: the neck
opening, a corner of the hood, the cod-
piece, the sleeve. The piece of cloth
developed into a small bag drawn up at the
top with strings and this, in turn, was
tucked into part of the costume.

From the sixteenth century, in men's
dress, a pocket in the form of a small pouch
was inserted into a seam in the trunk hose,
then into the breeches of the seventeenth
century. Coat pockets were introduced into
the justaucorps, first as vertical slits, then
horizontal near to the hem of the coat skirt.
From the late seventeenth century onwards

POCKET
Slashed pockets on hips and
breast-pocket, car coat, 1960

Sheepskin patch pockets, 1970

Slashed pocket with buttons
set low in coat skirt, 1685

Slashed coat pocket with gold
buttons and embroidery on flap,
1745.

Slashed pocket on hip, overcoat,
1950

coat pockets had flaps, usually richly decorated with braid and embroidery and they were set higher, near the hip bone. Soon they were introduced into the waistcoats also.

From the mid-seventeenth century women's dress contained pockets which were made in pairs attached to a tape which was tied round the waist under the skirt. They were reached through a placket slit in the skirt. In the years 1790–1815, because of the thin fabrics and few garments worn under the prevailing fashions, women carried their personal possessions in a reticule but returned to pockets tied round the waist as skirts became fuller again. By mid-nineteenth century pockets were sewn into the skirt seams and a watch pocket was inserted at the waist or in the bodice.

From the nineteenth century onwards a variety of named pocket designs have been incorporated in clothes for men, a few of which, especially in the twentieth century, have been adapted to women's fashions. These include:

Bellows – a patch pocket with buttoned flap and bellows pleat in the centre, that is, a vertical, unpressed pleat which expands to accommodate articles placed in the pocket. Worn especially in Norfolk jackets of the 1890s onwards.

Breast – worn inside a man's coat in the eighteenth century but on the left breast outside from the early nineteenth century onwards.

Fob – a small, horizontal pocket in the waistband of the breeches or pantaloons of the late eighteenth and early nineteenth centuries to take a fob watch. Often inserted in pairs.

French – term used in the later seventeenth century to describe horizontal pockets introduced into the justaucorps (a French style of coat).

Hare – a large pocket inserted inside a hunting or shooting jacket.

Hip – (also called a *caddie*) from the 1890s onwards, a pocket, with or without flap, inserted in the back of the trousers at hip level; to be distinguished from a pocket on the hips which was sewn into the skirts of a coat, over the hip.

Long – in the eighteenth and nineteenth centuries, a general term for a vertical pocket; a horizontal one was referred to as a *cross* pocket.

Panier – the pairs of pockets were hung outside the eighteenth-century paniers and were reached through a slit in the gown skirt.

Patch – a pocket, with or without flap, sewn on to the exterior of the garment.

Pleat – in the eighteenth and nineteenth centuries, a pocket in the pleats was one sewn into the back of the coat skirts under the pleats.

Skirt – in the eighteenth and nineteenth centuries, a pocket sewn into the lining of a man's coat skirts.

Slashed – a pocket on the inner side of a garment with a slash on the outer side finished by a bound edge and, sometimes, a flap.

Ticket – introduced for railway tickets and inserted into overcoats and coats from about 1860. Since the 1890s a ticket pocket has often been inserted into the jacket of a lounge suit above the right hand pocket.

Polish dress

Traditionally there has always been a great variety in Polish dress, the garments, styles and decoration differing from region to region. In mountain areas there is an affinity between Polish dress and that of similar terrain in neighbouring Rumania, Russia and Czechoslovakia as well as Baltic countries such as Albania, Greece and Bulgaria. This can be seen in the white coats and breeches decorated with black braid embroidery as well as in the boots and hats. In fashionable dress of the fifteenth to eighteenth centuries Polish attire evidenced regional characteristics as in the men's caftan style of coat worn with fur hat and feather, seen also in Russia and Hungary, and the elaborately decorative head-dresses worn by the women.

In peasant and regional dress brilliant, rich colours were used, evidencing great variety in both designs and motifs for the wealth of embroidered decoration. Cross-stitch designs using geometrical motifs were widely employed as well as conventionalized forms of birds, animals and human figures. Braid was used extensively in embroidered decoration, also buttons and beads. Beautiful lace was made and added as trimming. Stripes were a popular decorative medium, either straight or in zig-zag pattern. For both sexes the characteristic garment was the sheepskin coat worn with the wool inside and the exterior surface decorated by embroidery and appliqué motifs in wool and leather. These coats were generally loose-fitting and could be sleeveless or have long sleeves. Long, white cloth coats were also worn, especially by men in the region of Cracow.

Everyday dress for men consisted of full trousers, often striped, tucked into boots just below the knee, a long-sleeved shirt and, over this, a short jacket with sleeves or a longer, sleeveless coat, usually belted at the waist. Fringe and tassel trimming were common. Hats and caps were small, with feather decoration. Women wore simple dresses with full skirts. Often there were two skirts, one over the other, the outer one being knee-length, the other reaching the ankles. Alternatively, a fitting, decora-

Man from Cracow in white cloth coat with red trimming. Navy under coat, pink and white trousers and black boots. Red hat with black fur and peacock feather

Woman from Cracow. White blouse and white embroidered apron. Flowered skirt, black boots. Richly decorated bodice, several necklaces

Sheepskin coat with red trimming. Black and red striped skirt. Yellow bodice with black bands. Kerchief with ruched edging. Brown boots

White coat with brown binding. Black boots and hat. Green and red jacket and waistband. Deep purple trousers

POLISH DRESS

Fur-lined coat and cap, leather boots, c.1600

POMANDER
Silver gilt pomander, 1490–5

Gold pomander case decorated with pearls, 1535

Gold filigree pomander containing solid ambergris, 1650

Enamelled silver perfume case, c.1620

Polish noblewoman, 1532

Silver gilt perfume case, c.1700

Silver scent bottle, 1685

Silver gilt perfume case, 1645

tive bodice was worn with a skirt over an embroidered blouse which had full peasant sleeves. Shawls or kerchiefs were draped or tied round the head or a cap or bonnet was worn. For festive occasions the costume of both sexes was richly embroidered, jewellery was worn, men had elaborate feather decoration in their hats and women had complex head-dresses, especially the brides who wore tall erections composed of ribbons and flowers.

Pomade, pomatum

A perfumed ointment originally used for the skin but later applied especially for controlling and dressing the coiffure. The name derives from the original unguent which is said to have contained apple.

Pomander

A gold or silver hollow sphere, hinged to open, containing aromatic substances made up into a ball. The pomander depended from a lady's girdle or necklace; it was also carried by men, in the hand or in a garment, to perfume the atmosphere and to

POMPADOUR
Marquise de Pompadour, after
Boucher, 1758. Grey silk dress,
powdered hair

PONCHO
Hand-woven brightly-coloured
wool ponchos. South American
Indians

act as protection against infection. The
word derives from the old French *pome
ambre* and the medieval *pomme d'embre*=
apple of amber: ambergris was the usual
perfume base. Pomanders were mainly in
use during the sixteenth and early seventeenth centuries; after this perfume cases
and tiny bottles were carried or worn, at
the corsage or on the girdle. Such cases and
bottles were of precious metal in different
shapes and contained either solid or liquid
scent; they were decoratively incised or
ornamented with filigree and often jewelled
or enamelled (for perfumery, see *Cosmetics*).

Pompadour

Several features of costume have been
named after the Marquise de Pompadour
(1721–64), mistress of Louis XV of France,
features which have recurred since, especially in the second half of the nineteenth
century. Her elegant, unaffected coiffure,
the hair brushed up off the forehead and
at the back was seen again in the 1890s
and early years of the twentieth century
(see *Hairstyles*) and the Pompadour curving,

slender heel has returned to fashion more
than once. Other Pompadour features,
which were the fashionable mode of the
1750s, include ornamental aprons, a fitted
bodice, a summer coat and fabrics such as
Pompadour silk and Pompadour Duchesse
satin.

Poncho

An ancient form of very simple garment
with the dual purpose of cloak by day and
blanket by night (see *Cloak*). Traditional to
the South American Indian (see *Inca dress*),
the poncho is a square of woollen cloth,
generally hand-woven in brightly-coloured
stripes. Worn by both sexes, it has a hole
in the centre for the head to pass through
and hangs down to waist-level or longer.

Poodle cloth

A woven or knitted material made with a
looped and knotted surface resembling
that of the coat of a French poodle.

PRINCESS LINE
Princess day dress in mauve
taffeta, Swiss, 1879

Poplin

In the seventeenth century a fabric made of a silk warp and a worsted weft and having a corded surface. The name derives from the French *papalin*, in turn stemming from the Italian *papalino* referring to papal, because the fabric was, at that time, made in Avignon, seat of the Papacy. A double poplin was also made which was a heavier material. During the nineteenth century, poplins, then manufactured mainly in Ireland, could also be made of worsted and cotton or worsted and linen (usually termed poplinette) and, in more modern times, nylon is alternatively used. The fabric can be corded or have a watered or brocaded surface.

Porphyry

A beautifully marked stone used in jewellery, made of crystals of white or red felspar embedded in a reddish ground which contains crystals of a number of other minerals. Quarried near the Red Sea from the days of ancient Egypt.

Princess evening gown in cream tulle over pink silk taffeta. Cream lace sleeves and skirt hem ruffles. French, 1905

Postiche

A counterfeit article, one substituting for the real thing. Used in costume to refer to a hair piece or wig also to the false beard of the pharaohs (see *Egypt, ancient*).

Poulaine, pullayne, crakow, piked shoe

Poulaine, derived from the old French *Poulaine* = Poland, referring to shoes in the Polish style. These were the designs of footwear with extended, that is *piked*, toes fashionable in the fourteenth and fifteenth centuries but especially between 1380 and 1410 and 1460 to 1480: a fashionable trend which started early in Poland, then Italy and afterwards spread westwards. The term crakow derives from the name of the Polish city.

Powdering

An eighteenth century term given to a jacket, gown or dress put on over the clothes to protect them while powdering the wig.

Prétintailles

A French term for decorative cut-out pieces of lace and silks appliquéd to women's skirts in the later seventeenth century.

Princess line or cut

The princess gown was introduced in the 1860s at a time when the crinoline form had begun to flatten in front and at the sides, the fullness and interest of the dress being concentrated towards the back. The gown was cut in one piece in front, bodice and skirt together without a waist seam, in order to make the material lie flat over the waist and stomach and so emphasize the contrasting fullness at the rear. As the bustle styles took over from the crinoline, the princess line became sleeker and the flat, close fitting more important.

In the twentieth century the figure-flattening princess silhouette has often recurred. The dress or coat is cut in gores which hug the waist and hips and flare to the hem: there is no waist seam.

Punch, Pulcinella, Polichinelle

This universal character from the comedy stage has his origins in the theatre of ancient Rome. In combined characterization from Maccus and Bucco of Roman farce, he was seen as Pulcinella (Polliciniello) in sixteenth century Naples with a large, hooked nose, a hump, a protruding stomach (the peasecod-belly of the time) and thin legs. His dress was that of the peasant of the period: wide pantaloons, a linen shirt, a ruffled collar and conical hat.

In France in the seventeenth century he appeared as Polichinelle in breeches, stockings and jacket. By 1700 both hump and paunch had become more pronounced. As time passed the character was seen in all the countries of western Europe, as Punch in England, Pulzinella in Germany, Toneelget in Holland and Pulchinella in Spain. The costume stabilized and became traditional: a white ruff, conical or tricorne hat, face mask, wide pantaloons or breeches and stockings, jacket and contemporary shoes; the nose, hump and paunch were markedly exaggerated.

Puritan dress

Originally a term of disparagement, the word Puritan was coined about 1564 to denote those in England who regarded the reformation of the Church under Queen Elizabeth as inadequate and sought further 'purification' of its ritual and doctrine. The ideals of Puritanism were brought to England by English Protestants inspired by Swiss Calvinism and, in turn, these principles and way of thinking were taken to the New World in the early seventeenth century.

Puritans did not adopt a style of dress of their own but wore a sober version of the current mode without trimming or decoration, gaiety or fripperies. Under the Protectorate in England, between 1649 and 1660, their influence on dress was considerable and this made the clothes worn by most people during the years much plainer than, for example, their French

PUNCH ETC.
Polichinelle in red and green costume with gold braid and buttons, France, 1820

Pulcinella in red, yellow and green costume. Italy, 1690–1700. After Maurice Sand

PURITAN DRESS
Less extreme Puritan dress. Black felt hat with plumes. White band and cuffs. Dark cloth cloak with silk lining. Dark red jacket, grey breeches and buff leather boots and gloves, 1653.

Black cloak, cap and shoes. White band and cuffs. Brown wool jacket and breeches, 1650

White linen apron, cap, cuffs and falling band. Black felt hat, grey wool dress, 1650

RAINWEAR

Dark fawn waterproof trench coat, 1933

Green plastic mackintosh with hood, patch pockets and raglan sleeves, 1946

counterparts. The excessively severe dress, actually inspired by the middle class version of the mode of the day, was only adopted by Puritans of extreme views. In this men wore their hair short and uncurled, with a tall black hat set upon it; collars and cuffs were plain white, untrimmed. There was no lace or ribbon in the costume. Fabrics were of wool or linen and colours sombre – black, mauve, brown, grey. Women of similar views wore the same

style of hat over a white cap which concealed the hair, a large white but plain falling band and white apron and cuffs over an unornamented dress and black shoes or boots. Not all those of Puritan persuasion dressed in this sombre manner. The majority affected a compromise between this and the attire of the swash-buckling royalist, wearing fashionable dress with restrained trimming and in quiet colours.

Raffia
Soft fibre from the leaves of the raffia palm used to make hats and bags.

Rainwear
In the whole history of costume man has sought to find materials which would protect him from the rain and would be water-repellant or -proof. In more primitive societies capes and headcoverings were made of strips of animal intestines sewn together, or of shiny, water-repellant leaves tied on to a net base, or grass, reeds and rushes woven into a protective covering (see *Eskimo dress* and *Maori dress*). In more recent times natural fabrics have been treated with oil, gum or varnish to provide water-repellant materials for the outer garments of fishermen, sailors and for industrial use (see *Oiled fabrics*).

It was in the nineteenth century that research led to a means of waterproofing fabrics from which raincoats and capes could be made for normal use in everyday wear. In 1823 *Charles Macintosh*, the Scottish chemist (1776–1843), took out a patent for the waterproof fabric which he had invented. This process involved the cementing of two thicknesses of india rubber by means of naptha and the early

garments made from this were received with certain disfavour because of the unpleasant smell which they emitted. The word *mackintosh*, with slight variation in spelling, came later to mean any cloth made waterproof by a coating of india rubber and, thus, any garment made from such material.

Soon waterproof and weatherproof cloth for raincoats was being more widely produced. *Thomas Burberry*, a country draper, started up his business in the late 1830s. From his own mill his cloth was weatherproofed before and after weaving and was made up into rainwear, at first for men, but later for both sexes. The term 'Burberry' is still synonymous with a particular type of raincoat. The firm provided a wide range of protective wear for all weathers and, at the turn of the century, specialized in covering for travelling in the open motor car (see *Motoring wear*). In the mid-nineteenth century Aquascutum also supplied varied fashions for inclement weather, extending this to women's attire early in the twentieth century.

In the present century rainwear has been made from cotton, silk, wool and nylon rendered rainproof or showerproof by a variety of chemical processes. In general, the showerproof fabric is lightweight and

RAINWEAR

water-repellant but to be rainproof needs to be heavier, more closely woven and be treated with a more efficacious water-repellant compound. Rainwear fashions in the twentieth century follow those of other coats and overcoats. Ladies' rainwear often has an attached hood.

Rayle, rail
A piece of material draped around the neck: a neckerchief (see also *Headrail*). A *night rayle* (rail) was a loose wrap, cape or jacket, worn by women in the bedroom.

Ready-made, ready-to-wear, off-the-peg clothes
In the second half of the eighteenth century ready-made clothes of poor quality were being advertised for working class men and women but it was well into the nineteenth century before the middle classes would purchase garments of that type. An important event in the mechanization of dressmaking and tailoring was the introduction of the sewing machine (see *Sewing Machine*), which gave relief to the drudgery of handstitching by seamstresses. By the 1860s quantities of ready-made clothes were available and, after this, the quality began to improve so that, by 1875, the middle classes were beginning to look to the ready-made dress though, for the remainder of the century, middle class and professional men still had their clothes made to measure (see also *Department Store*).

Rep, repp
A firmly woven material of wool, silk or cotton with a transverse rib texture.

Revers
The turned back part of a coat, jacket or dress, which combines with the collar to lie flat round the neckline.

Rhinestone
A form of rock crystal which is facet cut to resemble a diamond and used in jewellery.

Aquascutum waterproof wool coat, 1910

Burberry weatherproof coat for motoring wear, 1904

Short white raincoat, 1967

Grey gabardine raincoat, 1950

RIBBON
Danish gentleman *c.*1655.
Ribbon rosette and loop
decoration to costume.

Ribbon

A band of fine material, such as silk, satin
or velvet, woven with selvedge edges.
Particularly fashionable as costume decoration in the seventeenth century when
ribbon loops, bows, rosettes and favours
ornamented all parts of the dress and
especially that of the men.

Riding costume

Clothes designed specifically for physically
active sports, especially for women, were
a feature of the later nineteenth century.
Riding, prior to this date, was not a sport
but an essential means of travel and so a
way of life. During the Middle Ages and
until well into the sixteenth century,
women rode astride a horse just as men
did. Adopting their normal dress to this
activity, women wore hose and boots of
the same type as those of the men, with
their everyday style of long gown on top.
In the sixteenth century these hose were
replaced by doublet and trunk hose or
breeches, again with the gown on top.
During the sixteenth century women began
to ride side saddle so their normal dress

was comparatively convenient for this
although the skirt shape was maintained
by underskirts only, the farthingale petticoat being quite unsuited to mounting a
horse. They also adopted an overskirt,
called a safeguard, for further protection
in inclement weather. Men wore their
normal clothes for riding, with boots, a hat
and a cloak; women adopted the boots and
cloak and confined their hair in a cap or
net under a hat or hood.

During the seventeenth and eighteenth
centuries men wore their normal attire for
riding according to fashion, breeches and
jacket, petticoat breeches, then justaucorps, vest and breeches and, finally,
habit à la française. Boots were preferred
to shoes, hats be-plumed and ribboned,
voluminous capes were wrapped round the
body in bad weather. Ladies continued to
wear their normal dress until the 1660s
when, with the advent of the masculine
justaucorps, they began to adopt men's
fashions for the top half of their attire,
retaining feminine styles for the lower.
From about 1665 until the end of the
eighteenth century they wore the man's
coat and waistcoat, wig, cravat and hat
then, below the coat, a long skirt to cover
their breeches and boots. Capes and cloaks
were replaced in the eighteenth century,
by long coats with collar and shoulder
capes, for both sexes.

From about 1790 women's riding dress
returned to a feminine style, not based
upon men's clothes, but following the
styles of the day, high-waisted at first
later, in the 1830s, with lower, slender
waistline, sloping shoulders and leg-of-
mutton sleeves. Throughout the nineteenth
century riding dress followed the vagaries
of feminine fashion though, of course, no
crinoline or bustle framework was feasible
for riding a horse, even side saddle. Under
the gown women wore the same leg-
coverings as men, though these were never
visible; at first breeches, then pantaloons
strapped under the instep and, finally,
trousers. Boots were worn with all of these.

In the second half of the nineteenth
century riding habits were more specifically designed for women to suit the

Riding habit of coat, waistcoat and skirt matching in pink silk with gold decoration. Tricorne hat, gloves, 1715

Green cloth coat and skirt, velvet collar and cuffs. Cream silk waistcoat. Black hat with gold edging, 1780

Lady's habit in green with black braid ornamentation. Black hat, plumes and boots, 1812. Man's habit of dark coat with white pantaloons inside boots. Top hat, 1806

Brown wool habit and bowler hat, c.1880

Dark grey waterproof cloth habit of cape and skirt over white cotton bodice. Black hat with veil, 1835

Dark blue cloth habit, top hat with veil, pantaloons strapped under boots, 1834

Man's riding coat of dark cloth over light corduroy breeches strapped on inner thigh. Leather gaiters, top hat, gloves, 1890. Lady's riding habit of grey tweed over silk waistcoat. Top hat and veil, gloves, 1896

Riding coat with
shoulder capes.
Hat with ribbon
decoration. Fichu.
Light dress, gloves,
1790

Modern jodhpurs,
jacket, pullover,
felt hat

position of riding side saddle and to ensure elegance and propriety so that, whether standing or seated in the saddle, the skirt fell gracefully and demurely covered the ankle. Specific materials were used which were suited to their purpose, for example, riding trousers were made of chamois leather, with the lower part below the knee of material to match the skirt. The trousers were fastened with a fly buttoning in front and buttoned to the corset or stays at the waist. The skirt on top had a draw string fastening and was buttoned at the waist to the jacket. From the late 1860s the riding habit was carefully tailored so that the skirt could be less full but was designed with a recess for the right knee when mounted. This was a pouch shaping so that when the rider was seated side saddle on the horse the garment still hung correctly as a skirt. With the 1880s the riding costume was tailored to fit even more accurately, fewer petticoats were worn, detachable apron fronts were added and the skirt had a train. The bodice to accompany this skirt was a fitting, waist-length jacket with long sleeves and a short peplum or 'tails' at the back. Ladies wore top hats or bowlers with veils draped elegantly round them. Safety skirts were introduced in the late 1870s. These had press stud or hook and eye fastenings at the back which could be closed when walking but unfastened when mounted on the horse, so avoiding the skirt being caught up if one was unseated.

Until the second half of the nineteenth century men had continued to ride in a version of their normal attire. With the introduction of the sack coat and lounge jacket these were adopted for riding, cut with a back vent or vents, like the modern hacking jacket. By the 1890s riding breeches had largely replaced trousers. These were cut full to just above the knee then were fitting and strapped with suède or leather on the inside of the thigh. Leather or cloth leggings covered the lower leg. By the turn of the century the wing-shape cut to the riding breeches had developed and a special riding jacket with a flared skirt and vent accompanied them.

At the beginning of the twentieth cen-

tury a few women began to ride astride, wearing a divided skirt or an apron front over breeches. These apron fronts hung down from the knee in front when the wearer was mounted but were open behind and could be removed on dismounting. It was the 1920s before women in general finally adopted men's riding breeches and rode astride. Later, riding trousers, *jodhpurs*, were worn by both sexes. These are cut full at the hips and tight-fitting from knee to ankle, ending in a cuff and a strap under the instep. Jodhpurs were an Indian garment named after a state in Rajputana.

Ring

Finger rings and, less commonly, those made for the thumb and the toes, have been an important item of jewellery in all civilizations. Made of precious metals, rings have been decorated with engraving and enamelling and set with jewels and all kinds of polished stones. Through the ages, the wearing of certain rings has denoted rank or a specific occasion, condition or significance as, for example, mourning rings, engagement, betrothal or love rings, wedding rings, signet rings or magic rings. The origin of most of these is ancient.

Robin, robing

An obsolete term referring to a decorative trimming in the form of a band round the edges of a garment.

Roll

A term describing a rounded, usually padded, part of a garment or a padding placed under or inside an item of clothing (see *Bourrelet* and *Bum-barrel*). A roll collar is a rounded design without notch or rever; a roll hem is one with a rolled edge fastened by tiny slip stitches. It is used for edging sheer fabrics such as gauze, silk or chiffon.

Rome (ancient)

The Roman Republic evolved from tribal kingdoms which were first set up in Italy in the eighth century BC. After 500 BC the republic was established and expanded, absorbing the adjacent peoples and country-

Sumerian. Gold with blue stones, c.2500 BC

Phoenician. Gold with semi-precious stone, seventh century BC

Minoan. Gold and lapis lazuli, seventeenth century BC

Greek. Gold, c.300 BC

Etruscan. Gold, fifth century BC

Roman. Silver, fifth century AD.

Roman. Gold and onyx, second century AD.

Roman Gold and beryl

Ostrogothic, Italy. Gold, sixth century

Anglo-Saxon. Gold rings, Britain, eighth to eleventh century

Medieval. Gold with blue stone, c.1200

Norman. Gilt bronze with blue stone.

Silver gilt, c.1130

Medieval. Gold and sapphire.

Gold with sapphire and amethysts, thirteenth century

Medieval. Magical ring

Medieval. Silver betrothal ring with clasped hands

Medieval. Gold and sapphire, c.1300

Medieval. Signet rings

Medieval. Silver inscribed ring.

Gold and amethyst, c.1380

Medieval, c.1450. Gold with diamonds and rubies.

Gold and amethyst. c.1450

c.1450 Silver gilt

Gold enamelled and gold and sapphire, c.1480

Inscribed gold, c.1480

Gold and pearls Medieval, c.1480.

Tudor, c.1530. Gold.

Tudor. Gold with turquoise and garnets.

Gold, enamelled, with diamond Tudor, c.1530.

Gold enamelled, and emerald, c.1550

Gold and sapphire, c.1550

Gold, enamelled, and diamond, c.1550

Inscribed silver, c.1550

Elizabethan, c.1580. Silver love ring

Gold and emerald Seventeenth century, c.1620.

Gold and diamond, c.1620

Gold enamelled with emerald, c.1620

Seventeenth century, c.1650. Gold, turquoise and garnets.

Gold and garnet, c.1650

Gold with crystal, c.1650

Gold with crystal, c.1650

Gold enamelled Seventeenth century, c.1680.

Seventeenth century, c.1695. Gold with ruby and diamonds.

Gold and garnet, c.1695

Gold with jacinth, c.1695

Eighteenth century, c.1725. Gold with diamonds.

Gold with diamonds, c.1725

Gold with diamonds, c.1725

Mourning ring with inscription inside

Eighteenth century, c.1750. Gold with rubies and diamonds.

Filigree gold with enamelled setting. Victorian

Victorian. Gold with opal and diamonds.

Gold with emerald and diamonds. Victorian

side. Area by area the country of Italy became a vassal state to the City of Rome. The Etruscans were absorbed, the Sicilians, then Carthage and North Africa and, in 146 BC, Greece also became a part of the Roman Republic. This was only the beginning. In 30 BC Egypt was absorbed and soon western Europe extending to most of Britain. For 400 years after this, the Romans enslaved, organized and civilized the peoples of the compass of their known world, extending all round the Mediterranean from Spain to the Black Sea and from Britain to Egypt.

The republic was severely shaken in 44 BC by the murder of Julius Caesar. The years of uncertainty and unrest were resolved when the republic developed into an empire with Augustus its first emperor in 27 BC. From this time, until 476 AD when the western empire collapsed, the Roman Empire was ruler and pace-setter to the known western world.

The story of costume under the direction of Rome is almost identical to the history of all the visual arts, architecture and crafts. The Romans inherited their designs from the Greeks. They continued in the same mode but the pattern slowly altered, becoming a mutation. The basis of design remained the same. What altered was the treatment and adaptation of the forms. In costume, as in art, the Roman version is more ornate, richly adorned, more varied and, under later Imperial Rome, most elaborate.

In dress this process was characterized by a more extensive use of ornament and jewellery, rich colours, the wearing of a greater number of garments, one on top of the others, the frequent bathing and changing of clothes during the course of the day and the introduction of richer fabrics. These materials were introduced as a result of the extension of the boundaries of empire and consequent expansion of trading relations. Cottons from India and silks from the east were freely available to the wealthy. They appeared in a wide range of colours and were then enriched further by the beautiful embroidery, ornamental braid and fringing. Heliogabalus

(218–222 AD) was the first Roman emperor to wear silk. Much later, looms were set up to weave silk but the raw material had still to be imported from the east (see *Silk*). Roman ladies developed the art of embroidery to a high degree. They used coloured wools intermixed with gold thread.

In *men's dress* the most characteristic and important of the Roman clothing was the *toga*. In Republican Rome, especially in the earlier years, it was the chief garment, worn directly on top of the underwear. This consisted, according to rank, of *feminalia* (femoralia), which was a kind of pants or short breeches and, for lower classes, the *subligaculum*, a piece of cloth wound round the waist and passed between the legs to form a loincloth. The toga soon became the mark of the Roman citizen, who alone was permitted to wear it. A slave may not don a toga though a freed man was allowed to do so.

The toga began by having a similar function to the Greek himation in that it was a large cloak wrapped round the body in a variety of ways according to the personality and inclination of the wearer and that it was draped, having no fastenings or pins. It differed only in that, instead of being rectangular in shape, it was a segment of a circle. It was partly this difference in shape which led to the complex and prescribed methods of draping. It was also a much larger piece of material, being about 18 feet in length along the chord of the segment and about five and a half feet at its greatest width. Usually made of wool, it was thus a heavy, unwieldy garment to handle and, in draping, might require the assistance of another person. The most usual method of draping in general use from about the second century BC onwards was to place some five feet of the straight edge of the fabric against the centre vertical line of the front of the body, with the extreme end at the feet and the curved edge to the left, outer side. The rest of the material, some 13 feet, was thrown across the left shoulder, passed loosely round the back, under the right arm and once again partly over the left shoulder but partly also over

Palla over stola

Dalmatica over
stola, veil

Second century AD

Roman empress.
Palla over stola

Emperor in toga,
sandals

Toga over tunica
with latus clavus,
calcei

Long, pleated tunic
with palla draped
on top. Veil

Double-girded
tunic, boots, cloak

Palla over pleated
tunic

Paenula over short
tunica, sandals

Purple paluda-
mentum with gold,
embroidered
border over tunica
talaris

the left arm, where the second end hung loose. The portion of cloth on the chest from the first layer was then pulled out a little to form folds which draped over the second layer. When desired, the looser material at the back could be pulled up to give covering to the head. Draped in this and similar ways, the toga is depicted in innumerable figure sculptures.

The toga acted as a denoter of rank within the Roman citizenry. White was worn by tribunes – the *toga pura* or *virilis*; purple, the symbol of power, was reserved for the emperor, who may also have had his toga decorated in gold. Those worn by magistrates and certain other ranks (*toga praetexta*) were characterized by a band of purple woven into the cloth along the chord of the material. The *toga gabiana* had one fold thrown round the head and the toga *trabea* was a shorter robe with purple band ornamentation. Under the Empire the wearing of a toga was reserved more and more for ceremonial use by important personages. The garment was of fine wool and, later, silk and was enriched with panels, bands of colour and gold embroidery. As its general use declined, the materials became richer and the methods of draping more complex.

By the second century AD ordinary citizens had abandoned the toga and turned to other, easier-to-handle types of cloak. In Rome, out-of-doors, it was the wearing of a cloak or mantle which distinguished a citizen from other people. There was a variety of designs to choose from and all these draped, outer garments came under the general heading of *amictus*. The *abolla*, *paludamentum* and *sagum* were mainly for military use. The abolla was a thick garment fastened at the neck and was full enough to be draped on top of a toga. The paludamentum was an officer's cloak, full and long and often richly decorated. The sagum was originally a Celtic cloak (see also *Saie*), worn by soldiers. Civilian cloaks were mostly similar to the Greek chlamys (see *Greece, ancient*). There was the *lacerna* which was long, flowing and very full. Fastened at the throat and hooded, it could be draped on top of the toga. It was

Palla used as
headcovering

derived from a Gaulish style and was used for riding. The *birrus* was also hooded but of rougher cloth and could be worn by all classes under the later empire. It continued in use during the Middle Ages as the byrrus. The *alicula* was short, more a cape, and was often a children's garment. The *paenula* was the bad weather covering. Made of heavy wool or leather, it had a hood and a hole for the head to pass through like a poncho. Romans living in Greek areas adopted the rectangular, draped cloak based on the himation (see *Greece, ancient*) and, unlike the other cloaks, worn without any fastening; it could also be pulled up on to the head. In the later years of empire this garment, the *pallium*, was folded lengthwise so that it resembled a long scarf; it was then draped round the shoulders, the ends hanging in front and was worn on top of another cloak. In this manner its evolution can be traced through the Byzantine and later civilizations to become, eventually, a vestment of the Christian Church.

Indoors the basic masculine garment was the *tunica*, made of wool or linen and, like the Greek prototype, the chiton (see *Greece, ancient*), a draped design. It was girded, often double-girded at waist and hip, the material bloused between belts and it reached to the knees. It consisted of two rectangular pieces of fabric sewn at the sides and either pinned or sewn on the shoulders. Some designs were sleeveless, others had short sleeves which were cut in one with the garment, not inset. Again, colours indicated the rank and position of the wearer. Upper classes wore white, others natural or brown.

Under the empire, especially in later years, it was customary to wear more than one tunica. Three might be worn, the one nearest to the body, the *subucula*, acted as a shirt. Important citizens, especially on ceremonial occasions, began, in the third century AD, to wear ankle-length tunicas on top of the shorter ones. These were termed *tunica talaris* after the Latin *talus* = of the ankles. A wide-sleeved, loose tunica appeared, introduced about 190 AD from Dalmatia, called a *dalmatica*. The tunicas of persons of rank and position were distinguished by bands of purple running vertically down the tunic. Such bands (*clavi*) could be broad, the *latus clavus* of the senator, or narrow, generally in pairs, the *angustus clavus*, of lesser ranks. In retirement, a senator exchanged his *latus clavus* for *angusti clavi* to denote his abandonment of public life.

Feminine Roman costume was closely modelled on the Greek, the Roman *stola* being like the Greek chiton (see *Greece, ancient*) and the equivalent of the masculine *tunica*. In the Imperial period the stola was of wool, cotton or silk; it had more material in the width than the Greek prototype. Ladies of rank wore it very long, forming a train at the back. Circling under the breasts and, sometimes, the hips as well, were beautiful, jewelled and embroidered girdles (the *cingulum*). The garment was usually richly embroidered and sometimes fringed. Bands of decorative gold embroidery, termed *segmentum*, ornamented the stola. Fine pleating was also often employed, especially for the train. Generally the stola was sleeved, either with sewn sleeves or pinned at intervals in the Greek manner. Fashionable colours included yellow, greyish-blue, white, red and green.

Under the stola women wore one or more tunics. These were similar but sleeveless and were often of wool. Under these the *supparum* was a linen garment worn on top of the *subucula*. Next to the skin were briefs and a linen or wool breast-band called the *mamillare*. An additional or alternative support to the breasts could be provided by the *strophium* which was a long, narrow piece of material wound round the torso on top of the supparum. Sometimes a stomach-band or girdle was also worn to control the figure.

The feminine equivalent of the masculine toga or pallium was the *palla*, which was the outer garment. A large, rectangular piece of material like the Greek prototype, this was brightly-coloured and embroidered on fine wool. It could be draped or, commonly, folded lengthwise and pinned on each shoulder by a fibula. The toilette of an elegant woman was completed by a shoulder cape or scarf, a fan and a handkerchief.

Roman footwear was based upon Greek designs but was more varied, several styles of shoe and boot being available. Customs too differed; the Greeks generally went barefoot in the house, Romans rarely did so, regarding the wearing of footwear a mark of class distinction (see *Boot, Sandal, Shoe*).

Both sexes gave great care and attention to their hair and complexion and spent a great deal of time on their toilette, bathing, perfuming their hair, bodies and attire as well as applying cosmetics to the face (see *Beard, Cosmetics, Hairstyles* and *Wig*). The feminine coiffure was such a feature of the toilette that a lady needed little further headcovering. In any case, like the Greeks, Roman ladies did not often go out. They enclosed part of their hair in gold or silver nets with pearls or bound it in a scarf or band. Sometimes they wore veils or draped the folds of the palla over the head. Men went bareheaded for most of the time. Hoods were worn, attached to the cloak or separate. There was a hat like the Greek petasos and a close-fitting cap, the *galerus* or *galeritus*, as well as the *pileus* (from the Greek pilos).

Under the republic, the wearing of *jewellery* was frowned upon and restricted. There are consequently not many examples surviving and these are based upon Etruscan and Greek designs. From the time of Augustus onwards the Roman love of jewellery was permitted to have full play. Designs were still derivative, based on Hellenic Greece and the quality of workmanship was less fine. As the empire was extended a greater elaboration and richness became apparent; pieces were heavier and there was an abundant use of gold and precious and semi-precious stones: sapphires, emeralds, aquamarines, opals and even diamonds, though the last were not cut. A great quantity of jewellery was worn by both sexes, particularly finger rings (more than one on a finger), fibulae, and bracelets. Women also adorned themselves freely with necklaces and pendants, anklets, fillets on their hair and earrings. Late

Black satin vlieger with padded rolls at shoulders, Dutch, 1590

Dark grey cloth vlieger with puff sleeves, Flemish, 1550–5

Dark green velvet ropa with jewelled, gold, embroidered edging and padded rolls at shoulder, English, c.1560

Imperial jewellery presaged the richness and quantity of Byzantine ornament (see *Bracelet, Byzantine dress, Earring, Fibula, Fillet, Necklace, Pendant, Ring*).

Ropa, marlotte, vlieger

The overgown or surcote worn by women in the sixteenth and early seventeenth centuries and thought to be of oriental origin. The garment was named and interpreted differently from one country to another (see also *Chamarre*). The Spanish version, the *ropa*, was the European prototype; this had a high collar under or outside the small ruff and padded or puffed short sleeves which sometimes continued as a fitting sleeve to the wrists. The garment could be worn unfastened or it was clasped at the neck then fell, unwaisted, to the ground. As an outer item of clothing, it was made of velvet, silk or cloth and was often richly embroidered and banded. The

English ropa was similar and the French *marlotte* could be half-length. The Dutch *vlieger* was usually worn unfastened and could have shoulder rolls or puff sleeves.

Rouleau (x)

French word for a rolled, coiled or twisted material. In costume, refers to a wide, full piping used for the trimming of garments, particularly the edges of hats and bonnets and for skirts.

Ruby

A precious stone which is a variety of corundum and is found in shades from deep crimson-purple to a pale rose colour. Found mainly in Asia.

Ruche, rouche, ruching

From the French word for bee-hive. A pleated or goffered, decorative trimming sewn to ladies' garments, made of self-material or in lace, gauze or ribbon. In this usage the name alludes to the construction bands of a straw hive.

Ruff

For both sexes, the square or boat-shaped neckline of the 1530s and 1540s developed, in Spain, in the 1550s into a high neckline closely encircling the throat. This design, applied equally to the man's doublet or jerkin and to the feminine gown, generally opened down the centre front from chin to waist and was fastened by buttons or clasps. Under this high-necked garment the shirt or chemise followed the same line and was decorated at throat and wrists by neat ruffles; at the neck the ruffle was open in front and divided by the chin, at the wrists the ruffles were circular bands extending all round. These ruffles were in the form of a strip of material gathered into a straight edge to make a frill and were attached to shirt or chemise.

This Spanish style was quickly adopted all over Europe and, as time passed, the ruffles became full-scale *ruffs*, which were termed bands (see *Band*). They were then separate items of wear, not attached to the shirt or chemise, and were made from linen, lawn or Holland cambric. The long strip of fabric was pleated and set into a neckband (also wristbands) and usually completely encircled the neck, being tied in front with tiny, tasselled cords called *band strings*.

After 1565, with the introduction of starch, ruffs became larger. They required frequent and expert laundering. They were washed, starched, then set while damp into form and *goffered* (gauffered) by inserting heated metal *setting* or *poking sticks* into the individual folds; these folds and ribs were known as *purls* or *sets*. When dry the ruff was placed in a low, wide *band box*. The fashionable ruff gradually increased in size until 1580–5, when it might extend nine inches on either side of the neck and consist of 18 yards of material. It would be starched, often in colour, and require a support underneath at the rear. The supporting structures, known as *underproppers*, *supportasse* or *rebato* (the name varying

according to design and region), could be wire frames fitting the back of the neck with the radiating wires being hidden in the ruff folds or were of pasteboard covered in white, pleated cotton. The edge of the ruff was often wired. Lace edging, or even a ruff entirely of lace, was fashionable in some countries, particularly England, France and Italy, while in Holland, northern Germany and Poland ruffs tended to be large but plain. Wrist ruffles were in matching sets with the ruff and this was termed a *suit of ruffs*. These sets might be embroidered in black, gold or silver thread and tiny jewels were sewn into the pattern; this was especially so in Spain, where ruffs were not over-large but were very elegant.

RUCHE
Ruched polonaise skirt, Swedish, 1778

Ruched cap and gown, German, 1780

Ruched dress over hoop skirt, English, 1773

Spanish and
Portuguese small
ruffs, 1560–70

Lace-edged ruff,
Flemish, 1610

Circular ruff,
Italian, 1581

Man in cartwheel
ruff and Queen
Elizabeth in open,
lace-edged ruff,
English, 1580–90

Ruff hanging on
wall peg

Goffering irons

Spanish
embroidered ruff,
1584

Plain cartwheel
ruff, Dutch, 1615

Falling ruff,
Hungarian, 1618

Queen Elizabeth in
lace-edged ruff,
c.1585

Wire framework
supportasse under
cartwheel ruff,
French, 1580

Cartwheel ruff,
French, 1581

Cartwheel ruff,
Danzig, c.1600

Plain ruff, Polish,
c.1610

Under propper of
pasteboard covered
in pleated white
cotton, Italian,
1620

Lace-edged ruff,
English, 1562

RUMANIAN DRESS
Man from Oltenia in white wool
jacket and trousers decorated
in black braid embroidery.
Black sheepskin clăbătul.

Some specific designs of ruff were named. The very large ones were *cartwheel ruffs*. Some were composed of two layers of folded material one above the other; these were *double ruffs*. Some styles were made with folds in unsymmetrical form, not in the traditional figure of eight pattern; because of their resemblance to the curling leaves of cabbage or lettuce, these were known as *cabbage* or *lettuce ruffs*.

In the late sixteenth and early seventeenth centuries women often wore the *open ruff*. This extended round the sides of a décolleté neckline, open in front and supported at the rear so that the ruff framed the head. Such open ruffs were often lace-edged and a small, circular ruff would encircle the throat inside the main design. In the seventeenth century the unstarched ruff became fashionable. Without the stiffening the folds drooped gently over the shoulders; this was the *falling ruff*.

Rumanian dress

Rumanian traditional costume has evolved over the centuries from that of many races, in the beginning from the Roman and Byzantine Empires, then influenced by the neighbouring Balkan countries of Greece, Bulgaria and Serbia, as well as Hungary and, later, from the Turkish Ottoman Empire. Rumanian dress varies from region to region, in particular between mountain and plain, but it is mainly the detail that differs rather than the fundamental style of dress. Traditional materials come from flax, hemp, wool and fur. Most striking is the colour and gaiety of the garments, furnished by rich, bright embroideries covering large areas of the costume and the use of striking colour combinations. Young people wear costumes with richer decoration and brighter colours than the old and spangles, coloured beads and gold and silver threads are widely used for ornamentation.

In the mountain areas, the Carpathians and the Transylvanian Alps, warmer clothes and materials are worn. Men have a loose, long shirt, bound at the waist with a deep, decorative cummerbund worn over the trousers. The feet are covered by shapeless socks under shoes of the simple carbatine type (see *Shoes*), which are laced on top and the laces continue up the leg binding over the socks and over or under the trousers. On top of the shirt is an open, sleeveless bolero or jacket, the *cojoc*, which is decoratively embroidered and, often, fur-lined. In cold weather a coat can be worn on top, which is long or hip-length. The longer version is, like the Hungarian *szür*, very decoratively embroidered and often slung round the shoulders, the sleeves hanging loose. A warmer coat or cloak of fur or sheepskin, the *suba*, is like the Hungarian version, also the Russian shuba. Various caps or hats are worn, the sheepskin cap, the *căciulă*, which is grey, black or white, the *clăbătul*, which has a point like a Phrygian cap, or a black felt hat with brim, a *pāsla* and, in very bad weather, a hood on top (*glugā*).

In the plains areas along the Danube or west in Oltenia, shirts are worn longer and trousers wider. Trousers, jackets and coats are often of white wool or felt and attractively decorated with black braid embroidery. Knickerbockers (*ţundra*) sometimes replace trousers.

Women's dress consists of a long shirt blouse like the men's, richly embroidered on shoulders and sleeves, especially in red, black and blue. On top of this is a one-piece wrap-round wool skirt, the *fota*, which is decoratively patterned, often all over. This is held in place at the waist by a deep cummerbund sometimes with a belt also. On top of the blouse is worn an ornamented *cojoc* which has sleeves and can be short or knee-length; it is often fur-lined. In some areas a pleated skirt, the *vālnic*, is worn instead of the fota and, on top of this, an ornamented apron; sometimes two aprons are tied on, one at the back, one in front. Another alternative is provided by the dress made of thick material and designed in two parts; the upper part, the *ciupag*, has wide raglan sleeves and is richly embroidered, the lower, the *poale*, a skirt, is decorated by vertical, embroidered bands. A heavily embroidered, sleeveless bolero is worn on top of the dress.

Woman from Banat with embroidered conciul decorated by gold coins. Blouse and skirt, white embroidered in red, blue, yellow and black. Two aprons, one back, one front

Woman from Banat in striped head kerchief and coloured and fringed aprons. Baby in basket strapped across chest

Woman in white skirt embroidered in black. Black pleated skirt with coloured border over red underskirt. White transparent, embroidered marama. Embroidered cummerbund.

Man from Moldavia in white shirt and trousers. Richly embroidered cojoc, colour on black. Similar deep belt. Felt hat

Man from Oltenia in black sheepskin căciulă, white shirt and white coat embroidered with black braid. White ţundra to match.

Man from Moldavia in jacket embroidered in colours, lined and edged with grey astrakhan fur over cojoc and shirt. White trousers, black felt hat, cummerbund.

The feet are shod with the same primitive type of lace-up shoes as those of the men, on top of stockings or socks. Headcoverings vary greatly and are often beautifully decorated. Most usual is the long, rectangular gauze veil, the *marama*, which can be worn in many different ways, its draperies reaching nearly to the ground. There is also a variety of coloured kerchiefs and fitting caps which enclose the whole head (*conciul*) and are attractively woven and decorated in silk with gold and silver thread. Necklaces of gold coin design are often worn. In Banat and Oltenia in western Rumania it was a tradition for women to carry their babies in a wicker basket on their backs, strapped across the chest.

Russet

A coarse homespun woollen cloth used for peasant dress in past centuries. It was of a dull hue, generally reddish-brown, grey or yellowish-brown.

Russian dress

There has been, over the centuries, a tremendous variation in the costume worn in the vast area which today comprises the USSR. This is due, even within the boundaries of Europe, to the extremes of climate and terrain, to different ethnic groupings and to a variation in historical development. In fashionable dress worn in the major cities of European Russia the influences previous to the eighteenth century were strongly Asiatic. Under Genghis Khan the Mongolian Empire had been extended in the thirteenth century as far west as the Danube delta in the south and Cracow further north. In the following century the Turks advanced to establish the Ottoman Empire over this area, taking Constantinople in 1453. The traditional dress for both sexes was a caftan style of coat. Fur-lined in winter, this was buttoned up to the neck in front and had long sleeves in varying styles. For men the coat was calf- or ankle-length and under it was worn a shirt, a shorter under-coat, trousers and, usually, boots pulled over these. Fur caps or fur-trimmed hats were most usual. Under the caftan women wore a long-sleeved blouse, bodice and long skirt or a gown. They had fur caps or decorative caps with veils.

Russia was slower to adopt French fashions than other European countries. In the first half of the eighteenth century beautiful fabrics were worn by the nobility, silks of all kinds, finely embroidered and jewelled, but the styles of garments were still influenced more by the East than by Paris. The fabrics themselves were imported from China, Persia and Turkey. From about 1730, fine silks were made in Russia and the Empress Elizabeth, who reigned 1741–62, began to import French clothes for her own wardrobe and for her Court. From mid-century the Russian nobility more and more adopted the French culture, its language, customs and dress. The Empress Catherine II tried more than once to introduce a simpler, national form of dress but, unlike King Gustav (see *Scandinavian dress*, Sweden), she was unsuccessful. The Russian aristocracy, having at last been introduced to the elegance of Western attire, was not going to abandon it so quickly.

In regional and peasant dress decoration was very beautiful, both in embroidery and printed designs. Women's dress, in particular, was ornamented with embroidery, especially so for festive costumes, and decorative jewellery was extensively worn. Characteristic items were chain and pearl collars, several rows of chain necklaces, earrings and hair ornaments. There was a great variety of types of head-dresses in different regions and many of these were intricate and beautiful designs made of rich materials such as gold or silver fabrics, velvet and silk with embroidery using pearls and metal thread. Most of the head-dresses were in fitted cap or bonnet form then elaborated by different shapes added to this basis. Out-of-doors veils were worn on top of the head-dress and these too were often embroidered and decorated with a fringe.

A characteristic garment was the *sarafan*, a long, full skirt attached to a fitted, sleeveless bodice, or it could be in the form of a separate skirt and jacket/bodice. It was

Russian nobleman, sixteenth century. Fur hat and fur-trimmed caftan, braid fastenings. Leather boots

Russian noblewoman, sixteenth century. Velvet coat with fur and braid trimming. Gold embroidered cap under white veil

Floral-patterned caftan, leather boots. Russian nobleman, 1560–1600

Russian woman in embroidered, stiffened headdress, embroidered jacket over white blouse and scarf. Striped apron over dark wool skirt. Leather boots

Woman from Lithuania. Check wool jacket with basque, kerchief to match. White apron, dark wool skirt, white blouse

Woman from Latvia. Red wool jacket over white blouse. Grey skirt with coloured borders. White stockings, shoes. Striped scarf, felt hat

Russian man in skin jacket (sarafan) with appliqué decoration and fur edging worn over rubashka. Striped trousers. Leather boots, felt hat worn on top of a full, long-sleeved blouse. Alternatively, a bodice with full, decorative sleeves could be worn with the skirt and blouse.

Men's dress was less elaborate and ornamented except on garments reserved for festive occasions. Characteristic was the full shirt (*rubashka*) made of heavy linen, usually white or light in colour, and decorated with woven or embroidered bands of colour at collar, cuffs and hem. The hip-length shirt was generally worn outside the full linen or cloth trousers. These trousers were often tucked into leather or felt boots or could be cross-banded from knee to ankle, with shoes below. A fur-lined, sleeveless jacket (*sarafan*) or a larger cloak was worn on top for warmth; the fur or sheep's fleece was turned inside and the outside was decorated with wool or leather appliqué and embroidery. A heavy sheepskin coat, the *shuba*, was worn in winter; this was a similar garment to the Rumanian suba (see *Overcoat* and *Rumanian dress*). Fur caps or felt hats were general wear.

In the Baltic States of Lithuania, Latvia and Estonia the ethnic origins and languages are different. Scandinavian, German and Polish influences are strong though the area is part of the USSR. The women's kerchief and white linen head-dresses show affinities with Scandinavian dress as do the metal breast buckles and tall hats. The striped and checked aprons and skirts are typically Baltic (see also *Caucasian dress* and *Ukrainian dress*).

Sackcloth
A coarse textile fabric of linen or cotton used for sacking also for some sports wear; in ancient times a material signifying mourning or penitence. The biblical term 'sackcloth and ashes' referred to being clothed in sackcloth and having ashes sprinkled on the head as a sign of extreme penitence and humility.

Saie, saye, sayon
1) *Saie* was a Celtic cloak made of a rough and hairy animal skin, pinned on the right shoulder and draped round the body. It was adapted under the Roman Empire as the sagum (see *Rome, ancient*).
2) In the Middle Ages the *saye* or *sayon* was a sleeveless jacket worn by ordinary people.

Sampot
A Cambodian garment for both sexes consisting of a piece of material wound round the waist and drawn up between the legs to form full trousers or pantaloons.

Sanbenito
A penitential garment made of yellow sackcloth worn by those condemned under the Spanish Inquisition (fifteenth and sixteenth centuries). The garment was so named because, in shape, it resembled the *scapular*, a cloak covering the shoulders prescribed by the Rule of Benedict to be worn by the monks when engaged in manual labour. The *sanbenito* was decorated by a St Andrew's cross at front and back and was worn by a confessed and penitent heretic. A similar garment, in black, was adopted for those condemned by auto-da-fé.

Sandal
Footwear in the form of a sole held to the foot by straps, ties or a knob grip for the toes. Because of their coolness and delicacy, sandals are traditional wear in countries

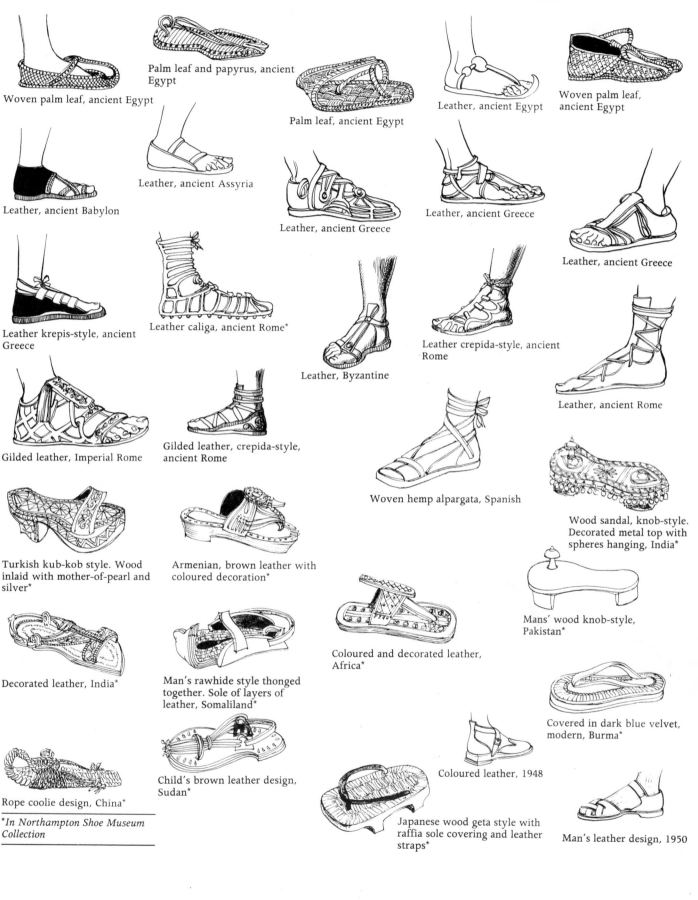

Woven palm leaf, ancient Egypt

Palm leaf and papyrus, ancient Egypt

Palm leaf, ancient Egypt

Leather, ancient Egypt

Woven palm leaf, ancient Egypt

Leather, ancient Babylon

Leather, ancient Assyria

Leather, ancient Greece

Leather, ancient Greece

Leather, ancient Greece

Leather krepis-style, ancient Greece

Leather caliga, ancient Rome*

Leather, Byzantine

Leather crepida-style, ancient Rome

Leather, ancient Rome

Gilded leather, Imperial Rome

Gilded leather, crepida-style, ancient Rome

Woven hemp alpargata, Spanish

Wood sandal, knob-style. Decorated metal top with spheres hanging, India*

Turkish kub-kob style. Wood inlaid with mother-of-pearl and silver*

Armenian, brown leather with coloured decoration*

Coloured and decorated leather, Africa*

Mans' wood knob-style, Pakistan*

Decorated leather, India*

Man's rawhide style thonged together. Sole of layers of leather, Somaliland*

Covered in dark blue velvet, modern, Burma*

Rope coolie design, China*

Child's brown leather design, Sudan*

Coloured leather, 1948

*In Northampton Shoe Museum Collection

Japanese wood geta style with raffia sole covering and leather straps*

Man's leather design, 1950

with a warm climate and, in Britain, have become fashionable only in the twentieth century. Sandals have been worn in Europe over the centuries in countries bordering the Mediterranean. In the classical world of Greece, Rome and Byzantium, the sandal was general footwear for both sexes. The sole was shaped to the foot and varied designs of leather straps or cords held it in place; the leather was dyed and decorated, even gilded. Typical was the Greek *krepis*, which became the Roman *crepida*; this had a thick sole and leather sides, decorated, then laced across the instep. The Roman *caliga* was a short, military, sandal-boot, very strong, the sole studded with nails, but with a latticed upper laced up the front to the calf with leather laces. The traditional Spanish rope sandal made from hemp or esparto grass, the *alpargata*, derives from the time of the Moorish occupation, when the Christians adopted the Arabic word for 'a pair' to become *el-par-korkat* and then *alpargate*. Still in use in the Pyrenees and, with modern dress, on the beach, the alpargata is a sandal version of the espadrille, the rope-soled canvas shoe, both of which are worn in Spain, France and Italy (see *Shoes, espadrille*).

The sandal has always been worn extensively in Turkey, the Middle East and Africa. Designs vary greatly but many are made from leather and are brightly coloured and elaborately and imaginatively decorated. Sandals in ancient Egypt were made from leather, papyrus and plaited or woven palm leaves and fibres. The toes were often turned up and the sandals worn by the nobility were embroidered and jewelled. The Assyrians and Babylonians also wore sandals but these were less open than the Egyptian ones and had a back piece covering the heel.

In the Orient, especially India, the knob form of sandal had been worn for centuries. This has a thick wood sole and is held to the foot by a decorative knob which is set between the big toe and the other toes, being gripped by them there. Far Eastern designs are also varied from the wooden-soled Japanese geta or clog style to the Chinese coolies' grass- or rope-woven

SANS-CULOTTE
Sans-culotte, 1792, in carmagnole and trousers

SARONG
Batik-patterned sarong, Indonesia

SASH
White silk hip sash over brocade justaucorps with gold frogging, French, c.1685

White silk sash round the body over grey velvet doublet, Swiss, 1608 design, which resembles the ancient Egyptian version.

Sans-culotte
Name given to the revolutionaries in France under the Convention by the aristocrats because they wore trousers, not the fashionable knee breeches. The term means literally 'without breeches' (see also *Carmagnole*).

Sapphire
A precious stone of a beautiful, transparent blue; the word is related to the Greek δίασπρος, lapis lazuli.

Sarong
A characteristic garment worn in Malaysia and Indonesia consisting of a rectangular piece of coloured, patterned cotton or silk, some four to five yards long and one yard wide, which is draped round the body to form a dress or skirt. Javanese women drape themselves from above the breasts to the ground. However, often, the sarong is a skirt worn by either sex. The ends can be sewn together and the top edge is held by a sash, making a draped skirt which can vary in length from knee to ankle.

Sash
A long, wide piece of soft material, in the form of a band or scarf, bound round the waist, hips or slung across the torso and the ends generally tied (see also *Cummerbund* and *Japanese dress*, obi). Sashes tied on the hip and crossing the body from the shoulder were fashionable wear for men in the later sixteenth and early seventeenth centuries. Men wore a broad waist sash in the first half of the seventeenth century and lower, to encircle the hips, on top of the justaucorps in the second half of the century. Sashes were intermittently fashionable on women's dresses, marking the waist or hips, from the nineteenth century onwards.

Sateen
A fabric resembling satin in its glossy face or silk or rayon but the major part of it of cotton or wool. A strong durable material used widely for linings.

Orange satin hip sash over grey-mauve satin dress covered by an overdress of pearled orange tulle. Evening gown, c.1925, French

Olive green taffeta dress with stripes of black and green. Matching sash. Day dress, 1865, Dutch

Black satin sash over black net overdress decorated with gold and black sequins, jet and rhinestones. Evening gown, 1911, French

Emerald green wool coat with sash tie to match, English, 1946

Golden silk sash wound round a pale blue silk doublet, Dutch, 1637

Satin

A silk or rayon fabric, worn for hundreds of years, of close texture with a glossy face and dull back. The smooth, glossy surface is produced by finishing the fabric between heated rollers. Many varieties and qualities of satin have been made over the centuries; these include:

Antique – a white satin woven to resemble an old material which has turned parchment-colour with the passing of time.

Crêpe-back – a satin finished with a crêpe back and satin-finished face so that the material can be used on either side.

Damask – a satin patterned in a floral, arabesque design.

De chine – satin de chine was the early European term for this lustrous silk fabric because it was originally made in China and came to Europe in the early Middle Ages.

De lyon – a ribbed-back satin.

Duchesse – a heavy, firm, exceptionally soft and lustrous satin.

Farmer's – a cotton and worsted backing but lustrous face.

Fontange – a satin with broad stripes of white and colour.

Foulard – a satin patterned with spots or stripes.

Jean – twilled-back satin.

Merveilleux – a soft, twilled satin.

Pompadour – a white satin embroidered with floral sprays in colour.

Satinesco – a poor quality satin.

Satinet – a lightweight satin.

Skinner's – an American fabric of the late nineteenth century.

Slipper – strong, durable, closely-woven satin with a dull back and semi-glossy surface.

Scandinavian dress

In the Middle Ages fashionable dress followed the general mode but, as a result of its geographical isolation, each style in Scandinavian attire lagged behind and was later in being introduced. Being nearer to the centre of European development Danish fashions, by the sixteenth century, were taken more directly from the prevailing Dutch and German styles but Norway, Sweden and Finland continued to be, due to their geographical position, on the fringe of the European scene so that fashions were indigenous apart from those of the nobility.

The Court of the Vasas was the first in Sweden to bring fashions there up to date. Under the founder of the dynasty, Gustav Vasa, 1523–60, German tailors were brought to Stockholm and German garments imported from Lübeck. Fabrics of all kinds were also imported; woollen cloth from England, Holland and Germany, fine linen from Holland and rich fabrics such as silks, velvets, brocades came from Italy, Spain and the East. The nobility and gentry wore imported fabrics chiefly. Plain linen was made in Sweden and a wide variety of furs were home produced. Until after 1580 men's dress was based on the German pattern, for example, the short gown with wide shoulders and the pluderhosen or Venetians. In the last quarter of the century Spanish styles reached Sweden but, though modish, were less popular as they were more fitting and less comfortable than the looser, German styles. The long gown, which had been worn in Sweden in the Middle Ages, continued to be seen during the sixteenth century, for colder weather and for wear by older men. Fur-lined, it was particularly suited to the climate of the Finnish and Swedish winter months. It had much in common with the Russian caftan in its braid decorations and fastenings on the chest.

Women's dress followed a simpler form than fashionable design. The bodice, often separate and sleeveless, was laced at the back and the separate sleeves were embroidered. Two skirts were worn; a luxuriously patterned underskirt and an overskirt open in front to display the other. Petticoats and bolster were generally preferred to the farthingale and the ropa style of surcote was popular.

During the seventeenth century Scandinavia followed current Dutch, German and then French modes. The Puritan influence from England had a marked effect in the 1650s. All quality materials were still imported.

From the later seventeenth century

Lapland woman in reindeer skin clothes. Baby carried in basket

Norwegian woman from Hardanger fjord. White head-dress, blouse and embroidered apron. Green and red bodice

Laplander in reindeer skin tunic, trousers, boots and cap. Scarf and mittens.

Swedish man in coat, waistcoat and breeches. Red wool cap, wool stockings

Norwegian man in green jacket and breeches with dark red edging. Patterned wool socks, embroidered cap

Swedish woman. White head-dress, blouse and kerchief. Black and red apron, navy skirt

Danish man in striped jacket and waistcoat. Wool cap

Finnish woman in white lace-edged cap, white apron and blouse. Brightly-coloured bodice and skirt

Danish woman in check apron and striped dress. Embroidered kerchief and headdress.

Swedish dress *c.*1550. King
Gustav Vasa in gown, doublet
and hose in black embroidered
in gold
Finnish noblewoman in ropa
worn over patterned gown,
1575

English Puritan influence on
Swedish costume, *c.*1665

Scandinavia, like the rest of Europe,
enthusiastically adopted French culture
and dress but, in the 1770s, King Gustav III
of Sweden introduced a national style of
dress which he decreed should be worn by
the Court, the nobility and the professional
classes. This was an attempt to curtail, in
Scandinavia, the excesses and luxury of the
French modes of the time, to introduce a
fashion more suited to the northern climate
and one which would patronize the home
textile industry.

The masculine style was to be based
upon early seventeenth century dress but
it became something of a mixture of past
styles adapted to the later eighteenth
century. It was, however, a specific mode
which consisted of a straight jacket with
broad sash on top encircling the waist.
Fitting breeches and stockings were worn
with ribbon rosettes at the knee. Shoes
were of seventeenth century design but
French types of current wig were worn.
The cloak was simple and straight. The
ladies' version of the national dress was
nearer to current French fashion. Most
typical were polonaise or circassienne
gowns, though an early seventeenth century design of ruff or collar often accompanied the high coiffure.

Denmark also introduced the Gustavian
style and it was published in the illustrated
journals in other countries in western
Europe. Though not an unqualified success,
it was worn extensively during the lifetime
of the king and achieved its purpose in
curtailing the excessive extravagances of
French dress of the 1770s to be seen elsewhere. It also led to increased consumption
of home-produced fabrics. Towards the
end of the century Scandinavia reverted to
the current European modes.

The wearing of peasant and regional
costumes in Scandinavia is now reserved
chiefly for folk dancing and festivals but
the rich heritage has been preserved and
can be studied in books and museums as
well as in rural communities. In *Denmark*
such costumes are worn only in remote areas
and on the islands and the men's dress,
which was based upon a rural version of
the fashionable dress of the day, has more

or less disappeared. Women's dress was characterized by a general popularity of check materials and a kerchief worn round the shoulders instead of a collar to the blouse. This kerchief was attached to the waistbelt or tied at the back. As elsewhere in Scandinavia, full, long aprons were worn and skirts were ankle-length with ample material pleated in wide accordion pleats preserved by being first damped then heated. Bodices were fitting, often laced across the blouse and had a basque at the back to conceal the waistline junction of bodice and skirt. There was a wide variety of embroidered and plain caps and bonnets, often stiffly shaped and folded.

Swedish regional dress has been carefully preserved and documented. It was rich in distinctive variety from one region to another. Many of the general characteristics are the same as in the rest of Scandinavia: the pleated skirts, decorative aprons, fitted bodices laced across the white blouse with turned-down collar and the hanging pockets attached, medieval-fashion, to the waistbelt. A great variety of caps and bonnets were worn, also kerchiefs which were tied round the head. A good deal of jewellery was popular, especially decorative buttons and buckles and chain and disc necklaces. As in Finland, many garments were made of striped material; in Finland these were generally placed vertically, in Sweden they could be horizontal also. Men's dress has survived less well. The shirts were the most distinctive part of the costume; these were fastened at the neck with a bow or buttons and were extensively embroidered. Trousers or knickerbockers were worn with jackets or coats and small hats or caps.

In *Finland* also men's national costume is rarely worn. Traditionally it consisted of a hip-length tunic with waistbelt from which hung a purse and weapon, accompanied by a shirt and knickerbockers. Finnish dress was less colourful and elaborate than that of other Scandinavian countries probably because of the long years of Russian domination when symbols of nationalism were firmly discouraged. Embroidery was more sparingly worked

Swedish national dress, 1778

and clothes tended to be of plain or striped materials. Decoration for head-dresses and bonnets was provided by lace and ribbons. The hanging purse was usual in Finland, generally with longer cords than in Sweden. Such purses could also contain keys and sewing materials. Moccasin footwear was generally worn.

Norwegian national costumes are the most decorative and colourful in northern Europe. They varied greatly from valley to valley and this distinction has been maintained more than elsewhere because of the mountainous, fjord terrain which, until comparatively recently, made access difficult. Decorative methods such as coloured knitting patterns (the prototype of Fair Isle knitting) and embroidery were traditionally very beautiful and complex. Hardanger embroidery, for example, was used particularly to decorate blouses and aprons (see *Embroidery*). Ornamental silver buttons and jewellery adorned the costume.

The dress of the *Laplanders* was dictated by the climate since these nomadic people inhabit the northern regions of Norway, Sweden and Finland within the Arctic Circle. Their costume has much in common with that of the Eskimos (see *Eskimo dress*). The reindeer provides skin for garments as well as leather and sewing thread. Both sexes dress similarly in a full tunic (*peski*) which is pulled on over the head then zipped up at the neck and pulled in by a waistbelt. The man's tunic is hip-length, the woman's reaches the ankles. With the tunic are worn trousers, which are tucked into boots or ankle wrappings, a cape, a scarf, a cap or bonnet, gloves or mittens. The garments are decorated only with coloured borders made by pieces of cloth appliquéd on to the skin which is worn with the fur inside. The women carry their babies around with them in wood or wicker cradles in a similar manner to the nomadic North American Indians (see *Babies' and Infants' Wear* and *North American Indian dress*).

Scarf

A piece of material worn round the neck for warmth or decoration. A sixteenth century term, originally the scarf was worn by men as a sash or baldric slung across the body from shoulder to hip and served to carry small articles (see *Sash*). In the nineteenth century the neckscarf was fashionable wear for men (see *Neckwear*). The headscarf of rural and modern use derived from the medieval coverchief (see *Couvrechef*).

Scarlet

A rich cloth made from the early Middle Ages first called escarlate and derived from the Persian *saqalāt*. It was made in various colours but, because it was so often dyed a brilliant red hue, the name became associated more with the colour than the material.

Schreinerize

A method of finishing mercerized cotton fabrics to give a lustre by passing the wet material between heated, heavy rollers engraved with a network of fine lines. The process is named after Ludwig Schreiner and was patented in 1895.

Scogger

A woven or knitted wool stocking or sleeve without foot or hand portion worn to protect the arm or placed over the footwear to prevent slipping on icy surfaces.

Scottish Highland dress

Before the Second World War it was generally believed that the traditional and familiar Scottish Highland dress was of ancient origin dating back over 1000 years to the Gaelic chieftains. Research carried out during the last 40 years has shown that this is not so and that the ensemble is of seventeenth century origin and the characteristic, specific clan tartans are of more recent date still though the clans themselves are of ancient origin dating back, in small district clans, to the sixth century. (The Gaelic word *clann* means children, so clan before a Highland name refers to the family of that group or tribe.) It is not certain what the people of Scotland wore in these early centuries but it is thought that they were clad in a similar manner to the other inhabitants of northern Europe at the time, in loose trousers or leg-bandings, tunics and cloaks. From the eleventh to the fifteenth century descriptions by travellers to Scotland mention an attire composed of a shirt or tunic, braies or shorts, bare feet and a cloak wrapped round the upper part of the body. In the sixteenth century the Scots, like the Irish, were wearing *trews*, a fitted, long trouser, or leg-bandings, rawhide shoes, a knee-length shirt with full sleeves and a short jacket on top. Over all was wrapped a dark wool mantle. Fynes Moryson (see bibliography) in his travels about 1600 refers to saffron-coloured loose shirts and coarse woollen cloaks of two or three different colours woven into a chequer pattern. He also refers to the broad, woollen, blue caps which the Scots wore.

It was in the seventeenth century that the Scottish tunic or shirt was superseded by the *belted plaid*, in Gaelic *feile-mor*. Simply a rectangle of woollen material some six yards by two (see *Plaid*), it was folded lengthwise into pleats. The wearer then fastened the lower part of the material to his body with a leather belt so that it became a full knee-length skirt and the remainder of the material was then draped around the upper part of the body as desired; it was often fastened on one shoulder, the rest of the fabric hanging down the back. At night the wearer un-

Earl of Eglinton,
1780s. Scarlet coat
with green edging,
white waistcoat.
Tartan plaid in
shades of green
with blue and
black. Red and
white hose, black
leather shoes.
Black plume in
bonnet. Leather
sporran. Sword
and dirk

A Highland
chieftain, c.1670.
Belted plaid, double
width about 5
yards long in
yellow, brown, red
and black tartan.
Black bonnet with
white plume. Gold
decorated doublet.
Gold hose sash
ties, red and black
hose. Black and
gold shoes. Musket,
dirk and pistol

Green and red
tartan doublet and
trews. Plaid of
red, green and
gold tartan.
Leather sporran.
Bonnet and
cockade. Broad-
sword and pistol.
Major Fraser,
Highlander, c.1720

Sir John Sinclair,
c.1800. Trews and
plaid in tartan of
two shades of
green, yellow and
red. Red jacket,
dark red sash.
White fur sporran,
black shoes

Alastair Macdonell,
c.1810. Jacket and
plaid in red and
green tartan. Red
and white hose,
red ties. White
waistcoat, white
fur sporran,
bonnet. Musket,
dirk

Modern day wear.
Tweed jacket, shirt,
tartan tie. Kilt,
leather sporran.
Tartan socks, black
shoes

Modern evening
wear. Black
doublet with
leather belt and
lace jabot and
wrist ruffles. Fur
sporran, kilt.
Dark stockings,
black shoes

fastened his belt and the plaid once more became a blanket. The modern *kilt* developed from the belted plaid, being simply the lower, pleated part on its own. This was worn from about 1725–30 onwards; it was not sewn but overlapped in front and was known as the little kilt (*feile-beag* in Gaelic). The word kilt is thought to derive from a Danish word *kilte*, meaning to gird or tuck up.

Trews continued to be worn instead of or as well as the plaid. Alternatively the kilt was worn with stockings or hose which were gartered below the knee. By about 1730 it became general for Highlanders to wear a plaid and bare knees with stockings below, while Lowlanders preferred trews and a small shoulder plaid. Accompanying the plaid or trews was a jacket over a doublet and under this a shirt. Shoes were heelless like slippers and the cap or bonnet was most often blue. Women also wore plaids and tied a white kerchief over their heads.

In the seventeenth century the belted plaid was tied or pinned on the shoulder with a wood or bone bodkin. By the eighteenth century silver pins and brooches were being worn and these became larger and more elaborate in the nineteenth century. Many were circular designs and were decorated with varied patterns of interlacing blended with floral and animal motifs. The *sporran* was originally a simple leather or cloth pouch fastened by thongs which pulled it together at the top. In the eighteenth century metal clasp fastenings were introduced and the very elaborate, large sporrans were a nineteenth century affectation. These were furry or hairy, made of badger or goat skin.

After the Highland defeat on Culloden Moor in 1746 Highland dress, as a symbol of the power of the clans, was proscribed by the English government but the dress style was not lost as its use was not forbidden to the military. Many Highlanders were recruited into the army, later becoming regiments in the British Army, notably the Black Watch, so the kilt, jacket, bonnet and stockings continued to be worn; the belted plaid was not adopted because it was regarded as being too unweildy for army use. The Proscription Act was repealed in 1782 and the wearing of Highland dress returned to civil use but this time as a fashion for English as well as Scots. Indeed, the English aristocracy took it up with such enthusiasm that it became permanently safe from threat of extinction. The seal of royal approval was set upon the wearing of both tartan and Highland dress with its adoption by George IV on his visit to Edinburgh in 1822; Prince Albert and Queen Victoria completed the conquest in mid-century.

The striped and checked pattern woven into symmetrical squares by a striped warp and weft is known as a *tartan*, though the word tartan originally referred to a type of material not its design. This chequer pattern is not, of course, unique to Scotland and has been a traditional type of decoration in many cultures in different parts of the world. Tartan fabrics were woven in Scotland from at least the later Middle Ages. The wool was prepared, dyed, spun and woven at home and, since warp and weft were not identical, the pattern produced was not necessarily regular or symmetrical. Dyes were mainly of vegetable origin and colours therefore soft and subtle.

The clan tartans are of much more recent introduction and date from the later eighteenth century, well after the '45. They were popularized by British Army regimental dress then later, in the nineteenth century, by the English monarchy and aristocracy. With the introduction of aniline dyes (see *Dyeing*) the brilliant colours of the tartans which we know today were produced. The making of tartans continued to be a cottage industry until the eighteenth century when the Wilson family of Bannockburn, which was a textile centre, began to make tartan fabrics on a commercial scale and, by the end of the century, were exporting them all over Scotland and, later, to Europe and the USA. In the nineteenth century new tartan patterns were designed in great numbers; there were even seven or eight versions of the Royal Stewart, some designed by Prince Albert.

Today Highland dress can be worn in

Scotland for most occasions. For day wear it consists of the kilt with sporran and belt, a tweed jacket over shirt and tie, tartan socks and leather shoes and a cap or bonnet; the smaller dagger or *skean dhu* is tucked into the top of one of the stockings. Evening wear can vary from a traditional type of black evening dress jacket (like 'tails' without the tails) to a velvet jacket or doublet accompanied by an evening dress bow tie and collared shirt or a lace cravat and wrist ruffles. Footwear consists of soft, black heelless slippers. The plaid, when worn, is fastened on the shoulder by a plaid brooch. Ladies also wear the plaid fastened in this way on top of a white evening dress.

Scye

A tailor's term for the shape and opening of the armhole.

Seam

A joining made by sewing together two pieces of material so that the raw edges are turned inwards and the flat seamed side faces outwards. There are several types of seam, notably the *French seam*, where the two edges are narrowly seamed together on the right side and the garment is then turned inside out and seamed again; this gives a neat seam with no unfinished edges. In a *welt seam* the material is first seamed with one edge projecting further forwards than the other. This wider piece is then folded over and basted under the narrow one, which gives a neat, raised seam, which can then be decoratively finished on the right side. In a *piped seam* a narrow strip of material is inserted between the two pieces of fabric to be seamed and this is then visible as a narrow piping on the right side of the garment; it can be of self-colour or decorative in a contrasting hue.

Seamstress

A person whose work is plain sewing and finishing in distinction from the wider field of the dressmaker or embroiderer.

Seersucker

A fine linen or cotton textile made in India, characterized by a puckered striped surface. The word is a corruption of the Persian *shir o shakka*, meaning literally 'milk and sugar', but referring to a striped linen fabric. Modern seersucker can be of cotton, silk or rayon. It is still characterized by its puckered striped surface which is produced by varying the tension of the warp threads.

Selvage, selvedge

The edge of a woven material which has been finished in a webbed weave in order to prevent unravelling.

Sennit

Plaited straw or palm leaves which are made into hats. The sennit straw used for making sailor hats was treated with shellac to make it firm and hard.

Separates

A modern term to describe the idea of designing various parts of a woman's costume so that they are interchangeable and co-ordinated in design and colour. Separates include, particularly, a jacket, blouse, jumper, top or shirt, skirt and trousers.

Serge

A durable, twilled worsted material. In the Middle Ages chiefly a furnishing material and in the seventeenth and eighteenth centuries a fabric in general use among the poorer classes for outer clothing because of its durability. From the nineteenth century on a quality, strong material used chiefly for men's and women's tailored suits and coats. Many varieties of serge have been manufactured and imported and a number of the latter have acquired names relating to their town or material of origin, for example, *serge de Ghent, serge de Nimes* or *sergenim* (see *Denim*) and *sergedusoy* (*serge du soie*).

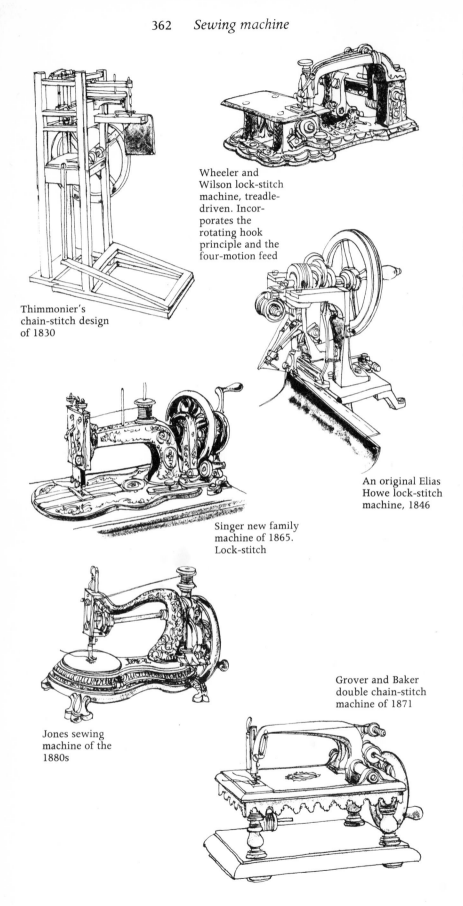

Thimmonier's chain-stitch design of 1830

Wheeler and Wilson lock-stitch machine, treadle-driven. Incorporates the rotating hook principle and the four-motion feed

An original Elias Howe lock-stitch machine, 1846

Singer new family machine of 1865. Lock-stitch

Grover and Baker double chain-stitch machine of 1871

Jones sewing machine of the 1880s

Sewing machine

A machine sews in a different manner from a hand-sewer. The latter passes the needle and thread through the material and pierces it again from the other side. It is difficult to design a machine which will imitate this process and, indeed, this was not achieved until the 1930s. In machine sewing the successful method, followed from the early designs onwards, has been to use an eye-pointed needle which will convey the thread through the cloth without having itself to pass through completely. There are three types of stitch: the simple chain or tambour stitch, the double chain and the lock stitch. In the first of these a single thread is used which is held by a looper as the needle rises and falls so that each stitch is secured by the one before. In the other two systems two threads are employed and the lock stitch has proved an excellent method especially for smaller and domestic machines. In this there is a needle thread above the material and a bobbin thread under it and these two are locked together at each stitch by the upper thread being passed round the lower and tightening it in position. In the double chain stitch method more thread is used but it was for many years more suited to large-scale industrial use and, from the beginning, many different types of machine have been designed for industrial sewing, for varied materials and purposes. Both stitch systems are still in use in modern machines.

The double-pointed needle with central eye was patented in 1755 by *Charles Weisenthal* but the earliest sewing machine was patented by the Englishman *Thomas Saint* in 1790. This machine was intended to sew, quilt and stitch but was chiefly designed for leatherwork and was fitted with an awl to pierce the material for the thread to follow. It was a single-thread, chain-stitch design which had a forked not eye-pointed needle. Although Saint invented the first sewing machine, patented it and made drawings and descriptions of how it worked, it is thought unlikely that he actually made the machine. His patent was forgotten for many years until found by Newton Wilson, a sewing machine manufacturer, in 1874. Wilson made a model from the drawings but had to alter parts of it to get it to work.

The first satisfactorily functioning single-thread, chain-stitch machine was invented in 1830 by the Frenchman *Barthélemy Thimmonier*, a tailor who lived near Lyons. Soon about 80 of his machines were in operation in Paris making army uniforms but opposition to this new mechanical threat to their employment made hand-workers so violent that they destroyed the machines and nearly murdered the inventor. The set-back was only temporary and Thimmonier developed his machine further from a clumsy wood one to an improved metal design which could work faster on a greater variety of fabrics. He obtained further patents for improvements in England and America as well as France.

The development of the double-thread, lock-stitch system with eye-pointed needle came chiefly from inventors in America, by *Walter Hunt*, 1832–4, *Elias Howe*, 1846, *Allan B. Wilson*, 1849–51 and *Isaac Merrit Singer*, 1851. Howe's invention had an under-thread shuttle but his needle had to be curved and the material held vertically. These drawbacks were countered by Singer, who developed a system using a straight needle and the material was supported on a horizontal table. Allan B. Wilson devised the rotary hook and bobbin construction which reduced the excessive noise made by the shuttle and later invented the four-motion feed which moved the work on after every stitch. Meanwhile *William O. Grover* with *William F. Baker* patented a double-chain stitch machine and *James E.A. Gibbs* and *J. Willcox* developed a design using a rotary hook to make a twisted single-chain stitch.

Since the 1850s many improvements have been made to the sewing machine, such as the introduction of positive take-up in 1872, the reversible feed of 1919, the introduction of varied and decorative stitches and, of course, the powering by electric motor; thousands of patents have been issued in the USA and Europe for such improvements. The machines have become easier to use and more efficient as a result

of all these improvements and added accessories but the underlying principles of operation remain unchanged.

Shag
A worsted or silk material with a long nap, woven between the late sixteenth and late eighteenth centuries.

Shank
1) A loop, or a protuberance with a hole inserted, attached to the back of some buttons by which the button may be sewn on.
2) Part of a shoe (see *Shoes*).

Shawl
A square or rectangular piece of material worn round the shoulders and upper part of the body. Shawls were especially fashionable during the nineteenth century, in the early decades to provide warmth and decoration to accompany the sheer dress fabrics of the day and, later, they were particularly suited to wear with the crinoline skirts as only the upper part of the body required extra layers of material. The shawl was of oriental origin (see *Indian dress*) and the word derives from the Persian *shāl*, which was adopted into Urdu and other Indian languages and, in the later eighteenth century, into most European ones.

The *cashmere shawl* was at first imported from Kashmir, where is was made from the wool of the Tibetan mountain goat, also known as the shawl-goat. By the early nineteenth century cashmere shawls were being made in Britain of soft wool. *Norwich square shawls* were also introduced early in the century; these had a silk warp and wool weft. The *Paisley shawl*, from 1808, could be made of silk, cotton or wool, or of mixed yarns. The characteristic Paisley design became highly fashionable (see *Paisley pattern*). *Spanish shawls* were also very popular, based on the manta and mantilla (see *Manta*). The *serape* (*sarape*) was of Mexican Spanish origin, dating back to Aztec design. The *rebozo* came from South America. By the mid-nineteenth century in Europe, shawls were made in

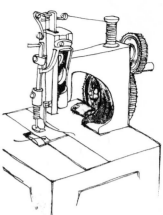

The original design of Singer machine, 1851. Lock-stitch design

SHAWL
Deep lavender silk shawl with
tiered, self-colour fringing,
English, 1848

White spotted muslin evening
shawl with lace edging, Russian,
1853

Black silk shawl with mauve
ruched bands and black
Chantilly lace flouncing,
English, 1860

all sizes, of all kinds of materials and with varied patterns and motifs as well as trimming. Very large shawls were fashionable with the full skirts of the 1860s.

Shirring
Close, narrow, parallel lines of stitching which make gathers in the textile material.

Shirt
An undergarment covering the upper part of the body, originally worn next to the skin but, from the nineteenth century on, a vest or undershirt often worn beneath it. Also referred to as a chemise (see *Chemise*), the shirt was common to both sexes until the nineteenth century when the name came to refer solely to the masculine garment. In modern dress a wide variety of shirts are available for all occasions from leisure to formal wear in all colours, materials, patterns and styles with easy-care shirts representing the majority of designs available. Before about 1950, apart from short-sleeved, open-necked sportswear, the day shirt always had long sleeves with cuffs closed by links or buttons and a neckband with separate collar fastened by studs, or an attached collar; the garment opened part way down the centre front which had a centre panel or yoke or, in the mid-twentieth century, could be of coat style, opening from neck to hem. It reached the hips and was slit at each side seam. Materials were different weights of cotton, flannelette or silk. Day shirts could be coloured and, traditionally were formally striped, checked or plain; evening shirts were white with pleated or stiff fronts. Named varieties include:
Aloha – an American fashion originating in the 1930s, of a brightly-coloured and patterned silk shirt based on the Hawaiian garment. A coat design, the shirt is worn outside the trousers or shorts.
Aquatic – a nineteenth century, informal shirt designed for boating and seaside wear and decorated with brightly-coloured stripes or checks.
Basque – a popular, informal shirt of the later nineteenth century based on the Basque fisherman's jersey, with round

neck and short sleeves.

Boiled – an American slang term for a white evening shirt with stiffly starched front.

Chitterlings – usual term for the frilled shirt front fashionable from the late eighteenth century until just after 1900.

Coat – a shirt opening all down the front and donned like a coat.

Pleated – a nineteenth century fashion for a pleated front for day or evening wear.

Polo – in England a shirt with a high polo neckline; in America, a summer shirt with round or collared neckline.

Shirt-waist or *shirt blouse* – an adaptation of the masculine shirt to a formal, feminine blouse in the years 1890–1910. The blouse was characterized by a masculine collar with tie or scarf. Shirtwaist is an American term (see *Blouse*).

Sports – worn without a tie, usually open at the neck and with long or short sleeves. Made from a varied selection of patterns and materials.

Sweat – for athletic wear, generally of heavy cotton, with round neck and sleeves.

T-shirt – an informal round-necked design with short sleeves cut in one with the garment; generally made of coloured or patterned cotton or a synthetic material.

Shoddy

A material made from reclaimed wool spun from torn-up woollen rags, with the addition of new wool.

Shoes and shoe-making

For the purpose of protecting the feet, apart from fashion, three types of footwear evolved in different parts of the world according to climate, terrain and the way of life of the people. Boots were customary with nomadic horseriding communities in cold mountainous regions as well as the open steppes and hot sandy desert conditions (see *Boot*). Sandals were the chief footwear in warm climates where the need was to protect the sole of the foot as well as keeping the foot cool (see *Sandal*). The shoe developed in colder regions where both warmth and protection were needed and was the footwear for northern Europe, Asia and the colder parts of North America.

The early form of footwear was a single piece of rawhide (see *Leather*), often with the hair attached and facing outwards. A leather thong or sinew was threaded through holes pierced round the edge of the material and when the foot was placed on the rawhide the thong was drawn up tight and tied on top of the foot, thus providing sole and upper in one piece of material. Known as the *carbatine* or carbatina, this simple shoe was worn all over northern Europe both before and after the coming of the Romans and could be found in use in more remote areas, such as the Aran Islands of Ireland, as late as the early years of the twentieth century, where it was known as a *pampootie*. A Scottish term for such rawhide shoes was *rullion* or rivelin. Of the same derivation is the *moccasin* of the North American Indian. In this design the leather is pleated on top into a decorative apron front (see *North American Indian dress*).

In classical dress the Greeks generally wore sandals but the *Etruscans* of both sexes are frequently depicted in a closed shoe or ankle-shoe, both with slightly upturned toes. Under the *Roman* and *Byzantine Empires* shoes were worn as well as sandals. There were several styles; the closed *calceus*, usually laced at the ankle and worn in the street in towns, was generally reserved for wear by Roman citizens, its colour denoting the rank of the wearer, for instance, senators at first wore black or white but later this was changed to red. The better quality Roman and Byzantine shoes were made in leather or cloth, dyed in various colours and decorated with gilt and embroidery. They were shaped to the foot and fastened by laces, or a button. The *gallica*, from Gaul, had a closed upper and was laced up on top of the foot; the *campagus* seems to have had a high back and be strapped across the front, with an open instep. The carbatine shoe of undressed hide was worn by ordinary people; such footwear had no left or right pattern, as had the calceus.

After the fall of the Roman Empire, Roman styles of shoes continued to be worn for many centuries in the Mediterranean

Pampootie, Isle of Aran More, nineteenth century*

Similar design, Iceland. Fur and flesh scraped off*

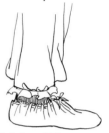

Britain, *c*.900 AD. Rawhide

Child's moccasin. North American Indian, Iroquois. Tan suède, orange and blue raffia decoration*

North American Indian moccasin of white leather, embroidered in orange and blue, Iroquois*

Lady's shoes, Etruscan, seventh century BC

Leather gallica, Roman, second century AD

Leather shoe, Germany, *c*.fourth century AD

areas but northern Europe held to a stronger, more closed shoe, often ankle-length and laced there. Better class shoes were shaped to the foot and were made of leather or fabric in all colours. By the late eleventh century shoes were being made with sole and upper stitched together with thread instead of being thonged and there was more variety in materials from which the shoe was made. Cordovan leather was widely used (see *Leather*) also coloured silk, damask and velvet with gold and extensive embroidered decoration. Shoes were fastened with laces, buttons or buckles and pattens protected delicate designs out-of-doors (see *Patten*). The pointed-toe shoe was introduced in the late eleventh century and for some time this was cut and shaped into the form of a scorpion's tail or ram's horns. In the twelfth century it settled down to a simple point which lasted for much of the Middle Ages and gave rise to excessive lengths in the fourteenth and fifteenth centuries (see *Poulaine*). During the Middle Ages the ankle-shoe was worn, especially in the twelfth and thirteenth centuries, fastened with a buckle or button, but lower cut designs with rolled tops or laced side slits were also worn. Soled hose with pattens replaced shoes for some time in the fourteenth and fifteenth centuries

The pointed toe ended its long fashion about 1490 and the more comfortable round toe, with welted shoe construction, took its place, to be ousted in the years 1515–20 onwards by the excessively wide toes which, for some years, were square ended or horned. Such shoes, for fashionable wear, were low cut in front and might be fastened by a strap across the top of the foot. Like other items of clothing at the time, shoes were decorated by slashes and embroidery. They were made of leather, velvet or satin in all colours. By 1550 a more natural-shaped elegant shoe fashion had returned, still slashed, jewelled and embroidered. By 1570 a higher, tongued front was usual with latchets tied over it and, in the 1580s, there developed the wedge cork shoes which led to the first signs of a heel being built up at the back by the end of the century.

For the first half of the seventeenth century shoes had tapering square or rounded toes and were decorated by a large ribbon rosette on top of the foot which hid much of the shoe. The heel was now established and grew in height from one inch to two or two and a half inches (see *Heel*). For men, boots were *de rigueur* from about 1625–30 until the 1650s (see *Boot*). After this, with the introduction of petticoat breeches and then the justaucorps, boots were clearly incongruous and shoes returned to fashion for over 100 years. In the 1650s and 1660s the shoe was open at the sides and was finished on top by a ribbon tie over an upstanding tongue; in the 1670s this tie was replaced by a metal buckle (see *Buckle*) and both tongue and heel became higher. In the last decade of the century shoes were often cut high, up to or above the ankle, the open sides had disappeared and, for ladies, the pointed toe returned.

During the eighteenth century designs for men's shoes diverged from those for ladies, a differentiation which was to be a permanent one. After about 1720 men's shoes were of leather, usually black, though heels were often still red. The buckle fastening was normal until the 1790s, the size and style varying from small, jewelled buckles in the early years to the large square, plain metal designs of the mid-century. From about 1785 shoes became almost slippers; they were cut lower with short fronts and low heels and were decorated only by a ribbon bow or a small jewelled ornament. Women's shoes were made of many different materials: kid, satin, brocade, velvet. They were richly embroidered and ornamented by gold or silver braid, ribbon ties, lace, ruching and jewelled buckles. They were as elaborate as the gown and in the 1760s and 1770s were visible below the shorter gown skirts of the time. By 1740–5 the heavier English heel began to give way to the slenderer French high styles (see *Heel*) and these only began to lower after 1775. Toes were pointed and slightly upturned. After the French Revolution heelless slippers, tied on with ribbons, were fashionable.

Byzantine, sixth century, coloured leather

Leather, English, 1080

Leather, English, 1310

Gold embroidered velvet, English, c.1450

Leather, Spanish, 1465

Leather, Oslo, eighth century

Stuffed scorpion tail toe, c.1110

Gold embroidered, English, 1260

Leather, English, 1355

Leather, Swiss, c.1450

Leather, Swedish, thirteenth century

Embroidered and slashed, German, 1570–90

Red velvet with ribbon rose, 1630

Brown suède with red bow, Spanish, c.1665

Slashed velvet, horned, English, c.1540

Velvet, eared, German, c.1540

Hungarian, 1602. Startup type

Leather with ribbon rose, 1620

Men's shoes, Danish, c.1700

Gold embroidered, Hungarian, c.1700

Blue satin, Spanish, c.1820

Blue silk, English, 1810

Man's shoe, brown cloth and leather, 1850

Cream satin evening, French, 1895

Pink satin with coloured silk embroidery, French, 1780

Black silk with diamanté buckle, Spanish, c.1780

Brown leather, English, 1912

Pink silk with silver lace, German, c.1750

Bronze kid, 1860–70

Black kid, 1868–70

Black patent leather and lizard skin, 1927

Black suède ankle-strap, 1950

Man's brown leather, 1948

Tan leather and white buckskin, 1946

Cream satin with glass beads, 1877

Yellow satin, 1865

Apple green suède, 1958

Leather 1924

Brown leather and suède, 1931

Black suède 1964

Crimson suède sling-back, 1950

Blue leather and white buckskin wedge, 1948

Gold kid evening, 1925

Turkish man's shoe, c.1830. Dark green leather with red heel*

Man's red Morocco leather shoe with blue cloth lining, Egyptian, 1860s*

Man's shoe of black and red plastic, 1976

Purple skin shoe. White and gold decoration. Eskimo*

Serbian leather*

Dark brown leather, Armenian, nineteenth century*

Dark red leather Greek shoe. Red silk pompon*

Rawhide Veldtschoen, Boer, 1900*

Black leather overshoe, Finland*

Czech leather shoe, wool pompons*

Canvas espadrille with rope sole

* In Northampton Shoe Museum Collection

Pink silk
embroidered lady's
shoe for bound
foot, Chinese*

Black satin man's
shoe with black
cord decoration,
Chinese*

Boy's shoe. Black
background,
embroidered in
green and gold,
Chinese*

Cotton tabi,
Japanese

Leather shoe with
brass wire
decoration. Indian
man's shoe*

Moroccan man's
shoe in red leather
with decoration in
blue and green*

Brown leather
stitched decoration.
Afghan man's
shoe*

Yellow leather   Two tones of
Nigerian man's   brown leather,
shoe, 1924*   cut edges. Indian
                  man's shoe*

In the nineteenth century, until about 1840, men wore boots rather then shoes (see *Boot*), reserving the black pump or slipper for evening and indoor wear. During the middle years of the century boots or shoes were worn under trousers and it was only from the 1860s that shoes became more popular, in Oxford or Derby designs. In general, men's shoes were made of leather though uppers could be partly or wholly of cloth. Until the 1820s ladies continued to wear the heelless pump or slipper, made of kid or silk, fastened by ribbons crossed over the foot and round the ankle. A low heel was reintroduced in the 1830s, though the square toe was retained till nearly the end of the century, when a pointed toe returned with higher heels. Coloured leather was fashionable for these shoes while evening wear was generally in black or bronze kid. For most of the nineteenth century ladies wore boots for out-of-doors or shoes with grey or fawn gaiters on top.

Men's shoes in the first 50 years of the twentieth century were conservative in style, made of leather or suède with laced-up fronts in Oxford or brogue designs; they had a rounded toe and low, stacked heel. In the 1920s and 1930s, especially in summer, a two-tone shoe was fashionable, usually in white buckskin and dark leather. Since the Second World War, as with the rest of the costume, men's footwear has become more varied. Different materials are used and plastic has become more common as the price of leather has soared. The extremely pointed toes of the 1950s (winkle-pickers) gave place in the 1960s to a more natural style but the 1970s have seen a protracted period of fashion for the high platform soles. At first a vogue for ladies' footwear, the fashion spread to men's and, with the modish flared trouser bottoms, soles and heels have become higher and higher, especially popular with the fashion-conscious young.

With the First World War shorter skirts, women's ankles became visible and shoes were elegant, with long pointed toes and high, slim heels. They were buttoned or laced high or were cut low and had ribbon bow decoration. The 1920s brought very pointed toes, high, curved heels and court styles or strap fastenings. Patent leather, kid or suède were used, with evening designs of gold or silver kid, satin or brocade. The 1930s and 1940s saw more comfortable, informal shoes with cuban heels, wedge and platform soles and low-heeled walking brogues. Court and strap shoes with slenderer, higher heels were worn in town. Austerity in the Second World War dictated the use of lower quality leathers, cork and wood soles and heels and, in the 1950s, came synthetic soling materials followed by general use of plastics in the 1960s. Styles and colours became varied. With the 'New Look' dresses, the cuban heels and wedge soles of the war-time fashions gave place to elegant, higher heels; ankle-strap and sling-back shoes were fashionable. Then followed the stiletto heels and very pointed toes of the late 1950s, when heels could be four inches high and tips only three-eighths of an inch in diameter – fatal to wood floor surfacing. Contemporaneously were worn flat casual shoes with low-cut fronts and pointed toes. The 1970s have been characterized by the chunky, broad toes and high platform soles. The more extreme versions of this style are patronized generally only by the young but a general clumpiness of design pervades most current designs of footwear.

For related articles on other forms of footwear see also *Beachwear, Boot, Buckle, Chopine, Clog, Galoshes, Heel, Patten, Poulaine, Sandal, Slipper, Snowshoe*. Among the many named varieties of shoe common in Europe and other parts of the world are included:

Ankle-strap – a fashion for children and adults with a button or buckle and strap fastening round the ankle.

Brogue – originally a rawhide shoe worn in the mountains of Scotland and Ireland. In more modern times brogues are flat-heeled, lace-up, leather shoes decorated by perforations, decorative stitching and gimped edging.

Co-respondent – a two-tone shoe made of white buckskin and coloured leather fashionable in the inter-war years.

Court – a shoe without fastening perennially fashionable. So-named because it was originally worn by both sexes at Court.

Derby – a tie-shoe with eyelets and laces, the eyelet tabs stitched on top of the vamp.

Duckbill – a name given to the broad-toed shoes of the first half of the sixteenth century.

Eared (also *horned*) – names applied to the more extreme square toes of the years 1535–50, when the corners of the toes extended sideways resembling ears or horns.

Espadrille – the traditional rope-soled, canvas shoe, tied round the ankle, worn by Spaniards and the French of the Mediterranean and Pyrenean areas. Now very popular as beach and boat wear (see *Sandal*, *alpargata*).

Ghillie – the name refers to a type of cross-lacing which passes through loops in the shoe and can extend from the vamp to the ankle. Originally a Scottish dancing shoe style but is now also to be seen in fashion shoes.

Monk – the usual name for a plain-fronted shoe fastened by a strap and buckle on the outer side of the instep. Sometimes a fringed leather flap covers this fastening.

Oxford – a traditional, closed, tie-front shoe with the eyelet tabs stitched under the vamp.

Peep-toe – a shoe cut away in front to display part of the toes.

Pump – a court shoe, usually heelless or with fairly low heel.

Sling-back – a shoe with a strap passing round the back of an open heel.

Sneaker – an American term for a canvas shoe with a rubber or rope sole which enables a person to walk silently.

Startup, startop – in the sixteenth and seventeenth centuries a peasant's ankle-shoe worn over leggings which extended to mid-calf or knee length.

Tabi – a sock-shoe worn with the geta (clog) by the Japanese (see *Clog* and *Japanese dress*).

Veldtshoen – from *veldt-shoe*, originally a South African shoe of untanned hide made so that the edges of the upper were turned outwards to form a flange which was stitched on to the sole or middle sole. In a welted veldtshoen construction the lining is welted to the insole and the flanged upper stitched to welt and sole.

Wedge-sole – where a wedge-shaped piece of cork, wood or plastic is inserted under the shoe in order to make heel and sole in one solid piece.

Winkle-picker – a style of shoe with excessively pointed toes fashionable in the 1950s.

SHOE-MAKING

There are four principal stages involved in making a shoe.

1) *Making the upper*. This includes designing the style, making a pattern, cutting the material to the pattern and seaming the parts together to make a complete top covering.

2) *Making the sole*. This may be a single piece of material as in an early moccasin or be in layers which include an insole and middle sole.

3) *Shaping the upper to the last*. The *last* is a shaped wooden or metal block which corresponds to the foot but incorporates variations according to the style of the shoe. The process of shaping the upper to this last and so creating a three-dimensional form out of two-dimensional pieces of material is called *lasting*. The *lasting margin* is the outer edge of the upper which is turned under during lasting and then fixed to the sole or insole.

4) *Joining the upper and sole together, a process known as attaching*. There are three chief methods of attaching, *a*) by nailing or pegging, *b*) by stitching, *c*) by welt construction. In *nailed construction* the upper is nailed to the sole and the nails pass through the lasting margin which is set between the insole and the sole. The Romans used this type of construction and, for military and hard wear, used nails with large heads which also reinforced the sole. This type of construction was re-introduced in the early nineteenth century when nailing machines were designed in order to make army boots. A stitching method, called *turnshoe construction*, was developed in northern Europe after the collapse of the Roman Empire. This footwear was

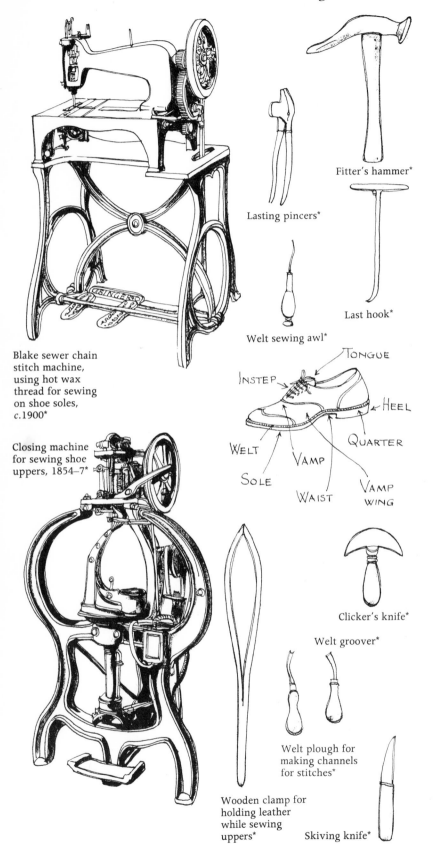

Blake sewer chain stitch machine, using hot wax thread for sewing on shoe soles, c.1900*

Closing machine for sewing shoe uppers, 1854–7*

Lasting pincers*

Fitter's hammer*

Last hook*

Welt sewing awl*

Tongue

Instep

Heel

Welt

Quarter

Vamp

Sole

Vamp Wing

Waist

Clicker's knife*

Welt groover*

Welt plough for making channels for stitches*

Wooden clamp for holding leather while sewing uppers*

Skiving knife*

generally made inside out with upper and sole attached to one another by thonging or thread stitching; the lasting margin of the upper was sewn to a sole composed of only one layer of material so that, when the shoe was turned right side out, the seam was inside as was also the flesh side of the leather. *Welted construction* was introduced to western Europe around the end of the fifteenth century and is still in use. A *welt* is a narrow strip of leather sewn to the lasting margin. In welting construction the upper, plus welt, is sewn to the insole, leaving an upstanding rib projecting a short distance from the upper; the sole can then be sewn to this welt.

Shoe-making was a cottage industry for many centuries. The materials were collected by the worker from the employer and the work was done by hand at home. In the early nineteenth century the hand-work was carried out more and more in factories, called *closing shops*, where child labour was widely used. The master craftsman in charge of such shops was the *clicker*, a man of great skill and experience who selected and cut up from the complete hides the pieces of leather for making uppers and soles. The early machines designed for stitching the parts of a shoe upper together began to operate in the late 1850s. The introduction of these *closing machines* was strongly resisted by the handworkers but, by 1870, the machines were being used in considerable numbers and child labour had virtually disappeared. Complete mechanization of shoe-making was slow to come. Manfield of Northampton was, in 1892, one of the first firms to organize the bulk of the processes to be carried out in purpose-built premises.

The chief parts of a shoe are shown in the diagram. Other common terms include:
Butted seam – where edges of sections of the upper are butted together and sewn.
Channel – stitching holes usually set in a groove.
Close seam – where the sections of leather to be seamed are opened out and flattened after stitching.
Closing – the stitching together of the sections of the upper.

Clump sole – a half sole added to a shoe as a repair, in contrast to long-soling where the entire sole is repaired.

Horn – a shaped piece of metal or plastic used to ease the foot into the shoe. Originally made of polished horn.

Insole – the sole inside the shoe next to the foot.

Lapped seam – where the edges of the two pieces of material to be sewn are overlapped and sewn through.

Latchet – a design which has often been fashionable as a means of shoe fastening. The quarters are extended to straps which can then be tied by strings or ribbons on the instep or fastened there by a buckle. Latchets can overlap or not quite meet one another.

Middle sole – an extra sole placed between insole and sole.

Sock – a lining material stuck to the inside of the insole of the shoe. This can be full length or cover the heel seat only.

Straights – shoes which are symmetrical and can be worn on either foot.

Trees – a form of metal, wood or plastic placed in the shoe when not being worn in order to preserve its shape.

Sicilian, Sicilienne

A fabric originating in Sicily and generally made of a mixture of mohair and cotton. In the nineteenth century especially it was more often of silk and wool.

Silk

The finest and most sought after of all natural fibres and the only one to be available in a natural, continuous filament. In the ancient world there were two sources of silk; the chief of these, producing the finest quality filament, was obtained from the cocoon of the silk moth, the *bombyx mori*. The grubs of the moth feed on mulberry leaves and they spin their cocoons, at the appropriate time in their life cycle, by exuding a viscous substance in a fine filament, one from each of two glands on either side of the body. The larva fastens one end of the filaments to a twig or branch and spins a cocoon round itself which is composed of a continuous thread 800–1200 yards in length. In the natural process the moth emerges by pushing the threads aside in order to make an opening. Such short or damaged threads can be made into spun or raw silk. Under sericulture the chrysalis is killed by suffocation with steam or hot air and the continuous cocoon thread can be unravelled. The second method was to scrape threads from the cocoons of wild silkworms which feed on the leaves of a number of different trees. This wild or tussah moth produces a coarser, less luxurious fibre.

The cultivation of silk originated in China in remote times, believed by some sources to be as far back in the past as 8000 years ago. The Empress Hsi Ling Shih is said to have developed a technique for rearing silkworms (2640 BC) and unravelling the long filaments from the cocoons and an orchard of mulberry trees was cultivated in the palace grounds under her personal supervision. The lady is also credited by the Chinese with the invention of the loom. The Chinese guarded their secret of the manufacture of silk for hundreds of years, retaining their monopoly and exporting silk as yarn, raw silk and finished, woven fabric to a world which prized this beautiful material and would pay exorbitantly for it. By about 1000 BC, or possibly earlier, silkworm culture and silk manufacture was established in India in the valley of the Brahmaputra river and, later, across the delta, in that of the Ganges. Knowledge of the process is thought to have spread overland from China and tradition recounts that some eggs of the moth and some seeds of the mulberry tree were carried to India by a Chinese princess, hidden in the folds of her head-dress. From the Ganges valley sericulture was slowly carried westward, to Persia and Central Asia. The Japanese acquired knowledge of the culture via Korea in the third century AD and silk manufacture became an important Japanese industry.

The first mention in western literature was by Aristotle who described a great, horned worm which changed into a caterpillar, then a bombylius and after that a chrysalis. He described the spinning of the

SKIRT
Harem skirt,
Lanvin gown, 1935

Bias cut skirt, 1931

thread and the unreeling of the cocoon and said that this was first done by Pamphile, daughter of Plates on the island of Cos. His account is vague and not very accurate but certainly raw silk was imported into Cos before Aristotle's time and woven into fabric. Pliny gave similarly vague descriptions of the process and referred to worms which 'weave webs like spiders producing a luxurious material, for women's dresses called silk (bombycina).' Certainly silks were finding their way to Rome by the first century AD and were exorbitantly expensive. The Romans acquired knowledge and experience of the fabric but were uninformed about its source and means of production. Despite attempts to ban its use and astronomic price levels, silk continued to be a prized material under the Roman Empire.

The Emperor Justinian in the sixth century AD tried, in vain, to divert the silk trade from its route from Persia into eastern Europe but soon afterwards, two Persian monks who had worked as missionaries in China and, while there, had studied sericulture and silk weaving, came to Justinian and offered him their knowledge and some silkworm eggs in exchange for a large monetary reward. Justinian accepted. The monks returned to China and, with eggs concealed in a hollow bamboo tube, brought them to Justinian in 550. From these eggs have been produced the strains and varieties used in western Europe since that time. The silkworms flourished in Constantinople. The Byzantine emperors, like the Chinese before them, kept secret the process and monopolized the silk industry in Europe. The factories there turned out some of the most magnificent silks ever produced, woven with gold and silver threads in coloured, figured and plain fabrics. Branch factories were set up outside Constantinople at Athens, Thebes and Corinth but the Imperial capital retained the silkworms.

Inevitably knowledge of sericulture and silk manufacture percolated to western Europe but it took many centuries before the secrets escaped from Constantinople. The Saracens learnt the process and took

their knowledge eastwards and westwards. Trade and manufacture were established in the eleventh and twelfth centuries in Asia Minor and Sicily. From here it spread to the north Italian cities and, in 1480, Louis XI began silk weaving at Tours while, in 1520, Francis I brought silkworm eggs from Milan and reared them in the Rhône valley. In England silk manufacture was introduced in the fifteenth century but serious manufacture only began in 1585 when Flemish weavers emigrated there because of their struggles with Spain. But it was the revocation of the Edict of Nantes which brought the French Huguenots flooding into Spitalfields in London to set up their silk looms there as well as in Germany and Switzerland. Named silk terms include:

Armozeen, Armazine, Armoisin – a heavy silk, generally black, used chiefly for clerical gowns and mourning scarves and bands.

Art – an abbreviation for artificial silk (see *Synthetic and Man-made fibres*).

Atlas – a silk satin made in the East. Derives from the Arabic word for smooth.

Caledonian – from the early nineteenth century, a silk patterned in a small check on a white ground.

Cappadine – a silk flock or waste left from the cocoon after the silk filament has been unravelled.

Cendal, Sendal – a sheer, rich silk used in the Middle Ages.

China – a soft light silk used mainly for linings.

Ducape – a plain, heavy silk widely used from the mid-seventeenth century, especially for dresses and outer wear.

Faille – a silk or rayon with horizontally ribbed surface.

Foulard – a light, twilled silk used chiefly for ties and scarves. Foulard can also be made of cotton, rayon or worsted.

Gauze – a sheer, transparent silk first made in Gaza. Can also be made of cotton, linen or rayon.

Gossamer – a soft, fine silk used for veils.

Grenadine – an open gauze of silk or cotton used in the nineteenth century especially for dresses.

Grosgrain – a heavy, closely-woven, corded

silk. Can now also be made from cotton or rayon. Varieties include gros de Londres, gros de Naples, gros de Suez and gros de Tours.

Kinkob – an Indian silk interwoven with gold or silver thread.

Levantine – a strong, twilled silk first made in the Levant.

Lisse – a fine silk gauze.

Lutestring, Lustring – a glossy silk fabric or ribbon.

Macclesfield – a quality, handwoven silk from the Cheshire town of that name.

Mogador – A Moroccan silk named after the seaport of that name (now Essaouira).

Peau d'Ange – a French silk of the early twentieth century.

Peau de Soie – a firm, double-faced, twilled silk with a dull finish to both sides.

Pekin – a dress silk made originally in China, with alternate stripes warp-wise of satin and velvet finish.

Pongee – a soft, unbleached Chinese silk made from the cocoon filaments of wild silkworms. Derives from a Chinese word, meaning 'home-made on one's own loom'.

Raw – a term for silk made from short fibres or waste, also called *wild silk*. A number of such silks are called after the place where they are made, for example, Habutai in Japan and Honan and Shantung in China.

Samite – a rich, medieval silk usually interwoven with threads of gold and silver.

Sarsenet, Sarcenet – a fine, soft silk used chiefly for linings. The medieval silk possibly derived from Saracen make.

Shantung – a pongee-type material made from wild silk.

Shot – a colour effect produced by using warp threads of one colour with weft threads of another.

Spun – silk made from yarn spun from short fibres taken from broken cocoons or waste.

Surah – a soft, twilled, lightweight silk named after Surat in India, its town of origin. A similar fabric in a heavier weight is called *silk serge* and one with a glossy finish, *satin surah*.

Tabby – a striped or watered silk taffeta named after Attābiy, a district in Bagdad where such material was first made.

Taffeta – in early times, a plainly-woven, glossy material, the name derived from the Persian tāftan, meaning to shine, also to spin. Known in England from the fourteenth century and soon began to refer to a thin silk with gleaming lustre. There are several varieties of taffeta, such as a moiré-patterned fabric or a cross-ribbed, faille taffeta. Today, taffeta can be made of a number of different fabrics, not only silk. *Tufttaffeta*, used especially in the sixteenth and seventeenth centuries, was a taffeta with a tufted pile.

Thai – a wild silk from Thailand, often patterned by tie and dye techniques or by weaving.

Tusser, Tussah, Tussore – from the Hindi and Urdū word *tasar*, meaning shuttle but probably referring to the shape of the cocoon. A natural silk woven from the short fibres of the wild silkworm of India.

Silver cloth or tissue

As with gold cloth (see *Gold cloth*), this costly material was made in past centuries by using a silver metal warp and a silk weft. Today, aluminium and plastic are used. In one method a laminate is made of two layers of plastic enclosing one of aluminium foil and the laminate is shredded. In another, a plastic film is plated with aluminium by a process undertaken in a vacuum. These methods are used in Lurex fabrics (an American trade name).

Skirt

A garment or part of a garment which hangs down and covers the body below the waist. The term can be applied to this part of a man's doublet or coat, a woman's dress or may be, in more modern times, a separate garment. Before the nineteenth century the term petticoat was often used to denote a woman's skirt or underskirt.

Until the later Middle Ages garments were generally cut in one piece longitudinally without a waist seam. In the first part of the sixteenth century men's doublets were made with pleated or gored skirts which were decorative and reached nearly to the knee. Until the twentieth century

Peg-top skirt, 1919

Peg-top evening skirt, 1964

Doublet skirt in gold and white, Flemish, 1522

Dirndl skirt, 1939

Green satin over-skirt tied back with red velvet bows showing grey silk lining and cream silk under-skirt, 1670

Cocktail dress with mini skirt, 1966

Black lace dinner gown with uneven skirt hemline, 1929

Pencil skirt, French, 1950

Blue velvet coat with maxi skirt over grey nylon mini skirt, 1969

Tunic and hobble skirt, Austrian, 1914

Panier or hoop skirt, English, 1750

Skirt over wheel or French farthingale with drum ruffle, English, c.1600

Skirt over Spanish farthingale, Spanish, c.1600

Two-colour bustle skirt with train, French, c.1875

Carriage dress with double skirt over crinoline, English, 1859

Evening dress with two-colour bustle skirt and train, English, 1886

Divided skirt, 1959

women's skirts were long, extending at least to the ankles and, recurrently, ground-length and with a train. Marked differences of shape were produced by the recurring theme of a framework of some kind worn under the skirt, either as a stiffened or whaleboned petticoat or as a padded roll or basket tied on at the waist (see *Bustle, Crinoline, Farthingale* and *Panier*). Over the centuries, a recurring fashion was for the overskirt to be open in front to display the underskirt which was equally decorative but of different colour and material. Sometimes, especially in the late seventeenth and early eighteenth centuries, the overskirt was looped back at the sides to display the lining and fastened there by brooches or sash ties.

From the 1890s onwards named, varied designs of skirts followed quickly upon one another. The *bell skirt* of the 1890s was a long, gored and flared design held into a bell form by tapes sewn into the lining. The bell-shape has recurred at intervals since as has also the *circular skirt*. This is cut as a circle of material with a hole left in the centre for the waist. It was worn in the 1890s and was revived in the late 1940s; the short version is worn by skaters. Between 1910 and 1920 skirt styles changed rapidly. There was the *harem* which was based upon Turkish trousers; it was a full design draped and gathered in to the ankles. The *peg-top* had a full draped *panier* effect on the hips diminishing in width towards the ankles. The *hobble skirt* at first had a wide band encircling it just below the knees; also based on Turkish trousers it was very restricted at the ankles making it difficult to walk and after a year or so was adapted to a more convenient style draped and tapered towards the ankle. *Tunic skirts* of varied design appeared; some had two or three tiers of tunic over a draped, narrow skirt. Evening dress tiers were flared and wired out like lampshades or minarets (see *Tunic*).

In the 1920s came the skirt with the uneven hemline, worn in the early years gently to break in the short skirts and, again in the later 1920s, to endeavour to bring back the longer hemlines once more.

Generally one or more longer floating panels were added to the skirt at the back or sides. In the 1930s the *bias cut*, introduced by Mme Vionnet in the 1920s, was fashionable. This led to skirts, long and calf-length, which clung to the figure. Very popular for informal wear in the late 1930s and the 1940s was the Austrian peasant *dirndl*, a very full skirt gathered into a tight waist-band. Since 1945 there have been the New Look, full, long skirts, the ballet-length evening skirts, the *pencil* or *sheath* fitted skirt and, for various periods of time and overlapping in date, the *mini*, the *midi* and the *maxi*.

Among specific named skirt designs are the Hawaiian *hula*, the grass skirt of the dancers, the fitted sheath slit at the sides based on the Chinese *cheongsam* (see *Chinese dress*). The pleated, *divided skirt* was introduced in the 1880s for bicycling. Of knee- or mid-calf-length, this design was popular between the wars for sports and leisure wear; also known as a *culotte skirt*, it is really a pair of full shorts, designed so that the division is not readily apparent. The *wrap-around skirt* has been a useful leisure or beach style during much of the twentieth century. It is wrapped round the body left open at the side but fastened at the waist; it can, alternatively, be buttoned nearly to the hem.

Slashed garments

Dress in the years from 1520–40 in Europe was strongly influenced by the strange fashion for slashed decoration. The idea came from the costume of the Swiss and Bavarian mercenary, the *lansquenet* or *landsknecht*. Several different explanations exist, putting forward reasons for the origins of this type of ornamentation. One tells of how, after the battle of 1477, when the Swiss mercenaries had defeated the Burgundians, they mended their tattered uniforms with strips of banners and hangings from the tents of the vanquished enemy, producing a multi-coloured attire, slashed and showing different materials through the slits. Another states that the clothes of the lansquenets were too tight and that they slashed them to make themselves more comfortable, thus displaying the undertunic or shirt beneath. Whatever the reason for the beginning of this custom, by 1520 the fashion had spread over Europe. All garments for men and women received this treatment from tunics, hose and gowns to hats, boots and shoes. The garment beneath was pulled through the slits to form a puff of a different coloured material. The edges of the slash were embroidered or braided and the ends held by points or a jewelled clasp. The slashes were made in the most complex patterns, especially on the doublet bodice.

Sleeves

All possible permutations of design have been introduced into sleeve styles over the centuries and these have been revived and reintroduced into fashion according to their suitability for the current mode of dress. Early medieval sleeve designs were generally cut in one with the garment, not set-in. Most usually the sleeve of the outer tunic or gown was cut fully; it could be short, elbow, three-quarter or full-length. If it was not full-length it displayed the wrist-length undersleeve which was usually fitting. If it was long it was often very wide and flaring at the wrist, decorated by embroidered banding there and hanging down.

The later Middle Ages, from about 1350 onwards, displayed great variety in sleeve styles, many of which were revived in later periods. In the fourteenth century the *tightly-fitting sleeve* was fashionable, that of the outer tunic often ending at the elbow in a cuff and hanging tippets, while the undersleeve was decorated by a row of buttons from elbow to wrist and extended to the first row of knuckles on the hand. With the houppelande came the very wide loose sleeve, its edges cut into daggers. Fifteenth-century styles included the *bishop sleeve*, full and long and gathered into a tight wristband, which had been worn intermittently since sixth century Byzantine dress, the fuller *bag* or *bagpipe sleeve*, also fitting at the wrist, and the padded shoulder style. The *dolman* or *batwing* sleeve was worn in the early Middle Ages

SLASHED GARMENTS
Swiss landsknecht in slashed costume, *c.*1525

Green cloth doublet slashed on chest and sleeves to display white shirt. Young Englishman, 1528

and has reappeared at intervals since. Dolman was generally used to describe the style in the nineteenth century while batwing is a modern term. This is cut very wide at the armhole, almost to the waist, and diminishes towards the wrist; it was most commonly cut in one with the garment. The *hanging sleeve* appeared in many guises. The thirteenth century version was slit in front at elbow-level and the arm passed through the slit to display the long sleeve of the undergarment. The remainder of the outer, hanging sleeve then fell in folds behind the arm. Fifteenth century versions were often padded in hanging bag sleeves or fell, decoratively pleated, as sleeve capes. Hanging sleeves of the late fifteenth century fell as long tubes nearly to ground level.

The sleeve cut in one with the garment and not set-in was more common in earlier centuries as the set-in sleeve required a higher standard of tailoring to be stylish

Crimson velvet houppelande with gold circle decoration. Bag or bag-pipe sleeve, English, 1410

Overgown with three-quarter sleeve over fitted sleeve of under-gown, c.1300

Crimson tunic, hanging, pleated sleeve of gold and black, Italian, 1455

Bag sleeves, Danish, 1410

Surcote with hanging sleeves, English, 1250

Hanging bag sleeve, grey fur, Italian, 1435

Tunic with bag-pipe sleeve, English, 1380

Gold, patterned houppelande with wide bag-pipe sleeves, French 1440

Bishop sleeve, 1971

Bishop sleeve, Spanish, 1435

Hanging sleeve to gown, Finestrella sleeves to doublet. English, 1495

Fitted sleeve, 1965

Puffed and banded sleeves, Swiss, 1514

Dolman sleeve, French, 1913

Dolman sleeve, English, thirteenth century

Padded puff sleeve to gown, English, 1532

Hanging bag sleeve, English, 1450

Marie de' Medici, ice-blue satin gown with slashed sleeve showing gold brocade undersleeve, 1615

Upper sleeves puffed, of purple and green/blue with gold decoration. Lower sleeves of purple with white puffs pulled through the slashes, Italian, 1535–40

Princess Mary, English, c.1545. Black silk gown with bell sleeve turned back to display black velvet lining and red satin padded false sleeve

Catherine Howard, English; c.1540. Padded sleeves of black silk and velvet, gold aglets

Marie de' Medici, 1610. Deep purple satin gown with puffed, padded and banded sleeves

Anne of Cleves, 1539. Pink gown with gold banding. Very wide sleeves banded on upper arm

Sleeve with epaulet, English, 1614

Puffed, slashed and banded sleeve, English, 1630

Revival of puffed, slashed and banded sleeve, Swedish, 1802

Pagoda or funnel sleeve with engageantes, Russian, 1755

Princess Mary, English, 1552. Puff sleeves in black velvet and white fur.

Queen Henrietta Maria, English, 1640

Engageantes, French, 1728

Leg-of-mutton (gigot) sleeve, Polish, 1828

Banded loose sleeve, English, 1680. Prototype of marino faliero

Balloon or melon sleeve, English, 1894

Elephant sleeve, Dutch, 1834

Wide, loose sleeve typical of 1850s, Hungarian

Deep crimson velvet puff sleeves, English, 1895

Leg-of-mutton sleeve, Dutch, 1896

and comfortable. The *kimono* style, with a wide sleeve, was one version (see *Japanese dress*) and the magyar another. The *magyar sleeve* stemmed from the Hungarian peasant style and this was usually cut more narrowly at the elbow and widened again towards the wrist.

With the Renaissance an infinite variety of sleeves were introduced which were banded at intervals creating puffs which in turn were padded and slashed to display linings and undergarments. The late fifteenth century Italian *finestrella sleeve* became fashionable in Europe. This was a fitted design made in two or three parts, the sections being laced together with points and leaving the full puffs of the chemise or shirt to be bloused out between the sections. Puffed sleeves were heavily padded in the men's gowns of the 1530s and 1540s and women's gowns had similarly padded puffs to the upper sleeve and innumerable, jewelled slashes to the lower, with the fabric of the undergarment pulled through the slashes in small puffs. In the 1590s sleeves were padded all the way down but diminishing towards the wrist. Very fashionable was the sleeve banded at intervals all the way down the arm leaving the material to puff out in between. This was a style sometimes called '*virago*' and was reintroduced under the French First Empire as a *mameluke sleeve*.

Especially typical of women's dress in the years 1530–55 was the *bell sleeve* to the gown displaying a *false sleeve* beneath. The outer sleeve was fitting on the upper arm and opened out into a wide bell shape. The material was then turned back and fastened to the sleeve of the upper arm so displaying the lining of contrasting colour and fabric. The false sleeve was generally of a third colour and material and was padded, embroidered and jewelled and was slashed to display the white chemise through the slashes. In the 1560s and 1570s an up-standing *puff sleeve* was fashionable.

With the seventeenth century came simpler designs. In the early years men wore sleeves with *epaulet shoulders*. With the 1620s and 1630s came the sleeve slashed vertically from shoulder to wrist displaying the white shirt or chemise. By 1635 ladies' sleeves were three-quarter length, very full but unpadded, and were finished by elegant ruffles or lace cuffs.

From the later seventeenth century onwards men's coats were tailored with fitting *set-in sleeves* which widened towards the large cuffs. Women's sleeves were still full and often banded on the upper arm to give a wide open bell sleeve on the forearm. This style was reintroduced as the marino faliero sleeve of the 1830s. Eighteenth-century sleeves for ladies' gowns were generally fitting to the elbow where they were finished by a deep cuff or, later, as *pagoda* or *funnel sleeves*. These had one or more tiers of flounces sewn to the fitted part at the elbow. Below this sleeve were the silk and lace ruffles called, in French, *engageantes*. *Peasant sleeves* were worn in less formal attire, especially in central and eastern Europe; these were very full and had a dropped, gathered shoulder line. The material was gathered in again at the wrists.

Ladies' sleeves of the early nineteenth century were short puff styles or puffed out at the top and long and fitting below. In the 1830s the puff sleeves became much larger developing into the *leg-of-mutton* (in French *gigot*) *sleeve*, a style which was reintroduced in the 1890s. Also fashionable in the 1830s was the *elephant sleeve* in which the fullness dropped to a lower line resembling an elephant's ear before being gathered into a fitting wristband. The mid-century style was usually wide and flaring at the bottom and only three-quarter or bracelet length. An alternative fashion in the 1890s to the leg-of-mutton sleeve was the *balloon* or *melon* style. This was also full at the top and tight on the forearm but was stiffened into a more rounded melon shape and was not gathered in at the shoulder. The *raglan sleeve*, with its sloping shoulder line, was worn for coats and suits from the mid-nineteenth century (see *Coat, Raglan* and *Rainwear*). Fashionable in the twentieth century, in addition to revivals of past styles, were the *cap sleeve*, just covering the shoulder and the *bracelet-length sleeve* extending to about two inches above the wrist bone.

Leg-of-mutton sleeve, Swedish, 1830

Sealskin coat with falling leg-of-mutton sleeve, English, 1893

SLIPPER

Lady's slipper. Red velvet with gold bands. German, seventeenth century

Man's slipper of white silk embroidered in silver. Spanish, eighteenth century

White kid mule embroidered in coloured silk and silver, French, 1750

Lady's mule in striped silk, Spanish, eighteenth century

Man's slipper of snakeskin and black leather, English, 1890

Man's slipper of blue silk, appliqué embroidery, Chinese*

Turkish leather slipper (babouche style). Decoration of spangles, beads and silver thread*

Moroccan slipper in red leather with gold thread embroidery*

Turkish mule and sock of yellow leather (babouche style)*
*In Northampton Shoe Museum Collection

Slip
1) An undergarment worn as a foundation to a dress. In modern times an alternative term for a petticoat.
2) A corset cover.
3) An under-waistcoat.

Slipper
A lightweight, low-cut shoe, without fastening, worn indoors and for comfort. The name derives from the ease with which this footwear can be slipped on and off. Such shoes have been worn for centuries and many designs have been of the *mule* type which has no back or quarters, so can be slipped on more easily (see also *Pantoffle*). Earlier designs were heelless but, from the later seventeenth century onwards, heels typical of the style of the period were fashionable. Modern mules can have elegant heels when worn by women (low, flat heels for men) but are also especially suited as bedroom slippers when they are often heelless and made of soft fluffy materials – fur, down or washable nylon fur; these are also called *scuffs*. The Oriental mule, the *babouche*, was originally a Turkish design which was made of decorative, coloured leather and had upturned toes. Modern slippers, especially for men, are sometimes based on this style but usually with a western-type toe finish. From the mid-nineteenth century onwards many styles of slipper have been introduced for both sexes especially designed for ease and comfort in the home. The *carpet slipper* was one of these. Originally it was made with a wool upper comprising vamp and quarters and often embroidered in coloured cross-stitch and beads; the soft sole had no heel.

Slop, sloppe, slops
A term used in the singular from the Middle Ages to refer to many different kinds of loose-fitting garments: in the fourteenth and fifteenth centuries, a magic bag or a cassock, jacket, mantle or cloak, gown or overdress, also a slipper. In the sixteenth and early seventeenth century *slops*, in the plural, were the full trunk hose or wide, baggy breeches of the time; one leg of such hose was called a slop (see *Hose*). The term was also especially applied in the seventeenth century to sailors' loose breeches which were ready-made from inferior quality material. From this slops came to designate particularly cheap, ready-made garments of any type. *Spanish slops* were the trunk hose made fashionable in Spain in the second half of the sixteenth century, *Dutch slops*, the Dutch or German pluderhosen of these years and the early seventeenth century, while *small slops* were plainer, less full breeches open at the knee.

Smallclothes
In the late eighteenth and the nineteenth century a term for men's breeches.

Smock
From Saxon times until the eighteenth century a term for a woman's chemise (see *Chemise*). Derived from the old Norse *smokkr* and North Friesian *smok* = a woman's shift or sheath. The word *smock* was also linked with other undergarments, for example, a *smock-petticoat* and *smock-shirt*. *Smock frock* was the term applied to the farm labourer's traditional smock of coarse homespun linen or cotton worn as a working protective garment. This had long, full sleeves, a square collar and, usually, a yoke; it was gathered or smocked in front and hung fully to below the knees (see *Embroidery, smocking*).

Snap fastener
This American term has now almost taken over from the English *press stud*. Snapper is an abbreviation. A metal or plastic fastening made in two parts to be sewn to either side of an opening to be closed in a garment. One part is in male form, the other female and these fit tightly into one another to make a firm closure.

Snowshoe
An oval framework of light, bent wood shaped like a tennis racquet, strung in a net pattern with strips of rawhide, intestine or waterproofed thongs. When the boot is strapped to this framework, the wearer can walk in soft snow without sinking.

Traditional wear in Arctic and other snowy lands by Eskimos, North American Indians, Siberians etc.

Snuff box and bottle

Snuff is a preparation of powdered tobacco. The practice of taking snuff, that is of taking a pinch between the finger and thumb and sniffing and inhaling it, became fashionable in Europe about 1670–80 and continued so for both sexes until the early decades of the nineteenth century. Snuff boxes containing the powdered tobacco were carried in pockets. Some of the containers were exquisitely made, masterpieces of the craftsman's art in ceramic, enamelling and metalwork. Some boxes were painted with miniature portraits or landscapes, others were jewelled or engraved. In the Orient snuff bottles were widely used as containers in the eighteenth and nineteenth centuries. In China there were some beautiful pocket bottles while, for social occasions, larger bottles were set on the table for guests to partake. The workmanship in glass, cameo and coloured stones was very fine.

Socks

From the old English *socc*, the Latin *soccus* and the old High German *soch*, referring, from the early eighth century onwards, to a soft shoe or slipper. In the seventeenth

SLOP
Spanish slops, 1559

German pluderhosen, *c.*1600

SNUFF BOTTLE
Chinese snuff bottle. Blue and white glass

SNOWSHOE
Canadian snowshoe of wood, gut and leather. Buff leather boot, nineteenth century*

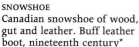

In Northampton Shoe Museum Collection

Japanese snowshoe of bent wood, about 21 inches long, 1900

SPANISH DRESS
Traditional capa and faja over breeches. Black felt hat.

century also used to refer to the Italian high chopine, the *zoccolo*. From the fourteenth century a sock was also a half-hose or short stocking, covering the foot and extending upwards to mid-calf level. In the nineteenth century men wore socks with pantaloons and trousers and, by the twentieth century, there were various lengths, styles and functions as, for example, bed-socks, golf-socks, ankle-socks, pop socks. (Knee-highs in the USA.)

Solitaire
1) A black neck ribbon worn by men on top of the stock in the eighteenth century (see *Stock*).
2) A single gemstone set in a ring or brooch.

Spanish dress
In the sixteenth century the colonization of the New World had given great wealth and power to Spain and the designs of dress established in the Iberian Peninsula influenced all of Europe not under Turkish rule. Initially there was strong resistance to Spanish dominance in dress from the areas of northern Europe under the influence of the Reformation but, by mid-century, Spanish styles were paramount. Spanish dress was characterized by its elegance, austerity, rigidity and superb decoration. Black was the dominant colour for normal wear; gayer colours were for special, festive occasions. Fabrics were rich and heavy, decoration was in gold and silver thread, with jewels and pearls. These qualities typified the Spanish way of life. Spanish rule was essentially that of the Roman Catholic Church which, in a restrictive, rigid manner, proscribed and opposed reform or change. The insistence upon traditional ceremonial at court, the limitations on the life of the people were epitomized in the elegant but profoundly uncomfortable constriction of the whaleboned and bombasted costume. These modes were beautiful works of art in themselves but artificial in form. The Moorish inheritance was still apparent especially in the textiles, the rich embroideries, the use of jewels and jewelled

buttons, points and ornaments as well as heavy girdles and collars. The jewelled buttons fastened to the centre front of the ladies' gowns stemmed from the Moorish style of coat dresses. This was a characteristic Spanish fashion unlike the long girdle chains terminating in pomander or pendant usual in France and England. The leather styles of shoes and chopine were decorated with Moorish motifs in silver or gold ornament and had slightly upturned pointed toes.

The Spanish contributed a number of innovations to sixteenth century costume. These included the cape, in all its varied forms, the corset and farthingale, the high neckline supporting a ruff and the bombasted doublet and trunk hose. During the century other nations took these up and extended and adapted them but Spain's use of these features was always restrained and austere (see *Cloak, Corset, Embroidery (Blackwork), Farthingale, Hose, Ruff*).

The shirt and chemise were white but often decorated with black silk embroidery – Spanish blackwork – sometimes intertwined with gold or silver thread. This decoration was employed especially at the edges of the elegant wrist ruffles and neck ruffle or collar. The Spanish were the first to take to the high neckline topped by the small ruff. The Spanish doublet accentuated a slim waist; it was pointed in front and was finished by narrow basques. Spanish slashing on chest and picadils was restrained and narrow, the undergarment barely showing through the slits. Padding was also restrained. With the doublet was worn the characteristic Spanish trunk hose.

Capes and cloaks had long been traditional Spanish garments. In the sixteenth century they came into their own and the fashion spread all over Europe. Spanish modes were greatly varied, in length, in fullness, the addition of hanging or open sleeves, the use of a wide collar or small turn-back one or none. The method of wearing differed also. The garment could be worn round both shoulders or only one or might be simply draped over an arm or slung round the body. The bullfighter's cloak, the *capa de paseo*, worn for his

Queen Isabella in black velvet gown over farthingale, gold fastenings to centre skirt opening. Jewelled girdle, buttons and neckchains. Ruff embroidered in black silk, 1565
Philip II in doublet, trunk hose, hose and shoes of yellow embroidered in silver. Brown satin gown with sable fur, 1553

Queen Isabella, 1615, in brocade gown over embroidered underskirt over farthingale. Lace-edged ruff
Man in brown and gold doublet, jerkin and trunk hose. Dark cape, 1600

The Infanta Maria Teresa, 1660. Pink and silver-grey dress over garde-infant framework

Torero in red satin attire richly decorated in gold. Black cap and shoes. Capa de paséo

Infanta Isabella Clara, 1584. White satin gown and under-gown with gold pattern over farthingale. Gold jewelled collar and girdle. Lace-edged ruff. Black hat with plumes and aigrette

SPATS
Grey cloth spat, 1920

SPENCER
Dark green silk spencer, English,
1820

ceremonial entry into the ring, was richly decorated and was cut in a semi-circle, with a collar. The rest of the torero's costume was made up of a silk or satin jacket and breeches, richly embroidered almost all over in gold or silver thread, and the characteristic black cap. Round his waist was wrapped that essentially Spanish article of apparel, the long sash, the *faja*. This was a traditional part of Spanish dress as was also the wide-brimmed sombrero, from which style were derived the Cavalier hats of the seventeenth century.

Sixteenth century women's dress was dominated by the corset and Spanish farthingale which, in Spain, was a bell shape. This form of skirt had been introduced in Spain as early as the fifteenth century and was maintained in fashion here later than elsewhere. Indeed, in the seventeenth century, time seemed to stand still in fashion and Spain, after leading European modes during the sixteenth century, now seemed to be in a backwater, unwilling to move forwards and clinging to the hieratic dress of the court with its corsetry, rigidity, heavy use of cosmetics and jewellery, its rich, be-jewelled fabrics. The contrast, in 1660, between the new modes now set by the French and the old-fashioned, formal approach of the Spanish was clearly apparent in the costumes worn by the French and Spanish courts for the wedding of Louis XIV and Maria Teresa, an event well recorded both in paint and written record. Maria Teresa herself wore the farthingale in its last phase, termed a *tontillo* or a *garde-infant*. As can be seen in Velasquez's portrait in the Prado, this is an immense framework skirt, flattened somewhat at back and front but extended widely at each side.

Spatterdashes, spats

Spatterdashes were leggings of leather or cloth, laced, buckled or buttoned on the outer side of the leg and worn to protect the stockings or trousers from being splashed while riding or walking. Worn from the seventeenth century onwards, *Spats* were a shortened version of these;

they were ankle-length, buttoned on the outer side and strapped under the shoe. They were fashionable from the mid-nineteenth century until the 1930s (see also *Gaiter*).

Spencer

1) A waist-length short jacket with collar, revers and long sleeves worn from about 1790 until 1825 (see *Coat* and *Jacket*).
2) A knitted, sleeveless undergarment worn for extra warmth from the late nineteenth century until the early twentieth century.

Spinel

A gem stone of a red or brownish-red colour resembling a ruby.

Spinning

The process of spinning is to draw out the fibres and twist them into a thread. Twisting is the important factor as this lays the fibres in a spiral formation and presses them together to form a thread. Natural fibres have irregularities and the spinning process hooks these into one another. For example, wool fibres are formed in overlapping scales, flax fibres have knots and cotton ones have bends or kinks. Silk is different in that it is already formed in a long continuous filament extruded from the worm (see *Silk*). The simplest and earliest method of spinning was by hand, pulling out the fibres, twisting them and winding the thread on to a spool. This was done in three separate processes. This very slow method was carried out in antiquity and by primitive peoples as was also spinning by means of a hooked stick, held between the fingers and twisted.

In all spinning there are three distinctive actions: the drawing out or attenuation of the raw material, twisting it and winding the thread on to a holder. The first equipment developed to speed up these processes was spinning by *spindle and whorl*, a method used throughout antiquity until the Middle Ages and one employed by most primitive peoples. The unspun fibre is carried on a large stick, the *distaff*, which can be held in one hand or stuck in the spinster's belt. The material is drawn out by hand from the distaff, teased between finger and thumb and attached by the twisted thread to the weighted, wooden stick, the spindle. This spindle is notched at one end to hold the yarn and has a disc of wood or pottery at the other to act as a flywheel and balance; this is the whorl which is set rotating to twist the thread. The spindle can be rotated in the hand, rested vertically on a support or, more commonly, be suspended in mid-air while the thread is being spun. After each section of thread has been spun it has to be wound by hand on to the spindle and the spinster secures the end of the thread again into the notch and repeats the process. Spinning could be carried out while walking, standing or sitting.

The invention of the *spinning wheel* greatly speeded up the process of spinning and increased its efficiency. It is not known when the wheel was first used but it is thought to have been introduced from the East and was in use in Europe from the fourteenth century. Known as the *great wheel* (also the *Jersey wheel* and the *Welsh farm spinning wheel*), it was first used to wind the thread, then to twist it but the two processes had to be carried out separately, one after the other. A groove was incised in the whorl and the spindle was mounted horizontally supported by bearings. It was rotated by means of a driving band from the large wheel which was also held by bearings. There was no treadle and the spinster stood, turning the wheel with the right hand and drawing out the fibre with the left; this sliver of wool was attached to the thread which was twisted as it was wound spirally off the end of the spindle. When a length of the thread had been spun the spinster held the yarn at a different angle to wind it on to the spindle, also using the motive power of the wheel.

The next development was the introduction of a flyer and bobbin so that the two processes of twisting and winding on could be carried out continuously without the spinster having to keep stopping spinning in order to wind on a spun length of thread. The *flyer* was a U-shaped piece of wood fitted with hooks along its curving arms. The flyer and the bobbin turned independently, each provided with a pulley but of different diameter. A driving cord passed twice in grooved channels in the wheel and continued round the two pulleys but, as the bobbin pulley was smaller, the bobbin revolved faster than the flyer which had the larger pulley; the difference in speeds meant that the yarn could be wound on to the bobbin continuously and, from time to time, the yarn was transferred to the next hook so that the bobbin was filled evenly. When the bobbin was full the flyer was unscrewed to enable it to be taken out and replaced. This type of spinning wheel with flyer and bobbin was known from about 1480 – Leonardo da Vinci designed such a wheel soon after this – but the *Saxony wheel*, as it was called, was based on a later design by Jurgens of Germany. In the sixteenth century a treadle was incorporated into the Saxony wheel which enabled the spinster to have both hands free to handle threads and raw material from the distaff. A further development with the treadle spinning wheel was to spin two threads at once one in each hand driven by two spindles. A variation, with doubling frame, produced a yarn of extra thickness as two yarns were twisted together. The parts of a treadle-driven Saxony wheel are shown in the illustrations of *Jurgens'* design and of an eighteenth-century English spinning wheel.

By 1760 it was becoming a matter of urgency to produce a machine which could speed up the process of spinning because, due to developments in the mechanization of weaving such as John Kay's flying shuttle (see *Weaving*), there was an acute shortage of spun yarn for the weavers to use so creating unemployment for them. A number of experimental 'spinning machines' had been designed but the first successful one was James Hargreaves' *Spinning Jenny*. The word 'jenny', like 'gin' and 'ginny', is a colloquialism for engine. *James Hargreaves* (1719–78) was a poor, illiterate Blackburn weaver in the cotton industry but a mechanical genius. In the

Ancient Egypt, 1300 BC

Sudan

Great wheel spindle

Hargreaves' spinning jenny spindle

Spinning mule spindle

Arkwright's water frame spindle

Spinning by spindle and whorl

Egyptian stone whorl

The Great wheel

early 1760s he designed a spinning machine with eight vertical spindles based on the great wheel principle. His spinning wheel, which was operated by the spinster's right hand, was placed on its side and had driving bands for each of the eight spindles. The turning of the wheel caused the spindles to rotate. The spinster's left hand operated the draw bar of the movable carriage which controlled the drawing out of the fibres from the distaff-tubes which held the slubbings of the corded material. The draw bar also controlled the lengths of twisted thread the distaff-tubes which held the slubbings of the corded material. The draw bar also controlled the lengths of twisted thread and the winding on of the spun yarn to the spindles. The tubes which held the slubbings were positioned vertically by two pieces of wood and the spindles twisted the threads powered by pulleys controlled by the driving bands on the wheel.

By 1766 Hargreaves had developed his jenny to take 16 spindles and the wheel was set in an upright position so that it was easier for the spinster to handle. By 1768 his home was being attacked by irate hand spinners and his jennies destroyed, so Hargreaves went to Nottingham where he ran a cotton spinning mill providing yarn for the local hosiery industry. He applied for a patent for his spinning jenny in 1770. The spinning jenny was widely used, especially in Lancashire, for producing cotton yarns. It was a simple machine which could be made without too great a cost and was popular both in the mill and with home cottage weavers.

The next development, almost contemporary with Hargreaves' jenny, was Arkwright's *Water Frame. Sir Richard Arkwright* was born in Preston in 1732. He came from a poor family and had little schooling but he was inventive, had a forceful personality and outstanding qualities as an entrepreneur. He studied a model of *Thomas Highs'* early spinning machine of 1763 and the roller drawing technique invented by *Lewis Paul* in 1738. He hired the services of John Kay and developed a roller spinning machine in 1768, taking out a patent the following year. This original experimental machine had four bobbins and flyers and the motive power was supplied by a horse mill.

After threats from local hand workers fearing unemployment, Arkwright moved to Nottingham where he went into partnership with *Jedediah Strutt* (see *Knitting*) and they established a mill there using a number of spinning machines, motivated by horse power, producing yarn for the hosiers. A horse mill was geared to a vertical shaft with a large pulley which drove the spindles by means of a belt; through a friction wheel the shaft gave motion to the rollers. In 1771 Arkwright moved to a larger mill at Cromford in Derbyshire which was driven by water power from the river Derwent. From about 1775 he developed larger machines which were improvements upon his earlier designs. Because of the water power these were known as water frames. From machines having eight spindles he went on to ones with 24 spindles and three pairs of weighted rollers. The upper rollers were

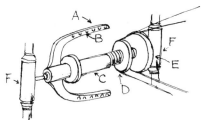

Detail of Jurgens' wheel
A Flyer
B Hooks
C Bobbin
D Bobbin pulley
E Flyer pulley
F supports

A Distaff to hold prepared fibres
B 2 cords, one to bobbin, one to bobbin screw
C The wheel, operated by treadle
D Spindle. Metal rod holding flyer, bobbin and bobbin screw
E Bobbin, for holding spun yarn
F Bobbin screw. A separate wheel which operates spindle and gives twist to yarn
G Maidens, which hold spindle
H Tension screw to adjust tension of driving bands
I Flyer. Distributes yarn evenly across bobbin
J Table
K Mother-of-all. Horizontal bar holding maidens and moved by tension screw
L Foot treadle
M Footman. Treadle arm
N Uprights. Hold axle for wheel

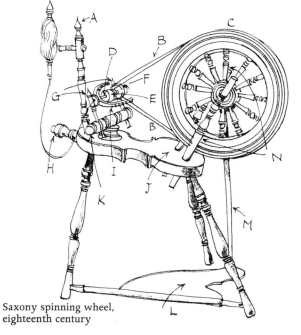

Saxony spinning wheel, eighteenth century

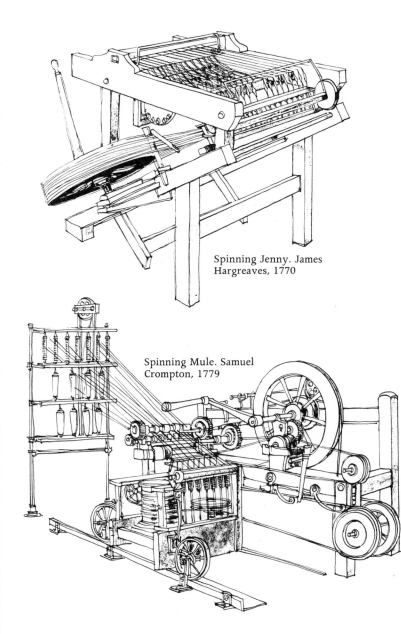

Spinning Jenny. James Hargreaves, 1770

Spinning Mule. Samuel Crompton, 1779

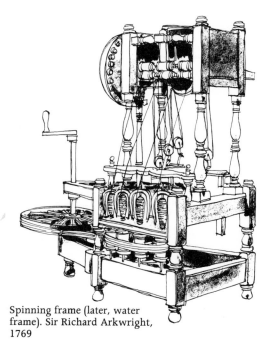

Spinning frame (later, water frame). Sir Richard Arkwright, 1769

Walking suit of
tweed with skirt
drawn up, 1886

All England Eleven
cricket attire, 1846.
White shirt and
trousers, black top
hat and belt

leather covered to give a cushioned surfacing and the lower ones were fluted. Great pressure could be applied so that the rollers could grip the cotton without injuring the fibres. The frame was driven from a vertical shaft which was powered by a water wheel; each shaft controlled two frames.

Like other inventors of the industrial revolution, Arkwright was many times threatened by angry workers and machine breakers. He built several mills and some were burnt down but he rebuilt and mobilized and armed his workers to defend themselves and their mill. A few years before he died, in 1790, Arkwright installed his first steam engine for driving power for his spinning machines.

The important characteristic of Arkwright's frame was his successful use of rollers which made finer yarn which was twisted and wound on to the bobbins by the same principle as the Saxony spinning wheel. The finished yarn was more evenly spun than that produced on Hargreaves' jenny.

In the 1770s a machine was devised which combined the principles of Arkwright's method of drawing out the material by rollers and Hargreaves' movable reciprocal carriage; this was Crompton's *Spinning Mule*. Samuel Crompton was born near Bolton in Lancashire in 1753. From boyhood he worked on the family cottage loom and at the age of 16 was spinning cotton yarn on one of Hargreaves' early small cottage jennies. Crompton was not pleased with the rather coarse and uneven yarn produced by the jenny so began to re-design it. He spent many years perfecting a spinning machine and by 1779 had produced a more complex design with rollers to draw out and attenuate the material and a carriage and system of stretching to give finer yarn. The travelling carriage supported a row of spindles set at an angle from the vertical which were driven by means of pulleys and drums.

Crompton sold the yarns which he produced on his machine and it was quickly appreciated that these were finer, softer and more even than any produced by

machine before. Because of their quality, which resembled Indian cottons, his machine was referred to as a *muslin wheel* but later it came to be called a spinning mule because of its hybrid nature, being a cross between a jenny and a water frame. Crompton's first mule had about 30 spindles but the design was soon enlarged and improved. As time passed larger machines were made, taking up to 1000 spindles, and the mule brought wealth and prosperity to Bolton because of its fame as a centre for spinning fine cotton yarns. Crompton, who died in poverty in 1827, had no share in this prosperity.

Crompton's mule was driven by hand but later it was operated by water power. In 1825 *Richard Roberts* of Manchester patented a shaper device, the cop, which made it into an automatic mule. After this most of the advances in techniques of spinning came from the USA, such as the *ring spinning frame*, developed by several inventors about 1830, and the later cap spinning frame, the tube frame and the fly frame.

Sports and recreational dress

Before the nineteenth century no special attire was devised for this purpose; on the whole ladies did not participate and men simply took off their coats and played cricket, for example, in shirt, waistcoat, breeches and stockings. During the first half of the nineteenth century men began to wear an accepted form of dress for sport and games through this was not specifically designed for the purpose. For cricket, from the 1820s, men usually wore white trousers with white shirts and boots. Short jackets with long sleeves could be worn on top and a hat was essential; this, until 1850, was a top hat and after this more usually a cap or round hat. Belts replaced braces.

More specific recommendations for sports and recreational costume came in the second half of the century. For men playing cricket striped, coloured blazers were introduced towards the end of the century also protective wear for the batsman and wicket keeper; before this the

White tennis dress, socks and shoes. Cap with shade, 1938.

White silk blouse, white belt and linen skirt, black tie, canvas shoes. Tennis, 1907

Striped cotton tennis dress, straw hat, 1884

Skating dress of dark green wool with crimson velvet and grey fur jacket. Pale green silk hat, gloves and accordion pleated skirt hem, 1875

Burberry jacket, cap and drawn-up skirt for golf, 1904

White blouse, black belt, navy skirt, straw hat, hockey, 1893

Cycling dress of 1892. Tweed cap, Norfolk jacket and knickerbockers. Socks, gaiters, shoes

Lady cricketer, 1890, in white blouse, skirt and rationals with coloured ribbon decoration. Red silk sash and bow. Cap, stockings, boots

Footballer of 1875 in striped jersey and socks, boots and plain knickerbockers

Navy serge gym
tunic, velvet neck-
band, white blouse,
black stockings
and shoes, 1930

Cycling costume of
tweed coat and
rationals, white
blouse, fawn
gaiters and gloves,
black boots, straw
hat, 1898

wearing of such padding was considered to be unsporting. W.G. Grace in 1888 recommended an outfit entirely in white, flannel trousers with belt or scarf to keep them up, shirt, jersey if needed, a cap and boots. Football was a game dating from medieval times but the modern sport developed from the public schools of the nineteenth century. Special attire stemmed from the 1860s when players wore knicker-bockers and jerseys with stockings, ankle boots and a pill-box cap. The knicker-bockers were slowly replaced by shorts, knee-length ones in the 1880s, shorter by 1900. Hockey costume followed a similar pattern.

From the 1870s onwards, for other games and sports, men adopted blazers with trousers or Norfolk jackets with knicker-bockers. For golf, blazers of certain colours were demanded by some clubs, red at Wimbledon, for example, but, in general, by the 1890s the Norfolk or lounge jacket with knickerbockers in matching tweed with cap and woollen socks were the usual attire. A similar costume was worn for bicycling, very popular from the 1890s, skating, walking, croquet and mountain climbing and walking.

For ladies the problem was much more difficult. Their everyday dress in the second half of the nineteenth century, when they began to participate seriously in such games, was one dominated by rigid cor-setry, crinolines and bustles covered by ample petticoats and very long skirts, all quite unsuitable for partaking of any form of energetic exercise. The only alleviation was provided in the 1860s, when ladies were trying to walk in the country and the mountains in crinoline skirts, by a device which raised up the skirt hem by eight cords or suspenders attached underneath at the waist. A further development in the 1870s was for buttons to be sewn round the waistband so that the hem of the skirt, which was provided with buttonholes, could be looped up to the waist. If a man should appear in the distance the buttons could quickly be unfastened and the skirt allowed to fall to ground level once more. By the 1880s some types of special attire

were being recommended for tennis, hockey and bicycling but these were of the Bloomer Tennis Costume variety, consist-ing of a knee-length, belted, long-sleeved dress worn over 'rationals', that is, knee-length bloomers, with stockings, gaiters and boots. Such an attire may have been less restrictive than the normal day dress but it was distinctly unattractive and un-feminine so most women opted for what they normally wore and struggled to run in long skirts and layers of petticoats.

A more desirable, yet not unfeminine, attire came in the 1890s and variations of it were worn for tennis, bicycling, cricket, hockey, golf, shooting and walking. Such costumes were not what a modern girl would call practicable but they were at least a step in the right direction towards that end. A navy serge skirt to the ground, a high-necked shirt blouse with masculine collar and tie, jacket and straw or felt hat, gloves and canvas shoes or leather boots could be worn for most sports. For bicycl-ing the attire varied from ordinary day dresses, where the skirt had to be held down by means of a loop of elastic sewn to the hem and kept in place by the feet on the pedals, or the special costume for the enthusiast, consisting of a knee-length coat on fashionable lines over rationals, gaiters and boots and a straw or felt hat. For certain games, specific costumes were recom-mended; in 1890, Lillywhite's supplied an officially approved ensemble for cricket consisting of a calf-length dress in fashion-able style with stockings, boots and peaked cap. By the late 1890s, the skirt had daring-ly been shortened to the knee.

For cycling and walking, in particular, various attempts were made in the 1890s to design a garment which would replace the ground-length skirt which was clearly unsuitable. A divided skirt was attempted but was so ornamented with flounces as to defeat its purpose. A skirt shortened to just above the ankles was worn with a jacket but the most comfortable covering for the legs were the loose knickerbockers. At first these 'unmentionables', as they were termed, were hidden beneath a skirt but towards the end of the decade they became visible, reaching to just below the knee and accompanied by a slightly shorter coat or jacket and skirt. These knicker-bockers were first known as bloomers (see *Bloomers*) but also as *rationals*.

For games and gymnastics in girls' schools the *gym tunic* made its appearance by 1890. In the early 1900s it was widely adopted for school and college teams and soon as a school uniform. The gym tunic was comfortable and allowed free move-ment in energetic pursuits. It had a square neckline and three box pleats back and front. It was knee-length and was tied at the waist with a braid girdle. Gym tunics were made in varied colours according to the school choice; underneath was worn a long-sleeved white blouse and long black or dark stockings.

With the twentieth century sports dress, especially for women, was becoming more practical. For tennis, hats were abandoned by 1908 and the costume was all white. Skirts were a little shorter – ankle-length – and long stockings were worn underneath. A calf-length navy skirt was usual for other games. A measure of the interest aroused in women in playing games is shown by the inclusion of sports attire in the fashion journals of the early twentieth century.

In the 1920s and 1930s there was a further increase in the popularity with both sexes in outdoor pursuits especially cycling and country walking (or hiking, as it was generally termed). Men wore open-necked, short-sleeved sports shirts, informal pull-overs and plus fours (see *Knickerbockers*); for summer, shorts were becoming popular. In ladies' wear shorts and slacks had come in by 1930. The early shorts were narrow and masculine-styled but pleated, fuller designs appeared by the mid-thirties. Wrap-over and divided skirts were fashionable by 1939. In tennis dress, it was Suzanne Lenglen who pioneered the head bandeau and knee-length white tennis dress, styled in characteristic 1920s line and worn over long white stockings and socks. By the 1930s a white blouse and shorts with bare legs and ankle socks was the accepted mode followed, just before the war, by the attrac-tive tennis dress with skirt above the knees

Bicycling dress of tweed jacket and skirt, white bodice, gaiters, boots, gloves, 1889

Hiking costume 1931. Orange wool jumper, green linen shorts, wool socks, black beret

White tennis dress, stockings, socks, canvas shoes and bandeau, 1927

(see also *Bathing dress* and *Beachwear and seaside dress*).

Starch
A substance made from flour and from certain plants which, when mixed with water, becomes a liquid gum or paste. Employed in costume to stiffen cotton, linen and lawn fabrics and used especially in the sixteenth century for collars, caps and ruffs (see *Ruff*).

Stayband
A headband with bib ends worn by young babies. When the ends were pinned down in front the band provided a support for the baby's head.

Stock
A stiffened neckcloth wrapped round the neck and fastened with a buckle or tie at the back. The stock was fashionable from about 1735, taking over from the cravat, until the 1840s, though it was occasionally worn later in the century. It continued in use with the riding habit of both men and women until well into the twentieth

STOCK
Black stock over white collar, King George IV, English

Black solitaire worn with bag wig and white stock

STOLE
White tulle stole with
embroidered edge, German,
1811

Yellow and tan striped stole
with tan fringe, Spanish, 1798

century. The stock was most often white but could be black or, rarely, coloured. In the eighteenth century a *solitaire* was fashionable, worn on top of the stock; this was a black ribbon tied round the neck to finish in a bow at the throat or with the ends tucked into the shirt front. Most commonly the solitaire accompanied the wearing of a bag wig (see *Solitaire* and *Wig*).

Stockinette, stockinet

Originally a knitted textile, usually cotton, having an elastic quality and used especially for underwear and stockings. Derives from stocking-net, that is, the stocking stitch mesh of the knitted fabric. Also a closely-woven textile, with elasticity, most generally of wool, resembling the knitted textile.

Stockings

A knitted or woven covering for the leg and foot. Such covering, made in different lengths, had been worn from the early centuries AD but was known by various other names; for the history before the later sixteenth century see *Chausses* and *Hose*. In the early sixteenth century the lower part of the hose were termed stocks or netherstocks, then stocken or stocking of hose; by about 1580 the word stocking had come into general use for the separate covering for the leg from the knee downwards and knitted stockings replaced the woven material tailored in sections to fit the leg (see *Knitting*). Seventeenth century stockings were made in various colours to suit the rest of the costume; the best quality ones were of silk and many of these were decorated with elaborate designs of clocks. Less expensive stockings were made of cotton or wool. Later, lisle stockings were produced which were made of cotton which had been given a silky texture by a mercerizing process.

During the sixteenth to the nineteenth centuries when men wore stockings, these were fastened by a garter round the leg just below the knee. In the 1820s and 1830s as trousers and pantaloons took over from breeches, stockings were replaced by socks. Over the centuries ladies had also kept their stockings up by means of garters. Alternatively the stocking could be fastened to the underwear until, in the nineteenth century, suspenders were attached to the corset for the purpose of supporting the stocking (see *Suspenders*).

The colour of ladies' stockings varied greatly from age to age. While gown skirts were long, reaching to ground level, ladies could please themselves about the colour of their stockings. When, in the 1770s and 1780s, the skirt rose a few inches above the ground, the stocking was either coloured to match the gown or could be red, white or a pastel shade. In the years 1820–50 stockings were most commonly white or flesh-coloured. A black net stocking worn over a flesh-tinted one was considered very fashionable. Coloured stockings were re-introduced in the 1860s, while by 1880, they were usually made to match the gown or petticoat; black net returned to favour in the 1890s.

It was during the First World War that ladies' skirts rose above the ankle and it became more important to choose a suitable stocking colour. For day wear these were generally beige, grey or black, while for evening it was preferable for them to match the gown. With the shorter skirts of the 1920s flesh-tinted stockings came into their own, in silk for preference, in lisle or wool otherwise. During the Second World War many women went bare-legged as much as possible because of a shortage of silk stockings, but when the war was over the nylon stocking began to replace the silk one. The first nylon stockings had been shown by Du Pont at the New York Fair of 1938 and were put on sale in the USA in 1939. The war interrupted the smooth process of development and marketing the nylon stocking but after 1945 it was only a question of building up sufficient supplies before the silk stocking was totally supplanted by nylon.

It was the mini-skirt of the 1960s which rendered the stocking an out-moded fashion and nylon tights (panty hose in America), essential for wearing with a mini-skirt, were also adopted by the vast majority of women for general wear because they were warmer and did away with the need for belts and suspenders to support them (see also *Leotard* for body stocking). Apart from the sheer nylon tights and stockings available in many shades, there has also been produced a wide range of heavier-weight, brightly coloured, lacy-patterned versions for winter wear.

Stole

In classical antiquity the stola was a long gown or robe (see *Rome, ancient*) and the term stole for a long time was used to describe such a garment. By the early Middle Ages a stole was an ecclesiastical vestment in the shape of a narrow strip of material worn round the shoulders. In this later form the stole was revived as a long scarf worn by women, especially in the years 1790–1820, when the vogue for classical dress was marked and when the wearer of the thin clothing required added warmth. Such stoles could be of fur, feathers or any fabric from transparent gauze to cashmere or velvet and were embroidered, fringed and decorated in a variety of ways. Some stoles were narrow strips of material, others broader, up to a yard in width. The custom of wearing a stole has been revived in the twentieth century for wear with evening dresses.

Stomacher

A decorative panel of a V or U shape worn attached to or separate from the front of a doublet or gown. Worn by men in the late fifteenth and the sixteenth centuries and women from about 1570 until the 1770s. In the sixteenth century the stomacher was characteristic of Spanish dress; it was part of a stiffened bodice front like a breastplate and was reinforced by strips of metal and/or whalebone to maintain the smooth, rigid form of the doublet or gown bodice. It was worn over the body garment (often laced to it) and descended to a sharp or rounded point at the waist. The stomacher was usually ornately decorated either all over or in part with lace, ribbons or jewelled embroidery and it was in a different material and colouring from the remainder of the costume. If the gown or

Figured black vlieger with black velvet edging over pink taffeta skirt and gold and black stomacher. Gold sleeves with black bands. Dutch, 1590–1600

Gold and brown gown embroidered all over, under-skirt striped red and gold, sleeves white with red ribbons, white stomacher. Spanish, *c*.1665

Blue taffeta gown over pale blue silk petticoat with pink and green sprig pattern, striped, brocaded stomacher. English, 1715–20

SUITS
Party suit in rose-
coloured velvet,
English, 1971

doublet was plain, the stomacher was patterned, if the gown was patterned all over, the stomacher might be plain. In the later seventeenth and first half of the eighteenth century the front of the stomacher was often decorated with graduated ribbon bows (see *Échelle* and *Plastron*).

Suède cloth, suede finish
A textile with the surface treated to imitate suède leather.

Suit
A complete costume usually made of one material and consisting of a jacket, waistcoat and trousers for men and a jacket, skirt and blouse for women. The tradition for a man's suit had its origins in the *habit à la française* of the eighteenth century, which comprised a coat, waistcoat and breeches, though these were not by any means commonly of the same material or colour. In the later eighteenth century and for the first half of the nineteenth men wore tail coats of varied design (see *Coat*), which did not match the breeches or trousers and it was only in the late 1850s that a jacket coat came to be worn and this was only made as a suit in matching fabric for all three garments from the 1860s. At this time the cut was poor and the attire somewhat ill-fitting but the suit was only intended for very informal and country wear. By the later 1870s the *lounge suit*, as it was termed, was worn more often and the cut was improved; the revers were still high, the collar small and the front edges were rounded off. With the 1890s the lounge suit became respectable wear for town as well as country and the rounded front edges had become square cut. An evening lounge suit, dinner jacket with trousers, had been introduced (see *Evening dress*).

During the twentieth century the lounge suit has gradually developed from being the normal office and city suit, worn for most other occasions also in a less formal material, apart from holiday and leisure wear, to being reserved for town and evening attire. Trousers have altered in cut during the twentieth century following the

general trend for these garments, through straight cut designs with turn-ups, wide Oxford bag styles to drainpipes and, finally, hipsters and bell-bottoms (see *Trousers*). Jackets have changed less, but length, revers styles, single or double-breasted designs and, above all, materials used, have kept pace with current trends. The movement towards richly-coloured velvets and corduroys for festive wear suits has brought men's fashion full circle back to eighteenth century preferences in reaction from the black and dark worsteds of the Victorians. Since the Second World War the waistcoat has gradually been worn less and less. For Norfolk jacket and knickerbocker suits see *Jacket, Knickerbockers* and *Sports dress*; for Eton suits see *Children's dress, Collar* and *Jacket*: for boiler suits and siren suit see *Jumpsuit*; for Mao suit see *Chinese dress*.

Tailored suits for *women* began to form part of the wardrobe from the 1880s, worn especially for walking, leisure wear and the office; since then, the suit in one design or another has been an essential part of a woman's wardrobe. The suit has varied in these years, over almost a century, in tune with the current fashion trends. In the years between 1880 and 1910 the skirts followed the silhouettes of the gowns, through bustle draperies to bell-shaped pleated skirts and gores. Jackets of the 1880s had a short, flared skirt or peplum in order to rest on the bustle at the back; by Edwardian times they were longer to cover the hips. In the 1890s and early years of the new century tailoring was of the highest standard and tailored suits, worn with softly feminine or masculine shirt blouses with ties, were very popular. By 1905 the suit was the accepted fashionable street wear. Navy, brown, green and black broadcloth and serge were fashionable, with white for summer.

The years 1914–20 saw great variety in styles, reflecting the bizarre skirts of these years but the twenties had a straight, waistless silhouette. Suits were especially fashionable after 1924; the shorter skirts were often pleated all round and blouses, generally of crêpe de chine or jersey wool or silk, were worn outside the skirt and

Green wool suit with dark green braid trimming, English, 1907

Plain gabardine suit with velvet collar, English, 1918

Brown tweed suit, German, 1885

Fawn tweed suit of jacket, waistcoat and skirt, English, 1893

Trouser suit in red, black and fawn patterned wool over red wool tunic with black belt, English, 1972

Black suit with black velvet collar, English, 1949

Mustard yellow woollen suit with yellow-green collar, cuffs and belt, English, 1926

Grey wool suit with hat to match, French, 1950

Striped wool suit in grey and bright green, green silk blouse, collar and cuffs, English, 1967

SUIT
Dark brown tweed
three-piece suit
for leisure wear,
English, 1860

Grey stripe mixture
lounge suit,
English, 1914

Light grey tweed
suit with braid
edging, English,
1885

Check worsted
brown suit,
English, 1968

ended on the hips, often with a belt (see *Fashion Designers*, Chanel).

The suits of the 1940s were chunky and square, with padded shoulder line and straight skirts just covering the knee but, with the New Look, the full, small-waisted, swinging skirt came in, accompanied by an elegant short, waisted jacket. From the 1960s onwards, the tailored suit was replaced by the informal, softer-line suit and the *trouser suit* has become more than an acceptable alternative (see *Fashion Designers*, Courrèges). For sunsuits (see *Beachwear*).

Sumptuary laws
Laws passed to regulate expenditure and curb excess. In costume, many such laws were passed in Britain and Europe over the 400 years between about 1300 and 1700. There were two specific purposes for such legislation; firstly, to restrain imports of what was usually a costly, foreign product in order to protect the home industry and, secondly, to maintain a social class structure by permitting only specific persons of rank and position to wear certain garments, fabrics and decoration. Examples of the first type of legislation were Edward III's Act of 1337 and Charles II's of 1666 restricting the import of foreign cloth in order to protect the English woollen trade and Jean-Baptiste Colbert's legislation of the 1660s to prohibit the importation of foreign lace into France in order to protect the infant French lace industry (see *Lace*). In the early fourteenth century Venice, the then leader of European fashion, became one of the first places in Europe to pass a number of sumptuary laws in order to endeavour to limit the natural instinct of its people to express their wealth and status in luxury apparel, an extravagance which threatened the economy of the city state.

A well-defined system of class status was a characteristic of the fourteenth and fifteenth centuries in Europe and sumptuary legislation, such as Edward III's Act of 1363, as well as those of many other countries, were passed to enumerate categorically which fabrics, furs and types of ornamentation were permitted to which

Red sideless
surcote with white
fur plastron and
edging. Blue
undergown with
jewelled hip belt,
Austrian, *c.*1410

Silver-grey sideless
surcote with
ermine trimming.
Red undergown
with gold design,
German, 1350–60

Parti-coloured
surcote, deep pink
on right, ultra-
marine and yellow
stripes on left,
German, 1310–30

Cyclas or surcote
of pink, under-
gown of spotted
blue, German,
1310–30

Cyclas or surcote
in white, Italian,
1305

Striped surcote in
strawberry pink
and purple stripes,
white lining,
German, 1310–30

classes of society. The most popular decorative material for the edges and linings of
garments in the fifteenth century was fur
and one's status was made evident by which
fur one was allowed to wear. In addition,
in countries such as England and France,
a restriction on the wearing and, therefore,
the importation of costly Russian and
eastern European furs would assist the
important home industries which traded
in hides and furs. For example, furs permitted for use by royalty and the wealthy
aristocracy included marten, vair and
ermine (see *Furs*). Descending the social
scale one comes to otter, fox, beaver, lamb,
goat and wolf.

Surcoat, surcote

A garment worn on top of the tunic or cote.
The medieval fashion for a super- or overtunic was introduced in the late twelfth
century as a tabard (see *Tabard*). By 1220
this had developed into a loose, sleeveless
garment with large armholes worn over the
tunic or gown. The masculine version was
often only three-quarter length, showing
the bliaud or cote below. Later in the
century the garment developed sleeves;
these were generally loose and long and
had a slit in front at elbow-level for the
arm to pass through so that they became
hanging sleeves (see *Sleeve*). A purse was
often attached to a waist or hip belt worn
round the bliaud beneath; slits, called
fitchets, were then made in the surcote (see
Fitchet). In the early fourteenth century
the belt was more commonly worn round
the outer garment, encircling the hips. The
surcote became a little less loose and three-
quarter sleeves were more usual than
hanging ones.

Women wore a surcoat in the thirteenth
century also. At this time the garment was
generally called a cyclas (see *Cyclas*); at

SURCOAT, SURCOTE
Sleeveless surcote,
French, thirteenth
century

Sideless surcote
with jewelled
plastron and fur
edging, French,
1390

first it was sleeveless, with wide armholes, but later had hanging or three-quarter sleeves like those of the men. In the early fourteenth century the cyclas became more waisted and fitting on the torso.

Between the years 1340 and 1460 the *sideless surcoat* was fashionable wear for women (see *Gown*). This had an almost off-the-shoulder wide neckline and immensely large armholes reaching to the hips. The neck and armholes were edged with fur or a band of jewelled embroidery and, in addition, down the front, was a fur plastron often set with jewelled buttons down the centre which attached it, for support, to the gown beneath. Sometimes the central fur strip was very narrow and required such assistance to take the weight of the immensely, full, long skirt, gathered into the 'armholes' at hip level. In some designs the plastron was wide and had deep fur edging round both armholes.

Suspenders
1) American and alternative term for braces (see *Braces*).
2) Sock suspenders introduced for men's socks in the late fifteenth century; these consisted of a band of woven elastic worn round the calf with a dependent suspender to attach to the sock.
3) From about 1880 elastic suspenders were attached to the lower edge of women's corsets by a shaped belt and supported the stockings (in the USA detachable garters). (see *Corset*).

Swansdown
1) The soft down feathers of a swan used for muffs, boas, pèlerines, also for powder puffs.
2) A warm cotton (also wool) fabric, first made in China and also known as Canton or cotton flannel.

Swatch
A sample or specimen of cloth to show colour, design and texture.

Synthetic and man-made fabrics
These are made from fibres which are not of natural origin such as wool, silk, flax and cotton, but have been produced by the chemical treatment of raw materials such as wood pulp and extracts and by-products of petroleum and coal. Such fibres have now become numerous and appear even more so as different countries give different names to designate their products. The manufacturing processes for man-made fibres are similar. The raw materials are chemically treated and, if necessary, melted by heating to produce a viscous liquid which can be extruded through a series of fine holes to form filaments which can then be twisted, woven or knitted into fabrics. Alternatively, such fibres can be made in staple form, that is, the filament lengths are cut into short staples which can be combed, drawn and spun into yarn in the same manner as natural fibres; they can also be blended, if desired, with natural fibres before spinning.

The theory of making an artificial fibre dates back to the seventeenth century when the Englishman Robert Hooke enunciated in his *Micrographia* of 1664 the possibility of making such a fibre which could be extruded in a similar manner to the process followed by the silkworm (see *Silk*). In 1734 the Frenchman René A.F. Réamur suggested possible ways in which gums and resins could be similarly handled. Further steps in the theory were provided by the English silk weaver Louis Schwabe in 1842 when he exhibited an apparatus with a nozzle containing fine holes through which filaments of glass could be spun, very much in the manner of the spinnerets through which were later spun filaments of rayon. The first patent for the manufacture of an artificial textile was issued in 1855 to the Swiss George Audemars who prepared fabrics from the inner bark of the mulberry and other trees and nitrated and dissolved them in a mixture of ether and alcohol then combined this with a rubber solution to form a spinning mixture. A further stage was advanced when the Englishman Sir Joseph Swann was seeking a more satisfactory carbon filament for electric light bulbs. He patented a process in 1883 to make such a filament by squeezing a nitro-cellulose solution into a coagulating medium and denitrated the filament.

None of these steps actually produced an artificial fabric but assisted in the route towards this. The process of doing this was enunciated by the Frenchman Comte Hilaire de Chardonnet, often referred to as 'the father of the rayon industry', who, after years of experimentation, produced his first fabric in 1884 from a nitrocellulose solution of mulberry leaf pulp. He exhibited articles made from this in the Paris Exposition of 1889 and so gained financial backing to set up a factory at Besançon where the first commercial production of rayon began in 1891. This nitrocellulose process was followed by a cuprammonium process but the most successful method for the production of rayon was the viscose process which derived from the researches of a group of chemists in the 1890s. In this method the cellulose material is produced from wood pulp. A fourth method, the acetate process, was developed after the others and the commercialization of this was carried out by Henri and Camille Dreyfus.

Known as artificial or art silk, this man-made fabric did not develop sufficiently attractive qualities until the 1920s to become an important costume material. By then it entered into general use for clothing, especially in the field of underwear. In 1924 the name *Rayon* was adopted in the USA to designate this synthetic textile made from a cellulose base.

Nylon was the first completely synthetic fibre and is produced entirely from mineral sources. It is a polyamide fibre composed of nitrogen and oxygen (derived from air), carbon and hydrogen, the two last-named being originally derived from coal but now from oil and natural gas. Nylon was developed in the USA in the Du Pont laboratories over a long period from 1927 to 1938, research which cost over 27 million dollars. This remarkable fibre was first made into stockings commercially in 1939 and later into other garments. Nylon was the first name for the fabric and describes a family of man-made fibres which are now available under a number of brand names according to type and country of origin; these include: Bri-Nylon, Enkalon, Antron, Perlon, Cantrece, Celon, Qiana and Nomex. Ban-lon is a textured, bulk nylon fabric.

The polyester fibres also sprang from work carried out in this field by the Du Pont laboratories in the 1930s but commercial development did not begin until 1950. A man's suit was displayed to the press in the USA in 1951 made in Dacron, Du Pont's trade name, and its remarkable crease-resistant and lightweight qualities were demonstrated in that it had been worn for 67 days without being pressed, had twice been worn for a dip in the swimming pool and had been washed in a washing machine, all without suffering undue ill effects. The British equivalent polyester fibre is Terylene, produced commercially by I.C.I. in 1955. These polyester fibres are derived from air, water and oil products and are now made by a number of countries, for example, Diolen and Trevira in Germany, Terlenka in Holland, Tergal in France, Terital in Italy, Tetoron in Japan and Spinlene in Scandinavia. Crimplene is a bulked form of Terylene.

Acrylic fibres are derived from an oil-refining and coal-carbonizing process and are ideal for making fabrics which give warmth while being lightweight. The material is used especially for blankets, carpets, fur-type pile fabrics and knitwear. First commercially manufactured in the USA by Du Pont as Orlon in 1952, there are now a number of acrylic and modacrylic fibres as, for instance, Britain's Courtelle and Teklan, Germany's Dolan and Dralon, France's Crylor and America's Acrilan, Sayelle and Dynel.

Metallic yarns have also been developed, notably the American Lamé, Lurex and Metlon and the French Rexor (see *Silver cloth*). Stretch fabrics include Lycra, developed in the USA and presented in 1959, Helanca, Vyrene, Spanzelle and Elura (see *Elastic, Elasticized materials, Elastomers*).

T

Tabard

Was introduced in the early Middle Ages as a covering for the Crusading knight's armour as a practical measure to conceal the sun's glare upon the metal in hot countries. It was adopted for civilian use in the twelfth century as a loose, rectangular garment hanging back and front over the tunic or bliaud (see *Surcoat*).

TABARD
Tabard over tunic, Danish, *c*.1200

TABLIER
Black silk day dress with black lace, buttons, fringe and bow trimming. Tablier skirt (apron front), 1872

Deep violet silk day dress with self-colour piping, fringe trimming, belt bows and buttons. Tablier skirt (apron front), 1868–70

Tablier

French for apron. The complex bustle skirts of the late 1860s and the 1870s were draped up towards the back. The overskirt was usually open in front and looped back at each side, leaving a decorative apron form in the centre. Alternatively, the open overskirt was allowed to fall on each side with one corner descending towards the hem of the underskirt; the back part of the overskirt was then fastened up under the bodice basque.

Tache

From old French *tache* = fibula, a mechanism for fastening two parts of a fitting together: a clasp, buckle, hook and eye, press stud etc.

Taj

Arabic word for crown. Used chiefly to denote a crown or head-dress of distinction. The open, circular, Middle Eastern design derives from the ancient Persian crown and that of Mesopotamia (see *Persian dress*).

Tapa cloth, bark fibre cloth, wood bast fabric

A fabric obtained by soaking in water the bark of certain trees, then beating it to the required size and thickness. The finished fabric was then dried and could be painted or dyed in coloured designs and used for clothing, hangings and bed-coverings. It was made in many parts of the world, notably north-west, central and southern America, equatorial Africa, Indonesia, Malaysia and Oceania; of these, the Pacific Polynesian fabric was of the best quality. *Tapa* is a Polynesian word meaning a fabric made from the inner bark of certain trees but the terms bark fibre cloth and wood bast fabric are used elsewhere. The making of tapa used to be one of the most important industries on islands such as Fiji, Tahiti, Hawaii, Samoa and Tonga but most examples of the material are now in the world's museums and production is rare. The best tapa was made from the paper mulberry tree which was especially cultivated in plantations but it could also be made from other sources such as the bread fruit tree, a native raspberry and the hibiscus bush.

The process of making bark fibre cloth was mainly carried out by women. First the bark was stripped from the tree and soaked in water to remove the coarse outer bark. The remaining inner bark fibres were then broken up by beating with hard wood beaters then felted together. Several pieces of material could be joined by lapping the edges together with taro starch then beating to fuse them; great lengths of fabric could be obtained in this manner. Different thicknesses were achieved by beating; these varied from a very fine, almost transparent, gauze-like fabric to a heavy material. There were two stages to beating the best tapa, the first done by plain or ridged beaters to break up the fibres but the second, later, was done by patterned beaters which then implanted a design on the material. When this process was carried out on the fine, gauze-like tapa it made it look like lace.

After the pattern had been impressed on the fabric it was stretched out to dry in the sun and afterwards was spread over moss to bleach it to near white. Patterns were then added to the material by painting with a brush or by dyeing. This latter process could be done by rubbing in the dye with a pad or by printing it by means of bamboo stamps. The considerable range of dye colours were of vegetable origin with the addition of black made from charcoal and red and yellow earth ochres. In Hawaii a final process was added which was to perfume the material with juice from various plants.

Tartarin, tartarine

From old French *tasel* or *tassel* and medieval fabric imported in the Middle Ages from the Orient (probably China) via Tartary.

Tassel

From old French *tasel* or *tassel* and Medieval Latin *tassellus*. Originally denoted a clasp or fibula fastening a cloak or tunic. Now a pendant ornamentation made of cord or yarn fringe which is held together by a round or oval cord knob at the top. Widely used in costume as decoration to all kinds of garments and accessories.

TASSET
Grey-blue doublet and breeches.
Slashes and tassets edged with
gold braid, Charles I, 1631

Tasset, tassette

Basques of the doublet which were especially prominent in the 1620s and 1630s (see *Basque*).

Textile processes

A number of processes are necessary to prepare the natural fibres of wool, linen, cotton and silk for spinning, also to finish the fabric after it has been woven. These

TAPA CLOTH
Wooden tapa beaters

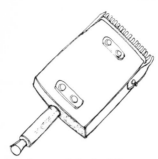

Wooden comb for hackling flax, fourth century AD

Hand card, leather pinned on wood

Teazle cross

Calico polisher, wood and metal

Linen glazer, wood

Wood and metal silk rubber

processes are described in this article, spinning is considered as a separate article under *Spinning* and warping and weaving under *Weaving*.

The first processes in preparing cotton, flax and wool for spinning are to clean the raw material and remove extraneous matter as well as to separate the fibrous material from its casing. In the case of wool received from the shearers, the material is sorted according to quality and this depends on the type of fleece and the part of the fleece from which it has come. The wool is then washed to remove the oil and dirt. With flax it is necessary to separate the fibrous material of the stems from the woody, outer rind, while with cotton, the boll or pod as well as the seeds must be removed. Over the centuries all these processes have been carried out by hand until, in the eighteenth century, machines were devised to reduce the labour. The flax was *hackled* by a flat wooden comb with a handle. The cotton was beaten to break up the pod and the seeds were picked out, this work being done by women and children.

In the second half of the eighteenth century a number of machines were devised to handle the problems of cleaning cotton. At this time the so-called 'triangular trade' (see *Cotton*) was at its height and the exporting of raw cotton from the southern states of America to mills in England was big business. It was very much in the interest of the American plantation owners to speed up the transportation of cotton and reduce their costs. Several machines, known as *batting machines*, were developed to open up the pods and clean the cotton. The principle was that of a rotating cylindrical cage made of cane which retained the cotton but permitted the seeds and fragments of pod to fall through a mesh. The Americans then began to ship the seedless cotton, compressed into bales, which reduced their costs considerably. In Britain then a machine known as a *devil* was evolved which would break up these bales. This comprised a cylinder with projecting spikes which revolved inside a stationary cage. An improved version of this idea was soon developed. It was

capable of maintaining a continuous action of feeding in raw cotton and expelling opened up cotton by means of feed rollers and a delivery mechanism.

Meanwhile, in America, by the end of the century, more advanced machines had been developed to remove the cotton seeds and impurities from the raw material. In the 1780s the *scutching and blowing machine* was perfected, where the cotton was passed between rollers to break up the bolls, then it was beaten up by metal bars to release the seeds which fell through a grid and, finally, a current of air was blown through the cotton to remove dirt particles. A marked advance was provided by the cotton gin (engine) devised by *Eli Whitney*, which consisted of a series of steel discs fitted with hooks projecting through slits in a metal grid. When the discs were rotated the hooks caught on the fibres and pulled them through the slots leaving the seeds behind. Whitney patented his gin in 1794. In 1796 the *saw gin* was developed which had saw teeth instead of hooks; it was driven by horse power and enabled one man in charge of the operation to replace 50 men who had been needed to carry out the same quantity of work with the roller gins.

After cleansing, the most important preliminary processes before spinning were carding and combing, both carried out in England from the early Middle Ages. The purpose of *carding* cotton and wool is to disentangle and straighten the fibres. Short fibres of cotton and some wool are left untangled but pointing in different directions still; longer wool fibres are left more nearly parallel with one another. Before the machine age carding was carried out by a pair of hand cards. These are made of wood faced with leather; small wire hooks are fitted closely together through the leather and fixed to the wood backing. The washed cotton or wool is pressed onto the wire teeth of one card and the other card, held in the opposite direction from the first, that is, with the handles pointing away from each other, is drawn across it. Thus each card holds some of the fibres, partly carded. The cards are then turned round so that the handles point in the same direction and are drawn across each other for the second time. This transfers all the carded fibres to one card in a soft cylinder called a rolag.

The carding process could be speeded up by using larger card surfaces on a bench or attaching one to a post and using a pulley and treadle operation for the other, but with the development of spinning machines (see *Spinning*), the carding operation lagged behind. Patents were taken out for two carding machines in the 1740s, one by *Daniel Bourn* and one by *Lewis Paul*. The idea was to use a cylinder, its surface fitted with wire points, which would rotate closely inside another cylinder and so card the fibres continuously. Several further engines incorporating improvements were devised, by *Hargreaves* and *Crompton* among others. *Sir Richard Arkwright* made such a machine about 1775; cotton was fed into this by fluted rollers on to a fast-moving large cylinder; the raw material was then carded between this cylinder and a series of flats which covered it, set between the first and third small rollers. By the end of the eighteenth century there were two chief designs of carding engine, one using flat cards and the other a roller and clearer card, in which pairs of rollers over the cylinder carried out the carding in conjunction with the cylinder. Eighteenth century carding machines were designed to card cotton but soon they were adapted for wool. In general, the flat carding machines were found to be more suitable for cotton and the roller and clearer designs for wool.

Combing is not quite the same process as carding. The latter has only a surface action which, for short-fibred materials, is enough to disentangle and straighten. For longer fibres such as wool it was better to comb them with combs made of three or four rows of long metal teeth which penetrated the mass of fibres and made them lie parallel as well as removing some of the natural waviness. With wool there was another function performed by combing which was to divide the longer fibres from the shorter ones and so separate

material suitable for wool yarn from that for worsted. The longer fibres are left by the combing process in parallel and suitable for spinning into smooth, compact worsted yarns. The shorter fibres rejected by the combing are made into softer, loosely twisted woollen yarns (see *Wool*).

Hand-combing was a cottage industry. The comber collected a stone of wool from the mill, washed it and wrung it out by rollers, more than once; he then took it home to comb it. In his cottage a post was set up affixed to the floor and with a lamp hanging high up one side while, lower down on the other, a fitting called a jenny was attached to which one comb was fixed (the static comb), its points facing vertically upwards. Combs were made with several graduated rows of steel teeth set into wooden blocks and so were more like steel brushes than combs. They were kept warm on a coal or charcoal stove as the heated metal combed better and damaged the fibres less than cold steel. A second comb was held in the hand, its spikes parallel to the ground. The wool was pulled on to the teeth of the static comb by hand then drawn off by the moving comb. This process, known as *jigging*, was repeated several times. The comber then drew off the longer, combed fibres by hand, placed them parallel to one another and twisted them into a ball. The *slivers*, as they were termed, were then washed again, placed on a bench and sprinkled with oil and a further combing was carried out. After this the final slivers were pulled off the comb through a horn disc (the *diz*).

Combing was hard and skilled work and there was a great deal of industrial unrest in the second half of the eighteenth century as combers repeatedly went on strike for higher rates of pay. Under pressure, employers sought a machine to replace their rebellious workers. A wool-combing machine was patented in 1792 by *Edmund Cartwright*, which produced combed wool as fast as 20 hand-combers could work but the results were not as good. Other inventions followed and further industrial unrest. Finally, in 1827, *Platt* produced a satisfactory combing machine with results as

Wood and iron cropping shears

Cropping shear weight for placing on lower blade and so giving a closer cut

Burling irons

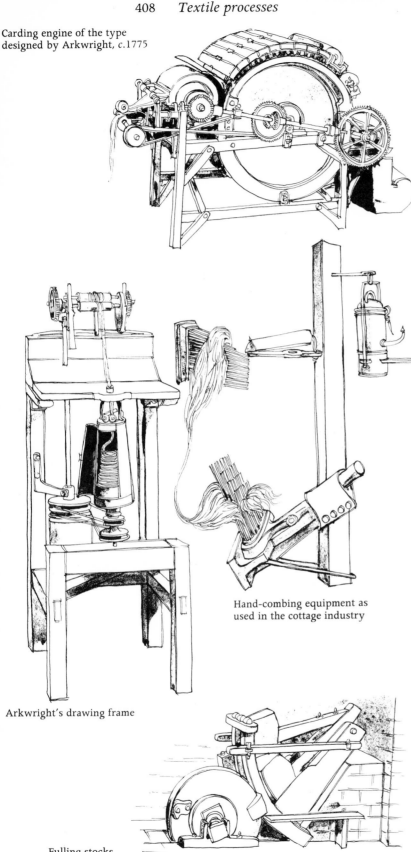

Carding engine of the type designed by Arkwright, *c.*1775

Hand-combing equipment as used in the cottage industry

Arkwright's drawing frame

Fulling stocks

good as work done by hand and gradually hand-combing was phased out. *James Noble's* machine of 1853 became the standard type of combing machine which operated with one large, horizontal, circular comb and two smaller ones inside. The wool was fed on to the larger comber and the smaller combs gradually took the wool from it.

A further preparatory process after carding cotton was found beneficial; this was *drawing*. A drawing frame was developed in the late 1770s by *Sir Richard Arkwright* which drew out the slivers and evened out their inequalities. Two carded slivers were fed on to a pair of rollers and then passed on to a second pair which were rotating at a faster speed. The slivers, then combined and attenuated, passed through a third pair of rollers into a cylindrical rotating can which coiled and slightly twisted the slubbing. The slivers were put through three drawing frames in succession, more slivers being joined at each repetition, and this later produced a spun yarn of greater evenness and regularity. Arkwright's machine was often known as a lantern frame because of the shape of the can which resembled a lantern.

After spinning, *woollen yarn* is counted by weight. Its thickness is recorded by the number of hanks, each of fixed length, which, gathered together, weigh one pound. The number of yards in a hank or skein varies from region to region; in Yorkshire it is 560 yards of worsted yarn and 256 yards of woollen.

The processes necessary to prepare *silk filaments* for weaving are different from those for wool, cotton and flax because the silk is already in the form of a long filament extruded by the silkworm into a cocoon (see *Silk*). When the silk filaments are unwound from the cocoon they are too fine and delicate to be woven individually so filaments from a number of cocoons have to be wound together and are then washed to remove the gummy sericin. During the eighteenth century a number of mechanical means were developed for winding the fine filaments together and then twisting them ready for weaving. *Thomas Lombe* was granted a patent in 1718 for machines to do this, based on Italian methods which had been in use since the Middle Ages. Further developments were made during the eighteenth century and by the 1780s the process involved reeling the filaments from 30 to 40 cocoons into a hank, in which form the silk was imported into Britain. The machine then tightly twisted these combined filaments by a 'throwing' process to make them suitable for weaving by means of a wheel and cross. The silk filaments were attached to 24 hooks on the wheel, were then taken round hooks on the cross and returned to the wheel hooks. By turning by hand a larger wheel attached to the smaller one, the threads were twisted and could then be formed into a skein by a reeler.

After a textile has been woven there are still a number of processes which it must undergo before it is in a condition to make up into garments; these all come under the heading of *finishing processes*. The material is washed after it is taken off the loom. A *polish* or *glaze* is often given to cottons, silks and linens. Hand glazers and polishers were generally made of wood with metal parts to accentuate the gloss (see drawings). Woollen cloth needs to be *fulled*, a process which thickens the warp and weft threads to make them thicker and less visible as individual threads; this is particularly necessary for felts and heavy woollens. In fulling the cloth is made wet then beaten with heavy hammers, washed again, then stretched out to dry. Some woollen materials and felts are also *napped*, a process which brings up a fuzzy surface on the fabric. Woollens also need to be cropped and finally burled and mended. After the fulled cloth has been dried it is then *teazled* to raise the loose fibres. This used to be done with a *teazle cross*, that is thistle heads held together in a wooden cross frame (see drawing). The teazled cloth was stretched out and cropped. This used to be undertaken by enormous hand cropping shears, about four feet long, made of wood and iron. The *cropping* leaves the cloth with an even pile. Finally, the cloth still contains some knots and mistakes in weaving.

These have to be corrected by hand, a process known as *burling* and *mending* and one which traditionally has been a home, piece-work process.

There are many different ways in which a woven fabric may be patterned. For centuries, *painting*, *tie-and-dye*, *batik* and simple *hand-block printing* methods have been used all over the world (see *Batik, Dyeing*). Simple woven patterns using different warp and weft colours are also of ancient origin, though with the Jacquard system, complex patterns could be woven (see *Weaving*). In modern times printed material is produced by a mass-production mechanical system, though hand-blocked and hand-screen methods are also used on a small scale for individual work. In *screen printing* the colour is applied through fine mesh screens, a different screen being needed for each colour. A further method is *warp-printing*, generally used on silk, wherein the warp threads are printed with a pattern before weaving and, when woven with a plain-coloured weft, give a shadow effect to the design.

Thimble

From Roman times leather and metal protective caps made for finger or thumb. The modern sewing thimble dates from the seventeenth century, then worn especially on the thumb and known as a thumble or thum-bell. At first made of leather but soon it was made from metal and called a thimble.

Thrums

Short ends of warp threads remaining on the loom after the piece of weaving has been cut off. A term also applied to a fringe of threads at the edge of a piece of woven material. From this the word thrums came to be applied to a cap or hat woven from such short pieces of unused warp threads.

Ticking

A heavy, closely-woven linen or cotton fabric, usually striped, from which pillow and mattress covers are made. In modern times also used for heavy, stiff, summer coats and jackets.

TIPPET
Patterned tunic with tippets,
English, 1365

Gown with tippets, Spanish,
1380

Tiffany
A transparent silk, muslin or lawn gauze used for underwear and blouses.

Tinsel
A fabric, usually silk, scintillating with interwoven metal threads. Tinsel embroidery is worked with such sparkling threads.

Tippet
1) In the Middle Ages the pendant streamer hanging from the elbow-length sleeve of the tunic or gown. The term was also sometimes applied to the liripipe (see *Liripipe*).
2) A woman's shoulder cape, most generally of fur, fashionable from the seventeenth century onwards.

Tobe
An Arab garment worn generally in North Africa, consisting of a straight length of cotton cloth draped round the body or slipped on over the head.

Tog
Plural togs. Derived from *togeman, togman*, from the sixteenth century onwards used as a colloquial term for a coat, an outer garment or, simply, clothes. More widely used in the nineteenth century when, it is suggested, there was a connection with the Latin *toga*. The past participle *togged* was similarly used to denote being booted, hatted or clothed.

Toilet
A piece of material or a wrapper worn round the shoulders while the hair was being dressed.

Toilinet
A fine woollen cloth used particularly for waistcoats in the early nineteenth century. The word probably derived from the French *toile* = linen, cloth.

Topaz
A semi-precious stone, a fluo-silicate of aluminium, transparent and lustrous, seen in shades of yellow, blue, green and white

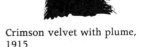

TOQUE
Toque style of hat
Brown straw with plaid band
and feather trimming, 1864

Crimson velvet with plume,
1915

and found in many areas from Scotland to the Urals and Germany to South America.

Toque
1) In the later Middle Ages a woman's coif or indoor cap. Later became a general term for a cap or bonnet. In more recent times a fitting, round, brimless hat.
2) In the 1820s and 1830s a pad used to support the elaborate coiffure of the time.

Torsade
A decoration for a head-dress or cap, made of twisted or plaited cord or ribbon.

Train
An elongation of the hem of a gown or robe so that it trails on the ground. Apart from ceremonial dress, of which trains have traditionally been a feature, the garments of both sexes swept the ground in the late eleventh and early twelfth centuries and the houppelande styles were also excessively full and long in the years 1380–1430. After this trains were fashionable on women's gowns in certain periods, notably the fifteenth century, the late seventeenth and early eighteenth centuries, returning again with the *fin de siècle* and the Empire style of the early 1800s. There was a further revival with the bustle gowns of the 1870s

Worth evening dress. Dark green velvet bodice, cream brocade skirt striped with pink sprays. White tulle overskirt and flouncing. Cream silk 'sweepers', French, 1891

Red floral-patterned over-gown with train over spotted light-coloured under-skirt, Austrian, *c*.1690

Patterned gown with velvet collar and belt, German, 1465

Plain white dress with decorative stole, Russian, 1796

Wine-red velvet ball gown, white lace decoration, bustle skirt. Hungarian, 1875

Evening gown of pale green lace decorated with bands of silver lamé. Jewelled shoulder straps, English, 1933

Houppelande, *c*.1380, Italian

TRAIN
Gold-brown velvet
houppelande
lined with white
fur, English, 1385

Evening gown of
coffee-coloured
brocade with
cabbage rose
design over black
georgette under-
skirt with fish-tail
train, English, 1913

and 1880s and this continued until the outbreak of the First World War; in the years 1910–14 these were generally of the narrow fish-tail or mermaid's tail variety. Since 1914 the train has been reserved for very formal gowns and for a few of the evening dresses of the 1930s.

Trousers, trowsers

A garment worn by both sexes which encloses the legs and body from waist to ankles.

In the context of world history of costume trousers have been worn since ancient times, chiefly in the colder areas and in the Orient. The traditional Chinese dress, dating back over many centuries, is for amply cut, warm trousers tied at the waist and often bound at the ankles also, padded in winter against the cold (see *Chinese dress*). The warrior horsemen of Asia introduced similar trousers to India and the garment, adapted over the centuries to the Indian

climate, but especially suited to the mountainous north, survives in several guises (see *Indian dress*). In Japan also the voluminous *hakama* were traditional wear (see *Japanese dress*). In Persia, as in the Far East, some type of trouser garment has been part of the costume since ancient times and worn, either as outer or undergarments, by women as much as by men (see *Persian dress*).

From these sources the wearing of trousers, for warmth or as richly decorative garments, spread to become an essential article of dress in Turkey (see *Turkish dress*) and, thence under the Ottoman Empire, to central Europe where, in Hungary for example, trousers continued to be worn until, in the nineteenth century, they became fashionable western dress for men (see *Hungarian dress*).

In the cultures which evolved around the Mediterranean shores the draped costume was paramount, in ancient Egypt, Greece and Rome, for instance, but in the eastern part of the Roman Empire, under Byzantium, trousers were worn by members of both sexes. These were elegantly cut and hugged the legs as in the medieval hose of western countries; they were then tucked into boots or worn over shoes (see *Byzantine dress*).

Earlier than this the nomad horsemen had travelled westwards from the Asian to the European steppes and had settled in a number of areas near the Caspian Sea, round the Black Sea and, by 400 BC, had extended as far westwards as Hungary, Bulgaria, Rumania and eastern Germany. The people of these nomad societies wore full, long trousers, sometimes tied at the ankle, sometimes worn loose and wide like the 'Oxford bags' of the 1920s in England. Such tribes included the Cimmerians, Sarmathians, Parthians and Dacians. This style of loose trouser, most commonly tied at the ankle, became general wear in Bronze and Iron Age northern Europe: a sensible, warm manner of dressing. They were worn by Celts, Gauls and Teutons before the coming of the Roman Empire and, after its collapse, continued as traditional nether garments until the bound braies and

Dacian King,
second century BC

Deep purple trousers to match
suede coat, English, 1969

Grey worsted suit,
English, 1967

Grey-blue trousers, Spanish,
1840–50

Bohemian,
c.1885

White corduroy trousers,
strapped, English, 1824

Toutonic tribesman,
1st century AD

Golden-coloured
polyester/wool
French-cut slacks,
1974

Iron Age Celt in Britain

Persian trousers,
fifth century BC

Light grey trousers,
strapped, English,
1842

chausses leg-coverings of the Merovingians and Carolingians replaced them and formed the foundation for medieval hose (see *Bronze Age dress in Europe, Carolingian dress, Frankish dress* and *Merovingian dress*). In a number of communities who were living in colder climates, some form of trousers continued to be worn through the centuries until the western nations adopted the trouser as fashionable dress in the nineteenth century. Examples of this include the Scottish and Irish *trews* (*truis*) and the North American Indian skin breeches which, in some instances, included foot covering also (see *North American Indian dress* and *Scottish Highland dress*).

The substitution of full-length breeches for the knee breeches, which had been worn by men for so long, dates from the French Revolution. Breeches and stockings were automatically associated with Court dress so supporters of the revolution adopted pantaloons worn with long socks. The aristocracy contemptuously referred to the wearers of such garments as *Sans-culottes* (see *Sans-culotte*).

After a few years, under Napoleon, culottes returned to fashion but only temporarily. From 1800 onwards, pantaloons began to replace breeches permanently. They were fitting and made from a stretch type of material such as stockinet or soft doeskin in grey, beige, lemon or white. Some were of finely striped cotton and, especially fashionable, was the buff or yellow nankeen fabric, a strong cotton imported from Nanking in China. Until 1820 both breeches and trousers continued in vogue, the former were always worn at Court and on formal occasions but the latter steadily gained in popularity. There was great opposition to the wearing of long pantaloons in England, where breeches and stockings were considered to be more dignified but, when George IV came to the throne in 1820, he gave a definite lead towards the adoption of trousers for wear on all occasions. By the early 1820s they had become general wear, either tucked into tall boots or strapped under the instep of the shoe. Peg-top styles were fashionable;

these were very full and padded at the hips and tight-fitting on the lower leg. They helped to accentuate the small waist, full chest and hip line fashionable at the time.

From the 1840s trousers became fuller on the lower leg and instep strapping tended to disappear; the upper part was correspondingly cut less fully. Also, the opening, which until now had been of the broad front flap or fall style, began to be of the fly front design. Styles of trouser did not change radically for the remainder of the nineteenth century but materials became heavier and colours darker. Black, dark grey or grey stripes were usual in the second half of the century and after 1870 suits all of one material were introduced (see *Suit*). In 1895 vertical creases were put into trouser legs and it became fashionable to turn up the hems. This was an English idea which quickly spread to France.

In the early twentieth century men's trouser styles changed little; there was a slow trend towards a looser cut and creases and turn-ups became more common. In the 1920s the slim line gave place to the excessively wide 'Oxford bags', which were up to 24 inches wide at the turn-up. Also, grey flannel trousers became popular for informal wear. After 1929 the trouser width was reduced but, until after the Second World War they continued to be cut very fully. In the 1950s trousers became narrower and lost their cuffs; zip fasteners took over from front fly buttons. In the 1960s trousers were more fitting still and were cut lower on the hips, a hipster design which continued through into the 1970s. Teen-age styles were extreme and young men looked as though they had been poured into their trousers (see also *Jean* and *Levis*). Chunky hip-belts became fashionable. In the 1970s, though the low-cut hipster style has continued, the narrow trouser has been replaced by the flared bottoms and cuffs have been reintroduced. Both variation in trouser width and cuffs are optional to suit personal preference. The wide, flared trouser bottoms are reminiscent of the traditional sailor's bell-bottom trousers. These, of regulation 25 inches in diameter and horizontally pleated for storage purposes, date back to the days when sailors made their own uniforms and found it easier and less wasteful to use a whole bolt of serge, which measured 54 inches across and which, allowing for turnings, gave two 25 inch trouser legs. These are being replaced from 1977 by the flared from the knee, vertically creased trousers of modern fashion.

Women adopted trousers for horseback riding in the nineteenth century but these were completely hidden under the full skirt of the riding habit (see *Riding dress*). It was in the late 1920s that trousers appeared on the beach known, by 1930, as *lido pyjamas* and later as *beach pyjamas* (see *Beachwear*). In the 1930s and 1940s trousers began to be worn for holiday use, sports and country walking and, in war-time, they were found to be useful for doing all kinds of work. They were adopted by the Services for certain trades and especially for night duty. After the Second World War women began to wear trousers more and more in the home and for informal occasions. In the 1950s these were fitting; stretch pants were fashionable with straps under the instep. Parallel with masculine styles the full flared bottoms replaced these and in the 1960s the trouser suit became acceptable fashionable wear (see *Suit*).

Trousses, trusses
In the seventeenth-century, close-fitting upper hose or breeches covering the buttocks and upper thigh.

Truss
To tie or fasten. Used especially with reference to tying the points or laces used in the Middle Ages to fasten the edge of one garment to another (see *Aglet*).

Tucker
In the seventeenth, eighteenth and nineteenth centuries, a yoke of lace, frilled or embroidered fabric inserted as a fill-in to a bodice with low décolletage.

Tuke, tewke
A buckram or canvas stiffening used in the sixteenth century.

Fawn trousers, strapped, German, 1839

Navy worsted suit, English, 1926

Dark grey trousers, German, 1874

Grey worsted suit, English, 1948

TUNIC
Three-quarter-length tunic over
long gown. Spanish nobleman,
twelfth century

Ancient Greek tunic (chiton),
double-girded, fifth century BC

Dark red tunic dress with key
pattern and fringe border hem,
white gown, gauze stole.
Ribbons and plumes in the hair.
English, 1810

Striped tunic over long gown.
British Celtic dress, first
century BC

Knee-length tunic for everyday
wear, English, c.1170

Golden brown velvet tunic
dress with black fur edging,
English, 1915

Tulle
A fine bobbin net made of silk or cotton thread. Used in the eighteenth century chiefly for indoor caps and in more modern times for veiling.

Tunic
A body garment of varied length, with or without sleeves, which is slipped on over the head and can be girded at the waist. The classical tunic was made of two rectangular pieces of material pinned or sewn at the shoulders then girded at waist and/or hips; this garment could be knee or ankle-length (see *Byzantine dress, Etruscan dress, Greece* and *Rome*). The tunic was the usual wear in Europe before, during and after the occupation by the Romans. For men it was generally knee-length for everyday use and ankle-length for the nobility and for important occasions. Women sometimes wore a knee-length tunic over a ground-length gown. The tunic, which was slipped on over the head, had a round neckline without collar and was often slit in front to facilitate passage of the head. It was finally replaced in the fourteenth century by the fitted body garment (see *Doublet*).

In more recent times tunics have been worn by women over a gown or trousers. The thin garments fashionable in the years 1790–1815 gave inadequate protection against the cold so knee-length tunics were worn over the long, white or pale dresses; these tunics were generally made of warmer materials, such as velvet, and were in stronger colours. Tunic dresses were also fashionable in the years 1910–18, a time when there was great variety in skirt styles, an outer skirt usually being fuller than the longer, slimmer, under one. Tunics have returned to fashion in the 1960s and 1970s when they are worn over blouses and jumpers to accompany skirts or trousers (see *Suit,* Trouser).

Turban
Originally a head-dress made up from a long piece of material wrapped around the head in many and varied ways. The name derives from the Persian word *dulbānd,*

Brown turban, Italian, 1505

Silk, soft turban, Italian, *c.*1450

White turban and liripipe, Swiss, 1460–70

Lady in turban with dagged tabs and liripipe, gentleman in swathed turban, Swiss, 1430–40

Beige velvet turban, 1929

Black turban with jewelled
ornament and white veil
wrapped round turban in
swathes, Flemish, 1480

Silk turban with jewelled
ornament, Spanish, *c.*1530

which later became tulband and finally turban. The head-dress is of Moslem origin, worn by men as a symbol of their profession of Mohammedanism and the turban has been widely worn since the early Middle Ages in the Orient, especially in the Indian sub-continent, in Persia, the Middle East and Turkey, where it is generally wrapped around a cap (see *Indian dress* and *Turkish dress*).

The turban was introduced into fashionable European dress in the early fifteenth century and was widely seen in decorative form from then until the early years of the sixteenth century. Padded or softly loose, it was mainly worn by women, decorated by a veil and/or attached liripipe though, at the height of the fashion, about 1440–50, men adopted it too. The turban was worn particularly in countries in central and eastern Europe, Italy and Austria for example, but it was also very popular in Switzerland and Flanders.

The fashion for wearing turban head-dresses has been revived at intervals since

Silk turban with feather,
English, 1826

the sixteenth century, most notably from 1790 and in the early decades of the nineteenth century, also from the 1920s onwards when short hairstyles have made it a particularly suitable headcovering. All kinds of materials have been used, trimmed usually with feathers and jewels.

Turkish dress

From the time of the collapse of Constantinople in 1453 there was a strong Byzantine influence on Turkish dress. The Turks, with their love of display, adopted with enthusiasm the rich silks, gold and silver fabrics, encrusted embroideries and furs which characterized the costume of the Byzantine Court. By the time of Suleiman in the sixteenth century, a series of sumptuary laws was passed, allocating to each rank of court and army officials their prescribed form of attire, colours, fabrics and decoration.

Over the centuries until the modernization of Turkey just after the First World War, the chief garments worn by the average man comprised a shirt and trousers, boots, a decorative jacket, a deep waist sash, the *kuşak*, a cap and turban. The trousers were of the baggy type descending to be fitting on the lower leg, cut on the *şalvar* pattern (see *Chalvar*) and the brightly-coloured leather boots had turned-up toes. The waist sash, the *kuşak*, was a long, wide piece of coloured material wound round the body on top of the trousers to keep the lumbar regions warm; it was also a decorative feature and varied in colour, pattern and material used. The jacket, usually worn open, was of cloth, wool or felt and gaily decorated. In cold weather a long caftan was worn on top. The *tarboosh* (fez), the traditional Moslem cap, was the flower-pot style which became part of the national dress of Turkey early in the nineteenth century; it was generally bound round on the brow by a turban on top (see *Cap*).

Professional men, court officials and men of rank wore similar garments but made of rich materials and, on top of the trousers, shirt and *kuşak*, they were clothed in a long caftan-style of coat; sometimes, more than one such coat was worn, a sleeveless or short-sleeved one, with long hanging sleeves behind, covered one with long fitting sleeves. Various names were used for these richly embroidered and ornamented coats: dolman, caftan, stambouline. The last name refers simply to a garment of Stamboul, the Turkish spelling for Istanbul (Constantinople). Such officials also wore very large turbans and especially wide sashes of beautifully decorated silks.

Out-of-doors, Moslem custom dictated that women were perforce completely covered from head to foot by an enveloping cloak and veil, the *çarşaf* or *tcharchaf*. There were several varieties of these garments according to region and rank and some were of heavier and darker materials than others (see *Chādar – çarşaf, mahramah, petche, yaşmak – Feridjé* and *Litham*).

Under this enveloping garment women wore a knee-length loose chemise of white silk, wool or linen, the *gömlek*, which was fastened at the neck with a brooch and had wide, loose sleeves, accompanied by linen drawers tied at the waist with a drawstring (*dislik*). An essential garment was the enveloping pair of trousers, the *şalvar* or *chalwar*, which were worn on top of or instead of the *dislik*. The *şalvar* were fastened at the waist by a belt, the *uçkar*, and were very full from waist to knee (see *Chalvar*). They could be made of beautiful materials, brocaded silks and gold and silver fabrics, and up to eight yards of this could be used to make a pair. On top of these garments was worn an embroidered silk, fitting waistcoat, the *yelek*, and a long gown or gowns, the *entari*, which was generally fitting at the back and open in front and buttoned. It had fitted and hanging sleeves. The decorative, wide sash, the *kuşak*, was worn on top and was elegantly tied in front or at the hip. Fur pelisses or padded jackets were added in cold weather.

The Turkish heelless house slippers were worn indoors and, out-of-doors, a leather shoe or ankle boot, all with turned-up toes. *Kub-kobs* kept the footwear dry in muddy streets or at the baths (see *Patten*). Jewelled caps, turbans and embroidered kerchiefs were among the usual head-dresses.

Man of high rank, sixteenth century. Caftan with hanging sleeves over brocaded gown. Boots, turban, tarboosh

Lady of rank, sixteenth century. Tarboosh, turban and veil. Coat with kuşak and hanging sleeves over salvar

Girl from seraglio, Istanbul, nineteenth century. Patterned yelek over white gömlek. Fringed decorative kuşak. Velvet, fur-edged gown. Şalvar, shoes and kub-kobs

Important dignitary, Istanbul, nineteenth century. Dark velvet gown, fur-edged and with hanging sleeves. Patterned caftan with striped kuşak. Official, white headdress

(*left*) Man from Angora. Jacket of embroidered felt over wool waistcoat. Striped wool trousers, red leather boots. Tarboosh with turban. Nineteenth century

(*right*) Man from Istanbul. White silk shirt, brightly-coloured waistcoat. White cotton trousers, black shoes, red tarboosh. Nineteenth century.

Turkish women of wealth and importance wore clothes made from beautiful fabrics ornamented with jewelled embroideries; their hair and person was similarly bejewelled. They used cosmetics heavily on their eyes, cheeks and lips and dyed their hair.

Turkish towelling
A cotton fabric woven with raised nap or loops on both sides and widely used for bathrobes, beachwear and towels. First woven in Britain but adopted in Turkey, where it was made extensively, then exported to Britain and known as Turkish towelling.

Turquoise
An opaque and sometimes translucent gem stone ranging in colour from blue to pale bluish-green: a hydrous phosphate of aluminium. So-named because it was first found in Turkestan, but later from Persia.

U

Ugly
In the mid-nineteenth century a term for a shade in the form of an extra brim attached to the front of a woman's bonnet to protect the eyes from bright sunlight.

Ukrainian dress
The national and peasant dress of the peoples of this southern part of the USSR, Ukrainians, Ruthenes, Cossacks, shows some influence from further west, from Hungary and Poland, and is elegant and more sophisticated than that of the regions further north. The costume is brightly coloured in some regions, with a wealth of embroidered decoration; in others, notably the central area, dark coloured garments contrasting with white blouses and shirts are more typical.

In general, men's dress consisted of full trousers tucked into leather boots, a white, long-sleeved shirt embroidered in colour at neck and sleeves and a sleeveless decorative jacket. For cold weather a cloak or caftan of homespun cloth was worn and a fur hat or cap. Women also wore full, long-sleeved blouses with embroidered decoration, a bodice and a full skirt. Sometimes two skirts were worn, the upper one flared out only to knee-level. Women also usually adopted boots and, only occasionally, shoes. They covered their hair with stiff decorative caps with veils. A coat of caftan or pelisse style was usual in winter.

Umbrella, parasol, sunshade
A portable,. usually folding, protection against rain or sun, generally circular in

UKRAINIAN DRESS
Red velvet sleeveless coat with brown fur, white embroidered blouse, two skirts – one blue, one white, black boots, flower and ribbon headdress

Sheepskin waistcoat, shirt with sash, dark trousers, black boots and astrakhan cap

UMBRELLA, PARASOL, SUNSHADE

Silk umbrella, Swedish, 1906

Lace-edged parasol, Spanish, *c*.1800

Long, walking umbrella, Austrian, *c*.1880

Lace and velvet parasol, Russian, *c*.1893

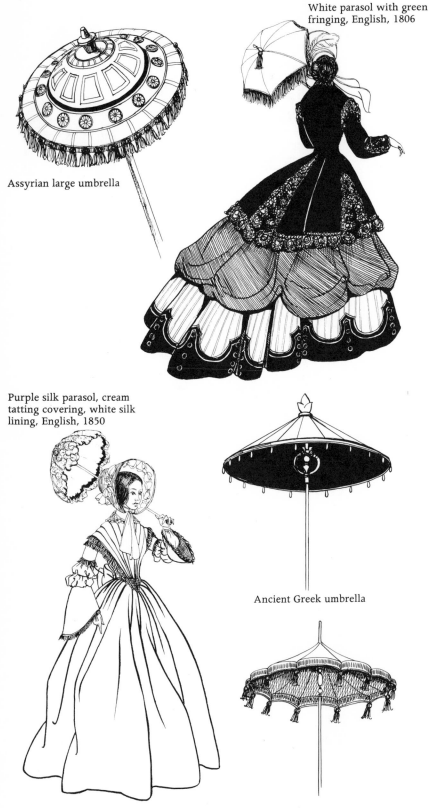

Assyrian large umbrella

White parasol with green fringing, English, 1806

Purple silk parasol, cream tatting covering, white silk lining, English, 1850

Ancient Greek umbrella

Red silk pagoda parasol, cord edging and tassels, English, 1805

shape with folding ribs and a handle at the axis. In antiquity, in ancient Egypt, Assyria, Babylon, Persia and Greece the umbrella was made principally as a protection from the sun and large, decorative umbrellas with long handles were carried by slaves or bearers to shade persons of rank. In Rome also the umbrella was used as a shade from the sun, the word deriving from the Latin *umbraculum*, denoting a shady place or bower but later coming to refer to an umbrella. In the Orient and the Middle East the umbrella has long been used as protection from rain as well as sun and it was often made of leather as well as other materials.

The modern umbrella was used in Italy as long ago as the late sixteenth century and its use spread to the rest of Europe. At first it was made of leather but soon other, lighter materials were used. The umbrella became an article of fashion, carried by women, in the eighteenth century. It was carried at first in France, where rigid parasols (for shading the face) were small and made from dainty materials, silks, lace and satin, while the *parapluie* (for protection against the rain) opened and closed and was made from stronger fabrics.

The parasol, in particular, remained an important article in feminine attire throughout the nineteenth century. Designed sometimes to open and close, the pagoda shape was fashionable in the early decades and small, dainty rounded shapes accompanied the later immense crinoline skirts. The *tilting parasol* with hinged stick was in vogue from about 1795 while the *en tout cas* was a later nineteenth century innovation. The name derived from the French term, this design served all eventualities, being an elegant parasol when the sun shone yet being strong enough to withstand a summer shower as an umbrella. The umbrella acquired the nickname of 'gamp' in the 1840s, named after Charles Dickens' Mrs Gamp.

Fashionable men began to carry umbrellas from the middle of the nineteenth century; before this the use of an umbrella had been considered to be effeminate. Men's umbrellas were large, with long handles and were carefully rolled and secured. From the 1880s women also began to carry long, walking, rolled umbrellas.

Underwear, lingerie

Prior to the nineteenth century underwear was comparatively simple, consisting of a loose chemise or shirt, some type of drawers or pants, stockings and, especially for women in periods when it was fashionable to constrict or support the figure, foundation garments designed to flatten, slim or distend and emphasize the breasts, waist and stomach. See also articles upon specific subjects: *Brassière, Chemise, Corset, Drawers, Elastic (Elasticized Fabrics), Greece (ancient), Pantaloons (Pantalettes), Petticoat, Rome (ancient).*

In the early nineteenth century very little underwear was worn with the thin, simple gowns of the day, but from the 1830s until the 1870s an increasing weight of garments had to be borne underneath the dresses and skirts. There seemed to be a pathological fear of catching a chill so men, women and children all wore many layers of material so that no part of the body except the face was exposed to the air. Women especially had to endure a quantity of clothes which included as a minimum a long-sleeved, voluminous chemise, a corset, corset cover, camisole, drawers or pantalettes and several petticoats. Underwear was white, partly starched and was made chiefly from cambric, batiste, calico and flannel. There was much coyness about referring to underwear which, over the years, was subject to varied euphemisms: underpinnings, unmentionables, indescribables, unwhisperables to name a few. The more glamorous word lingerie entered the English vocabulary in the second half of the century.

From the 1860s undergarments for women began to be more attractive. Broderie anglaise decorated the neck, sleeve and hem edges, lace edging was introduced and, in the 1880s, silk began to be used as an underwear material. By the end of the century undergarments were beautifully embroidered, lace and ribbon trimmed and made from a variety of soft cottons and

White cotton camisole, 1880

White cotton bosom amplifier with lace and ribbon trimming, 1905

Blue silk combinations with lace and ribbon trimming, 1903

Crêpe de chine cami-knickers, embroidered decoration, 1920s

Silk vest and directoire knickers, 1920

Suspender belt, 1925

Silk cami-knickers, bias cut, 1930s

Nylon and Lycra bra and pantee girdle, 1970

White wool combinations, 1910

White cotton combinations, 1926

Cotton vest and briefs, 1955

silks. Styles became more attractive also; sleeves became shorter, hemlines rose and garments were less voluminous and more shaped to the figure. From the late nineteenth century it became customary to combine two garments in one and 'combinations' had arrived. These became popular for men as well as women as they reduced the number of garments to be worn. For men the undervest and long drawers or pants became one garment, for women the chemise and drawers were similarly combined. By the first decade of the twentieth century men's combinations (union suit in the USA) had a high, round neck, short sleeves, were buttoned down the centre front and had pants reaching to the ankles. By the second decade the garment could be sleeveless with a lower neckline and the legs had become 'shorts'. Despite this, many men preferred to retain short sleeves and long pants, either for warmth or through conservatism, in combinations until the Second World War.

In the 1880s new principles of health and hygiene were being advocated in dress and especially in underwear. One of the proponents of this was Dr Jaeger, Professor of Physiology at Stuttgart University. Dr Jaeger believed in the efficacy of wearing wool next to the skin and, from 1884, woollen underwear was manufactured in Britain under the Jaeger name. Within a few years undervests, combinations and drawers were being made in wool in a stockinette weave and the material was even used for corsets and petticoats but these, not unnaturally, were less successful commercially. Dr Jaeger advocated the use of wool for underwear because it was porous and allowed the body to 'breathe'. Soon, in 1887, the idea of an open textured cotton material was put forward by Lewis Haslam. This cellular material was soon marketed as Aertex which, like Jaeger, is still a household word. A third, equally long-lived name is Viyella, which was a fabric made from a blend of cotton and wool; it was produced by William Hollins and Co. in the 1890s, at first intended for men's shirts and nightwear but was soon adopted for all kinds of underwear.

In the first decade of the twentieth century fashionable feminine underwear had become elegant and expensive. Now generally referred to as lingerie, the garments were tailored to the figure in silk, taffeta and satin, trimmed with a quantity of lace and ribbon. Combinations still had legs reaching to below the knees but were not as voluminous or heavy as previously. Drawers, now known as knickers, were equally elaborately trimmed with lace frilling and inserts. The shape of the fashionable figure was maintained with, apart from the corset (see *Corset*), flounced and lace-trimmed bosom amplifiers, the current version of the nineteenth century practical camisole. Lingerie was now often made in sets. The 'set' comprised knickers, bust bodice, chemise and petticoat, all in one material and decoration.

After 1920 the trend in underwear was for simpler, more natural styles and greater freedom of movement. In men's underwear of the 1920s and 1930s combinations were retained in cellular cotton or wool knit but gradually the separate undervest and trunks replaced them. Sleeves were seen less often and trunks became shorter. In the post-war years underwear became scantier with either a vest not being worn or the round-necked, sleeveless type, often of the open mesh 'string' material and briefs replacing underpants. All colours, plain or patterned, were seen with man-made fibres generally taking over from cottons.

After 1910 women's underwear became less bulky, straighter in line and less lavishly trimmed. It was 'slimmed down' to suit the gown skirts of the years 1910–20, then shortened to accommodate the 1920s styles. The combination garment of knickers and chemise had become cami-knickers by 1916, though separate chemise with directoire knickers (full with elastic at waist and legs) or French knickers (with flared open legs) were also worn. With the 1920s and the fashionably boyish figure, underwear at last was restricted in sheer size. The voluminousness totally disappeared and slips, chemises and knickers were fitting and very simple in style. Many different combination garments became fashionable: the cami-knickers still but also the combined bust bodice, hip belt, knickers and slip also the chemise, knickers, corset and camisole. Materials included lawn, crêpe de chine, satin, cotton and silk tricot. All these garments were comfortable and sparingly trimmed. With the 1920s names of garments were simplified also; lingerie became generally 'undies', petticoats became first 'petties' then slips, knickers turned into pants or panties in the 1930s and combinations 'combs'.

The development of new, man-made fibres was a vital factor in changing the design and form of underwear from the 1920s onwards (see *Elastic, elasticized fabrics* and *Synthetic and man-made fabrics*). In the field of corsetry (see *Corset*), the natural, easy-support foundation garments revolutionized design. The boned corset gradually vanished to be replaced by elastic stretch belts and girdles, suspender belts, pantee girdles and corselettes all in Lycra-type elastic net and nylon. All lengths of foundation garment, from the long-leg corselette to the diminutive suspender belt, were available though, with the natural 'young' lines of the 1960s and 1970s and the ubiquitousness of trouser wearing, fewer and fewer women wear foundation garments at all.

The new materials revolutionized the design of all other underwear also. Beginning with the locknit (knitted rayon) fabrics of the 1930s and 1940s the field opened up to all the possibilities of nylon in the post-war years. The fashionable line of the clothes of the day were reflected in the underwear. In the late 1920s and the 1930s the bias cut was applied to French knickers, cami-knickers and slips, all of which became more fitting and shorter. Pretty colours were available, plain and patterned, with narrow lace-edge trimming. With the post-war 'New Look' these garments became fuller and more feminine, more elaborately decorated and with flounced, ruched skirts. Simplicity and brevity returned with the mini-skirt and, in the 1960s, co-ordinates became fashionable, supplying a set with a range of bra, briefs, pantee girdle, waist petticoat and slip all in the same material and pattern.

Uni-sex clothes

A development in clothes for the young of the 1960s and 1970s when almost identical garments were designed for both sexes. These styles have a limited following which generally means the girl wearing her boy friend's type of clothes rather than the other way round.

Patterned nylon matching briefs and bra, 1970

Valona

In Spain, ruffs were replaced by the valona by order of Philip IV. This was a simple, white collar favoured by Philip. It was made of gauze, starched and untrimmed and was supported by a golilla (see *Golilla*).

Veil

One of the most ancient articles of feminine dress which has been associated over the

ages with elegance, modesty, humility, subservience, marriage and death and has represented a specific significance in different world religions.

In ancient times veils were made of linen, cotton, silk, even wool but, as it became possible to weave very fine, semi-transparent materials, these were quickly adopted for long, flowing veils. Other styles were stiffened and wired to stand

VALONA
Spanish valona, 1625

Veil over turban, Byzantine, eleventh century

White veil, *c*.1200

Horned, wired veil over jewelled caul, *c*.1450

Turban and veil, 1470

Silk pill box hat and veil, 1943

Anglo-Saxon queen. White veil held in position by crown

Queen Elizabeth I. Wired, jewelled, gauze butterfly wing veil, 1592

Gold headdress, wired butterfly veil, English, 1480

Steeple headdress with veil, Burgundian, 1480

out in wing-like shapes. In the East the veil had traditionally represented humility and subservience. With the coming of the Moslem religion, women were expected to cover their heads and part of their faces with its folds when out-of-doors. As time passed, in countries of the Middle East, in Turkey and Persia especially, rules made by man, rather than Mahomet, became stricter and only the eyes were permitted to be uncovered and even these peered through a mesh window (see *Chādar* etc. and *Turkish dress*).

In Europe the veil, made in varied sizes, materials and colours, was worn by the ancient Greeks, Romans, under Byzantine rule and throughout the Middle Ages. In early times it was simply a piece of material, large or small, which was held in place by a fillet or ribbon encircling the brow or by being pinned to the hair. In the later Middle Ages, from the fourteenth century onwards, the veil accompanied the head-dress, being draped round it, over it or simply flowing down the back. It was especially fashionable in the fifteenth century when it was worn with turbans, cauls, horned and steeple head-dresses. Sometimes it was long and flowing, sometimes wired into butterfly wings.

With the hood designs of head-dress of the sixteenth century the veil went out of fashion but returned for a brief period in the years 1580–1610 in the form of two wired, circular wings, one worn on each side of the back of the head; these were filled with white gauze or silk and edged with pearls or jewels. Accompanying these was a white transparent veil which draped over the shoulders and fell to the ground at the back.

The veil disappeared from fashionable dress once more in the early seventeenth century and returned only in the nineteenth century when short, decorative veils were attached to or draped over bonnets and hats. They were particularly modish in the years 1795–1830 and in the 1890s. In the former period the veils generally hung free, in the latter, spotted and patterned veils enclosed the face and were tied under the chin or at the back of

Gold and jewelled horned head-dress with white transparent veil, English, 1440

Steeple headdress with white, wired veil, 1460

Gold headdress with white veil, Flemish Burgundian, *c.*1435

Black velvet hat trimmed with pale blue and black ribbons, pink roses and black lace veil, English, 1895

VEIL
Roman veil, second century AD

Red headdress with black velvet edging, white veil, Flemish, 1480

the neck. Short veils continued to be attached to hats until the Second World War.

Veils have continued to be an important part of peasant and national dress until recent times as well as in bridal and mourning wear (see *Mourning dress* and *Wedding dress*). They were also worn during the nineteenth century for riding (see *Riding dress*) and at the turn of the century for motoring (see *Motoring wear*).

Velvet

A silk textile with a short, dense, smooth pile. A luxury fabric imported into Europe originally from India but made in Italy (notably in Genoa, Milan, Florence and Venice) from the Middle Ages. Italian workers set up workshops in France and Flanders from about 1500 onwards. *Velours* is the French word for velvet but, in English, the term signifies a velvet pile fabric made from linen, cotton or wool, used for upholstery and furnishing and, in the nineteenth century, manufactured chiefly in Prussia. There are many named velvets, notably:

Bagheera – a crush-resistant velvet with uncut pile.
Branched – a late medieval figured velvet.
Broché – a satin figured velvet.
Chiffon – a soft, very fine velvet.
Ciselé – a velvet figuring on a satin ground.
Corduroy – a corded, cotton velvet. The name is of English invention derived from *corde du roi* but this is not a term which was used in France. Used in the eighteenth century for labourers' clothes as it is very hardwearing. Now a fashion fabric.
Cut – a brocaded velvet design upon a chiffon or georgette ground.
De Laine – a velvet pattern upon a wool ground.
Du Dauphin – an eighteenth century Spitalfields striped velvet.
Imperial – a striped silk and velvet fabric.
Lyons – a rich, stiff velvet with a silk, cotton or rayon back.
Mirror – a watered velvet.
Muscovite – a velvet brocade.
Nacré – an iridescent velvet.

VEST
Blue and silver brocaded vest under red velvet coat embroidered in silver, Danish, 1695

Salmon-coloured silk vest embroidered all over in soft colours, French, 1738

Panne – velvet with a lustrous, flattened pile.

Raised – a velvet with the pile cut to leave a raised design.

Stamped – velvet with a design stamped upon the pile.

Transparent – a sheer velvet with a design printed upon its rayon pile.

There are a number of imitation or mock velvets. These include:

Mockado – also known as mock velvet. A deep-piled fabric made in the sixteenth to eighteenth centuries chiefly from wool.

Tripe – a fabric woven as velvet but made from wool or other thread. In the fifteenth to eighteenth centuries also known as velure or Naples fustian. So-called because of its resemblance to edible tripe.

Velveret – in the eighteenth and nineteenth centuries made of cotton weave with a silk pile.

Velveteen – a cotton velvet.

Venetian

A fine-textured woollen cloth with a twilled surface.

Vent

An opening or slit made in a garment for ease of wear or donning as in, for example, the back of a coat or jacket.

Vest, veste

1) A robe or gown worn in antiquity and in the East.

2) Forerunner of the waistcoat, a body garment which evolved from the sixteenth century doublet, worn under the jerkin. In the second half of the seventeenth century the jerkin developed into the justaucorps (coat). By the 1670s this was knee-length and had long sleeves with large, turned-back cuffs. The vest (veste) worn under it was similar in style but had long fitting sleeves and its skirt was a few inches shorter. It could be worn indoors without the justaucorps on top. During the first half of the eighteenth century the vest continued to be similar to the coat (now the *habit à la française*) but about six inches shorter; it was made of a rich, brocaded or embroidered fabric, often decorated all

over. After mid-century it became a sleeveless waistcoat (see *Waistcoat*).

3) From the mid-nineteenth century onwards the term has been used in England for an undervest (see *Underwear*). In the USA this is generally referred to as an undershirt.

Vestings

Material for making up men's vests or waistcoats.

Vigogne

A fabric made from the wool of the vicuña (see *Furs*). Vigogne yarn includes some cotton and other wools.

Visite

A nineteenth-century term for a sleeveless or part-sleeve cape or mantle worn by ladies. The style of the visite varied during the years of the 1840s to 1890s at which time it was fashionable for summer and winter wear as a covering for the shoulders and back.

Voile

A thin, transparent, plain material made from wool, cotton, silk or man-made fibres.

VISITE
White muslin visite, English, 1840

WAISTCOAT
Striped waistcoat, English, 1780

White piqué waistcoat under
dark brown cloth coat, English,
1806

Waistcoat

A body garment fastened up the centre front. In men's wear the sleeved seventeenth and eighteenth-century waistcoat was usually referred to as a vest (see *Vest* also *Gilet*). After mid-century the garment became sleeveless (in conjunction with the more fitting sleeve of the coat) and gradually grew shorter. After 1785 the waistcoat was more often cut straight across at waist level and sometimes had revers. The material contrasted with that used for the coat but was now plainer; stripes or spots had replaced embroidered and brocaded decoration.

During the nineteenth century the waistcoat followed the same lines as the coat being, for example, tight-waisted but full on the chest in the years 1820–40. With the plainer, heavier materials and more sombre colour schemes of the mid-century waistcoats were generally unpatterned, in white, grey or fawn. With the advent of the suit in the 1870s the waistcoat was then made from the same material as the coat and trousers. Double- and single-breasted styles were worn all century though in the second half the pointed waistline style tended to replace the straight across cut. Waistcoats continued in fashion in the twentieth century but the three-piece suit has been worn less and less since the Second World War, chiefly due to the spread of central heating for buildings.

Women have also worn waistcoats for certain occasions since the later seventeenth century. They have been incorporated into the design of riding habits (see *Riding dress*) and have been worn for extra warmth, then often as an undergarment. The tailored suits of the 1880s and 1890s generally included a waistcoat together with the blouse, jacket and skirt (see *Suit*). Waistcoats are also often incorporated into modern skirt and trouser ensembles.

Wale

A ridge or raised rib in a textile fabric, for example, the striped effect in corduroy.

Wamus

An American term used especially in the nineteenth century for a woollen, knitted jacket. Derives from a woollen body garment worn under armour.

Wardrobe

In the Middle Ages the term referred to a room in which clothes were kept, also the stock of clothes belonging to a person. From the late eighteenth century the term has also been used to denote a cupboard which contains clothes.

Watch

Portable timepieces were first made in Europe in the late fifteenth century. They were like miniature clocks enclosed in boxes and were made in Germany; because of their rounded shape, they were known as Nuremberg eggs. These watches were too large to carry in a pocket so generally hung from the belt. Sixteenth century watches were enclosed in beautifully made decorative metal and jewelled cases designed in many forms: crosses, small books, shells and even skulls.

Watches were very costly until the later eighteenth century when, as they became less expensive, they were more frequently owned. Men wore fob watches hanging over the trousers below the waistcoat; a pair was fashionable, one known as a *fausse montre* as it was a dummy. Alternatively, small watches could be set into the decorative waistcoat buttons. This fashion for fob watches continued until well into the nineteenth century when it was more usual to carry a larger, flat, round hunter watch in the waistcoat pocket. The hunter had a metal cover front and back; the front lid protected the glass and could be snapped open and shut to reveal the watch face as required. A watch chain was later worn across the front of the waistcoat attached to the watch and secured to a waistcoat chain hole. In England this chain was often known as an Albert.

Ladies wore fob watches pinned to the gown or coat bodice in the nineteenth century; alternatively, the watch could be worn as a pendant to a necklace chain or hung from a chain attached to the waistbelt. Later the bracelet watch became fashionable and this design was taken up by men from the early years of the twentieth century.

Weave

A term given to the characteristic surface pattern of a piece of woven material. Considerable variation can be imparted to the form of the weave according to the handling of the two sets of interlacing threads, the warp and the weft (see *Weaving*). Among the best known weaves are:

Herringbone – a zig-zag form of twill weave resembling a fishbone design. Similar patterns are known as *chevron, fishbone* and *broken twill* weaves.

Honeycomb – a pattern of all-over regular indentations similar to those of a honeycomb. Specific honeycomb weaves include *piqué* and *waffle cloth*.

Pebble – a rough-surfaced fabric.

Tabby – the simplest possible weave with the warp and weft threads interlacing one another alternately. Also known as *plain* or *taffeta weave*.

Twill – the strongest weave with a perceptible diagonal line extending from selvedge to selvedge. There are many varieties of twill weave such as *cavalry twill*, which has a strong, clearly patterned line and is traditionally used for uniforms, *middy twill*, generally of cotton and *Poiret twill*, named after the couturier, a fine dress material.

Weaving, warping

Before weaving can begin the loom has to be prepared. All woven fabric consists of two sets of threads crossing one another at right angles. One set, the *warp* is fixed to the loom, the other, the *weft*, creates the woven fabric by being interlaced across the warp by means of a shuttle. Before this weaving can be carried out the warp must be affixed to the loom.

Warp threads need a good deal of preparation before they are ready for the weaving to begin; the yarn needs to be cut into pieces of the correct length (probably each 90–100 yards) and then the correct number must be placed side by side and untangled so that they may be wound on to the roller or beam. There may be 6000 or more of such warp threads and to handle this number in such lengths required skill and experience in the days of handweaving.

The process of measuring the yarn into the required lengths and number of lengths is known as *warping*. In the days before machines were available this was done by using a peg board and was known as *wallwarping*. The peg board, leaning against or attached to a wall, had two vertical timbers set some distance apart and each was fitted with wooden pegs or dowels, one above the other. The weaver attached a thread to one dowel then walked backwards and forwards taking his thread round the dowels. These were spaced apart so that the correct length of warp thread was provided. The weaver repeated the process until he had the correct number of warp threads. The threads on the peg board were arranged there in crosses; this crossing of the yarn threads made the warping up, that is the winding on of the warp to the loom and its threading through the heddles of the loom, much easier.

In the seventeenth century the *warping mill* was invented which converted the yarn from single threads into a rope of untwisted threads which would constitute the warp.

Striped silk waistcoat under black frock coat, English, 1855

White and gold striped waistcoat under red coat, Belgian, 1790

Hand thrown shuttle for use with silk, English, nineteenth century

Flying shuttle, English

Warper's horn comb, English

A chained warp

A weaver's wooden comb, ancient Egypt

The yarn to be warped was wound on to bobbins held in a stationary frame or creel. The mill was a large, circular framework which rotated on a vertical axis. The operator turned the mill by means of a handle attached to ropes and pulley wheels. The yarn was run off from the bobbins and fed to the mill via an iron bar and further wooden bobbins and thence on to pegs fixed at required intervals to the mill frame. The warp threads were wound round the mill framework, backwards and forwards, until the required number had been reached. Later, hand-operated mills were adapted to other forms of power.

Warp threads are subjected to considerable wear by friction in the process of weaving as the heddles lift first one set of threads then another to provide an opening (shed) for the shuttle to pass through. To offset wear caused by this friction the warp was sized before it was attached to the loom. After being warped the ropes of threads were removed from the warping board or mill then were *chained*, that is plaited, to avoid entanglement, and drawn through a sizing trough containing glue size. In order to remove excess liquid the chained warp was then squeezed through a pottery throat or was spun (whuzzed). In this process the wet yarn was placed in a *whuzzing basket* which was then spun on a stick or rod so that the liquid was driven out by centrifugal force in rather the same manner as a modern spin dryer. Despite the sizing process and the chaining of the warp rope, some entanglement was inevitable so the weaver used a comb to remove these tangles before attaching the warp to the loom.

The actual weaving process interlaces the two sets of threads, warp and weft. The *plain* or *tabby weave* is the simplest form of this, where each alternate warp thread is raised and the weft thread is passed between these and the alternate ones, which are lowered. The process is then reversed and the weft thread passed through once more. In more complex weaves specific threads are raised and lowered and there are many possible permutations to this process. All over the world weaving has been carried out for centuries with the use of hand looms. These were fairly simple structures set up in cottages for weavers to work in a home-based industry. A drawing of a typical European loom of this type is shown, with the principal parts lettered, for reference.

First the prepared warp had to be attached to the loom and threaded ready for weaving. The warp threads were wound on to a roller, the *warp beam* (A), so that they formed a sheet of threads closely packed, and evenly spaced, side by side. The next stage was the drawing-in process. In this each warp yarn had to be threaded through an eyelet hole in the heddle (heald) leash. The *heddle* (B) was a rectangular wooden frame containing cords or wires set vertically into it. Each cord (leash, G) had an eyelet in the centre of it and each warp thread had its own eyelet. For a plain weave two heddles were needed, threaded with alternate warp yarns so that when one heddle was raised and the other lowered, a space was created between the groups of threads so that the shuttle containing the weft thread could be passed through; this space is known as a *shed*. Two people were needed to thread the warp through the heddle leashes, one to hold the thread and one to pull it through with the aid of a threading hook. The process had to be carefully done as any errors in threading would repeat the mistake throughout the piece of weaving.

After this each warp thread had to be passed through the *reed* (C). This was a rectangular enclosed comb, so-called because it was originally made of split reeds but later of metal wires. The vertical openings in the reed were known as *dents* and each thread had to be passed through, generally one per dent; a reeding hook was used for this. The function of the reed was to act as a separator for the warp threads and a beater for the weft. The drawing-in process was completed by the warp threads being tied to the *cloth beam* (D) so that weaving could commence. As the finished cloth was woven it was gradually wound on to this beam.

The heddles were tied to pulleys known

Hand loom with jacquard
apparatus, 1832 (Crown
Copyright. Science Museum,
London)

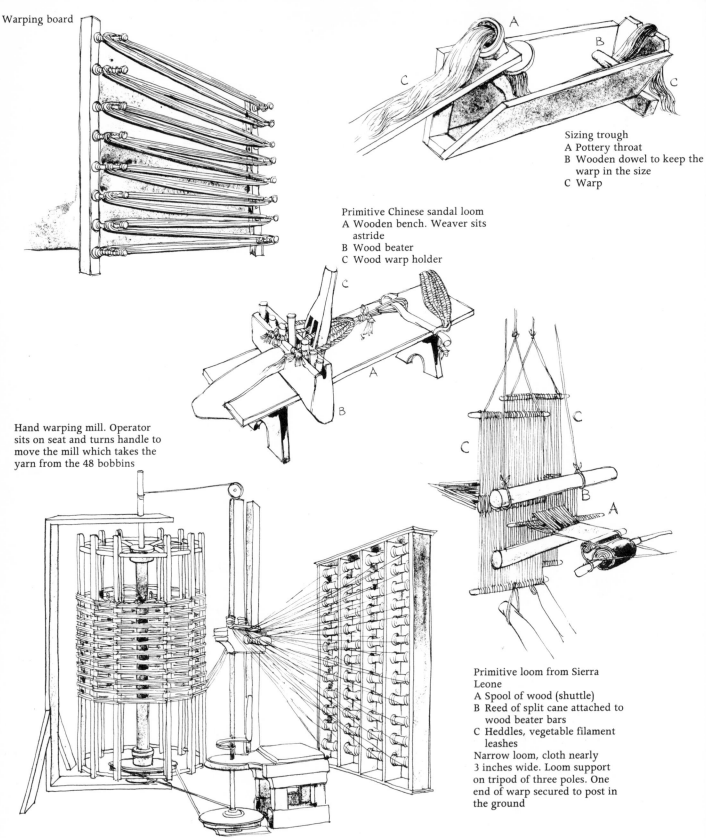

Warping board

Sizing trough
A Pottery throat
B Wooden dowel to keep the
  warp in the size
C Warp

Primitive Chinese sandal loom
A Wooden bench. Weaver sits
  astride
B Wood beater
C Wood warp holder

Hand warping mill. Operator
sits on seat and turns handle to
move the mill which takes the
yarn from the 48 bobbins

Primitive loom from Sierra
Leone
A Spool of wood (shuttle)
B Reed of split cane attached to
  wood beater bars
C Heddles, vegetable filament
  leashes
Narrow loom, cloth nearly
3 inches wide. Loom support
on tripod of three poles. One
end of warp secured to post in
the ground

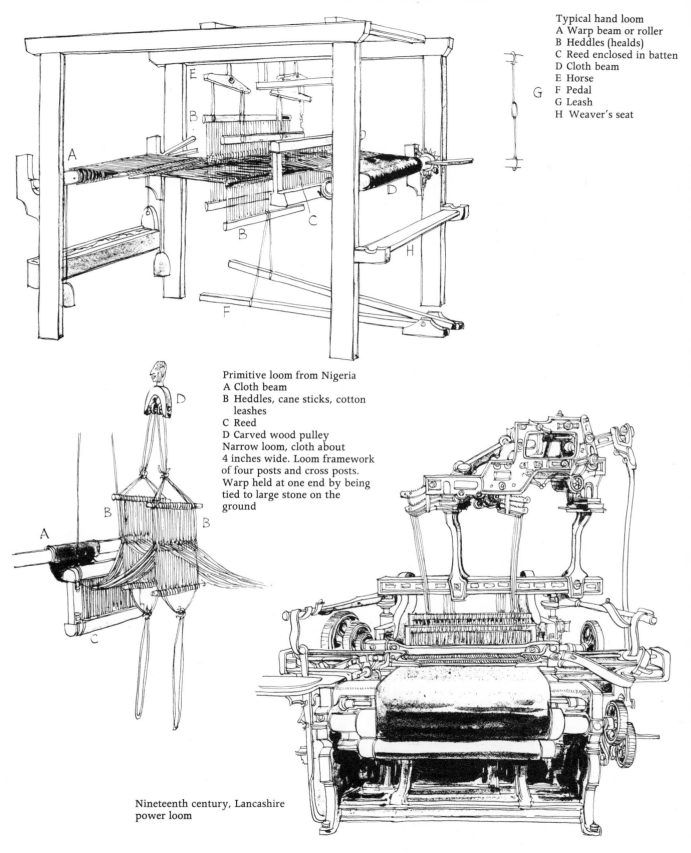

Typical hand loom
A Warp beam or roller
B Heddles (healds)
C Reed enclosed in batten
D Cloth beam
E Horse
F Pedal
G Leash
H Weaver's seat

Primitive loom from Nigeria
A Cloth beam
B Heddles, cane sticks, cotton
   leashes
C Reed
D Carved wood pulley
Narrow loom, cloth about
4 inches wide. Loom framework
of four posts and cross posts.
Warp held at one end by being
tied to large stone on the
ground

Nineteenth century, Lancashire
power loom

Wrap reel invented by Sir Richard Arkwright for winding yarn into hanks of measured length. One revolution of the index represents a hank of 840 yards.

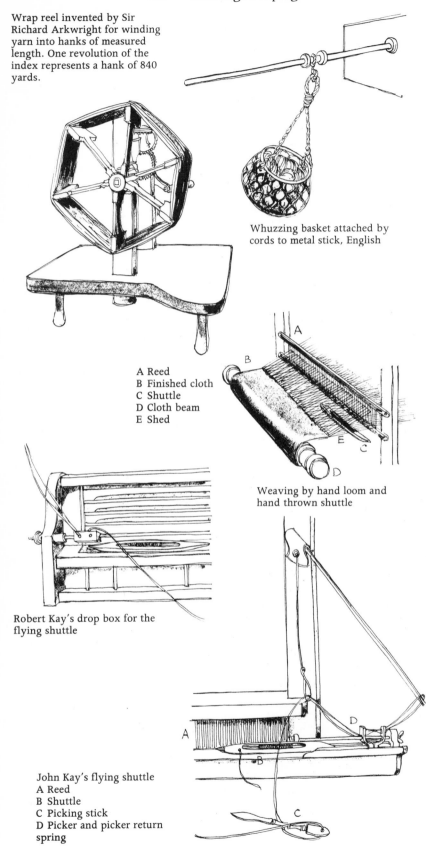

Whuzzing basket attached by cords to metal stick, English

A Reed
B Finished cloth
C Shuttle
D Cloth beam
E Shed

Weaving by hand loom and hand thrown shuttle

Robert Kay's drop box for the flying shuttle

John Kay's flying shuttle
A Reed
B Shuttle
C Picking stick
D Picker and picker return spring

as *horses* (E), which in turn were attached to pedals (F). The pedals, operated by the weaver's feet as he sat at his bench (H), raised and lowered the heddles, so creating the shed for the shuttle to be passed through. The *shuttle* (see drawings) contained the weft yarn wound on to a bobbin which rotated as the yarn was unwound and this thread passed out through an eye in the shuttle. After the shuttle had been passed (*thrown*) through the shed, the reed was pulled forward to beat and push the weft thread up to the woven cloth. A weaver's wooden comb was also used to beat the weft thread close. The heddles were then reversed, changing the shed, and the shuttle was returned.

Many variations in the weave could be produced by using a number of heddles and arranging a careful selection for raising and lowering different threads (see *Weave*). Plaid, check or striped materials were produced by using warp and/or weft threads of different colours. Pile fabrics, such as velvet, were made by the warp or weft yarns being passed over gauge wires, so creating loops which could later be cut to make the pile.

Although, in Europe, the industrial revolution brought mechanization and more complex and faster power looms, hand loom weaving continued in more primitive areas of the world. The principles of these primitive looms are the same as those just described for European hand loom weaving but these were less advanced and were not necessarily set in a rigid, wooden frame construction but held in a simpler manner (see examples illustrated). Materials to hand were used to make the loom, wood strips for the reed, for instance, and weaving was often only in narrow strips (see also *Braid* for tablet braid weaving).

For centuries the slow awkward method of throwing the shuttle continued. Weaving a wider piece of cloth on a wider loom needed two operators, one on each side of the loom to pass the shuttle back and forth. Faster weaving and wider pieces of cloth became possible with the invention by

John Kay in 1733 of the *flying* or *wheel shuttle*. *John Kay* was a Lancashire reed maker, first using reeds in his construction, then replacing these with wire which caused less wear to the warp threads. His flying shuttle consisted of a *shuttle box* constructed on each side of the loom, the two being connected by a board or batten called a *shuttle race,* to which the reed was attached. Each box was fitted with a metal spindle with a *picker,* which could slide along it. The weaver held a *picking stick,* which was attached by cords to the pickers. He jerked the stick from side to side, making each picker in turn slide along the spindle, taking the shuttle with it, so that it was thrown across the loom and back again from one shuttle box to the other. Kay's shuttle invention not only speeded up the action of the shuttle but made it run a true and correct course from one side to the other and so reduced friction on the warp threads.

John Kay's shuttle only allowed one coloured weft thread to be used at a time. His son *Robert Kay* invented a multiple shuttle box in 1760. This *drop box* could be raised and lowered as required and so enabled the weaver to use more than one coloured weft thread at a time, which was a great assistance for check fabrics.

Attempts to design *power-driven looms* had been made since the sixteenth century. Indeed, Leonardo da Vinci had made sketches for one as early as the 1490s and the Frenchmen de Gennes and Vaucanson each designed a device in 1678 and 1745 respectively. Power looms were made as early as the late sixteenth century but they could only weave narrow tapes and ribbons as it had not been discovered how to make the shuttle travel mechanically across the loom for more than a few inches. There was also, in the seventeenth and early eighteenth centuries, great industrial unrest caused by the threat to employment posed by the power looms; riots, destruction of property, even attacks on individuals, followed this threat to the weavers' employment. It was the same pattern of violence and threat of violence which John Kay had suffered due

to his flying shuttle invention and had caused him to take his design to France.

It was *Dr Edmund Cartwright,* a Leicestershire rural rector, who finally succeeded in designing and patenting a practical power loom. Dr Cartwright had no experience of weaving and little of machinery but was impelled to try to produce a satisfactory machine after discussions with some Manchester manufacturers about their difficulties in obtaining one. His first machine was patented in 1786, followed by improved designs in the two succeeding years. The looms made to his designs were a success and were used by firms who powered them by water and by steam.

Both the mills using the machines and the machines themselves were destroyed more than once by rioting and burning but it was a temporary setback. New mills were set up and improved looms followed in the late eighteenth and the nineteenth centuries. These improvements included an automatic stopping device if the weft supply failed, a warp-protector motion and better means for producing tufted and pile fabrics. One outstanding problem remained in the later nineteenth century: a method of automatically replenishing the weft in the shuttle. A successful invention to deal with this difficulty was made by *James H. Northrop* in the 1890s. Northrop was a Keighley man who had emigrated to the USA. His *Northrop loom* became a term synonymous with an *automatic loom* and was the most important invention since Cartwright's first power loom. In it, when the shuttle ran short of weft, a full bobbin was automatically inserted. A thread cutter cut the weft off the nearly empty bobbin and, as it was ejected from the shuttle, continued with the new one.

Since 1945 labour shortages and high wages have led to further automation including shuttleless looms and looms in which the weft is carried through the warp shed by a jet of air or water. These and other new techniques have made modern looms quieter, faster, more reliable and efficient and they need a minimum of supervision.

Apart from checks and stripes, *patterned weaving* was slow to develop; the problems in devising a mechanism to achieve a figured material were considerable. In hand loom weaving skilled weavers could handle several heddles and, with the advent of the power loom, a greater number of heddles were introduced giving more elaborate patterns, but changes in pattern still required a major operation. An attachment to the loom called a *dobby* helped to make such changes of pattern quicker; this equipment was able to select the heddles which needed to be raised and lowered and, with connections to the loom, could move them as required. The dobby was employed in simple form on hand looms but was only fully developed mechanically in the nineteenth century; it was introduced into silk weaving in the 1830s.

The eighteenth century development of the punched card system was primarily a French contribution. In 1725 *Bouchon* invented the system for using holes punched in lengths of paper and, three years later, *Falcon* developed the idea of using punched cards attached to a continuous chain to control the loom; each card determined one line of the pattern. The draw boy, the weaver's assistant, would offer up one of the cards to the wires or needles controlling the warp thread system before each throw of the shuttle. Only when the wires encountered holes in the card was the system engaged and the required warp threads were raised. In 1745 *Jacques de Vaucanson* designed a loom to weave figured cloth which combined the ideas of Bouchon and Falcon together with de Gennes' 1678 shuttle mechanism.

It was *Joseph Marie Jacquard* who introduced in 1801 an apparatus using the punched card principle by which all the motions of the loom were brought about by the weaver without need for a draw boy. Like the earlier designs, the punched cards, one for each pick or shuttle throw, forming a line in the pattern, were laced into a continuous chain held by a cradle but these passed in succession over a cylinder or prism pressing in turn against the needles and operating the system according to whether a hole or a blank was encountered. The cards were held in the correct position on the cylinder face by pegs which entered the holes on the card. Each card was brought up automatically to face the needles. There were several shuttle boxes to provide changes in colour for the weft, each box being brought into line as required by a hand lever.

The purpose of the jacquard system, which was used with hand and power looms, was to direct the movement of the warp threads required to produce the figured pattern. The warp threads followed a predetermined pattern according to the holes punched in the cards. The pattern to be woven was drawn on squared paper and the punched cards were prepared from this. The jacquard attachment was used chiefly at first for silk, where provision was made for selecting several hundred warp threads using as many as 1200 individual cards. As the design of looms was improved, the use of the system was extended to weaving figured cotton, linen and worsted. Jacquard's invention was taken over by the French government in 1806 and a royalty and pension were paid to the inventor.

Wedding dress

The special clothes and, particularly, the 'white wedding' were very much a nineteenth century tradition. In general, over the centuries before this bride and bridegroom wore garments of a style fashionable at that time but of a quality and decoration which was more lavish and special than their usual wear. In ancient Rome yellow was the normal wedding colour and the characteristic bridal adornment a bright yellow or flame-coloured veil, the *flammeum*, under which the bride's coiffure was elaborately dressed and garlanded with flowers. After this, in the Middle Ages, no specific colour was accepted as bridal wear and the richness of dress depended upon the wealth and social position of the couple.

By the end of the sixteenth century the wearing of white had become established as a symbol of purity and virginity and, from

Bride, 1805. Embroidered white batiste dress. White embroidered veil and gloves. Flowers. Poland

Bride and bridegroom, 1835. Bride in white silk and lace dress with embroidered white veil. Handkerchief and gloves. Bridegroom in black tail coat and trousers, grey satin waistcoat, black top hat and slippers. White shirt and bow tie. France

Bride, 1927. White velvet dress with white lace and net overskirt. White veil, stockings and shoes. Flowers. White ostrich feather fan. Bridesmaid in white lace and net dress. White socks and shoes. Holland

Bride, 1893. Pale peach silk dress. White veil and gloves. Flowers. Bridesmaid in dress of white silk and lace. Dark green velvet ribbons. White boots. Page in black velvet suit with black corded silk tie and knee ribbons. White socks, shirt and collar. Holland

CORBEILLES DE MARIAGE
White satin and lace, cord and
ribbons

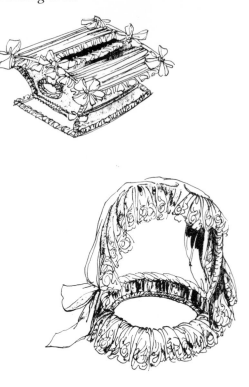

Oyster satin lining and ribbons,
white lace. To contain gloves,
handkerchief, fan, reticule,
flowers etc.

this time onwards, some brides wore white but it was only in this context, not as a bridal colour. Indeed, in the seventeenth and early eighteenth centuries, a white wedding gown would occasion comment rather than be accepted as the norm. The association of white as a colour symbol for a bride as well as denoting innocence gradually became a tradition from the late eighteenth century. Partly this was because at that time many fashionable gowns were white anyway, a mode which had been based on the mistaken theory that all classical dress had been white (the excavated classical statues were white as the colour had worn away) and partly because in the second half of the eighteenth century, the weddings of royalty and the aristocracy had often been dressed in white or silver. By 1800 white was accepted as the ideal for a wedding gown and in 1813 the first fashion plate of a white wedding dress appeared in the *Journal des Dames*. After this the white wedding, with its specially designed gown for wear on just one occasion had become customary.

The style of the wedding gown continued to follow that of the current fashion but a train was nearly always worn except with the crinoline gowns of the 1850s and 1860s. In the earlier part of the nineteenth century necklines were décolleté as in evening gowns but from mid-century onwards the neckline followed the neat high line and gowns had long sleeves also; the emphasis was on discretion and modesty. The same theme of neckline up to the throat and sleeves down to the hand continued into the 1930s (apart from a few years in the 1920s).

The wedding veil is also a tradition of the nineteenth century. Roman brides wore veils and the veil was an item of medieval headcovering in normal wear but later, especially in the eighteenth century, brides wore the styles of cap, bonnet or hat, decorated with lace falls, typical of the current mode. From 1800 though, a white veil became an essential part of the bridal attire. These varied greatly in size and shape during the nineteenth century from the decorative classical designs of the early years to triangular ones with the immense skirts of the mid-century. These were small and dainty, in lace, just covering the head and draped to the shoulders. From the 1870s, almost to the present day, the very long veils made of transparent net or tulle, held on the brow by a garland of orange blossom, cascaded over the shoulders and down the back to cover the gown's long train. This raiment for a wedding solemnized in a Christian church had now come into line with the Jewish custom for a bridal veil which was held in place by a fillet and covered the head completely.

Flowers had always been a decorative and symbolic feature at weddings but the artificial flowers made into a chaplet to hold the veil in place or carried as a bouquet were a nineteenth century custom as was also the prevalence of orange blossom as a bridal flower; this symbolized chastity and fertility and was a tradition extending well into the twentieth century. English brides had been accustomed to wearing chaplets of white roses in the earlier nineteenth century; the orange blossoms had been a French tradition which spread to America then back to Britain where by

Bride, 1937. White satin dress, bias cut. White veil and orange blossom. Holland

Bride, 1914. White satin dress with lace edging. White veil and gloves. White lace reticule. Flowers. Holland

Bride, 1825. White satin dress with white gauze trimming. White veil and gloves. Flowers in hair. White slippers. Holland

Bride, 1974. White linen dress with black-edged linen flowers. White veil and gloves. Holland

Bride, 1854. White tarlatan dress over white satin. White bonnet and veil, orange blossom. White gloves, handkerchief and shoes. Sweden.

Bride, 1883. Overdress of pale gold silk damask, underdress of white satin. White cap, veil and gloves. Flowers. England

Brown flannel short bedgown, back view. Worn with skirt and apron

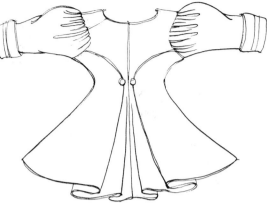

1840 it was an established custom.

Until the mid-nineteenth century the bridegroom's attire was less prescribed than that of the bride. Before this, formal fashionable dress of the day was worn, in a richer version of materials and ornamentation. Breeches and stockings remained usual wear until the 1830s when pantaloons and trousers became acceptable wedding attire. Around mid-century the evening dress mode of black tail coat and trousers with light, decorative waistcoat and white shirt, tie and gloves became the correct wear. From the 1870s a morning coat with striped grey and black trousers could be worn, alternatively a black frock coat with lighter trousers. A top hat always accompanied a wedding suit. A flower buttonhole had become fashionable by the 1860s. Since 1900 the grey top hat, grey or black morning coat, striped grey and black trousers and white accessories have been *de rigueur* wedding dress though, since 1945, tail coats have often been replaced by lounge suits or shorter coats.

The wedding ring has been, by tradition, a symbol of eternity and constancy. The plain gold or jewelled band, placed on the bride's hand during the wedding ceremony, has been set on the third finger of the left hand in Britain since the Reformation. On the Continent of Europe, this is sometimes the third finger of the right hand while, for a Jewish girl, it was placed on the index finger of her right hand. In the sixteenth and seventeenth centuries the wedding ring could be worn on the thumb.

Welsh dress

The ensemble which is often (mistakenly) believed to represent Welsh national costume worn by women was based originally on the seventeenth and eighteenth century peasant dress worn generally in Britain and Europe. It became fossilized in Wales in the later eighteenth century then converted during the nineteenth into what has become a fancy dress worn for the stage and the festival. There is no evidence that the Welsh people in the seventeenth and eighteenth centuries wore clothes which differed in any way from those of England. The well-to-do followed the current European, that is, French fashion. Everyone else adopted such styles after varied periods of time and in simpler, less luxurious manner. Ordinary people made their own garments from fabrics manufactured in Wales, often locally, and this usually meant striped or plain flannel.

It was in the early nineteenth century that an interest was taken and studies made of Welsh rural dress. Writers described a romanticized version and paintings and drawings were published showing this and presenting it as a traditional, national costume. Such writers were following the general, current Romantic movement. One of the most energetic and zealous moving spirits behind the establishment of this style of dress as a national one was Lady Llanover who, from 1830 onwards, publicized the dress in her descriptions and water colours. She offered prizes and organized competitions for such costumes, she wore the dress herself and encouraged her fashionable friends to do likewise. Later in the century the movement snowballed and in the twentieth century became popular as a tourist attraction. The costume was worn for festivals, folk dancing and at *eisteddfodau* and, depicted in coloured postcards, it was accepted as a national dress: one based not on tradition but upon a fallacy. Lady Llanover and her fellow enthusiasts were not interested in male costume so when men appeared at such festival events they wore a version of eighteenth century peasant dress.

The so-called Welsh national dress consists of an open gown, a petticoat, an apron, shawl or kerchief round the shoulders and, most characteristic, a white cap surmounted by a tall, black hat. Apart from the hat, which has become distorted over the years to a travesty of its original seventeenth-century shape, the remainder of the costume is very much that worn by women of rural communities in the eighteenth century which stemmed from fashionable town dress of the seventeenth century and one which, in these areas of Wales, was retained longer than in similar districts in England.

The basis was the bedgown which, originally, was put on by all women in the mornings as a loose house gown, and was worn by working women as normal dress combined with a petticoat and an apron (see *Bedgown* and *Petticoat*). The Welsh rural bedgown was generally of Welsh flannel in various colours, plain or striped. The long version was an open gown, long and cut away from the waist in front. It had elbow-length sleeves, with which could be worn long mittens or extra sleeves on the forearm, and a low neckline showing an underbodice and over which a shoulder shawl was pinned or tied. These shawls were generally rectangular, of flannel, wool or cotton and usually brightly coloured. A petticoat of contrasting-coloured flannel was worn with the long bedgown; the shorter style was accompanied by a long, full skirt as it ended in a peplum on the hips.

The apron was a traditional seventeenth and eighteenth century item of dress and was part of peasant costume all over Europe. The Welsh apron was of flannel or cotton, striped, or more often, in check design. The white cap was made in various styles, with or without lappets and generally tied under the chin. The black hat was originally low-crowned with ribbon and buckle but it grew taller as the nineteenth century advanced. For out-of-doors, the long, full, hooded cloak, traditional in Wales for centuries, completed the costume. The hood was always large, the material gathered round and shaped to fit into the collar (see *Cloak*).

Flannel bedgown with red and black stripes, black apron with white lines, dark red scarf, white bodice and cap, c.1820–30

Dark brown cotton bedgown with floral pattern in white, pinks and blues. White apron, cap and scarf. Pink petticoat, 1790

Long flannel bedgown striped in black and red. Worn with petticoat and apron

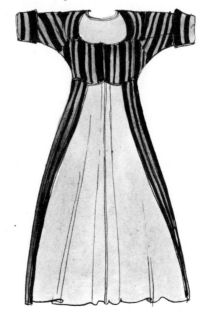

So-called Welsh costume made especially for Liverpool Eisteddfod of 1900. Green woollen bedgown with darker green velvet cuffs and edging. Apron striped in blue, red and yellow. Petticoat striped in blue, red, gold and brown. Black hat over white cap. Yellow and brown scarf. Black buckled shoes

WHISK
Lace whisk, English, 1616

WHISKERS
Piccadilly Weepers, English, 1865

Lace and lawn whisk, Anne of Denmark, 1617

Whalebone
In the Middle Ages the term referred to ivory obtained from the walrus. The material used in strips for stiffening various parts of the costume is taken from certain whales, particularly the baleen whale. It is a springy, horny substance which grows in the upper jaw in layers instead of teeth. The chief use of whalebone in costume through the ages has been to stiffen the seams of corsets, fitted bodices and doublets.

Whipcord
A twill cloth with diagonal weave. A hard-wearing, heavy fabric used especially for riding breeches, uniforms and sportswear.

Whisk
A lace or lace-edged white lawn collar, stiffened with starch or wire edging or supported on an under-collar, fashionable in the early decades of the seventeenth century. A more decorative version of the Spanish golilla, worn especially in England, Germany and Flanders (see *Golilla, Valona*).

Whiskers, facial hair
Hair grown on the face, now usually referring to hair on the cheeks and the angle of the jaw. The custom of growing such hair, not in conjunction with a beard, was particularly a fashion of the middle years of the nineteenth century, from the 1840s to the 1870s. These whiskers, or sidewhiskers, which left the chin free, were especially long in the 1860s when they were known by various names in different countries: in England, Piccadilly weepers, in France, cutlets, in America, dundrearies after Lord Dundreary, a character in a play, and burnsides after General Burnside. Sidewhiskers (sideburns in the USA) are grown only on the upper cheek; they have become fashionable again, especially with younger men, since the 1960s (see also *Beard, Hairstyles, Moustache* and *Jewish dress*, peoth).

Wig
An artificial covering for the head made of human or animal hair, wool or synthetic materials, dyed or powdered in a variety of colours. Wigs have been worn since ancient times to hide an insufficiency of natural hair, to provide a different style of coiffure, for fashion or decorative reasons as well as to designate certain professions, for ceremonial purposes, as disguise, or for reasons of religion or royal status.

Apart from the purpose of augmenting the insufficiency of natural hair or as a disguise, the wearing of wigs has been associated more with certain cultures and in specific periods. Of the ancient civilizations, the Egyptians were particularly noted for the wearing of wigs, shaving their heads or cutting the hair very short and covering the head with a wig varying in size and splendour according to rank (see *Egypt, ancient*). Greek and Roman women also wore wigs, in order to alter the colour and form of their coiffure. Under the Empire Roman women adopted complex coiffure styles many of which were achieved with the aid of a wig. Blond wigs were especially favoured during the Gallic and Teuton campaigns when they were made from the hair of captured slaves.

In Europe, Italians of the later fifteenth and early sixteenth centuries, men and women, wore wigs of different colours to vary their coiffure styles. Such wigs could be made of human hair but were often of silk thread. In the later sixteenth century and early years of the seventeenth, aristocratic women wore neat wigs dressed in small curls piled up on top of the head. Queen Elizabeth I possessed a number of wigs in her wardrobe and favoured these in red or golden shades and ladies of her court emulated her.

In Europe and the West the wig was widely adopted in place of the natural hair (which was generally cut very short) in the years 1660–1800. During the seventeenth century this *periwig* (*peruke, perwyke*), as it was called and later abbreviated to wig, was of *full-bottomed* style and worn by men. At first, in the 1660s and 1670s, it was dressed in a similar manner to the natural hair styles of the time, long, curled and flowing. By 1680 it had become very large and began to be arranged with a centre parting and a mass of curls and ringlets which rose to a peak on each side of the parting. These then cascaded over the shoulders and down the back nearly to the waist. The wig was of natural hair colours from blond to black, according to taste. The French were the chief European wigmakers; they imported the hair and made up the wigs in France then exported them to all countries. The *Duvillier wig* was named after a French perruquier of about 1700. The fine quality wig made of human hair was the status symbol of the well-to-do. In England, Samuel Pepys tells of fears that, owing to shortage of supply during the Plague of 1665, rumours were rife that the hair of plague victims was being used in the manufacture of periwigs. Men who could not accord these costly wigs (as much as £5 each) wore ones made of goat or horse hair or of wool.

The full-bottomed wig continued in fashion until the early eighteenth century though smaller wigs, tied at the nape with a ribbon bow, were worn for travelling and sport. Most wigs were in natural colours until about 1715 but grey powdering was introduced about 1708 as a prelude to the white powdering which soon followed.

Men wore wigs for most of the eighteenth century but, by about 1710, for greater

Dark brown periwig, *c.*1680, English

Black periwig, Charles II, 1684

William III, 1700

Black periwig, *c.*1670, English

White powdered tie wig, pigeon's wings, 1735, English

White powdered pigtail wig, pigeon's wings, *c.*1740

White powdered tie wig, 1740, Italian

Pigtail wig, English, 1750

Ramillie wig, English, 1755

Bag wig, English, 1770

Beech wig stand, 18 inches high, late eighteenth century

Fruit wood and ivory head scratcher for a late eighteenth century wig.

White powdered wig decorated with ribbons, jewel and ostrich plumes, Swedish, 1780

Ancient Egypt

White powdered wig, jewelled ornament, Italian, 1770

White ramillie wig, English, 1753

Powdered wig, cadogan style, decorated with ribbons and ostrich plumes, 1778

White pigtail wig, English, c.1768

Roman lady, c.90 AD

White powdered wig, cadogan style, pearl and ribbon decoration, 1780

Powdered hedgehog wig, English, 1787

comfort, younger men were tying back the curls of the full-bottomed wig with a black ribbon into a bow. At the same time the wig became smaller and neater and the peaks on each side of the parting were replaced by a style brushed back from the forehead over a pad: a *toupee* (toupet) style. The sides, over the temples, were dressed in soft waves or curls known as *pigeon's wings*. The tail of the wig which hung down the back, known in French as a *queue*, in England as a *cue* or *cue-peruke*, was, for the rest of the century, dressed in a variety of ways. In the first half of the century the style which was simply tied back with a ribbon bow at the nape leaving the curls to hang down the back was known as a *tie* (tye) *wig*. A long, bushy, white wig was the *Adonis*. Soon the wig began to be replaced by a plaited queue; this could be in a simple plait or two or three. The *pig-tail wig* was one in which the plait was encased in black silk with a black bow at the nape and another near the tip. A *ramillie(s) wig* was similar but was not covered in black silk; this was named after the Duke of Marlborough's battle of Ramillies.

Towards mid-century the softly curled side parts of the wigs were replaced by formal, horizontal curls on the temples; at first there were three curls, one above the other, then two and finally only one. These were known as *buckled wigs*, the name derived from the French *boucle* = curl. Further variations in dressing the queue appeared. There was the *bag wig*, where the tail was encased in a black silk bag drawn up with cords at the nape and finished with a black bow; this kept the powder from the coat and was also useful when growing the natural hair, for some men wore their own hair powdered to imitate wig styles. Also fashionable later in the century was the *cadogan* (said to be named after the Earl of Cadogan), also called catogan or *club wig*, where the queue was looped under and over and tied in place with a black ribbon bow. This ribbon was often carried round to the front of the neck to form the solitaire (see *Solitaire*). Other variations were provided by the

major wig, where the queue was finished in two corkscrew curls (a similar style was the *brigadier wig*), the *campaigne wig*, worn chiefly for travelling which had bushy sides and a short queue and the different versions of the *bob wig*. The bob wig was one which did not have a queue and, as the name suggests, was shaped in a bushy bob. A short, curled version of this was the *cauliflower wig*, a plain, neat one was the *cut wig*, while the *scratch wig* was shorter still, covering only the back part of the head with the natural hair brushed over it at the front.

In the 1770s, when women were wearing excessively high coiffures, men also, for a short time, had their wigs dressed up high in front. The last phase in the fashion for wigs was the *hedgehog* style (*a l'hérisson*), which was the mode of the 1780s. In this the hair was cut raggedly all over so that the ends stuck out like a hedgehog's quills. The back hair was dressed as before. After 1785 most men returned to natural hair, unpowdered.

Women took to wearing wigs especially in the second half of the eighteenth century. From 1750 onwards the hair was dressed with pomatum and powdered white. The sticky pomatum with the powder on top held the coiffure in place; it was the eighteenth century equivalent of hair lacquer. The coiffure grew larger and, from 1760, was either a wig or natural hair dressed up over pads (see *Hairstyles*). In the 1770s and early 1780s coiffures reached absurd heights with extravagant decoration. After this women took to hedgehog wigs then, by 1790, abandoned wigs for neat coiffures of natural hair. Only in the early years of the nineteenth century did they adopt the *cache-folie*, an appropriately-named small wig worn to hide the Titus, cropped hairstyles which had been fashionable just after the Revolution.

Wimple, guimple, gwimple
A woman's head-dress of the Middle Ages, worn chiefly from the late twelfth to the mid-fourteenth century and, less fashionably, in the fifteenth century, consisting of a piece of linen or silk, usually white,

WIMPLE
Wimple, German, 1460

White veil and wimple, Spanish, 1300–40

Couvrechef and wimple, English, 1320

fastened to the hair on the crown or on each side above the ears and draped to cover the chin, neck and throat; the lower edge was often tucked into the gown neckline. The wimple head-dress was completed by a couvrechef or veil (see also *Barbette, Couvrechef, Gorget*).

Wincey, winsey

A hard-wearing fabric with a cotton or linen warp and woollen weft used especially for shirts and nightwear (see also *Linsey-Woolsey*).

Windcheater, windbreaker

A jacket made of heavy or impermeable material, lined and/or quilted, worn for sports or mountain walking to resist the wind. A term in general use in the 1930s but now largely replaced by parka (see *Anorak*).

Witzchoura, witchoura

A warm, winter coat worn by women from 1808 and into the 1830s for use over the thin dresses of the period. Fur trimmed and lined, the witzchoura derived from the Polish wolf-skin coat, the *wilczura*. It

was an ankle-length garment styled, as an overcoat or mantle, with the currently fashionable high waistline. It had long sleeves and, usually, a shoulder cape or high collar; some designs were hooded.

Wool

One of the most important of natural textile fibres, wool is obtained from the domesticated sheep; it has been spun and woven since the days of antiquity. Most animal fibres are in the form of hair, some animals being covered with hair only and some having an inner coat of wool and an outer one of hair. Most breeds of domesticated sheep carry a fleece of wool only, though the primitive wild sheep, as well as some later, domesticated breeds, have both hair and wool coats (see also *Furs*). Woollen fabric can also be woven from mixtures of hair and wool from other animals including the alpaca, the angora goat and the llama.

The ancient Egyptians made woollen cloaks from their coarse, dark-coloured sheep and the Greeks and Romans produced finer woollens to make into draped garments as well as outer wear. A lightweight, fine wool was being woven in India several centuries before the coming of Christ. In Britain the making of woollen cloth has always been a staple industry. The sheep was domesticated here before the coming of the Romans and, from the early Middle Ages until the development of the cotton trade in the second half of the eighteenth century, it was the country's greatest revenue earner. English wool was, during the Middle Ages, regarded as of fine and lustrous quality. A finer wool was developed in the eighteenth century by cross-breeding the natural English stock with the Spanish merino sheep. Though not fully successful, this led to the breeding of a fairly fine-woolled sheep of which the Southdown is the modern descendant. Other breeds have produced quality wools also, notably the Hampshire, Oxford, Lincoln, Suffolk and Romney Marsh sheep. Some sheep have produced wools suited for specific purposes, for example, the blackface wool for carpet yarns, Welsh wool for flannels, Shetland wool for knitting yarns and Cheviot wool for tweeds. This breed is said to have been perfected by a cross between the indigenous Cheviot sheep and some merino sheep carried in the Armada ships of 1588.

Outside Britain the Spanish merino sheep had traditionally produced the finest wool since it was brought into the peninsula by the Moors. From the eighteenth century onwards the breed was introduced into France, Germany and Hungary as well as Britain and, among the crosses made between the merinos and indigenous flocks, was produced the famous Saxony breed. The merino was also introduced into the Americas, South Africa and Australasia. In South America and Australia in particular, enormous quantities of fine wool have been produced by the cross-breeding of this and other types of sheep. In Australia these fine wools were first shipped from Botany Bay, hence the use of the term Botany wool which has become a synonym for such yarns. The colour of a sheep's fleece is most often white but wool from black, brown, fawn and grey fleeces is also used, being especially suited to the rougher tweeds and knitting yarns.

Wool is graded and sorted according to the length and quality of the fibres and its felting (see *Felting*) propensities. In general, the shorter fibres are made into *woollen yarns* and the longer, lustrous ones into *worsted yarns* (see also *Textile Processes*). Worsted is named after a Norfolk village, north of Norwich, which was called Wurthstede, Worthstede and later Worthsted but has now become Worstead. *Tweed* is a twilled woollen cloth made in many qualities from coarse homespun to the finest of wools. It originated in southern Scotland, its manufacture still being predominantly Scottish, and often two or more colours are combined to make the yarn. The word tweed appeared in the first half of the nineteenth century and seems to have derived from an error caused by the mis-reading of the word *tweel* (Scottish for twill). The nearby River Tweed also possibly influenced the adoption of the term as a trade name for woollen weaves of the area.

Among the varieties of named woollen materials produced over the centuries are included:

Angora – the goat from this area of Asia Minor which has a coat of long, silken wool (see *Angora*).

Baize – a coarse, woollen cloth with a long nap made from the sixteenth century in different colours but later predominantly green.

Barège – a very fine, lightweight wool named after Barèges in France (see *Barège*).

Batiste – an extremely fine, lightweight wool fabric (see *Batiste*).

Botany – a fine worsted made from the wool of the merino sheep in Australia and first exported from Botany Bay. Later the term came to refer to any high quality wool or worsted.

Bure – (see *Bure*).

Caddis – a plain-woven woollen fabric made since the Middle Ages, used for garments and for padding.

Cashmere – a fine, soft wool originally made in Kashmir from the wool of the Tibetan wild goat. Similar goats are now bred in the west and cashmere is made from this wool mixed with sheep's wool.

Cassimere, Kerseymere – a soft, lightweight woollen cloth, often twilled.

Cheviot – a woollen cloth or tweed made from the wool of the Cheviot sheep and used for suits and coats.

Cotswold – fine quality wool from Cotswold sheep.

Crêpe – a lightweight worsted.

Donegal tweed – originally a heavy homespun tweed made in Ireland. Now machine-made and used for heavy suits and overcoats.

Duffel, Duffle – a heavy woollen cloth with a thick nap named after the Belgian town of Duffel. Warm coats and cloaks were made from duffel from the seventeenth century onwards and duffle coats were worn in the early days of motoring (see *Overcoat*).

Estamin – at first an open woollen fabric but later a finer, twilled dress material.

Flannel – a warm, soft woollen fabric of plain or twill weave (see *Flannel*).

Frieze – a coarse, thick woollen cloth with a nap, made particularly in Ireland and

WITZCHOURA
Dark blue velvet witzchoura with grey fur trimming, collar and cape. Plush hat with fur and ostrich plume decoration, muff

used primarily for outdoor wear.

Harris – a famous tweed woven on the islands of the Outer Hebrides.

Heather mixture – a combination of coloured fibres intermingled in the yarn and used especially for tweeds and knitting wools to resemble heather colouring.

Kelt – a homespun woollen frieze generally made of mixed black and white yarn and used especially in Scotland and northern England in the sixteenth to eighteenth century.

Kendal – a green, woollen cloth named after its town of origin in north-west England.

Kersey – a coarse, ribbed woollen cloth made in narrow widths suitable for stockings from the Middle Ages onwards. Possibly named after the Suffolk village of Kersey.

Kilmarnock – a woollen serge named after its town of origin.

Melton – a heavy, felted woollen cloth with a short nap, originally made in England. Suitable for outdoor wear as protection in cold weather.

Merino – a soft, fine woollen or worsted material or knitting yarn made from the wool of the merino sheep. A high quality yarn, resembling cashmere in its woven form.

Penniston, Pennystone – a coarse, heavy woollen cloth originating at Penistone in Yorkshire and made into outdoor wear in the sixteenth to eighteenth century.

Perpetuana, Perpets, Petuna – a durable (hence everlasting), glossy-surfaced woollen cloth made in England from the late sixteenth century. Worn especially by the Puritans of the seventeenth century in England and also later in the American Colonies.

Petersham cloth – a heavy wool overcoating with a knotted surface finish.

Prunella – a fine, durable worsted in smooth or twill weave used from the seventeenth century especially for academic, legal and ecclesiastical gowns and vestments.

Rapcloth – a coarse, rough, undyed, homespun woollen cloth made in Britain from the sixteenth century.

Rateen, Ratinet – a coarse, friezed cloth of the seventeenth and eighteenth centuries. Ratinet was a thinner version.

Satara – a ribbed, lustred woollen cloth from Satara in the Bombay district of India.

Saxony cloth – the name given, in the later eighteenth century, to a fabric made from merino wool produced in Saxony. Later the term came to apply to any fine, smooth woollen material of merino or botany quality.

Serge – a twilled worsted (see *Serge*).

Shalloon – a lightweight, fine, closely-woven woollen fabric, twilled on both sides and used chiefly for linings.

Shetland – a knitting yarn and a woven fabric made from the wool of Shetland sheep, both lightweight and warm.

Stamin, Stammel – a coarse woollen or worsted cloth, usually dyed red, made from the early Middle Ages and used especially for underwear.

Vicuña – wool from the vicuña, a member of the llama family, very soft, fine and expensive due to the rarity of the animal (see *Furs*).

Wadmal – from the Middle Ages a coarse woollen cloth used for rough clothing and bed coverings.

Witney – a heavy woollen cloth with a nap, made in Witney, Oxfordshire from the eighteenth century and used chiefly for men's overcoats.

Wrapper

1) A woman's negligée or informal house gown from the eighteenth century onwards. Made in a variety of materials and designs, either belted or hanging loose with a front fastening.

2) A man's overcoat of the nineteenth century (see *Overcoat*).

Yarn
Spun fibre for use in knitting, sewing, weaving etc. For preparation see *Spinning* and *Textile Processes*.

Yoke
A part of the bodice of a blouse or dress which contains the neckline and covers part of the shoulders or, in a skirt or trousers, extends from waist to hip. In both instances the yoke is fitting to the body and supports the material of the rest of the garment which is often much fuller and gathered, pleated or shaped into it. The yoke is sometimes of double fabric and frequently decorated and of different material from the remainder of the garment.

YOKE
Pale blue satin evening gown with yoke and undersleeves in a deeper shade, 1873

Yoke skirt in golden brown wool with cream blouse and black belt, 1963

Zephyr
The term can be applied to a number of lightweight garments such as a thin shawl or a sweater, also to fabrics which are light and delicate: in particular, zephyr gingham, zephyr barège, zephyr yarn.

Zibeline, zibelline
A soft, rich woollen fabric with a furry, long nap.

Zip fastener, zipper
A mechanical slide fastener with inter-locking teeth first manufactured in the 1920s which has become steadily more popular and useful ever since as the neatest method of closure for all types of garments. With the passing of time zippers have become slimmer and plastic has largely replaced metal.

Zircon
A mineral composed of zirconium silicate which, in its transparent form, is used as a gem stone. The zircon is rarely completely colourless and is found in shades of brown, red, orange, yellow, green and blue. The name is believed to derive from the Arabic *zargun* and certain varieties are named jargoon. The gem stone quality of zircon is found chiefly in Sri Lanka and Australia.

Sources of Information on Costume

The chief sources for the years before the seventeenth century are the churches, museums and galleries which have collections of sculpture, paintings, portraits, mosaics, relief carving, coloured glass, drawings and engravings, jewellery, medallions, effigies, embroidered textiles and illuminated manuscripts.

From AD 1600 onwards there exist many collections of actual garments and complete costumes. A few examples have survived from before this date and these comprise particularly articles made from leather. Many costume collections are devoted to national and regional dress, others to fashionable wear.

For the student who requires extensive and detailed information on the costume museums in Europe, it is helpful to consult the comprehensive guide, published in four languages by the Palazzo Grassi in Venice, which is available in major libraries: *Guida Internazionale ai Musei e alle Collezione Pubbliche di Costumi e di Tessuti*, published by the Centro Internazionale delle Arti e del Costume, Palazzo Grassi, Venezia, 1970.

The quality and quantity of actual costumes to be seen in collections varies greatly from country to country. It bears little relation to the importance of the country concerned in the history of costume. The majority of costume collections have been assembled over the years by individuals and have later been donated to museums and cities. Countries which possess excellent and extensive collections include Great Britain, Spain, Sweden, Switzerland and Holland. Several countries, such as France and Italy, possess good collections but lack suitable available buildings in which to display them. Others, such as Germany and Poland, lost much of their collections in the Second World War and are now re-establishing them. The more important costume and textile sources relating to articles in this encyclopaedia to be found in Britain are listed below:

Bath
Museum of Costume, Assembly Rooms A fine collection of costumes from 1610 to the present day, displayed attractively and with imagination. Twentieth-century dress is comprehensive for all decades – an unusual and useful feature.
Costume and Fashion Research Centre, No. 4, the Circus Place for reference and study.

Belfast, Northern Ireland
Ulster Museum Costume collection mainly from Northern Ireland c.1750–1930. Serious loss in recent times due to civil disorder.

Birmingham
City Museum and Art Gallery Costume collection from eighteenth century onwards. Also Manchu robes and jewellery from Egypt and India; and Japanese netsuke.

Blackburn, Lancashire
Lewis Textile Museum Collection of textile machinery and equipment through the ages.

Broadway, Worcestershire
Snowshill Manor Costumes late seventeenth to the nineteenth century.

Cambridge
Fitzwilliam Museum Paintings.

Cardiff
National Museum of Wales, Welsh Folk Museum, St Fagan's Collection of Welsh costume.

Edinburgh
Royal Scottish Museum Large collection of European costume seventeenth to twentieth century. Also Eskimo, North American and South American Indian, Afghan, Chinese, Arab and Japanese dress and accessories. Good lace, needlework and textile sections.
National Museum of Antiquities Mainly Scottish dress, accessories and jewellery from very early times.
National Gallery of Scotland and
National Portrait Gallery of Scotland containing many portraits of Scottish Highland dress.

Glasgow
Glasgow Art Gallery and Museum British costumes from 1760 to 1935.

Gloucester
City Museum and Art Gallery Mid-eighteenth century onwards.

Halifax
Bankfield Museum Remarkable collection of textile equipment and machinery, primitive looms from all parts of the world. Some regional European costumes, textiles, lace, bark cloth and accessories.

Hereford
City Museum and Art Gallery Costume and accessories 1750–1930.

Leicester
Museum and Art Gallery Sixteenth century onwards.

London
The Victoria and Albert Museum A very large costume collection. Display in the Costume Court of dress from 1580 onwards. Fashion dolls; also fashion plates mounted in leaf form round the Court. The museum also contains a fine collection of portrait miniatures, textiles, stained glass, sculpture and carvings as well as its outstanding library. A branch of the Victoria and Albert Museum is at the *Bethnal Green Museum* where there are costumes from 1750 to 1935 on display as well as children's costumes from 1780 to 1890. There is also a large collection of fashion dolls, mainly from the nineteenth century.
The British Museum A superb collection of jewellery from Minoan, Greek, Etruscan, Roman, prehistoric, Saxon and medieval periods. Equally fine collection of illuminated manuscripts and antique sculpture. The library.
The Museum of London Excellent collection of costumes and accessories from 1575.
The Science Museum Extensive collection of textile machinery through the ages.
Industrial Health and Safety Centre Display of protective dress.
The National Gallery Paintings.
The National Portrait Gallery Portraits.

Manchester
Gallery of English Costume, Platt Hall An excellent display of costumes from the eighteenth century onwards.

Northampton
Central Museum An extensive collection of all kinds of footwear from the earliest times from all parts of the world.

Nottingham
The Lace Museum A new centre for the display and study of lace.

Oxford
The Pitt Rivers Museum Ethnographical collection from all parts of the world including Eskimo, Maori and North American Indian dress, footwear, jewellery and accessories.

Paisley
Museum Shawls and other items.

Saffron Walden, Essex
Museum Eskimo, Maori and North American Indian dress; also footwear and accessories.

Worthing
Museum and Art Gallery English costume seventeenth century onwards.

York
Castle Museum English costume 1740–1930.

Bibliography

Classified list of books recommended for further study. Books are available in the English language unless stated otherwise.

Encyclopaedias and Dictionaries
BECK, S.W., *The Drapers' Dictionary: a manual of textile fabrics, their history and applications,* The Warehousemen and Drapers' Journal, 1886.
CUNNINGTON, C.W. and P., and BEARD, C., *A Dictionary of English Costume,* Black, 1972.
DOZY, P.A. REINHART, *Dictionnaire détaillé des noms des vêtements chez les Arabes,* Jean Müller, Amsterdam, 1845 (French text).
ENCYCLOPAEDIA BRITANNICA
GAY, V., *Glossaire Archéologique du Moyen Age et de la Renaissance* (2 vols): vol. I, Librairie de la Societé Bibliographique, Paris, 1882; vol. II, Auguste Picard, Paris, 1928 (French text).
IRONSIDE, J., *A Fashion Alphabet,* Michael Joseph, 1968.

KYBALOVA, L., HERBENOVA, O., and LAMAROVA, M., *A Pictorial Encyclopaedia of Fashion,* Paul Hamlyn, 1968.
LAMBERT, E., *World of Fashion: People, Places and Resources,* Bowker, 1976.
LELOIR, M., *Dictionnaire du Costume et ses Accessoires, des Armes et des Etoffes des Origines à nos Jours,* Librairie Gründ, 1951.
PICKEN, M.B., *The Fashion Dictionary,* Funk and Wagnall, 1973.
SCHOEFFLER, O.E., and GALE, W., *Esquire's Encyclopaedia of 20th Century Men's Fashions,* McGraw-Hill, USA, 1973.
WILCOX, R.T., *The Dictionary of Costume,* Batsford, 1970.
WILSON, G.B.L., *The Dictionary of Ballet,* Black, 1957.

History, General
ARNOLD, J., *A Handbook of Costume,* Macmillan, 1973.
ASSAILLY, G.D., *Ages of Elegance, 5000 Years of Fashion and Frivolity,* Macmillan, 1973.

BOEHN, M. VON, *Modes and Manners* (4 vols), *Decline of the Ancient World to 1800*, Harrap, 1932–35.

BOEHN, M. VON and FISCHEL, O., *Modes and Manners of the 19th century* (4 vols), Dent, 1927.

BOUCHER, F., *A History of Costume in the West*, Thames and Hudson, 1967.

BRAUN and SCHNEIDER, *Historic Costume in Pictures*, Dover Publications, New York, 1975.

BRAUN-RONSDORF, M., *The Wheel of Fashion: Costume since the French Revolution, 1789–1929*, Thames and Hudson, 1964.

BROBY-JOHANSEN, R., *An Illustrated History of Costume*, Faber, 1968.

BRUHN, W., and TILKE, M., *A Pictorial History of Costume*, Zwemmer, 1955.

CARTER, E., *Twentieth Century Fashion, 1900 to Today*, Eyre Methuen, 1975.

CONTINI, M., *Fashion from Ancient Egypt to the Present Day*, Paul Hamlyn, 1967.

DAVENPORT, M., *The Book of Costume*, Crown Publishers, New York, 1968.

DORNER, J., *Fashion: the Changing Shape of Fashion through the Years*, Octopus, 1974; *Fashion in the Twenties and Thirties*, Ian Allen, 1973; *Fashion in the Forties and Fifties*, Ian Allen, 1975.

EVANS, M., *Costume Throughout the Ages*, Lippincott, USA, 1950.

EWING, E., *History of Twentieth Century Fashion*, Batsford, 1974.

FABRE, M., *History of Fashion*, Leisure Arts, 1967.

GARLAND, M., *The Changing Face of Beauty*, Weidenfeld and Nicolson, 1957; *The Changing Form of Fashion*, Dent, 1970.

GARLAND, M., and BLACK, J.A., *A History of Fashion*, Orbis, 1975.

HAMILTON HILL, M., and BUCKNELL, P.A., *The Evolution of Fashion*, Batsford, 1967.

HANSEN, H.H., *Costume Cavalcade*, Methuen, 1956.

HOTTENROTH, F., *Le Costume chez les Peuples Anciens et Modernes* (2 vols), Armand Guérinet, 1884; also reprint, New York, 1947.

HOUSTON, M.G., *Medieval Costume in England and France*, Black, 1965.

HOWELL, G., *In Vogue: Six Decades of Fashion*, Allen Lane, 1975.

KELLY, F.M., and SCHWABE, R., *Historic Costume 1490–1790*, Blum, 1968; *A Short History of Costume and Armour, 1066–1800*, David and Charles, 1972.

KLEPPER, E., and LAVER, J., *Costume Through the Ages*, Thames and Hudson, 1963.

KOHLER, C., and SICHART, E. VON, *A History of Costume*, Harrap, 1928; reprinted Dover paperback, 1963.

LAVER, J., *A Concise History of Costume*, Thames and Hudson, 1969; *Costume*, Cassell, 1963.

LISTER, M., *Costume*, Barrie and Jenkins, 1974; *Costumes of everyday life, working clothes 900–1910*, Barrie and Jenkins, 1972.

MOORE, D.L., *Fashion through Fashion Plates, 1770–1970*, Ward Lock, 1971.

MORYSON, F., *An Itinerary Containing His Ten Yeeres Travell through the Twelve Dominions of Germany, Bohmerland, Sweitzerland, Netherland, Denmarke, Poland, Italy, Turky, France, England, Scotland and Ireland*, James MacLelose and Sons, Glasgow University Press, 1907 (first printed John Beale, London 1617).

NORRIS, H., *Costume and Fashion* (4 vols), Dent, 1924–38.

PAYNE, B., *History of Costume from the Ancient Egyptians to the Twentieth Century*, Harper and Row, New York, 1965.

PISTOLESE, R., and HORSTING, R., *History of Fashions*, John Wiley, 1970.

RUPPERT, J., *Le Costume* (5 vols), Flammarion, 1958.

STAVRIDI, M., *The Hugh Evelyn History of Costume*, Hugh Evelyn, 1970.

THIEL, E., *Geschichte des Kostüms*, Berlin, 1963 (German text).

The Ancient World

This section includes various races and civilisations up to AD 1000.

BROHOLM, H.C., and HALD, M., *Costumes of the Bronze Age in Denmark*, Nyt Nordisk Forlag, Copenhagen, 1940.

EVANS, M.M., and ABRAHAMS, E., *Ancient Greek Dress*, Argonaut, Chicago, 1964.

HALD, M., *Olddanske Tekstiler*, Nordisk Forlag, Copenhagen, 1950 (Danish text, English summary).

HOPE, T., *Costume of the Greeks and Romans*, 1812; Dover paperback, 1962.

HOUSTON, M.G., *Ancient Egyptian, Mesopotamian and Persian Costume*, Black, 1972; *Ancient Greek, Roman and Byzantine Costume*, Black, 1966.

LAVER, J., and KLEPPER, E., *Costume in Antiquity*, Thames and Hudson, 1964.

LUTZ, H., *Textiles and Costumes among the Peoples of the Ancient Near East*, Leipzig, 1923.

PIGOTT, S. (ed.), *The Dawn of Civilisation*, Thames and Hudson, 1961.

TACITUS (Tr. H. Mattingley), *The Agricola and the Germania*, Penguin Books, 1970.

TALBOT-RICE, T., *The Scythians*, Thames and Hudson, 1971.

WILSON, L.M., *The Clothing of the Ancient Romans*, John Hopkins Press, USA, 1938; *The Roman Toga*, John Hopkins Press, USA, 1924.

Britain

ADBURGHAM, A., *Liberty's: A Biography of a Shop*, Allen and Unwin, 1975.

ANTHONY, I.E., *Costumes of the Welsh People*, Welsh Folk Museum, 1975.

BENNETT-ENGLAND, R., *Dress Optional*, Peter Owen, 1967.

BINDER, P., *The Pearlies*, Jupiter Books, 1975.

BOUQUET, A.C., *Church Brasses*, Batsford, 1956.

BRADFIELD, N., *Historical Costumes of England, 1066–1968*, Harrap, 1970; *Costume in Detail 1730–1930*, Harrap, 1968.

BROBY-JOHANSEN, R., *Body and Clothes*, Faber, 1976.

BROOKE, I., *English Costume, Middle Ages to 19th Century* (6 vols), Black, 1964; *Dress and Undress, the Restoration and 18th Century*, Methuen, 1958.

BUCK, A., *Victorian Costume and Costume Accessories*, Herbert Jenkins, 1961.

CLAYTON, M., *Catalogue of Rubbings of Brasses and Incised Slabs*, Victoria and Albert Museum, H.M.S.O., 1968.

CLINCH, G., *English Costume from Prehistoric Times to the end of the 18th Century*, 1809; Reprint E.P. Publishing, 1975.

CUNNINGTON, C.W., *Englishwomen's Clothing in the 19th Century*, Faber, 1952; *Englishwomen's Clothing in the Present Century*, Faber, 1952.

CUNNINGTON, C.W. and P., *Handbook of English Costume* (4 vols), *Medieval to 19th Century*, Faber, 1973; *Costume in Pictures*, Dutton Vista, 1964; *Your Book of Costume*, Faber, 1973.

CUNNINGTON, P., *Costume of Household Servants, Middle Ages to 1900*, Black, 1974.

CUNNINGTON, P., and LUCAS, C., *Occupational Costume in England, 11th century to 1914*, Black, 1976; *Charity Costume*, Black, 1977.

CUNNINGTON, P., and MANSFIELD, A., *Handbook of English Costume in the Twentieth Century, 1900–1950*, Faber, 1976.

DUNBAR, J.T., *History of Highland Dress*, Oliver and Boyd, 1962.

ELLIS, M., *Welsh Costume and Customs*, National Library of Wales, 1951.

GIBBS-SMITH, C., *The Fashionable Lady of the 19th Century*, Victoria and Albert Museum, H.M.S.O., 1960.

HALLS, Z., *Women's Costume 1600–1750; Women's Costume 1750–1800; Men's Costume 1580–1750; Men's Costume 1750–1800*, Museum of London, H.M.S.O., 1970.

LANGBRIDGE, R.H., *Edwardian Shopping: Army and Navy Stores Catalogues, 1893–1913*, David and Charles, 1975.

LANSDELL, A., *The Clothes of the Cut*, British Waterways Board, 1975.

LAVER, J., *Nineteenth Century Costume*, Victoria and Albert Museum, H.M.S.O., 1947; *Taste and Fashion – from the French Revolution until Today*, Harrap, 1937.

MAXWELL, S., and HUTCHINSON, R., *Scottish Costume 1550–1850*, Black, 1958.

OAKES, A., and HAMILTON HILL, M., *Rural Costume in Western Europe and the British Isles*, Batsford, 1970.

PAYNE, F.G., *Welsh Peasant Costume*, Welsh Folk Museum, 1969.

STANILAND, K., *Costume in Miniature*, Gallery of English Costume, Manchester, 1970.

TAYLOR, J., *It's a Small, Medium and Outsize World*, Hugh Evelyn, 1966.

YARWOOD, D., *English Costume*, Batsford, 1975; *Outline of English Costume*, Batsford, 1977.

Europe

ALEXIANU, A., *Mode și veșminte din trecut*, Editura Meridiane, Bucharest (Rumanian text).

ANDERSEN, E., *Folk Costume in the National Museum*, National Museum, Copenhagen, 1971.

ATLAS OF POLISH FOLK COSTUME (many vols), Lublin, 1949–70 (Polish text, English summaries).

BANATEANU, T., *Folk Costumes, Woven Textiles and Embroideries of Rumania*, State Publishing House, Bucharest, 1958.

BAUR-HEINHOLD, M., *Deutsche Trachten*, Langewiesche, 1958 (German text).

BENTIVEGNA, F.C., *Abbigliamento e Costume nella Pittura* (2 vols). *15th–18th century*, Bestetti, Roma, 1962 (Italian text).

BERGMAN, E., *Nationella Dräkten* (18th Century National Dress in Sweden), Nordiska Museet, Stockholm, 1938 (Swedish Text, English summaries).

BERNIS MADRAZO, C., *Indumentaria Española en tiempos de Carlo V, 1500–1600*, Madrid, 1962; *Indumentaria Medieval Española, 7th Century to 1500*, Madrid, 1966 (both Spanish text).

BIRBARI, E., *Dress in Italian Painting 1460–1500*, John Murray, 1975.

BLUM, A., *Costume of the Western World 1515–1643* (2 vols), Harrap, 1951.

BRADSHAW, A., *World Costumes*, Black, 1977.

CHRISTENSEN, S.F., *Kongedragterne, 17th and 18th Century* (2 vols), Danish royal collection at Rosenborg Castle, Copenhagen, 1940 (Danish text, notes in English).

DIEDERICHS, E., *Deutsches Leben der Vergangenheit in Bildern* (2 vols), *15th–18th Century*, 1908.

EGYED, E., *Three Centuries of Fashion* (Hungarian Costumes), Museum of Decorative Arts, Budapest, 1965 (French summary).

ENACHESCU-CANTEMIR, A., *Popular Roumanian Dress*, Scrisul Romanesc, Bucharest (notes in English).

EVANS, J., *Dress in Medieval France*, Oxford University Press, 1952.

FOX, L., *Folk Costumes of Western Europe*, Boyd and Oliver, 1972; *Folk Costumes of Southern Europe*, Chatto, Boyd and Oliver, 1972.

GABORJAN, A., *Hungarian Peasant Costumes*, Corvina Press, 1969.

GILBERT, J., *National Costumes of the World*, Hamlyn, 1972.

GOTLICH, G.G., *Costumi Populari Italiani* (3 vols), Milan, 1951–58 (Italian text).

GUDJOHNSSON, E.E., *National Costumes of Women in Iceland from the 16th Century to the Present Day*, Reykjavik, 1969.

GUTKOWSKA-RYCHLEWSKA, M., and TASZYCKA, M., *Fashionable Clothes and Accessories of the 19th Century*, Narodowe Museum, Cracow, 1967 (Polish text, French captions).

HAZELIUS-BERG, G., *Women's Costume, 1600–1900*, Nordiska Museet, Stockholm, 1952 (Swedish text, English summary).

HOTTENROTH, F., *Handbuch der Deutsche Tracht*, Gustav Weise, Stuttgart, 1895–96 (German).

HUXLEY, F., *Peoples of the World in Colour*, Blandford, 1975.

KOSVEN, M.O., *Peoples of the Caucasus* (2 vols), 1961–62.

KROGH, K.J., *Viking Greenland*, National Museum, Copenhagen, 1967.

LEVINSON-NECIAIEVA, *Costume of the 17th and 18th Centuries*, Kremlin, Moscow, 1929–30 (Russian text).

LEVI-PISETZKY, R., *Storia del Costume in Italia* (5 vols), *Medieval– 19th Century*, Milan, 1964–69 (Italian text).

MANN, K., *Peasant Costume in Europe*, Black, 1950.

MANUGIEWICZ, J., *Polskie Stroje Ludowe*, Warsaw (Polish text, English notes).

MARKOV, J., *The Slovak National Dress through the Centuries*, Artia, 1956.

MBORJA, D., and ZOIZI, R., *Popular Art in Albania: Costume, Textiles, Clothing*, Tirana State University, 1959.

ORTIZ ECHAGUE, J., *España: Tipos y Trajes*, Madrid, 1971 (Spanish text).

PATRIK, A.N., *Armenian Dress from Antiquity to the Present Day*, Erevan, 1967.

PENZER, N.M., *The Harem* (Turkish Dress under Ottoman Empire), Spring Books, 1967.

PETTIGREW, D.W., *Peasant Costume of the Black Forest*, Black, 1937.

PRIMMER, K., *Scandinavian Peasant Costume*, Black, 1939.

PYLKANEN, R., *The Costume of the Nobility, Clergy and Burghers of the earlier Vasa Period 1550–1620; Baroque Costume in Finland 1620–1720*, National Museum of Finland, Helsinki, 1970 (Finnish text, English summary).

ROCAMORA, M., *Costume Collection*, Rocamora Museum, Barcelona (Spanish text).

RYBAKOV, B.A., *Treasures in the Kremlin*, Nevill, 1962.

RYNDIN, V., and KOZLINSKY, V., *Russian Costume* (Town and Regional Dress), Moscow, 1960.

SHARAYA, N.M., and MOISCENKO, E.I., *Russian Dress from the 18th to the end of the 19th Century*, Hermitage Museum, Leningrad, 1962 (Russian text).

SKROŇKOVÁ, O., *Fashions through the Centuries* (Czech Costume), Spring Books, 1959.

SLAVA, M.K., *Baltic Nations and their Dress*, Moscow, 1964.

STUBENRAUCH, P. VON, *Wiener Moden*, Vienna, 1826.

THIENEN, F. VAN, *Das Kostüm der Blütezeit Hollands, 1600–1660*, Berlin, 1930 (German text).

THIENEN, F. VAN, and DUYVETTER, F., *Traditional Dutch Costumes*, Amsterdam, 1968.

VARAGNAC, A., *Costumes Nationaux*, Hypérion, Paris, 1939 (French text).

VELEVA, M.G., and LEPANTSOVA, E., *Bulgarian Folk Costumes; Bulgarian National Dress*, Sofia, 1961 and 1969.

VILPPULA, H., *Folk Costumes and Textiles*, National Museum of Finland, Helsinki.

VINOGRADOVA, N., *Russian Traditional Dress*, Moscow, 1969.

WEIDITZ, C., *Das Trachtenbuch des Christoph Weiditz von seinen reisen nach Spanien und den Niederlanden, 1529–32*, Berlin, 1927.

YARWOOD, D., *European Costume*, Batsford, 1975.

The Americas

ARTS COUNCIL, THE, Catalogue, *Sacred Circles: 2000 Years of North American Art*, 1976 (Actual costumes, jewellery and accessories of the North American Indian and Eskimo).

BRAINERD, G.W., *The Maya Civilisation*, Southwest Museum, Los Angeles, 1954.

CORDRY, D. and D., *Mexican Indian Costume*, University of Texas, 1968.

EARLE, A.M., *Two Centuries of Costume in America* (2 vols), Reprint of 1903, Dover Books, New York, 1971.

MCCLELLAN, E., *History of American Costume 1607–1870*, Reprint of 1904, Tudor Publishing, New York, 1969.

THOMPSON, J.E.S., *The Rise and Fall of Maya Civilisation*, University of Oklahoma Press.

WARWICK, E., and PITZ, H., *Early American Costume*, Reprint of 1929, Blom, New York, 1965.

WILCOX, R.T., *Five Centuries of American Costume*, Black, 1966.

Asia

ATKINSON, J., *Character and Costumes of Afghaunistan*, Graves, 1843.

AYER, J., *Oriental Costume*, Studio Vista, 1974.

CAMMAN, A.C., *China's Dragon Robes*, Ronald Press, New York, 1952.

DAR, S.N., *Costume of India and Pakistan*, Bombay, 1969.

GHURYE, G.S., *Indian Costume*, Luzac, 1967.

MINNICH, H.B., *Japanese Costume and the Makers of its elegant tradition*, Tokyo, 1963.

NEEDHAM, J., *Science and Civilisation in China*, Cambridge University Press, 1962.

NOMA, S., *Japanese Costume and Textiles*, Weatherhill, 1974.

PRIEST, A., *Costumes from the Forbidden City*, Metropolitan Museum of Art, New York, 1945.

RUBENS, A., *A History of Jewish Costume*, Weidenfeld and Nicolson, 1973.

RUPPERT, J., *Le Costume Juif*, Paris, 1939 (French text).

SCOTT, A.C., *Chinese Costume in Transition*, Singapore, 1958.

Polynesia, Maori etc.

BEAGLEHOLE, J.C. (ed.), *The Journals of Captain Cook on his Voyages of Discovery* (4 vols), Cambridge University Press, 1967.

BUCK, P., *Arts and Crafts of Hawaii*, Bishop Museum Press, 1957; *The Coming of the Maori*, New Zealand, 1949.

MEAD, S.M., *Traditional Maori Clothing*, New Zealand, 1969.

Fashion and Haute Couture

AMIES, H., *Just so far*, Collins, 1954.

BAILLEN, C., *Chanel Solitaire*, Collins, 1973.

BALMAIN, P., *My Years and Seasons*, Cassell, 1964.

BATTERSBY, M., *Art Deco Fashion* (Couturier's Creations 1908–25), Academy Editions, 1974.

BEATON, C., *The Glass of Fashion*, Weidenfeld and Nicolson, 1954.

BROGDEN, J., *Fashion Design*, Studio Vista, 1971.

CHARLES-ROUX, E., *Chanel*, Cope, 1976.

DIOR, C., *Dior: the autobiography of Christian Dior*, Weidenfeld and Nicolson, 1957.

GARLAND, M., *Fashion*, Penguin, 1962.

LATOUR, A., *Kings of Fashion*, Weidenfeld and Nicolson, 1958.

LYNAM, R., *Paris Fashion*, Michael Joseph, 1972.

PEACOCK, J., *Fashion Sketchbook 1920–60*, Thames and Hudson, 1977.

PENN, I., *Inventive Paris Clothes 1909–39*, Thames and Hudson, 1977.

QUANT, M., *Quant by Quant*, Cassell, 1966.

SCHIAPARELLI, E., *Shocking life*, Dent, 1954.

TORRENS, D., *Fashion Illustrated*, Studio Vista, 1974.

WATKINS, J.E., *Who's Who in Fashion*, Fairchild, 1975.

WHITE, P., *Poiret*, Studio Vista, 1973.

Construction and Patterns of Garments

ARNOLD, J., *Patterns of Fashion 1660–1860*, also *1860–1940*, Macmillan, 1972.

FERNALD, M., and SHENTON, E., *Costume Design and Making*, Black, 1937.

HILL, M.H., *The Evolution of Fashion: Pattern and Cut 1066–1930*, Batsford, 1967.

WAUGH, N., *The Cut of Men's Clothes 1600–1900*, Faber, 1964; *The Cut of Women's Clothes 1600–1930*, Faber, 1968.

Children's Dress

BROOKE, I., *English Children's Costume since 1775*, Black, 1964.

Children's Costume, The Gallery of English Costume, Manchester, 1959.

CUNNINGTON, P., and BUCK, A., *Children's Costume in England 1300–1900*, Black, 1965.

EWING, E., *History of Children's Costume*, Batsford, 1977.

GARLAND, M., *The Changing Face of Childhood*, Hutchinson, 1963.

LAVER, J., *Children's Fashions of the 19th Century*, Batsford, 1951.

Academical Dress

HARGREAVES-MAWDSLEY, W.N., *A History of Academical Dress in Europe until the end of the 18th Century*, Clarendon Press, Oxford, 1963.

HAYCRAFT, F.W., *The Degrees and Hoods of the World's Universities and Colleges*, Reprinted 1972.

SHAW, G.W., *Academical Dress of British Universities*, Heffer, Cambridge, 1966.

VENABLES, D.R., and CLIFFORD, R.E., *Academic Dress of the University of Oxford*, University of Oxford, 1957.

Costume for Weddings, Births, Deaths, Nursing and Maternity Wear

AUDIAT, P., *Vingt-cinq siècles de Mariage*, Hachette, 1963 (French text).

CUNNINGTON, P., and LUCAS, C., *Costume for Births, Marriages and Deaths*, Black, 1972.

DE JONG, M.C., *Marrying in White, Two Centuries of Bridal Apparel, 1765–1976*, The Costume Museum, The Hague, 1976.

DENEKE, B., *Hochzeit*, Munich, 1971 (German text).

MONSARRAT, A., *And the Bride Wore . . .*, Gentry, 1973.

Costume for Sport, Recreation and Leisure

Costume for Sport, Gallery of English Costume, Manchester, 1963.

CUNNINGTON, P., and MANSFIELD, A., *English Costume for Sports and Outdoor Recreations 16th–19th Centuries*, Black, 1969.

KIDWELL, C., *Women's Bathing and Swimming Costume in the United States*, USA, 1968.

Masque, Ball and Comedy Costume

DUCHARTRE, P.L., *The Italian Comedy*, Harrap, 1929.

SAND, M., *Masques et Bouffons* (2 vols), Paris, 1860 (French text).

Footwear

BROOKE, I., *Footwear: A Short History of European and American Shoes*, Pitman, 1972.

Deutsches Ledermuseum und Deutsches Schuhmuseum, Catalogue, Offenbach-am-Main, 1961.

FORRER, R., *Archäologisches zur Geschichte des Schuhes aller Zeiten*, Bally-Schuhmuseums in Schönenwerd, 1942.

Picture Book of Boots and Shoes, Northampton Shoe Museum, 1975.

SWANN, J., *Shoes Concealed in Buildings*, Northampton Shoe Museum, 1970; *A History of Shoe Fashions*, Northampton Shoe Museum, 1975.

THORNTON, J.H., *Textbook of Footwear Manufacture*, National Trade Press, 1964.

WILCOX, R.T., *The Mode of Footwear*, Scribner, New York, 1948.

WILSON, E., *A History of Shoe Fashions*, Pitman, 1969.

Headwear, Hairstyles, Wigs and Facial Hair

AMPHLETT, H., *Hats: A History of Fashion in Headwear*, Sadler, 1974.

ARNOLD, J., *Perukes and Periwigs c.1660–1740*, from portraits in the National Portrait Gallery.

CHARLES, A., and DE ANFRASIO, R., *The History of Hair*, Bonanza, New York, 1970.

CORSON, R., *Fashion in Hair*, Peter Owen, 1965.

COURTAIS, G. DE, *Women's Headdress and Hairstyles in England from* AD *600 to the Present Day*, Batsford, 1973.

STEVENS-COX, F., *An Illustrated Dictionary of Hairdressing and Wig-making*, Hairdresser's Technical Council, 1966.

WILCOX, R.T., *The Mode in Hats and Headdresses*, Scribner, New York, 1959.

WOODFORDE, J., *The Strange Story of False Hair*, Routledge and Kegan Paul, 1971.

Underwear

CUNNINGTON, C.W. and P., *A History of Underclothes*, Michael Joseph, 1951.

EWING, E., *Fashion in Underwear*, Batsford, 1971.

REYBURN, W., *Bust up: the uplifting tale of Otto Tilzling and the development of the bra*, Macdonald, 1971.

SAINT-LAURENT, C., *A History of Ladies' Underwear*, Michael Joseph, 1968.

WAUGH, N., *Corsets and Crinolines*, Batsford, 1970.

Accessories

ARMSTRONG, H., *A Collector's History of Fans*, Studio Vista, 1974.

BRAUN-RONSDORF, M., *A History of the Handkerchief*, Lewis, 1967.

CLABBURN, P., *Norwich Shawls*, Norfolk Museum, 1975.

COLLE, D., *Collars, Stocks, Cravats* (Men's neckwear 1655–1900), New York, 1974.

CORSON, R., *Fashions in Eyeglasses*, Peter Owen, 1967.

CRAWFORD, T.S., *A History of the Umbrella*, David and Charles, 1970.

DAVEY, N.D., *Netsuke*, Faber, 1974.

GREEN, B. DE V., *A Collector's Guide to Fans over the Ages*, Muller, 1975.

LAVER, J., *The Book of Ties*, Seeley Service, 1968.

LUSCOMB, S.C., *The Collector's Encyclopaedia of Buttons*, Crown, New York, 1968.

PEACOCK, P., *Buttons for the Collector*, 1972.

ROCK, C.H., *Paisley Shawls*, Paisley Museum, 1966.

Jewellery

ALDRED, C., *Jewels of the Pharaohs*, 1972.

CLIFFORD, A., *Cut Steel and Berlin Iron Jewellery*, Adams and Dent, 1971.

DICKINSON, J.Y., *The Book of Pearls*, Bonanza, New York, 1968.
EVANS, J., *A History of Jewellery 1100–1870*, Faber, 1970.
HINKS, P., *Nineteenth Century Jewellery*, Faber, 1977.
KUNZ, G.F., *Rings for the Finger*, Constable, 1973.
LEWIS, M.D.S., *Antique Paste Jewellery*, Faber, 1970.
SMITH, H.C., *Jewellery*, E.P. Publishing, 1973.

Cosmetics and Perfumery

CORSON, R., *Fashions in Make-up*, Peter Owen, 1972.
LEWIS, A.A., and WOODWORTH, C., *Miss Elizabeth Arden*, Allen, 1973.
PERUTZ, K., *Beyond the Looking Glass: Life in the Beauty Culture*, Hodder and Stoughton, 1970.
SIMON, R., *The Price of Beauty*, Longmans, 1971.
TRUEMAN, J., *The Romantic Story of Scent*, Jupiter, 1975.

Materials: Textile Fabrics, Leather, Furs and Hides

CUNNINGTON, C.W. and P., and BEARD, C., *A Dictionary of English Costume, Glossary of Materials*, Black, 1972.
EMERY, I., *The Primary Structures of Fabrics*, The Textile Museum, Washington, 1966.
FLANAGAN, J.F., *Spitalfields Silks of the 18th and 19th Centuries*, Lewis, 1965.
IRWIN, J., and BRETT, K.B., *Origins of Chintz*, H.M.S.O., 1970.
MONTGOMERY, F.M., *Printed Textiles*, Thames and Hudson, 1970.
OXFORD ENGLISH DICTIONARY, THE (COMPACT), 1971.
ROTHSTEIN, N., *The English Silk Industry 1700–1825*, Adams and Dart, 1974.
SANTANGELO, A., *The Development of Italian Textile Design from the 12th to the 18th Century*, Zwemmer, 1964.
WATERER, J.W., *Leather Craftsmanship*, Bell, 1968; *Leather in Life, Art and Industry*, Faber, 1946; *Leather*, Oxford Clarendon Press.
WILCOX, R.T., *The Mode in Furs*, Scribner, New York, 1951; *The Dictionary of Costume*, Batsford, 1970.

Textiles: Dyeing, Printing, Spinning, Weaving and other processes

CROWFOOT, G.M., and ROTH, H.L., *Hand Spinning and Wool Combing*, Bean, 1974.
ENGLISH, W., *The Textile Industry*, Longmans, 1969.
GILBERT, K.R., *Textile Machinery*, Science Museum booklet, H.M.S.O., 1971.
INNES, R.A., *Non-European Looms*, Bankfield Museum, Halifax, 1959.
LEGGETT, W.F., *Ancient and Medieval Dyes*, New York, 1944.
ROBINSON, S., *A History of Dyed Textiles*, Studio Vista, London, 1969.
WEIR, S., *Spinning and Weaving in Palestine*, The British Museum, 1970.

WILKINSON, W., and DIMELOR, J.S., *Handbook of the Lewis Textile Museum*, Blackburn.

Knitting and Knitted Textiles

GRASS, M.N., *A History of Hosiery*, Fairchild, New York, 1955; *Stockings for a Queen*, Heinemann, 1967.
HARTLEY, M., and INGILBY, J., *The Old Hand-knitters of the Dales*, Dalesman, 1951.
KIEWE, H.E., *The Sacred History of Knitting*, Art Needlework Industries, 1967.
THOMAS, M., *Mary Thomas's Knitting Book*, Hodder and Stoughton, 1938.

Lace

FREEMAN, C., *Pillow Lace in the East Midlands*, Luton Museum, 1958.
HALLS, Z., *Nottingham Lace*, Nottingham Museum, 1973.
HOPEWELL, J., *Pillow Lace and Bobbins*, Shire Publications, 1975.
HUETSON, T.L., *Lace and Bobbins*, David and Charles, 1973.
JACKSON, F.N., *A History of Hand-made Lace*, Scribner, New York, 1900.
PALLISER, F.B., *A History of Lace*, originally 1875, revised edition, 1902.
WARDLE, P., *Victorian Lace*, Herbert Jenkins, 1968.

Embroidery

Bayeux Tapestry of Queen Matilda, Musée Tapisserie de la Reine Mathilde, Bayeux, France.
COATS, J. and P., *Anchor Manual of Needlework*, Batsford, 1974.
DIGBY, G.W., *Elizabethan Embroidery*, Faber, 1963.
DONGERKERY, K.S., *The Romance of Indian Embroidery*, Bombay, 1951.
EDWARDS, J., *Bead Embroidery*, Batsford, 1966.
JONES, M.E., *A History of Western Embroidery*, Studio Vista, 1969.
NEVINSON, J.L., *Catalogue of English Domestic Embroidery of the 16th and 17th Centuries*, Victoria and Albert Museum, 1938.
PETERSEN, G., and SVENNÅS, E., *Handbook of Stitches*, Batsford, 1970.
SWAIN, M., *Historical Needlework*, Barrie and Jenkins, 1970.
THOMAS, M., *Mary Thomas's Dictionary of Embroidery Stitches*, Hodder and Stoughton, 1934.
VICTORIA AND ALBERT MUSEUM, *Brief Guide to the Persian Embroideries*, 1929; *Brief Guide to the Chinese Embroideries*, 1931; *Elizabethan Embroideries*, 1948.
WACE, A., and J.B., *Catalogue of Algerian Embroideries*, Victoria and Albert Museum, 1935.
WADE, N.V., *The Basic Stitches of Embroidery*, H.M.S.O., 1966.
WARDLE, P., *Guide to English Embroidery*, H.M.S.O., 1970.

Index